PHILOSOPHY,
CULTURE AND RELIGION

Mind, Language and World

PHILOSOPHY, CULTURE AND RELIGION

The Collected Essays of Bimal Krishna Matilal

Mind, Language and World

Edited by
Jonardon Ganeri

MOTILAL BANARSIDASS
PUBLISHERS PRIVATE LIMITED

OXFORD
UNIVERSITY PRESS

OXFORD
UNIVERSITY PRESS

Oxford University Press is a department of the University of Oxford. It furthers the University's objective of excellence in research, scholarship, and education by publishing worldwide. Oxford is a registered trademark of Oxford University Press in the UK and in certain other countries

Published in India by
Oxford University Press
2/11 Ground Floor, Ansari Road,Daryaganj New Delhi-110002, India

First published 2002
Oxford India Paperbacks 2015
Second impression 2017

ISBN: 978-208-4136-9

Printed in India by Repro Knowledgecast Limited, Thane

The Matilal Trust

The Matilal Trust is a foundation set up at King's College London with a generous donation made by Mrs Karabi Matilal. The purpose of this Trust is to promote Matilal's work by making Indian Philosophy accessible to the general philosophical community. It has sought to do this by creating a post in Indian Philosophy at King's College London for the provision of undergraduate and graduate teaching in Indian Philosophy, and by sponsoring a series of conferences on Indian Philosophy in London. The Trust does not yet have the funds to make a full-time appointment, and its Trustees are actively raising further sponsorship. More information on the activities of the Trust can be gained from Professor Richard Sorabji, Department of Philosophy, King's College London, WC2R 2LS, UK.

Acknowledgements

I would like to thank, first of all, my assistant, Joerg Tuske, for his diligent and painstaking labours, in helping me locate references and correct the text, and for keeping me sane with amusing email messages. The funds for this assistance were kindly provided by the Matilal Trust, a foundation set up at King's College London to promote Matilal's work.

I should like to thank Karabi Matilal herself, who made available to me Matilal's unpublished writings for the purposes of these volumes, and who has been a constant source of encouragement. I would also like to thank Dr Heeraman Tiwari, to whom the original idea for these volumes owes a very great deal, and also the Trustees of the Matilal Trust, Professors Richard Sorabji, Gayatri Chakravorty Spivak, and Amartya Sen. I am also grateful to my department at the University of Nottingham for their support. Finally, I must express particular thanks to the editors at OUP Delhi. They have been hugely supportive, and have taken upon themselves such onerous duties as obtaining copyright permissions for all the articles. Having published Matilal's *The Word and the World* (1990), and a commemoration volume, *Relativism, Suffering and Beyond: Essays in Memory of B.K. Matilal* (P. Bilimoria and J.N. Mohanty eds, 1997), OUP India has also produced, in addition to his *Philosophy, Culture and Religion*, an imprint of Matilal's *The Character of Logic in India* (SUNY Press 1998). The most onerous task of all has been the retyping and setting of the text, and for this I thank most warmly the typists and copy-editors involved in the project.

Jonardan Ganeri, October 1998

Contents

Mind, Language and World

Ethics and Epics

PART I. *DHARMA*, RATIONALITY AND MORAL DILEMMAS

PART II. EPICS AND ETHICS

PART III. PLURALISM, RELATIVISM AND INTERACTION BETWEEN CULTURES

PART IV. IDEAS FROM THE EAST

PART V. CONCEPTS IN INDIAN RELIGIONS

Introduction

Bimal Krishna Matilal (1935–91) became Spalding Professor of Eastern Religions and Ethics at the University of Oxford and Fellow of All Souls College in 1976, before which he held teaching positions at the University of Toronto for eleven years. He was born in Joynagar, West Bengal, and left for Calcutta at the age of fourteen, where he studied first at the Islamia College and then at the Sanskrit Department of the University of Calcutta. In 1957 he was appointed as lecturer in the Government Sanskrit College. He continued to study Nyāya there with a number of eminent pandits, and under their guidance completed a traditional degree, that of Tarkatīrtha, Master of Logic and Argument, in 1962. For some time prior to this, Matilal had been in correspondence with Daniel Ingalls, who suggested to him the possibility of moving to Harvard in order to acquaint himself with the work being done by W.V.O. Quine in philosophical and mathematical logic. Breaking with the tradition in which he was trained, Matilal followed this advice, completing his Ph.D. at Harvard in 1965 having taken Quine's classes, and continuing his studies in mathematical logic with D. Føllesdal. In his doctoral thesis, *The Navya-Nyāya Doctrine of Negation*, published by Harvard University Press in 1968, he gives voice to his growing conviction that 'India should not, indeed cannot, be left out of any general study of the history of logic and philosophy'. This was to be the first statement of a thesis to the defence of which he devoted his academic life, that our philosophical understanding of fundamental problems is enriched if the ideas of the philosophers of classical India are brought to bear in the modern discussion.

These volumes have a double function. The first is to bring together many articles that have been published before in journals, anthologies and *Festschriften*. Many of Matilal's articles from before 1985 have already been reprinted, sometimes in a revised form, in his earlier collection, *Logic, Language and Reality* (Delhi: Motilal Banarsidass, 1985; 2nd edition, 1990), and for that reason are not included here. Nor have I included articles which have appeared as chapters in one of Matilal's other books, notably *The Word and the World* (Delhi: Oxford University Press, 1990). In the section 'The Provenance of the Essays', I have given details of the original place of publication of all of Matilal's essays, and where they can be found, if not in *Philosophy, Culture and Religion* then as chapters in one of these books.

The second function of these volumes is to publish for the first time a set of essays on which Matilal was working at the end of his life. Matilal was engaged principally on three projects (I do not include here his preparation of *The Character of Logic in India*, published by SUNY Press, 1998 and OUP Delhi). One project *Epics and Ethics*, sought to uncover the dynamic moral theorizing implicit in the epic, narrative and *dharmaśāstra* literature. This literature, he argues, redresses the classical philosophers' failure to fully discuss moral philosophy. Some essays from this project have already been published, but several are new. A second project was to study the role perceptions India had in the rise of the 'guru culture' of the sixties, in the movements founded by Maharishi Mahesh Yogi, Prabhupāda and Yogi Bhajan. This project was entitled *Ideas from the East*, and resulted in the four long essays under that heading in Volume 2. Finally, Matilal had begun work on a new introductory book to Buddhism, in which philosophical ideas were to have a central place. The part he completed is now 17-1 (Essay 17, Volume 1). Several other previously unpublished essays, some of which have their origin as conference papers or talks, are included here too for the first time.

Collected together, Matilal's essays reveal the extraordinary depth of his philosophical interest in India. His reputation as one of the leading exponents of Indian logic and epistemology is, of course, reflected here. Yet those who know of him through his major books in these areas, *The Navya-Nyāya Doctrine of Negation* (Harvard: Harvard University Press, 1968), *Epistemology, Logic and Grammar in Indian Philosophical Analysis* (The Hague: Mouton, 1971), and *Perception: An Essay on Classical Indian Theories of Knowledge* (Oxford: Clarendon Press, 1986; 2nd edition 1991), may be surprised to discover the range of his other writings. The essays here deal, in general, with every aspect of the relation between philosophical theory and Indian thought: from analysis of the arguments of the classical philosophers to evaluation of the role of philosophy in classical Indian society, from diagnosis of western perceptions of Indian philosophy to analysis of the thought of past Indian intellectuals like Bankimchandra and Radhakrishnan. Matilal, strikingly, is willing to look at a great range of sources for philosophical theory. As well as the writings of the classical Indian philosophical schools, he uses material from the grammatical literature, the epics, *dharmaśāstras*, medical literature, poetics and literary criticism. This eclecticism is no accident but has important methodological motivations. Matilal argues that it is only in the study of such diversity of literature that one can discover the mechanisms of the internal criticism to which a dynamic culture necessarily subjects itself in the process of revising and reinterpreting its values and the meaning of its fundamental concepts, and to be sure that one's own evaluation and criticism is immersed in, and not detached from, the practices and perceptions of the culture (27-1, 28-1). He also observes that a selective attention to particular aspects of Indian culture is part of what has generated a set of myths and misperceptions about Indian philosophy, most notably the popular idea that Indian philosophy is primarily spiritual and intuitive, in contrast to the rational West. Explicitly recognizing this risk of bias produced by selective attention, Matilal extends as widely as possible the 'observational basis' from which his conclusions are drawn (25-1).

While the great majority of the essays appeal to classical Indian sources, Matilal's treatment is neither historical nor philological. He does not engage in the reconstruction of the original Ur-texts, nor in descriptions of the intellectual development of a person or the evolution and chronology of a school. Instead, Matilal approaches the Indian materials with a methodology that is explicitly, if moderately, comparative-philosophical. In one essay (23-1), he describes the aims of this approach in the following terms: 'the purpose of the Indian philosopher today, who chooses to work on the classical systems, is to interpret, and thereby offer a medium where philosophers . . ., both Indian and Western, may converse.' Behind this modest statement lay a bold intellectual programme, a reinterpretation of the relationship between contemporary philosophy and the classical traditions, the main features of which I shall attempt briefly to describe.

The history of Indian philosophical studies in the twentieth century has been a history of comparisons, comparisons between Indian philosophy on the one hand, and whatever philosophical system was in vogue on the other. British idealism, logical positivism, neo-Kantian philosophy, the ordinary language school, and many other theories have all been used as counterpoints for a comparison with Indian theory. Matilal, an Oxford philosopher himself, depended mainly on the developments in contemporary anglo-american philosophy. Is Matilal's work, then, simply the latest in a long line of fashionable but transient comparisons, this time between Indian philosophy and the western analytical school? Matilal himself responded to this criticism, arguing that, if nothing else, his work was a much needed 'corrective', a way of displacing prevalent myths about the irrational and mystical nature of the Indian philosophers (*Perception*, pp. 4–5). He also criticized early comparativists for 'misunderstanding the nature and extent of the problem' they were addressing (23-1). The early comparativists were unclear first of all about the *purpose* of making the comparison, and in consequence rarely got further than merely juxtaposing doctrines, making priority claims in the history of ideas, or, at best, arguing that a doctrine acquires *prima facie* support if it can be shown to have arisen independently in different places. They could supply, however, no criterion for determining when a point of comparison is significant and when merely superficial. Indeed, the very existence of such a criterion is cast in doubt by J.N. Mohanty's observation that, in practice, 'just when an exciting point of agreement is identified and pursued, surprising differences erupt; and just when you have the feeling that no two ideas could be further apart, identities catch you off guard' (Mohanty, 1993, p. 216). Comparison is always a process of simplification, in which allegedly 'accidental' differences in formulation or context are eliminated, but without a criterion for distinguishing the accidental from the essential, the comparison lacks proper grounding. Another objection to the early approach is that the Indian theories were mostly treated as the *objects* of the comparison, to be placed in correspondence with some sub-set of western theory, an approach which necessarily denied to them the possibility of original content.

In Matilal's work, on the other hand, the goal is not merely to compare. It is informed, first and foremost, by a deep humanism, a conviction that the classical thinkers should not be thought of as mysterious, exotic or tradition-bound creatures, but as rational agents trying to understand their cultures and societies with as little prejudice as possible: 'we may discover in this way that in the past we were not all gods or spiritual dolls, but we were at least humans with all their glories and shortcomings, their ambitions and aspirations, their reasons and emotions' (24-1). It is this humanism in Matilal's approach which is brought out in his claim that the comparativist should create the means whereby philosophers of different ages and societies may converse. The point is to establish the prerequisites for a debate or an interaction, something which can sustain, in Amartya Sen's apt phrase, an 'intellectual connecting' between philosophers and traditions (Sen, 1992, p. 5). The basis for such an interaction is a shared commitment to a set of evaluative principles, norms on reasoned argument, the assessment of evidence and value, rather than to any particular shared body of doctrine. A little like the *adhyakṣa* or 'supervisor' in a traditional Indian debate, the comparativist's role in Matilal's conception is to set out and oversee those ground-rules, adherence to which is a precondition for the conversation to take place. The same commitment to rational inquiry can be found elsewhere—for example, in Greek and medieval philosophy, phenomenalism and elsewhere. Matilal's field of expertise was analytical philosophy, however, and so he sought to open the conversation between the classical Indian philosophers and their contemporary analytical colleagues. Where he succeeds so well here is in charting the philosophical terrain, identifying the salient groups of texts appropriate for the analytical enquiry (most notably, the *pramāṇa-śāstra*), and pin-pointing the topics in which Indian theory can be expected to make a substantial contribution. A good example of the latter is the epistemology of testimony, where the extensive Indian discussions have a real prospect of informing contemporary debates. A volume of articles co-edited by Arindam Chakrabarti and B.K. Matilal (*Knowing from Words*, Dordrecht: Kluwer, 1994) brings together the leading Indian and western philosophers in the area, and is an impressive illustration of the sort of philosophical 'interconnecting' Matilal sought for and believed to be possible.

Matilal stresses that it is essential for the modern comparativist to have, in addition to sound linguistic and philological skills, a good understanding of 'what counts as a philosophical problem in the classical texts' (23-1; cf. *Logic, Language and Reality*, p. xi). How does one know, when reading a classical text, what is to count as a *philosophical* problem? Broadly speaking, there have been two sorts of response to this question: those of universalism and those of relativism. Universalism, in its extreme form, is the doctrine that philosophical problems are global, that diverse philosophical traditions are addressing the same questions, and that the differences between them are ones of style rather than content. A more moderate universalism claims only that there is a single 'logical space' of philosophical problems, in which different traditions explore overlapping but not necessarily coextensive regions. Universalists believe that there is a *philosophia perennis*, a global philosophy, whose nature will be revealed by a synthesis or amalgamation of the ideas of East and West. The opposing doctrine, relativism, states in its extreme form that philosophical problems are entirely culture-specific, that each tradition has its own private conceptual scheme, incommensurable with all others. A more moderate relativism permits a 'notional' commensuration of the ideas of diverse cultures, but insists that the similarities are in style alone, and not in content. The doctrines of the East can be made to look familiar, similar enough indeed to seem intelligible; but in substance, they are radically different.

Matilal rejects completely the kind of relativism that would regard ideas and values as inevitably indexed by cultural context, and he offers both a critique and an alternative. The alternative, a form of pluralism, is most clearly formulated in his later work on relativism in moral theory. He formulates there the thesis of 'minimal universal morality', the doctrine that there are certain basic and universally applicable values, a 'minimal moral fabric underlying all societies and all groups of human beings' (18-2). The minimal universal morals are values which attach to the 'naked man' stripped of specific cultural context; they are, perhaps, the basic capacities and needs associated with being a human being in a society. These are values which the comparativist can identify, if he approaches the other culture with humanity and imagination (cf. 24-1, 25-1). The existence of such raw human values is consistent with there being substantive and even incommensurable local differences, and for this reason Matilal regards his position as combining pluralism with moral realism. The relativist, mistaking the local, context-specific values of a given society with the totality of its values, overlooks the existence of a commonality which can serve as the basis of real confrontation, interaction and exchange between cultures: 'to transform two monologues into a dialogue we need a common ground, some common thought patterns between the participants, as well as a willingness to listen to each other' (14-2).

At the same time, it is the local, culture-specific values which characterize or individuate a given culture, distinguish it from others (an example is Louis Dumont's idea that social hierarchy is a *value* in traditional societies; cf. 28-1, 4-2). It is the characteristic values of a culture, religion or society that are often the interesting and important things to explore, but it is the existence of a common framework that makes it possible to explore them: 'I do not say that different Indian religions talk simply about the same thing in different languages and idioms . . . Rather, I would say that they talk about different things while standing on a common ground' (15-1). Underlying Matilal's humane pluralism is a bold recognition that 'human nature is manifold and is expressed through diverse values, ways of thinking, acting and feeling' (27-2), that global human values can coexist with culture-specific constraints, that genuinely conflicting values are possible, and that they are possible because of the existence of a common set of values.

The idea has a specific application in Matilal's approach to comparative philosophy. Here the universal principles are the norms governing rational argument. Any conversation between Indian and western philosophers depends on there being a minimum of agreement, or at least a 'limit on difference', about what counts as a rational argument or a well-conducted investigation into a philosophical problem. Rationality in a minimal sense is itself a universal value. When he has identified the idioms for these shared principles of rational argument, a comparativist has a common ground from which to explore differences. Matilal's pluralism acknowledges what is right about both universalism and relativism, without being reducible to either. His essays are indeed the 'marvellous conversations of mankind' (Mohanty, 1986), between Sextus Empiricus and Sañjaya, Strawson and Udayana, or Bhartṛhari and Quine. They are demonstrations of an exciting and original way of approaching our global intellectual history.

Matilal sought in his work to bring classical India into the philosophical mainstream, thereby 'transforming the exile into companion' (the phrase is from Schwab, 1950, p. 1). If the Sanskrit philosophical literature had indeed been excluded from the philosophical curriculum, it was because of a myth, the myth that there are two philosophical cultures—one Eastern, spiritual, atavistic, the other Western, rational, materialistic—having incommensurable values, doctrines and standards. As H.H. Price, while Wykeham Professor of Logic at Oxford, put the matter: 'we seem to be confronted with two entirely different worlds of thought, so different that there is not even the possibility of disagreement between them. The one looks outward, and is concerned with Logic and with the presuppositions of scientific knowledge; the other inward, into the "deep yet dazzling darkness" of the mystical consciousness' (Price, 1955, p. 228). Matilal ruefully comments, in a slightly different context (20-2), that in this strange mixture of fact and imagination, it is as if the Westerner is set on conquering the other (foreign lands, the material world), and the Indian on conquering himself (his inner world). In any case, the effect of the division was to deny to 'Orientals' the status of being people-like-us: 'the Oriental man is either subhuman or superhuman, never human. He is either a snake-charmer, a native, an outlandish species, or else a Bhagawan, a Maharishi, a Mahārāja, an exotic person, a Prabhupāda. The implication of the presupposition is that there cannot be any *horizontal relationship* between East and West' (25-1).

Matilal regards the very idea that there are independently bounded and closed philosophical cultures as a 'dogma of orientalism', albeit a self-sustaining one which has served the historical interests of Indian and western philosophers alike. Mysticism and spirituality, the properties projected onto the East, do not fit the western self-image as rational and scientific: 'it is as if our Western man is embarrassed to acknowledge anything that is even remotely irrational or mystical as part of his indigenous heritage' (20-2). So mystical systems such as neoplatonism have been regarded as marginal in western thought. In no less measure, Indian authors like Radhakrishnan have wished to downplay the rationalist streams in the Indian traditions in their desire to represent Indian culture as distinctively spiritual and intuitive, a desire at one with the nationalist search for an autonomous Indian identity (26-1). Anthropologists and 'colonial liberals' have also found the relativist dogma convenient, for it absolved them of the need to make value judgements on the practices of the society being governed or observed. The platitude, however, is a myth: 'the fact of the matter is that materialism and spiritualism, rationality and irrationalism-cum-intuitionism, are monopolies of neither India nor the West' (2-2). Matilal's argument against the dogma (and indeed against other expressions of cultural relativism) is that it is impossible to individuate cultures in any such way as would give them sharp boundaries; cultures are always mixing and merging with each other, identities are being enriched or revised by adoption and absorption (18-2, 19-2). Indeed, it is for Matilal the very mutability of cultures which shows real confrontation between them to be possible. If relativism were true, the only confrontation that could occur would be 'notional', and would have no impact on the values of either culture. Cultures do not, however, have unchanging, immutable essences; even what seem to be the most characteristic and embedded values of a culture are subject to gradual trade-offs, rejections and modifications in the course of time.

I have spoken so far of Matilal's methodological framework. In the remainder of this introduction, I will look at the detail in Matilal's programme, as reflected in the principal themes of the essays collected here. The unifying motif in his work is the study of rational traditions in Indian thought. Matilal's sustained analysis of the logical grounds of mysticism (1-1 to 5-1; see also Appendix 1 of *The Word and the World*, and Chapter 4 of *Logical and Ethical Issues in Religious Belief*, Calcutta: University of Calcutta, 1982) represents therefore a powerful engagement with prevalent but misconceived ideas about the mystical nature of Indian thought. He seeks to demonstrate that even the so-called 'mystical' philosophers (such as Sañjaya, Nāgārjuna and Śrīharṣa) defend their views with carefully reasoned argument, and do not let them rest merely on spiritual insight or intuition. In particular, Matilal perceives and seeks an explanation for close ties between mysticism and scepticism. Both agree that our beliefs about the empirical world, as ordinarily understood, lack warrant. Both defend this thesis with the help of carefully reasoned argument—'mysticism' is no less rational than scepticism. Where they differ is in their attitude towards the possibility of knowledge gained through unusual means of unusual matters. Here, as Matilal puts it in 5-1, the sceptic is a *pessimist* while the mystic is an *optimist*. Unlike the sceptic, the mystic does not regard the failure of our everyday methods of acquiring knowledge as entailing that there is no knowledge to be had. Knowledge is possible, albeit knowledge of an unusual type, a type typically described as ineffable and unstructured. Scepticism leads to mysticism when the state of mind engendered by the sceptic's *ataraxia* or suspension of judgement is regarded as peculiarly suitable for the occurrence of experiences characterised as 'mystical'.

Matilal's own philosophical sympathies lie with neither mysticism nor scepticism but with a form of realism. Several articles here continue his celebrated defence of the Nyāya position in his magnum opus, *Perception*, and most are written after its publication in 1986 (6-1 is an exception, for it is a *précis* of the leading argument in *Perception*). The common-sense realism of the Nyāya philosophers asserts that we do indeed see the objects we take ourselves to see, that those objects exist by having parts without being merely the sum of their parts, and that they fall into objective, natural categories. Two ingredients in Matilal's defence of this theory have a particular significance: the doctrine that perception is non-partitive, and an interpretation of the concept of objectivity. To say that perception is non-partitive is to say that we can see objects without *seeing* their parts (e.g. their front-surfaces) or their properties (e.g. their colour and shape). That is not to deny that the parts and properties of an object figure in the explanation of our coming to see it—it is part of the explanation for our seeing an object that light reflecting from the surface of the object causes stimulation of the retina. What the non-partitivity thesis does deny is that the parts or properties of the object can enter that explanation only if they themselves become *objects* of perceptual awareness. If this is correct, Matilal points out, then the move typically made by the Buddhist phenomenalist, that the 'support' (*ālambana*) for perceptual awareness must be unstructured and immediately given, is blocked. This leads, however, to what Matilal (6-1) claims is the hardest problem for the Nyāya realist. If phenomenal entities like sense-data and *svalakṣaṇas* have no explanatory role in perception, how do we account for such apparently purely phenomenal illusions as seeing the blue dome of the sky, a rainbow, or a circular disk as elliptical?

Matilal's innovative solution introduces a new concept of objectivity (6-1, 9-1, 12-1). To be objective is to be independent of minds. Being 'mind-dependent,' however, need not mean being a private, intentional object in the way that sense-data and other purely phenomenal entities are. It can mean simply having a mental event as a causal condition, an event on whose continuing existence the object depends. Although illusory, the blueness of the sky and the ellipticality of the disk are objective at least in the sense that they are not purely private objects of sensation, but are produced by, and shared by, the perception of any observer located in the right position. Matilal observes (8-1) that the Nyāya exploit such a notion of objectivity in their theory of number, for numbers are thought to be objective properties, and yet dependent for their existence on mental acts of counting. The realism which such a notion of objectivity grounds is softer than that to which sceptics (and at least some mystics) are committed, according to which objects can exist independently of anyone's capacity to know they exist. We might note too that a concept of objectivity as an invariance between subjects, rather than as an independence from any subject, is particularly suitable to the realism Matilal espouses in his moral theory, based as it is on the idea that there is a set of minimal, culture-invariant, moral values (cf. 16-2). The two issues are indeed intertwined in his critique of the sort of 'commitment-free understanding' of languages or cultures that is presupposed by much ethnography, and which rests on the idea that the existence of propositions is independent of the languages in which they are expressed (11-1; cf. 21-1).

Matilal's disclosure of philosophical connections is not limited to the conversation between classical Indian and contemporary Western philosophers, but extends to the interaction between the classical philosophical schools themselves. Argument and attempted refutation are the overt modes of this interaction, but cross-fertilization and absorption of ideas were the inevitable, if usually unremarked, effects. Matilal regards the sparring match between Naiyāyikas and Buddhists as a fundamental axis in the history of classical Indian philosophical thought (14-1, 15-1, 18-1). In two essays here on Mādhyamika Buddhism (13-1, 16-1), Matilal considers again the question: what is the status of Nāgārjuna's claim to reject all theses without thereby having a thesis (namely, that all theses are false)? Matilal's well-known strategy in other work has been to interpret the Mādhyamika 'rejection' as an illocutionary refusal to assent, a speech-act which is distinct from and does not entail asserting the proposition's negation. In 13-1, however, he considers a different solution: the doctrine of emptiness is not a thesis precisely because it is a *comment* on all theses. This move, taking the Mādhyamika claim to be on a different level to ordinary propositions, is correlated with the doctrine of 'two truths' in Buddhism. In 16-1, Matilal considers whether there is an analogy to be drawn between the Mādhyamika *prasaṅga* technique for reducing a thesis to absurdity, and Derrida's notion of the deconstruction of a text. Another essay, 'What is Buddhism?' (17-1), was to have been the basis of a book, and is one of Matilal's last written pieces. It is a survey of the canon and chief philosophical doctrines of the Buddhists, as well as of the life of Buddha.

The section in this collection on 'Sanskrit Semantics' contains some articles not included in Matilal's book on Indian philosophy of language, *The Word and the World.* Two essays (19-1, 20-1) discuss concepts employed in Pāṇinian grammatical theory: the *ekaśeṣa* rule and the 'locative' *kāraka.* In 21-1, Matilal considers the notion of translation. He argues that Bhartṛhari would have agreed with Quine that there are no such things as meanings as translation-invariants, not on the grounds of an indeterminacy of translation, but because 'meaning' (*sphoṭa*) is inseparable from the 'utterance' (*nāda*) that conveys it. In a manner reminiscent of his argument that relativism is false because cultures are not isolated wholes, Matilal points out that the thought experiment on which Quine's argument rests depends on a technical notion of language as a closed system, whereas natural languages overlap, grow and change, whence his conclusion that 'translation, understanding and communication are all of a piece and are made possible by a commonly shared world, as well as by the creative power of each 'living' language.' Essay 22-1, apparently delivered to an audience of linguists, suggests a new way to think about the notions of expectancy (*ākāṅkṣā*) and compatibility (*yogyatā*) in Indian grammatical theory, namely as rules on the combination of grammatical categories. A verb 'expects' an item of a particular type to be its direct object (it 'expects' a noun and not, say, another verb); and the verb is then also 'compatible' only with nouns of a particular type (nouns of liquid and not say of fire, if the verb is 'drinks'). It is for this reason, Matilal suggests, that the apparently semantic notion of compatibility is given a place in Indian grammatical theory.

In a series of essays on images of Indian philosophy, Matilal identifies a set of myths and perceptions, which have come to constitute the belief that there is an almost 'ontological distinction' (25-1) between Indian and western philosophy. Among these myths are: that 'the East is irrational and emotional, the West rational and logical'; that 'concepts such as justice and fairness, privacy and individual freedom, are foreign to the Indian mind [*sic*], which is at best familiar with a sort of crude intuition as a guide to ethical and moral sensitivity'; that the 'caste-oriented hierarchical society in India has remained well-integrated and thereby for a long time has been tension-free and stable' (28-1). Matilal rejects the argument that these ideas are entirely a product of European romanticization of the East, and agrees even that they have an 'observational basis' (with a glance at Berkeley, he jokes that it is because every idea must be caused by an impression!). Perceptions become myths, however, when a selective attention to certain facets of Indian culture is overgeneralized, and other aspects and characteristics of Indian thought ignored. Matilal also rejects as exaggerated Edward Said's thesis that western Orientalist scholarship was driven entirely by the politics of power. The Orientalists did at least bring a commendably scientific outlook to their study of the East; however, what should have been a rigorous but also humanistic study, combining scientific precision with an understanding of the humanity in the cultures and societies under investigation, became instead a dry collation of facts and figures into neat systems of categorization and classification (25-1).

Another issue turns on the classical Indian author's own conception of philosophical activity; specifically, the precise meaning of the terms *darśana* and *ānvīkṣikī*, and the relation between the study of philosophy and the goals of practical life. Referring to Kauṭilya's *Arthaśāstra*, Uddyotakara's *Nyāyavārttika* and to other texts, Matilal forcefully argues that the ancient Indians had a clear conception of philosophy as an independent discipline which 'primarily concerned itself with rational inquiry and consciously wanted to avoid religious dogmas' (24-1). Philosophy is the study of the means of knowing (*pramāṇa*), by virtue of which our actions are rewarded with success, we are turned away from the sources of suffering, and so towards the final goal of life, which is described cagily in Nyāya as that 'than which there is nothing better' (*niḥśreyasa*).

Study of Indian theories of rationality, including the demonstration that there do exist rational traditions in Indian thought, is, as I have noted, a key unifying theme in Matilal's work. To be rational is, minimally, to ground one's beliefs on proper evidence, and to determine the course of one's actions on the basis of suitable rules or action-guides. While the concept of proper evidence is the subject matter of the *pramāṇaśāstra*, a body of literature whose philosophical contours Matilal did much to map, it is he claims in the epic literature and *dharmaśāstra* that one can find the Indian accounts of practical reason and moral theory. (This distinction is reflected to a considerable extent in the division of articles between the two volumes.) The focus of his journeys into this massive literature is the concept of a moral dilemma. Matilal defines a moral dilemma in terms of conflicting principles of moral obligation—as a situation in which 'the agent cannot do everything that is morally obligatory for him to do in that situation' (1-2). He reviews a number of instances in the Indian epics. In each of his examples, the structure is similar: typically, a formal ethical duty (*dharma*) conflicts with another such duty, or else with a conventional moral obligation. In one example from the *Mahābhārata*, which was the subject of a celebrated controversy between Rabindranatha Tagore and Bankimchandra Chattopadhyay, Arjuna is faced with a stark choice between belying an earlier promise (to kill anybody who insults his *gāṇḍīva* bow), or else committing fratricide (against Yudhiṣṭhira, who insulted the bow in a moment of rage). It is again Arjuna, who, in the story of the *Bhagavadgītā*, is faced with the dilemma of reneging on his caste duty to fight, or going ahead and thereby killing his respected elders and family members. Matilal contrasts the 'formalistic' ethics advocated in the *Rāmāyaṇa*, in which telling the truth, keeping a promise, or doing one's caste duty, is an 'unconditional obligation' (7-2), with the 'devious diplomacy' of Kṛṣṇa in the *Mahābhārata* (1-2, 3-2, 8-2), for whom formal obligations need not override all other moral and non-moral considerations. In an astonishing metaphor, Matilal likens Kṛṣṇa's attitude to formal moral codes to that of a poet, who 'accepts the constraints of metre . . . but has absolute control over them . . . who governs from above but does not dictate' (3-2). Responding to situational constraints, Kṛṣṇa breaches rigid moral codes and in doing so creates new ethical paradigms. The moral insight to be drawn, Matilal suggests, is that the experience of genuine moral dilemmas enriches an agent's practical wisdom. More generally, the epics give prominence to two important aspects of *dharma*-ethics: the vulnerability of moral virtues, and the elusiveness of moral truth (5-2). John Brockington, in his definitive study, *The Sanskrit Epics*, comments that 'if Matilal's ideas are taken seriously, as surely they should be, the concept of *dharma* in the *Mahābhārata* gains a far deeper dimension' (1998, p. 64).

The authors of the medieval *dharmaśāstra*, notably Manu and Yājñavalkya, though frequently criticized for devising apologia of unjust social institutions and caste inequalities, nevertheless realized that 'the full extent of *dharma*-morality can be sustained only if it can be given a rational basis' (5-2). When confronted with a genuine moral dilemma—an irreconcilable conflict in one's moral obligations—these authors say that one should do what is 'approved by the heart', which Matilal interprets with approval as an appeal to the dictates of a moral conscience, 'impartial and not biased by any baser emotions'. In matters of public morality, the moral conscience of a suitably constituted assembly is recommended by Manu as the arbiter, where the assembly should include scholars versed in the three Vedas, a logician, an exegete, an etymologist, and an ordinary person from each of the three groups, student, householder and retired person. Matilal suggests that a careful study of the treatment of *dharma* in such texts, as well as in the later retellings of the epic stories, would reveal how the changing ethos of a self critical tradition attempted to reconcile the tensions and volatilities which are part and parcel of *dharma*-ethics (4-2, cf. 28-1, 5-2).

Matilal stresses that the final course of action a moral agent chooses, when confronted with a genuine moral dilemma, will inevitably be accompanied with regret, remorse, guilt and shame (the 'moral emotions'), for the moral agent has to live with the consequence of violating one moral duty in choosing to act in accordance with another (5-2, 6-2). It is in this context of moral conflict that Matilal places the *Bhagavadgītā* discussion of *karma* (10-2, 11-2). Three 'ways of life' or 'action-guides' are distinguished: acting-with-desire (*karma*), non-action (*akarma*), and acting-without-desire (*niṣkāmakarma*). The first two are the ways recommended by *brāhmaṇas* and *śramaṇas* respectively. The former is based on performing Vedic rites and sacrifices in the hope of getting rewards, or, more generally, on acting even in situations of moral conflict and accepting the consequences. The latter is the way of renunciation, the idea being that choosing the path of renunciation saves one from moral lapses, even in conflict situations, as one prefers not to act than to act and thereby violate a moral duty. The third alternative is the one recommended by Kṛṣṇa in the *Gītā*: to act but abandon all desire for the outcome of one's actions. Matilal points out that there are certainly philosophical problems with the notion of desireless action, for instance to do with the coherence of saying that one should act without desire if one *desires* to live a good or moral life, and he considers the available solutions (10-2). He argues, more generally, that the introduction of the *karma* doctrine and the notion of caste rationalized *dharma*-ethics and gave it an appearance at least of consistency, but did not really stabilize it or remove the inner conflicts and tensions which gave it life. Matilal's emphasis on the internal dynamism and inherent instability of the *dharma* system is a radical departure from traditional Indological scholarship, which saw in the hierarchy of caste and *karma* a highly stable, and thereby static and unevolving, societal structure.

Matilal sees the primary source of moral conflict as lying in real confrontations between different value systems. This leads him into a more general discussion of the competing claims of different value systems, religions and cultures. He is critical of relativism, the doctrine that distinct value systems do not in fact genuinely conflict. It is a doctrine Matilal particularly associates with the 'colonial liberal,' who refuses to condone or condemn the practices and values of another culture, on the grounds that they are incommensurable with western cultural values. In a sustained attack on relativist claims about religions (15-2, 16-2), Matilal agues instead that minimal 'common elements' in all religions can be isolated at a suitable level of description. He tentatively suggests, among others, respect for life or commitment to non-violence, and a prohibition on lying, as two candidates; another (27-2) is the quest for immortality. This does not imply that different religions are simply talking about the same thing in different ways; rather they talk about different things while standing on a common ground. Matilal often refers to Tagore's idea that there is a 'surplus in man', a capacity to be more than machines, to think about and question our own values, and so to reach a kind of self-understanding of our place in nature. The different world religions all, perhaps, address this surplus, and in doing so become 'alternative hypotheses to render the universe comprehensible and our life in it meaningful' (16-2). The target of 18-2 and 19-2 is cultural relativism. Matilal again argues that there are minimal, culture-invariant values, shared by all cultures, based perhaps on basic human needs and capacities, such as the need for food, shelter, the alleviation of pain, and interaction with others. The purpose of these essays is to show that cultures and religions *do* interact, that there is a common basis for conversation, meaningful connections, genuine conflicts and moral dilemmas.

The myth that the East embodies values alien to the West took a new form in the sixties and seventies, as a growing discontent with western 'materialism' led to a 'turning East', in search of a more spiritual alternative to the values of the Enlightenment. In a set of essays on 'Ideas from the East' (20-2, 23-2), Matilal examines in detail the extensive debates over the value of psychedelic drugs as short-cuts to mystical experience (Huxley, Zaehner), and the claim that all religions originate from drug-cults (Wasson). He looks too at the 'guru culture', the spread of movements like ISKCON and the popularity of Maharishi Mahesh Yogi's school of transcendental meditation. The tone of his account is 'critical and debunking', but is intended as a preliminary to a discussion of what has lasting worth and contemporary value in the religious doctrines of the East. For, he comments, 'as regards to turning East, there is always . . . a distinction between how not to do it and how to do it' (23-2). That leads into Matilal's analysis of Indian philosophy of religion. Concepts which had been 'reinterpreted' by the leaders of the new movements are here examined with reference to their proper textual context. Matilal discusses the central ideas in Indian soteriology (a term he is willing to use in the Indian context with certain qualifications; see 17-1). He isolates a commitment to the 'thesis of universal suffering (*duḥkha*)' as a trademark of Indian religious belief. Rejecting the psychologistic reading of this thesis, which make Indian religions pessimistic, he instead interprets the thesis as asserting that ordinary life-experience, when reflected on in a certain way, lacks value or significance (25-2, 26-2). Another trademark, however, is that there is a separate and higher mode of experience, *nirvāṇa*, a cessation of suffering and, perhaps, a transcendental value. Matilal argues that the thesis of universal suffering generates an Indian version of the problem of evil, in which the fact of suffering is seen as incompatible with a belief in God's omnipotence and benevolence (24-2), and he goes on to consider Śaṃkara's attempt to resolve the problem, and so to the connection between theodicy and the *karma* hypothesis (28-2, 29-2). If the problem of evil was not regarded by Indian theologians as a major difficulty, it is because God was not typically conceived of as absolutely omnipotent; His powers are circumscribed by the laws of *karma* or retributive moral causation. In Matilal's view the *karma* doctrine underwent, over the course of its development, a *volte face*, when, having originally been propounded to oppose the fatalism of the Ājīvikas and to encourage a kind of moral responsibility, it later degenerated into a doctrine of rigid determinism.

When Tagore spoke of the 'surplus in man', he had in mind our capacity to question and transcend our own values, and eventually to reach the dignity that comes with self-understanding. Matilal had a deep intellectual respect for Tagore's humanism, and suggests (12-1) that 'it may be necessary to revive, within modern Western analytical philosophy circles, the old classical Indian or . . . 'premodern' concern for the dignity of human nature . . . making the 'Surplus in Man' more visible to us in our perception of the self'. This, he says, is the context in which analysis and understanding of classical Indian theories about the sense of self have their true significance. I would generalize his remark a little, and conclude by saying that central to much of his philosophical programme is Matilal's conviction that, with a better understanding of 'premodern' traditions, there comes too a clearer understanding of the importance of old concepts like those of 'human dignity', 'duty' and 'rational self-wisdom'. In the same essay, Tagore likened the cultures of the world to several mountain peaks 'having different altitude, temperature, flora and fauna, and yet belonging to the same chain of hills'. There are, he says, 'no absolute barriers of communication' between different cultures, because in each case 'their foundation is the same' (1920, p. 34). Matilal would have agreed wholeheartedly with these sentiments, and confirmed in his scholarship and erudition what Tagore had earlier, and indeed at a time of enormous cultural confrontation and upheaval, already discerned.

JONARDON GANERI

NOTES AND REFERENCES

Brockington, John (1998), *The Sanskrit Epics* (Leiden: E.J. Brill).

Mohanty, J.N. (1986), 'A Conversation of Mankind', Review of B.K. Matilal, *Perception: An Essay on Classical Indian Theories of Knowledge*, *Times Literary Supplement*, 10 October 1986.

Mohanty, J.N. (1993), 'On Interpreting Indian Philosophy: Some Problems and Concerns', in P. Bilimoria (ed.), *Essays on Indian Philosophy* (Delhi: Oxford University Press), pp. 207–19.

Price, H.H. (1955), 'The Present Relations between Eastern and Western Philosophy', *The Hibbert Journal*, vol. liii, pp. 222–9.

Schwab, Raymond (1950), *The Oriental Renaissance: Europe's Rediscovery of India and the East, 1680–1880.* Translated by G. Patterson-Black and V. Reinking, foreword by E.W. Said (New York: Columbia University Press, 1984).

Sen, Amartya (1992), 'Address' delivered on the occasion of a Commemoration of Bimal Krishna Matilal at All Souls College, Oxford, 6 June 1992.

Tagore, Rabindranath (1920), 'The Surplus in Man', in *The Religion of Man* (Oxford: Oxford University Press), pp. 31–9.

The Provenance of the Essays

ARTICLES INCLUDED IN THESE VOLUMES

Many of the essays collected here have been published before. I should like to thank the respective copyright-holders, for their permission to reproduce the articles. The details of publication are as follows:

1-1. 'Mysticism and Reality: Ineffability', *Journal of Indian Philosophy*,3, 1975, pp. 217–52.

2-1. *The Logical Illumination of Indian Mysticism.* Inaugural Address, University of Oxford, Clarendon Press. 1977.

3-1. 'The Ineffable', in H. Coward (ed.), *Language in Indian Philosophy and Religion.* Studies in Religion, supplement 5. Wilfred Laurier University Press, Ontario. 1978, pp. 55–62.

4-1. 'Scepticism and Mysticism', *Journal of the American Oriental Society* (*Ingalls Felicitation volume*), 105, 1985, pp. 479–84.

7-1. 'Awareness and Meaning in Navya-Nyāya', in B.K. Matilal and J.L. Shaw (eds), *Analytical Philosophy in Comparative Perspective*, Dordrecht: Reidel, 1985, pp. 373–92.

8-1. 'On the Theory of Numbers and the *Paryāpti* Relation', *The Journal of the Asiatic Society*, 27, 1987, pp. 13–21.

10-1. 'Knowledge, Truth and *Pramātva*', in Daya Krishna and K.L. Sharma (eds), *The Philosophy of J.N. Mohanty*, New Delhi: Indian Council of Philosophical Research, 1991, pp. 169–82.

11-1. 'Understanding, Knowing and Justification', in B.K. Matilal and A. Chakrabarti (eds), *Knowing from Words: Western and Indian Philosophical Analysis of Understanding and Testimony* (Dordrecht: Kluwer), 1994, pp. 347–66.

12-1. 'A Realist View of Perception', P.K. Sen and R.R. Verma (eds), *The Philosophy of P.F. Strawson*, New Delhi: Indian Council of Philosophical Research, 1995, pp. 305–26.

13-1. 'A Critique of the Mādhyamika Position', in M. Sprung (ed.), *The Problem of Two Truths in Buddhism and Vedānta*, Dordrecht: Reidel, 1973, pp. 54–63.

14-1. 'Nyāya Critique of the Buddhist Doctrine of Non-Soul', *Journal of Indian Philosophy*, 17, 1989, pp. 61–79. Reprinted in Augustine Thottakara (ed.), *Self and Consciousness: Indian Interpretations*, Centre of Indian and Inter-religious Studies, Rome (Bangalore: Dharmaram Publications), 1989, pp. 173–92.

15-1. '*Apoha*: Diṅnāga as Interpreted by Uddyotakara', *Indian Journal of Buddhist Studies*, 1, 1989, pp. 53–60, Part 1.

16-1. 'Is *Prasaṅga* a Form of Deconstruction?', *Journal of Indian Philosophy* 20, 1992, pp. 345–62. Contains the text of 'Mādhyamika', *Annals of the Bhandarkar Oriental Research Institute*, 68 (R.G. Bhandarkar 150th Birth Anniversary volume), 1987, pp. 215–24.

18-1. 'The Perception of the Self in Indian Tradition', R.T. Ames (ed.), *Self as Person in Asian Theory and Practice*, New York: SUNY Press. 1994, pp. 279–96.

19-1. 'Some Comments of Patanjali under 1.2.64', in S.D. Joshi and S.D. Laddu (eds), *Proceedings of the International Seminar on Studies in the Aṣṭādhyāyī of Pāṇini*. Pune: University of Poona, 1983, pp. 119–26.

20-1. 'On the Notion of the Locative in Sanskrit', *Indian Journal of Linguistics* (*Praci-Bhasa-Vijnan*) 10, 1983, pp. 160–8.

23-1. 'Indian Philosophy: Is There a Problem Today?' in S.S. Rama Rao Pappu and R. Puligandla (eds), *Indian Philosophy: Past and Future*, Motilal Banarsidass, 1982, pp. 253–9.

24-1. 'On the Concept of Philosophy in India', delivered under the title 'Pramāṇa as evidence,' to the 32nd International Congress for Asian and North African Studies, Hamburg 1986 (abstract in *Zeitschrift der Deutschen Morgenländischen Gesellschaft*, supplement 9, 1992). Reprinted in *Philosophical Essays: Anantalal Thakur Felicitation Volume*, Calcutta: Sanskrit Pustak Bhandar, 1987, pp. 190–8.

25-1. 'On Dogmas of Orientalism', in K.K. Dasgupta, P.K. Bhattacharya, and R.D. Choudhury (eds), *Sraddhanjali: Studies in Ancient Indian History, D.C. Sircar Commemoration Volume*, Delhi: Sundeep Prakashan 1988, pp. 15–21.

26-1. 'Ideas and Values in Radhakrishnan's Thought', in G. Parthasarathi and D.P. Chattopadhyaya (eds), *Radhakrishnan Centenary Volume*, Delhi: OUP, 1989, pp. 20–9.

27-1. 'Indian Without Mystification: Comments on Nussbaum and Sen', presented at a conference entitled 'Development and Technological Transformation in Traditional Societies: Alternative Approaches', United Nations University, World Institute for Development Economics Research (WIDER), Helsinki, 4–7 August 1986.

28-1. 'Images of India: Perceptions and Problems', in M. Chatterjee (ed.), *The Philosophy of Nikunja Vihari Banerjee*. Delhi: Indian Council of Philosophical Research, 1990, pp. 1–15. A shorter version is reprinted in B. Chatterjee (ed.), *Bankimchandra Chatterjee: Perceptions and Problems*, New Delhi: Sahitya Akademi, 1994, pp. 242–5. Parts of the paper are also in the *Oxford Majlis Society Commemoration Volume*, 1987.

30-1. 'Radhakrishnan and the Problem of Modernity in Indian Philosophy', in S.S. Ram Rao Pappu (ed.), *New Essays on the Philosophy of Sarvepalli Radhakrishnan*, Delhi: Sri Satguru Publ., 1995, pp. 55–63.

1-2. 'Moral Dilemmas and Religious Dogmas', *Bulletin of the Rama Krishna Mission Institute of Culture*, 34, 1983, pp. 243–50. A summary of six lectures given at the Rama Krishna Mission Institute of Culture in 1982 as the Malatmala-Bankubehari Memorial Lectures.

2-2. 'Sri Ramakrishna: Simplicity with Profundity', *Bulletin of the Ramakrishna Mission Institute of Culture*, 38, 1987, pp. 27–30. A lecture delivered on Sri Ramakrishna's 150th Birth Anniversary.

3-2. 'Moral Dilemmas: Insights from Indian Epics', in B.K. Matilal (ed.), *Moral Dilemmas in the Mahābhārata*, Shimla: Indian Institute of Advanced Study, 1989, pp. 1–9.

5-2. 'Dharma and Rationality', in Shlomo Biderman and Ben-Ami Scharfstein (eds), *Rationality in Question: On Eastern and Western Views of Rationality*, Leiden: E.J. Brill, 1989, pp. 191–216.

7-2. 'Rāma's Moral Decisions', *The Adyar Library Bulletin* 44–5, 1980, pp. 344–51.

8-2. 'Kṛṣṇa: In Defence of a Devious Divinity', in A. Sharma (ed.), *Essays in the Mahābhārata*, Leiden: E.J. Brill, 1991, pp. 401–18.

11-2. 'Caste, Karma and the *Gītā*', in Roy W. Perrett (ed.), *Indian Philosophy of Religion*, Dordrecht: Kluwer, 1989, pp. 195–202.

14-2. 'The Problem of Inter-Faith Studies', in T.A. Aykara (ed.), *Meeting of Religions: New Orientations and Perspectives*, Bangalore:

Dharmaram Publications, 1978, pp. 1-6. Reprinted in *Sophia* 34, 1995, pp. 167–72.

15-2. 'Towards Defining Religion in the Indian Context', in T.A. Aykara (ed.), *Meeting of Religions: New Orientations and Perspectives*, Bangalore: Dharmaram Publications, 1978, pp. 31–41.

17-2. 'Between Peace and Deterrence', in E. Kaye (ed.), *Peace Studies: The Hard Questions*, Oxford Peace Lectures 1984–5, Rex Collins, London, 1987, pp. 59–82.

18-2. 'Ethical Relativism and Confrontation of Cultures', in M. Krausz (ed.) *Relativism: Interpretation and Confrontation*. Notre Dame: University of Notre Dame Press, 1989, pp. 339–62. Revised version of 'Confrontation of Cultures', *S.G. Deuskar Lectures on Indian History and Culture*, Centre for Studies in Social Sciences, Calcutta, 1986.

19-2. 'Pluralism, Relativism and Interaction Between Cultures', in E. Deutsch (ed.), *Culture and Modernity: East-West Philosophical Perspectives*, Honolulu: University of Hawaii Press, 1991, pp. 141–60.

24-2. 'On Omnipotence', *Our Heritage*, vol. xxviii, 1980, pp. 3–20. Partly reprinted as 'On God's Omnipotence,' in *Bulletin of the Rama Krishna Mission Institute of Culture*, 33, 1982, pp. 3–7.

26-2. 'On the University of Suffering', in K.N. Tiwari (ed.), *Suffering: Indian Perspectives*, Delhi: Motilal Banarsidass, 1986, pp. 12–22.

29-2. 'A Note on Śaṃkara's Theodicy', *Journal of Indian Philosophy* 20, 1992, pp. 363–76.

INDEX TO THE PAPERS IN *LOGIC, LANGUAGE AND REALITY*

Many of Matilal's pre-1985 articles are reprinted in his earlier collection, *Logic, Language and Reality: An Introduction to Indian Philosophical Studies* (Delhi: Motilal Banarsidass, 1985). Unfortunately, there is no indication there of the provenance of the sections. I list the original sources here.

§1.1 'Aristotle and the Question of his Influence on Indian Logic', *Proceedings of a Round Table Conference* (*UNESCO celebration of the 2500th anniversary of Aristotle*), Paris, 1979.

§1.2 'Debate and Dialectic in Ancient India', *Philosophical Essays: Prof. Anantalal Thakur Felicitation Volume*, Calcutta: Sanskrit Pustak Bhandar, 1987, pp. 53–66. This article also appears in

Perception as §§3.3–3.4, and in *The Character of Logic in India*, as §1.1.

§1.3 'The Doctrine of *Nyāyābhāsa*', *The Calcutta Review*, 152, 1959, pp. 69–73.

§1.5 'A note on the Nyāya fallacy *sādhyamasama* and *petitio principii*', *Journal of Indian Philosophy*, 2, 1974, pp. 211–24.

§1.6 'Diṅnāga's remarks on the concept of *anumeya*', *Journal of the Ganganatha Jha Research Institute*, 24 (Umesha Mishra Commemoration Volume), 1968, pp. 151–9.

§1.7 'Buddhist Logic and Epistemology' in J.D.G. Evans and B.K. Matilal (eds), *Buddhist Logic and Epistemology: Studies in the Buddhist Analysis of Inference and Language*, Dordrecht: Reidel, 1985, pp. 1–30. This article also appears in *The Character of Logic in India*, as chapter 4.

§2.1 'A Discourse on Self-Contradictory Terms', *The Calcutta Review*, 158, 1961, pp. 10–16.

§2.2 'Reference and Existence in Nyāya and Buddhism', *Journal of Indian Philosophy*, 1, 1970, pp. 83–110. This article also appears in *Epistemology, Logic and Grammar*, as chapter 4.

§2.3 'On the Navya-Nyāya logic of property and location', in *Proceedings of the 1975 International Symposium of Multiple-valued Logic*, Bloomington: Indiana University, pp. 450–61.

§2.4 'Gaṅgeśa on the Concept of Universal property (*kevalānvayin*)', *Philosophy East and West* 18, 1968, pp. 151–61. Reprinted in *The Character of Logic in India*, as part of chapter 7, pp. 143–68.

§2.5 'Review of C. Goekoop, *The Logic of Invariable Concomitance in the Tattvacintāmaṇi: Gaṅgeśa's Anumitinirūpaṇa and Vyāptivāda*', *Journal of the American Oriental Society*, vol. 92, no. 1, 1972, pp. 169–73.

§2.6 'Double Negation in Navya-Nyāya', M. Nagatomi et al. (eds), *Sanskrit and Indian Studies: Essays in Honour of Daniel H.H. Ingalls*, 1980, pp. 1–10.

§2.7 'A Note on the Difference of Difference', in G. Bhattacharya et al. (eds), *A Corpus of Indian Studies: Essays in Honour of Gaurinath Sastri*, Calcutta, 1980, pp. 69–78.

§2.8 'The Intensional Character of *lakṣaṇa* and *saṃkara* in Navya-Nyāya', *Indo-Iranian Journal* 8,1964, pp. 85–95.

§3.1 'Indian Theories of Truth and Knowledge (review of J.N. Mohanty's *Gaṅgeśa's Theory of Truth*)', *Philosophy East and West*, 18, 1968, pp. 321–33.

§3.2 'Error and Truth—Classical Indian Theories', *Philosophy East and West*, 31, 1981, pp. 215–24.

§3.3 'A Critique of Buddhist Idealism', in L. Cousins, A. Kunst and R. Norman (eds), *Buddhist Studies in Honour of I.B. Horner*, Dordrecht: Reidel. 1974, pp. 139–69.

§3.4 'Memory', in D. Malvania et al. (eds), *Studies in Indian Philosophy: A Memorial Volume in Honour of Pandit Sukhlalji Sanghavi*, Ahmedabad, 1981, pp. 125–34.

§4.1 'Ontological Problems in Nyāya, Buddhism and Jainism: A Comparative Study', *Journal of Indian Philosophy*, 5, 1977, pp. 91–106.

§4.2 'Causality in the Nyāya-Vaiśeṣika school', *Philosophy East and West*, 25, 1975, pp. 41–8.

§4.3 'A Note on the Jaina Conception of Substance', *Sambodhi*, 5, 1976, pp. 3–12.

§4.4 'Saptabhaṅgī', in J.N. Mohanty and S.P. Banerjee (eds), *Self, Knowledge and Freedom: Essays for Kalidas Bhattacharya*, Calcutta: World Press, 1978, pp. 159–72.

§4.6 'Ignorance or Misconception? A Note on *avidyā* in Buddhism', in S. Balasooriya et al. (eds), *Buddhist Studies in Honour of W. Rahula*, London: Gordon Fraser, 1980, pp. 154–64.

§4.7 (pp. 333–46): 'Ālayavijñāna, Transmigration and Absolutism', *Journal of Oriental Research* (Madras), 40–1, 1970–1, pp. 151–66. Reprinted in S. Janaki (ed.), *M. Kuppuswami Sastri Birth Centenary Volume*, Madras 1981.

§4.7 (pp. 346–51): 'The Enigmas of Buddhism: *duḥkha* and *nirvāṇa*', *Journal of Dharma* 2, 1977, pp. 302–6.

§4.8 (pp. 351–62): 'Transmigration and the Causal Chain in Nyāya and Buddhism', in R.C. Amore (ed.), *Developments in Buddhist Thought: Canadian Contributions to Buddhist Studies*, 1979, pp. 83–92.

§4.8 (pp. 362–78): 'Karma: A Metaphysical Hypothesis in Moral Causation', in T.M.P. Mahadevan et al. (eds), *Contemporary Indian Philosophers of History*, Calcutta, 1977, pp. 233–47.

§5.1 'The Doctrine of *karaṇa* in Grammar and Logic', *Journal of the Ganganatha Jha Research Institute*, 17, 1960–1, pp. 63–9.

§5.2 'The Notion of Substance and Quality in Ancient Indian Grammar', *Acta et Commentationes Universitatis Tartuensis* (Finland), II, 1973, 384–405.

§5.3 'Jagadīśa's Classification of Grammatical Categories', in R.N. Dandekar et al. (ed.), *Sanskrit and Indological Studies: Dr V. Raghavan Felicitation Volume*, Delhi: Motilal Banarsidass, 1975, pp. 221–9.

§5.4 'Indian Theorists on the Nature of the Sentence (*vākya*)', *Foundation of Language*, 2, 1966, pp. 377–93.

§5.5 'Grammaticality and Meaningfulness', in S.D. Joshi (ed.), *Amṛtadhārā: Prof. R.N. Dandekar Felicitation Volume*, 1984, pp. 263–71.

INDEX TO PAPERS PUBLISHED IN
THE WORD AND THE WORLD

Some well-known articles are reprinted as chapters in Matilal's *The Word and the World: India's Contribution to the Study of Language* (Delhi: Oxford University Press, 1990). They are as follows.

Chapter 5: 'Bhavānanda on "What is a *kāraka*"', in M. Deshpande et al. (eds), *S.D. Joshi Felicitation Volume*, Poona.

Chapter 6: '*Śābdabodha* and the Problem of Knowledge Representation in Sanskrit', *Journal of Indian Philosophy*, 16, 1988, pp. 107–22.

Chapter 10: 'The Context Principle and Some Indian Controversies Over Meaning', co-written with P.K. Sen, *Mind*, 1988, pp. 73–97.

Chapter 12: 'On Bhartṛhari's Philosophical Insight', in B.K. Matilal and P. Bilimoria (eds), *Sanskrit and Related Studies: Contemporary Researches and Reflections*, Delhi: Sri Satguru Publications, 1990, pp. 3–13.

Appendix 1: 'Mysticism and Ineffability: Some Problems of Indian Logic and Language', in B.S. Alton (ed.), *Toronto Studies in Religion*, New York: Peter Lang, 1988, pp. 115–24.

OTHER ARTICLES

The article 'Dharmakīrti and the Universally Negative Inference', in Ernest Stenkellner (ed.), *Studies in the Buddhist Epistemological Tradition: Proceedings of the Second International Dharmakīrti Conference*, Vienna (Vienna: Verlag der Oesterreichischen Akademie der Wissenschaften, 1991, pp. 161–18), is reprinted in *The Character of Logic in India*, 1998, pp. 118–26. A slightly abbreviated version of the article 'Buddhist Logic and Epistemology', in Bimal K. Matilal and Robert D. Evans (eds), *Buddhist Logic and Epistemology: Studies in the Buddhist Analysis of Inference and Language* (Dordrecht: Reidel, 1986), pp. 1–31, is also reprinted there, pp. 88–105.

None of the articles Matilal wrote as encyclopedia entries are included in *Philosophy, Culture and Religion.* 'Indian Philosophy', in J.R. Burr (ed.), *Handbook of World Philosophy: Contemporary Developments Since 1945* (Westport: Greenwood Press, 1980, pp. 437–70), is a useful survey of the secondary literature in Indian philosophy between 1950 and 1980. Another encyclopedia article is 'Jainism', *World Encyclopedia of Peace* (Oxford: Permagon Press, 1987, pp. 495–8). There are entries too in Longman's *Encyclopedia of Religion* (New York: Columbia University Press, 1989); and in A.J. Ayer and J. O'Grady (eds), *A Dictionary of Philosophical Quotations* (Oxford: Blackwell, 1994). Four other published articles are not included here, since their interest is mainly biographical: 'Dialectical Materialism Viewed through an Indian Eye', *The Calcutta Review* (145, 1957, pp. 10–14; Matilal's first published piece!); 'On Marxist Dialectics: Comments on Hao Wang's Article', *Philosophy East and West* (1974, pp. 321–8); 'Religion as the Principle of Unity in a Global Community', in I. Nagami (ed.), *Proceedings of the First International Conference of Scientists and Religious Leaders on Shaping the Future of Mankind*, Kyoto, 1978, Kyo Bun Kwan, Tokyo, 1979, pp. 103–10; 'The Surplus in Man', in *Philosophical Papers* (Department of Philosophy, University of North Bengal, vol. 2, 1987, pp. 1–7).

PART I
Scepticism and Mysticism

1
Mysticism and Reality: Ineffability

Wherefrom words turn back,
Along with the mind, without reaching
The bliss of Brahman, (but) he who knows
Fears nothing at any time.

(2.4, Tr. E.H. Hume)

This is how the *Taittirīya Upaniṣad* describes the bliss of Brahman as something indescribable in words. An echo of the same idea is found in the *Katha Upaniṣad*: 5.14:

'This is it'—thus they recognize
The highest happiness that is ineffable.

The point is that the peak experience in Brahman realization, the supreme joy or happiness, is something that cannot be put into words. The mystical consciousness is an ecstatic feeling that is ineffable.

The ineffability of mystical experience or mysticism is a doctrine which seems to be unanimously accepted by most modern writers on mysticism. William James (1902) in his important study of religion and mysticism, noted four distinctive marks of any 'mystical' experience, the first and the most important of which was ineffability. He called it 'the handiest of the marks' by which one could classify a state of mind as mystical. The four common characteristics noted by James were: (1) Ineffability, (2) Noetic Quality, which James explained as the experiencer's feeling that the mystical experience is a deeper insight into truth and an authority on truth, (3) Transiency, and (4) Passivity (pp. 292–4).

James thought that the first two characters were all important for they would allow one to classify an experience as mystical. For the present, we should concentrate only on the first character, ineffability. D.T. Suzuki mentioned some common characters of *satori* in Zen Buddhism such as 'irrationality, inexplicability and incommunicability'. By these expressions, most probably, he wanted to carry the same sense as ineffability.

W.T. Stace (1960) has dealt at some length with the notion of ineffability of mystical experience. He has argued that this alleged ineffability of the mystical experience need not be taken seriously, for the mystics, in his opinion, had generally mistaken the 'paradoxicality' of mysticism as ineffability. Stace is one of the few modern philosophers who have tried to give a philosophic justification of mysticism and have examined its alleged ineffability. Stace's book has been influential. Thus, for example, modern researchers on the psychology of drug experience like W.N. Pahnke (1967) and A. Deikman (1967) have mainly depended upon Stace for their exploration and categorization of LSD-induced mystical experience. But unfortunately, Stace misstated the problem of mysticism in general and misinterpreted the problem of ineffability in particular. In fact, his criticism of the ineffability doctrine as well as justification of mysticism is wrong in more ways than I can hope to mention here. One specimen, I believe, will do.

Stace begins on the ineffability problem as follows: (p. 277)

> One of the best known facts about mystics is that they feel that language is inadequate, or even wholly useless, as a means of communicating their experiences or their insights to others. They say that what they experience is unutterable or ineffable. They use language but then declare that the words they have used do not say what they want to say and that all words as such are inherently incapable of doing so.

Stace then goes on to refer to the unanimity of different mystics like Eckhart, Plotinus, R.M. Bucke, J.A. Symonds and Arthur Koestler about the ineffability of mystical experience. Stace says that James only gave a name to the problem by calling it ineffability but did not offer any solution nor did he contribute anything to our understanding of the problem. But this is an unfair criticism of James, for he did comment on the problem briefly (pp. 292–3), from which one can easily see how he understood the ineffability question. He said:

> . . . mystical states are more like states of feeling than like states of intellect. No one can make clear to another who has never had a certain feeling, in what the quality or worth of it consists.

Before we proceed any further, I wish to underline a distinction which is often confused in the discussion of the problem of ineffability of mysticism. It is one thing to say of a particular piece of experience that it is effable or ineffable, and it is another thing to say that whatever is experienced in such an experience is ineffable. I suggest that in the context of 'mystical experience' a distinction between an experience and its 'content' is quite useful. True, such a distinction has been from the point of view of epistemology, often controversial among philosophers all over the world through the ages. But without entering into this philosophers all over the world through the ages. But without entering into this philosophic dispute, I would simply urge the reader to keep this distinction in mind. For such a distinction of experience and its content, I think, will facilitate our theoretical understanding of the situation in mysticism.

'Experience' is a word which needs some explanation. In philosophical and religious literature, the term is used sometimes ambiguously to include not only the immediate experience (sensation) or mediate experience (perception) but also feelings (pleasures and pains), i.e., subjective impressions disassociated from cognition or representation of objects. Although pleasure and pain are often regarded as 'qualities' of experience rather than the experience itself (for we say 'painful experience' or 'pleasurable experience'), the distinction of the quality and the qualified in this case does not make much sense, and 'a painful experience' is often regarded as a stylistic variation of 'a feeling of pain'. It is often said that pleasure and pain represent nothing actual in the objects, but reveal the state or condition of the subject. This observation is generally true. But it may open the door for idealism or subjectivism.

The Sanskrit term *vedanā*, under which pleasure and pain are subsumed in Buddhism, shares the same ambiguity as the English term 'feeling'. This bit of cross-cultural agreement is interesting, for it only shows the general feeling of ambivalence of ordinary people about the meaning of 'feeling'. Let us note also in this connection that some Buddhists (following of Diṅnāga) have argued against the Nyāya view by asserting that pleasure and pain are not distinguishable from the cognitive states that reveal them. (Cf. Srīdhara, 1963, ed., pp. 218–20).

It is true that our observation about 'experience' will be contested by a *monistic* philosopher who seeks to obliterate the usual distinction between subjectivity and objectivity. But to simplify our understanding at the moment let us talk from the point of view of a person who has not yet accepted monistic epistemology. At this level, it would be useful to remember that a piece of experience (for we shall call it a piece of experience) that is alleged to be mystical can be called ineffable without thereby implying that what is experienced or revealed in that experience is also ineffable. What is called the Ultimate Reality (be it God or Brahman or Suchness or Emptiness) is usually claimed to be revealed in a mystical experience. And this Ultimate Reality is said to be also ineffable because it cannot be properly described in words or characterized by description. We have thus to distinguish between 'ineffability' applied as a predicate to the mystical experience itself and 'ineffability' applied as a predicate to the Ultimate Reality. In the first case, it is the ineffability of a special kind of feeling, and hence comparable to the more *mundane* form of ineffability applied to a feeling of love, art experience or appreciation of music. In the second case, it is comparable to the ineffability of a *thing* (if the Ultimate Reality can be called a *thing*), which, for example, happens to be such a unique thing that our language apparatus cannot describe it adequately. It cannot be claimed always that for each unique thing in this world, there exists a proper description in a given language. Thus, from the point of view of a given language, we may reasonably contend that a particular thing is ineffable in that language. In this way, we can see that the second type of ineffability is also not an entirely unfamiliar notion.

When James called mysticism ineffable, he clearly meant the first kind of ineffability. For he described mystical experience as more like 'states of feeling,' i.e., emotive states comparable to love or a lover's state of mind. He argued (p. 293): 'One must have been in love one's self to understand a lover's state of mind.' This is what Stace has described as 'The Emotion Theory.' It is, according to Stace, one of the possible explanations of the alleged ineffability of the mystical experience. But Stace has found this theory to be inadequate (pp. 281–3).

It is well known that certain emotions in us run too deep for words. Emotions are, in fact, classifiable only under some general names as love, hate, hope, etc., but a particular emotive feeling with its peculiar shade or intensity may very well be such that words cannot describe it properly. The situation is comparable to the relation between colour words and the colour world. Admittedly we have a class of colour predicates to which we can also add probably a few more. But each shade (and tone) of a colour that artists produce or nature presents to us cannot always be adequately described in words. A particular emotion likewise shares the same fate. Probably in this sense Stace has claimed that emotions are more 'shadowy and elusive, less sharply outlined, than the conceptual structure of thought when these latter are clear and distinct.' And for this reason, he says, 'words tend to fit them poorly.' But emotions in this sense are no more shadowy and elusive than particular shades of colour. Thus, if some emotions are ineffable, so are some peculiar shades of colour.

A mystical experience can be regarded as a special kind of emotive feeling. For the usual expressions of the mystics are 'ecstasy', 'joy', 'rapture', 'bliss', etc. Thus it may very well be an emotive feeling. If this is so then it is not at all difficult to understand that some would be inclined to call it ineffable. This 'Emotion' Theory can, of course, be criticized and refuted (and I shall give below the criticism of a very distinguished Indian thinker, Ānandavardhana, of the ninth century AD). But I disagree with the way Stace has attempted to reject it.

Stace has argued that mystical experience is more like perception than emotion, and not only the hyperemotional mystics like St Theresa and Suso but also the calm and serene ones like Eckhart and the Buddha are reputed to have had mystical experiences. Thus, Stace thinks, the Emotion Theory is wrong because it over-emphasizes the role of emotion in the mystical consciousness and pays no attention to its other aspects. Stace also claims that both Eckhart and the Buddha found mystical consciousness ineffable.

But the above argument is wrong. First, it is not clear whether the Buddha himself claimed any mystical experience to be ineffable. So it is not fair to compare him with Meister Eckhart with regard to the role of emotion (or the lack of it) in their respective mystical experiences. In early Buddhism, *nirvāṇa*, which Stace claims to be 'invariably represented as beyond experience,' is usually described as *asaṃkhata* (*asaṃskṛta*) meaning 'unconditioned' or 'uncompounded' and as 'extinction' of thirst or craving (*tṛṣṇā*). It is not also clear whether the early (Theravādin) Buddhist meant by *nirvāṇa* anything like an experience that is ineffable. In fact, we have evidence to the contrary. (Such evidence will be cited below.)

Second, an experience can be unmoved by 'emotional storm' and still be ineffable in principle, if it happens to be a unique kind of experience. It is the uniqueness that accounts for its alleged ineffability, not its emotional association (or lack of it). Thus, it is better to settle for a multiplicity of grounds accounting for the alleged ineffability of mystical experiences. In one case it may be due to the emotional overburden, as in the case of love and art experience or aesthetic pleasure, and in another case it maybe due to the uniqueness of the experience itself. Thus, the idea of a common cause accounting for the alleged ineffability of all types of mystical experience, an idea which Stace has put forward in criticizing the so-called Emotion Theory—should be discarded.

The closest notion to mystical states in early Buddhism would be the talk of mental states developed in what is called *bhāvanā* 'meditation'.

Usually there are two types of meditation mentioned in the Buddhist canons, *samatha* (or *samādhi*) and *vipassanā* (or *vipaśyanā*). The first kind was prevalent in India before the time of the Buddha. The second kind was what the Buddha was supposed to have discovered. The first kind leads through extreme mental concentration to the highest mystical states such as the mind conforming to the sphere of Infinite Space, the sphere of Nothingness, or the sphere of Neither perception Nor non-perception. But all these mystical states, according to the Buddha, are conditioned by the mind. They are not 'unconditioned' (*a-saṃskṛta*), and not Truth. Nirvāṇa is Truth because *nirvāṇa* is unconditioned. This is described in the Buddha's dialogue with Pukkusati in the *Majjhimanikāya, Dhātuvibhaṅga-sutta* (No. 140). As the story is interesting, let me relate it briefly:

In a potter's shed the Buddha was staying overnight while he saw another young recluse who had arrived there earlier. They were not familiar with each other. So the Buddha thought to himself: Pleasant are the ways of this young man. Let me ask him about his mission. So the Buddha asked: 'O bhikkhu, in whose name have you left home? Who is your master? Whose doctrine do you admire?'

'O friend,' answered the young man, 'there is the recluse Gotama, a Śākyan descendant, who left the Śākya family to become a recluse. He has a high reputation as an Arhant, a Fully-enlightened One. In the name of that Blessed One I have become a recluse. He is my Master. I admire his doctrine.'

'Where does that Blessed One, the Arhant, the Fully-enlightened One live at the present moment?'

'In the country to the north, friend, there is a city called Savatthi. It is there that the Blessed One, the Arhant, the Fully-enlightened One, is living now.'

'Have you seen him, that Blessed One? Would you recognize him if you saw him?'

'I have never seen that Blessed One. Nor should I recognize him if I saw him.'

The Buddha realized that the young man had left home in order to become a monk under him. But without divulging his own identity, he said, 'O bhikkhu, I will teach you the doctrine. Listen and pay attention. I will speak.'

'Very well, friend,' the young man answered.

Then the Buddha delivered a remarkable discourse, in the quiet night of the potter's shed, about the Truth:

'A man is composed of six elements—solidity, fluidity, heat, motion, space and consciousness. He analyses them and finds that none of them can be really said 'mine' or 'my self'. He sees how consciousness appears and disappears. Therefore, through this knowledge his mind becomes detached. Detachment gives him a pure spiritual equanimity (*upekkhā*), which he directs towards the attainment of any high spiritual (mystical) state. But then he thinks: 'If I focus this purified and cleansed equanimity on the sphere of Infinite Space and develop a mind conforming thereto, that will be mind-conditioned (a mental creation). If I focus this purified and cleansed equanimity on the sphere of Infinite Consciousness . . . or on the sphere of Nothingness . . . or on the sphere of Neither perception Nor non-perception, and develop a mind conforming thereto, that will also be mind-conditioned.' (But *nirvāṇa* is unconditioned, *asaṃkhata*.) Then that man neither creates anything mentally nor wills continuity and becoming (*bhava*) and non-becoming (*vi-bhava*). He does not construct, does not cling to anything in this world. He is completely calmed, and . . . knows: Finished is birth, lived is pure life, what should be done is done, nothing more is left to be done. At this stage, when he experiences a pleasant, unpleasant or neutral sensation, he sees it as impermanent, and knows that it does not bind him. He knows that all those sensations will be pacified with the dissolution of the body, just as the flame of a lamp goes out when the oil and wick give out.'

It is clear from the above discourse that the Buddha regarded all mystic states developed through the form of meditation called *samatha* as mind-conditioned. They did not give to the Buddha insight in to the Ultimate Reality. He practiced them and found that these mystic states were 'mere happy living in this existence' and 'peaceful living, but nothing more' (Rahula, 1959, p. 68).

The Buddha is said to have discovered and preached the second type of meditation called *vipassanā*, which give *Insight* into the real nature of things leading to the complete liberation of mind—to the realization of the Ultimate Truth, Nirvāṇa. The system of this meditation is discussed in the Nikāyas. The above will be sufficient to show what the Buddha thought about the mystical trances and other mystical states. Since these states are said to be mind-conditioned, they cannot be regarded as beyond linguistic expression or ineffable. For it is conceded in Buddhism that whatever is mind-conditioned is also expressible in language. Even the *nirvāṇa* consciousness is not clearly stated to be ineffable in early Buddhism. It is only claimed to be an insight—the deepest insight in to the nature of things. What is, however, claimed to be beyond verbal knowledge or language in Buddhism, particularly in different forms of Mahāyāna Buddhism, is the so-called Ultimate Reality or *Tattva*. We should now recall that this is then the alleged ineffability of what is realized or grasped in the mystical experience rather than the experience itself. And I might add that Stace's explanation and criticism of the so-called Emotion Theory of ineffability blurs this distinction, among other things.

The Emotion Theory, however, can be criticized on just grounds, as I have indicated above. A lesson from Ānandavardhana, the great protagonist of the theory of Suggestion (*dhvani*) in literature and art experience, is in order here. Ānandavardhana's *Dhvānyāloka* is the most outstanding work in the history of Indian literary criticism. The key concept of all Sanskrit literary critics, the concept that sums up the essence of Sanskrit critical literature, is *rasa*, aesthetic rapture or imaginative experience. Ānandavardana was the first author to make *rasa* the pivotal point around which his discussion of literature (*kāvya*) revolves. He developed the idea of *rasa-dhvani*, according to which our aesthetic delight is multiplied thousand-fold when it is realized through the suggestivity of the poem.

That the aesthetic experience is very closely related to the mystical experience has been realized in India quite early in the history. The *Taittirīya Upaniṣad* used the term *rasa* to express the ultimate bliss, the Brahman experience (*Taittirīya*, II.7). Even Bharata (*c*. AD second century) has stated that the aesthetic experience derived from a poem or a drama is comparable to the mystical experience of a Yogin absorbed in meditation (*Nāṭyaśāstra*, VII.30). There is also a beautiful simile in the *Bṛhadāraṇyaka Upaniṣad* (IV.3.21), which compares mystical experience with climactic sexual pleasure:

> Just as a man, when closely embraced by a woman he loves, knows nothing of the outside world, nor even of the inner one, so also does the ego (*puruṣa*) know nothing of the outside or of the inner when it is closely embraced by pure consciousness, the Self.

Another text, the Vijñānabhairava, puts the same point as follows: (v.69):

> The pleasure which terminates in the infusion of the power of bliss in a person on the achievement of sexual intercourse—that pleasure is one's own pleasure on the realization of the essence of Brahman.

Abhinavagupta is well-known in the Indian tradition as a celebrated writer on aesthetics as well as an expert on Tantra, who frequently compared sexual experiences with ecstatic experiences and thus with the ultimate bliss (Masson and Patwardhan, 1969, pp. 24–34). In fact, the ultimate goal as expounded in the Buddhist Tantras (frequently called Mantrayāna or Vajrayāna which developed out of Mahāyāna Buddhism) as well as in Hindu theistic systems like Vaiṣṇavism and Śaivism is described in no uncertain terms as an exalted ecstasy the like of which is only to be found in the culmination of sexual or love experience. And it does not take a professional Freudian analyst to say that metaphors and similes in this connection are only outward garb and these religious systems probably achieved successful 'sublimation' of the basic instinctual drive for pleasure. Thus their connection with the aesthetic system described by Ānandavardhana and Abhinavagupta was not just incidental or irrelevant.

Art experience or aesthetic experience has been described by even such later writers as Viśvanātha (*c.* fourteenth century AD) as an exclusive and unique experience and 'genetically' comparable to the Brahman experience (*Sāhityadarpana*, III.2). In Sanskrit literary criticism, *rasa* carries a multitude of senses and hence a consistent translation becomes almost impossible. But it is clear that *rasa* always involves emotion. So the best way to describe it would be to call it aesthetic rapture or imaginative experience realized through a poem or a work of art derived from certain common emotive states of human mind such as the emotion of love, fear, anger, hate and humour. Incidentally, the *rasa* theory of art experience is a very important and momentous discovery of the Indian poeticians. Thus, modern writers have commented as follows (Masson and Patwardhan, 1969, p. 25):

> Judging Sanskrit literary criticism by standards of universal application, there can be no doubt that *rasa* is the greatest contribution that India has made to world literature.

Ānandavardhana first established the *rasa* theory and its suggestivity as the essence of poetry. He then proceeded to reject some wrong views about the nature of aesthetic experience. At the end of Uddyota I of the *Dhvānyāloka*, Ānandavardhana noted that many sincere critics admitted the importance of suggestivity of *rasa*, but said that it lay beyond the realm of speech, and one would do well to keep quiet about it:

> Those who say that the essence of *dhvani* (*rasa* experience) is patent only to the minds of sensitive readers, and (thus) ineffable, speak without having given careful thought to the matter. The general characteristics of *dhvani* have been given already (in the earlier part of the book), and the specific characteristics will be given in the sequel (in the later part of the book). If (one should still persist in claiming that) it is ineffable, then this would hold true of all (other) things (in the world). But if these people only mean this as a hyperbolic statement to show that the real nature of *dhvani* surpasses all other types of poetry, then they will be quite correct in what they say. (p. 162)

At the end of Uddyota III, Ānandavardhana came back to the issue of ineffability and indefinability of the aesthetic experience. He argued as follows:

> As for the definition of *dhvani* that someone has given, which is as follows: 'That is a case of *dhvani* when in poetry an indefinable beauty of certain words and meanings appears, that is only knowable by special experts, like the intrinsic

values (*jātyatva*) of certain jewels,' well, that definition is wrong and does not deserve to be considered here. For, the unique beauty of the phonetic forms of words consists in their property of being pleasant to the ears and absence of repetition. The unique beauty of meaningful words consists in clarity and suggestiveness. The uniqueness of the literal meanings is that they be clearly understood, that they be aimed at the suggested element, and that they be beautified by the suggested sense. Both types of qualities (i.e., uniqueness mentioned above) *can be spoken of* and have (in fact) been explained (by us) in some detail.

To assume some special qualities altogether different (from those already defined and explained by us) and to say that they are ineffable is simply the result of the breakdown of the power of discrimination, since *ineffability, in the sense that something is beyond the reach of all words, is impossible.* For in the last analysis, it is possible to speak of that which is (supposedly) ineffable by the word 'ineffable' itself. (My italics.)

As for what is some times said, namely that ineffability exists in the sense that it is the revelation of a thing (in consciousness) which is beyond the range of conceptual words expressing universals, this also cannot apply either to the charm of particular poems or to that of particular jewels. For, the properties of charming poems have in fact been explained by literary critics. In the case of particular jewels also, it is possible to fix a price for them on the basis of the appreciation of their generic features. However (we do admit that) in both cases the true worth (or nature) can only be known by particular experts. For only jewellers have real knowledge of gems and only sensitive critics can really appreciate the *rasa* of poems. How can anyone doubt this?

As for the well-known doctrine of the Buddhists (viz., the Dinnāga school) that all things are ineffable, we will deal with the views of the Buddhist in another book. We do not want to take up this subject here since to deal with a subject that belongs to another work would surely create boredom for the sensitive reader. (But we can say this much): Just as the Buddhists (in spite of their doctrine) are able to define perception, etc. (from the *vyavahāra* 'conventional' level), we can also do so in the case of *dhvani*. Therefore, since no other characteristic of *dhvani* stands to reason, and since *dhvani* is not identical with the literal meaning, the correct definition is the one we have given. Thus, it is said:

'It is no definition of *dhvani* to say that it is ineffable, since *dhvani* can be completely expounded. The correct definition of *dhvani* is the one already given.'

If the *rasa*-experience, despite its high emotional overtone, cannot be said to be ineffable, the religious/mystical experience, for the same reasons, cannot be described as ineffable. What Ānandavardhana says in order to criticize the contention of ineffability of the *rasa*-experience can be extrapolated to criticize the so-called 'Emotion' Theory about the ineffability of mystical experience. The usual function of a word applied to describe a thing (or an experience) is to classify it with similar things and to distinguish it from dissimilar things. Now a jeweller, in order to be able to evaluate or set an individual price on a particular jewel, must be able to classify it and distinguish its specific features. Thus, a jeweller who can evaluate a jewel can also describe the value of it in words. But if a mystic claims that his mystical experience is certainly valuable but it is ineffable, his position is like that of the jeweller who says that he can set a value on a particular jewel but cannot tell why he sets that particular value on that particular jewel. Or, we can say that the mystic is like a poet who has not uttered a word but claims to have written a very beautiful poem.

Stace mentions a second possible explanation of the alleged ineffability of mysticism, which he calls 'The Spiritual Blindness Theory'. Just as an experience of red cannot be communicated to a man born blind, mystical experience cannot be communicated through words to a non-mystic. This theory has been criticized by Stace. And he is probably right in doing so. I will skip here these rather trivial explanations of the alleged ineffability of mysticism and their equally trivial refutations by Stace.

A serious formulation of the ineffability of mysticism would concern the ineffability of the 'content' of mystical experience rather than the mystical experience itself. In other words, it is about the alleged ineffability of what we may call the Ultimate Reality, what true mystics assert to have experienced, although it may be named differently by different mystics, God, Brahman, Śūnyatā or Suchness. Let us now review Stace's own position on the problem of ineffability and examine what he calls a 'New theory'—a theory of his own (pp. 295–306).

Stace wants to distinguish here between ineffability as applied to the mystical experience *during* the experience itself and the same applied to the *remembered* mystical experience after the experience is over. He thinks that a confusion between these two 'has been disastrous' (p. 298). But this is, in our opinion, not an important distinction. For it is only in a trivial sense that a mystical experience cannot be called effable during the experience. A mystic may remain speechless during the experience much in the same way a lover may be speechless at the height of his emotion. This is, however, a recourse to 'The Emotion Theory' which Stace has already rejected. Thus it would be quite improper for Stace to emphasize that a mystical experience may be ineffable during the experience itself.

Stace concludes that the *remembered* mystical experience is speakable, for the mystics often talk about it. The notion of ineffability, he argues, is generated by the logical paradoxicality of the language used by mystics to describe the remembered experience. In their embarrassment, the mystics often call their experience ineffable. In Stace's own words, the mystic 'confuses the paradoxicality of mystical experience with ineffability' (p. 305).

As far as I can see, what Stace calls the *remembered* mystical experience could very well be equivalent to what I have called the 'content' of mystical experience. For a mystic usually tries to explain or express in language, at a later time, *what* he has experienced rather than the *experience itself*. The supposed paradoxicality, in that case, would apply to the 'content' of the mystical experience, i.e., the Ultimate Reality. Before I present my own critique of the doctrine of ineffability of mysticism, I wish to review another modern analysis of the 'ineffability' doctrine—that of Arthur Deikman, who has tried to present a psychological explanation of it with his concept of *deautomatization*. (Deikman, 1967).

Deikman contends that in our normal consciousness we work with the acquired, hierarchically organized psychic structures, with autonomic processes of perception and cognition. But mystical techniques like meditation or psychedelic drugs introduces a process which he calls 'deautomatization' (Deikman, 1967). It is the undoing of autonomic processes of perception and cognition 'resulting in, temporarily, a capacity for perception and cognition that is less efficient but potentially of wider range' (p. 58, 1967). Regarding the 'ineffability' problem, he proposes a psychological explanation by separating at least three types of mystical experience, all of which are claimed to be 'indescribable' (Deikman, 1967). I shall recount below Deikman's arguments.

The first type of mystical experience is based on primitive and infantile memories and related to fantasies of a pre-verbal or non-verbal sensory experience. This type of experience is usually explained by psychoanalysts as the 'oceanic feeling' (Freud, 1930). It is like the memory of the undifferentiated infantile ego state. In psychoanalytic terms, it is a regression to the early infant-mother symbiotic relationship, or more specifically the state of the union of infant and mother's breast. Now, since such an experience is a regression to a pre-verbal stage of experience, it is easy to see why it would be claimed to be ineffable.

The second type of mystical experience is claimed to be ineffable because it is 'too complex' or too out of the ordinary way to be verbalized. A typical example would be the drug induced-mystical states. A state like this can presumably be described as a very sudden expansion of the ordinary field of consciousness (as William James suggested, pp. 300–28), and hence the acquired language skill of the subject may for the time being be inadequate for expressing the experience.

The third type is called by Deikman as the 'trained-transcendent' mystical experience. Mystics like the author of *The Cloud of Unknowing*, and St. John of the Cross, fall, according to Deikman, into this category. Here the experience is claimed to be not blank or empty but intense, profound and positive—'vividly perceptual'. It is the experience which the mystics claim to be the 'ultimate goal of mystic path'.

We may easily understand the distinction between the first and the second types. But how is the first type to be distinguished from the third type? According to Deikman, the third type, if we believe in the 'phenomenological' accuracy of the mystics, 'does not include feeling of warmth, sweetness, visions, or any other elements of familiar sensory or intellectual experience' (p. 42). The said experience is claimed to be 'perceptual' but it lies so much outside of customary verbal or sensory reference that it becomes unidentifiable and ineffable. Deikman explains this type with his 'deautomatization' theory.

As far as I can see, the basis of the so-called 'phenomenological' distinction between the first type and the third type appears to be dubious. The motivation as well as the value-system internalized by the mystic is what seems to account for the so-called difference in the phenomenological descriptions of these experiences. There may be other psychological elements that account for the said difference in descriptions. Even Deikman is aware of the problem, for he says that 'the mystic,' in such cases (i.e., in the third type), 'is intensely *motivated* to *perceive* something' (p. 42, italics mine). And the mystic follows meditation or some such technique to obtain this state. Thus, if there are certain 'perceptual' capacities, as it is claimed, that we never attend to or utilize in our normal life, they are likely to appear under this condition. Besides, the mystic is already convinced about the ultimate goal of the mystical path and hence attaches highest moral value to the experience he obtains through his technique.

I hesitate to accept Deikman's distinction. That the first type of experience is more like a receptive feeling while the third type is claimed to be perceptual, should not make a great difference from the psychoanalytic point of view. There are mystics who prefer the first type, i.e., the complete absorption of the individuality in an undifferentiated consciousness. And these mystics would attach highest religious and moral values to such an experience. Atheist mystics however, prefer 'visions' to 'perceptual' experience of 'God'. And this is only a matter of taste.

As long as we are discussing the 'ineffability' problem, Deikman's emphasis on the 'perceptuality' of the third type of experience may point to another aspect of our problem. Most religious systems that recommend meditation as the best path to attain the Ultimate Reality describe the mystic revelation as a perceptual experience. We shall see presently that there is a sense in which one can say a perceptual experience is ineffable or unutterable in ordinary language (viz., Diṅnāga's theory of perception and mystical perception, see below). Such an experience is said to be inexpressible in language because the demand on language in such cases is that it expresses most adequately the uniqueness of the experience as well as of what is experienced.

Incidentally, Deikman's concluding remarks are worth quoting, for they are probably closer to the truth. 'Such an explanation (deautomatization) says nothing conclusive about the source of 'transcendent' stimuli. God or the Unconscious share equal possibilities here and one's interpretation will reflect one's presuppositions and beliefs' (p. 43).

So much for the alleged ineffability of the mystical experience itself. Let us now attend to the problem of the ineffability of the Ultimate Reality, the supposed 'content' of a true mystical experience. I shall try first to give the traditional Indian formulation of the 'Ineffability' doctrine—a philosophically, i.e., epistemologically, oriented doctrine, which is found primarily in Mahāyāna Buddhism and monistic Vedānta. A critique of this doctrine will be given at the end. Let us start with an imaginary dialogue between a mystic and a non-mystic:

MYSTIC: The true reality, the Essence, the Absolute, the pure Existence, the pure Consciousness, Emptiness, that is what I call the Ultimate Reality.

NON-MYSTIC: If you only would tell me somewhat plainly, what that means: the Ultimate Reality.

M: That I shall never succeed in doing. The plainest talk would be that it cannot be talked about. Is it not good enough for you?

N: It is not sober enough for me. Could it not be that there you have fallen into some kind of lofty rhapsodizing? Besides, you do talk about it when you call it the Ultimate Reality, and hence you would be able to indicate what it is you are talking about.

M: The problem is that I cannot actually say anything except uttering that phrase 'the Ultimate Reality'. One must try to think that to which this phrase points, that to which it can only point but which it cannot actually say.

N: What is a phrase for if it cannot *say* anything, if through it one cannot understand?

M: It is an innate difficulty, or a defeat, of our language that it cannot express what you are asking me to express.

(For a dialogue in a similar vein, see Constantine Brunner, 1968, pp. 341–2).

The above imaginary dialogue may very well have taken place between a Buddhist and a Naiyāyika in the Indian tradition. Whether the Buddha himself supported the ineffability doctrine or not, is not known. Evidence is not available to prove the point. But it is true that the Buddha was responsible for mobilizing what may be called a thorough-going 'de-personalization' of the philosophic language or discourse. Thus, he rejected terms like 'soul', 'self', 'person', or 'living being' (*ātman, pudgala, jīva* or *sattva*) as not meaning anything. Instead of posing meaningless questions such as 'who desires' or 'who acts' or 'who experiences' one should re-formulate them properly as 'depending on what desire arises' and so on (*Saṃyutta Nikāya*, II, 13). This might have led to the development, in later schools, of a distinction between what is ultimately real and what is merely conceptual (cf. *Prajñapti* school, A.K. Warder, 1970, p. 278), and finally to the distinction of two levels of truth—the ultimate or final truth (*paramārtha satya*) and the 'concealing' or conventional truth (*saṃvṛti satya*). When this tradition of the two levels of truth—a tradition that was not unknown in non-Buddhist schools (Matilal, 1973)—became well-established, it was generally contended that language deals with imagination (*vikalpa*) and concept. Conceptualization belongs to the conventional level. The Ultimate Reality cannot be described or expressed in words or language. The Ultimate Reality is beyond the realm of language, is ineffable. Words cannot express it although they may indicate it through indirection. Thus, any linguistic discourse on the Ultimate Reality should be understood in this indirect sense (although some discourses were, perhaps, *less* indirect than others, and there was thus the distinction between *nītārtha* and *neyārtha* in the Yogācāra school of Buddhism). Āryadeva explained the position as follows:

> Just as a *mleccha* (one speaking a foreign tongue) cannot be made to understand by any other language but his own, so also (ordinary) people cannot be made to understand by anything except the conventional language.

The *Laṅkāvatāra-sūtra* expresses the same position with a nice simile: (The Buddha says):

> Just as a king or merchant (at first) attracts his children with the help of beautiful clay animals for play, and then (at the right time) presents them with real animals, I attract similarly my disciples with various shadow characteristics of the dharmas, and then instruct them (when the right time comes) the *bhūtakoti*, which is to be experienced by each of them personally. (ed. Vaidya, p. 37)

This is the general Mahāyāna Buddhist position about the Ultimate Reality. Some modern scholars (viz., Murti, 1953) have surmised that the Buddha's approval of the 'ineffability' doctrine can be inferred from his classification in the *Nikāya*, of certain questions as *ṭhapanīya* 'to be set aside' or 'not to be answered' (*Aṅguttara Nikāya*, II.46). Sometimes these questions are called *avyākata*-questions, on which the Buddha refused to express an opinion. A good specimen of such questions is whether the Tathāgata exists after death or not (Jayatilleke, pp. 281–90). It appears that such questions are meaningless or unanswerable because any possible alternative answer will involve tacit assumption of a wrong viewpoint or a false position. The situation is comparable to such questions as 'When did you stop beating your wife?' The best way to tackle such a question is to refuse to answer it and maintain silence. This does not, however, lead to 'ineffability' doctrine as that doctrine was understood in late Buddhism. We have on the other hand a curious dialogue in *Majjhima Nikāya*, II.32, which seems to ridicule indirectly the 'ineffability' doctrine. I quote the dialogue below:

Buddha: What, Udayi, is your teacher's teaching?

Udayi: Our teacher's teaching is that this is the highest colour, this is the highest colour.

B: What is that colour?

U: That colour than which there is no other colour which is higher or better, is the highest colour.

B: What is that colour than which there is no colour higher or better?

U: That colour than which there is no other colour which is higher or better, is the highest colour.

B: You say that the highest colour is that than which there is no other colour, which is higher or better. But you do not specify that colour. It is like a person saying, 'I like and am in love with the "beauty queen" of this country' (cf. *imasmim janapade janapada-kalyāni*).

One can remove 'colour' from the above and substitute 'bliss' in its place, and then *the highest bliss*—the goal of mystical experience—can be similarly criticized *à la* Buddha. In other words, one can say that the Buddha in the above dialogue does not come out in favour of the 'ineffability' doctrine, i.e. ineffability of the ultimate goal of mystical experience. The Buddha seems to have been critical of such a doctrine. To consider the highest bliss or highest state of consciousness as the goal of mystical experience without *specifying* that state in words, is like being in love with the beauty queen of a country without having seen her at all!

Since the Ultimate is ineffable, silence would be the best way to teach it or instruct it. This need not be taken as a joke, for the Mahāyāna

Buddhist asserted such a position quite seriously. A verse ascribed to Nāgārjuna runs thus (G. Tucci, 1932, p. 314):

> Not a word was uttered by you, O Master, and (yet) all the disciples were refreshed (satisfied) by the *dharma*-shower.

Similar ideas about imparting instruction through silence are found in later non-Buddhist tradition too. The following verse is found in the *Dakṣināmūrtistotra*.

> How strange! Under the Banyan tree are old men. Their teacher is only a boy (a young man). His explanation consists in silence. Yet the disciples have been made free from doubts (through correct understanding).

We may mention in passing that the *Yogavāsiṣtha* (a popular text in India heavily influenced by Vedānta and Buddhism) also mentions that ultimately silence only remains (to relate itself to the Absolute) (VI B.83, 29).

In the Mahāyāna tradition, we find various formulations of the 'ineffability' doctrine. Let us quote from the *Prajñāpāramitā-sūtra* (E. Conze, tr., 1973):

> Chap. xxi, 20: 'As a magically created man, or one who has made his body invisible, cannot be defined by words, just so the Bodhisattva who courses in the doors to freedom can also not be defined by words.'
>
> Chap. xviii: 'Subhūti: It is wonderful to see the extent to which the Tathāgata has demonstrated the true nature of all these dharmas and yet one cannot properly talk about the true nature of all these dharmas. As I understand the meaning of the Tathāgata's teaching, evẹn all dharmas cannot be talked about, in any proper sense.
>
> Buddha: So it is, for one cannot properly express the emptiness of all dharmas in words.
>
> S: Can something have growth or diminution, if it is beyond all distinctive words?
>
> B: No, Subhūti . . .
>
> S: What is then the supreme enlightenment?
>
> B: It is Suchness.'

The *tathatā* or reality is repeatedly described in the Mahāyāna sutras as *anakṣara* 'without letters or words,' i.e., ineffable. In the *Lankāvatāra*, the Buddha is said to be saying (p. 37):

> But the 'Ultimate Reality,' O Mahāmati, is experienced by each enlightened individual and it is not within the domain of speech and conceptualization. Thus, conceptual construction does not express the Ultimate Reality.

In the Mādhyamika school, the 'ineffability' doctrine is expressed as follows. Nāgārjuna says (*Madhyamaka-kārikā*, 18.9) that the characteristic of *tattva* 'reality' (the Ultimate Reality) is 'free from conceptual construction' and non-diversified by discursive thought or language.' Again, in his comments on *nirvāṇa* (25.24), Nāgārjuna says that *nirvāṇa* is the cessation of *prapañca*. Candrakīrti gives several explanations of *prapañca*, one of which, he says, is speech. It is our speech or language that diversifies the un-differentiated reality and it is concerned with imaginative construction. Thus, Candrakīrti argues that *nirvāna* or the Ultimate Reality is beyond *prapañça* or linguistic construction. He quotes a passage from the *Tathāgata-gūhya-sūtra*, where it is said that the Tathāgata did neither utter a letter or word, nor does he utter now, nor will he utter in the future a single letter to instruct *nirvāṇa*. Why then do we seem to have so many instructions of the Buddha in the sūtras? Candrakīrti replies that they are not real but only what we, ordinary human beings, have constructed ourselves in our imagination, just as one constructs a separate world in one's dream. The Ultimate is, for Candrakīrti, *avacaḥ* 'beyond speech' and *anakṣara* 'beyond letters'. There is no dharma that can be spoken about.

In the Yogācāra school of Buddhism too, the Ultimate Reality is said to be ineffable because it is declared as completely devoid of the duality between the subject and the object, between 'apprehension' *grāhaka* and the 'apprehensible' *grāhya*—duality between words and the things they designate. This duality belongs to the conventional level of reality. The Ultimate Reality thus cannot be taught or talked about. Both the Yogācāra and the Mādhyamika argue, however, that the Ultimate Reality is known or revealed in the mystical experience, or apprehended through *prajñā* or the 'mystical insight' gained in the highest concentration of the mind. *Prajñā* is said to be 'seeing by way of not seeing' (cf. *a-darśana-yogena*). It is the way of understanding or apprehending the ineffable truth.

In the Pramāṇa school of Diṅnāga and Dharmakīrti, the 'ineffability' doctrine is formulated with the help of epistemology. Diṅnāga's epistemology or *pramāṇa* theory is based upon the crucial notion of *vikalpa* 'conceptual construction'—a notion which Bhartṛhari had shown before Diṅnāga to be the ground of speech or linguistic usage (Matilal, 1971, pp. 29–49). The notion of conceptual construction (or discursive language) signals, in Diṅnāga's system, the crucial distinction between cognitions which are mediated through concepts and words and cognitions which are immediate and direct, i.e., perception. In fact, Diṅnāga divides the world into two: the imaginative constructs or universals and the exclusive particulars or *svalakṣaṇa*. Perception or direct awareness is what grasps the exclusive particulars and what is completely untouched by conceptual construction or language. What is grasped in perception can never be expressed in language. In other words, the exclusive or unique particulars are unspeakable reals (as distinct from imaginative constructs), are ineffable. This amounts very closely to saying that what we directly experience cannot be talked about in language, and what we do talk about cannot be *directly* experienced and hence results from fictitious abstraction.

It may be pointed out also that the Ultimate Reality, in Diṅnāga's system, will tentatively be the exclusive particulars, which are simply individual and self-sufficient consciousness-moments. In the case of ordinary human beings, such perceptions are immediately followed by an influx of imaginative constructions and linguistic descriptions. This happens because of our congenital tendency to objectify fictions. But only the Yogins by their mystical power and meditation practice can put a stop to this influx of unreal concepts. They *see* reality as it is. They experience the Ultimate Reality in their Yogic perception, which is, in principle, beyond words and concepts.

In non-Buddhist tradition, Advaita Vedānta is the foremost to accept the 'ineffability' doctrine. We have seen the Upaniṣadic passages about the ineffability of the Brahman as well as Brahman experience. Yājñavalkya explained to Maitreyī in the Bṛhadāraṇyaka as follows:

> For where there is a duality, as it were, there one sees another; there one smells another; there one tastes another, there one speaks to another; there one hears another; there one thinks of another; there one touches another; one understands another. But where everything has become just one's own self, then whereby and whom would one see? then whereby and whom would one smell? then whereby and whom would one taste? then whereby and to whom would one speak? then whereby and whom would one hear? then whereby and of whom would one think? then whereby and whom would one touch? then whereby and whom would one understand? Whereby would one understand him by means of whom one understands this All? (R.E. Hume, tr., p. 147).

The moral of this teaching is, perhaps, that Brahman is the undifferentiated consciousness which is all-inclusive. It is the goal of mystical intuition—the 'uncuttable' whole, which cannot be expressed in words, for the use of a word implies duality or differentiation.

In the later Advaita tradition, Madhusūdana Sarasvatī has argued in favour of the ineffability of Brahman as follows: (pp. 784–7)

Brahman is without any dharma or characteristic, and unknowable (through our discursive thought). Hence Brahman is only *indicated* by such words (in the Scriptures) as 'the (ultimate) Bliss.' These words cannot *express* Brahman, for the cognitive ground for application of these words to denote Brahman does not exist.

Madhusūdana's elaborate discussion of the doctrine of ineffability is couched in the highly technical language of an Indian logician. It can be summarized as follows: The 'ground' for applying a word to denote an object is, according to the Indian semanticist, a quality or a property of that object. A denoting word can be said to be 'grounded' in the quality of the object it denotes (Matilal, 1971, pp. 106–22). Thus, an object COW is denoted by the word '(a) cow' because it has the quality *cow-ness*. But since Brahman lacks any quality, no word can be used to denote Brahman. In other words, Brahman is ineffable because it is devoid of all qualifications, all characteristics. Words like 'Brahman' and 'The Ultimate Reality' only *indicate* what is, in principle, ineffable.

We have seen thus different formulations of the 'ineffability' doctrine in the Indian tradition. One thing is, however, common to all of them. They all do not feel that they should refrain from talking about the 'ineffable' Ultimate Reality. In fact, this is no ground for embarrassment for them. First, they agree, all discourses about the Ultimate Reality are provisional. Besides, they all contend that such a discourse has a soteriological purpose to serve. There are indirect discourses by which people should be convinced. In other words, they all agree that their religious or philosophical discourse is only a game, but a worthwhile game or play leading to a goal. They even try to devise different acceptable means by which this GAME—i.e., their religio-philosophical discourse about the ineffable Ultimate Reality—should be effectively conducted. Broadly speaking, they resort to *three* such means. I shall describe them individually.

The first of these three methods is what is generally known as the method *via negativa*. This method in the Indian tradition goes as far back as Yājñavalkya in the *Bṛhadāraṇyaka Upaniṣad*, where the oft-quoted doctrine '*neti, neti*' ('not this, not that') was first propounded (III.9.26). Gauḍapāda commented on this doctrine as follows (*Āgamaśāstra*):

> The scripture, 'This is not, this is not', denies whatever is explained (about the Ultimate Reality), and thus reveals the truth that nothing originates, for (otherwise) origination would be incomprehensible.

Stated in simple language, the method consists in this: Although we cannot ascribe any predicate to the Ultimate Reality, we might very well say what the Ultimate Reality is not. Some Mādhyamika writers like

Bhāvaviveka used this method with the interesting stipulation that negation should be understood in this context as an extreme form of 'exclusion' negation. In Indian terminology, this is called 'denial of what could have been' (*prasajya pratiṣedha*, see Matilal, 1971, pp. 162–7).

Ordinarily, denial of a predicate or a property with regard to subject implies tacit acceptance of the *opposite* predicate or property. Thus, if we say that something is not *P* we should be prepared to accept some other property as applicable to that thing. But Bhāvaviveka develops the concept of a denial which means *just denial*—a denial which should not imply acceptance of a rival possibility. Thus, if the mystic says that the Ultimate Reality is not this, or not that, he is not prepared thereby to say what it is. The mystic cannot really say what the Ultimate Reality is because it is ineffable.

Diṅnāga developed his *apoha* 'exclusion' theory of word-meaning, which was based upon the same principle of negation. According to Diṅnāga, words express only imaginative constructs, universals, and the unique particulars, the ultimately reals, cannot be directly expressed by them. A word, when it is applied to a unique particular, can only mean the negation of what that particular thing is not, an *apoha* 'exclusion' of other possibilities. To put it another way, words cannot directly express the unique particular but can certainly point out to it through indirection, through negation. The meaning of a word is always 'a negation of other possibilities' *anyāpoha* (Matilal, 1971, pp. 39–46). Thus, the 'ineffability' doctrine is also vindicated by Diṅnāga's theory of 'exclusion' or *apoha*.

The second method used by the upholders of the 'ineffability' doctrine consists in bestowing contradictory attributes or predicates on the Ultimate Reality. This method is widely in use by the mystics of all countries and of all ages. To begin with, the early Upaniṣadic thinkers of India were champions of this method.

It moves, It moves not.
It is far, and it is near.
It is within all this,
And it is outside of all this. (*Īśa*, 5)

What that is, know as Being and Non-being
As the object of desire, higher than understanding,
As what is the best of creatures. (*Muṇḍaka* 2.2.1)

A slightly different method is found in the Mādhyamika dialectics, i.e., in the Mādhyamika doctrine of emptiness based upon the *denial* of the four-fold (sometimes two-fold) alternatives, e.g., Nāgārjuna says:

In the Instruction to Kātyāyana, the Glorious One refuted both 'it is' and 'it is not' by ascertaining (the true nature of) 'existence' and 'non-existence'. (*Mādhyamika-kārikā*, 15.7)

The existent things do neither originate from themselves, nor from something else, nor from both, nor from neither. (Ibid., 1.1)

Gauḍapāda used the same method:

That which is already existent does not come into being, and that which is non-existent does not also come into being; disputing thus the followers of the doctrine of non-dualism assert (the theory of) absolute non-becoming. (*Āgamaśāstra*, IV.4)

It is because of the use of this method by the mystics that mysticism is sometimes criticized as defying the laws of ordinary logic. The law that is supposed to have been defied by the mystics is the law of non-contradiction, which is roughly that a proposition and its contradiction cannot both be true together. The above method also tries to assign a *new* meaning to 'negation' or 'denial'. It is seen that both the mystics and their critics are equally emphatic in their claim that mysticism defies rationality. But the mystic considers this defiance a merit rather than a demerit or shortcoming. (To use the Sanskrit terminology, this defiance is considered a *bhūṣana* 'embellishment', not a *dūṣaṇa* 'fault'.) The logicians, on the other hand, tend to think of this defiance as a mark of irrationality, and therefore something deplorable. B. Russell has seen this situation as a 'conflict between two very different human impulses' (Russell, 1917, p. 1)—a conflict between what Russell has called 'the scientific impulse' and 'the mystical impulse.' This very feature is, I believe, the same as what W. T. Stace (and following him, W.N. Pahnke in 1967, p. 64) has called the 'essential paradoxicality' of mystical consciousness (Stace, 1960, p. 253).

Stace, in fact, is one of those who think that the defiance of logic by mysticism is only to be expected and that 'conscientious philosophers' should welcome this fact in view of the insight that they are supposed to derive from it about the true nature of logic. For one thing, Stace argues, the recognition of the paradoxicality of mystical consciousness as real shows that certain contemporary views about the philosophy of logic are simply dogmas and should better be rejected. One such dogma among contemporary philosophers, Stace thinks, is that no experience could ever conceivably contravene the law of logic. Another such related dogma, according to Stace, is that the laws of logic are only linguistic or verbal rules and say nothing about the world. Such dogmas, Stace recommends, should better be discarded in the light of the 'authentic' reports about mystical experience. Stace argues that only by discarding such 'dogmas' will we be in a position to distinguish between the areas of logic and non-logic—logic applying to our everyday world and also to other possible worlds where there is a multiplicity of objects and 'non-logic' or mystical paradoxes applying to the sphere of the One where there is no multiplicity. Stace defines logical rules as 'necessary rules for thinking of or dealing with a *multiplicity* of separate items, not verbal or 'semantic' rules' (p. 270).

There is an implicit circularity in Stace's argument here. First, logical rules are defined as being applicable only to a world where there is a multiplicity of objects. Then it is claimed that logic cannot be applied to mysticism because multiplicity is dismissed from mystical consciousness which experiences only one undifferentiated reality. It is very much like saying that logic does not apply to mysticism because logic is logic and mysticism is mysticism. Earlier writers on mysticism used to say that mysticism *transcends*, goes beyond, logic and hence logical rules do not apply to it. Stace has made very little improvement on this earlier claim.

Besides, I am not sure whether all the mystics themselves will agree with Stace about the area of mystical experience being the territory of the illogic. The very fact that most mystics try to rationalize their experience in terms of everyday logic (Stace himself cited many examples, such as Śaṃkara and Meister Eckhart) proves only the contrary. The Mādhyamika, for example, uses logic and applies it to our everyday experience in order to show that if we take our ordinary experience to be revealing some metaphysical or final truth we will be invariable led into some kind of contradiction. This is the Mādhyamika way of proving the non-finality of our everyday world, a way which should point to some supersensible reality, the Ultimate Reality that is beyond. Stace explains that the mystic's attempt to rationalize his mystical experience results from an internal conflict in the mystic between his rational and mystical consciousness. This explanation is hardly satisfactory. For such arguments can have some strength only when it has been shown, on independent grounds, that there is a separate world of an undifferentiated reality, a world of One, to which the 'illogic' of mysticism applies. I do not think that Stace or any other proponent of mysticism has been successful in demonstrating the existence of this world on independent grounds.

The real issue is not just the opposition of logical laws and mystical paradoxes, but consists in the puzzlement of the rational component of the human mind before the alleged paradoxicality of mystical experience. Nobody, however, claims that rationality is the only component of the human mind. There are, of course, other non-rational, emotive or affective, or non-cognitive components of the human mind. Art, literature, poetry and music appeal considerably to these sides of our mind. Thus, if Stace's claim about the mystical realm being the territory of the 'illogic' amounts to saying only that there is a non-rational component of the mind, no one will dispute it. But obviously Stace claims much more. He argues that there is a separate, and better, world of undifferentiated unity which is ultimately real. The only important argument that he cites in favour of his claim is the following:

> But how are we to explain it when Eckhart and Ruysbroeck agree in their descriptions with the *Upaniṣads*, since these two groups were independent of one another, had no contact, and had never even heard of one another. Yet the very language of the *Mandukya Upaniṣad* in describing the unitary consciousness is almost identical with the language in which Eckhart and Ruysbroeck describe the consciousness of the undifferentiated unity. And how can one explain by mutual influence the fact that the empty nothingness of pure consciousness as described by Christian mystics is identical in meaning with the Void of the Mahāyāna Buddhists. These are but two instances of the *independent* corroboration of the world's mystics by one another. The instances could be multiplied. (Stace's italic, p. 259)

The strength of such argument is dubious since it is based solely on the condition of corroboration. People use such argument too often to support their religious belief or faith in God. Recently supporters of drug-mysticism use a similar argument based on the common character of the drug-induced mystical experience and other types of mystical experience to support the claim that psychedelic drugs are the best gift of science to religion. R.E.L. Masters and Jean Houston, who apparently have been heavily influenced by the writing of Stace in matters of religion and philosophy, have appealed to a similar argument:

> Reports from the subjects concerning the structure and development of their mystical experience show a remarkable similarity. Along with generally confirming the characteristics of the introvertive mystical experience as Stace describes . . ., they also agree as to many particulars met with, too, in the classical literature of mysticism. In almost every case the experience is initiated with a sense of the ego dissolving into boundless being. This process is almost always attended by an experience of the subject being caught up in a torrent of preternatural light. (p. 307)

To counter such argument one may refer to the cautionary note of Ben-Ami Scharfstein (1973, p. 117): 'The likeness of drug-states to mystical ones should not give us the illusion of understanding the latter, for we do not understand the former.' But the hollowness of such argument is best shown by citing some analogous arguments the validity of which will not even be acceptable to the proponents of mysticism. For example, most people argue: There must be an afterlife, for, otherwise, why should so many people of different ages and different traditions worry about it Or, consider the following argument: There must be some superhuman creatures who could fly or move about freely as birds with or without wings, for, otherwise, why would mythologies of completely different religious traditions, which could not have influenced mutually one another, talk about such creatures? Or, to take a repulsive example: The devil must exist, for people set apart by time, space, culture and tradition feel that there is such an evil spirit to whom all the wrongs in the world are due. We should note that all these arguments are basically using the same principle: the condition of corroboration by widely different authorities.

Besides, corroboration of different descriptions of mystical experience one by the other is very much like searching for parallel passages, or lines, or similes, or metaphors in world literature. Any student of comparative literature knows that for some beautiful line in a Sanskrit poem (for example), it is possible to find sometimes a strikingly parallel line in some Western or other literature. Surely such parallelism cannot prove the objectivity of the poet's imagination any more than the parallelism between reports of mystical experience from different traditions can prove the objectivity of the relevant mystical experience. If it is said in answer to this criticism that poets sometimes think alike then I see no harm in accepting that mystics sometimes think alike. But then why is the poet's experience called imagination or fantasy while the mystic's experience is claimed to be real? If it is argued that poets indulge in fantasy consciously and deliberately while the mystics do not do so, then my question is: Are not there many cases also where someone fantasizes without being aware that he is fantasizing? On what grounds could we distinguish such fantasies from mystical experience? Stace has claimed that we cannot reject the testimony of many mystics 'unless we reject the whole of mysticism as a fraud' (p. 265). It should be pointed out that a third possibility exists between fraudulence and absolute truthfulness. This is the case of illusion. It happens when a man sincerely believes (for whatever reasons) that he is telling the truth although he is basically mistaken and under an illusion.

I have devoted a great deal of space to the discussion of Stace's arguments mainly for two reasons. First, Stace's arguments are quite typical of the arguments formulated by most proponents of mysticism. Second,

Stace's book, *Mysticism and Philosophy* (1960), has indeed exerted considerable influence upon the renewed effort and interest in the study of mysticism today. Most people like Masters, Houston, Panhke, Deikman and Prince today have accepted without question Stace's seven-point typology of mystical experience along with many other things mentioned in that book. It is rather unfortunate that the so-called philosophical arguments presented in the book suffer from serious defects and shortcomings. It could be noted in passing that one of the very few things that I agree with what Stace has said in this book is his repudiation of Hegel's idea that there is a superlogic, based on the identity of opposites, which people like Rudolf Otto and D.T. Suzuki think to be relevant to the study of mysticism. It is an illusion which should be repudiated. There is no superlogic. There is only one kind of logic, namely the logic described by the logicians (Stace, p. 268).

Now we come to discuss the third method used by the mystics to convince us about the ineffability of the Ultimate Reality. This method consists in the use of metaphor and rhetoric to convey the notion of ineffability. In the Sanskrit tradition of philosophical semantics, a very important place has been assigned to what is called *lakṣaṇā 'indication'* (= the *indicative* function of the world) by which the word gets an indirect or secondary meaning. Madhusūdana obviously resorted to this method. In the above account of Madhusūdana's method I have used 'indication' as a translation of *lakṣaṇā*. In English rhetoric, probably, the notion of metaphorical meaning is broad enough to include what I have meant by *indicated* meaning in the above passages. Roughly speaking, 'indication', *lakṣaṇā* means this. A word has usually a conventionally accepted meaning in isolation, which we can call its *direct* meaning. But sometimes, in a given context, the direct meaning of the same word may not fit in. That is, a combined, acceptable meaning of the phrase or sentence in question cannot be derived from the direct meanings of the individual component words. In such cases, we resort to an *indicated* meaning, a metaphorical meaning, of some particular word or words in order to derive a combined, acceptable meaning of the phrase or sentence in question. Most Sanskrit semanticists say that the word has a second power or function called 'indication' *lakṣaṇā* which gives its *indicated* meaning under such condition. But this is not all. The rule of the language requires that the indicated or metaphorical meaning must be related in some way or other with the primary or direct meaning of the word in question.

An example from the English language will make our point clear. We often say, 'the chair speaks' or 'the House unanimously agrees', but obviously we do not mean that an actual chair speaks. We can say following the convention of the Sanskrit semanticist that the *indicated* or secondary meanings in these contexts are the Chairman for 'the chair' and members of the house for 'the House'. Note also that 'the chair' means the Chairman who is related to the chair, and not just any man in the street. Similarly, there is a definite relation between the members of the House and House itself. Thus, even the indicated meaning of a word cannot depend simply on the whim of the speaker.

Philosophers like Madhusūdana Sarasvatī use this device of 'indication' *lakṣaṇā* to defend their position on the ineffability of the Ultimate Reality in the following manner: Words like 'the Ultimate Reality,' 'Brahman' and Ānanda' (and one can add 'Śūnyatā', 'Tathatā', and 'Bhūtakoṭi' of Mahāyāna Buddhism) are used by the mystics to *mean* the Ultimate Reality only through indication. In other words, they can only point to what the Ultimate Reality is, instead of *expressing* it directly. This pointing is done indirectly.

The Indian mystics explain this method sometimes by a popular example of showing or pointing a very dimly lighted star in the sky called Arundhatī. It is almost impossible to point to this particular star in the vast sky. But one may proceed as follows: Arundhatī is situated beside a bright star which is one of the seven stars in the constellation called the Ursa Major ('the Seven Saints' in Indian terminology). This bright star is the sixth star in the constellation, which is named by the Indians as Vasiṣṭha (in Indian mythology, Vasiṣṭha and Arundhatī are names of husband and wife—a sage and his wife who figure in the Rāmāyaṇa.) One may thus say: Look at that Ursa Major (or the Great Bear), and then look at that sixth star there, and then you can see Arundhatī by its side. In other words, it is not a direct ostentation but an indirect pointing. The so-called words for the Ultimate Reality mentioned above can point, in the same manner, to it through indirection.

The matter, however, is not so simple. For the words do not really function as pointers. They express or mean something in a given context. The Indian mystics resort to the theory of *lakṣaṇā* 'or 'indicative function' of words in order to get out of the quandary created by the notion of ineffability. But this position can hardly be defended on the acceptable theory of meaning. Remember that even the *indicative* function does not allow us to derive any meaning from a word according to our whims. In other words, it is not a license like that of Humpty Dumpty in Lewis Carroll's *Alice's Adventures Through the Looking Glass.* We may recall what Humpty Dumpty said to Alice:

'When *I* use a word,' Humpty Dumpty said in rather a scornful tone, 'it means just what I choose it to mean—neither more nor less.' 'The question is,' said Alice, 'whether you *can* make words mean different things.' 'The question is,' said Humpty Dumpty, 'which is to be master—that is all.'

We may very well ask, as Alice did, whether the mystic *can* make a word mean, even through indirection, what he chooses it to mean, i.e., his Ultimate Reality or the ineffable. Remember that even to derive an *indicated* meaning of a word to fit a given context we have to follow certain rules of idioms of the language. 'The chair' in 'the chair speaks' cannot mean just any odd unrelated thing in the world. It means 'the Chairman' who is related to the primary meaning, the chair. Besides, the indicated meaning is sought after only when the direct meaning or primary meaning is understood but fails to give a combined meaning of the entire expression, 'the chair speaks'.

Thus, we may ask: what are the direct meanings of such expressions like 'Brahman', 'Suchness', 'Highest Bliss' and 'the Ultimate Reality'? If they mean the goal of all mystic paths, the Ultimate Reality, through indication or indirection, what do they mean directly? One can see that these expressions are very much like 'the highest number that exceeds all other numbers' in Mathematics, which, to use the modern Western terminology, has a *meaning* all right but no *reference*. Without getting involved here into the now well-known problem of meaning and reference which G. Frege (1892) introduced in Western philosophy, or into the Russellian Theory of Descriptions (B. Russell, 1905), one can say that these meanings (*direct* meanings of these expressions) are not real, or at least, not as much real as an item of this everyday world. They may be real in some Platonic world of ideas. Now, to fulfil the condition of *indication*, the mystic has to show that his Ultimate Reality is related in some definite way to these direct meanings of the above expressions—meanings that are, as far as we know, denizens of the Platonic world. Just as the indicated meaning, the Chairman, is derived from 'the chair' on the basis of an existent relationship between the chair and the Chairman, the mystic will similarly have to specify a relationship between his Ultimate Reality—the ineffable Ultimate Reality—and the 'shadow' meanings of the above expressions. What could be this relation that the mystic supposes to exist between the Ultimate Reality and the direct meanings of the above expressions? In hindsight and not entirely facetiously one may remark that unless we reduce our everyday world into a shadow play, we cannot make any good sense of the mystic's justification of the ineffability doctrine on the basis of the theory of *lakṣaṇā* 'indication'.

This brings us to our more fundamental criticism of mysticism and its ineffability doctrine. In the Indian tradition, the Nyāya-Vaiśeṣika school has been strongly opposed to mysticism and its ineffability doctrine. The fundamental thesis of the Nyāya-Vaiśeṣika school can be stated as a combination of the following two propositions:

(a) If anything is or exists, it is, in principle, knowable, and nameable.

(b) Whatever is knowable is also nameable or expressible in language.

The first proposition is sometimes misunderstood by the modern interpreters as implying its converted from: Every nameable exists. But it is actually a universal affirmative of the form: Every existent is nameable or knowable. And, we know from Aristotle that universal affirmatives cannot be simply converted without altering their sense. For 'not every animal is a man; every man is an animal' (*Prior Analytics*, i, 2 [25^a25]). Thus, the Nyāya claims: not every nameable is existent, but every existent is nameable. For example, the son of a barren woman, which is nameable, does not exist.

It is clear that the Nyāya-Vaiśeṣika thesis is a good antidote to mysticism and the ineffability doctrine. It should also remove the modern (overwhelmingly Western) misunderstanding that Indian philosophy is invariably mystical. The business of most classical philosophers of India was solid and down-to-earth philosophic argumentation, not the creation of mystical illusion or poetic description of mystical experiences. Even the ineffability doctrine was defended and criticized by both proponents and opponents with serious and sophisticated reasonings. It is unfortunate that in a modern discussion of Indian or Oriental mysticism, these texts usually go unnoticed or unrecognized. Thus, any book today which purports to be about mysticism and Indian thought generally represents Indian philosophy as a heterogenous congeries of primitive religion, dogmas, pantheisms and bizarre animisms. But this only perpetuates the illusion about Indian mysticism.

If the Ultimate Reality is claimed to be accessible only to the mystical experience and no other accredited means of knowledge is of any help, then I do not see how such an Ultimate Reality can be expressible in language in order to be communicable to others. To avoid the quandary, the Buddhist (specially of the Dinnāga school) makes a further claim that the mystical experience is another means of knowledge—an accredited means like perception (*pratyakṣa*). It is in fact said to be a special kind of perceptual experience. This, however, does not avoid the problem of ineffability but only tries to establish the validity of the experience by subsuming it under the perceptual experience. And then the Buddhist epistemologists go on to say that the objects of even the ordinary (non-mystical) perception are ineffable because they are uniquely particular and momentary in nature. Such an epistemological hypothesis finds some support from the sense-data philosophers in the West, but it has not won universal acclamation. In fact, this move of the Buddhist epistemologists, instead of throwing more light on the nature of mystical experience, tries to mystify unduly the nature of ordinary perception. It is difficult to see why all objects of ordinary perception should be regarded as ineffable. Even a Mādhyamika Buddhist, Candrakīrti, has taken the Buddhist epistemologists to task for making such a claim in epistemology (pp. 21–3).

Since the validity of the mystical experience itself is in question here, neither accumulation of millions of cases of such experience nor corroboration of one such experience by another can take us very far by way of establishing its validity. For, any psychologist can tell that there is a general pattern or agreement among the dream experiences of different people living under similar conditions. But certainly that cannot prove the reality of dream objects. Corroboration in cases of mystical experiences would very much be like what the Indian critics call the case of a blind man guiding another blind man. Thus, the status of the Ultimate Reality revealed in some 'mystical experiences' is very dubious because such an experience can hardly be claimed to be knowledge. For no other means of knowledge, except the mystical experience itself (whose validity is under consideration), can establish its existence. Thus, the attempt to even *indirectly* describe the Ultimate Reality with the help of negation or negative properties or with metaphors and indicated meaning loses its significance. For what Udayana said about entities like the rabbit's horn can be equally applicable here:

> If no body has even seen or *known* a person called 'Devadatta' anywhere at any time, then the question 'Is Devadatta white, or is he black?' results simply from some outrageous perversion. And if, without caring to understand what this is all about, someone answers the question by saying 'he is white', another person has as much right to answer by saying, 'he is black'. Nothing is established by such questions and answers. (p. 69)

One can only add here the comment of the Buddha himself on a similar question. To say that I teach the highest or ultimate colour (see before for such a dialogue of the Buddha with Udayi) or the Ultimate Reality, is like saying that I am in love with the Beauty Queen of this country when I do not know or have never seen that Beauty Queen!

Mysticism and therefore the ineffability doctrine, in most cases, though probably not in all cases are sustained and supported by a belief—a religious belief, to all intents and purposes—in 'A Separate Reality'. This 'separate' reality is claimed sometimes to be the Ultimate Reality that is beyond or behind the ordinary everyday world. Fascination for such 'a separate reality' is widespread throughout the ages (witness the modern popularity of *Don Juan* and Carlos Castañeda's book with the same title). Huxley wanted to see this separate reality through his 'doors of perception'. William James called it 'an altogether other dimension of existence from the sensible and merely 'understandable' world.' (p. 389) He also proposed to call it a 'reality': 'But that which produces effects within another reality must be termed a reality itself, so I feel as we had no philosophic excuse for calling the unseen or mystical world unreal.' (Ibid.)

Whether such a 'separate' reality exists or not, we cannot tell. And the mystic cannot prove it either. It does not exist, at least, in the same way the world around us exists. There are certainly many *separate ways* of seeing or looking at things and the world around us. It should also be admitted that part of the way of our *seeing* the world is considerably conditioned by our culture, training, up-bringing and society. And different ways of *seeing* the world are results of different internalized conceptual apparatus. But if the mystic is trying to make only this point through his ineffability doctrine, it would be a trivial point. Of course, if a person is religiously and mystically inclined he can see religious and mystical significance in everything around him. Much in the same way, an artist sees artistic significance in everyday objects.

Implied in the notion of the Ultimate Reality or a supersensible world as well as in the claim that such a world is more REAL or even more VALUABLE than the ordinary world, is a theory that regards the material and external world as unreal and dream-like, as not final but a mere appearance. Most mystic reinforce this theory about the illusory nature of this world by asserting their belief in the position that reality is one and indivisible, multiplicity or diversity is only an appearance. It is true that unity is a concept against which we understand the visibility of this world. But if, for this reason, we assign the highest reality or ultimacy to unity over multiplicity, should we then be justified in assigning ultimacy or finality to invisibility over visibility?

The pertinent question is: Why is multiplicity of plurality or the world not to be regarded as real? The mystic answers: Because it does not make sense. Why? The mystic, e.g., the Buddhist, answers;

Its nature cannot be ascertained by our discriminating intellect (by dialectical process of reasoning). Things collapse into nothing as we analyse them with reasoning. (*Lankāvatārasūtra*, 2.173, 2.163)

Udayana, the Naiyāyika, has sarcastically remarked of the so-called analytical or dialectical argument of the Buddhist, as follows:

Your criticism of the multiplicity and the status of the phenomenal world in order to expose its unreality (emptiness) is like the argument of someone possessed by a spirit. (*Ātmatattvaviveka*, p. 230 f)

Udayana then goes on to cite a humorous argument as an example: Suppose a man (who is apparently possessed by a ghost) sees an elephant standing near the courthouse and starts wondering about it: what could this dark thing be? He 'discovers' four alternative possibilities. It could be 'solidified' darkness, or a rain-cloud, or just a 'friend', or only a 'shadow' of a thing lying on the ground. The first two alternatives are suggested for the obvious similarity of appearance. The third alternative is suggested because the ancient teacher, Kauṭilya, defined a 'friend' as someone who waits for you at the courthouse (or at the cremation ground). The fourth alternative is a humorous illustration of confusing the shadow for the real thing and the thing for the shadow. Then this man proceeds to reject all these four alternatives with his so-called dialectical reasoning and concludes:

I, therefore, conclude that there is no such *thing* that I see out there (it is only my imagination)!

After citing this argument, Udayana asks:

By such reasonings shall we consider that the existence of the elephant has been refuted? Or, shall we say that another who is equally possessed by a ghost (or obsessed) is doing better, for he says, 'What it is, it is', without committing himself to the existence of an elephant. (p. 231)

Apart from sarcasm, I think Udayana here points to a very valid and genuine difficulty inherent in the so-called dialectical arguments of the mystic and idealist philosophers who try to prove the hollowness of the phenomenal world. It is true that sometimes with a dialectical argument we can demolish a theory or proposition about the world. The Mādhyamikas are well-known for demolishing a concept or a theory by examining its four-fold (or two-fold) alternative construal. Udayana points out that such alternative construals are suitably chosen by the arguer himself so that he can refute them easily in the manner of the 'possessed' person mentioned above. Udayana suggests that by such pseudo-arguments the mystic might persuade himself to believe in one of the two alternatives: (a) The outside world is unreal and dream-like, and (b) The outside world is what it is (position of non-commitment in language as we find in the case of the Mādhyamika).

It is true that sometimes, in the light of certain overwhelming experiences or in a peculiar state of mind, we feel that many things in this world are meaningless, senseless and phantom-like. But this cannot constitute an over-all rejection of everything real and material in the world unless we are in a psychotic condition. It is also true that sometimes for someone who is undergoing unspeakable pain and suffering it is worthwhile to tell him to think that pain is unreal and the world where such pain exists and fear of pain exists is unreal. But that is a physician's privilege (or the privilege of the Buddha, the great physician) to comfort his patient, and not certainly a tested view of reality. Such a doctrine can have a value only in context, just as drugs and anaesthesia have values in removing painful feelings. But this cannot be taken to be a valid, or the ultimate, description of Reality.

One further point. Just as the so-called skeptic in Western philosophy since the time of Plato works with a strict concept of knowledge while denying the possibility of knowledge, so the mystic seems to reject the reality of the world—the phenomenal world—only by holding to a firm view about the nature of reality (J.W. Yolton, 1974). Thus, the Mādhyamika refutes the reality of the phenomenal world because it is dependently originating, and he implies that reality is independently existent and unconditioned. Most mystics argue that reality is the undifferentiated unity and therefore the phenomenal world because of its multiplicity is unreal.

Finally, if the moral of the mystic's ineffability doctrine is that our comprehension or experience always outruns our language or linguistic capacities, then such a doctrine can be highly educational. It might challenge us to clarify, modify and reorganize our ordinary experience and understanding of the world. It might warn us against being dogmatic in our comprehension of reality or against our having a complacent attitude about many things that we do not know. For although human knowledge (and science) is progressing everyday, there are many more things that we still do not know about the world around us. The progress of knowledge must be maintained and kept going. Complacence destroys this progress. Thus, we should be wary of complacence. But if the moral to be derived from mysticism is that the world around us is unreal, shadowy and phantom-like, or that the initial undifferentiated, uncategorized consciousness that we all experience at our birth or at our infantile stage is what is ultimately real and most valuable because it is blissful, then we will find ourselves some day back where we started—primitive human society or the Garden of Eden before our eating of the tree of knowledge.

References

Ānandavardhana, *Dhvānyāloka*, ed. by P. Sastri, Chowkhamba, Benares, 1940.

Aṅguttaranikāya, eds, by Richard Morris and by E. Hardy (in 5 vols), 1885–1900, Froude (Pali Text Society), London.

Aristotle, *The Basic Works of Aristotle*, ed. by R. McKeon, Random House, New York, 1941.

Bharata, *Nāṭyaśāstra*, ed. by M.R. Kavi *et al.*, 4 vols, Oriental Institute Gaekward Oriental Series, Baroda, 1938–64.

Bṛhadāraṇyaka Upaniṣad, ed. by S. Sastri *et al.*, Anandasrama, Poona, 1911.

Brunner, Constantine, *Science, Spirit & Superstition*, Tr. by A. Suhl and W. Bernard, University of Toronto Press, Toronto, 1968.

Candrakīrti, *Prasannapadā*, comm. on Nāgārjuna; see Nāgārjuna.

Carroll, Lewis. (pseudon.) Dodgson, C.L., *Annotated Alice*, New York, 1960.

Castañeda, C., *A Separate Reality*, Bodley Head, New York, 1971.

Conze, E. (Tr.), *The Perfection of Wisdom in Eight Thousand Lines*, Four Seasons Foundation, Bolinas, 1973.

Deikman, A.J., 'The Overestimation of the Mystical Experience', *Do Psychedelics Have Religious Implication*?, ed. by Salman and Prince, Quebec City, 1967, pp. 57–61.

Frege, G., 'Sense and Reference' (1892), *Philosophical Writings of G. Frege*, ed. by P.T. Geach and M. Black, Blackwell, Oxford, 1952.

Gauḍapāda, *Āgamaśāstra*, ed. by V. Bhattacharya, University of Calcutta, Calcutta, 1943.

Hume, R.E., *Thirteen Principal Upaniṣads*, Oxford University Press, Oxford, 1921.

Huxley, A., *The Doors of Perception*, Chatto & Windus, London, 1954.

Īśā Upaniṣad, in *Ekādaśopaniṣadaḥ*, ed. by V.S. Sastri, Motilal Banarsidass, Delhi, 1966.

James, W., *The Varieties of Religious Experience*, Longmans, London, 1902.

Kaṭha Upaniṣad, see *Īśā*.

Laṅkāvatāra-sūtra, ed. by P.L. Vaidya, Mithila Institute, Darbhanga, 1963.

Madhusūdana Sarasvatī, *Advaitasiddhi*, ed. by A.K. Sastri, Nirnayasagar, Bombay, 1917.

Majjhima Nikāya, ed. by Trenckner and Chalmers, 3 vols, Froude (Pali Text Society), London, 1888–99.

Masson and Patwardhan, *Śāntarasa and Abhinavagupta's Philosophy of Aesthetics*, Bhandarkar Institute, Poona, 1969.

Masters, R.E.L. and J. Houston, *The Varieties of Psychedelic Experience*, Delta paperback, 1967.

Matilal, B.K., *Epistemology, Logic and Grammar in Indian Philosophical Analysis*, Mouton & Co., The Hague/Paris, 1971.

———, 'A Critique of the Mādhyamika Position' *The Problems of Two Truths in Buddhism and Vedānta*, D. Reidel, Dordrecht, 1973, pp. 54–63.

Muṇḍaka Upaniṣad, see Īśā.

Nāgārjuna, *Madhyamakaśāstra*, with comm. of Candrakīrti, ed. by P.L. Vaidya, Mithila Institute, Darbhanga, 1960.

Pahnke, W.N., 'LSD and Religious Experience', *LSD, Man and Society*, ed. by De Bold and Leaf, Wesleyan University Press, Middletown, 1967.

Rahula, W., *What The Buddha Taught*, Gordon Fraser, London, 1959.

Russell, B., 'On Denoting', *Mind* 14 (1905), 479–93.

———, *Mysticism and Logic*, Doubleday Anchor paperback, New York, 1917.

Scharfstein, Ben-Ami, *Mystical Experience*, Blackwell, Oxford, 1973.

Srīdhara, *Nyāyakandalī*, Comm. on Praśastapāda, ed. by D. Jha. Research Institute. Varanasya Sanskrit Vaishvavidyalaya, Benares, 1963.

Stace, W.T., *Mysticism and Philosophy*, J.B. Lippincott, New York, 1960.

Suzuki, D.T., *Essays in Zen Buddhism*, Harper & Row, New York, 1949.

Taittirīya Upaniṣad, see *Īśā*.

Tucci, G., 'The Hymn to the Incomparable One', *Journal of the Royal Asiatic Society*, New Series, 27, 1932, pp. 312–14.

Udayana, *Ātmatattvaviveka*, ed. by D. Sastri, Chowkhamba, Benares, 1940.

Warder, A.K., *Indian Buddhism*, Motilal Banarsidass, Delhi, 1970.

Yolton, J.W., Review of B.K. Matilal's *Epistemology, Logic and Grammar in Indian Philosophical Analysis*, *Journal of Indian Philosophy*, 2 (1974), 384–96.

2

The Logical Illumination of Indian Mysticism

It is sad that death has taken Professor Zaehner so suddenly from our midst. During his time as Spalding Professor of Eastern Religions and Ethics, Professor Zaehner published a large number of books and articles, and actively participated in many live issues of today in the field of religion, philosophy, morality, and mysticism. He initiated many controversial discussions in the field of drugs, the typology of mysticism, and religion and modern society. Of his many concerns, I wish to choose two main problems for discussion this evening. My choice has been guided by considering not only the purpose of the Spalding Professorship at Oxford but also the avowed interest of my two predecessors, R.C. Zaehner and Sarvepalli Radhakrishnan.

First, Professor Zaehner profoundly, and I think justifiably, disagreed with such persons as Aldous Huxley concerning the value of mysticism ('oriental mysticism', to be sure) as a *philosophia perennis*. Second, Professor Zaehner entertained some deep-seated misgivings about the implicit amorality of a monistic metaphysical position, which is regarded as the bedrock of Eastern mysticism. My comments this evening will be broadly related to these two major issues.

Mystical doctrines that arise from Vedānta, Buddhism, Zen, and Taoism, Professor Zaehner argued, speak of a timeless state of Being, which transcends good and evil, right and wrong, and all the opposites and contradictions, that bedevil human life. The thinking of the Pre-Socratic philosophers of ancient Greece was, in this respect, remarkably similar to that of the Indian philosophers and mystics. But a very important and striking contrast between Eastern mysticism and mysticism in the Christian tradition is that the latter, unlike the former, is overwhelmingly God-orientated. The metaphysical foundation of Eastern mysticism is centered upon beliefs that are often expressed as 'All is One and One is All' and 'The One IS, all else is illusion'. Professor Zaehner argued that there is a moral ambivalence in these thoughts so deep-seated that it may lead to disastrous results in our everyday behaviour. He contended, for instance, that the gruesome murders perpetrated by Charles Manson and the 'Family', which shocked the world in 1969, were simply an example of the extremes to which we can be led by the amorality of monism expressed in such phrases as 'the union of opposites' and 'transcendence of good and evil'.[1]

I will start with a remark made by Professor Zaehner in his last book. Observing that the so called perennial philosophy of the union of opposites is expounded alike by Heraclitus and the Upaniṣads, he went on to say, 'But it (the perennial philosophy) needs to be rigorously checked by the rational mind which it would destroy' (*Our Savage God*, p. 102). In the same vein, he glorified Aristotle as the intellectual father of the Western world, 'for he was the first to think analytically about mystical experience, finding thereby the only truly human answer to the mystery because his answer was reached by thought, which alone distinguishes man from other animals, not by ecstasy and Platonic madness.'[2] Following the lead suggested in the few lines just quoted, I wish to attempt a rational presentation of some philosophical doctrines of India that are usually associated with mysticism: Advaita Vedānta and Māhāyana Buddhism. Although my own philosophic conviction is different and forces me to be critical of monistic metaphysics (and in this regard, I find myself in agreement with my immediate predecessor), it seems undeniable that a number of respectable writers on Advaita and Mādhyamika in ancient and medieval India examined their own doctrines as well as those of their rivals in the light of reason and logic. My attempt here is to show how this has been done, and with what success.

The idea of mysticism has mystified many of us, including Professor Zaehner. His attempt to understand the phenomenon was commendable. In today's world, we have a bewildering variety of publications on Advaita Vedānta and Māhāyana Buddhism along with a widespread proliferation of some popular forms of these two religious system—so bewildering, that an academic or professional philosopher today may hesitate to embark on a serious discussion of these two systems. This is a pity, for these two systems of Indian philosophy were in fact as serious as any philosophical system, either in the East or in the West. When one reads any standard original text of either Advaita or Mādhyamika philosophy, one cannot but admire greatly the intellectual honesty and professional sophistication of its author. In contrast, numerous modern publications are remarkable for the sheer obscurity and inanity of their presentation, and, as Professor Zaehner has regretted,[3] the intelligent layman in the West (and, I might add, in the East too) seems to be swallowing book after book of this kind. And this only lends support to the well-known maxim of Tertullian: *Credo quia absurdum*, 'I believe it because it is absurd'.

To prove my point about the seriousness and professionalism of Indian mystical philosophers, I will deal with two standard texts, in particular: Nāgārjuna's *Vigrahavyāvartanī* and Śrīharṣa's *Khaṇḍanakhaṇḍa-khādya*. A brief review of a few points described in either of these two texts will, I think, dispel any illusion that the so called Indian mysticism is fairly represented by the vague generalities and naive beliefs that we often hear today.

Whatever one may feel about the content of the doctrines of the philosophers I have mentioned, one cannot help appreciating and thinking highly of the form in which they were put. One can go even further: the form itself tells us something that is generally overlooked in present-day discussions of these doctrines, and that is that these authors intended their writing to be available for rational discussion. They were in fact writing for intelligent and critically minded readers and not pleading for the silence of mystic communion. I firmly believe that the very form in which these texts have been cast acts as an invitation to scholars and intellectuals to examine them dispassionately and in the light of reason.

First of all, let us note that these texts were written in correct and technical Sanskrit. And Sanskrit is a very difficult language (in all probability, it was not a spoken language when these texts were composed). It was a language that could be learned, not in any transcendental state of euphoria, but only after years of formal study of its grammar and syntax.[4] This, in my opinion, already acted as a 'corrective' check on the class of people whom these authors were addressing and writing for.

Second, these authors used formal arguments—Indian syllogistic forms, to be sure—at almost every step of their discourse. They clothed their doctrines in a technical (logical) vocabulary that presupposed a thorough-going and systematic training in logic and the *pramāṇa-śāstra* (epistemology or the study of the means of knowledge). In fact the vocabulary of the *pramāṇa-śāstra* implies a universe of discourse that not only is commonly shared by all the different schools of Indian philosophy but also tends to be global in its meaning. If we use 'logic' in a broad and liberal sense, then, as I have argued elsewhere, it would be difficult to talk about any inherent distinction between Indian logic and Western logic.[5] And these authors, apart from everything else, were astute logicians (in, at least, an Indian sense of the term). Thus, nobody who had not spent several years in formal study of the technical vocabularies of Indian logic would find it easy to follow these texts, much less to comprehend and criticize these doctrines. This probably acted as an additional corrective check upon readers. In brief, these texts were very far from being rhapsodies of mystical experience, or what Professor Zaehner called 'ecstacy and Platonic madness'.

While I stress the value of the form of these texts, I am nevertheless aware that human beings crave content. And I am certainly not one to shirk the substance of these texts while only praising their form. For indeed these works do intend to convey a message, and that message is often more than strictly philosophical. I consider it my duty as a scholar to make this message as clear and as forceful as it must originally have appeared to these authors themselves. This is by no means a simple task.

Nāgārjuna wrote his *Mādhyamika-kārikā* primarily to show the essentially conditional and provisional nature of the *dharma* theory of the Abhidharma school, and along with this he wanted to expose the necessarily provisional nature of any philosophic theory of reality. Nāgārjuna argued: A thing is always without its own-nature (*svabhāva*), empty or devoid of what may be termed its essence or being. For the assumption that a thing has its own-nature runs contrary to our empirical evidence as well as to our reasoning. Experience reveals the happening of events only, no own-nature, no essence. The own-nature (which, with some reservations, can be rendered as the essence) of a thing is conceived as the unchanging, underlying core, and this conception is held by Nāgārjuna to be incompatible with the commonsense notion as well as the philosophic notion of change.

Nāgārjuna used the familiar paradox of causation, i.e., the paradox of change and permanence. This paradox, according to Nāgārjuna, shows that a thing cannot possess its own-nature; its essence. If a thing has its own-nature it cannot change, for that would go against the presumed unchangeability of own-nature; and if the thing does not have its own-nature then change cannot take place either, for 'change' means transformation of the own-nature into something else.[6]

Nāgārjuna's argument can be briefly stated as follows. Everything is empty or devoid of its own-nature because everything is 'dependently originating'. The implicit premise is that the own-nature of things and the fact of their dependent origination cannot go together. The presence of one implies the absence of the other. It is also suggested by Nāgārjuna's argument that the fact of dependent origination of things (viz., A arises when B is there) is given to us by experience (and the Buddhist is simply drawing our attention to this fact of experience), and the own-nature is an *a priori* assumption. And thus, since one contradicts the other the Mādhyamika draws the conclusion that all things are empty (of their own-nature).

In the *Vigrahavyāvartanī*, Nāgārjuna raises a fundamental issue in philosophy. It is in fact a basic problem in the philosophy of logic, Indian logic, to be sure. Posing as a Nyāya opponent Nāgārjuna asks the following question: If everything (including statements) is empty then the statement that states that everything is empty is also empty and thus loses its assertive force or its claim to truth. And, if this latter statement is not intended to be empty then one has to state the ground for such a preferential treatment of this particular statement (i.e., one has to explain why, while all other statements are empty, this particular one is not so).[7] Nāgārjuna says that a disputant in this case can formulate three pairs of alternatives (*ṣaṭkoṭika-vāda*),[8] which I shall expound below. 'Everything is empty' is actually a negative statement, a negation (*pratiṣedha*), for it is a rephrasing of 'nothing has its own-nature'. Now the first two alternatives are suggested as follows.[9] (If everything is empty then):

1. The above negation is itself empty, does not have its own-nature, and thus it is improper (*anupapanna*), FALSE.

or 2. The negation itself is not empty, it does have its own-nature, and thus it is not improper, it is TRUE.

Note that if 1 is accepted, Nāgārjuna fails to convey the truth that he is supposed to convey. If, however, 2 is accepted then we have a *partially* paradoxical situation, viz., if this negation is true then it is also false because the negation is also included in 'everything'.

The second pair of alternatives is formulated as follows:

3. Everything is empty, but this negation is not empty (i.e., TRUE); 'Everything' does not include this negation.

or 4. This negation, along with everything else, lacks its own-nature, is FALSE.

Note that 3 accords a special status to the negation in question, for it says, in fact, that everything *except* this negation is empty. Thus, the opponent is justified in asking for the ground on which such exception is to be made (*viśeṣahetuś ca vaktavyaḥ*). With 4; we are back to the same problem as with 1, namely, Nāgārjuna fails to communicate his message.

The third pair is stated as follows:

5. The negation is also empty (false) just as everything else, but even so it successfully conveys its meaning.

or 6. Everything except this negation is empty, and therefore the negation successfully conveys its meaning.

There is very little difference between 3 and 6. But 5 obviously leads to the awkward position that even a false negation can successfully negate. If this is admitted then one might as well stipulate that even a false thing can function successfully.

To simplify matters for our discussion, let me substitute for the statement of Nāgārjuna, 'Nothing has its own-nature' (I will call it NS), the statement 'No statement is true' or 'All statements are false'. Instead of talking about *things* we talk about statements. As far as I can see, this does not misinterpret his philosophical motivation, for instead of referring to the 'world of things' we are referring to the 'world of statements'. Thus, the 'own-nature' of a thing is represented here by the *truth* of a statement, and the lack of 'own-nature' by the *falsity* (lack of truth) of the statement. In fact, a Nāgārjunian might happily agree to translate 'Everything is empty' as 'Every statement is false', for all statements may be viewed as *prapañca* and therefore belonging to the *saṁvṛti* level, which will imply that they are false from the point of view of the *paramārtha* or Ultimate Reality.

Let us assume that NS = 'No statement is true'.

We will now be in a better position to locate the logical difficulties which the 'emptiness' doctrine of Nāgārjuna might possibly face and also to find a way out of those difficulties. It is difficult not to recall the ancient Liar paradox of Epimenides, who apparently said, himself being a Cretan, that all Cretans are liars (this is, at least, taken to be one version of the Liar paradox). But I shall try to avoid any facile comparison between the two, and instead limit myself to the logical problems raised by NS in the Indian context. It will be noted that NS may be paradoxical but is not a proper antinomy.[10]

If NS is asserted to be true, we have already a counter-example which will make NS false. In other words, as long as NS is itself counted as a statement, if we claim it to be true, we will be forced to admit its falsity. But this is not properly antinomical, for if we assume NS to be false, we do not have any way of deducing from this assumption that it is true. Thus, we can, and obviously Nāgārjuna can, consistently hold NS to be false. But then we are obliged (and so is Nāgārjuna) to answer at least two further questions. First, if NS is false, it fails to communicate the message of Nāgārjuna. Note this is what is actually claimed by the opponent of Nāgārjuna in the above alternatives 1 and 4. In Indian terminology, NS, under this interpretation, is no longer a *deśanā*, it does not serve any purpose. Second, to suppose that NS is false is also to suppose logically its contradictory, i.e., 'Some statement is true' to be true. Translated back in the 'thing-talk', we will have to say that if we suppose 'Everything is empty' to be itself empty, we will have to admit at least one non-empty thing, i.e., one thing that does not lack its own-nature. Now, to hold that some statement is true, we are committed to presuppose the existence of a true statement, different from NS. If the argument so far has been right, it will then seem possible for us to settle an empirical question on logical grounds. Note that there is no logical incompatibility in supposing that NS is the only statement in a Nāgārjunian world. But we cannot count NS to be false unless there exists another true statement in that world (a contingent fact). Note that although the opponent to alternative 5 above does not explicitly raise this point it is nevertheless an implicit difficulty in alternative 5.

To avoid the above problem, we might use an *exceptive* clause (see alternative 3 and 6), and say that NS is:

No statement except this one is true.

This way of avoiding the problem arising from self-reference will not lead us to any logical difficulties;[12] but the opponent will still press Nāgārjuna to supply a factual reason for this exception. Nāgārjuna, in this respect, does not enjoy the privilege that is apparently available to Epimenides. Epimenides, for example, can claim that all Cretans except himself are liars, and hence the paradox will disappear. But Nāgārjuna's situation is different. If NS is said to have a special, in fact unique, status of being true while all other statements are false, the opponent will insist that NS cannot in that case be considered to be a statement. This is what is actually meant by the technical fault called *dṛṣṭāntāsiddhi*. The said fault has at least two consequences. First, the NS in this case would be an entirely solipsistic statement which nobody will be able to understand. Second, if all statements except NS are false, then falsity becomes a necessary character of a statement, and thus it would not be proper any more to call NS a statement. The underlying principle is this: if all members except one, say *a*, of a class possess a property, then there is a very strong reason to disqualify *a* from the membership of that class. This argument is sound as long as we talk in terms of natural classes (where membership is subject to empirical discovery).

To assist Nāgārjuna, we may note that he has a very easy way out. For he can consistently hold that no statement is true without every asserting NS.[13] Although this seems to be his final position, it is interesting to see how he eventually reaches it. He observes:

'Therefore, just as my statement is empty, all things are empty. And hence the lack of own-nature of all things is proven in both ways.' *Vv.*, p. 127, II.6–7.

This would appear to be a quibble. Is Nāgārjuna saying that if a negation (*pratiṣedha*) is false, it only intensifies the force of that negation? No, for that would be a very odd view and would deny the practical validity and utility of logic. Nāgārjuna is in fact trying to say something else:

If I had propounded a thesis to be proven (*pratijñā*), certainly then I would be at fault. But I do not propound any thesis to be proven, and therefore I am surely not at fault. *Vv.*, v. 29.

If this is not satisfactory, Nāgārjuna continues:

Thus, as long as all things are empty, completely unarising (*?upaśānta*) and devoid of any essence, how can a statement qualify to be a thesis to be proven? And if so, how can any fault attach to us—a fault such as the disqualification of a statement from being considered as a thesis? *Vv.*, p. 127, II.19–20.

Briefly, if NS is claimed to be a thesis, it can be either proved or disproved, be either accepted or rejected. But since Nāgārjuna does not make such a claim, the attack of the opponent would be wide of the mark. Moreover:

If I (wish to) establish any fact through such means of knowledge as perception, I would offer it for either acceptance or rejection. But since I do not, you cannot refute my point. *Vv.*, v. 30.

Nāgārjuna's point seems to be this. Only a proposition can be true or false. But since NS is not claimed as a proposition, we cannot even begin to think of its contradictory, viz., 'some statement is true'. Thus, Nāgārjuna has almost turned the tables against his opponent. But one may now suspect that he is trying to score a point only by leaving us in the quicksand of a very strange philosophic debate—a debate where the winner wins only by violating the ground rules! If Nāgārjuna did not have any position or proposition to defend, why did he enter the debate in the first place? He has two different answers to this charge. The first answer is somewhat illuminating, for it explains what the Mādhyamika philosophy is all about, while the second is posed as a counter-question.

Nāgārjuna first says that NS can provisionally be proposed as a thesis for a debate only from the point of view of *saṃvyavahāra*, conventional or provisional reality.

We do not, in fact cannot, make our point without having recourse to *saṃvyavahāra* (= *saṁvṛti*). *Vv.*, v. 28cd.

In the *Mādhyamika-kārikā*, he has already emphasized that there are two levels of truth: the *saṁvṛti* or the provisional and the *paramārtha* or the ultimate. The Buddha has taught his doctrine in terms of these two levels of truth. Nāgārjuna repeats here:

We cannot state that all things are empty without recourse to ordinary human behaviour (i.e. an utterance). For the teaching of the doctrine (*dharma-deśanā*) cannot be conducted without recourse to *vyavahāra*. *Vv.*, p. 127, II.1–3.

To explain: The teacher-philosopher has only two choices. He can remain silent, but then he fails in his duty as a teacher and no longer remains true to his profession. Or, he can teach his doctrine using the ordinary vehicle of communication, i.e., speech, but he can do so only at the risk of being misunderstood and misinterpreted. In the first case, he cannot instruct the disciples at all, and in the second case, he runs the risk of misleading his disciples. Nāgārjuna clearly prefers the second alternative: the risk of a wrong lead is better than no lead at all! Thus, the force of *vyavahāra* is admitted, and Nāgārjuna enters into the debate. Now, if he seems to be misleading or not following the ground rules, it is, according to him, the fault of the medium he has chosen, and the medium has been chosen in the absence of any better alternative.

Nāgārjuna's second reply comes in terms of a counter-offensive. The opponent accepts certain ad hoc rules of a philosophic debate. The debater states his position, viz., a thesis to be proven or disproven. He also accepts a system of *pramāṇas*, means of knowledge, by means of which he intends to prove (or disprove) his thesis. His crucial assumption is that there are means of knowledge or *pramāṇas*, which establish facts or truths (*arthas* or *prameyas*) expressed by the thesis. Nāgārjuna argues:

If those facts are established through the means of knowledge (*pramāṇas*), tell me then how those means of knowledge are themselves established?

If the means of knowledge are established by another set of means of knowledge, infinite regress follows. For the first cannot be established, nor the middle, nor the last. *Vv.*, vv. 31, 32.

To avoid this quandary, the opponent might say that the means of knowledge are self-validating or self-established, and hence they do not need anything else to establish or validate them. But then, Nāgārjuna argues, the means of knowledge would enjoy a unique status in this world, for while everything else stands in need of being proven by a means of knowledge, they themselves do not. Now the tables seem to be turned against the opponent, for Nāgārjuna can ask him to explain the ground for according such a unique status to the *pramāṇas*, means of knowledge. Remember Nāgārjuna himself did not claim anything more than this for NS, viz., a special status, so that NS can convey its meaning without itself being considered as either true or false.

The opponent apparently has two other alternatives open to him: (a) He may say that one means of knowledge is validated[14] by another means of knowledge. But then he will have to admit that at least one means of knowledge is self-validating. (b) He may claim that a means of knowledge is validated by the truth or fact it reveals, and the fact it reveals is validated by that very means of knowledge. But then Nāgārjuna has placed his opponent where he actually wanted him to be. The means of knowledge and the truths they reveal thus stand together and fall together. To establish a truth you need the means of knowledge, and to validate the means of knowledge you need a truth. This, Nāgārjuna insists, spells out only a variety of the vicious circle.[15]

This may remind us of the old and rather trivial controversy of the chicken and the egg. But Nāgārjuna's point is not necessarily trivial. He is not asking 'Which came first? the chicken or the egg?' He raises instead a pertinent question, viz., if one asserts that the *pramāṇas* (means of knowledge) establish the *prameyas* (truth), is it not then equally possible to assert that the *prameyas* validate the *pramāṇas*? Or, to use the well-known simile of Nāgārjuna, if one can say that the father generates the son, it is then equally sayable that the son generates the father, for without a son how could one be a father?[16] The point of all this is that the opponent's almost unflinching confidence in the *pramāṇa* system as the best method of establishing truths, is hereby shown to be based upon some very questionable hypotheses, and he is forced to abandon his insistence that a philosophic debate should strictly be conducted and regulated by a *pramāṇa* system.

The textual tradition of ancient India speaks generally of three types of 'formal' philosophic debate: *vāda*, *jalpa*, and *vitaṇḍā*.[17] The first is said to be characterized by what may be called the philosopher's search for the truth. This type of debate is used to explain and clarify some philosophic position (thesis) to those who wish to understand it (e.g., the pupils). Each debate has two sides: the proponent and opponent. In the *vāda* type of debate, however, both sides are committed to find a correct position and establish the same with the help of accredited means of knowledge (*pramāṇa*) as well as by valid hypothetical, or inductive, or dialectical reasoning (*tarka*). Here, a position is defended only with valid reasoning and refutation is conducted by locating fallacies in the counter thesis. This debate is concluded as soon as the truth is established.

The second type of debate (*jalpa*) is characterized not so much by the philosopher's search for the truth as by the disputant's drive for victory. Thus, in the second type, not only valid reasonings, etc., are applied, but also, to ensure victory over the opponent, sophistry and trickery become part of the rules of the game. Each side tries to establish a thesis and refute a counter thesis, and victory can be achieved, as in war, by either fair or unfair means. A false rejoinder or a criticism to confuse the opponent or to confute the issue is permissible in this debate.

The third type of debate (*vitaṇḍā*) is cryptically described in the Nyāyasūtra 1.2.44 as one that is concerned with only the refutation of the thesis but not with the establishment of any counter thesis or counter position. It is a negative debate where the disputant's responsibility lies only in refutation. Commentators from Vātsyāyana onwards remarked that *vitaṇḍā*, i.e. this third kind, is no better than useless wrangling and is a very disreputable form of debate. In other words, this debate has all the faults of the second form of debate (*jalpa*) but lacks all the virtues of the first type. Vātsyāyana maintained that *vitaṇḍā* is actually an embarrassment to the philosophers, and that it is even worse than *jalpa*, for the victory in this form of debate is not only unfair but also undeserved. It is an inglorious victory, for the debater in this case enjoys an unfair advantage which is not allowed to his opponent. The debater is exclusively concerned with finding fault with the opponent's thesis, but the opponent cannot do the same, for the debater may have no thesis of his own or no position to defend.[18]

But in spite of the denunciation of *vitaṇḍā* by Vātsyāyana, many respectable philosophers regarded this negative form of debate as a very useful and effective philosophic method. In fact, *vitaṇḍā* is not necessarily a futile wrangling. Even Akṣapāda Gotama did not think so. According to him, as we have seen above, a *vitaṇḍā* consists not in defending any view but in refuting another view. Thus, while determination of truth is the goal of the first type (*vāda*) and victory is the goal of the second type (*jalpa*), the goal of the third type (*vitaṇḍā*) is either of them or both. For, the mystic or the monistic philosopher may take the position that the refutation of wrong views will be tantamount to the establishment of the truth. In other words, for the mystic, the truth is self-evident as soon as the veils of wrong views are lifted. And if truth is established in this negative way, victory is also achieved. This interpretation of *vitaṇḍā* (contrary to Vātsyāyana's comment) is supported even by some Naiyāyikas, e.g., Sānātanī.[19]

Mystics and monistic philosophers of India used *vitaṇḍā* or negative argumentation as a very fruitful philosophic activity. And in this regard they were joined by the Cārvāka sceptics and the agnostics. Monistic philosophers generally believed in an Ultimate Reality which is ineffable in principle. Thus, the Ultimate Reality cannot directly be the subject of any philosophic discourse (which is only *prapañca*). Faced with this problem, the monistic philosophers chose *vitaṇḍā*, i.e. the respectable form of the negative argumentation that I have discussed above, as an expedient to communicate their message. We may doubt whether Nāgārjuna can strictly be called a mystic. But we cannot doubt that he expounded the *tattva* (truth) simply by not talking about it:

> Not a word was uttered by you, O Master, and (yet) all the disciples are refreshed (satisfied) by the shower of (your teaching of) *dharma*.[20]

One of the effective ways of conducting *vitaṇḍā*, i.e., the negative form of philosophic debate, is to use the well-known pattern of philosophic argument called *prasaṅga*. That Nāgārjuna greatly favoured the use of *prasaṅga* can hardly be denied.[21] The *prasaṅga* form of argument, which I am inclined to translate as *reductio ad absurdum*, is very suitable for the destructive use which the debater in *vitaṇḍā* is particularly interested in. Briefly the method is this. The debater takes the purported thesis of the opponent, or a set of interrelated ideas or concepts accepted by the opponent (such as, motion, time, and causality), and deduces from it (logical) consequences which would be shown to be *either* inconsistent with the original thesis or the original set of concepts, *or* decidedly absurd in the light of our everyday experience. Thus, the original position of the opponent will be reduced to a nonsensical claim. I recommend *reductio ad absurdum* as a translation of *prasaṅga*, for the method is strikingly similar to the *reductio ad absurdum* described by Professor Gilbert Ryle in his Inaugural Lecture at Oxford: 'A pattern of argument which is proper and even proprietary to philosophy is the *reductio ad absurdum*. This argument moves by extracting contradictions or logical paradoxes from its material.'[22] Ryle distinguished the weak Euclidean *reductio* from the strong *reductio* that is generally used by philosophers. In Euclidean reduction, the truth of a theorem is proved by deducing from it contradictory consequences which are in conflict with the axioms of the system or with consequences drawn from them. Here the truth of the theorem is made dependent upon the assumption of the truth of the axioms. It is weak in the sense that it shows only that either the theorem is true if the axioms are true or that both are false.

Prasaṅga, like the strong reduction, is a tool for the refutation of the opponent's position in a debate. Ryle compared strong reduction with 'destruction-tests' of the engineers and physicists to determine the strength and usefulness of metals etc. He has, however, argued that there is a constructive side to the strong *reductio*. For, he says, 'Absurdities are the original goad to philosophical thinking; they continue to be its scalpel' (p. 12). He also compared strong *reductio* with the threshing operation by which chaff is separated and discarded and grain is collected. But I believe, a Nāgārjuna or a Śrīharṣa would hesitate to assign such a positive character to the *prasaṅga* as 'collecting the grain' after the threshing. Rather, it would be urged by an Indian *prāsaṅgika* that after the flail with its winnowing fan has blown away the chaff of misconception and wrong thesis, the truth will shine by itself in its own glory. *Prasaṅga* and *vitaṇḍā* cannot tell us what is true or what exists, but they can certainly tell us, if they are properly employed, what is not true and what does not exist.

Śrīharṣa in the Advaita Vedānta tradition was a worthy successor of Nāgārjuna in the use of the above method as an essential part of philosophic activity. Śrīharṣa was an original thinker of the Vedānta school. He had the boldness to claim—and he made good his claim—that as far as philosophical method is concerned there exists very little difference between a Mādhyamika and a Advaita Vedāntin, or even between a mystic and a Cārvāka nihilist.

The *reductio* is not the only form of argument used by philosophers, a point already conceded by Ryle.[23] We can think of philosophers as divided into two main groups: the *prāsaṅgika* (the *vitaṇḍin*) and the *pramāṇa-vādin*. The first group consists of those who use only the *reductio* and the negative form of debate, while the second group comprises those who would establish, in addition to the *reductio*, a system of *pramāṇas* or accredited means of knowledge on the basis of which they would construct a system. One of the platitudes of the *pramāṇa-vādin*, i.e. the second group of philosophers, is that a philosophic debate cannot properly begin unless both parties entering it first admit that *pramāṇas*—i.e. means of knowledge such as perception and inference, and logical fallacies—are acceptable realities. For it is only with the help of such concepts that a philosophic debate can properly proceed. This was the well expressed view of Vātsyāyana and many *pramāṇa-vādins* against the negative form of debate.

Śrīharṣa, in the beginning of his *Khaṇḍanakhaṇḍakhādya*, attacks the above platitude and, in order to reject it, he first resolves it into four possible alternative meanings: the platitude may mean:

1. That debaters who do not admit a *pramāṇa* system are unable to start a debate,

or, 2. That the *pramāṇas* are directly related to the debate as cause to its effect,

or, 3. That it is the practice of all people and philosophers alike first to accept a system of *pramāṇas* and then to enter a philosophic debate,

or, 4. That without the acceptance of *pramāṇas* and logical fallacies, the twin goals of a debate, viz., the establishment of truth and determination of victory, will never be achieved. (*Kk*., p. 6)

Śrīharṣa rejects, as anyone could have guessed, all the four alternatives.

> The first alternative is untenable, for such philosophers as Cārvāka and Mādhyamika do enter into serious philosophic debates despite their refusal to admit the existence of a *pramāṇa* system. Indeed, if such debates did not exist, your attempt (i.e., the attempt of a *pramāṇa-vādin*) to refute such debates (viz., *vitaṇḍā*) would be the most unusual behaviour (on your part). (*Kk*., p. 7)

Śrīharṣa argues that it is in fact unfair to shut the door of the philosophic debating room to someone just because of his prior refusal to accept a *pramāṇa* system. (*Kk*., p. 7)

> You seem to be using the refusal to admit the existence of *pramāṇas* as a new kind of silencing charm. But did not Bṛhaspati, in spite of this charm, write the *Lokāyata-sūtras*? Did not the Buddha also teach the Mādhyamika texts (debating against the rival philosophers)? And did not Śaṅkara write his commentary on the *sūtras* of Bādarāyaṇa?

One may note that citation of the above counter examples by Śrīharṣa eventually proves that alternatives 2 and 3 are also wrong.

The opponent might rejoin that these counter examples do not constitute real philosophical debates since they are incapable of proving or disproving anything. For as long as the *pramāṇas*, etc., are not admitted nothing can strictly be proved or disproved. Anticipating this rejoinder, Śrīharṣa replies as follows. First, one may enter a debate only by *provisionally* accepting some *pramāṇas* and logical fallacies. But this provisional acceptance (*abhyupagama*) on his part does not entail acceptance of the existence of *pramāṇas*, etc. For, by using *prasaṅga* or *reductio* the debater can show that if the opponent accepts a *pramāṇa*, say *p*, then the logical consequence of *p* will *either* be inconsistent with *p* (directly or indirectly) *or* it will be patently absurd. This expedient of provisional acceptance seems to be an echo of Nāgārjuna's appeal to the *vyavahāra* level of truth for making possible a philosophical discourse.

Second, Śrīharṣa insists that even such a provisional acceptance is not essential to the debater's position. True, in the context of a debate, we need to determine what counts as good and successful argument and what counts as bad and unsuccessful argument. But a Mādhyamika or a Cārvāka will remain satisfied as long as he can determine that certain arguments are invalid. Thus, a Mādhyamika or a Cārvāka is qualified to enter into a debate if he is capable of locating some logical defects (fallacies) in the opponent's argument. He can very well maintain an indifferent attitude (*udāsīna*) toward the *pramāṇas*. For it is the opponent who will need the service of *pramāṇas* to establish the truth of his claim. The opponent such as the Naiyāyika cannot be satisfied, as apparently Mādhyamika or the Vedāntin debater can, with devising a refutation of the refutation devised already by his rival. For while inconsistency (or absurdity) may guarantee the falsity of one's claim, consistency does not guarantee its truth, Only a *pramāṇa* can establish such a truth.

Moreover, Śrīharṣa argues, even the fourth alternative given above is wrong. For, in debate there will be a neutral judge (*madhyastha*) who will decide who has won. If he finds that one debater (be he a Mādhyamika or a Cārvāka) has not violated the conventional rules of the debate while the other has done so, he will declare the first as victorious. And this does not entail, as far as Śrīharṣa can see, that the victorious debater must first accept a system of *pramāṇas*. If you now ask the victorious debater how then the truth is to be established, he will shrug it off by pointing out that truths are self-evident. When the chaff is winnowed away, only the grain of truth remains.

I have now concluded my illustrative exposition of the uses of logic and arguments made by the so called mystical philosophers of India. Let me come back to my original theme. My personal philosophical view does not, I must admit, coincide with that of either Māhāyana Buddhism or Advaita Vedānta. But I must emphasize at the same time that these two philosophical systems of the East were not the work of fools. I think I have given enough evidence already to show that neither of the two systems constituted a philosophy of 'woolly ideas', as is sometimes thought today. Of course, there are texts containing a popular and poetic presentation of these systems. And the emotional appeal of such presentation can strike chords untouched by the debate of Śrīharṣa or rational arguments of Nāgārjuna. The religious literature of the East is very rich in this respect. There are unique passages from the Upaniṣads, for example, which are grand, elevating and enjoyable irrespective of their claim to truth. For many they represent genuine expressions of mystical experience. For others, they embody metaphysical speculations, for still others poetry. Thousands of other religious texts have been written in this manner. There is naturally a danger that uncritical appraisal of these texts may degenerate into inanities. But the critical philosophers of India, who were also mystically inclined, often made mysticism philosophically attractive and intellectually stimulating. I have tried to show how serious was their attempt, and how near they came to succeeding in it. Even without sharing the philosophical views of Buddhism and Vedānta, one can very well appreciate their aesthetic appeal, their beauty, and their grandeur.

From a philosophical point of view, one may argue that no dispassionate judgement is possible without proper analysis and clarification of the doctrine we wish to judge. In order even to criticize these doctrines, one needs to understand them clearly. Thus the spirit of what I have called in another context 'intellectual non-violence' has been shown surprisingly and conspicuously by the Jaina philosophers of India: any criticism must be preceded by a proper and total understanding of the doctrine one tries to criticize. It is, of course, possible, though perhaps not probable, that if one *fully* understands these mystical doctrines, one would find very little in them to be critical about. One may still reasonably assume that a rational comprehension of them is possible. But my feeling is that total understanding in this case will probably be ever elusive. Using an analogy which Freud applied to his own theories, I am tempted to say that they are like the paintings of Rembrandt—a little light and a great deal of darkness.

If total understanding through rational means will always be elusive, one may argue, why try at all? Why, indeed? It is a fact that Śrīharṣa, Nāgārjuna, and Diṅnāga have been accused by fellow-Buddhists and fellow-Vedāntins of indulging in a profane and debased enterprise. The Taoist says, 'The fish trap exists because of the fish, once you have got the fish you can forget the trap.'

The above charge, I think, is mistaken on at least two counts. First, the logical arguments are useful, for they illuminate the mystical instead of deepening its mystery. In fact, the logical is indispensable (to, at least, a large number of people) for the illumination of the mystical. One needs the fish trap if one hopes to catch the fish at all. You can kick the ladder away only when you have climbed up the wall, not before. Or, to use the analogy mentioned by Candrakīrti, one can forget the raft after one has crossed to the other shore. Second, the human mind is an incurably restless organ. One can repeat the parable of the Monkey and the Crooked Hair (where in order to prevent the monkey from engaging in mischief the master ordered him to straighten a naturally crooked hair, in which task he had since then been constantly engaged). Professor B. Scharfstein has put it very nicely:

> Who with the wit to use it (the mind) can keep it still for long? A daydreaming pianist will hammer with his fingers on invisible keys, a poet will mutter with fragmentary eloquence, a bright man will reason, quietly if he must, but impatient to express himself aloud. And just as a rationalist may sometimes break out into mystical poetry, mystics, unable or unwilling to check themselves, break out into reason, and some of them, after they have tasted the forbidden pleasure, go on enjoying it until one is led to suspect that they are anti-rational mystics by name but reasoners by nature, with the normal, unmystical lust to defeat the enemy.[24]

Thus we have to reckon with the force of the rational component of human mind. The rational component will go on performing its function even if it is only to justify the so-called 'irrational' propensities. For example, many people feel that it is not enough to have a religious faith, but that such faith requires, or must admit of, rational support. Belief in *theos* (God) is often not enough, and hence theology becomes, along with it, a very useful enterprise. *Rasa*, or aesthetic pleasure that is derived from a poem, music, or a painting, is not always satisfying by itself. For a theory of beauty or aesthetics plays often an important role in such enjoyment. In the same way we see that the taste of mystical experience was not enough for many ancient Indians, for they fabricated or constructed the most amazing illumination of mysticism through the use of logic. They wished to comprehend rationally what they apparently experienced through mystical insight. Or, as some would like to put it, they were driven to their mystical conclusion by the force of their logic.

Let me turn now to the second concern of Professor Zaehner. Do the mystical philosophers of the East, by preaching the doctrine of an ineffable Ultimate Reality, blur the all-important distinction between good and evil? Do they develop a completely amoral position by asking one to transcend good and evil? In a bitter vein, Professor Zaehner stated in his last book that in the light of such an amoral philosophy of monism, it would be impossible to distinguish between a Charles Manson and Mother Theresa. The question of relation (or the lack of it) between morality and the so-called monistic mysticism is a very intricate one. Many issues have to be resolved first and more technical distinctions have to be introduced and emphasized before we can even meaningfully address ourselves to this important question. So I will not go into it here.

While I concede that the salvational aim of Indian mysticism is not always compatible with a moral aim, I must emphasize that the so-called monistic philosophy of the East certainly cannot endorse a Charles Manson, as my predecessor feared. Charles Manson's quoting of the *Bhagavadgītā* is no more surprising than the devil's quoting the Bible. In defence of monism, one can add that no Vedāntic or Buddhist philosophers of repute ever suggested that men should abandon the good-evil distinction before they have achieved *nirvāṇa*. Rather it has always been emphasized that one cannot gain liberating knowledge without having lived a perfectly moral life. Any mystic of the past or the present will no doubt agree. The mystic claims simply that when one realizes the Ultimate Reality—the 'cosmic consciousness'—the good-evil distinction sloughs itself off as an inessential and unnecessary detail, for 'evil has been overcome' and without 'evil' 'good' loses its original meaning.

The above idea, as far as I can see, is not quite foreign to the Christian tradition. It was, for example, St Augustine who rejected the Manichaean conception of an ultimate dualism of good and evil (which was probably borrowed from Zoroastrianism) and formulated his theodicy. Augustine argued that evil has no independent existence, since it is only a privation or perversion of something good. And man is said to be intrinsically good, though corruptible. The Indian mystic, however, solves the problem in a slightly different way. He argues that good exists at two levels, which we may distinguish as $good_1$ and $good_2$. What is $good_1$ is contrasted with evil, and at the ordinary level, dualism of good and evil prevails. But $good_1$ and evil are also intimately related to each other. They, like light and darkness, stand together and fall together. Thus, when evil is eliminated, $good_2$ then makes its presence felt. This is the ultimate good which is said to be beyond $good_1$ and evil. When *avidyā* is destroyed, suffering or *duḥkha* vanishes itself, not because it is an illusion but because it is conditioned by *avidyā*. To use a simile; as long as there is night, darkness and light (from lamps, etc.) fight each other, but when the sun appears and destroys darkness, lamp-light, etc., are also rendered insignificant.

Thus, the mystical transcendence of good and evil does not have any immoral, moral, or even amoral sense. Each mystic (whether a Vedāntin or a Buddhist), on the other hand, has been deeply concerned with moral life in the everyday world. He always emphasizes that there are two quite different levels of reality—the provisional or conventional, and the ultimate. Nāgārjuna says quite explicitly:[25]

He who does not understand the distinction of the two levels of truth (reality), does not understand the truth of the doctrine of the Buddha.

Like a snake grasped at the wrong end, or a craft wrongly learnt, the emptiness doctrine, when it is wrongly understood, destroys a person of poor intelligence.

At the everyday level of reality, the good-evil distinction is, of course, very important, indeed vital. Thus, morality is as much a concern for the mystical philosopher as it is for any non-mystical thinker.

Even the so-called illusory or fictional nature of the everyday world should not foster amorality in our everyday behaviour. For the everyday level of reality (i.e. *saṁvṛti*) is no less important for the mystic in his striving for salvation or *nirvāṇa*. Nāgārjuna insists:[26]

The Ultimate Reality cannot be taught without recourse to everyday reality. And *nirvāṇa* cannot be attained without the understanding of Ultimate Reality.

In fact, it is a common mistake—a mistake that is unfortunately being perpetuated by many today—to describe the *saṁvṛti*, i.e., the everyday world, as an illusion or even an appearance. It is, I think, improper to assume that the so-called appearance-reality distinction, so well-known in Western philosophy, will also hold for Nāgārjuna and Śaṅkara. Of course, it is said that the everyday world is not real. But an object can be said to be *not real* in two very different senses. The so-called object may be non-existent, and hence deserves to be called 'not real'. On the other hand, a toy gun, for example, can be said to be 'not real' because it is a toy gun. A toy elephant (to use an image of the *Laṅkāvatāra-sūtra*) does not possess the own-nature or *svabhāva* that it is supposed to possess or that it professes to possess.

Similarly, the everyday world, it is argued, does not embody the *svabhāva* or essence it professes to embody. It falls short of the ideal of *svabhāva*, and in this sense it is unreal. Thus, *saṁsāra* or *saṁvṛti* is not a mere appearance, still less an illusion—it is something that is not quite successful in embodying an own-nature, *svabhāva*.[27] It seems to be misrepresentation to call the everyday world an illusion, or identical with the Red King's dream in Alice's adventures.

Proper understanding of the distinction between *saṁvṛti* and *paramārtha*, between the everyday reality and the Ultimate Reality, is, as has already been emphasized, the key to the understanding of the nature of Indian mysticism. *Saṁvṛti* is not identical with illusion although it may be inclusive of that which we call illusion. Thus, some philosophers (cf. Bhāvaviveka, Prajñākaramati, etc.) try to distinguish between the true *saṁvṛti* and the false *saṁvṛti* (*tathya* and *mithyā*). False *saṁvṛti* refers to the illusory appearance of things (mirage, etc.) But true *saṁvṛti* is the everyday world where a spade appears as a spade and we are allowed to call a spade a spade. This is called *saṁvṛti* only because it covers and conceals the ultimate nature of the object we see. This is justifiable since *saṁvṛti* etymologically means covering and concealing. In fact, each thing is said by the mystic to have two natures or aspects, one that is grasped by our ordinary perception and intellect, and the other that lies concealed or hidden by the first but is revealed only to the perfect wisdom or *prajñā-pāramitā*. Our worldly behaviour operates with the first nature or the first aspect, while the second is operative only in *nirvāṇa*. But the Indian mystic warns at the same time that it is the first alone that can lead us to the second. And when one penetrates the second, the previous duality of nature merges into one. That is what is called the mystic 'unity' or oneness of reality.

The everyday world is therefore vitally important to the mystic, it is important for his pursuit of *nirvāṇa*. And consequently, morality is part and parcel of the same pursuit. Thus, I believe that it is possible fully to vindicate morality in mysticism, even in the monistic mysticism of the East.

Before I conclude, I wish to make some general observations about the aim and purpose of the Spalding Professorship at the University of Oxford. The express aim of the late Mr Spalding was to bring together the world's great religions 'in closer understanding, harmony and friendship'. Professor Zaehner in his inaugural address said (p. 17): 'The only common ground is that the function of religion is to provide release. There is no agreement at all as to what it is that man must be released from. The great religions are talking at cross purposes.' While I do not disagree for a moment that the great religions of East and West differ greatly one from another, I cannot help feeling that one is over-stating the case for distinction and antagonism if one thinks that they work 'at cross purposes'. Here again there is a lesson to be learnt from the Jainas of India. The central philosophy of Jainism is sometimes described as the non-onesidedness of truth (*anekāntavāda*). In my opinion, this very important philosophic attitude derives its force from the value the early Jainas put on *ahiṁsā* 'non-violence'. As I have already pointed out, the

Jainas carried the principle of non-violence from the physical and practical plane to the intellectual plane. Thus, 'respect for the life of others' was eventually transformed into an obligatory respect for the views and beliefs of others. The Jainas claim that when two or several parties are seriously and sincerely arguing regarding the truth, it is seldom that one side is absolutely wrong, while the other side is absolutely right. The world is not divided only into black and white, for there are innumerable shades of grey in between. The Jainas contend that one should try to understand the particular point of view of each disputing party if one wishes to grasp completely the truth of the situation. The *total* truth, the Jainas emphasize, may be derived from the integration of all different viewpoints (*nayas*).[28]

If the problem of the divergence of the world's great religions is presented to a Jaina, he will comment as follows: One can overstate the divergence and thereby undermine their common ground. This will foster antagonism and probably violence. Or, one can overstate the similarity and thereby blur the vital distinction, which will result in intellectual dishonesty and barrenness. But we need not be caught between these two extremes. Our Jaina friend will humbly ask us to remember that there are many other sides of the question besides the one we, in this particular moment, have in mind. The total truth, the Jaina claims, is ever elusive for a single individual (or a single creed) unless he happens to be omniscient. Or, following the Buddha, one might say that emphasis on the similarity and sameness will be another form of eternalism or *śāśvatavāda*, and emphasis on the ultimate difference will be a form of annihilationism (*ucchedavāda*). But a follower of the Tathāgata should avoid both extremes and follow the Middle Way.

My intention here, I wish to emphasize is not to refute the views of my predecessors. I have tried only to add a new dimension to their thoughts by deriving lessons from my study of the Jaina and the Buddhist philosophy.

If the world's great religions do have a 'common ground', then it will be possible to define the term *religion*. But the definition of religion has proved to be a notoriously difficult task. The problem is further complicated by the existence of such non-theistic Eastern religions as Buddhism, Jainism, and Vedānta. But the difficulty of defining religion adequately is not, I think, insurmountable. An adequate definition must underline the common characteristics underlying the diverse religious traditions of East and West. If such a definition can be formulated it will already be a step towards bringing the world's great religions to what may be called a 'closer understanding'. This is not, however, the place to indulge in attempting to frame a definition. Besides, it would be too ambitious at this stage when there is much groundwork yet to be done.

I wish to make only an impressionistic suggestion.

One of the common factors in all the world's great religions is, as I see it, a belief that the unexamined life is not worth living. In this sense, then, Socrates was a religious philosopher. All great religions, it seems to me, contain a belief that a certain control of the instincts is necessary for our civilized living—a belief that the cultivation of certain positive emotions, e.g., compassion and concern for other people or other beings, is a necessary concomitant of any search for personal *nirvāṇa*, freedom or salvation. In this sense, then Yuddhiṣṭhira of the *Mahābhārata* was an incarnation of *dharma* 'religious duty', for he lived a truly religious life, as Professor Zaehner rightly pointed out in his *Hinduism*, and refused to enter heaven, the so-called highest prize of his religious life, without the animal, a dog, that loyally followed him to the doors of heaven. This incident was, perhaps, the highest expression of the religiosity that Yuddhiṣṭhira had in him. All great religions also include a belief that purely external circumstances cannot constitute the be-all and end-all of human existence—a belief that the world we see only with our senses is not all that there can possibly be. Thus to me, to be religious means to have a humility about what else there is. Moreover, all great religions contain a belief that people can be better than they are as well as a belief that people can experience more than they do.

One may claim that any adequate definition of religion will contain, among many other things, a reference to a higher plane of existence, a 'deathless, painless' existence, or in Buddhist terms, an unconditioned existence, which is in sharp contrast with the existing conditions of life, the mechanical, the existential, the trivial, the non-final, or the non-essential world. Man's religious urge is invariably characterized by a quest for this higher mode of existence. In Indian terminology, it would be stated as a contrast between the *paramārtha* and the *vyavahāra*, between *nirvāṇa* and *saṁsāra*. Some philosophers would call it a contrast between the spiritual and the material, between the fragile and the immortal, between the infinite and the finite. Some historians of religions have called it a distinction between the sacred and profane. Controversy as well as scepticism about such religious concepts as God, an after-life or *nirvāṇa* centres around the question whether such a different (higher) plane of existence exists in some acceptable sense. But after many centuries of controversy it is now reasonably clear that its supposed existence can be neither proved nor disproved through our accredited means of knowledge. Even the ancient Mīmāṃsaka observed that ordinary *pramāṇas*, perception and inference, are powerless either to validate or to invalidate religious concepts, and hence any attempt in this direction would yield very little at the end.

Man's quest and concern for the sacred takes different forms and has different expressions all over the world. Hence the diversities of the world's great religions. The sociologist will probably connect this concern with the realities of the human situation, man's powerlessness and frustration concerning scarcity and uncertainty, his lack of prevision of, and control over, events that are crucially important to his safety, happiness, and welfare. Classical psychoananlysis will give a genetic explanation for this urge in terms of unconscious wish-fulfilment as well as in terms of a number of technical and clinical concepts such as anxiety, the defence-mechanisms, the Oedipus situation and the problems of obsessional neurosis. But again, a genetic explanation (whether sociological or psychological) of our concern for the sacred and the higher form of existence does nothing either to prove or to disprove the sacred. A comment of Ernest Jones, whom Freud described as the greatest psychoanalyst of the English speaking world, illustrates the point nicely:

> . . . religious beliefs, whether savage, mythological or Christian, may or may not be true—in their nature they are not capable of proof or disproof—but it is highly probable that they would have arisen in their identical forms whether they were true or not. . . But we must not forget that neurosis is an expression of the same forces and conflicts that have led to the loftiest aspirations and profoundest achievements of our race, and that neurotics are often the torch-bearers of civilization. They may strain themselves in the effort, but without that effort there would be no civilization.[29]

The Vedic seer raised the question, 'Which god is really there, to whom we must offer oblation?' This shows that scepticism is as old as the birth of civilization. But so is man's attempt to comprehend rationally the religious and the mystical. Both the religious man and the rational man in our society today raise their eyebrows at the question of 'rational comprehension' of the religious and the mystical. For the rational man believes that religion is basically irrational; it is, at its best, above and beyond reason, and, at its worst, is below reason. The religious man will hesitate because, for him, religion is based on experience or on faith or on both. Hence, he would argue, it is impossible for an agnostic, who lacks any experience, either religious or mystical, to have a rational comprehension of religion or mysticism. For a man may understand the definition of drunkenness, but will never rationally understand what it *really* is to be drunk.

But I think that this is another dichotomy that my Jaina friend will advise us to avoid, for he believes that it is mistaken. Man is a rational animal, but, what is more interesting, he is not exclusively rational. Hence, he continues to search for the 'promised' land, for the 'sacred', for *nirvāṇa*. It has been claimed by the sociologist that human civilization is but a fabrication of a child afraid to be alone in the dark. And religion is part of that civilization. Man also has a monkey inside him, which prompts him to ask rational questions and demand rational answers. Otherwise, we would not have a Socrates, or an Aristotle, or a Buddha, or a Nāgārjuna, or a Śrīharṣa. As my predecessor used often to say, quoting a phrase of Al-Ghazali, 'for reason is God's scale on earth'.[30]

I shall conclude, in a rather lighter vein, by referring to a few well-known metaphors. The ordinary man is probably a counter-example to the concept of Buridan's ass. We all know what Buridan's ass[31] did. He was given a choice to eat from two equal bales of hay situated at equal distance from him. But being unable to decide between the two equally balanced alternatives, he chose to starve himself to death. The main purpose of this story is to illustrate the problem of reasoned choice in the absence of preference. But my point is slightly different.

Buridan's ass was most probably a philosopher, certainly a logician. But an ordinary man even with reason chooses to act randomly under the circumstances. In fact, the ordinary man is worse off than Buridan's ass in this matter. He is torn and tormented by the conflict between the taste of 'the tree of life' and that of 'the tree of knowledge'. And reason cannot show any evaluative preference of one over the other. His condition is comparable to that of one who is placed between two equally tempting glasses of juice—one containing, say, the juice of religion and mysticism and the other that of rationality and scepticism—and being attracted to both, tries, perhaps not unreasonably, to partake a little of both. Thus, he may ask much in the same way the Vedic seer asked,

'To what god shall we offer oblation?'

'KASMAI DEVĀYA HAVIṢĀ VIDHEMA?'

Notes and References

Vv. *Vigrahavyāvartanī*, Nāgārjuna. Edited by E.H. Johnston and Arnold Kunst, *Melanges chinois et bouddhiques*, vol. IX, 1948–51, pp. 99–152.
Dr K. Bhattacharya translated this text with Introduction and Notes, 'The Dialectical Methods of Nāgārjuna' in *Journal of Indian Philosophy* (D. Reidel, Dordrecht, 1971), vol. I, no. 3, 1971. Passages quoted here are, however, from my own translation.

Kk. *Khandanakhandakhādya*, Śrīharṣa. Edited by Dr Navikānta Jhā. Kashi Sanskrit Series, Chowkhamba: Varanasi, 1970.
An English translation of the Introductory portions of this text has been prepared with elaborate notes and explanation by Dr Phyllis Granoff. 'Philosophy and Argument in Late Vedata', *Classical India Monograph Series* (D. Reidel, Dordrecht, 1978). Passages quoted here are, however, from my own translation.

1. R.C. Zaehner: *Our Savage God* (London, Collins, 1974): '. . . and in our everyday world this ambivalence can have disastrous results', p. 15.
2. Ibid., p. 294.
3. Ibid., pp. 14–15
4. I am tempted to quote the passage from *Pañcatantra* (Kathāmukha, beginning with *'dvādasabhih varṣaih kila vyākaraṇaṃ śrūyate'*. See F. Edgerton's *The Pañcatantra Reconstructed* (A.O.S., New Haven, 1924), p. 4. The passage makes the point that before a pupil should start learning a *śāstra*, he must first spend twelve years in the study of grammar, etc.
5. See my 'Double Negation in Navyanyāya', M. Nagatomi *et al.* eds, *Sanskrit and Indian Studies: Essays in Honour of Gaurinath Sastri*, Calcutta, 1980. pp. 69–78.
6. *Mādhyamika-śāstra*, ch. 15, verses 8, 9 (ed. P.L. Vaidya, 1960).
   We may note that the concept of 'own-nature' in Nāgārjuna's writings is almost as ambiguous as the concept of essence of Aristotle or the theory of Forms in Plato. The following comment from the *Mādhyamika-kārikā*, ch. 15, verse 2, may be of some help:

   > How could "own-nature" be something created? For 'own-nature' is (surely) uncreated (literally, "non-artificial" = *akṛtrima*) and independent of others as well.

7. *Vv.*, p. 108.
8. *Nyāyasūtras,* 5.1.39–43 (ed. G. Jha, Poona Oriental Series, Oriental Book Agency, Poona, 1939).
9. *Vv.*, pp. 109–10.
10. I have the following distinction of paradox and antinomy in my mind. A paradox packs a surprise, but the surprise quickly dissipates itself as we

ponder the proof. This is how W.V. Quine defines what he calls 'veridical paradox'. A 'falsidical paradox', according to Quine, packs a surprise, but it is seen as a false alarm when we solve the underlying fallacy. 'An antinomy, however, packs a surprise that can be accommodated by nothing less than a repudiation of part of our conceptual heritage.' *The Ways of Paradox and Other Essays*, Revised and Enlarged Edition (Harvard University Press, Cambridge, 1976), p. 9.

11. This is similar to the point raised by Alonzo Church regarding the Liar Paradox in his review of A. Koyré's, *The Liar* in *The Journal of Symbolic Logic*, vol. 12 (1946), p. 131.
12. This point is mentioned by Nicholas Rescher in 'Self-referential Statement'. See his *Topics in Philosophical Logic* (D. Reidel, Dordrecht, 1968), p. 16.
13. This point is derived from the comments of A.N. Prior. 'Fearing that nothing we fear is the case, asserting that nothing we assert is the case and so on, must be more difficult performances than we at first take them to be' (p. 74). Prior suggests that our problem may be over with the statement of Epimenides if we do *not* suppose that it is *asserted* by him. Prior actually follows here a suggestion of John Buridan. One of John Buridan's examples was 'No proposition is negative'. According to Prior, Buridan insists that the said proposition should be classified as a 'possible' one because things could be as it signified, even though it could not possibly be true. Prior contends, '. . . it can be that no proposition is negative, though it cannot be that 'No proposition is negative' is true (p. 144).

    See 'Epimenides the Cretan', and 'Some problems of self-reference in John Buridan', in A.N. Prior's *Papers in Logic and Ethics* (eds P.T. Geach and A.J.P. Kenny—London, Duckworth, 1976). The present note owes much to an informal discussion I had with my friend Professor Hans Herzberger regarding the problem of self-reference.
14. The Sanskrit word '*siddha*' literally means 'accomplished'. It can be translated either as 'validated' or 'established' depending upon the context. I have taken some liberty in translation to make the point clear.
15. Faults like *ātmāśraya, anyonyāśraya*, and *cakraka* can roughly be called varieties of vicious circle. See my *The Navya-nyāya Doctrine of Negation* (Harvard University Press, Cambridge, Mass., 1968), pp. 82–4.
16. *Vv.*, verses 49, 50.
17. See *Nyāyasūtras* 1.2.1–3.
18. See Vātsyāyana's comments under *Nyāyasūtra* 1.1.1, beginning with '*vitaṇḍā tu parīksyate*', p. 4 (Jha's edition).
19. The work of this author is unfortunately lost. Udayana referred to him as 'an ancient Gauḍa Naiyāyika', and so probably he hailed from Bengal. His independent view about *vitaṇḍā* has been preserved by Udayana. See my *Nyāya-Vaiśeṣika* (Otto Harrassowitz, Wiesbaden, 1977), in *A History of Indian Literature*, ed. Jan Gonda, vol. VI, fasc, p. 92.

20. See G. Tucci, 'The Hymn to the Incomparable One', *Journal of the Royal Asiatic Society*, New Series, 27 (1932), pp. 312–14.
21. See the chapters of the *Kk.*
22. Gilbert Ryle, *Philosophical Arguments*, Inaugural Lecture at Oxford (Oxford, Clarendon Press, 1945), p. 6.
23. Ibid., p. 6. 'I am not trying to prove that no other types of argument are proper to philosophy.'
24. Ben-Ami Scharfstein, *Mystical Experience* (Blackwell, 1973; Penguin Book Inc., Baltimore, Maryland, 1974), p. 44.
25. *Mādhyamika-śāstra*, ch. 24, verses 9, 11.
26. Ibid., verse 10
27. Ibid., verses 15–19.
28. See my *The Central Philosophy of Jainism: Anekāntavāda* (1981, L.D. Indological Institute, Ahmedabad).
29. Ernest Jones, *What is Psychoanalysis*? (London, Allen & Unwin, 1949), p. 105.
30. Zaehner, R.C., *At Sundry Times* (London, Faber & Faber, 1958), p. 12.
31. The example, according to Nicholas Rescher, does not occur in Buridan's extant writings. But it is based on an illustration in Aristotle's *De Caelo* (295b32) that became a standard illustration in the Aristotelian tradition. Rescher, however, has traced the example in its essentially ultimate form in the Arabic philosopher Ghazali and cited a passage from Averroe's *Tahfut-al-Tahafut*. See Rescher's essay 'Buridan, Jean' in *The Encyclopedia of Philosophy*, ed. P. Edwards (Macmillan, London, 1967), vol. I.

3

The Ineffable

Not a word was uttered by you, O Master, and (yet) all the disciples were refreshed by the Dharma-Shower.

(Ascribed to Nāgārjuna)

How strange! Under the banyan tree are old men. Their teacher is only a boy. His explanation consists in silence. Yet the disciples have been made free from doubts (through correct understanding).

(*Dakṣiṇamurtistotra*)

The two verses quoted above are from two different streams of Indian tradition. The first is taken from the tradition of Mahāyāna Buddhism, while the second is from Advaita Vedānta of Saṃkara. Taken together they present us with the classic, and in every sense, poetic formulation of what I shall call here the *Ineffability* doctrine. Simply stated, the *Ineffability* doctrine means that (a) the Ultimate Reality is ineffable, and (b) the mystical experience in which the Ultimate Reality is supposed to be revealed is also beyond words. The Upaniṣadic mysticism of ancient India was eloquent about the ineffability of the bliss of Brahman. Thus the Taittiriya says,[1]

Where from words turn back
Along with the mind, without reaching
The bliss of Brahman.

And the Kaṭha notes: [2]

'This is it'—thus they recognize
The highest happiness that is ineffable.

In both these passages, the authors insist that the peak experience in Brahmin realization is something that cannot be put into words. It is *too deep* for words.

It seems to be a matter of curious coincidence that the ancient philosophers of religion and the mystics are apparently in agreement with some modern philosophers of language who, under the influence of Ludwig Wittgenstein, hold to the doctrine of *Ineffability* in some form or other. It is, however, true that the Western mystics and theologians in the Judeo-Christian tradition propound the *Ineffability* doctrine in the sense that there is something called God or the divine but nothing in principle can be said about its nature. And this is not exactly the same as the position of Wittgenstein in *Tractatus*, according to which philosophical sentences do not say anything but only 'signify what cannot be said, by presenting clearly what can be said'.[3] But when we think of the *Ineffability* thesis which has been apparently supported by Nāgārjuna and his followers, it does not seem to be very remote from the contention of Wittgenstein. Āryadeva, disciple of Nāgārjuna, thus contends that although silence (*āryatuṣnīmbhāva*) is the best method to instruct the Ultimate Reality, philosophic discourses are not entirely useless.[4]

Just as a *mleccha* (one speaking a foreign tongue) cannot be made to understand by any other language but his own, so also (ordinary) people cannot be made to understand by anything except the conventional language.

In the *Laṅkāvatāra-sūtra*, the Tathāgata says this with the help of a simile:[5]

Just as a king or merchant (at first) attracts his children with the help of beautiful clay animals for play, and then (at the right time) presents them with real animals, I attract similarly my disciples with various shadow characteristics of the dharmas and then instruct them (when the right time comes) the *Bhūtakoṭi* which is to be experienced by each of them personally.

One is obviously reminded here of the 'ladder' analogy of Wittgenstein:[6]

My propositions serve as elucidations in the following way: anyone who understands me eventually recognizes them as nonsensical, when he has used them—as steps—to climb up beyond. (He must, so to speak, throw away the latter after he has climbed up it.)

Even Diṅnāga, who rejected Nāgārjuna's critique of the *pramāṇa* theory, believed the *svalakṣaṇas* to be ultimately beyond words. This is, at least, how Diṅnāga was interpreted by his later interpreter, Dharmakīrti. To use Diṅnāga's own words, the *svalakṣaṇas* (the ultimate particulars) are self-manifesting (*sva-saṃvedya*), inexpressible in words (*anirdeśya*) and visible to the respective sense-organs (*indriya-gocaraḥ*).[7] While I concede that Diṅnāga's line admits of alternative interpretations, I wish to point out that at least one of the traditional interpretations believes that for Diṅnāga the *svalakṣaṇas*, which are ultimately real and are revealed in perceptual consciousness, are ineffable. What *can* be seen, *cannot* be said.

Indian philosophers who hold to the doctrine of *Ineffability* in some form or other, agree that all philosophic discourses about the Ultimate Reality are provisional, but not useless. A religious or philosophic discourse that is based upon a belief of the *Ineffability* thesis is considered by Indian philosophers to be a game or play leading to a goal, but it is to be sure a worthwhile game. There are various means by which this game can be played. Broadly speaking, Indian philosophers resort to three different methods by which they think the notion of the Ineffable Ultimate Reality may be effectively conveyed. I shall discuss them accordingly.

First, there is the method *via negativa*. This method is familiar to the Western theologians as the negative theology, according to which it is believed that although there is God nothing *affirmative* can be said about its nature. In the Indian tradition, this method is as old as Yājñavalkya of the *Bṛhadāraṇyaka Upaniṣad*. Yājñavalkya's much-acclaimed method is nick-named *neti neti*: [8]

This Self is (simply described as) *not, not.*

Even Nāgārjuna defines *tattva—that-ness* (reality) with the help of this method:[9]

The characteristic of *tattva—that-ness* is such that it is independent of being instructed by others, not diversified by diversifying speech, devoid of thought-construction, and non-dual (unambiguous) in meaning.

The method, in fact, consists in saying that although no positive characterization of the Ultimate Reality is possible, a negative characterization may be in order.

An objection to this method will take us deeper into the logical (philosophical) problem of negation. Negation is usually understood as the opposite of affirmation. It is generally presumed that there cannot be any bare negation. Whenever anything is denied, some positive ground of denial is assumed. From this rather trivially true premise, it is sometimes argued that each denial involves us into some form of commitment, some form of positive presupposition. The presupposition may be in the form of assuring the existence of a subject of the denial (as the existence of the subject in the denial, *this is not a pot*). Or it may be in the form of our implicitly assuming some other predicate to be true of the subject (as *red* or *green* in the denial, *the pot is not blue*).

Indian logicians from very ancient times used to make a distinction between the two types of negation: *paryudāsa privation of terms* and *prasajya-pratiṣedha—denial of what could have been*, roughly corresponding to the term-negation and propositional negation or denial of a predication.[10] The Sanskrit grammarians rightly noted that formation of Sanskrit compounds is allowed generally in the first case, but not in the second. It is also pointed out that positive presupposition is very prominent in the first case, but not so in the second. Bhāvaviveka, a follower of Nāgārjuna, argued that in presenting the Ineffable through the *via negativa* method the second type of negation was involved. In fact, it would be an extreme form of the second type of negation—a negation where the positive presupposition is practically avoided.[11] The second type of negation, as it was understood by Bhāvaviveka, always played an important role in Buddhist philosophy. Thus, even a follower of Diṅnāga would interpret his *apoha* doctrine as involving negation where the presuppositional ground is suspended.[12] One may further argue that if, in Diṅnāga's system, *svalakṣaṇas* are ineffable, then it is only natural that a Diṅnāgian would say that the ineffable *svalakṣaṇas* are presented through this type of *apoha* or double negation. For this will simply be a more sophisticated use of the *via negativa* method.

The second method consists in assigning contradictory attributes or predicates to the Ultimate Reality. Mystics of all ages and of all countries are very fond of this method. To quote from ancient Indian sources:

It is not coarse, not fine, not short, not long. (*Bṛhadāraṇyaka III.8*)

It moves, it moves not, it is far, and it is near. (*Iśa*)

The Mādhyamikas, in fact, combine the first, and the second method and expound their doctrine of Emptiness as the *denial* of the fourfold or twofold alternatives. Instead of asserting that the Ultimate Reality is both *A* and not *A*, it is said that it is neither.

The usual objection to this method is that it defies the laws of ordinary logic. This feeling is generally reflected in the slogan: *mysticism defies rationality*. Many things can be said in favour as well as against this contention, but we will not go into them here.[13] Briefly, it may be stated that it is futile to construct a *super logic* in order to justify mysticism. Rather, it may be a reasonable move if we concede that mysticism is concerned with the non-rational, emotive or affective components of the human mind.

The third method consists in the use of metaphor and rhetoric to convey the notion of ineffability. This is not to be confused with the *Ineffability* thesis in Aesthetics, according to which a work of art succeeds in expressing something (an emotion or feeling) which ordinary language fails to do.[14] Some Indian philosophers of language argue that although the Ultimate Reality is, in principle, ineffable, it can be conveyed through what they call the operation of *lakṣaṇā—indicative function of a word.* Indian semantic theory states that a word occurring in a sentence contributes to the sentence-meaning in either of the two ways: it may *express* a meaning (which would be its primary meaning, generally the lexical meaning) or it may *indicate* a meaning (directly or indirectly connected with the lexical meaning). Thus Madhusūdana Sarasvatī argues that words like *Brahman, God*, or *The Ultimate Reality* are not entirely meaningless, for although they cannot, in principle, *express* the ineffable, they can very well *indicate* it through the indicative function of a word.

Critics of this method, however, point out that it is rather odd that a word that lacks any *express* meaning or lexical meaning, in principle, will be able to have an *indicated* meaning. Generally the rule is: when the lexical meaning of a word is incompatible with the intended meaning of the sentence in which it occurs, we resort to its *indicated* or metaphorical meaning (e.g., *the village is on the river*). Now, if words like *Brahman* mean through *indication* the Ineffable, what do they mean directly? Further, what is the relation between this indicated meaning of the word *Brahman* and its direct lexical meaning?

These objections, however, can be answered with some stipulations, but I will not go into them here. The important.thing to remember is that the acceptance of the indicative function of a word is not to be treated as a license which will allow us to derive any meaning from the word according to our whims. It is only a device to account for the already understood sentence-meaning, to explain why a successful communication has taken place between the speaker and the listener when such a communication has already taken place. Thus, it is not like the license of Lewis Carroll's Humpty Dumpty in *Alice's Adventures Through the Looking Glass*:

> 'When *I* use a word' Humpty Dumpty said in rather a scornful tone, 'it means just what I choose it to mean—neither more nor less'. 'The question is,' said Alice, 'whether you *can* make words mean different things.' 'The question is', said Humpty Dumpty, 'which is to be master—that is all.'

The question is: whether we can call something *Brahman* and again claim it to be ineffable.

Let me conclude by showing that the above is not really a logical paradox. In other words, there is a perfectly good interpretation of the Ineffability thesis which is logically unproblematic. One may say, 'There is something *x* or some fact which cannot be put into words,' for to say this is not to put *x* into words. And this statement is not the same as saying 'there is some *x* about which nothing can *literally* be said.' Again, the second statement appears paradoxical only on the surface. If we allow the distinction between the object language and metalanguage then, perhaps, the second version may also be interpreted non-paradoxically.

Notes

1. *Taittirīya* 2.4 (Translation E.H. Hume).
2. *Kaṭha* 5.14.
3. Wittgenstein Tractatus 4.115.
4. Quoted by Candrakīrti, p. 157.
5. *Laṅkavatāra-sūtra*, p. 37.
6. Wittgenstein, pp. 6–54.
7. See Hattori, p. 27.
8. *Bṛhadāraṇyaka* IV, 4.
9. *Madhyamika-śāstra*, pp. 18–19.
10. See Matilal (1968), pp. 156–7. I have called the first ***nominally bound negative***, and the second ***verbally bound negative***.
11. See Matilal (1971), pp. 162–5.
12. See Herzberger, pp. 11–14.
13. See Matilal (1975).
14. Ānandavardhana, in the Indian tradition of literary criticism, criticized and rejected the thesis that *Rasa* (aesthetic) experience is ineffable. See Matilal (1975).

References

Hattori, M. *Dignāga, On Perception*, Cambridge (Mass): Harvard University Press, 1968.

Herzberger, H., 'Double Negation in Buddhist Logic', *Journal of Indian Philosophy*, 3 (1975), pp. 1–16.

Laṅkāvatārā-sūtra, ed. P.L. Vaidya, Darbhanga: Mithila Institute, 1963.

Masson, J.L. and Patwardhan, M.V. *Aesthetic Rapture* (2 vols), Poona: Deccan College, 1970.

Matilal, B.K. (1968), *The Navya-nyāya Doctrine of Negation*, Cambridge (Mass.): Harvard University Press 1968.

———, (1971), *Epistemology, Logic and Grammar in Indian Philosophical Analysis*, The Hague: Mouton, 1971.

———, (1975), 'Mysticism and Reality: Ineffability', *Journal of Indian Philosophy*, 3 (1975), nos 3, 4.

Nāgārjuna *Madhyamika-śāstra* with Candrakīrti's Comm., ed. P.L. Vaidya, Darbhanga; Mithila Institute, 1960.

Wittgenstein, L., *Tractatus Logic-Philosophicus*, Tr. D.F. Pears and B.F. McGuinness, London: Kegan Paul, 1922.

Upaniṣads: *Eighteen Principal Upaniṣads*, eds V.P. Limaye and R.D. Vadekar, Poona: Vaidika Samsodhana Mandala, 1968.

4

Scepticism and Mysticism

Professor Daniel Ingalls is neither a sceptic nor a mystic. But it is obvious to some of us that he has sympathy for both. It may be that he has more sympathy for the sceptic than for the mystic. In my study of the history of scepticism in India I have often been struck by the following phenomenon: The outstanding and even extreme sceptical arguments are usually to be found in the writings of the authors who were initially mystically inclined or who would like to push philosophical or dialectical argumentation to its utmost limit, so that rational means would prove to be bankrupt! I propose to deal with this phenomenon here. It is hoped that an 'empathetic' understanding of such a phenomenon is possible even when one does neither have a sceptical point of view nor even a mystical one. In this I have only followed the line which Professor Ingalls has taken in many other similar studies.

It will be seen at the end that the connection that I believe to be there between the sceptical attitude and the mystical is a contingent one. A sceptic does not necessarily become a mystic. Or, to put the matter in another way, it is not true, at least not always true, that the end of the path for a true and serious sceptic is mysticism. Sceptics do not always take a plunge into the 'oceanic feeling' of mysticism. At least I do not hold such a thesis. But that is why it seems more interesting and more intriguing to find the above phenomenon: why did the sceptical tradition form a very important, and almost an inseparable, component of the major mystical traditions of India? What did the mystics have to do with the use of logic and rational means that would have been more appropriate for scepticism? Why is this craving for attempts at rational explanation using logic and dialectics if at the end all this would be superceded by some irrational, inexplicable and ineffable consciousness? If I am going to enjoy poetry would it matter much if I discover that the poet used bad logic and fallacious arguments? The answer to such questions is not immediately obvious.

A philosophical sceptic is not an iconoclast or an aggressor in the Temple of Truth, but because of his extreme concern for truth he is reluctant to accept anything less. He persists in seeking and probing. If a philosopher is one who tries to expound or defend a view about the world or the way the world is or appears to us, a sceptic takes the position of his opponent. Scepticism has in fact formed an important part of philosophic activity in almost all ages everywhere. Indeed, philosophy today is more commonly understood as a kind of activity, and sceptical questions and doubts supply the vital moving force of such activity.

It is difficult to define scepticism. But some broad characterizations can be offered. If the word 'sceptic' means simply 'an inquirer' or 'an investigator' (as has been noted by R.G. Bury in his introduction to *Outlines of Pyrrhonism*)[1] then many philosophers could be called 'sceptics'. But obviously the word has a more specific sense. Scepticism can be understood as a critical philosophical attitude consistently maintained throughout. However, scepticism has acquired a negative connotation. A sceptic rejects the validity of any knowledge-claim or truth-claim.

The spirit of scepticism can be carried on to the fields of morality, religion and politics. The concern of the sceptic in such fields is not so much with truth as with the justification or rightness of certain principles, concepts or ideas. Scepticism usually aligns itself with pessimism as well as 'passivism'. It is difficult for a sceptic to be an optimist or a political activist or a revolutionary, for his scepticism would not be consistent with his activity. But activism and scepticism would not be an impossible combination in some humans, for consistency is not an inalienable trait of all humans. A sceptic's positive characterization is that he is a seeker after truth. In practice, however, a sceptic may be a *conformist* with the prevailing social and political norms. He may live by the existing rules and standards while not believing in their absolute validity. He is not, as I have already said, a revolutionary, for he lacks conviction about the truth or the goal of such actions. A sceptic has to be a good dialectician, skilful in the art of argumentation. He can be a 'sophist' in a non-pejorative sense. He is like a well-armed man, always on guard and ready for the argument, but he never provokes any. Or, he may be a man who carefully avoids arguments and renounces contentions, for it may be that 'philosophic problems *completely* disappear' for him (as Wittgenstein notes in *Philosophical Investigation* I, 133).[2] I shall argue that a sceptic can also be a mystic.

Who deserves to be called 'sceptic' according to the above characterizations? In the Indian context, we can mention Sañjaya and a few other *śramaṇas* who were contemporaries of the Buddha (563–483 BC). In the history of Western thought, Sextus Empiricus (*c.* AD 200) is often regarded as the most well-known of those who call themselves sceptics. In developing the position of Indian scepticism, I shall draw mainly from the writings of three different philosophers, Nāgārjuna (*c.* AD 150), Jāyarāśi (*c.* AD 800) and Śrīharṣa (*c.* AD 1000). They represent three different philosophic traditions of India. The first is a Mādhyamika Buddhist, the second was either a materialist or an agnostic, the third was an Advaita Vedāntin (a mystic). But inspite of these differences, they shared a common style of philosophizing as well as a common attitude toward the discovery of truth. Śrīharṣa, the last named philosopher, noted explicitly this common style and argued that in spite of the well-known differences in their metaphysical beliefs, their philosophical style was bound to be in the same way critical, sceptical, refutative and destructive.

A philosophical position can hardly be vindicated or established unless it has answered its critics and responded to the objections of its opponents. In the Indian tradition, the opponents' criticisms and objections are usually grouped under the rubric *pūrvapakṣa*. To build up the *pūrvapakṣa* in a greatly meticulous manner has been the general practice of all systematic philosophers of India since AD first century. It has been claimed that if the *pūrvapakṣa* is not properly understood, the philosopher's own position will hardly make any sense. Our understanding fight of a doctrine deepens by our understanding of not so much what it says as what it refutes and rejects.

An opponent is not always a sceptic. For usually the opponent refutes a rival position and gives at the same time arguments to sustain his own position. But if the opponent does not have a position of his own or he does not want to argue for his own position but is simply interested in refuting all other positions or theses, then he becomes a sceptic or a follower of sceptical methodology. A sceptic cannot have a position of his own in principle, for to be consistent he has to be sceptical of all theses, all positions. Scepticism in other words has to be paradoxical in order to be consistent. But the air of paradoxicality, I suggest, can be removed.

Refutation of a philosophical position usually implies acceptance of its negation, i.e., a counter-position, a counter-thesis. But a sceptic cannot maintain his scepticism by assenting to a counter-thesis. It is his duty to disagree with both the thesis and its anti-thesis or counter-thesis by assigning reasons in both cases. He has to suspend his judgement in favour of either. It is however not easy to maintain such all round scepticism. It is rather easy to be a non-believer in some particular doctrine or other. But philosophical scepticism is of a different breed. A sceptic has to be well-conversant with the art of philosophic debate. For scepticism can be sustained only by a master-debater, a dialectician. He has to employ skilfully his *pro*-arguments as well as his *contra*-argument so that his sceptical position, if it is a position at all, would remain uncompromised. For any *pro*-argument for a doctrine, he has to find an equally strong *contra*-argument so that the tug of war of pro's and con's comes to a standstill and balances one another. It is therefore obvious that such scepticism can hardly flourish unless in a *mileau* where the art as well as the theory of disputation or dialectic has reached a well-developed form. Such a situation did obtain in ancient and classical India, as it did in Greece. Hence the sceptics were not far behind.

Sañjaya

Professor H. Ui has described Sañjaya's philosophy as a sort of scepticism on the one hand and a primitive step towards a critique of knowledge on the other.[3] This assessment of Sañjaya seems to me to be fairly correct. This tradition must have been the precursor of the later-day scepticism about knowledge and perception as reflected in the writings of Nāgārjuna, Jāyarāśi and Śrīharṣa.

Sañjaya questioned the knowledge-claims of other *śramaṇas* and *brāhmaṇas* regarding certain moral, religious and metaphysical matters. Typical questions asked in those days (see *Dīgha-Nikāya*) were: 'Is there a soul?' 'Is there an after-life?' and 'What is right and what is wrong?' Sañjaya and his followers argued that it is impossible to *know* correct answers to such questions.[4]

It should be noted that these early Indian sceptics attached higher value to ethical development and final salvation than to resolution of the philosophical questions. They apparently maintained that it would be wrong or morally reprehensible to make false claims, whether knowingly or unknowingly. Thus, Sañjaya said that since he did not (and in fact nobody did) *know* the answers to such questions he would not claim that he knew, for that would be a false claim and would mislead people (which would be immoral). The Jaina canonical literature, as Hermann Jacobi pointed out, noted that these *śramaṇa* sceptics maintained that no knowledge but *tapas* (ascetic austerity) was necessary for salvation or final beatitude. These sceptics were similar to those described by Sextus, who resorted to their *epochē* (suspending all judgements) to gain the state of unperturbedness or *ataraxia*. Sextus says.[5]

The man who determines nothing as to what is naturally good or bad neither shuns nor pursues anything eagerly; and, in consequence, he is unperturbed.

In the Indian context, these sceptics were also recluses (*śramaṇas*) and hence were committed to the ascetic way of life practicing austerities (*tapas*) to achieve quietude.

Some of the *śramaṇas* were however astute debaters. In this regard, they can be placed somewhere in the midway between the Greek sophists and the Greek sceptics. The early canonical literature of Buddhism and Jainism bears ample witness to this fact. Oldenberg has put the point nicely in his outstanding book, *The Buddha* (tr. W. Holms):[6]

Certain phenomena which developed themselves in the busy bustle of the ascetic and philosophizing circles, may be described as a species of Indian *sophistic*; wherever a Socrates appears, sophists cannot fail to follow. The condition under which these sophistic arose were quite similar to those which gave birth to their Greek counterpart . . . there followed Gorgiases, and Protagorases, and a whole host of ingenious species, somewhat frivolous virtuosi, dealers in dialectic and rhetoric.

Even if we discount Oldenberg's enthusiasm for comparison of East and West, his general point is correct, as the later history of the art of philosophical disputation in India shows.

The concerns of the early Indian recluse-sceptic were mainly spiritual, moral and religious. Hence unlike the Greek sophists, they did not go to the extent of teaching the art of debate and rhetoric to the rich young men in exchange for money. Nor did they (with a few exceptions, e.g. Jābāli in the *Rāmāyaṇa*) 'meddle' in politics or public affairs of the government.

The principles of the art of argumentation that were developed in classical India made room for the kind of debate that a sceptic had to adopt in order to refute all theses without asserting any of his own. This type of debate was called *vitaṇḍā* later in the *Nyāyasūtras*. In the early period, Sañjaya developed a crude technique of what may be called a five-fold rejection of a position: (1) 'Not so,' (2) 'Not thus', (3) 'Not otherwise,' (4) 'Not not so,' (5) 'Not *no* to not so,' The upshot of this rather clumsy negation and double negation was to maintain an attitude of 'non-assertion.' Sañjaya used this method in its crude form, but Nāgārjuna perfected it with his tetralemmas, dilemmas and reductions (*prasaṅga*).

Notice that this does not amount strictly to 'anti-rationalism' or illogicality. Refutation in this context can be taken to be an 'illocutionary' negation (distinct from a 'propositional' negation), as it is done in the Speech-Act theory of John Searle.[7] Sañjaya said about the existence of the after-life: 'Neither do I say that there is an after-life nor do I say that there is none.' This seems consistent, for it is not a conjunction of a proposition and its negation as. '(∃x) (x is F) and ~ (∃x) (x is F)', but conjunction of the negation of two Speech Acts: ~ Ass (∃x) (x is F) and ~ Ass ~ (∃x) (x is F).

Nāgārjuna

I shall take this opportunity to reformulate a Nāgārjunnian tetralemma in order to show how sceptical arguments of this kind lead to the direction of mysticism and the ineffability doctrine. Consider the following debate modelled after the first verse of Nāgārjuna's *Mādhyamika Kārikā*.

1. Is a thing produced from itself?
1a. No.
2. It is produced from something other than itself?
2a. No.
3. It is produced from both itself and others?
3a. No.
4. Is it produced from neither (or nothing)?
4a. No.

It is clear that 1 and 2 are not at least contradictories, for it is possible for a thing to be produced partly from itself and partly from others. Hence 3 is a possible formulation not exhausted by the rejection of 1 and 2. Now the question arises: have we exhausted all possibilities by three rejections 1a, 2a and 3a? If we have, the fourth must be construed as a question about production itself: Is it *not* produced at all? But Nāgārjuna asks us to reject this also by 4a! How to make sense of this rejection? The problem is this. If refutation of the refutation of production amounts to production itself, then we are back in the game, i.e., with one of the three alternatives, 1, 2 or 3. But they have been already rejected! Therefore 4a cannot be regarded as an ordinary refutation. I intend to call it 'the Nāgārjunian refutation' or 'the mystic's refusal' to talk or to play the ball-game. It rejects the context of the debate, the dichotomy of production and non-production. In other words, the sceptic-debater returns the ball to the opponent's court in the first three cases. But in 4a, he refuses to play. Scepticism thus points up to mysticism, to the ineffability of the ultimates.

One can achieve the same goal by using dialectical arguments and reductions. Nāgārjuna, Śrīharṣa and Jāyarāśi were champions of this method. Let me explain it very briefly. The idea is to construe all the possible positions about a philosophical topic or a concept, and reject them one by one by reducing them to some sort of absurdity or showing some contradiction within the concept. When all the positions are in this way refuted, the sceptic debater can then say that he has no position or thesis of his own to defend nor can he assert any. Thus Nāgārjuna answered when he was confronted with the paradoxicality of his own position:[8] 'I have no (philosophical) thesis to defend.' A thesis (*pratijñā*) is technically defined in Nyāya as the statement of a position or a view to be proved. Hence the above remark can ambiguously mean either that he has no position of his own or that his position is not stateable. I argue that it is this ingrained ambiguity that transforms scepticism into mysticism.

Nāgārjuna developed a systematic critique of the concepts of knowledge and the knowable. He attacked the idea that there are *prāmāṇas*, i.e., accredited means of knowledge. The argument is rather well-known. Roughly it is this. If there are accredited means of knowing, either we know them or we don't. If we know them, we need further accredited means to know that we know them and to know the second set of means we need another, and so on. This is *regressus ad infinitum*:

> Each dog has on its own back a little flea to bite him. And on that flea another flea and so *ad infinitum*.

In Sanskrit, the fault is called *anavasthā*, which means that we are on a slippery ground, slipping ever backward without stopping. Russell has said about such a paradox.

> . . . the process is like trying to jump on the shadow of your head (*My Philosophical Development*, p. 82).[9]

But suppose we do not *know* the means. Now if so, how is it established that they are *valid* means, and not tricks? Who or what validates them? There is an old village parable about a witch doctor in Bengal who was a successful exorcist because he used to exorcise persons or objects possessed of evil spirits with the help of a handful of mustard seeds. One day the evil spirit, in order to baffle the exorcism, entered into those seeds themselves. Our situation would be similar if the means were invalid or defective. In reply we may say that certain means are self-validating and self-established. But Nāgārjuna counters this as follows: (a) The notion of self-validation suffers from circularity; (b) if certain means cannot be known then it contradicts the original thesis of the philosopher about knowledge: we know everything by knowledge (*hīyate vādaḥ*); and (c) we need to give a satisfactory answer to the question: why certain objects are self-validating while others are not? What differentiates them? (*viśeṣa-hetuś ca vaktavyaḥ*). I shall leave the matter here.

Jayarāśi and Śrīharṣa

Jāyarāśi was not a Buddhist. He is usually taken to be a follower of Bṛhaspati, the materialist, the anti-religious sceptic. Professor Walter Ruben is reluctant to call him a materialist because, except for paying only a lip-service to Bṛhaspati, he does not propound any positive materialist doctrine. I agree with Ruben, who calls Jāyarāśi an agnostic. Jāyarāśi critically examined the available definitions of such means of knowledge as perception and inference. In this way he developed the general thesis: it is not possible for us to have 'knowledge' in the required sense. For all the available definitions are fundamentally flawed. Definability of concepts ensures their intelligibility. Hence if these concepts lack definability they lack intelligibility. Scepticism thus wins the day.

To illustrate another argument of Jāyarāśi. Roughly, the received doctrine about knowledge is that while not all our cognitive experiences would amount to knowledge, some would become knowledge. Let us say that whenever a cognitive experience has the character E it amounts to knowledge. Now, how do we know that a cognitive experience has E? For if we don't, we would never know that we have knowledge. And if we know E through another cognitive experience, then we need to know another E that characterizes this cognitive experience. And so on *ad infinitum*.[10]

Śrīharṣa continued the debate (300 hundred years later) almost in a similar vein. In the course of his argumentation, he developed also a sceptical paradox which has kinship with what is called today 'Gettier's sceptical paradox' about the concept of knowledge as justified true belief. Śrīharṣa was arguing against the concept of knowledge as the object-corresponding (true) cognitive experience derived from reliable evidence (*prāmāṇa*). He said that this is faulty for we can have *true* cognitive experience ('there is fire') from reliable evidence, viz., the premise or the awareness that there is smoke, where such awareness is falsely derived from the misperception of a dust-storm as smoke, and where by accident there is fire. Here the evidence is reliable, a deductive inference, for the falsity of the premises has nothing to do with soundness of inference, but such evidence again is not connected with the *truth* of the cognitive experience in the relevant way. Scepticism wins again for knowledge cannot be defined in this way.[11]

Śrīharṣa also takes up the cue from Nāgārjuna and continues to defend the position that a sceptic can participate in logical debate without asserting and defending any position of his own, i.e., without forfeiting his sceptic claims. Here the paradox is this. If all philosophical theses are, as the sceptical claims, wrong or 'empty' (*śūnya*) of any substance or essence, then this very thesis suffers from the same fate. And if it does, it cannot do its role, i.e., assert or state anything. And if it does not, we have a counter-example to prove that the thesis is wrong. The way out of this suggested by the sceptic as follows: It may be that all these are empty, but such a thesis cannot itself be asserted or stated. A.N. Prior, in explaining J. Buridan's paradox about 'no proposition is true' suggested a similar way out:

> But if God were to annihilate all negative propositions, there would in fact be no negative propositions, even if this were not then being asserted by any proposition at all. In short, *it can be that no proposition is negative, though it cannot be that 'no proposition is negative' is true.*[12]

Making a 'parody' of this, a Buddhist might say: if the Buddha were to empty each proposition of its own meaning-essence, there would be in fact no non-empty proposition, even if *this* remains unasserted or unstateable.

A logician like a Naiyāyika may say to a sceptic: 'You have to believe in the principles of argument and reasoning. For if you don't, you cannot use them to derive your sceptical conclusion. You should remain silent.' In reply, Śrīharṣa has said that this is indeed a poor argument, given in desperation. For the history of philosophy shows that no sceptic, not even a mystic, remained silent without arguing or debating. The choice is open to the sceptic to accept the principles of debate only provisionally. The above argument Śrīharṣa says, cannot be a new kind of 'silencing charm' to set the matter at rest. In short, the sceptics do argue; the onus (of making him silent) lies with the opponent, not with them.

It has been facetiously suggested that the practical life of a true sceptic would be impossible, for if he did not even believe that the floor would not melt under his feet or that food would satisfy his hunger, he would not be able to walk or eat to survive. This point is easily answered. Jāyarāśi has said that those who are wise recommend that we follow the ordinary worldly behaviour, for 'with regard to practical behaviour the wise resemble the fool or the child.' An echo of this is found in the comment of Sextus:

We live in accordance with the normal rules of life, undogmatically, seeing that we cannot remain wholly inactive.[13]

Mysticism

William James in his *Varieties of Religious Experience* (1902) noted four common distinctive marks of any 'mystical' experience: 1) Ineffability, 2) Noetic quality, 3) Transiency, and 4) Passivity. W.T. Stace in his *Mysticism and Philosophy* (1960) has mentioned several other characteristics of a mystical experience. Of all these, I have concentrated upon only one crucial concept: ineffability. In the above therefore I have referred to this one characteristic of mysticism whenever I have shown how a transition from scepticism to mysticism might eventually take place. I shall conclude by elaborating upon this issue.

A sceptic is not necessarily a mystic. At least he is not so initially. And the mystic cannot always be a thoroughgoing sceptic. But the following situation might obtain. A sceptic might keep his mind free of any dogmas, dicta and doctrines. His attitude is something like this. If the mind is free then truth, if there is any, will dawn upon the person automatically. It is sometimes put metaphorically: If the darkness is dispelled, encumbrances of false views and ignorance are removed, then truth will shine in its own glory. No other effort is needed. Sextus has put the point in a different manner. Arne Naess has said:

The mature sceptic decides neither for the positive nor for the negative in relation to any doctrine, but allows both possibilities to stand open . . . To his surprise he eventually finds that *epochē* (suspension of judgment) leads to, or is accompanied by, just that peace of mind (*ataraxia*) which he sets out to achieve by finding truth. The mature sceptic will not, of course, claim that there is a necessary connection between *epochē* and *ataraxia*.[14]

Śrīharṣa argued that truth or the Ultimate Truth is either self-evident or unknowable. In either case, it stands to reason for us to keep our minds purged of all the false views, conceptions and dogmas about such ultimate truth. The sceptic's use of logic and dialectic is instrumental. So is the mystic's use of philosophical argumentation. Negative dialectic is like the ladder to be kicked away when the purpose is served. Or to change the metaphor of Wittgenstein to that of Candrakīrti, this use of arguments, etc. is like the raft that one uses to cross the river. But once you are on the other side, you should forget about the raft. Or, as the Buddha said in one of his dialogue: You need the medicine to cure your disease, but once you are cured, you must get the medicine itself purged out of your system. For otherwise you get rid of one disease (one false view) to make room only for another.

It may be that connection between scepticism and mysticism was not as pronounced in the Western tradition as it surely was in the Indian tradition. But this may be just a matter of emphasis. For the connection is obviously not a necessary one. It is contingent. And such contingency does arise. Let us notice still that Sextus has compared the sceptic with Apelles, the court painter of Alexander the Great. Once Apelles was painting a horse and wanted to paint the foam in the mouth of the running horse. Being unsuccessful several times, in despair he flung a wiping sponge at the canvas. And lo and behold, the foam was all of a sudden there as a result of the marks of the sponge.[15] Sceptics get their *ataraxia* in this way suddenly. One can easily be reminded of the *sudden illumination theory* of the Indian mystics!

Notes and References

1. See R.G. Bury, *Sextus Empiricus*, I: *Outlines of Pyrrhonism*, Loeb Classical Library, London, 1933, p. xxix.
2. L. Wittgenstein, *Philosophical Investigations*, I, para 133, Blackwell, Oxford, 1958.
3. H. Ui, *Vaiśeṣika Philosophy* (ed. F.W. Thomas), 1917, p. 23, New edn., Varanasi, 1962.
4. See *Dīgha Nikāya*, I, 27.
5. *Sextus*, I, 28.
6. H. Oldenberg, *The Buddha*, 1882 edn., William and Norgate, London, 1882, p. 68.
7. J. Searle, *Speech-Acts*, Cambridge, 1969, pp. 32–3.
8. See *Vigravyāvartanī*, verse 29.
9. B. Russell, *My Philosophical Development*, Alex and Unwin, London, 1959, p. 82.
10. Jayarāśi's *Tattvopaplavasiṃha* is a remarkable book to reconstruct the history of scepticism in India. He has been usually characterized by scholars as an agnostic.
11. Śrīharṣa's *Khaṇḍanakhaṇḍakhādya* provides an important landmark to trace the history of Indian dialectics and scepticism. See Phyllis Granoff's *Philosophy and Argument in Late Vedānta*, D. Reidel, Dordrecht, 1978.

12. See A.N. Prior, *Papers in Logic and Ethics* (eds. P. Geach and A. Kenny), Duckworth, London, 1976, p. 144.
13. *Sextus*, I, p. 23.
14. A. Naess, *Scepticism*, Kegan Paul, London, 1968, p. 5.
15. *Sextus*, I, 28.

5

Scepticism, Mysticism and Sri Aurobindo's Optimism

I

Mystics are, in my opinion, 'optimist-passivist' while revolutionaries are 'optimist-activists'. Both burn with enthusiasm, but while the former look inward, the latter look outside to the world around us. Sri Aurobindo was formerly a revolutionary, and then became a mystic. One may thus say that from being an optimist-activist, he turned into an optimist-passivist, a transformation that is not entirely unusual.

Sri Aurobindo was a mystic. He was also a sceptic to some extent, as all mystics are in some way or other. As I have shown elsewhere, the translation from scepticism to mysticism was the hallmark of the classical Indian sceptical tradition beginning with Sañjaya, and developing through the Buddha, Nāgārjuna, Jayarāśi and Śrīharsa. Of these, Sañjaya and Jayarāśi remained sceptical, perhaps only to become 'mature' sceptics who would have *ataraxia* out of their *epoché* (my ch. 4 'Scepticism and Mysticism'). But the others seem to have *used* sceptical arguments, and to have maintained the general sceptical attitude towards any metaphysical truth or philosophical theory as constituting the springboard for their mystical way of life. Even the 'mature' sceptic is a mystic in the minimal sense. He must keep his mind open and free of dogmas, for when discriminating knowledge or discursive thought fails, it is claimed, insight into the ultimate nature of things may arise all of a sudden. Truth, as the cliché goes, dawns upon a person when he can rid himself of all false and unwarranted beliefs. Śrīharsa claimed that Brahman does not need to be established, proven or shown through any means—it will illuminate and show itself as soon as the fabricated walls of misconceptions and false beliefs, dogmas and delusions, are destroyed. Other usual analogies are that when the cloud of unknowing is dispersed, truth shines forth by itself—when the disease is cured, normalcy is restored automatically, when the cover of *saṃvṛti* is removed, the jewel of *paramārtha* sparkles by itself.

A true sceptic is not really a drop-out from the rat-race of life. As Jayarāśi would say, for him all philosophic questions remain unproven and open, but in practical life, the sceptic must follow commonsense and ordinary worldly behaviour (cf. *laukika-mārga*), for, he said:

> With regard to ordinary behaviour, the wise resembles the fool or the child.

The ideal of the Greek sceptic, as delineated by Sextus Empiricus, was not very far from this. Sextus says:

> We live in accordance with the normal rules of life, undogmatically, seeing that we cannot remain wholly inactive.[1]

It may be countered that my comparison with the Greek sceptic is misleading. For *ataraxia* may be very different from what we understand by the mystical insight or even the mystical delight in having a pure, 'objectless' experience. *Ataraxia* means only that the sceptic is at peace with himself: no oscillation, no disturbance. But I am not fully convinced by such arguments. For there are, it is claimed, a variety of ways by which the mystical state of mind can be reached. It is not always an ecstatic delight. It may be an undisturbed peace with oneself, or an experience of the 'emptiness', a blissful state or a state of perfect poise. It may be the state of a '*sthitaprajña*', as the *Śrīmad-Bhagavad-Gītā* describes it. If such varieties of mystical states are recognized, then transition from pure scepticism to the quietude of mysticism seems natural enough.

An illustration from Sextus would be relevant to support the point:

> The sceptic, in fact, had the same experience which is said to have befallen the painter Apelles. Once, they say, when he was painting a horse and wished to represent in the painting the horse's foam, he was so unsuccessful that he gave up the attempt and flung at the picture the sponge on which he used to wipe the paint off his brush, and the mark of the sponge produced the effect of a horse's foam.[2]

This seems to be very similar to the 'sudden illumination' theory of the Indian mystics. A Buddhist Zen master would also love this analogy!

I have said that Sri Aurobindo belongs to the mystical tradition of India, and claimed that all mystics in this tradition were to some degree sceptics or agnostics. Further, I have characterized the mystics as optimists. This may seem to be a contradiction. For scepticism inspires pessimism, if anything. Optimism is a different kettle off fish, it will be said, one that goes along with gullibility and credulousness. Besides, are not those people, who travel for many days from Los Angeles to the Himalayas to seek mystical illumination from an Indian holy man, gullible and credulous? Are not the 'inanities' uttered by any modern guru taken to be highly significant by those who are aspirant after going on the upward and onward, mystical, trip? Is it not also a fact that even the most intelligent person can follow a guru, and when pressed for an explanation, answer in the manner of the Patristic father: I believe it because it is absurd, I believe it because it is impossible?

I concede the point that mostly gullible people search after a guru, and aspire to obtain the formula for 'instant' *nirvāṇa*. It may even true that those who have had what we call mystical experience are especially gullible; for they cannot, it has been generally claimed, help believing in its veridicality. But both of these points, I shall argue, do not affect what I have claimed to be the almost inborn sceptical tendency of the mystic, and its coexistence with the burning optimism about a better, and perhaps a more real possibility for Man and the Universe. Let us first follow the sceptical route.

II

There are many varieties of scepticism. Here, however, we are concerned with a rather fundamental form of scepticism about the possibility of knowledge regarding what is ultimately real, and what is most valuable. In the ultimate sense, I believe, reality and value coincide (the 'whole' or the unlimited is both meaningful and valuable in itself) and hence the two questions, viz., what is ultimately real and what is most valuable, seem to converge in an integrated search. A sceptic in this sense is not an intruder in the Temple of Truth, but because of his utmost concern for the truth, for knowledge, he is unable to accept anything less. He starts off by arguing that we do not know what we think we do. And if he does not completely succeed in making all of us sceptical, he scores nevertheless a point or two. He does just enough to disrupt our complacency about the possibility of knowledge, and he shows that none of us should be so cocksure that we do know. The sceptic may use destructive dilemmas and *reductio ad absurdum* arguments to destroy the subjective feeling of the persons who claim that they do know. Or, he may construct arguments to show that there are other logical possibilities, so that our claim that we know is simply ad hoc, and without the required absolute guarantee for its being infallible. In the Indian context, philosophers like Nāgārjuna,

Jayarāśi and Śrīharsa chose the first method for exposing contradiction and incoherence in our system of beliefs and assumptions. It is constantly shown in this *prasaṅga-koṭivikalpa-vitaṇḍā* style of philosophizing that our non-empirical beliefs and assumptions about the world we experience are always in conflict with the strict experiential evidence that we may adduce when we are pressed to defend such beliefs. Thus, our belief in the veridicality of our experience is unfounded. For, as the *Laṅkāvatāra-Sūtra* says (repeated several times):

> As we logically analyse the objects through intellect, their essential nature remains indeterminate. Therefore, they have been described (by me, the Buddha) as lacking essence and appellation.

In another version, we have from Dharmakīrti:[3]

> As we analyse, they (i.e. the objects) fall apart.

In other words, the objects, like bubbles, burst under the prick of logical scrutiny.

The second method, formulation of arguments to show sceptical possibilities, was also used by philosophers such as Vasubandhu and his followers. It was shown here, much in the manner of a Cartesian sceptic, that it is consistent to hold that all our ordinary waking experiences have a dream-like character (in the sense that from the fact that we have an experience, no inference about the existence of the experienced object is logically possible), although we may invariably believe in the veridicality of such experiences. The situation is not very different when we conduct the argument in terms of an evil *genié* or a mad scientist or (the science fiction possibility of) the case of the brain in a vat. Vasubandhu puts the point about the possibility of a universal delusion in an amazingly simple language:

> In a dream, that the objects of our sight etc. do not exist, is not known until one wakes up.[4]

My purpose here, however, is neither to repeat well-known sceptical arguments nor to analyse or answer them. The reason for introducing the sceptical questions is to underline the fact that the theme of universal delusion (the so-called knowledge being only veiled ignorance), has been very commonplace with the mystical philosophers. Sri Aurobindo called it the 'eternal paradox' and used the theme effectively in his philosophical activity, presupposing, I believe, all the sceptical arguments and formulations to show that the existing state of affairs is not ultimately satisfactory. As a Sanskrit philosopher would say: *tataḥ kim*? ('What else is there?') The search which we all humans must undertake, according to Sri Aurobindo, is not quite different from the Socratic ideal: the unexamined life is not worth living.

Scepticism will serve its full purpose for the mystics and mystical philosophers as soon as the challenge to our accepted dogma about our knowledge of the world around us and of the 'meaning' and value of life in this world is sustained. And in spite of the untiring attempts of the philosophers and thinkers over the centuries to either nullify or neutralize the challenge, it has been sustained in some form or other. In fact, it has demonstrated wonderful resilience. We may dismiss scepticism for various practical reasons and disdain those who try to say that when we are eating an apple, it is not *really* an apple that we may be eating etc. But the nagging sceptical doubt about such dim possibilities would still be hard to overcome. The mystics, therefore, can easily make it their point of departure.

It may be that we have not paid, in the above comments, due heed to the formidable arguments of the anti-sceptical philosophers who have given 'final' answers to scepticism. It may, therefore, very well be the case that along with the mystics, we have been too gullible in the opposite way in acknowledging the persuasive force of the sceptical arguments. But it is really difficult to see how this could be so. For, radical scepticism, described by Kant as a 'scandal' in philosophy, is not refutable in its own terms. It is an almost unassailable (theoretical) position. One may counter that this is a much magnified picture of a very negligible doubt. For beyond a certain point, scepticism would cease to be interesting. Besides, sceptical arguments may not be entirely flawless.

Let us pursue this line of thought a little further. The problem with the sceptical possibility of this life being a super-dream (or of our being only brains in a vat stimulated by mad scientists so as to make us experience always the way we do), is not that we are not able to dismiss it under various circumstances, but that we *do not know* that such a possibility *does not* obtain. Let us refer to a modern refutation of the sceptical argument by Hilary Putnam in his *Reason, Truth and History*.

Putnam has argued that the supposition that we are brains in a vat is a self-refuting one, for if we can consider whether it is true or false, it becomes false thereby. Through a sophisticated use of the theory of reference, it has been claimed that if we can successfully describe the possibility, using constituent terms to refer, then it would not hold true. In other words, given our practice of reference, we can finally show with involved arguments that the so-called sceptical possibility is incoherent. This is a very serious charge against scepticism: scepticism is not even (theoretically) coherent.

It is indeed difficult to see how Putnam's argument against the sceptic succeeds completely. As long as we concede that there could be 'transcendental' manipulators who are NOT floating in the vat as we presumably do, we cannot exclude the possibility that we may very well be brains in the vat, and still use terms whose reference would be only parasitical upon those used by the manipulators.

One can reformulate a Nyāya critique of the Nāgārjunian position to show also that pure scepticism is not even coherent. To wit (from the *Vigrahavyāvartanī*): if everything lacks essence, then this assertion that everything lacks essence (which is, no doubt, part of 'everything') also lacks essence. And if it does not, we have already a counter-example to disprove the thesis. In other words, if the 'emptiness' position is statable it becomes, by the same token, false; because it is thereby rendered incoherent. The usual sceptical, Nāgārjunian or Śrīharṣa-like answer is: Be it so. The position of universal scepticism is not statable or assertable—*nāsti ca mama pratijñā kācana*. A.N. Prior gave a similar explanation of John Buridan's discussion of similar paradoxes. He contended:

> . . . it can be that no position is negative, though it cannot be that 'No proposition is negative' is true.[5]

If, for example, God annihilated all negative propositions, then there would be no negative propositions, but by God's decree, nobody would then be formulating the proposition, 'No proposition is negative'.

Modern theologians have often argued that the concept of an almighty God in theism can be made coherent in spite of the problems presented by the predominance of evil, and paradoxes of omniscience and omnipotence. The non-believers and agnostics may counter that coherence is not enough. For coherence may be a necessary criterion for there being an almighty and benevolent God, it is certainly not a sufficient one. Using a similar argument, one can very well turn the table against the sceptics of the above kind, who use the supposition of a super-dream, an evil demon or mad scientists. The anti-sceptic may say that the supposition of the sceptical possibilities may be coherent, but that is not sufficient to show that those transcendental manipulations are really facts. In the absence of any other positive evidence, the matter cannot be decided either way. Our super-sceptic may, however, still remain unimpressed. For he would say that his job is finished by showing such possibilities alone.

Another line of argument against scepticism has been to claim that the sceptic or the super-sceptic does not really know what he himself is talking about. He introduces a notion of knowledge, let us call it *knowledge-special*, which is highly restrictive and demanding. To put it in a pat statement, if we have to know anything exactly in the way the sceptic wants us to know, we would agree with the sceptic that we cannot know anything. Those who combat scepticism would, however, operate with a notion of knowledge—call it *knowledge-normal*, which is much less restrictive or demanding, and therefore, according to such a notion of knowledge, we would know various things and facts. Once we draw a distinction between *knowledge-special* and *knowledge-normal*, we may reasonably ask the question: Why does the mystic find the sceptical possibilities so attractive?

III

The answer to the question posed above may, in my opinion, be found if we can appreciate the motivation of the mystic, which springs from the eternal human quest for value and meaning, coupled with man's natural dissatisfaction with the familiar and the apparent. The façade seems to conceal the real object, instead of revealing it. If we break through the veil of ideas, we are supposed to reach reality. The world as it is presented to us is, for the mystic, like Rembrandt's paintings: a little light and a great deal of darkness. As Sri Aurobindo would say, our ordinary experiences allow only a little knowledge, and a great deal of darkness. If we could penetrate through the cover of *samvṛti*, we would reach *paramārtha*.

Dissatisfaction with the ordinary, day-to-day world, or with what I have called *knowledge-normal*, is quite universal. The sceptic annoys us so that we may focus upon it. Moreover, are we not all born-sceptics in some way or other? Is not such scepticism an essential factor of our human predicament? It was Śaṅkara's well-known contention (supported by several passages in the Upaniṣads) that what we call *knowledge-normal*, knowledge that gives us information about the world we live in, knowledge that is derived from such means of knowing (*pramāṇa*) as perception, inference and scriptures, is to be down-graded as *a-vidyā*, which I translate (consistently with the dictum of the Sanskrit grammarians regarding the various meanings of the negative particle) as 'bad knowledge'. Indeed, the negative particle '*a*' in '*a-vidyā*' can be, in many of its occurences, only evaluative instead of descriptive, at least that would justify our calling it *knowledge-normal.* Indeed, Sri Aurobindo has called it 'mixed knowledge-ignorance'.[6] In his commentary on *Brahmasūtra* 1.1.1., Śaṅkara says:

(Therefore) sense-perception and other means of knowledge, as well as the scriptures, have their locations falling under the domain of 'bad knowledge'. For men do not differ from animals in this respect. Animals, when sounds or other sensible qualities affect their sense of hearing and other senses, recede or advance according as the object appears to be desirable or undesirable. [Here, I have slightly departed from the traditional interpretation.]

The idea is that even with our gift of rationality, it is seldom that we can rise above the level of animal behaviour, and the knowledge that we derive from our senses and reason is of the same kind as, though, perhaps, million-times better and mightier than, the animal knowledge. In other words, as long as man confines himself to this type of *knowledge-normal*, the value and meaning of his life, the worth of his human existence would always elude him. Sri Aurobindo has not really debunked this *knowledge-normal.* In fact, it has been recognized rightly as the first step forward:

To correct the errors of the sense-mind by the use of reason is one of the most valuable powers developed by man, and the chief cause of his superiority among terrestrial beings.[7]

Human reason, claims Sri Aurobindo, has another function, a 'pure or sovereign' function—which 'brings us finally from physical to metaphysical knowledge. Here, I think, we reach the notion of knowledge *knowledge-special*, the one that I have argued to have been envisioned by the sceptics, though never actualized. This knowledge, it is claimed, is 'beyond the perception of the senses, but seizable by the perception of the intellect' (*Bhagavad-Gītā* VI.21, translated in *The Life Divine*, vol. I, p. 77). Sri Aurobindo says that this is the knowledge of the 'supraphysical' (ibid., I, p. 74). If our *knowledge-normal* is what yields information, *knowledge-special* yields revelation. Our *knowledge-normal* is barren as far as the meaning and value of our corporeal existence is concerned. Left to itself, it leads, the mystic claims, to a dead-end. But being unified with *knowledge-special*, it serves the most useful purpose. The 'information' which it then yields becomes impregnated with value and meaning. According to Sri Aurobindo, the mystic, therefore, need not, in fact should not, ignore or debunk our *knowledge-normal*, but he should evaluate it only for what it is. In this way, the mystic transcends the sceptic. Dissatisfaction with *knowledge-normal*, a reflex of inborn human scepticism, leads in this way to the search for the perfect knowledge, *knowledge-special*, knowledge of the unlimited. It is believed that mystical insight ushers in such knowledge of the unlimited.

IV

A knowledge by identity, a knowledge by intimate direct contact, a knowledge by separative direct contact, a wholly separative knowledge by indirect contact are the four cognitive methods of Nature.[8]

In these words, Sri Aurobindo underlines a process and a fourfold order of knowledge, which enables him to distinguish finally between *knowledge-normal* (he calls it 'separative knowledge' where identification in various degrees may take place) and *knowledge-special* (which he calls 'knowledge by identity' in its purest form). Such Upaniṣadic passages as 'He who sees all existences in the Self,' 'He who sees the Self in all existences', 'He in whom the Self has become all existences' are cited (ibid., p. 306) in support of the second type of knowledge. It transpires to be a sort of mystical self-awareness of an undifferentiated whole, the alleged goal of mystical consciousness.

Sri Aurobindo does not posit this kind of knowledge simply as the goal of those individual human beings who are motivated and inclined to follow the path of mysticism. He declares with firm conviction that this has already been determined as the destiny of man. The Universal Spirit, which permeates every being including human and other lower forms of life, would indeed find another of its self-fulfillments when through evolutionary process every man would be awakened from his materialistic slumber, and thereby transformed into the spiritual MAN. There will then be the ascent towards the Supermind. This is what I have said to be the burning optimism of Sri Aurobindo's philosophy. The process is described in detail in volume II of *The Life Divine*.

Some general observations can be made here on the reality-claim of the mystic's insight. William James called it the 'noetic quality' of mystical experience, the quality by virtue of which a high percentage of those who have access to the experience, not only believe in the veridicality of the experience, but attach greater value to it than to anything else.[9] Can this simply be ascribed to the gullibility of those experiencers? The anti-mystic is often cocksure, and therefore hasty in rejecting the claim of the mystics. But in this way he often becomes guilty of an easy reductionism, and a simplistic belief that 'knowledge' that does not conform to *knowledge-normal* is at best an illusion, and at worst, a neurotic fantasy. But must every unfamiliar thing be reduced to something we know and can handle better? Can a Rembrandt be only a number of brush-strokes on a canvas? Ernest Jones writes:

But we must not forget that neurosis is an expression of the same forces and conflicts that have led to the loftiest aspirations and profoundest achievements of our race, and that neurotics are often the torch-bearers of civilization. They may strain themselves in the effort, but without that effort there would be no civilization.[10]

Wittgenstein comments:

What it says does not add to our knowledge in any sense. But it is a document of a tendency in the human mind which I personally cannot help respecting deeply, and I would not for my life ridicule it.[11]

Nozick offers the following comment on reductionism:

Reductionism is not simply a theoretical mistake, it is a moral failing.[12]

It may be said that the mystics themselves do not offer much help for us (who lack first hand acquaintance with mystical experience) in understanding mysticism. There are so many different, often conflicting, theories about, and descriptions of, the experience (as well as the experienced reality) that we feel baffled even if we sincerely try to make some sense of them. But this difficulty need not be insuperable. The said different theories and descriptions are, I believe, results of the sincere attempts by the mystics (when they are no longer undergoing mystical experience) to offer a connected, 'rational' explanation of *knowledge-special* in terms of *knowledge-normal*. They, therefore, share the general character of theoretical explanation as such: They are essentially underdetermined even by all the empirical data supplied by experience. A consequence of Quine's theory about indeterminacy of translation has been that different (sometimes even conflicting) theories can be supported by the totality of empirical evidence, for there is no 'fact of the matter' for one of the two conflicting theories being true rather than the other. In Quine's words:

. . . they can be logically incompatible and empirically equivalent.[13]

If this view is right, then under such a superficial interpretation (that Quine may not approve of) the divergent claims about the nature and content of mystical experience may be put in their place. And therefore we need not worry about such questions as to whether the Ultimate Reality revealed inn mystical experience is fullness or emptiness, Brahman or *śūnyatā*.

It may very well be that the mystics themselves add value and meaning (or, perhaps, 'super-value' and 'super-meaning') to the experiential content of mysticism. It may be that such meanings are invented and forged together, rather than discovered. J.L. Mackie has argued in his book *Ethics* that there are no objective values, and that we 'invent' right and wrong. This may generally be true. But a pragmatic approach in such cases is always advisable. It has been claimed that mysticism has been influential in changing the views and life-styles of most of those who have had such experiences. It is further claimed that this change has been mostly for the better. We may still ask: Better? In what sense? But if we grant the most obvious distinction between what William James has called the *diabolical* mysticism and the most benign one,[14] I do not see how we can suspend all judgement and remain neutral. James once said, referring to the mystical reality of the 'unseen region':

> Yet the unseen region in question is not merely ideal, for it produces effects in this world.[15]

We do not really know that it produces such effects. Nor do we know that it does not. Hence, as Nyāya would say, *saṃśayād api pravṛttiḥ*: Action can sometimes take place even when we are dubious about the outcome.

Notes and References

1. *Outlines of Pyrrhonism*, I, Loeb edn., ed. R.G. Bury, 1933, p. 23.
2. Ibid., pp. 20–1.
3. *Pramāṇavārttika*, ch. 2, v.209.
4. *Vijñaptimātratā, siddhi-viṃśatikā*, v.17 cd.
5. *Papers in Logic and Ethics* (eds. P. Geach & A. Gerry), London, Duckworth, 1976, p. 144.
6. *The Life Divine*, New York: Sri Aurobindo Library, 1949, II, p. 286.
7. Ibid., I, p. 73.
8. Ibid., II, p. 280.
9. *Varieties of Religious Experience*, London, Longmans, 1902, p. 193.
10. *What is Psychoanalysis*? London: Allen & Unwin, 1949, p. 105.
11. *Lectures on Ethics*, p. 12.
12. *Philosophical Explanations*, Oxford: Clarendon, 1981, p. 631.
13. 'On the Reasons for the Indeterminacy of Translation', *Journal of Philosophy*, 1970, p. 179.
14. *Varieties of Religious Experiences*, p. 326.
15. Ibid., p. 389.

PART II
Nyāya Realism

6

Naïve Realism, Nyāya Realism and the Causal Theory

Philosophers today generally accept some form of the causal theory of perception. Hence talk of naïve realism may understandably raise some eyebrows; it is usually taken for granted that science has somehow corrected our commonsense, uncritical assumptions about perception and perceptual objects. Russell, for example, wrote in 1940:

> Naïve realism leads to physics, and physics, if true, shows that naïve realism is false. Therefore, naïve realism, if true, is false. Therefore, it is false. (p. 15)

In Indian philosophical vocabulary, this is a *prasaṅga* argument. A *prasaṅga* argument at best destroys a certainty, it renders a tacit assumption dubious. But it seldom establishes any truth. It is, to use modern jargon, 'deconstructive', it is therapeutic. For surely, if physics or science starts with commonsense or naïve realism, naïve realism cannot be simply false. We must stay afloat in our ocean of commonsense, while we reconstruct the boat (in Neurath's metaphor) plank by plank. We cannot turn the ocean into land.

Our commonsense or naïve view-point may not be infallible, but we have little better to go on, if we denounce it completely. There is a certain 'perversity', as Quine once called it, if we keep insisting upon finding indubitable evidence for the reality of our most familiar physical things. The word 'naïve' is an unfortunate coinage, for surely naïve realism is a queer name for a philosophical position, even if the position be that of an opponent. Other philosophers have proposed a change in the name: call it Direct Realism. D.M. Armstrong is one of the few defenders of this position. Regarding the change of name, Wilfred Sellars has said:

> To avoid confusion—and the paradox of calling anything as sophisticated as an ably defended philosophical position 'naïve'—I will use the phrase 'direct realism' instead. (p. 61)

I believe at least two theses about naïve realism are defensible. First, naïve realism is not naïve. Second, any defensible theory of perception tries to assimilate part of the philosophical insight provided by the naïve theory. The first point has already been made by philosophers like Sellars and Armstrong. In fact, despite the use of the adjective 'naïve' the view has for a considerable length of time gained philosophical respectability, if only to be used as a counterpoint to other forms of realism, such as sophisticated realism or the casual theory. The second point is tied to the first. Although the naïve view has often been ridiculed by the philosophical heirs of John Locke and David Hume, and although sometimes it is summarily rejected as an 'infantile' obsession, which fails to distinguish between 'perceptions' (in the Humean sense) and the independently existing objects, it has been pretty resilient. Even Strawson (1979), while developing his own version of the causal theory, deriving some ideas from an earlier paper by Grice (1961), has given a very sympathetic hearing to the naïve concept of perception. Most recently, Colin McGinn, in his *The Subjective View* (1983) has argued that his subjectivist theory of the secondary properties does not seem to be incompatible with the philosophical insight found in the naïve theory.

The idea of naïvete probably began in the thought that people in their pre-philosophical or pre-reflective mood always take a realistic stance, and when they see a tomato for instance, they presumably naively take it to be a whole tomato, an independently existing, three-dimensional object with a colour *directly* grasped by the perceiver. Why this is called naïve? The answer probably is that a little reflection, a little challenge, would show instantly that this is an unreflective and perhaps wrong assumption—the assumption that the perceiver grasps directly a material object, that he does not perceive it in virtue of perceiving anything else. There are various tricks, several familiar moves, by which the perceiver can be persuaded to give up his commonsensical claim or belief that the immediate object of his perception is a material object, say a tomato. (For example, he may be suggestively told that he sees only a *red bulgy shape* which he takes to be a tomato, and he would readily agree.) When we give up such claim, what is left to us? Presumably, we have several alternatives. I shall consider at least three of them.

1. The immediate object of perception is the front surface or a facade of the tomato, i.e., the opaque surface of the body. This is the kind of direct realism which Moore once defended. According to some, this is also a variety of naïve realism, for perception (or mind) directly grasps a material object, an opaque surface. But now we have probably added a

new meaning to naïve realism. Naïvete consists in allowing the mind to grasp the non-mental, material things, and in not appreciating the obvious difficulties of what we may call 'connection'. The connection must be *close* enough to make non-mediated grasping possible. According to one well-entrenched view, the close connection is possible if both the mind and the material body belong to the same ontological category or exemplify the same universal, e.g., substancehood. However, when the required connection is specified, we face other difficulties, the foremost of which is that of explaining misperception. How could the mind-substance be connected with or even be causally dependent on the non-material fictitious snake that we see? This is perhaps one of the consequences of the platitude that goes by the name of 'argument from illusion' and it is supposed to refute the naïve view.

Moore, however, talked about 'directly seeing *x*' in the sense of 'seeing every bit of *x*', and also insisted that the criterion for 'directly seeing *x*' is 'could not be mistaken about *x*'. In this way, we may *see* the after image. Even some physical bodies, Moore claimed, can be seen *directly* in this sense (a spot of ink, a drop of clear water). But Moore avoided our earlier version of naïvete by claiming that we do not see bodies in this way generally, we see opaque surfaces; we see bodies by virtue of our seeing the opaque surface.

2. The immediate object of our perception is a sense-datum, or the Lockean idea of sensation. We see non-mediately the sense-data, and the material object is seen in virtue of our seeing such sense-data. Notice that if these sense-data are non-material, then the problem of connecting mind with the material object non-mediately has been somehow circumvented. On this view, however, when something looks red it is only a red sense-datum, and presumably the material object, our tomato, has only a disposition to cause the required experience of red. If we do not further reify sense-data, no further question arises, for as J. Bennett has argued, we may avoid a number of 'mildly lunatic conundrums' in this way. There are, however, other problems to be faced here. One is a not so lunatic conundrum of a possible mismatch between phenomenology and ontology, which might favour idealism. The other is a dilemma: either regard all such sensory properties as subjective or reduce them to dispositional traits of the corresponding material object.

3. The immediate object of perception is a sense-datum, but it is a mental object. Our perception of material objects is derivative upon our perception of these mental data. One rather odd consequence of this view is that it is the mental object that I take to be red, not the tomato before

me. It may be somewhat counterintuitive, but this is inadvertently supported by theory of secondary qualities or the relativity of our secondary quality perception. It is argued that since qualities are not genuinely, according to the scientifically informed view (here we get another meaning of naïvete; 'naïve' because 'unscientific'), ascribable to the material objects, and yet they must belong in something or somewhere, it is concluded that they belong to the mental.

All three try to save realism while avoiding naïvete. But the first is probably still naïve, for reasons already given. The second is not naïve, but still it is somewhat non-committal. The third by virtue of its open commitment to the mental sense-data, becomes a dubious form of representational realism. According to some it may be a short step to idealism or anti-realism from here. The tension between idealism and realism becomes obvious when too much emphasis is put on the scientific view in disregard of the commonsense picture. To quote Russell again: 'Science seems to be at war with itself: when it most means to be objective, it finds itself plunged into subjectivity against its will.' (1940)

If mind is said to grasp directly only what is mental, then: (a) we have lost the categorial closeness as well as communicative connection between the mind and the material things out there, and (b) we have fallen into the trap of subjectivism where mind grasps what it *creates* or *posits*. As Frege has warned us:

> If we want to emerge from subjectivism at all, we must conceive of knowledge as an activity that does not create what it knows, but grasps what is already there. (Preface, *Grundgetze*)

That is why for Frege the thoughts we grasp are mind-independent somewhere out there if you like, but not created by mind. In any case, our flight from naïvete has often proven to be hazardous.

I shall now talk about Nyāya realism. First, I will settle the banality of a terminological problem. Is 'perception' an acceptable English rendering of the Sanskrit term *pratyakṣa*? Some have doubted the exactness of this usual rendering. Etymologically, *pratyakṣa* (where *prati* means 'each' and *akṣa* means a sensory faculty) is closer to the notion of sensation or sensory experience, where perception is what 'goes beyond' (in A.J. Ayer's language) such sensory experience as gives rise to it. I concede the ground for hesitation. But I still prefer 'perception'. Among other things, talking about etymology, Vātsyāyana (*c.* AD 150) has added the word *vṛtti*, which can conceivably mean 'going out' for objects, and *pratyakṣa* would be the grasping of the sensible object. Second, *pratyakṣa* in Sanskrit includes inner perceptions, i.e., grasping of the inner states or events, such as cognitions, pleasure and pain, for mind (*manas*) is also an *akṣa*, a sense, an inner sense or faculty. Even the Buddhists, who seem to favour the 'sensation' view of perception, have argued that mind is an inner sense (Diṅnāga).

Further, I believe the well-entrenched distinction between sensation and perception has sometimes been overrated. To partly substantiate the claim, it may be pointed out that our perceptual capacity must lie with the our information-processing capacity. But even this 'machine' model does not fully justify the separation of sensation as input or data from perception as the processing of such input. For without the said processing there cannot be any input or information, and without information there cannot be any processing; unprocessed information is virtually non-existent in practical terms. This is not a modern argument but, I believe a modern translation of an old Nāgārjunian argument, i.e., a Mādhyamika argument (*c.* AD 150). At least I have used it as my primary source. Furthermore, the human machine is *sensitive* (no pun intended); it is self-monitored, and self-conscious. Hence the idea of an 'unprocessed' sensation is more a myth than a reality. The genesis of this idea has fallen into disrepute today. The idea is generated by a sort of perverse foundationalism, by the intense search for infallibility and incorrigibility. Foundationalism in classical India had various ramifications. Even Diṅnāga (*c.* AD 450) said that the mind-mediated (i.e., inference-mediated in modern terms) character of perceptual judgement is solely responsible for error, and hence if we strip off this character from perception completely, we can ensure impossibility of error. Hence the well-entrenched (both in India and the West) and overrated distinction between the given and the interpretation, sensation and perception, content and scheme, the optical picture and the phrasing of it by the organ or the brain, has been called in question. When the rationale is questioned, the alleged 'epistemological model' that is sustained by it may collapse or need radical re-modelling.

The Nyāya view of perception is a sort of naïve realism, but it has certain unique features. It fights both representationalism and phenomenalism. Besides, it also develops a sort of *causal* theory of its own. We must distinguish, however. Nyāya direct realism is different from what G.E. Moore once defended. For one thing, a Moorean would argue that we do not see the opaque bodies directly, by seeing say, *every bit of it*. Our actual seeing of the table, on Moore's view, is based upon our seeing 'much less', i.e., the opaque front surfaces.

Uddyotakara (*c.* AD 500), expounding the Nyāya view, has insistently argued that we see bodies *directly*, not in virtue of seeing the front surfaces. For bodies are both physical realities and *wholes*. Wholes are on this view, contained in the parts, not the other way around. The table as a whole is considered a locatee of the parts which jointly constitute its location or locus, the container. Instead of asking 'How can we see the whole body without seeing its parts or surface?' we should rather ask 'How can we see the locus without first seeing the locatee?' Or, what amounts to the same thing, 'How can we see the part or the surface without seeing what it is a part or the surface of?' Of course, we can be cheated by a tricky representation of the surface only, as the mythical king Udayana was by a trick elephant. But such misfirings only presuppose the presence of cases where firing is just on target. If there were no targets, there would be no misfires.

Uddyotakara concedes that we do see the surface simply because it is there to be seen or grasped. In Nyāya terminology, this means that the perception-generating connection between the sense-organ, the eye, and thence the mind on the one hand, and the opaque surface, a material reality, on the other, is as much possible as between the same organ, the eye-cum-mind and the whole table, since both the relata are substances or belong to the same substantial category. Hence the strict, water-tight, dualism of the mental and the non-mental, or in Indian terms, the inert (*jaḍa*) and the conscious (*a-jaḍa*), is not tenable here. Be that as it may, the opaque surface may be perceived, but occasionally it will be possible to see the whole without noticing the surface. For example, I may see a whole horse running by without seeing the peculiarity of its front surface. In fact, according to the Nyāya view of causation, the opaque surface (or having an opaque surface), its mere presence, and not necessarily a sensible experience of it, is what is causally depended upon for the perception of the body to arise. This is in accord with the causal analysis given by Praśastapāda (*c.* AD 450), which Uddyotakara repeats in this context with approval. Thus the connection between the perception of the opaque surface and that of the whole body is merely contingent. The former is not causally necessary for the latter. Similarly, on this view, having a colour, or a colour-disposition, i.e., the required opacity, is only what is necessary (causally) for the perception of the whole body to arise, not the actual sensible experience of that opacity, or the colour itself. Such sensible experience of colour etc., may and does arise, but is only contingently connected with the seeing of the opaque body as a whole.

The so-called naïvete of the Nyāya view must also be distinguished from the naïvete of D.M. Armstrong's view. On Armstrong's view of direct realism, we can *hear* a train, *taste* sugar, and *smell* flowers directly, not just the sensible properties of these material bodies, viz, the sound of the train, sweetness of the sugar or fragrance of flowers. The Nyāya view is rather modest in this regard, It is argued in Nyāya that the senses of sight and touch enjoy a special status in our sensory life. While other sense-organs (of hearing, smelling and tasting) directly grasp only the sensible qualities of the material objects, sight and touch can do both, grasp directly the bodies themselves as well as their sensible qualities. We can *hear* a train only metaphorically, i.e., perceive it through ascription of the sound to the locus of its origin.

Strawson is a causal theorist. In one of his papers, he talks about the criteria of difference or differential treatment of the sense of sight and that of touch from those of smell, taste and hearing. He uses a notion of what he calls 'categorial homogeneity'—the excess of such homogeneities on his view underlines the relevant difference of sounds and smells from the objects of touch. The objects of touch, he concludes, are necessarily fluid or solid bodies. This spells out a sort of direct realism regarding the sense of touch, and hence it coincides with the Nyāya view, provided we add the adjective 'immediate' to the word 'object'. Non-metaphorically and non-elliptically, I can say 'I touch the table' but I cannot say in the same way (par contra Armstrong) 'I hear the train'. The Nyāya believes, however, par contra Strawson, the sense of sight is also on par in this regard with the sense of touch. We grasp the table directly by sight as well as by touch. In fact this concurrence between sight and touch, i.e., that we can touch the same material body which we can see, is used as a premise to prove the unity of not only the spatial occupant but also the perceiver, the person. This concurrence is believed to be self-evident. There is another requirement of the Nyāya theory. The perceiver and the perceived material body must *instantiate* the same substantial *form* to render the account of the 'causal' interaction between them somewhat unproblematic.

H.P. Grice has defended a modern version of CTP (the causal theory of perception), which states that it is a necessary condition of one's perceiving a material reality *M* that one's sense-impression leading to the perception in question should be causally dependent upon some state of affairs involving that object *M*. Here if we replace 'sense-impression' by an expression for some sort of substantial material interaction or interconnection (cf. *sannikarṣa*) with the material body in question, then we have a close enough formulation of the Nyāya view of perception. Causation in perception in some form or other is the shared feature of both the naïve (as well as Nyāya) and the representationalist views. Strawson has given a modified and generalized version of the Gricean CTP, which seems to be quite unobjectionable from the Nyāya point of view, as long as the explicit aim of this formulation (as Strawson himself admits, p. 75) is also to fit it into the 'naïve concept of perception'.

The word 'causal' in 'causal dependence' is very intriguing. In a strictly dualistic framework of the Cartesian variety, some sort of interactionism is to be invoked, lest the theory of causal process becomes guilty of categorial promiscuity. If the causal process is, as is commonly understood, of a mechanistic type, then the physical sensory reaction through sensory reaction through confrontation with the material body belongs in the domain of material causation, while the sensory experience caused by the same physical event, leading to perception, belongs in the domain of mental events. This transition from the material to the mental domain may present some explanatory problems, unless the philosopher is also inclined to accept some from of identity theory. But the dualist may resort to interactionism.

Does the Nyāya view of causation fare any better in this regard? I believe it does. I have already indicated that on this view there is categorial similarity between the material and the mental. Even the Buddhist, who rejects the notion of an enduring subject, a soul substance, believes that the percepts, the perceptual awareness and the perceptual faculty, all three, belong to a homogenous group, so that there can be concurrence, interaction and causal dependence among them. The Nyāya view explicitly rejects the physical mechanistic sense of causation, according to which causal potency (*śakti*) involves emission of force from the causal to the effect. For Nyāya, a causal condition is one that is endowed with a 'transparent' set of properties; it the invariable, relevant and immediate antecedent. All these adjectives require comment, which I shall skip in this context.

The alleged transparency may be a bit clouded by some 'counterfactual' requirements, when we try to explain such terms as 'relevant' and 'invariable'. But that is not the issue here. A mental event on this view will have a set of *relevant* and immediate antecedents, which may include both mental and material antecedents. Thus, it is possible to include sensory reaction, the object's presence, a memory, presence of light etc., in the set of the relevant antecedents, related causally to the suitable sensory experience that takes place as a mental event immediately after. If causation is reduced to mere relevance, immediate and antecedent, then no transmission of energy from the material to the mental domain would be needed to be postulated. Besides as far as the succession of events is concerned, there is also the already noted categorial homogeneity, or uniformity, between the mental and the material.

The Buddhist philosopher, Diṅnāga, in order to refute realism in Nyāya and other theories of perception, formulated the following criterion as the hallmark of any kind of realism worth defending. This is called the examination of the *ālambana*, 'the objective support' in perception. The *ālambana*, says Diṅnāga, must fulfill at least the following two conditions—so that we can save realism: (a) it must be causally depended upon by the perception in question, and (b) it must also be phenomenologically given in that perceptual awareness. If there is thus the concurrence of the phenomenologically given with the ontologically construed causal ancestry, we have then saved realism. But if there is a mismatch, we have refuted realism, or externalism, the theory that an external, material object is grasped in perception. Diṅnāga has argued that it is impossible to claim that an external (real) object fulfills both conditions; it may fulfill the first, causality, but not the second, phenomenology. And the phenomenologically given obviously fulfills the second, not the first. Hence the non-concurrence or mismatch. The well-known phenomenal objects, the rainbow, the shadow, the blue dome of the sky, the blur, the continuous green spread of the forest, cannot be said to cause anything.

Faced with this dilemma of the alleged phenomenology-ontology mismatch, the Nyāya realist moves to obliterate the gap, and reject altogether the concept of the phenomenological content of the experience as distinct from the ontological object outside. The Nyāya naïve realism is thus of a piece with a radical move against the 'content' theory. The object *in* perception is also the object outside, nothing like forms, images (*ākāra*), representations contents, intervene between perception and its objects. There is no 'veil of ideas' of the Lockean or any other kind.

This brings us to the most crucial issue in Nyāya realism. If we repudiate representation or phenomenological content altogether, how are we to account for objects in illusions, dreams etc. The problem seems to be more general and radical. One of the questions frequently discussed by the Indian philosophers of different persuasions, is: Whether an awareness is intrinsically with-a-form, or without-a-form? The Buddhist answer was that it is essentially with-a-form, and then there was a fight between the Buddhist representationalist (Sautrāntika) and the Buddhist idealist (Yogācāra) to decide whether that form is a contribution from the object outside, or not. In fact, in this type of representationalism, idealism remains unrefuted, since the so-called *form* or representation is constitutive of the awareness event, unique in each case, and determined by the ongoing mechanism of the awareness-series, the idea of its being *caused* by the external object may become superfluous, and hence may be ignored. This was the line taken by Dharmakīrti (*c.* AD 630).

The two realist schools, the Nyāya and the Prābhākara, answered that awareness is without-a-form, only the objects grasped differentiate them, one from the other. The objects are not *in* the awareness, but only affectively present in the vicinity, to affect the awareness and to qualify it, much as the blue of a blue lotus affects and qualifies the crystal piece due to proximity.

The anti-naïve theorists may argue that there are at least two outstanding cases where this 'against-content' doctrine would not be very successful: (a) where the awareness (perceptual) misrepresents the object, a rope appears as a snake, and (b) where the object of awareness is simply non-existent, in dreams, hallucinations, etc. The Nyāya puts forward its doctrine of 'misplacement' or 'misconnection' to explain such cases. If what looks like a snake is not a snake but a rope, Nyāya invokes the idea of a remembered snake. We perceive the rope as a snake, the verbal report is 'This is a snake' where 'This' refers to the snake outside, but it is misidentified with a remembered snake, or the remembered feature snakehood is misascribed to it. Thus, here too, the phenomenologically given snake concurs or matches with the ontological snake which generated past experiences. We have only misconnected the present rope with the remembered snake or *misplaced* on the rope-locus the remembered character of snakehood. The dream objects, it is argued, are all composite in character, and hence analysable into bits and pieces, each of which the subject must have experienced before in some way or other. Hence dreams are only revived memories where objects of past experience are indiscriminately disjoined and them misconnected in various *odd* ways. So the chain of causal connection of the ontological object with the phenomenological is still maintained.

How about hallucinations, and experiences of many phenomenal objects, the blur at a distance, the rainbow, the shadow, etc.? The Nyāya. explanation here is also in terms of memory and misconnection of various bits and pieces of the actual. Sometimes, this explanation becomes too tortuous. Hence either the explanation becomes too involved, or the Nyāya radical move against all sorts of contents, representations etc., becomes defeated. Taking some liberty with the Nyāya view, but working strictly within the general theoretical framework of Nyāya, I propose the following solution. These alleged phenomenal objects may be taken to be real, ontological objects. They can be regarded as temporary parts of the external reality. Some of them may be *objective* particulars, produced by a set of causal factors which include both the material and the mental. The intrusion of a mental event into the causal set of an effect does not always render the effect subjective. They can just be the momentary features of the external. The blur that I see without my glasses on vanishes when I put my glasses on; also, it does not exist when I am not looking at the book. On this theory, the blur is not in my head, but somewhere out there. This is not a sense-datum, unless sense-data are physical realities and also particulars for each perceptual sensory grasp. To admit these type of entities may be somewhat unorthodox in Nyāya, but Nyāya does admit a similar sort of external realities, viz., numbers higher than one, such as two and three. Such numbers, according to the Nyāya theory, are produced in the counted objects by the counting agent's count-oriented cognition (*apekṣabuddhi*). Such numbers, Nyāya asserts, are objective properties of the counted objects and they disappear as soon as the count-oriented cognition disappear. I invoke this peculiarity of the Nyāya view to support my contention that the so-called phenomenal objects may be taken to be real, non-subjective objects, if a similar causal account is given. There may be phenomenal objects which are persistently present even without a perceiver, they shadow etc., They are to be regarded as of a piece with the material reality, being caused by a set of such factors. There are others, for which presence of a perceiver needed for causing them, but still they may be non-subjective.

Part of the oddity may be resolved if we try to connect these particular (phenomenal) features to the categorial bases in the material object—to a particular disposition or trait to produce experiences of such features. As Nyāya has argued, there must be *two* objects to produce our experience of two, but two-ness belongs to the objects, produced only when one is counting. Such numbers seem to be on a par with secondary properties, if we take an objective view of them. This possibility of reduction to the causal ground in the objects shows its non-subjectivity. There may, however, be another kind of case, where it is more natural to say that the *subject* is disposed to have experiences of certain qualities under certain conditions, in which the contribution of the object to produce such experience would be minimal. But those would be cases of error finally, the explanation would be again in terms of psychological and physiological factors as before. The cases I have separated here for a differential treatment are not separately recognized in the Nyāya tradition. I believe the traditional explanation of *misplacement* may become too complicated for these cases, or a failure may threaten this type of direct realism of Nyāya. Hence I have suggested an alternative approach.

Could we take this set of features that we grasp to be the intentional content of the respective experience? Professor Anscombe has suggested that we could successfully avoid talk of sense-data, if we keep in mind the intentionality of sensation. She argues that there must always be an intentional object of seeing, but there need not always be a material object. In fact the thesis of intentionality (that we must admit an intentional object even when there is no actual object) provides the strongest challenge to naivete of Nyāya; Can Nyāya defend itself? I believe it can. We cannot simply describe or verbalize any intended object of sight etc. without using some material object language. As Quine has remarked regarding the sense-data, we take sidelong glances at the material objects while talking about sense-data. The same seems to hold for the intentional objects. Nyāya claims there is always some material object, or a set of material object components, bits and pieces, at the end of the line, near or far, past or present, in any so-called intentional use of seeing or sensing. When I see a 'shiny blur' when there is a watch there, the blur belongs, if not in the watch itself, in the physical world situation, distance, lighting condition, my poor eye-sight, etc. According to the standard interpretation, the intentional objects are repeatable, but these phenomenal-cum-real objects are unique to each occurrence of its experience. In the case of the propositional seeing however, the analysis would be different. Nyāya admits a sort of quasi-intentional structural description of such cognitive episodes, and the context becomes opaque and they are treated essentially in the manner of the modern treatment of propositional attitudes. I do not wish to enter into it here.

The duality of the 'manifest image' and the 'scientific image' and their alleged conflict are by now well-known. Most philosophers try to reconcile the conflict with stipulations and other such moves. Others argue that there is no real conflict, only two different domains, two discourses, to be kept separate, and statements about realities are to be relitivized. This issue has obviously a parallel in the classical Indian tradition. The Sautrāntika Buddhist introduced a distinction between what is nominally existent and what is substantially existent. The normal or phenomenal objects (all normal objects are phenomenal in his view) of perception, bodies, chair, stones, persons, are nominally existent. For they appear only when there is combination of their atomic constituents; the latter, the atoms, are however substantially existent—they are ultimates. Hence what is phenomenologically presented to perception cannot be causally related to such events, and what are causally responsible, the ultimates, the atoms, are not what we see. Thus our robust sense of realism suffers, for there is the said mismatch between phenomenology and ontology. Idealism wins the day.

A reflex of basically the same argument is found, paradoxically enough, among the hard-liners in scientific realism. To avoid contradiction between the two 'images', the commonsense and the scientific, the hard-liners, on pain of conceding incoherence, resolve that the manifest image is subjective, that commonsense suffers from congenital illusion. Anti-realisms of various kinds win the day.

To avoid the Sautrāntika quandary over the duality of the 'image', Nyāya takes a bold step to make the so-called phenomenal, bodies etc., also the real. The atoms may be the ultimate constituents, but when they combine a new ontological object is created thereby, the bodies, the wholes. Hence the phenomenological is also the ontological. The commonsense objects for Nyāya are also real. They emerge from or are created by the imperceptible or not ordinarily perceptible, ultimate elements, but science only explains this causal route, and does not repudiate their reality. Commonsense is not an illusion, much as science is not.

I have wilfully mixed separate disciplines in this presentation of classical Indian philosophy, the domain of the Sanskritists and the Indianists, and modern Western analytical philosophy. This has been done with the conviction that such an eclectic approach would be eventually profitable, and I believe, even philosophically rewarding. I have translated back and forth the philosophical issues that faced the classical Indian philosophers, in the vocabulary of modern philosophy, and vice-versa, for I have also attempted to translate the modern issues in the vocabulary of the classical Indian philosophers. In spite of some apparent undercommensurability, and since I also believe total incommensurability does not exist here, I believe such translations are both possible and fruitful for *both* kinds of philosophers today. I think it gives better insight into the nature of the philosophical problems as such (if historical relativity is not the main issue)—problems the classical people were trying to grapple with. And the reverse translation it is hoped, may illuminate some modern issues, some unrecognized aspects of these issues at least, and by doing so, may stimulate creative thinking all the more. Philosophical discourse need not be a dead-end, where intrusion of fresh ideas from outside as well as from the past would not be allowed. All points made here are only suggestive. Further explorations, I believe firmly, are bound to uncover many worthwhile and substantive issues.

APPENDIX: MARGINALIA ON NYĀYA REALISM AND STRAWSON

Strawson's realism in many significant ways coincides with that of the Nyāya. Regarding the alleged conflict of the 'scientific image' and the 'manifest image', Strawson advocates a sort of tolerance. He thinks that contradiction vanishes once we recognise the relativity in our conception of the real. Nyāya also accepts a proto-scientific image of the world, where gross bodies (the manifest image) are in fact made of real atoms or particles. But these bodies are not phenomenal objects, for the whole is a newly created thing, a real entity apart from the constituents, parts or atoms. Hence it is deemed to have both causal properties and representedness in perception. The independent reality of the wholes is thus seen to be an important ploy used by Nyāya to save its own form of realism.

The ontological thesis of Nyāya (and I believe of Strawson also) can be put in exceedingly simple language: There are particulars and there are also kinds of particulars. The first part coincides with the Lockean claim of the nominalists. It is the second part that meets the special claim of the Nyāya realists as well as Strawson. Universals are admitted as commonly shared real features or properties, as principles of classification for the particulars. Strawson finds Quine's criterion—'no entity without identity'—too narrow, but perhaps a liberal interpretation of the 'identification' principle can be given to admit abstract universals, as entities identified as objects of developed thought alone not found in Nature. They exist, however, if instances are found.

Nyāya accepts objective (real) universals, universals which are located out there in their instances, and such universals are concrete enough even to be perceptible in their perceptible instances. If I can see a dog, a particular, I can also see that it *is* a dog, that is, as characterised by dog-hood, just as I can see that it has four legs or a tail. I can see a man is healthy just as I can see that he is a man, but not necessarily that he is wealthy. Hence universals of this kind are more like shared features and are perceptible accordingly. This idea, I believe, somewhat peculiar as it may seem initially, tries to avoid the well-entrenched problem of traditional empiricism, according to which our access to universals can never be through observational means, but universals are arrived at through rational thinking and construction. Nyāya argues that at least some universals are our 'perceptual firsts', and hence other universals can be arrived at through analogical inference. I am not sure how Strawson would react to this view. Perhaps favourably.

The discussion of universals can take us from the domain of ontology through epistemology to the domain of logic. One of the persistent concerns of Strawson has been the philosophy of logic, notably the problem of singular reference and predication, which is connected with the notions of grammatical (and logical) subject and predicate. In Strawson's philosophy, the subject of predication coincides (almost) with the object of reference, and universals are involved in the act of predication. He tries to support the traditional idea that, while the universals can play the role of both subject and predicate, the particulars can be subjects only.

The Nyāya notion of predication is, however, different. The 'basic combination' is usually written in Western logic as '*Fa*' or '*a* is *F*'. The predicate term, according to Quine, is a syncategoramatic term, which has a blank place to be filled by a term purported to have a singular reference. For Nyāya, however, the basic combination seems to have the form '*Fab*' or '*a* is qualified by *b*', where '*a*' is called the qualificand and '*b*' is the qualifier. Perhaps we may call the syncategoramatic term for the qualification relation the predicate, while the other two terms are purported to have singular reference. In fact, in Nyāya logic, this blanket dyadic relation, qualification, occupies a fundamental position, much like the relation of class-membership in the logic of classes. In this way of looking at things, there cannot be any old-style subject-predicate distinction, based upon the category-criterion and role-playing. Logically speaking. Nyāya would reduce all types of expressions to this structure involving a single syncategoramatic dyadic relational term '. . . is qualified by—', where the first blank is to be filled up by the logical or grammatical subject and the second by the qualifier. A qualifier can be a concrete or abstract object, as long as the combinatory qualifying relation is spelled out to suit the description. Consider the much discussed example: 'Wisdom Socratizes'. We cannot say 'Wisdom is Socrates'. The Nyāya would say that 'Socratizes' hides the special qualificatory relation, locushood, and combines it with the singular term 'Socrates' referring to a spatiotemporal particular: '*Lws*'—to be read as 'Wisdom is located in Socrates.'

The Nyāya view of universal is, however, both reductionist and revisionist. In spirit, their universals are more akin to the natural kind universals. Real universals are *ultimate* and *simples*, they are also atemporal, but locatable in spatio-temporal particulars. It is also believed that these real universals are organisable in the form of an inverted tree-diagram (the highest being Existence), where any given universal is either included in or inclusive of (or both, in the case of intermediate ones) some other real universal. This apparently resists any cross-classification of natural kinds. In fact, many other ultimate and simple properties could have the same logical status as the real universals, but since they cannot form part of this hierarchical natural classification, they would not have any ontological status.

Another outstanding feature of the Nyāya theory is that if the application of a general term, while claiming a place in the natural classification, can be shown to be ascribable to some manifest feature or features of its instances, then it is not a real universal. It is what they call 'analysable', not a simple or ultimate. Thus, if the word *paśu* ('beast') is shown to be used to apply to such animals as are furry and have tails, etc., it does not constitute a real universal; but words like 'dog', 'cat', etc. do. In short, the Nyāya view is that the world of particulars is necessarily enclosed by a thin but essential domain of universals which are ontologically real, for otherwise we cannot make sense of 'kinds of particulars'.

I shall conclude with some parallels. Both Nyāya and Strawson seem to admit the thesis that everything that is, is knowable. Both seem to endorse the view that the relation between the 'scientific image' of the world and the 'manifest image' is one of ancestry and dependence. But for Strawson, science remains dependent upon common-sense, while for Nyāya (if I am allowed to speculate), the perceptibles, the manifest image, are off-spring of the imperceptible reals, although they are not unknowable. The reality status of both would be the same, however. Unlike the hard-liners among the scientific realists, Nyāya would not accept the consequence that each of us suffers from a persistent and inescapable illusion. Neither would Strawson. For Nyāya, the off-springs (i.e. the wholes) are as much real as the parents (parts, atoms). The manifest is not a phenomenal object, and hence by its mere presence it can *cause* perceptions. Thus the Diṅnāga criterion for realism is fulfilled. The Vedāntins like Bhartṛhari, who believe in the prevalence of a persistent and inescapable illusion, insist also that we are led to truths from the untruth, from illusion. In this respect, the Vedāntins, paradoxically, would agree with the scientific realist hard-liners. Both Nyāya realism and Strawson's realism seem to avoid this anomaly. The naïve is proven to be not naïve after all!

NOTES

1. Anscombe, E.M. (1981), 'The Intentionality of Sensation: A Grammatical Feature', in *The Collected Philosophical Papers of G.E.M. Anscombe: II, Metaphysics and the Philosophy of Mind*, Oxford: Blackwell.
2. Armstrong, D.M. (1961), *Perception and the Physical World*, London: Kegan Paul.

References

Grice, H.P. (1961), 'The Causal Theory of Perception', in R.J. Swartz (ed.), *Perceiving, Sensing and Knowing*, New York: Anchor Books.

McGinn, C. (1983), *The Subjective View*, Oxford: Oxford University Press.

Russell, B. (1940), *An Inquiry into Meaning and Truth*, London: Allen & Unwin.

Sellars, W. (1963), *Perception and Reality*, London: Kegan Paul.

Strawson, P.F. (1979), 'Perception and Its Objects', in G.F. Macdonald (ed.), *Perception and Identity*, London: Macmillan.

7

Awareness and Meaning in Navya-Nyāya

1. AWARENESS OF THE OBJECT AS QUALIFIED

In this paper, I shall try to formulate and examine two inter-related Nyāya principles about knowledge, and show how a tension evolved in the system as a result of their interaction. These two fundamental principles had far-reaching effects in shaping the Nyāya theory of meaning as well as its theory of verbal knowledge derived from linguistic utterance. This latter part, however, will not be fully discussed here, for I shall devote this paper mainly to the clarification of the said principles and what, if anything, could be done with them.

The first principle that I shall take up for examination could be very roughly stated as follows: Whenever an object *x* figures (for floats, or swims = *avagāhate*) in my awareness, it figures there as something, i.e., under some guise or mode, distinguished in some way or other. The second principle may also be stated, using similar metaphorical expressions as is usual with the Sanskrit writers, as follows: A precondition for having a clear and distinct, i.e. qualificative, awareness of the above kind is a further awareness of the qualifier or distinguishing element (*viśeṣaṇa*). To indulge in the elaboration of the implicit metaphor, we may say: When an object *x* features or floats distinctly in our awareness, it is invariably distinguished by a 'cloak' that may either be put upon it by us, or that may belong there initially, and be recognized by us as such. The second principle demands that to have such a distinguishing awareness (and a piece of knowledge is only a special case of such a distinguishing or qualificative or 'propositional' awareness in this theory) we need to have a prior awareness of the distinguisher or the cloak or the guise.

Let us formulate the first principle as follows:

P1: If something *x* is presented in my awareness or knowledge, it is presented there under the cloak of a purported property.

Here 'the cloak of a purported property' is called a *mode* (*prakāra*). In what follows, I shall call the purported property the qualifier, and the object *x* the qualificand. This qualifier-qualificand structure is regarded as implicit in the content of any cognitive episode that has a claim to be regarded as knowledge (in the episodic sense). An exception can be made for the cases of 'simple' awareness or the so-called non-constructive (*nir-vikalpa*) awareness (if there are any) where the object shines in its nakedness, in its guiseless glory. But such awareness is not called knowledge in Nyāya.

The above principle, if true, has several implications. First, if seeing or perceiving is also a species of knowing, then we have to say that all seeing is seeing-as. It has been generally held by the Buddhist epistemologists that there are pure cases of seeing where we see the object in its nakedness, the unique particular datum untinged with any qualifier. But such a case of seeing or sensing would not be counted, under the view we are examining, as a 'distinguishing' cognitive episode, which, when it is proven to be correct, may be claimed to be a knowing episode.

Secondly, the above principle seems to suggest that the usual distinction which philosophers make between our *knowledge-that* and *knowledge-what* (knowledge of things) does not present two irreducible alternatives. For, *knowledge-that* can be taken to be more fundamental, and in all cases of so-called *knowledge-what* there is, it may be argued, an implicit propositional structure: $F(a)$ or a as qualified by or distinguished by F-ness. We may say that someone's knowledge of F is actually unpackable as his knowledge of what is an F, i.e. that which is distinguished by the purported property F-ness. (In this context, I am ignoring presumably the complication due to the fact that in representing a *knowledge-that* in language, we invariably introduce an 'assertion' element in it. For the moment, we focus upon only the content of such 'assertions'.)

In view of the point just made, my knowledge of the pen I am now writing with is to be spelled out, in the minimal sense, as my knowledge of the thing *as* a pen. Alternatively, it could be my knowledge of the thing as a solid substance, as a shiny object, as an object made of silver and so on. But there cannot be any knowledge of the thing as totally unqualified (even 'thing-hood' would be a qualifing character in this view, and hence I can know it simply *as* a thing).

I may verbalize my knowledge as 'a pen', but this would only be an elliptical expression in this theory: '(It is) a pen' or 'Something characterized by pen-hood'. Here is an indication of how a linguistic expression, in this theory, would yield its *meaning*. The word 'pen', even when it is in a referential position in an expression, would not present the object directly—it would present the particular as qualified by the purported property, penhood.

A pragmatic transformation of the above principle (PI) in the context of a word-generated awareness would be:

> P' 1: If something *x* is denoted by a word, then in the awareness (of the object *x*) generated by the word (in the hearer) the object *x* is presented under the cloak of a purported property.

This is acceptable provided we add the following explanatory notes: (a) We may change 'denoted by' to 'designated by' if the word is a singular term or a proper name; (b) 'A word denotes *x*' means that at the utterance of the word an awareness of the object *x* is generated in a competent hearer by the familiar causal law; (c) 'The familiar causal law' refers either to the fact that the word has been learnt in a 'dubbing' situation and is thereby *infused* with a 'power' (*śakti*) to denote an object or that the word is learnt in some other way as infused with the 'power' to denote the same way. And by 'word-generated awareness' we mean that the word being uttered generates in the hearer the relevant awareness of the object by virtue of the said 'power'. The upshot of all this is that what is denoted by the word is presented in the awareness of the hearer under a cloak or a mode. I shall come back to talk about the word-generated awareness in Section 4. For the moment let me concentrate upon awareness in general and perceptual awareness in particular.

There is a well-entrenched philosophical view that says that perception of the thing *per se*, of the pure, 'uncoloured' existent, is what yields a piece of knowledge (*pramā*) in the basic sense, for it has not only psychological certainty, but also logical incorrigibility. If the (above) second point is conceded, it would go directly against such a contention of the epistemologists. Diṅnāga and many others have claimed that a sensation of blue, for example, when the object shines in its own glory and the subject grasps it directly, the purity of the object being not contaminated by anything, yields a very respectable piece of knowledge. If such an awareness cannot be called knowledge, what else would there be left for us to rely upon as the foundation of our knowledge?

In reply, the upholder of the above position may say that he does not dispute the fact that such episodes of pure sensation arise in us. What is in dispute is the cognitive character of such episodes. They are not pieces of empirical knowledge. To call them knowledge would be an inadvertent smuggling of an *a priori* character into what are essentially episodes of empirical knowledge. It is an important mark of our empirical understanding that it is liable to error. If we preclude any chance of our being in error with respect to the sensing of an object (and this is what 'logical incorrigibility' apparently means), then we forfeit its claim to be considered as a piece of empirical knowledge. The general idea behind this point is this: In order to be either true or false, an awareness must be an awareness of something *x* as *F*, i.e., as distinguished by a qualifier, *F*-ness, or (simply) by *f*. A true awareness is knowledge, and a false one an error, according to the terminology of the theory we are discussing here. Notice that in this theory, if I say 'I sense *F*-ly' I may be reporting a cognitive event where the object *grasped* is a particular sensation *x* which is distinguished by the distinguisher, *f*. In the same vein, in most cases of my awareness of blue, it can be unpacked as that of the wall as blue, the sky as blue, or the *śārī* of my beloved as blue. Only with such unpackings, the relevant episode can make knowledge-claims. For they are, in each case, liable to be false. For example, if the wall is white, the sky is colourless and my beloved wears a red *śārī*, I would be in error in each case. Such knowledge claims can be entertained only when the facts are liable to be different.[1]

We normally do talk about knowledge of things, and hence such usages must be explained. According to this theory, when I know the thing in my hand as a dot-pen, I can talk about this knowledge-episode in either of two ways: I can call it either my knowledge of the dot-pen or my knowledge of the purported property, viz., being a dot-pen; and in either case we may pick out the same episode. My knowledge of the thing thus seldom arises in isolation *from* my knowledge of the *way* the thing is presented in my awareness.

P1 raises the following problem. If I know *x* as distinguished by a property, *f*, then *f* is also a part of what I know. This implies that *f* also *floats* in my knowledge as much as *x* does, and hence one can argue that we need a further distinguisher for qualifying *f*. If I knew a piece as a piece of gold, then *being gold* is also what I know. It would be absurd to claim that I do not know what gold is or what *being gold* is like, then by our P1 we must say that if I know *being gold* (or gold-ness), I should know it under a further characterization. This leads to the peril of infinite regress: If *x* figures in my awareness by way of being gold, and being gold figures there by way of being something else, then there will be no stopping. To avoid this problem, an exception to P1 is formulated.

E1: When I am aware of an ultimate universal, a *simple* property (a *jāti* or an *akhaṇḍa upādhi*), I may be aware of it as such (unqualified). But if in the *verbal report* of the awareness the simple property is mentioned by a name it needs to be presented there under a further cloak of a purported property.[2]

Two observations are needed in this context. First, our sense of such expressions as 'purported property', 'ultimate universal' and 'simple property' may be taken to be ontologically neutral. Such properties may or may not be separately real, or existent in the mind-independent objective world. It may be that there are only chairs in this world, but no separate thing called 'chairhood'. Our talk of chairhood is restricted only to its being a recognizable distinguisher (*viśeṣaṇa*). It is significant that Nyāya does not make any distinction *in this context* between a real (objective) universal (*jāti*) and a nominal universal in so far as they play the logical role of 'simple' properties. A simple property is ultimate in the sense of being a property that is further unanalysable (unbreakable).

This leads to the second observation. We can have, according to E1, a very direct 'communion' with such simple properties, an uncoloured, non-mediated acquaintance. The distinction between such a knowledge of a simple property and the pure sensation of the uncoloured, unpropertied, naked object (about which knowledge-claim has been previously denied) is this: The former is being called here 'knowledge' only in virtue of its being an integral part of a knowledge-episode, such as knowledge of *x* as distinguished by a qualifier *f*, a simple property; but the latter has to stand apart, and be counted. Whether or not a purported awareness of a simple property can also stand apart and be counted (i.e. be a separate episode) is a controversial issue to which I shall now turn.

2. AWARENESS OF THE QUALIFIER

Our second principle mentioned in the beginning says that if there arises a qualificative awareness where an object *x* is distinguished by a qualifier *f*, in the above manner, one of its necessary pre-conditions is a prior awareness of *f*, the qualifier.

P2: To generate an awareness in which the object *x* is presented as qualified by *f*, a prior awareness of *f* is needed.

In order for me to be able to characterize or qualify *x* by *f* in my awareness, or attribute *f* to *x*, I must be in possession of an awareness of *f* prior to it. Unless I know what 'blue' of *being blue* is, I cannot judge something to be blue.

This principle is appealed to by the Navya-Naiyāyikas in order to settle an intricate controversy in their traditional theory of perception and knowledge. Previously we have noted the Nyāya ambivalence about the status of a pure, pre-linguistic, conception-free, sensory grasp of the object in its theory of perception. Nyāya denies knowledge-hood of such episodes, and argues, further that we are never 'consciously' aware that such a sensation has arisen. In other words, one is never aware that one is sensorily aware of anything in this pre-linguistic, conception-free manner. Powerful arguments of Bhartṛhari have well persuaded the Naiyāyikas to recognize the 'word-impregnated', conception-laden nature of our awareness, our thoughts, which are properly formed, employed and communicated.[3] But the Older Naiyāyikas did talk about a non-conceptual sensory grasp. In order to resolve the issue whether or not such graspings do arise in us, the New Naiyāyikas (Udayana, Gaṅgeśa etc.) emphasized the fact that only an inference can help us in deciding this matter. Roughly, the procedure is this: if we believe in P2, then my perceptual awareness of something x (say a piece of metal) as qualified by f (being gold, or goldness) must be preceded by my awareness of f (what it is to be gold, or goldness). Combining P1, E1 and P2, we may then say that as long as goldness is a 'simple' property according to our definition, it is possible for us to have a non-qualificative, non-mediated, perceptual awareness of goldness prior to the proper judgmental perception. The word 'perceptual' need not raise our eyebrows, for Nyāya maintains that if the individuals are perceptible, the so-called universals or simple properties residing therein may also be perceived, unless there is some stronger reason to believe them to be imperceptible. The only other difficulty in this is that universals like goldness or cowness are thought to be 'abstract' in some sense, while their locations, the individuals, are 'concrete' and hence, perceptible. But this 'concrete-abstract' division will cut no ice with Nyāya, for such a distinction does not exist in this system. It will be further argued that just as I can *see* that the chair has four legs (which is nothing but the property four-legged-ness), I can also see that this has chairness. Hence it can be called perception of chairness mediated, of course, by conception. But enough of this digression. Let me return to an examination of P2.

We may say that we need simply a conception of f (goldness), in order to be able to have an awareness of x as qualified by f. This can be supported by arguments of the following kind. Unless some awareness (or conception) of fire is already present in a person, he cannot infer that the hill has fire there because there is smoke there. If I have never been aware of what it is for an object to be a camel, I cannot certainly be aware, all of a sudden, of an object as being a camel. Even a colour-blind person must understand the meaning of 'green' as a compatible colour, in order to be able to comprehend what is meant by the sentence 'This is green'. In this way, only a prior conception of the qualifier as such needs to be postulated for making a qualificative awareness possible.

It may be countered that the above argument is faulty. For, even if we concede the point about the conception of the qualifier in the case of a non-perceptual awareness, in perception such a prior stage may not be needed. For, it is argued, the contact of my sense-organ with the qualifier, 'colour', would be enough to generate the awareness of the object as coloured. Gaṅgeśa, in fact, has conceded all this, if only implicitly.[4] For him, all that we need is a notion of the qualifier *f*, somehow presented prior to our being aware of something as qualified or distinguished by *f*. In some cases, such a presentation may be made possible through the revival of some memory-impression. In the case of inferred knowledge of 'verbal' (sentence-generated) knowledge, such a requirement is supplied by what is technically called *sādhyaprasiddhi* (literally, familiarity of the predicate property). I can neither infer something to be an abracadabra, nor understand the meaning of, i.e., have a knowledge from the utterance of, the sentence 'It is an abracadabra', unless I am already familiar with what it is for a thing to be an abracadabra. But cases of perception are certainly different.

An example is considered by Gaṅgeśa to get around the difficulty in a perceptual situation. I shall however reformulate the example to make the point clear. Suppose, a disc has just turned blue, and I am looking at it. Further suppose that it has a particular blue-tint, the like of which I have never seen before. Now, for Nyāya, the qualifier can be either a universal property or a particular one; and in this case, the particular blue-tint would be the relevant qualifier. (But such a particular has to play the role of a property, i.e., it has to become universal-like, in the context a propositional combination: it *has* blue-tint *b*.) The argument continues by pointing out that I would in this case first *see* the blue-tint, the particular, in conception-free awareness before I could become perceptually aware that the disc is qualified by that particular blue-tint. In other words I would have no other access to the *idea* of that blue-tint (obviously it cannot be remembered, because it has never been experienced before) except what my senses will yield. Here, therefore, we have a possible case for a simple perceptual awareness of a 'simple' entity, although this entity here is not a universal. The opponent may still argue that the particular blue-tint, in effect, will be seen, according to our P1, as a blue-tint, this means that this will be a complex awareness of the particular colour as being blue. I cannot simply have an awareness of the tint without seeing it as blue. The notion of being blue, an ultimate universal, would in that case be supplied by a memory-revival. But we can still say that this memory-revival, if it has occurred, is occasioned in such cases (compare: *prāthamika-go-pratyakṣa*—Gaṅgeśa, *jāgarādya-kālīna-go-pratyakṣa*—Vardhamāna) by the sensory apparatus (sense-object intercourse); and since the object, the particular blue-tint, is only visually given, it would not be a case of remembering, but a case of simple perceptual awareness.[5]

A follower of Bhartṛhari may continue the debate in another way. It may be claimed that the notion of cowness, horseness or goldness may be *congenital* to us, and this will be postulated on the basis of the pan-Indian belief in transmigration and previous briths. The notion of many 'simple' properties, the universals or natural kinds, may be only retention of memory from previous births. This is the nearest equivalent of the 'innate idea' theory in the Indian context. Unlike the Western rationalists, the Indian thinkers never say that there are some innate ideas in us; instead, the hypothesis that is put forward in this regard is that the ideas which seem to be congenital (innate) are acquired through experiences over countless previous existences. Hence, when a child first recognizes a cow as a cow, he may be aided simply by the memory-traces of his previous births. Some verbal instruction is however needed to revive his memory-traces. This cannot ultimately rule out a primary perceptual experience at some time in the past. In any case, we can ignore the hypothesis of previous births in this context, and endorse the nearly conclusive argument of Gaṅgeśa that at some point there could be cases of pure perceptual grasp of the simple properties, the qualifiers as such, which will then precede some of our qualificative perceptual knowledge of the object as qualified by such properties. Such 'simple' properties are mostly universals or properties of natural kinds, but in some cases they may even be non-universals, which are then combined with another particular in a qualificative awareness. It is the awareness itself that combines two such particulars into a *qualifier-qualified* tie.

3. PREDICATE-PROPERTY AND THE QUALIFIER OF THE SUBJECT

It is important to distinguish the present issues from certain parallel problems of distinguishing between the immediate and the mediate perception, the direct and indirect knowledge-problems that are usually current in philosophical writings on perception. We are trying to outline here a general theory of cognition or awareness, following the Nyāya principles; and this, I think, may throw some light on the intricate problems connected with meaning and denotation of words.

A critique of P2 can be formulated in a very general way. If a prior awareness, in some form or other, of the qualifying entity is necessary for the arising of a cognitive awareness (a supposition, or a knowledge) of an object (the qualificand) as qualified by such a qualifier, i.e., as distinguished by a purported property, why is it not equally necessary to have a prior awareness of the object itself, the qualificand? The general principle of thought seems to be that it is not possible for a person to have a thought about something that it is *F* or that it is qualified by *F*-ness, unless he knows which particular individual in the world he is thinking about. If, for example, I suppose or judge or know that a particular cow is white, then it is not only needed that I should already possess an awareness or knowledge of what it is for something to be white, but also that I should know that such a cow exists. Hence if it is emphasized that a prior awareness of white colour is needed, it may be equally emphasized that a prior awareness of such a cow is also needed.

This, however, is not a criticism of the Nyāya view, for, with a little twist, this criticism can be turned into a clarification of the Nyāya position. Let us consider the verbalized version of a knowledge-episode such as:

A cow is dark.

(I shall not consider the more usual '*The* cow is dark'. For one thing, the Sanskrit philosophers seldom discuss such formulations. For another, this presupposes that the object *x* is identified in more than one way: (i) by being qualified by cowness, as well as (ii) by being a previously identified object in the discussion or context.) Nyāya would say that the qualifier here is not only the dark shade or being dark, but also cowness. Cowness is called (in this context) the *dharmitāvacchedaka*, the delimiting character of the object *x* to which another qualifier, or attribute, has been attributed. We have to know both qualified by them. Under the usual interpretation, the above mentioned knowledge would be explained as that of an object *x* which is first qualified by cowness and then, being so qualified, it is further qualified by a dark shade, and this dark shade, in its turn, is qualified by being a dark shade (a universal, a simple property). Notice that being a dark shade is not a qualifier of *x*, rather it qualifies one of the qualifiers of *x*, and in this respect, that qualifier of *x* is playing the role of a qualificand, another object, viz., the dark shade.

One of the implications of the above critique and reply is that P1 actually leads to a theory of identification of objects through descriptions or information about them. I cannot identify an object unless I already possess some information about it. Part of this information may be perceptually given as in the case of being a cow when a child (*à la* Gaṅgeśa) first perceives a cow and then identifies it as a cow. Here 'perceives a cow' would be interpreted by Naiyāyika as the direct grasp of the three-dimensional 'cow-substance' (cf. *go-piṇḍa*) plus the cow-feature—the universal—but without any awareness of their connectedness. Similarly, 'identifies it as a cow' is to be interpreted as knowing or supposing that it is a cow. But the first direct grasp of two discrete (unconnected) entities is too quick to be captured in the person's introspective awareness (*anuvyavasāya*). The direct grasp, if it arises at all, arises as almost an 'unconscious' awareness.

The (second) structured awareness is however not unconscious. Moreover its structure (*a* as *F*) presupposes a prior awareness of the qualifier, the attribute cowness, which is supplied by the first awareness here. It is however not emphasized in Nyāya that the said structure would need also a prior awareness of the subject entity, the 'cow-substance' (*piṇḍa*). Just as the (unconnected) cowness is present there in the first awareness the awareness of the (again unconnected) cow-substance is also present there as an epistemic fact. But while the former is also required to contribute to the formation of the structural content of the introspectable awareness (the second), the latter is not necessary in the same way. For although it is not possible for a person to have a thought about something that is *F* unless he knows which particular individual in the world he is thinking about, to have a (visual) perceptual awareness that something is *F* it is not needed that one must have a prior knowledge of the subject entity as such. The perceptual event itself would identify (single out) the subject entity and qualify it with the *available* qualifier at the same time.

We identify (pick out, single out) an object *x* in various ways, and a particular *way* (a particular *mode* of singling out) in a given context would be called the *dharmitāvacchedaka*, the delimiting character of the qualifiable object. These ways or modes are usually governed by bits and pieces of information the person has gathered about the object. In a perceptual context however the object may be singled out by the perceptual event itself without the ostensive aid of such bits and pieces of presumably previously gathered information in order that it may be instantly qualified by the available qualifier (cowness). Such a qualificative awareness is one where the qualifiable object does not appear under any (other) distinguisher except the main qualifier, cowness. Roughly speaking, this awareness associates *F* with the *naked* object identified as such.

Most bits and pieces of information are perceptually gathered continuously by a person, and retained in his possession until some later time. Another important source of information is the exercise of reason upon the existing information. A third source is speech or language where the speaker wishes to transmit the information already in his possession. In this way all the *pramānas* can be seen as information-gathering instruments to help us identify the object. We would presently see how, according to Nyāya, a word would transmit information and help the hearer identify or know the object.

One further point before I proceed any further. When following Nyāya I am talking about an object that *floats in* our awareness, I am not talking about an *idea* in the mind or even what is called the 'content of consciousness'. Also I am not talking about a so-called mental image. For Nyāya, there is no such thing, no 'veil of ideas' between us and the things outside, and no mental images. In other words, the object is not 'mental' unless we are talking about such objects as internal states or psychological events, e.g. a desire, a feeling of pain, etc. According to Nyāya, an external object, when it is connected with awareness, stays the same—no novel object, no image, not even an idea, is created in the awareness; when an awareness arises in the subject, we can only say that a connection, called *cognizedness*, has been established momentarily between the object and the awareness. Nothing more need be conceded here.

4. LANGUAGE-GENERATED AWARENESS AND MEANING

I shall now try to explain the nature of a language-generated awareness or what is called *śābdabodha* in Nyāya. It is the awareness presumably of the competent hearer from the utterance of words or sentences. Although we shall be concerned here only with words and what they signify for the hearer, these words are always to be regarded as parts of some sentence or other. The theory presupposes the existence of a language community where speakers utter words and sentences to convey thoughts, intentions, commands, etc., and there are hearers who understand them from the *knowledge* they derive from such utterances. It is this knowledge that is called *śābdabodha*, and is distinguished from perception etc.

The process of acquiring this knowledge is described as follows. First, the utterance of words would directly generate knowledge of such words. This knowledge of the words leads to the awareness of the objects *meant* by them, and in this way, parallel to the grammatical connection of the words in the sentence, a knowledge of a connected *meaning* arises, which is called the product (*phala*) of the entire process. I shall concentrate here upon the knowledge generated by words rather than sentences.

In order to have awareness of the object *meant* from the knowledge of words, a special meaning-linkage between the word and its meaning is needed, and the hearer must be well aware of such a linkage in each case. We may call this meaning-linkage the 'denoting power of the word' (translating thereby the term *śakti* in Sanskrit). Besides the denoting power, the words may have another power by virtue of which it would help generating the knowledge of its meaning or the object meant. This is called 'metaphor' (cf. *lakṣaṇā*), which simply extends or contracts the denotative domain so that the right object may be picked up to suit the context or intention of the speaker. An example will make the point clear. The word 'river' generally means a mass of flowing water. In our terminology, it presents to the hearer, through the denoting power, an object qualified by the property riverhood, i.e., being a mass of flowing water. But in the sentence, 'The village is on the river', the word has a metaphorical use. It presents to the hearer (if he understands idioms and metaphors of the language) an object that is not the river itself, but only the bank of the river. How? By virtue of its being connected with some river.

How does the word get its denoting power? Indian philosophers are divided on this issue. According to some, it is 'natural' to the word. According to Nyāya, however, the word is invested with the power either by God's decree (in the case of words where nobody knows how the meaning was fixed) or modern stipulative definitions. In either case, however, the structure of the stipulation is the same. It is of the form of a will, 'From the word 'A' let us be informed of *B*', or 'Let this word 'A' inform (us) about *B*'. The competence of the hearer means that he has gathered information about such stipulations. Being infused with such stipulated denoting power, the word 'cow', for example, will be competent to generate the awareness of the object cow, but if we follow our previous principle, P1, the object will float in our awareness only as being qualified by cowness, as being delimited by cowness.

To cut a long story short, the hearer must acquire the knowledge of such denoting power of words (cf. *śaktigraha*) either by watching (as a child does) the speakers and the hearers in the community, their actions, responses, etc. (the child generally watches the behaviour of those giving commands, and those obeying or disobeying them, cf. *prayojakavṛddha* and *prayojya-vṛddha*) or through instructions from grammar, lexicon, intelligent guesses etc.

The knowledge of the denoting power, it is claimed, takes the following form 'The word X is empowered to present . . .' What fills the gap here would be called *śakya.* For convenience, I will call it the object *meant.* There are usually several views about what is exactly the object that is meant by such words as 'cow'. I shall refer to these three views. According to one, the word 'cow' means the universal 'cowness'. According to others, it is the individual cow, the object *x*, that is meant. According to Nyāya, the word 'cow' means, i.e., presents in the awareness of the hearer in the way described above, what is qualified by cowness, the object *x* as distinguished or delimited by cowness. In this way, cowness functions as the delimitor or distinguisher of the object meant by 'cow'. The older grammarians used to call it the 'occasioning ground for the use of the word' (*pravṛttinimitta*).

So far we have not said anything about proper names and descriptive phrases. It is clear that in this theory the proper name cannot present the object *meant* to the awareness of the hearer in an unqualified manner. Jagadīśa has called such words *pāribhāsika.*[6] In order to save P1, one can always think of some *nominal* property to qualify the object presented. In the case of descriptive phrases, the object is identified or presented to the awareness of the hearer as qualified by some purported property, some observable feature etc. called *upalakṣaṇa.* For example, 'cook' would mean an object, a person, which is marked off by the profession of cooking.

5. PROPER NAMES AND INDEXICALS

I shall conclude by noting several consequences of the theory of awareness and language mentioned above. First, it seems to me that there cannot be any genuine proper name in language, if the above theory is strictly adhered to. By a genuine proper name, I mean a name that will fulfil at least two conditions: (i) it names or identifies only one object, a single individual, (ii) it is directly latched on to the object such that the object would be presented as such, unqualified, to our awareness (as soon as the word is uttered) and not as qualified by some qualifier. In this regard, awareness due to the use of a proper name would resemble the purported sensory grasp of the 'naked' object, and we have already seen how difficult it is to make sense of such a non-qualificative awareness in the Nyāya view. Some older Naiyāyikas (as reported by Gadādhara) believe that a non-qualificative revival of the memory of the object *per se* is possible from the utterance of the name. But this would not be a *śābdabodha* or language-generated awareness, for there would be other elements in the actual language (e.g. use of a singular suffix etc.) so that the object would be presented in our resulting awareness as qualified by such singularity etc.

Another view is that all singular terms be introduced by definition (*paribhāṣā*, Jagadīśa), and the purported defining property be the qualifying character when the object is presented in our awareness by such a term. But this will certainly lead to further problems, as Gadādhara points out, with regard to such definition-sentences, among other things.[7] For example, the definition-sentence:

The moon is the satellite of the earth,

cannot generate awareness in the usual way. For, the object, viz. the moon, is to be presented or identified *per se* so that the property, viz. being the satellite of the earth, can be attributed to it. But a sentence-generated awareness cannot be such that the qualificand entity figures in it as totally unqualified (*nir-dharmitāvacchedakaka*, Gadādhara). As I have already noted, a perceptual awareness may be different in this respect from a word-generated awareness.

A third suggestion is to let the uniqueness of the individual be the qualifying character when it is presented in our awareness by the utterance of the name. It is presumed that during the name-giving ceremony, the linkage is established between such uniqueness of the object named and the name itself. But, it is argued, such uniqueness in the final analysis is nothing but the individual itself (this is how I interpret Jagadīśa's comment: *tad-vyaktitvañca tādātmyena saiva vyaktiḥ*).[8] Hence, the suggestion does not get us any further.

Gadādhara's suggestion is that we have to treat proper names differently from general names in that the latter designate things as qualified by the purported properties, but the former designate the unqualified objects, although when such objects are presented in our language-generated awareness they may be distinguished by some variable property or other. We may identify Rāma sometimes as the eldest son of Daśaratha, sometimes as the husband of Sītā and sometimes as the king of Ayodhyā. The proper name is thus not directly presenting the object in the hearer's awareness. The important thing to remember is that such distinguishers are no part of the *meaning* or the denoting power of such names. In the above example, when I hear the sentence, the moon may float in my awareness as the bright thing I see in the evening sky, but this qualifier or distinguisher, although it serves to distinguish the object presented, is no part of the denoting power of the expression 'the moon'. The expression may directly designate the moon, but the hearer captures it in his awareness always under some variable guise.

There are two other related consequences. One is that, according to this theory, the language-generated knowledge must be informative. It is therefore claimed that tautologous sentences, such as 'A is A', do not give rise to any such knowledge, for they do not contain any information. Such sentences would then be non-significant (meaningless?) in this theory, because they do not impart knowledge. One of the criteria for the significance of a sentence (such that it generates a *śābdabodha*) is that the delimiting character (qualifying property) of the subject-entity should not be identical with the main qualifier, the predicate-property. 'A is A' is a sentence where A-ness is both the predicate property and the character delimiting the subject. Hence its utterance does not generate knowledge in the hearer. This may be quite in keeping with the sentiment expressed by some philosophers that to say of any *one* thing that it is identical with itself is to say nothing.[9] But the Nyāya criterion is even stricter than what appears here. Of course, one may say that 'statement of identity consisting of *unlike* singular terms may be non-idle and hence significant'.[10] But Nyāya claims that this would not do. For, in the definition-sentence (see the above sentence) we have two unlike singular terms, but still its interpretation, according to Nyāya, runs into problems. Apparently the definition is supposed to supply the essential attribute of the moon and thereby give the delimiting character of the moon. But the subject-entity, the moon, is presented as qualified by the delimiting character, viz., being the satellite of the earth; and since it is the same property that we ascribe to it by the predicate expression, we face the same impasse as we do while dealing with 'A is A'. To resolve the impasse, Gadādhara introduced the important distinction between two types of distinguishers or properties used to identify or single out an object.

This brings me to the last consequence that I shall discuss here. A distinguisher or qualifier may identify an object in a totally irrelevant way, or it may be very pertinent to the identification of the object in the context of the further attribution of properties to it. I may grab an object by hand (cf. *śṛṅgagrāhikā vyavasthā*) and say that it is *F*, or understand it as being qualified by *F*-ness; but the manner of identification, viz., grabbing by hand, is totally irrelevant to the object's being *F*. I can identify an object as the man with the whisky-glass in hand, and go on to say that he is a logician, where the distinguisher, viz. having a whisky-glass in hand, is totally irrelevant to his being a logician (cf. *kākavad gṛham, jaṭābhiḥ tāpasaḥ*). But if I go on to say that he is going to get drunk very soon, then at least the audience may understand (or misunderstand) that the identifying qualifier, having a whisky-glass in hand, is relevant. Nyāya underlines the distinction by calling the relevant distinguishers *viśeṣaṇa*, and the irrelevant ones, *upalakṣaṇa*. One can, in this way, identify an object by an irrelevant qualifier, and assign a proper name to it. This would mean that there may be an irrelevant qualifier of the object presented to the awareness of a hearer by the utterance of a proper name. The connection between the name and the qualifier of the object presented by the name to the hearer is entirely arbitrary.

This expedient can also be used to explain part of the puzzlement about two different uses of the same sentence such as 'Smith's murderer is insane'. On one occasion it is said when no murderer has been apprehended, and there is no suspect, the observation is being made by looking at the way the murder has been committed. In the second, it is said when a person, say John, is already apprehended, and the observation is made on the basis of his behaviour. In both cases, we have the same qualifier to capture or identify the subject-entity, the object; but in the latter case, this property, that of being seemingly the murderer of Smith, is an irrelevant distinguisher or qualifier, a *upalakṣaṇa*, while in the former, it is a relevant one, a *viśeṣaṇa*.

How does the distinction between *viśeṣaṇa* and *upalakṣaṇa* compare with the traditional Western distinction between essence and accident? A brief comment on this point is in order here. Both *upalakṣaṇa* and *viseṣaṇa* are called 'distinguisher' (*vyavartaka*), and this undoubtedly underlines the epistemological character of the pair. In this context, Nyāya was not interested in the ontological question of essence and accident. On the other hand, the Naiyāyikas in general work within the framework of a metaphysic of substance, in which context, however, the notions of essence and accident are pertinent. Their doctrine of objective universal seems to be of a piece with the notion of essence.

A *viśeṣaṇa* or what I have called a *relevant* distinguisher need not however be an essential attribute in any ontological sense but simply be an attribute required for the application of a term. It is strictly related to our language, our vocabulary. It is meaningless to speak of a *viśesana* or relevant distinguisher except relative to the object's being denoted by a particular term. Sometimes it might coincide with the ontological essences or the objective universal but that is not the issue here. An *upalakṣaṇa* or what I have called an *irrelevant* distinguisher is not even related to the general terms (or singular terms) commonly used to denote (or designate) such objects. For example, the distinguisher that distinguishes the object designated by 'the moon' in the above sentence is not related to the particular term, the designator itself. It is only an ad hoc or ad hominem way of distinguishing the object by any suitable property.

Gadādhara has used this expedient quite convincingly to resolve some of our puzzles about pronouns, or indexicals like 'it' (*'tat'*), to which I can make only a very brief reference here. One of the problems with the use of 'it', as Nyāya sees it, is that it presents or captures a different object each time we use the expression, and we cannot talk about a property 'it-ness' (in the way we talk about cow-ness for different cases of using the word 'cow') as the qualifier by virtue of which the word 'it' would present the object each time to the awareness of the hearer. On the other hand, 'it' cannot be regarded as one of the homophonic words (accidents of most natural languages) with different meaning in each time of its use. It is also not a proper name where the speaker could possibly stipulate as to what it means. There is some intuitive reason to believe that it is one of the 'natural' words of the language, like the word 'cow' or 'beast', where we need a common feature (such as cowness for 'cow' and having a hairy tail for 'beast') to capture each time the object it refers to by qualifying the presented object by such a qualifier.

One suggestion is that we take the property, viz., being in the thought of the speaker, as the purported common feature which will qualify whichever object the word 'it' refers to in any of its uses. Thus, when a chair is meant by the use of 'it', the object will be presented not as qualified by chairhood, but by being in the thought of the speaker. Similarly, when a horse is meant, the object will be qualified by the same common feature. But this seems to be counter-intuitive. For, there are strong reasons for believing that in the following sentence the word 'it' presents the chair, the object, as having a necessary connection with chairhood:

There is a chair, bring it.

For nobody would claim here that the hearer who understands the sentence could bring a non-chair, something else that may be qualified by being in the thought of the speaker, and still be said to behave correctly. For successful behaviour the hearer must be aware, from the utterance of 'it', of the actual chair qualified by chairhood.

Gadādhara says that of course the 'it' in the above sentence presents the chair, i.e., the object qualified by chairhood, in the awareness of the hearer, but the hearer's route to capture this object is rather an *irrelevant* qualifier or distinguisher, that of being in the thought of the speaker. The latter property is an irrelevant distinguisher or identifier of the object (an *upalakṣaṇa*) in the sense already described; after the object has been identified, its function as a distinguisher comes to an end. The said property certainly provides the unifying character needed for our acquiring the knowledge of the denoting power of 'it', but it is not part of its *meaning*. It is only a catalyst-agent, being not relevant to what is said or what we may continue to say. After helping the hearer to identify the object of bringing, it ceases to be operative. There are, of course, many other problems that arise in the case of such indexicals, and Gadādhara discusses them to some extent.[11] But I forbear to enter into them here.

Notes and References

1. This is an appeal to the usual Sanskrit dictum: *saṃbhave vyabhicāre vā syād viśeṣaṇam arthavat* (an adjective is significant provided it is possible for it to be true or false of the object to which it is applied).
2. This rider is needed for the Naiyāyikas say that a 'simple' property may be cognised as such provided it is not *mentioned* by name (*ullikhyamāna*) in the verbal report of the cognition. If the verbal report of an awareness mentions 'cow' then we have to infer that cowness, which appears as a qualifier of the object mentioned by 'cow', itself appears as such (unqualified) in that cognition. If however the verbal report mentions cowness by name we have to say that it has appeared in the relevant cognition under another mode or qualifier.
3. For Bhartṛhari's view on this point, see *Vākyapadīya*, Kāṇḍa I, verses 1·15–16 (ed. S. Iyer, Poona, Deccan College, 1966).
4. Gaṅgeśa, *Tattvacintāmaṇi*, Pratyakṣa khaṇḍa (ed. Pt K. Tarkavagisa, Calcutta, Bibliotheca Indica, 1897), *Nirvikalpa-vāda*, pp. 817 ff.
5. Consult Gaṅgeśa, ibid., p. 817. For Vardhamāna, see his commentary on Udayana's *Tātparya-pariśuddhi*, eds. L.S. Dravid and V.P. Dvivedin, Calcutta: Bibliotheca Indica, 1911, pp. 533–5.
6. Jagadīśa, *Śabdaśaktiprakāśikā* (Kashi Sanskrit Series 109, ed. Pt D. Sastri, Benares, 1973), pp. 122 ff., verse 23.
7. For Gadādhara's view see his *Śaktivāda* (Kashi Sanskrit Series, Chowkhamba, ed. G.D. Sastri, Benares), p. 54 f.
8. This is from Jagadīśa's comment on the *Pakṣatā* section of *Tattvacintāmani*, (see Gaṅgeśa, Anumāna khaṇḍa, ed. S. Nyāyopadhyaya, Chowkhamba, Benares, 1906–8).
9. L. Wittgenstein, *Tractus Logico-Philosophicus*, London, 1963, 5.5305.
10. W.V. Quine, *Word and Object*, Cambridge, Mass., 1960, p. 117.

11. While discussing the problems connected with such singular terms as '*ākāśa*' (= the sky), Gadādhara discussed the problem of meaning connected with such pronouns as 'it', 'that', 'we', 'I' and 'you'. A discussion of these issues will take us far beyond the scope of this paper.

8

On the Theory of Number and *Paryāpti* in Navya-Nyāya

There has been some controversy about the notion of *paryāpti* as a relation among the modern interpreters of Navya-nyāya. Even the exponents of Navya-nyāya, such as Gadādhara, Jagadīśa and Mathuranātha, were not unanimous about the exact interpretation of *paryāpti*. The problem is of course related to old Nyāya-Vaiśeṣika theory of number. A number has been treated as a quality or a quality-particular (*guna*), an ontological category, and hence, according to the received doctrine of the Nyāya-Vaiśeṣika ontological scheme, it must be said to reside in the things or substances (counted one, two, three and so on) by a connector that is called inherence or *samavāya* in the system. But that is the beginning of our trouble. For one thing items, other than substances are also counted as one, two and three and the technical notion of *samavāya* would not be available for uniting numbers with such numbered items. For another, if for example duality inheres (i.e. resides by 'inherence') in two things counted as two then it must inhere also in either of them separately, and hence we must tolerate the oddity of saying that, of a pair, say the sky and the earth, the sky has duality!

The first problem is usually avoided by Nyāya by constructing a chain' relation. When we count qualities, actions or universals rather than things having properties, we do it on the basis of such 'chain' relations. In other words, we connect such numbers as two or three with the qualities and actions through the intermediary of the substances having them. This 'chain' relation may be variously formulated and in the context of 'two qualities' it is technically called '*svāśraya-samavetatva*' or locus-cum-inherence. This explanation is tolerated as long as we take a very generous view about 'residence'. For two-ness or duality does not actually *reside*, according to this explanation, in the qualities counted, but is connected with them because it resides in the substances (or substance) where these properties reside. This explanation can be called in question, but I shall have leave this problem here for the present.

Faced with the second problem, some exponents of Navya-nyāya have suggested that we should talk about two different ways by which numbers are connected with things numbered. One is the relation of inherence. To understand this we may think of a similar situation of a particular taste (*rasa*) residing by inherence in a substance like a mango. The taste inheres in the mango pervasively such that a part of the mango is also the place where the taste resides. Similarly, if duality inheres in the sky and the earth when counted as two it would be wrong to say in one sense that duality does not inhere in the sky at that time. In other words, just as in the case of the mango taste inheres also in its part, duality belonging to the two, the sky and the earth, must inhere also in one (part). This of course does not allow us to say that the sky is two for that would obviously be a false awareness and hence a false sense but we may say 'The sky has two-ness or duality (*dritva-vat gaganam*)' for it would be a verbal report of a correct awareness (for which the argument has already been given). This is one of the exceptions to the general rule by which the 'has' relationship is easily transformable into an 'is' relationship. Consider:

'A has B-ness' is equivalent to 'A is B'.

But 'The sky has two-ness' is not equivalent to 'The sky is two'.

The second way of connecting numbers with the numbered items is by a connection that would allow only such expressions as correct as: 'The sky and the earth are two', 'two sticks' and 'three mangoes' but would not allow such wrong inference as:

(1) 'Three mangoes';
therefore (2) 'Three-ness resides in these (three) mangoes'; and
therefore (3) 'Three-ness resides in each (of those mangoes).'

The connection called *paryāpti* is posted as a relation that allows the passage from (1) to (2) but blocks the passage from (2) to (3). This relation is thus supposed to distinguish itself from inherence. Three-ness or the number three is connected with all three items together (counted as three) by this relation and not with just one of them. It is an 'all or nothing' sort of connection. The problem is also connected with the peculiarity of the Nyāya-Vaiśeṣika theory of number, as we shall see below. In sum: numbers (like two-ness, three-ness), by inherence relation, reside not only in the things numbered jointly but also in each member of the group by the same token, but by *paryāpti* relation, they can reside in the numbered things grouped together, *not* in the individual members in the same way or by the same token.[1]

This is however not equivalent to Frege's definition of number as a set of sets. Viz., the number two is the set of sets of two things. There is however very distant resonance here with the distinction made in the Western tradition between the membership relation (of element, with the set) by virtue of which either of the two elements is said to be a member of the set of those two things and the relation of member two defined as a set of all sets of two things to its member sets. The number two or duality (two-ness) can also be seen as a property belonging to the totality consisting of two things. Now if this means that duality belongs to the totality of two things without belonging to either elements of the totality, then we seem to come very close to postulating the *paryāpti* relation. One however need not make too much of this superficial similarity. D.H.H. Ingalls was the first to point this out.[2] But his account was sketchy and incomplete. Perhaps, it was also based upon a misunderstanding of the exact significance of the *paryāpti* relation in the Navya-nyāya programme for the analysis of cognitions. Superficial similarity, it seems, had misled Ingalls into ascribing a significance to the *paryāpti* relation which was not there.[3]

D.C. Guha has put the matter in the right context. His account of *paryāpti* relation is fairly correct and properly contextualized although it is unfortunately loaded with Navya-nyāya (Sanskrit) technical terminology.[4] Guha rightly points out that the technical vocabulary of involving *paryāpti* is resorted to so that the number of delimiting properties (*avacchedaka*) on one side can be exactly matched by the same number of delimiting properties on the other side: they should be neither more nor less.

This needs some explanation. The pervasion (*vyāpti*) relation is formulated as one of co-location of *s* (*sādhya*) with *h* (*hetu*) provided the delimiting property of being such as *s* is not the delimiting property of the absenteehood of an absence which (absence) is colocated with *h*. In the usual example of inferring fire (our *s*) from smoke (our *h*) there is pervasion of smoke with fire because the delimiting property of being *s*, firehood, is not the delimiting property of the absenteehood of such absences as absence of pot or absence of cot that are colocated with smoke. Now it is possible to say that absence of all (kinds of) fire or the absence of two (kinds of) fire (i.e., grass-fire and non-grass fire) is also colocatable with smoke. If this is so, then the delimiting property of such absenteehood would be all-ness belonging to all types of fire or duality belonging to the two kinds of fire. These properties, all-ness of duality, are, however, pervaders of firehood. That is, firehood does not reside anywhere when such properties are not present. They occur in various bodies of fire, and so does firehood! This upsets the previous formulation of the 'pervasion' relation. For the said delimiting property of the absenteehood must include, according to Raghunātha's explanation, not only such pervaded properties as all-ness or duality but also those properties that are pervaded by them, viz. firehood in the present case. Now firehood is also the delimiting property of *s*, not different from it. Hence the above formulation fails.

To avoid this problem, Raghunātha has added that the said delimiting property (of the absenteehood) should be such that it should occur in the same and equal number of places or substrata as does any other pervaded property (such as firehood). Compare:[5] *svasamānavṛttikatvam.* This is further explained by Raghunātha as: *sva-paryāpty-adhikaraṇa-paryāpti-vṛttikatvam*. The said delimiting property should be such that it should be the adjunct of such a *paryāpti* relation as would be delimited by that very property as would also delimit the subjuncthood (*anyayogita-adhikaraṇatā*) of the *paryāpti* relation of the would be pervaded property (of the said delimiting property). Now firehood cannot be the pervaded property of the said delimiting property such as all-ness or duality (in such absences as 'all kinds of fire are absent' or 'both kinds of fire are absent'). For firehood exists in each individual body of fire by *paryāpti* relation while the said duality or all-ness cannot so exist by *paryāpti* relation. When we say, 'this is one body of fire' (or 'this is one pot) both firehood and unity exist in the particular (referred to by 'this') by *paryāpti* relation, the residence being delimited by the particularity of that particular (*idaṃtva*). When we say, 'These are two bodies of fire' both duality and firehood exist in those two particulars taken together by *paryāpti* relation.

Raghunātha was the first to give the seminal account of *paryāpti* as a relation in his *Avacchedakatva-nirukti*, part of *Tattvacintāmaṇīdidhiti*:[6]

> *paryāptiś cāyam eka imau dvāv ityādi-pratītisākṣika svarūpa-sambandha-viśeṣaḥ.*

This means that the relation we call *paryāpti* is a self-linking connector (a *svarūpa saṃbandha*)—that is evidenced by such specific case of awareness as 'this is one' and 'these are two'. According to the usual Nyāya-Vaiśeṣika ontological scheme, there is the relation of *samavāya* or 'inherence' between the numbers and the numbered entities (things). But since this cannot account for such differences in awareness as 'two mangoes' and 'two-ness or duality is present in or 'shared' by one (of the two)', it is argued by Raghunātha and others that we have to accept another connection between numbers (and many other properties) and the numbered entities or substrata that allow such first usage ('two mangoes') but not the second.

Let us consider the following case. It is possible to say that in a kitchen where smoke is present, there is absence of both (kinds of fire), gas fire and non-gas fire, and the absentee here is fire and the delimiting property of the absenteehood is also both-ness (belonging to both kinds of fire). Since this both-ness also pervades firehood, we cannot expect the correct inference of fire from smoke to go through for the formulation of the definition it has been said that fire-ness should not be the delimiting property of the said absenteehood. To block this drifting of the definition we have to tighten it by introducing the separate relation *paryāpti.*

The duality or both-ness is the delimitor. Hence the delimitorship is present in it by *paryāpti* relation of which the other term or the subjunct is duality. Duality is also present in the locus of duality by *paryāpti* relation of which the subjunct would be those dual delimiting properties. Hence this duality belonging to both kinds cannot share the same number of substrata with firehood because each body of fire is a substratum of firehood (even by *paryāpti* relation) while duality needs both kinds together to reside in. Hence the above drifting is blocked. This is a very rough sketch of the background for introducing a new relation like *paryāpti.*

If a property exists in many things jointly but it is not possible to deduce from it that such a property is also shared singly by each number of this group, then it is called a *vyāsajya-vṛtti* property (jointly-occurring property). Such properties invariably exist by *paryāpti* relation in their substrata. Duality, three-ness, quadruplicity and all-ness (*yāvattva*) are such properties. By extension even a non-*vyāsajya-vṛtti* property like unity (one-ness) and pothood (and firehood) is said to occur in its substratum by *paryāpti* relation as well (apart from the inherence relation). Of course the delimiting properties of their substratum-hood would be different in each case. As Jagadīśa has insisted in his *Avacchedakatva-nirukti.*[7]

'This is one pot'—this is to show that pothood is present by *paryāpti* being delimited by a property that can exist only in one substratum.

The possible implication is that when pothood is present in a pot by inherence no such delimitation is needed. Or, one may say that pothood is present by inherence in a pot, its substratumhood being delimited by pothood-ness. Jagadīśa has further commented that in 'This is one body of fire' either of the properties, firehood or one-ness, is present by *paryāpti* in the particular body, being delimited by the particularity belonging to the substratum (*idaṃtva*).

The Nyāya-Vaiśeṣika school entertains a rather peculiar notion of number—peculiar, that is, as far as our modern notion of number goes. A brief note on this issue may be in order here. All numbers are recognized as objective realities, in fact objective properties resident in the things numbered. All members except unity or one-ness (according to some) are transitory entities created in such numbered objects and then destroyed when one of their crucial causal factor is however a cognitive event—which is technically called *apekṣā buddhi* a conjunctive—count-oriented cognition. This cognitive event tacitly arises in the observer (count-er) and may be expressed verbally as 'this is one and that is one (which makes two)'. This emergent 'counting cognition continues to exist until the observer or count-er has perceived the two-ness, three-ness etc. in two things or three things. After such perceptions, this count-oriented cognitive event perishes (as all events must), and when such a crucial factor disappears there is no reason, as the Nyāya argument goes, for us to think that two-ness or three-ness continues to exist. This two-ness is thus unique (particular) in two ways, due to its own unique causal history as well as due to the uniqueness of the items counted. Universals are, however, said to inhere in particulars and hence a universal of two-ness is also posited as resident by inherence in each instance of duality (as we count two objects).

The usual English number-words, one, two etc. have a slightly ambiguous syntactical function. They are used mostly as adjectives or qualifiers: two mangoes, one man. We can also say 'two is a number' etc. This substantival use of 'two' can be designative of properties or locatees (*dharma*). Hence to dispel such ambiguity we may follow the Sanṣkrit style and use 'two-ness' or 'duality' as designative of the property that we call number two.

One cannot fail to notice the strain of 'subjectivity' in the above Nyāya conception of numbers as 'objective' properties. They are caused by a cognitive event that arises in the observer and the same event also accounts for its perception by the observer. They arise as particular occurrents and disappear from the objective world as soon as the said cognitive event is over. They seem to be very strange sort of objective properties, if we can call them *objective* at all. They are not mental and it may be wrong to call them material in the usual sense. Two points are suggested to explain the oddity. First, here as elsewhere, Navya-nyāya does not choose to talk in terms of such a mental-material dichotomy. But the exponent of Navya-nyāya would resist all attempts to describe numbers as *mental* entities, if such descriptions mean that they are not 'out there' in the things. Secondly, even a cognitive event in Nyāya is treated as an object and its causation may deliver, 'objective' realities. In fact, even the self in Nyāya can hardly be called 'subject-dependent' or 'subjective'.

The situation is comparable with the old dispute that centred around the status of sense-data among the Western philosophers of this century. The sense-data (according to some) are neither mental nor material or physical. They can be called simply 'Phenomena' to cut across the mental-material dichotomy.

The introduction of *paryāpti* relation did not go unchallenged in Navya-nyāya. Professor Sibajivan Bhattacharyya[8] in his forthcoming book has presented the essential points of this controversy, which I do not wish to repeat here. Some would like to explain residence of two-ness in two things jointly without resorting to the positing of *paryāpti* as a connector. Inherence is supposed to do the job just as well. A difficulty arises even among the exponents of *paryāpti* due to the tacit rule that if a property belongs to two or many, it cannot fail to belong to each separately. Mathuranātha and Gadādhara think that this rule does not apply here. For numbers can belong to the numbered without belonging to each individual. Jagadiīsa thinks that this cannot be so. The rule remains: if a property does not belong to each by a relation it cannot *eo ipso* belong to the group (many) by the same relation. Hence if two-ness does not belong to either (of the two), it would be absent from both (by *paryāpti* relation) which means that the awareness 'these (two) are not two' would have to be a (correct) knowledge—an absurd consequence. On the contrary, if two-ness belongs by *paryāpti* to either (this or that), we cannot say that 'this is two' is what expresses a piece of knowledge (is true). For the residence (by *paryāpti*) of two-ness in one (this) object is predicated here on the basis of the delimitor of such residence, which is unity or uniqueness of this object. And hence it is a false awareness. This however raises questions about the relative merit of *paryāpti* over inherence.

From one point of view, however, *paryāpti* is simpler and ontologically less burdensome. By *paryāpti* the numbered entity has the number but the entity *has* the *paryāpti* of the number by itself (*svarūpa*), just as a thing *has* in it, the inherence (of colour, say) by itself (*svarūpa*). We need three ontic entities for the complex, number-inherence-substance (numbered). But for the complex, number-*paryāpti*-substance (numbered), we need only two.

For some strange reason, however, some Navya-nyāya exponents insist that the collection or whole-ness is not a separate entity. It is neither here nor there. For if the number of the collected items (where a count-oriented cognition is bound to arise) is a separate reality then we have already admitted something else as real (although a transitory one) over and above the collected items themselves. Besides, Nyāya accepts whole or *avayavin* as distinct from parts. Uddyotakara asserted that many-ness (*bahutva*) is also a number and sometimes the distinctness of the whole (from parts) is but the distinctness of this many-ness as a number from the collected parts. This remark of Uddyotakara raises further questions which I forbear to answer here.

Notes and References

1. This has also been challenged. For some would argue that duality may reside in either of the pair by *paryāpti* relation to enable itself to reside in both by the same relation. But residence in the members of the group by *paryāpti* relation cannot generate the correct awareness of the sort, 'Either is both or dual'.
2. D.H.H. Ingalls, *Materials for the Study of Navya-nyāya Logic*, Harvard University Press, Cambridge (Mass.), 1951, pp. 76–8.
3. See the remark of Ingalls in the Foreword of D.C. Guha's book, *Navya-nyāya System of Logic*, Varanasi, 1968, 'For example, I see from his remark on the distinction between *dvitva* in one context and *dvitva* in another that an analogy which I made some years ago in print between *paryāpti* and Frege's theory of number should now be amended', p. xx.
4. Notice the following remark of Guha:

   To cite an example it may be said, according to the theory of the Navya Naiyāyikas that through the 'Paryāpti' relation 'Dvitva' or duality or for the matter of that any other property which exists in more than one object remain in more than one object alone, which may be known as two or three etc., but not in any one of the objects which taken together comprise the whole.' (p. 226)

   This is a clumsy statement, but it gets the matter right.
5. *Raghunātha's Avacchedakatva-nirukti* (with Jagadīśa), ed. Pandit Rajanarayan Shukla, Benares, 2005 V.S., pp. 34–6.
6. Ibid., p. 38.
7. Ibid., p. 38.
8. Sibajivan Bhattacharyya, *Introduction to Navya-nyāya Concept* (forthcoming).

9

Some Issues of Nyāya Realism

I shall start by considering a by now 'classic' paper of Donald Davidson, 'On the Very Idea of a Conceptual Scheme' (1974). This was an attack on one of the prevailing moods in modern philosophical circles, that of relativism or incommensurabilism. Davidson has reasserted recently:

> If by conceptual relativism we mean the idea that conceptual schemes and moral systems, or the languages associated with them, can differ massively—to the extent of being mutually unintelligible or incommensurable, or forever beyond rational resolve—then I reject conceptual relativism (1989, pp. 159–60).

The argument presented in Davidson (1974) would, if valid, explode a number of myths of modern philosophy: the myth of the given, the myth of a framework, of a paradigm, and the myth of the subjective. The conclusion at the same time lends a very strong support to what is now called external realism, or in Putnam's words, metaphysical realism. In this context, I would like to deal with the implication of Davidson's doctrine—his rejection of the third dogma of empiricism—for this type of realism. Besides, I wish to note that, in the Indian context, the Nyāya-Vaiśeṣika philosophers upheld a very strong form of realism which is similar to what has been called externalism or metaphysical realism. Hence it was also the case that the Naiyāyikas later in their history (thirteenth-fourteenth century AD) had serious misgivings about the idea of the completely uninterpreted given, or the completely uncategorized contents of experience. Of course, the Indian story of the interaction between Nyāya and Buddhism, Realism versus Non-realism, is very different in detail. However there are indubitable resonances there of what is partly going on now in the contemporary scene.

The 'dogma of scheme and reality (or content)' has been so ingrained in the philosophical tradition of empiricism that it seems strange even for a realist to question the epistemological model in which our knowledge is taken to ultimately depend upon clues provided by the stimulations of our sense organs. This epistemological model was also implicitly adopted in India by almost all the *pramāṇa*-theorists beginning with Diṅnāga, the Buddhist (*c.* AD 500), who was probably the prime mover in this direction. It is surprising, however, to note that Diṅnāga and his followers drew idealistic/reductionist conclusions from this premise. The ultimate source of evidence is the sensory input, and since it is impossible to be certain about the external world—the world outside the mind—our knowledge cannot get any further than this sensory experience, the uninterpreted data uncontaminated by the mind's play of imagination. In fact, Diṅnāga called sensory experience of this sort (also called 'perception': that which is free of any conceptualization) knowledge par excellence. Constructive thoughts or judgements (or conception-loaded cognitions) are really not knowledge, for (a) they destroy or contaminate the 'wholeness' of the sensory core, and (b) they attribute concepts to objects—which concepts are always imaginative constructs, being dependent upon the interests, beliefs, desires and preferences of the subject—they are always theory-bound and context-dependent. However, judgements can amount to knowledge only if they are based upon a sound inference. It is knowledge, not because it is error-immune, but because it prompts us to act and behave in a particular way and such actions and behaviour are largely successful. If the judgement attributes firehood to something, the expected results follow—we can cook our food with such an object, light a cigarette, etc.

This judgement however does not tell us exactly what the actual world outside the mind is like, for it simply shows that one concept-attribution is interrelated with some other concept-attributions, and a set of interrelated concepts form a conceptual scheme. There may be alternative schemes, which may also 'work'. Besides, the inference leading to a judgement of the above sort does not have the alleged sensory core as its evidence, instead it is dependent upon another judgement of the same sort attributing another concept—smokehood. The invariable connection between these concepts forces the inference.

The real objects for Diṅnāga were self-characterized, self-existent (momentary) particulars, grasped in our sensory or other experiences. They are actually at par with sense-data, percepts, or uninterpreted sensations. They are supposed to give objective support to each sensory awareness. However, Diṅnāga had an argument to show that they can only be the subjective core of our experience, they cannot lie outside the mind. The argument in brief is as follows. To be an objective support (*ālambana*), an entity must fulfil two conditions: it must be *causally connected* with that particular awareness (experience) and it must also *appear* in that awareness. The external object, if it is there, cannot fulfil both. For the external objects are nothing but supposed conglomerations of atoms—a pot or a chair is nothing but an imagined form or a shape to which we attribute a concept. What results from concept-attribution cannot cause anything. Concepts cannot cause. And the atoms, although they can cause the awareness, cannot appear in our experience. For we do not have sensations of atoms. Hence only the internal core, the self-characterized given, can fulfil both conditions and it lends the so-called 'objective support' to experience.

These self-characterized objects which are similar to sense-data or percepts and which some philosophers in the modern West have described in language by such a verbless complex as 'Red here now' are unanimously regarded by Diṅnāga and other Indian philosophers as virtually and actually ineffable. This obviously depended upon a view of language. Use of language depends upon shared properties, which are results of the synthesizing aspect of mental construction. For language is a social affair (as Quine has once said). The private sensory core, which are unique particulars, cannot therefore be expressed in language. This is also reminiscent of the argument against the notion of a private language *à la* Wittgenstein in modern times.

Later Indian philosophers of both realistic and non-realistic traditions agreed with the point that there may be a sensory core which is not capturable by language. However it was disputed whether this could be knowledge or even foundation for knowledge. The Nyāya realists argued that since this is not falsifiable because it lacks attribution of any sort, this could be neither knowledge nor error. Later on in the same realistic tradition, even its cognitive role was called in question. For there was a prevalent theory of language (ascribed to Bhartṛhari) which maintained that language and thought are inextricably intertwined such that language anchors thought and *vice versa*. Being influenced by this theory, the Nyāya realist claimed that any cognitive experience must be expressible in language. The ineffable sensory core, if there is any, should be little more than the physiological surface irritation, and hence non-cognitive. Besides, by its very nature, it would be even introspectable or amenable to inner perception. All introspectable states have a judgemental structure.

Judgements or structured thoughts constitute the starting point of knowledge, for only they can be true or false. They involve attribution and if the attribution is wrong, the corresponding belief is false, otherwise it is true. In this way, in Nyāya epistemology, the notion of the raw data or sensory core was found almost superfluous. Structured thoughts or judgements are not therefore interpretations or organizations of these raw data, for we have no conscious verbal access to such data. However, the structured thought that something is *F* may need a prior acquaintance with the *F*-attribute (a resonance of the Russellian view in his *Problems of Philosophy*) and Gaṅgeśa, the famous author of Navya-nyāya in fourteenth century AD, conceded the point. Notice that the requirement here in Nyāya was a prior knowledge of only the attributed predicate property (of cowhood in the judgement '*x* is a cow'), and not the prior knowledge of the subject element. In any case, it was argued that we need to posit a non-constructive bare acquaintance with the *F*-attribute at the previous moment (although such a state remains for ever unintrospectable in the above sense) for the (perceptual) judgement that something is an *F* to arise. Notice that such riders as 'non-constructive' and 'bare' emphasise the fact that the '*F*-attribute', whatever it is, is cognized or grasped *as such*, not as an attribute of anything, at this stage. This answers the paradox of having to know the attribute of the attribute in order that we may cognize the attribute, and so on ad infinitum. Hence, the rule is: to cognize the attribute or the subject, i.e. the locus of the attribute, we need to cognize the attribute of the attribute or the attribute of the subject. But when we reach the simples, the universals or unanalysable properties, they could be grasped *as such* (without qualifiers) by some act of cognition. I have discussed this issue in some detail in my *Perception* (1986, pp. 342–54). If this is not necessary for all our adult perceptions, in the case of a child first constructing a perceptual judgement that something is a cow, a prior state of bare acquaintance with what it takes to be a cow would be needed. This is however a far cry from the sensory core, or a sensation of blue that allegedly precedes perception of a blue patch.

Thus by questioning the role of the sensory core in the construction of judgemental knowledge, by exploding the myth of the given as the Buddhist would like to have it to maintain the pristine purity of the uninterpreted sensory data, by claiming that the sensory experience of the unstructured or pre-structured data, can neither be knowledge nor error, and by claiming further that such unstructured experience, if it happens at all, is by its very nature inaccessible to introspection in the given sense and it cannot be the evidential support for the structured knowledge to arise, Gaṅgeśa gave a very strong defence of Nyāya metaphysical realism.

It seems that Gaṅgeśa here almost struck at the root of what is called today the third dogma of empiricism. Davidson's familiar argument against this dogma, the dualism of scheme and content, has by now been discussed in detail by philosophers. Doubts have been raised and criticisms have been made of Davidson's argument. However, the argument or its criticism is not my concern here. I find a support to Davidson's conclusion in Gaṅgeśa's clever move to direct out attention to the logical prerequisite of a propositional knowledge or judgement and omit our talk of the unstructured data or the pure pre-linguistic content of our perceptual experience.

What seems to be involved in the Indian context are two very different ways of looking at language, or the 'theories' of language. One is enshrined in what I wish to call the 'linguaphobia' of Buddhism, particularly of Diṅnāga. The oft-quoted line ascribed to Diṅnāga is: 'Language issues from imaginative construction and vice versa'. Mind has the wordless grasp of the particulars, and use of language distorts reality, for it involves thought or imaginative construction (*vikalpa*) which does not, for it cannot, 'touch' reality. Mind is given here two different functions: that of completely passive reception and of active thought-construction being propelled by desires, preferences, and dispositions of the agent. It is even argued (by Dharmakīrti) that we can by forcing ourselves stop our mind from all constructive activities and arrest it in its passivity when pure data will shine forth. Intrusion of language contaminates and drives us to act in accordance with the *constructed* reality.

The other way of looking at language was first championed by Bhartṛhari and accepted with a great deal of modification by the Naiyāyikas. The strong interpretation of the Bhartṛhari thesis is that any cognitive awareness worth the name is interpenetrated with language or use of words. Words and concepts are two sides of the same coin. The idea of 'wordless grasp' seems to be a myth for the moment our sensation (Bhartṛhari's example was one of the touching the grass while walking on the meadow) punctuates the cognitive level, it penetrates the linguistic level, although the actual utterance of the relevant word may remain inarticulate. The world as we know it is *linguistically* given to us. The whole world is what language makes us aware of. It is an inalienable property of our souls. This is implicit in the very first verse of Bhartṛhari's *Of Words and Sentences* (*Vakyapadiya*).

The above view goes against the idea that there is a structureless world (or even the inchoate data) beyond our cognition or linguistic awareness, and on this we impose a structure by use of language. The structure that our cognition or linguistic awareness reveals is, on the second view, identical with, barring misfires, the structure of what *is* there. It is this part of the doctrine that Naiyāyikas like Gaṅgeśa accept and elaborate. Nor does our propositional awareness or judgement *re-present* or reflect the reality: it grasps the latter directly. The Naiyāyika has also a theory of truth, explicated by Gaṅgeśa, which is compatible with their doctrine of 'direct grasp' which eliminates any mediation of 'intentional content' between cognitive awareness or occurrent beliefs and what they are about. They however do not talk directly about the truth or falsity of sentences. Instead, they talk about the truth of the corresponding occurrent beliefs. A belief is true if and only if it recognizes a 'feature' in a place where it belongs. Thus we need an apparatus to describe a belief by identifying the 'feature' it recognizes or 'attributes' to a place and the place or locus where such a feature is recognized or attributed. Armed with such an apparatus we can say (and Gaṅgeśa did say) that an occurrent belief which (attributes or) recognizes white in snow is true if and only if white belongs to snow. There might be a distant resonance here of Convention T, which is worth exploring. I am however not going into it here.

The Naiyāyikas were in head-on collision course with the 'idealists' or 'relativists' in India. It is significant to note that their mistrust in the availability of the pure, structureless data as well as their outright rejection of any form of representation, of intentional content or propositional entities intervening between us and the world seems to be not only compatible with but also conducive to their brand of realism (if we can omit some minor details). On their view, there are no mental entities except the individual feelings of pleasure and pain, such psychological states or events as desires and cognitions and memory. In fact, they went further in this direction to embrace at least two other extreme and somewhat unusual views about our cognitive states and knowledge. They even questioned the first personal certification of our knowledge-states. First, they argued that it is possible for someone to be aware that *p* without his being aware, by the same token, that he is aware that *p*. In other words, a cognitive episode may arise in a subject in one moment and perish afterwards without always or necessarily being cognized by the subject.

This unselfconscious arising of a cognitive episode (belief-episode) may be explained by introducing a number of distinctions in the way an awareness arises in a subject. First, 'awareness that *p*' and 'knowledge that *p*' are distinguished on this theory such that 'awareness' is the generic name for any cognitive episode including doubts, etc., and that for an awareness to be knowledge it must be true and non-dubious and it could be, if challenged, supported by evidence, etc. Second, we may distinguish between the two following verbal descriptions of the two (presumably) distinct awareness episodes:

(1) The cup is blue.

(2) I know that the cup is blue.

This is not a distinction without a difference. The first, that is (1), may be an observer's (a third person's) description of somebody's (*S*'s) awareness. But (2) is a first personal description of his own assertion that *p*. *S* may be unself consciously aware that *p* and this awareness episode may pass away *unnoticed* by *S*. However, according to Nyāya, if *S* asserts that *p* (gives a verbal description of it by saying (1) or (2)) then *S* must be (self-consciously) aware that he is aware. On this view, there is another interesting detail here. *S* has an episodic belief or awareness at one moment, t_1 say and only in the next moment, t_2, *S* can *observe* that he is aware that *p*.

Further *S* may know that *p* at a given moment but by the same token he may not know that he knows that *p*. For the causal condition for his knowing that he knows is different from that for his simply knowing that *p*. A person may believe (truly) that *p*, which means on this theory that an occurrent belief that *p* has taken place in the subject, and *p* is true, and this, if unchallenged, would constitute his knowledge that *p*. However, if he claims or asserts that he knows that *p* [as in (2)], presumably he would have to know that he knows that *p*. Since knowing that *p* and knowing that knowing that *p* are two distinct episodes, for the second episode the subject needs evidence, such as successful activity, corroboration etc. Knowledge of knowledge is thus an inference by the agent at a later moment, detached from the episode of knowledge simpliciter.

This is a very unusual interpretation of the concept of consciousness in defiance of all the prevailing opinions. For example, if we can have unconscious awareness and after it has occurred the agent as an 'observer' cognizes it then awareness that *p* or an occurrent thought becomes 'objectified', being on a par with the other objects of cognition. No special privilege is enjoyed by the agent except that he can know what he has thought and meant (in the preceding moment) even when he is mistaken about such beliefs and meanings. However, the challenge to subjectivism is too pronounced in this view to be missed. On the other hand, our intuition about the first person authority is not threatened by this stance. For it concedes that I can know that I believe that *p* even when the belief happens to be wrong. (The point made by Davidson with the 'echidna-porcupine' example would seem to be acceptable to Nyāya.) Besides, by conceding that all thoughts, etc. are expressible in words, the Nyāya view avoids the reduction of the public concepts finally to the inexpressible phenomenal criteria. They are identified in terms of causal relations between agents and the world (there being nothing in between on this view).

All these, the Naiyāyikas asserted, were needed to remain true to their view of metaphysical realism. It remains for us to examine whether they are indeed necessary. However, I am not going to undertake this project here.

If consciousness loses its reflexivity, that is, if I can be aware of anything without automatically being self-aware or self-conscious that I am aware of it, then the traditional role that the ego plays in an act of consciousness is undermined and 'self-consciousness' acquires a new meaning. 'I am self-consciously aware that *p*' means that I had an unconscious awareness that *p* in the immediately preceding moment and now I am an 'observer' of that awareness, that is, I am aware that I am aware that *p*. An act of consciousness is on a par with an external event I may observe. This view of mind, one may suggest, comes very close to materialism. The Naiyāyikas however are not believers in the materialistic theory of mind, for it rejects the identity-theory. Mental events and physical events are distinct facts, but they may be very *similar* as far as their causal antecedents are concerned. They stop short of identifying mental events with brain-states, or with physical or bodily behaviour, although they agree that our speech behaviour or other behaviour gives the only clue to what the subject is experiencing. In any case, it seems that if we look at things in this way, the myth of the subjective is exploded.

Notes and References

Davidson, D. (1974). 'On the Very Idea of a Conceptual Scheme', *Proceedings and Addresses of the American Philosophical Association*, 47.

——— (1989), 'The Myth of the Subjective', in M. Krausz (ed.), *Relativism: Interpretation and Confrontation*, Notre Dame, Indiana: University of Notre Dame Press.

Matilal, B.K. (1986). *Perception: An Essay on Classical Indian Theories of Knowledge*, Oxford: Clarendon Press.

10

Knowledge, Truth and *Pramātva*

My acquaintance with Prof. J.N. Mohanty goes a long way back. In 1957 when I first started teaching at Government Sanskrit College, Calcutta, Prof. Mohanty was a research professor in the Post-Graduate Department of the College. We had a common teacher, one of the leading Naiyāyikas of our country, Late Pandit Śrī Anantakumāra Tarkatīrtha. Prof. Mohanty's *Gaṅgeśa's Theory of Truth* was hatched during his stay in Sanskrit College, a book on which I wrote a review article later in *Philosophy East and West*. Therefore, when I was requested to write a paper for a volume in honour of Prof. Mohanty, the first thing that came to my mind was *prāmānya* and *pramātva*. From my point of view, this would be most suitable for the volume.

The Sanskrit term *pramā* is usually translated by a careful translator today as 'knowledge'. This is certainly an improvement upon the older and wrong translation of *pramā* as 'valid knowledge'. It may be of some interest to see why such a mistaken phrase was offered by earlier (mostly Indian) scholars as a translation of *pramā*. A *pramā* is usually regarded as special kind of *jñāna* whose truth is guaranteed. This is mostly, though not always, true in Sanskrit (classical) philosophical literature. The word '*jñāna*', however, is sometimes used for 'knowledge' in ordinary Sanskrit. A knowledgeable person is called *jñānin*. Even in philosophical Sanskrit the distinction between *jñāna* (which can be better translated as a cognitive event or an awareness-episode) and *pramā* is not always maintained, and hence we see the *jñāna* is used indiscriminately for *pramā*; and it is left to us to gather from the context whether an ordinary cognitive event or a piece of knowledge is being referred to. This interchangeability of *jñāna* for *pramā* has apparently led the modern interpreters of Indian philosophy to confuse the issue, and most of them have felt the need for some adjective like 'valid' to qualify 'knowledge' in order apparently to gain the full force of *pramā* which is distinct from ordinary awareness. This was at best misleading and at worst a blunder that perpetuated misunderstanding of Indian philosophical doctrines by the English readers.

Mistranslation apart, there may be another side to this confusion, and this side may not sound so banal. What do we understand by 'knowledge' in the Western tradition? The traditional view is that it is justified true belief. The notion of knowledge invites scepticism, for, among other things, our justified beliefs are also *defeasible* in general. In simple language, it means that we may be justified in believing that *p*, while acknowledge at the same time that should certain things turn up differently we would not be justified in believing that *p*. This is a point our philosophy of knowledge concedes to the sceptics. But, if this is initially conceded, some form of scepticism would be hard to eradicate. I am, for example, justified in believing that I am eating an apple now for here it is, the apple I am holding in my right palm and taking bites from; but if this turns out to be a perfect dream, I should not be so justified and be prepared to abandon this belief.

The 'defeasibility' property of justified beliefs applies *mutatis mutandis* to the notion of episodic awareness. A proper awareness, if it is not a case of explicit doubt or unformed feeling, may be treated as a (justified) belief without much loss of perspicuity in our analytical study. It is true that belief and knowledge as justified true belief are usually taken to be dispositional properties, but for the sake of making our philosophical account relevant to the traditional Indian philosophical treatises, I shall treat them here in their episodic sense. For our purpose, therefore, there is a preference for talking in terms of cognitive events or awareness-episodes and knowledge-episodes. A cognitive episode may be *defeasible* in the above sense. But a *pramā* (which I shall translate as 'a knowledge-episode') lacks this feature conspicuously. And awareness-episode is either true or not true, and each time we have a non-dubious awareness we can assign some evidence, causal or logical, to account for its genesis. Assignment of evidence is a sort of justification, and, should it prove to be wrong later on, we would be ready to judge the awareness as false. But a true awareness by definition cannot be shown to be false. Hence, if *pramā* is only a non-dubious true awareness, it would not be *defeasible* in the way a piece of knowledge (as it is usually understood in the Western tradition) could be. This is probably the advantage (or disadvantage) of taking about knowledge in terms of justified belief rather than true, non-dubious awareness.

It is acknowledged that translation of *pramā* as 'knowledge' is not entirely satisfactory. The reason will be gradually made clear. But at the same time we cannot be too fastidious about translation in this respect. For, unless we give up our attempts at explanation and give in to some cheap version of the 'incommensurability' thesis, we have to accept some translation which is least unsatisfactory. In fact, we might take some comfort here, for the intuitive concept of 'knowledge' by and large coincides with the intuitive sense of *pramā* in Sanskrit despite some minor discrepancies.

What are these minor discrepancies? First, as I have already noted, a *pramā* is to be understood always as an episode in the person, an awareness-episode which is true and non-dubious. It is either a perceptual episode or it is comparable to thought-episodes arising in the person. But knowledge as justified true belief is not usually understood in the episodic sense. Second, since an episode is treated as an effect (*kārya*), Indian philosophers, mainly the Naiyāyikas, usually gave an account of *pramā* by introducing a causal analysis of the awareness-episode that amounted to knowledge. Some of the following questions were raised and discussed seriously: whether the totality of causal factors that causes an awareness-episode *that the snow is white* could also ensure its knowledge-hood (*pramātva*) or there are or should be additional factors to turn such a particular awareness-episode into a knowledge-episode or *pramā*? In the same vein it was asked: does a knowledge-episode *show* or expose (reveal) its own knowledge-hood? or is knowledge-hood of an awareness extrinsically determined (i.e. by another knowledge-episode)? While the first type of question is seldom, if ever, met with in the Western account of such issues as whether knowledge *simpliciter* ('*a* knows that *p*') is virtually equivalent to knowledge of that knowledge ('*a* knows that *a* knows that *p*').

The 'justified true belief' account of knowledge, which has been dominant since Plato in the West (until very recently), directs its attention to determining what constitutes justification for a belief which is true in order that it can be claimed to be knowledge. Western philosophers, therefore, have been concerned more with the finding of evidence or reason for a belief that is true than with its causal explanation even when a belief is treated as an episode. In a very general sense of the word 'cause', an evidential justification may on occasion coincide with the causal explanation. A much more recent view (A. Goldman) has held that, if there is a proper sort of causal connection between our belief and what we know or believe in, then our belief amounts to knowledge. The idea is to show in most cases that there is a common cause shared by the belief and the state of affairs believed in. This is an interesting direction of enquiry into knowledge, for the concerns of the *pramāṇa* theorists of India, despite their different origins, come here very close. Again the conceptual affinity between *pramā* and knowledge can be safely underlined. In fact, the notion of *pramāṇa* as the 'causal instrument' to *pramā* or knowledge-event has this dual character. It is both causal and evidential. Justification of a perceptual knowledge (this is a chair) is accomplished by citation of its causal connection with the sense-object contact. Although it is not the same cause as the presence of the chair in the room causes my perceptual knowledge of it, it is the evidence of the senses which justifies its knowledge-claim as well as accounts for its origin.

To talk about evidence for justifying true beliefs amounts to regarding knowledge as an inferred conclusion from evidence adduced. The truth of a true belief must, in this theory, be significantly connected with and be dependent upon the evidence adduced. If such connections are missing, we have Gettier-like sceptical counter-examples where one may have a justified true belief, but fails to have 'knowledge'. *A* has a justified true belief that one of his friends owns a car by seeing (evidence of the sense) that *B*, a friend of *A*, is driving a car. But this car is actually owned by *C*, another friend of *A*, a fact that is unknown to *A*. In this case *A* does not *know* that one of his friends owns a car. Obviously, the truth of the belief is not connected with the evidence adduced—a false belief used for inferring a further belief. What would be the reaction of the traditional *pramāṇa* philosophers of India when they are faced with such cases? A partial answer to this will be developed at the end of this paper.

If we take knowledge to be one's being in a special (infallible) state of mind, then justification would mean an explanation of how the subject came to be in this special state of mind. Importance is attached here not to where the subject has reached but how he got there. In such knowledge-claims, the knower must not only be sure but also, as it is often urged, must have a right to be sure. I shall call this feature the subjective moorings of the origin of knowledge. A belief may in a given situation be either true or false, but the subject should be capable, if required, of articulating how the belief was acquired. On demand he should be prepared to give reason, cite evidence, authority, etc. A belief is defeasible (in the sense already explained) in the way knowledge is not. But we can mistakenly assume a state of mind, belief (or even a cognitive event), to be knowledge when it is only a belief (or mere awareness), even a true belief. Knowledge, as Socrates insisted, 'cannot run away'. But one might be easily misled into believing that there is a mouse in the hole by somebody's trick, and later on if the trick is revealed and at the same time it also comes to light that there was a real mouse in the hole, one cannot claim that one had knowledge before although one *thought* that one had. This focuses upon the point that it is not only *what* we believe that sustains its knowledge-claim but also how we came to believe it.

When we consider the concept of *pramā* or *pramātva* in the Indian context, the picture is slightly different. For the sake of convenience I shall translate *pramātva* by 'knowledge-hood', by which is meant a property that turns an ordinary awareness-event into a knowledge-event. The question of how the subject acquires a piece of knowledge is reformulated here as a question about how the knowledge-event arises in the subject. A further question is raised: how does the subject become aware that an awareness-episode (which can very well be a knowledge-episode) has arisen in him? And further, how does he come to know or how is it revealed to him that his awareness constitutes a piece of knowledge? Different schools of Indian philosophy give different answers to these questions, and this only shows the implicit difference in their theories of knowledge. There is, obviously, a connection here with the discussion of the point raised in the previous paragraph which is often discussed in the Western tradition. When somebody adduces reasons or cites evidence for justifying the belief he has, he is already aware, in our way of looking at things, that he has a belief which he rightly or wrongly assumes to be true. This (second) awareness or (episodic) belief about belief may or may not be episodically concurrent with or indistinguishable from the first belief-episode. Indian philosophers held a variety of views in this regard. Further, since knowledge is an inferred conclusion from the evidence adduced, if the evidence is adequate and sound and properly connected with the truth of the belief, the subject knows thereby not only that he has a belief but that his belief has knowledge-hood. This may be an odd way of putting things, but, in the Indian context, such questions become very pertinent: knowledge of the knowledge-hood of the knowledge *simpliciter* may or may not be distinguishable from knowledge *simpliciter*. Again, different Indian philosophers give different answers. I shall clarify these points further.

When a cognitive event arises in a person, it purports to be a knowledge-episode. Even when it is infected with doubt or a dubious or uncertain attitude, there is a natural inclination in it to fit the truth, i.e., to be a knowledge-episode, for otherwise even the genesis of doubt cannot have any point. We become doubtful, because our goal is the non-dubious awareness of the truth. In the case of belief, the situation is also not very different; for example, when we believe something, we believe it to be true. If we assert our belief (as we commonly do), then we cannot say in the same breath, that we do not believe it to be true. (This is at least one way to understand the paradoxicality of G.E. Moore's puzzle: '*p* but I do not believe that *p*' *Ethics*, 1947, edn., p. 78.) Negatively, we may say that if we know something to be false, it would be impossible for us to believe it. Even in the Patristic formula *Credo quia absurdum* ('I believe it because it is absurd'), the believed content is said to be absurd, not *false*. Absurdity is not always a logical mark of falsity. Many absurd things have been found to be true. Hence one can, even *à la* the Patristic fathers, believe something that may be absurd but purported to be true.

Guided by such considerations about awareness-events (the same considerations may be projected towards the belief-event), some philosophers have claimed that it is only *natural* for an awareness to be a piece of knowledge (in the episodic sense). This means that knowledge-hood (*pramātva*) is an intrinsic, natural, and non-derivative or unconditional property of any awareness-event. The other half of the doctrine would then obviously be that the lack of knowledge-hood in an awareness-event is conditional and extrinsic (*aupādhika*). Such a lack is regarded as a defect caused by what may be termed as extrinsic conditions. An awareness is either true or untrue. A true awareness amounts to knowledge. An untrue one is either an error, an illusion, an opinion, a dream or even a doubt. In each case there are, in this way of looking at things, external or extrinsic causal factors that cause these individual defects in any given awareness which does not amount to knowledge. The so-called defects (*doṣa*) in the causal mechanism *retard*, so to say, the natural genesis of an awareness as knowledge. It is like saying that man is naturally good but culpable by external influences. When a man is born he is expected to be good by nature, but external conditions may destroy this natural quality, goodness, and in this way we have bad, evil men.

If the above constitutes one plausible account of knowledge and awareness, then we have been successful in underlining the view of the *Mīmāṃsā* school of classical India, according to which knowledge-hood characterizes an awareness naturally, i.e., unaided by anything else, or by itself (*svataḥ*). A further explanation of the view is this. An awareness-episode is causally conditioned by a number of factors, and it is the same set of causal factors that would deliver a knowledge-episode (the same awareness would be called knowledge), provided no extrinsic (destructive) causal factors intervene so when an awareness-event fails to be a knowledge-event, this failure is due to the additional and extraneous factors.

Under controlled situation such contaminating factors may not supposedly be allowed to intervene or interfere, and then knowledge-hood will automatically shine forth! In the same vein, the Mīmāṃsakas establish the scriptural authority or the infallibility of the Vedas (although they are not regarded as the Word of God). The scriptural infallibility or the knowledge-hood of the scriptural knowledge is beyond doubt, because it is revelation, i.e., unveiling of truth under controlled situation where no extraneous factors are allowed to interfere.

The view that opposes this view is a view of knowledge according to which awareness is a generic name under which such mental events as perceptual errors, doubts, verbal thoughts and knowledge-events are to be subsumed. In other words, a knowledge-event is a species of awareness-event. There are many kinds of awareness-events, and a knowledge-event is only one among many. This would mean that knowledge-hood is a contingent characteristic of a class of awareness-events, not a necessary or a natural one. A drink, for example, may not be naturally sweet unless we sweeten it with other ingredients. This view of knowledge is ascribable to the Nyāya-Vaiséṣikas. For the sake of convenience, we may call the former view the 'naturalistic' conception of knowledge and the latter the 'non-naturalistic' conception. According to the latter, the set of causal factors that produces the awareness-episode must be compounded with other extrinsic factors or conditions to generate the property, knowledge-hood, in that awareness. Knowledge-hood is conditioned by extrinsic factors, and hence it is extrinsic. This is what is meant by the claim that knowledge-hood arises (*utpadyate*) from *other* (external) conditions (cf. *parataḥ*), not out of itself. To revert to our previous analogy. Man is by nature neither good nor evil, but he is both culpable and perfectible, depending upon the causal factors that influence him.

So far I have been dealing with the genesis (*utpatti*) of knowledge-hood. The question was: how or under what conditions does an awareness-episode arise as a knowledge-episode or is endowed with the property, knowledge-hood? Briefly, under what conditions does it 'hit' the truth? Having cognitions, under the second view, is like taking shots at the bull's eye. Sometimes we hit it, at other times we miss. When we hit it, a knowledge-episode arises. When we fail, it does not. A related and perhaps more interesting question is: how is the knowledge-hood of a knowledge-event revealed, exposed or known to the knower? In other words, how do we have knowledge of knowledge?

If knowing something is an episode or an event, then like all other events it is possible to become aware of it. The person or the knower has a very special connection, a privileged communication, with the event we are calling knowledge. He is the *owner* of it. Therefore, it makes sense to ask: how does he know that a knowledge-event, not simply an awareness-event, has arisen in him? To put it differently, how is the knowledge-hood of the event exposed or revealed to him? The language in which these questions are formulated here presupposes the concept of the owner of thoughts. But this is not necessary. For a Buddhist (or a Humean) may formulate the same question differently: how does a knowledge-event become aware of itself? How does it *know* itself, i.e., its own knowledge-hood? These two are, however, separate questions. For a knowledge-event to be *aware* of itself is different from its being aware of itself as a piece of knowledge. In the first case, it is aware of itself as a piece of awareness; in the second, it knows itself as a knowledge-event. That is to say, in the second case, the property knowledge-hood is also revealed, exposed or known, while in the first case such a property remains unrevealed, unexposed.

Besides this, there is a further complication. If a knowledge-event is aware of itself, does it remain unexposed or unrevealed. Or, one needs another awareness-event to expose or reveal it? So if the 'self-exposition' view is not accepted, we have to fall back upon the 'exposition-by-other' theory (*svataḥ* vs. *parataḥ prakāśa*). This is the way the Nyāya-Vaiśeṣika and the Mīmāṃsā schools disputed in traditional India: revelation or exposition by itself or by another. If we now introduce the distinction made previously about how knowledge-hood of knowledge is known, we can tabulate four positions:

(1) A knowledge-event is exposed by itself as an awareness.
(2) It is exposed by itself as a piece of knowledge.
(3) It is exposed by another event as an awareness.
(4) It is exposed by another event as a piece of knowledge.

But this is not quite right. If we look at the different views of rival philosophers of traditional India, we realize that the more pertinent question from their point of view was:

Q. Whether or not whatever exposes/reveals a knowledge-event as an awareness, exposes it also (by the same token) as a piece of knowledge?

If the answer is yes, we have been able to capture the basic tenet of the Mīmāṃsā school, which takes knowledge-hood to be an intrinsic quality of awareness and asserts that, when an awareness is exposed, revealed to the knower, its knowledge-hood, if it had it, is also revealed thereby. This is called the *svataḥ prāmāṇya* theory. The present formulation allows difference of opinion among the Mīmāṃsakas themselves. The Prābhākara school of Mīmāṃsā obviously accepted the combined thesis of (1) and (2) above. (This is how Śālikanātha represented the view.) The Bhāṭṭa school of Mīmāṃsā, on the other hand, did not think that a knowledge-event or any awareness-event, for that matter, can be exposed or perceived by itself. When a perceiver perceives something, he becomes aware of the fact he perceives from the evidence of the *perceivedness* of the objects he perceives. This is the view of the Bhāṭṭas. An awareness or a piece of knowledge (as an event) is by itself imperceptible even to the subject himself, but its occurrence is inferred (and that is how an awareness is exposed or revealed to the subject) from the 'knownness' or 'cognized-ness' of the objects he is aware of. But when the subject is aware of (in this way, by an inference) his own awareness, he also knows its knowledge-hood (provided it is a piece of knowledge). Thus, the Bhāṭṭas say 'yes' to *Q* and reject (1) and (2), but accept (3). There is a third sub-school of Mīmāṃsā (Murāri Miśra), which accepts (3), rejecting (1) and (2), but maintains that each awareness-event is perceived (and this is the way it is exposed to the subject) by another inward perceptual event, called *anuvyavasāya*, that follows immediately. But this view is in agreement with the Bhāṭṭas and the Prābhākaras in saying 'yes' to *Q*. It maintains that the independent (inner) perceptual event that exposes the immediately preceding awareness-event exposes also its knowledge-hood (provided it is a piece of knowledge). All the three schools of Mīmāṃsā are also in agreement about the 'naturalistic' conception of knowledge.

The Buddhists, however, agree with the Prābhākara in accepting (1) (any awareness is self-exposed), but hold a non-naturalistic view of knowledge. They give a negative answer to *Q*, and accept (4) knowledge-hood of an awareness is exposed or established by another event, in fact, an inference from the evidence of conformity to behaviour. (This inference of the property, knowledge-hood, of an awareness is, however, very different from the inference by which the subject, according to the Bhāṭṭas, becomes aware of his own awareness. In the second case, the evidence is the subject's awareness that such and such object has been cognized.)

The Naiyāyikas give also a negative answer to *Q*. They are non-naturalist as far as knowledge-hood is concerned. They accept (3) and (4). An awareness-episode is exposed by another episode, i.e. by an inner perception (called *anuvyavasāya*) immediately following the episode. But the knowledge-hood of that awareness (if it happens to be knowledge) is not exposed or known thereby. Knowledge-hood is an extrinsic property, and it is exposed or revealed to the knower by an inference. The subject infers the knowledge-hood of his knowledge from some suitable and adequate evidence.

This position has several implications:

(a) Knowledge-hood is extrinsic, for an awareness does not have a natural claim to it;
(b) Knowledge-hood is a property contributed to an awareness by a set of contingent 'congenial' (cf. *guṇa*) factors;
(c) In perception, it pertains only to its awareness-hood, not to its knowledge-hood;
(d) Knowledge-hood is exposed or revealed by an inference based upon adequate and reliable evidence.

It is believed that this view can give a better answer to the sceptics, who despair about the possibility of knowledge, than the answer that is based upon the rather subjective claim that once you have knowledge you will necessarily *know* that you have knowledge. The Naiyāyikas argue that such a claim cannot be substantiated, for it is like claiming that if I have a pot of gold I must know that it is gold!

There is also another significance which may be noted. The sceptic's attack on the possibility of knowledge sometimes conflates two issues: knowledge *simpliciter* and knowing that one knows. This is, however, an entirely defensible distinction. In fact, this might lead us to find an important way to separate 'subjective' factors from 'objective' events. One of the sceptics' (simplified) strategy is this: since many times when you assume (believe) that you have knowledge you are proven to be wrong, as further evidence proves otherwise, and since even when you are absolutely sure and, therefore, assume that you know that you are sitting in a chair you are also ready to discard this belief, if it could be shown that all this is a dream or mass hallucination, you have to admit that you cannot assign any other reason for your knowledge-claim except your subjective certainty.

Those who hold the 'naturalistic' view of knowledge concede most of what the sceptic says about the subjective certainty but reinforce their claim by insisting that an awareness is always to be taken as true, i.e., a piece of knowledge, unless proven otherwise. Its innocence, i.e., knowledge-hood, shines through by itself. So, evidence is required only to prove guilt (lack of knowledge-hood), not innocence. Those who hold the 'non-naturalistic' view of knowledge, make capital of the suggested distinction, and argue that both innocence and guilt are to be proved with evidence. The subject can know neither the innocence (knowledge-hood) nor guilt (lack of knowledge-hood) of his awareness unless he is aided by evidence. It is possible on the basis of the distinction suggested above, to be aware of a knowledge-event without knowing of its knowledge-hood, if the evidence to support it is not forthcoming. One may know (inwardly perceive) that he has an awareness, but that will not expose its knowledge-hood, for he may entertain a doubt whether his awareness is true or not. The genesis of this second-order doubt (doubt regarding knowledge-hood) shows that the 'naturalistic' conception of knowledge-hood fails. Alternately, one may even be sure on some evidence or other that one's awareness is knowledge (that one has knowledge *simpliciter*), but, if, later on, further evidence proves the contrary, one is prepared to give up his false certainty (second-order certainty) about knowledge-hood. This may happen even when the said (first) awareness was true, i.e., there was a fact corresponding to it. Notice that in this theory when we are talking about evidence or justification of our knowledge, we are referring to the second-order awareness, knowledge of knowledge (or awareness of knowledge), not knowledge *simpliciter*. The main point to remember here is that recognition of the awareness-hood of an awareness does not necessarily imply recognition of its knowledge-hood. The two events are separate and produced by different causal factors. I underline this separation here, for it may be used to resolve partially certain sceptical puzzles about knowledge.

Śrīharṣa in the Indian tradition (eleventh century AD) formulated several sceptical counter-examples to dispute the Nyāya-Vaiśeṣika definition of knowledge. His first example was that of a lucky guess of some gambler, which happened to be true (and the gambler was absolutely certain). His second example was that of a conclusion which happened to be true but derived from false premises. Mistaking a cloud of dust to be smoke one infers fire to be present, and accidentally fire is there. If, however, we become too fastidious to call this conclusion true, for after all it is not the kind of fire we have inferred that is present there, Śrīharṣa gave the third example. Looking at the horns of an animal lying at a distance, we identify it as a bull; but later we discover that those were 'plastic' horns, for the real horns were cut off and replaced by these phoney ones long ago! Here our identification of the animal as a bull was correct, but did we have knowledge then?

The above (modified) examples of Śrīharṣa may well be reminiscent of what are called Gettier examples in modern (Western) discussion (originally triggered off by Edmund Gettier's 1967 paper, 'Is Justified True Belief Knowledge?'). But let us stay with Śrīharṣa for the moment. Navya-Nyāya would like to resolve Śrīharṣa's puzzle by suggesting certain terminological and conceptual adjustments. If knowledge is defined simply as a true awareness or an awareness which attributes a right predicate to a right place (cf. *tad-vati tat-prakāraka*), then, in all the above cases, we have to say that the subject had knowledge, because, willy-nilly, they hit the truth. In fact, Vācaspati Miśra II commented upon Śrīharṣa's question and said that these cognitive episodes deserved to be called 'knowledge', for they coincided with God's perception (which was always true). How can we then explain the hesitation on the part of the subjects themselves to accept their awareness as a piece of knowledge when falsity of the evidence or their mistake in deriving the so-called knowledge was exposed to them? Armed with the conceptual apparatus discussed before, a follower of Navya-Nyāya may answer as follows. When I realize that my identification of the animal as a bull was based upon a false evidence, I could say that my identification was true (and hence it was a piece of knowledge *simpliciter*), but the evidence upon which I based my second-order certitude (a purported knowledge of the knowledge-hood of the knowledge *simpliciter*) was false; and hence I did not know that I knew, although I knew it (a first-order awareness).

The oddity of the last part of the sentence is obvious. But is it entirely counter-intuitive? In other words, is it possible for somebody to know that *p* without knowing by the same token that he knows that *p*? The above Nyāya exercise has been to give an affirmative answer to the question. If we change from the 'first person' description to the 'third person' description, the point does not seem to be counter-intuitive any longer. Many a time by looking at the behaviour of another a person, a baby, for example, we can and do say; 'He knows, but does he know that he knows? He may not.'

Consider another case. *A* sees *B* stealing a book from the library but later a false evidence is given claiming that it was *B*'s (identical) twin brother whom *A* saw, not *B*. In this case, *A*, not knowing the falsity of this evidence, would be forced to withdraw his previous knowledge-claim, although what he saw was true. If we subject this example (which is due to G. Harman) to the analysis suggested by a follower of Navya-Nyāya, we may very well say: '*A* knows but does not know that he knows'.

The above analysis, however, raises a more important question. If a truth-hitting episode, a true awareness, amounts to knowledge, then do we not thereby obliterate the distinction between truth and knowledge-hood? Navya-Nyāya seems to accept this consequence and agree with such reduction as far as our first-order knowledge or knowledge *simpliciter* is concerned. This is one way of cutting off the so-called 'subjective moorings' from the conception of knowledge-hood. However, the second-order awareness or knowledge of knowledge should be treated differently. Knowledge of knowledge-hood is, in fact, an inference. False or inadequate evidence for such an inference affects the conclusion. That is, we cannot accept this conclusion as knowledge, even if it is a true conclusion, when the evidence adduced or used is shown to be false or inadequate. The subjective moorings of the conception of knowledge in this theory is transferred to the second-order knowledge or awareness.

In Navya-Nyāya, a knowledge-event is a true awareness which is not infected with a dubious attitude. This is a negative condition which brings back the subjective mooring. It is not claimed here that an awareness must have certainty in order to be knowledge. It should be *non-dubious*, which is further explained as its being 'not overwhelmed by a doubt about its lack of knowledge-hood' (cf. *aprāmāṇya-jñānānaskandita*). It is argued by the Navya-Naiyāyikas that if an awareness which happens to be true and hence have knowledge-hood is infected by a doubt about its knowledge-hood or the lack of it, then the resultant state cannot perform all the functions that a piece of knowledge is supposed to perform. But it may be maintained that the knowledge-hood of such an awareness is not destroyed thereby. Only the external causal factors here interfere to render certain functional powers of knowledge inert. For example, using such an awareness as a premise we cannot derive any further knowledge by inference, although there may be logical connection between the two pieces of knowledge.

Although it is not absolutely clear whether this proposed analysis resolves all the problems raised by Śrīharṣa when he formulated the counter-examples, there is no doubt that some progress has been made towards the clarification of our philosophical conceptions of knowledge. Could this analysis point up to a direction by following which a reasonable explanation of some of the puzzles created by the Gettier examples may be given? I think it could, provided we use the insight contained in the above analysis somewhat liberally.

11

Understanding, Knowing and Justification

1. UNDERSTANDING AND COMMITMENT

In today's world, with the spread of the study of social anthropology and/or ethnography as well as our resultant acquaintance with other cultures, we are trained to assert our understanding of a culture or a religion or a world-view that is not our own. In this context the world 'understanding' takes on a new meaning. When we say that we have an understanding, that is, a non-committal comprehension, of a religious doctrine, we are guarding ourselves from saying that we *believe* in such a doctrine. Inter-cultural studies open up the possibility of such commitment-less understanding.

Some fundamental questions arise regarding this claim of belief-free understanding. Is it possible to have an understanding without our having the slightest commitment to what it is that we understand in this way? Suppose the native believes that an eclipse of the sun brings misfortune to the inhabitants of a particular land. We can easily say that this is part of the belief-system of the native, while we have a much more scientific approach to the explanation of such natural phenomena. In other words, the native interprets the phenomenon in his own way, and we do not have to believe in such things. But there are other areas of the native's belief-system which need not be so outrageous as this one, and in such cases our own interpretation of natural phenomena may not be very different from that of the native. When the native claims that a lump of clay is a lump of clay, rainfall is good for crops, and that when seeds are sown they sprout, we cannot find any better interpretation except perhaps saddling the native with implicit knowledge of *some* scientific details of how a seed becomes a sprout and so on.

The point here is not that our interpretation (understanding) of some of the native's statements may coincide with the beliefs or knowledge-claims of the native, but a more general question—can we really understand and interpret even part of the native's belief-system expressed through his statements, without forming an idea of how and under which conditions these statements will hold true? This may or may not be the same as the Davidsonian point. There is no need to quibble over that issue. Unless we attribute a modicum of rationality to the general way a native thinks, talks, and expresses his beliefs and knowledge-claims, we would not even know how to proceed in our attempt to interpret the native. That we generally do so and succeed, even to a limited extent, would at least indicate that we maintain, probably at a very implicit level, a basic trust that the native acts and thinks for the most part somewhat rationally (the way we are trained to do so by the community).

Lexicographers note various meanings of the attitudinal verb 'understand', of which one at least is—'to know and comprehend the nature of the meaning of' some statement or object. It is frequently heard said, 'I understand what you mean,' and along with it comes the disclaimer—'but I do not accept it.' As knowledge or belief is based upon total acceptance, such an understanding of what the speaker means can hardly amount to knowledge on the part of the auditor. If this way of viewing the matter makes it imperative that we must first analyse our understanding of the meaning of a given expression as a primary attitude—a simple non-committal comprehension of what has been intended and communicated by the speaker—then understanding (and the attendant interpretation) can be the intermediate stage in providing us with the final knowledge or belief that we may possibly derive from the testimony of the native or any other knowledgeable person. However, there is another way of reading the matter—this is the view which the Naiyāyikas of India, specially Gaṅgeśa, expounded and upheld. Let us turn to their side of the story.

The speaker does not always utter a sentence in order to communicate the *literal* meaning. The opposite of 'literal' need not be 'metaphorical'. For Nyāya thinks that the *combination* of literal and metaphorical is what generally gives the *normal* meaning of an utterance. But there are many other contextual factors which determine the communication-intention of the speaker, and thereby modify the *import* of what he is trying to communicate. Suppose I enter my language class and say, 'Translate into Sanskrit, "you owe me a million dollars".' Here the students must first understand and interpret the sub-sentence, without raising any question about its truth-value. Not that the conditions under which it would be true would be in any way difficult to know (although there are sentences, e.g. 'A bridge will never be built in this place,' and such other Dummettian examples, which can and do present difficulties), nor is it the one where the speaker's communication-intention tends to be obscure or unfathomable by the auditor. The context, however, forewarns the auditor that here a belief or a knowledge-claim is not intended to be transmitted, although we must have a 'knowledge' of what the sentence means or a commitment-less understanding of the meaning of the expression from the syntactic and semantic structure permitted by the rules of the language in which the expression is given. A student who follows these rules will be successful eventually in producing the translation.

Here, it may be claimed, is a case of understanding which does not commit the auditor to the belief that he or she owes me a million dollars. But is it really a case where only a simple understanding is called for, and there is no commitment on the part of the auditor to believe anything else? At least two points are pertinent here. First, the student in my class is already aware that this is a class for translation and my first utterance 'translate' would certainly forewarn that the teacher is not trying to communicate knowledge by verbal testimony in this case. Hence, he cannot conceivably mistake my utterance as an attempt on my part to communicate my intention that he should believe that he owes me one million dollars. There are all sorts of safeguards against such an odd understanding. On the other hand, towards the last part of my utterance, i.e., the sub-sentence, he may wonder whether the uttered sentence is a part of a big joke, or even whether it is well-formed, for it certainly lacks what the Naiyāyikas called *semantic fitness*. According to Nyāya a sentence is not a well-formed one unless it fulfils at least three conditions: (a) the sentence must be formulated following the syntactical and grammatical *rules* of the language; (b) the semantic representations of two or more parts of the sentence must fit each other as such elements do *fit* in the actual world; (c) the world-elements of the sentence must also be spatio-temporally *proximate* to each other. The second condition is a strict requirement on the well-formedness of a sentence for, generally, the property of grammaticalness and the neatness of the world-elements would be regarded as sufficient. I shall come back to these points later.

Suppose we go back to ethnography. The ethnographers supposedly present us with, let us say, impartial description of an alien culture, which includes the alien's religious beliefs, his world-view, and various practices he is engaged in. Our ethnographer must take care to have the proper and correct understanding of the alien culture but should neither commit himself to the way of life the alien is engaged in nor take the belief-system of the alien to be ultimately valid. He can go as far as asserting that this belief-system is true for the alien but not for him. That is, he may embrace a sort of relativism, which will avoid commitment or any conflict with his own belief-system. Hence, at a deeper level, he may need a fundamental attitude of commitment-free understanding so that he can extend the horizon of his knowledge of other competing cultures on this earth. There is connection here between the meaning and translatability of the alien sentences and our study of ethnography.

This is, however, a different way of making a case for the epistemology of understanding. And it may be claimed, from a certain point of view, that testimony in general may suffer from a drawback. Our testifier may try to transmit his fanciful beliefs, which are factually false, but the speaker, due to his upbringing or ignorance or whatever, may be impervious to the truth-claim of his beliefs. And our auditor, coming from a different culture or upbringing, where fanciful factual beliefs are discouraged, and some sort of scientific or rational explanation is regarded as the norm, may reject the testimony of our old friend and thereby testimony as a source of knowledge may not fare any better. This is, however, not a very serious objection against testimony. For there are many obvious cases where the beliefs to be transmitted are transparent enough, such that the auditor may and sometimes does take them to be constituting knowledge episodes.

The main question is, however, whether understanding without commitment in such cases is at all possible in our first-hand reading of the alien culture. Of course, if we hear the alien saying or claiming that the eclipse of the sun is an evil omen, we would beg to differ. We will have to prefix his statement with such phrases: the native believes that . . .,' or 'he believes that . . .'. Now these innocent-looking phrases have some not so innocent-looking significances. The auditor must first *understand* that this speaker is expressing a deep-seated belief of his own and since this does not match any belief of the auditor's own we have to qualify such an attitude expressed by the speaker as the belief of the speaker, such that the auditor should not have any commitment to it.

But is this tenable? 'Understanding' is a difficult word to understand. Lexicons are not very helpful. 'Comprehension', and I am tempted to say 'comprehension in the right way as the speaker intends it,' would be the nearest equivalent offered. The qualification I wish to add to 'comprehension' must also be transferred there. If this is the right way of proceeding in this matter, then there is an argument against the notion of understanding discussed in the immediately previous paragraph. People do say (a) 'I understand you' and 'I agree', and also (b) 'I understand you but I do not agree.' In this age of disagreement (and this should be welcome, for without disagreement progress of thought may be retarded or arrested), we hear more of (b) than (a). But this does not completely obscure the original meaning of 'understanding'.

Ethnography was started as a subject in our universities for extending our understanding (and we should not hesitate to call it our knowledge, even in the ordinary sense) of the alternative belief-systems, world views, etc., other cultures, of our 'brothers.' Whatever might have been the original motive—perhaps conversion to Christianity, or to find a new world-order, one world with one set of beliefs, one particular religion, living under the same legal democratic culture and freedom (and, as rationality demanded according to the eighteenth-century AD European conquerors, one 'harmonious' universe should be the goal and hence everybody should be brought even by force, into the same line of thinking; see, for references to such views, Berlin 1969, and also Matilal 1991)—we cannot preclude the fact that the enquiry was initiated, at least a basic level, by a genuine desire to know about a foreign culture. I believe if this initial basis is completely removed then ethnography, which may be as non-committal as possible, and may not require any belief or faith in what the informants tell us (why should it be required at all in any case?), would seem to lose its direction and purpose. That is why I believe this view to be not tenable. Ethnographical understanding today may be regarded, without much difficulty, as a deliberate and conscious 'step-back' attitude, where we deliberately remove our commitment, belief, etc., and take it to be a non-committal but a correct comprehension of the alien cultural statement. This is a rather sophisticated attitude of understanding. It may be called a secondary attitude, carefully cultivated and properly held by the modern ethnographers.

Grammatically the verb 'to understand' takes a singular term as object when it is used non-committally. However, when used committally it takes a clause as object. Another meaning of 'understanding' is to grasp the meanings or purport of the words. It is the last-named meaning which prompts such uses as that of understanding an utterance without commitment. Whether this is a fundamental attitude or a complex attitude, where we suspend our commitment, is what is in dispute here.

Let us, for the sake of analogy, refer again to the case of the student in my hypothetical translation-revision class. He will not raise an eyebrow when asked to translate a sentence, for he is well aware that belief in the *truth* of any of these sentences to be translated is entirely unnecessary and even ridiculous. The context takes care of that. Hence simple non-committal understanding of the meaning is automatic and uninterrupted and natural. Our ethnographers are sailing in the same boat.

So far we have been avoiding facing a very serious and perhaps philosophically more important charge—the charge that would spring from Frege's dictum (and its enthusiastic interpretation by Dummett and others) that we can *grasp* a thought without judging it to be true or false. Grasping a thought in Frege's language might mean by extension that we can *understand* the meaning of a false statement or whatever, but withhold our belief in it. This is a moot point. In the usual (Dummettian) interpretation of Frege's *sense*, we may have a sense-centred grasping of the meaning of the given sentence, but not have any commitment to judge it to be true or false. The claim therefore transpires as this: understanding can be a basic attitude as soon as a sentence is heard from the speaker—it may be simply grasping the thought expressed.

2. SENSE AND *NIMITTA*

Since Frege, the sense-reference distinction in the philosophy of meaning has been so pervasive and, sometimes, over-emphasized that it is unthinkable today that if we talk about the Indian theories of meaning, questions will not be asked whether Indians made any distinction between sense and reference (especially when we talk about the meaning of singular terms etc.) In the sixties and early seventies, Mohanty and I (unconsciously following the new trend), got involved in a controversy about this issue of a sense-reference distinction in the classical Indian context. Mohanty, in the first edition of his book, *Gaṅgeśa's Theory of Truth* (1966), seemed to have summarily rejected the idea that the classical Indians had any idea of a *sense* of a term. In my review of this book (1968a), as well as in my (1968b) book, I protested and said that the Indians operated with the old 'property' component in the meaning-complex assignable to a singular term, and what for centuries they called *pravṛtti-nimitta*, 'the ground or basis for the application' of a term, or for designating an object by that term, could very well be their answer to some of the functions that Frege's *sense* is supposed to perform. In Navya-Nyāya, this 'ground' or 'basis' was reinterpreted as the 'delimiting property of the designatumhood in the object referred to.' This, however, would not fit *all* the way, the concept of Fregean sense, as Dummett interpreted it.

In any case, Mohanty, in his reply, gave a lukewarm support to my comments (and criticism). Later (1971), I tried to explain this rather enigmatic term 'basis' or 'ground,' sometimes with the help of the 'supposition' theory of the Western scholastics (see also I. Copi on properties as intensions; 1972, pp. 124–8). In any case, things were not made very clear by either of us at that time. Mohanty has now strongly put forward his negative thesis—there is no conception of sense among the classical Indians (cf. Mohanty 1992, pp. 65–7, 253–4). I believe Mohanty's negative thesis is based entirely on Dummett's interpretation of *sense*. Hence it can be rejected if we reject the stereotyped Dummettian version of Fregean sense.

Serious controversy over the interpretation of Fregean sense started in the seventies and eighties. There are now formidable opponents of the Dummettian interpretation of sense (G. Evans, S. Kripke and many others). In view of all these, we might skip our local problem, i.e. the controversy between Mohanty and me, and make some general comments instead.

Our issue here is the thin line to be (or not to be) drawn between understanding and knowing. Knowledge has traditionally been defined as justified true belief, although this has been questioned in recent times. In fact, we have today two different ways of defining knowledge. One is justificationism, the other is reliabilism. These two views of knowledge are regarded as rival views, although it is not always clear whether one view can totally ignore the intuition that is found acceptable in the rival view. The Indian *pramāṇa* theory appears to be somewhat neutral to this dispute. On the face of it, however, *pramāṇas* appear to be more akin to reliable and accredited sources of knowledge. However, this would be misleading for *pramāṇas* have an implicit characteristic of justification.

3. UNDERSTANDING AT A DEEPER LEVEL

It has been held by J. McDowell that in any communication process 'knowledge rubs off' on others like a contagious disease. In fact, we, as Naiyāyikas, tend to accept the picture where because a cosmic 'perspective' is denied, we take in the total stranger who is trying to communicate as 'one of us.' In this way of looking at things we would be able to *understand* his utterances, and even if we do understand them we know that they are part of the pattern whose earlier and later parts we would find familiar.

This picture appears in some cases to be quite normal and automatic. A charge of gullibility or even blindness to truth, that we tend thereby to accept everything that the speaker tells us, can be met. However, this is not an important point. What is important in our argument, at least so far, is the following point. By deploying a notion of *prima facie* understanding of the meaning of an utterance, which does not commit us to the truth or falsity of a judgement, we do not get very far. For as commitment-free understanding is a construction or an abstraction from what actually goes on within the hearer as part of his psychological causal processes, we may construct or abstract the concept of a certain understanding, and recognize that this is not how we first thought of the meaning of the utterance before we judged its truth value. In fact, the Naiyāyikas' point is that understand the 'meaning' of the other and their *prima facie* belief-claims or knowledge-claims go hand in hand. The notion of meaning constructed out of senses, or the contributions made by the senses of component expressions, justifiable under a Dummettian interpretation of sense. If a different interpretation of a Fregean sense is accepted (such as that suggested by G. Evans in his criticism of Dummett) then the picture changes dramatically.

There are obvious cases of tautologies; for example, 'A = A,' where it would be somewhat silly to claim that our understanding of the meaning of the utterance has to be intervened by a sense-based interpretation of the sentence. Consider the following two sentences:

(1) Phosphorus = Hesperus
(2) Phosphorus = Phosphorus

The argument of the Naiyāyikas is this. Just as in (2) we make a straightforward knowledge-claim the moment we understand the utterance, we also make a similar knowledge-claim the moment we understand the utterance (1). Although Frege argued that the meaning of these two utterance cannot be the same, for our cognitive experience of (1) cannot be the same as that of (2), this does not affect the Naiyāyikas argument that in both cases we make a knowledge-claim, and that the cognitive difference between (1) and (2) can be explained otherwise.

We have tried to show that it is not essential to talk about a *prima facie* understanding of the meaning of a sentence before we can judge it to be true or false. The Naiyāyikas were against the deployment of such a basic attitude prior to the belief-claim or knowledge-claim that arises in the hearer. The belief-claim or knowledge-claim should arise in the hearer, according to the Naiyāyikas, as soon as a *well-formed* utterance is heard. It can only leave certain conditions unfulfilled. What is important to note in this connection is that the Naiyāyikas do not think that the perception of the speaker's qualities, such as competence and reliability, play any role to generate belief-claims. Hence knowledge from testimony would be more or less automatic, if the uttered sentence fulfils (as already mentioned) three conditions. First, the words uttered must be grammatically acceptable. In other words, the words and inflexions must be juxtaposed following the conventional rules of grammar and syntax of the language. This property has been sometimes called syntactic expectancy. The second condition is that the word-elements must be proximate to each other such that interconnections between them would be transparent. This property is sometimes called 'proximity' in time and space of the word-elements. The third condition, however, is more important. It is called the semantic fitness. The word-elements constituting the utterance should be such that the meaning of one should *fit* the meaning of the other. In other words, words cannot be juxtaposed at random so as to produce nonsensical utterances such as 'pigs fly' and 'drink bananas.' These utterances lack semantic fitness or compatibility. This property of fitness is very important as far as knowledge by testimony is concerned. The Naiyāyikas claim that this would be enough for the hearer to judge whether the thought expressed is true or false and, if the hearer can grasp the thought as well as judge it to be true or false, then the hearer's understanding of the meaning of the utterance would amount to the hearer's knowledge of what has been conveyed by the word.

4. ON THE FITNESS CONDITION

The fitness condition is broadly defined by the Naiyāyikas to take care of at least two important cases of misfires in testimony, cases where testimony would mislead the hearer. These cases of 'misfires' in testimony can be understood as follow. Suppose we have an impossible condition: 'the child of a barren woman.' Obviously the fitness condition is not fulfilled here and we can easily reject the possibility of knowledge from such a combination. But the more important case would be to decide where the two words have *some sort* of semantic fitness, i.e., they are not incompatible, but the combination is not something that we find in the actual world. It would then be very difficult to decide whether the combination would be true or false. Consider the following sentence: 'There is an elephant in the next room'. Now it is possible that there is an elephant in the next room but the hearer has not seen it. The question arises whether the utterance would have semantic fitness. The Naiyāyikas would say that as long as the hearer cannot rule out the possibility of there being an elephant in the next room, he would have to accept it as semantically fit and therefore he must have a belief-claim from such utterances, provided that even the slightest doubt does not *infect* his attitude.

When an utterance is understood non-committally one expects the following special features to be present in the context—a belief or a doubt that the speaker is a liar, or the suspected impossibility of connection between the word elements. Nyāya believes that if the fitness condition is fulfilled then committed understanding or knowledge from the utterance would be our first reaction. This, however, invites the following problems.

How can we grasp the fitness condition unless we already have a non-committal grasp of what would be a possible combination? This question, according to Nyāya, is a pointer to the right direction where the solution of the puzzle lies.

The notion of fitness must be understood by considering not only the context of the utterance but also the hearer's belief system, and the social factors in the linguistic practice, that is the division of linguistic labour (I owe this point to my student. J. Ganeri). It is the pervasive practice according to which the hearer defers to others, in particular the speaker, to fix the meaning of the utterance. This will resolve the question whether it is possible for an elephant to be in the next room. The hearer takes the speaker to be an 'expert' in having a background knowledge and, hence, the utterance would have no obstacle in being accepted as true. Although both are fallible, the speaker and the hearer, it is granted that the hearer's acceptance of what the speaker says is not mitigated by the usual factors, doubt, prior knowledge to the contrary, unreliability of the speaker, etc.

In the example, 'there is an elephant in the next room', since the elephant is an observational concept, such that every one is an 'expert', as far as its meaning is concerned, the hearer need not doubt the veracity of the statement. So the fact remains that the meaning is socially determined by division of linguistic labour and this leads to the conclusion that such utterances are understood committally and they are semantically fit.

The Naiyāyikas (e.g., Gaṅgeśa) argued that the hearer need not bother to study such speaker-oriented qualities as sincerity and commitment. For even a well-formed sentence may be presented accidentally to the hearer (where the speaker may not be known to the hearer at all) and communication will take place without difficulty.

The Naiyāyikas insist that even the conscious knowledge of fitness is not necessary. Lack of knowledge to the contrary is all that we need for generating belief or knowledge-claim from testimony. This lack will take care of all the 'misfires':

(a) The speaker may be lying, in which case knowledge-claim will be withdrawn when further evidence is unfolded.
(b) The speaker may be mistakenly speaking the truth while he wants to mislead the audience;
(c) The speaker, a compulsive liar, is trying to communicate knowledge to his audience, as it generally happens.

Whether or not the above argument (gleaned mainly from Gaṅgeśa) can finally show that we directly have knowledge-or belief-claims by testimony without the intervention of non-committal understanding of the meaning of the utterance, is a matter that may still be disputed. However, some advantage has been shown to exist in the Naiyāyika's claim, which avoids the problem of studying or guessing the psychological qualities of the speaker.

5. PROPOSITIONS AND COGNITIVE CONTENT

The idea of a commitment-free understanding is sustained sometimes by the notion of a proposition or (Fregean) thought grasped by such an attitude. Nyāya sees the matter in a different way. The Naiyāyikas do not accept a proposition or a third realm of reality such as Frege's 'thought'. The content of cognition either belongs (as a property) to the cognition itself, or it is identical with the qualified objects or fact grasped by being causally related to the cognition itself. This, however, creates a difficulty in the Nyāya explanation of the content of a false belief, false statements, make-believe, etc. Nyāya, therefore, talks about two types of content, simple and complex. The complex content is what is constructed by compounding simple atomic contents.

We analyse the cognition of a pot belonging to the subject *S* as the simple content, i.e., the pot. This pot is identical with the pot outside.

S cognizes that the flower is red.

Here, the content of the cognition can be analysed as follows: The contenthood in the flower is qualified by contenthood in red. For short, we can write this as:

Q (that flower, red)

This is an example of a complex content. Here too a content should be identical with a fact in the real world that is causally related to the cognition.

The *complex* content according to Nyāya is of two types, the 'qualified' content and the 'conditioned' content. The above is an example of a 'qualified content', for the contenthood in that flower is qualified by the same in red. The content of a false belief would be a 'conditioned content.'

Suppose that flower is not red but *S* mistakenly thinks that it is red. Then '*S* thinks that that flower is red' can be represented as involving a contenthood where one part is *conditioned* but not *qualified* by another part. This can be represented as:

Q (*S*, *Q* (thought, *C* (that flower, red))

Here '*C* (that flower, red)' should be read as: Contenthood in that flower is *conditioned cognitively* by the contenthood in red. Therefore it does not matter if the flower in question is not objectively qualified by red. The element expressed by such description as '. . . is conditioned by . . .' is property of the cognitive event itself, and not of the world outside.

This notion of a conditioned content can be regarded as the Nyāya substitute for a proposition or thought grasped by cognition. But it is not identical with the notion of a proposition.

6. IS TESTIMONY-BASED KNOWLEDGE A CASE OF PERCEPTION?

There are those who, though in favour of allowing testimony-based knowledge, and who answer the sceptics by various sorts of replies and evidence, still think that, as knowledge, it is not *sui generis*, i.e., it is not an independent type of knowledge, such as perception and inference. If the knowledge types are already exhausted by this two-fold classification, on whatever grounds, then the story ends there. We can conveniently define and articulate a ground or criterion for the distinction of the two subclasses of knowledge, and any other candidate for knowledge that we are prepared to take in should be pushed into these two available pigeonholes. However, if we are prepared to take a less drastic attitude towards counting types or sub-types or towards groupings and base classificatory principles upon discoverable properties or features or causal conditionings or whatever, we may be reluctant to saddle ourselves with the most well-known two-fold classification of knowledge, perception and inference. However, it will be still open to us to examine and compare any putative candidate against the available definitional criteria of perception and inference and we may then decide (or not) to include or subsume the candidate into either of the classes.

Testimony-based knowledge is a candidate, let us say, which can be confronted with such a tentative procedure. The prevailing opinions differ whether to call testimony-based knowledge a special case of perception or, in fact, an inference. Turning to the classical Indian side of the picture, we see much more complexity on this issue. The two well-entrenched philosophical traditions, the Vaiśeṣika and the Buddhist, allow knowledge from words (*śabda*), but include it under inference. The former expended more energy over the years for this purpose, specially because their sister tradition, the Naiyāyika or the Nyāya system, disagreed. Almost all the other traditions were in favour of according a separate status to testimony, although the *Mīmāṃsakās* contended that the non-scriptural testimony may and does impart information about the world, but it could hardly amount to knowledge, according to their preferred definition of knowledge. Scriptural testimony, however, does yield knowledge—this thesis was accepted by most parties concerned.

If we first consider the Indian problem of reducibility to perception, we may start with some further comments. This problem is discussed by the thirteenth century-sixteenth century philosophers, Naiyāyikas like Gaṅgeśa and Jagadīśa. But it would be impossible to find out who actually held this view, for historical evidence—texts—are not available. Speculation among the modern Sanskrit pandits is that it was held by Cārvākas, the materialists, for in their view, all knowledge is perceptual and inference deals with only probabilities.and lucky guesses. However, we may safely ignore this. For there is not a single text of the Cārvāka school where the problem has been dealt with. Our best bet is to see how Gaṅgeśa and his followers would construct such a position in order to refute it.

Very briefly, then, let us run over the argument presented. A superficial way to call testimony perceptual is to designate it as a 'mental' perception. Since the objects presented by words are not presented to our ken in (external) perception, and consequently the sensory input is not possible, we may think of the 'inner' eye, the mind organ. Many things are perceived in this way—such as our inner states, pain, desire and even the more 'mental' image or content of such states. Hence, words present the meanings or objects to the mind and we perceive it. But this will not do. For external objects, i.e., bits of the meaning of our language, cannot be 'mentalized' so easily. Nyāya does not contribute to any form of representationalism in their realism, and hence the sophisticated form of mental representation of objects is unavailable to do justice to the claim of mental perceptual grasp of the word-represented objects. If anything, it would be like an actualized bit of memory with a new construction—a case similar to remembering. But it would be presumptuous to call it a perception.

There is, however, a more serious way, conceded by Nyāya, to expose the perceptual character of knowledge due to testimony. Memory-based elements, i.e., elements of the content of a perception contributed by our own memory-bank, are admitted without much ado by Nyāya in many well-known cases. In a perceptual error, e.g., 'This is a snake', the snakehood is admitted by Nyāya to be a memory-borne particular snake, experienced in a previous encounter, and identified, through a mental operation called 'superimposition' (*āropa*), with the object present in the visual field, a rope, and then perceptually grasped. Even a correct or veridical case of perception can be serviced by memory in the same way. My perceptual judgement, 'I see cold ice outside', consists of the property coldness, which invariably and necessarily characterizes ice, and is automatically presented within my perceptual ken, *maybe* internally. In any case, through habituated constant association of cold and ice in our adult life for a long time we are conditioned to take the ice in along with its dominant quality, coldness, despite the fact that cold touch is grasped usually by the tactile organ, not by the visual one. Since there is a propensity to take this judgement to be perceptual, the difficulty in explanation is removed by holding that memory presents with the required element to our perceptual ken. Such a capacity is admitted, for in such limited cases it is predicated with proper care and caution and our usual cases of misperception, where the so-called absent elements, the properly represented characteristics etc., are frequently grasped, and we would not budge to include them in our description of the content of the erroneous perception.

One safeguard against taking this alleged looseness in the theory to support such things as guesswork as having a perceptual claim is, according to Nyāya, to insist upon some peculiarities that the above examples do possess, and thereby facilitate their perceptual status. One may not count such claims as 'I see the hand once shaken by the queen' or 'I see the dog that bit John yesterday' as perceptual. For the general conditioning of the subject, through constant conjunction in repeated (and repeatable) past experiences, has not taken place in the counter examples. The verb 'see' used, by metaphorical extension, to mean 'cognition' in general. Besides, only certain specific properties or appendages of the substrate-object that is given already in perception can be dragged to the perceptual ken in order to qualify or characterize it. The presentation of the substrate-object, the rope or the ice, carries with it *some of the physically* unpresented characteristics, and riding on the shoulder of a memory of its previously experienced form, such a characteristic is also presented to the subject, not to his 'inner' eye to be sure, but to his physical eye. In grasping the substrate-object, eye cannot but grasp also, due to the peculiarities of the circumstances, the most of overt properties as characterizing the former.

Now, we are ready to test the perceptual claim of testimony-based knowledge in this way. The words present the objects to the perceiver-hearer via memory, which puts a construction upon them to form a connected whole, the alleged content of the resulting knowledge or understanding. This view may appear similar to another (modern) view, well argued on different grounds. Arguing against the possibility of comprehension of our full linguistic behaviour from 'the cosmic exile's perspective,' McDowell remarks that to avoid the Dummettian dilemma—of psychologism on the one hand and the difficulty of recognizing the unproblematicaly detectable facts on the other, we can exercise our 'perceptual capacity' and describe our full perceptual intake on the occasion of testimony, in terms of knowledge, in a non-question begging way, that is, what we ascribe to the subject—the hearers, when we say that they are competent language-users and understand the sentence uttered.

One argument is based upon the fact that our command of a language provides us, though not necessarily universally, with an additional perceptual capacity. Exploiting the slogan 'working one's way into language is working one's way into a conception of the world', as well as other comments by Wittgenstein in *On Certainty*, McDowell asserts:

> Command of a language is partly constituted by just such a perceptual capacity; one whose acquisition makes a new range of facts, not hitherto within one's perceptual ken, available to one's awareness (1981, p. 239).

Acquisition of such a perceptual capacity through the acquisition of a linguistic ability is admitted as a fact. Hence, the idea would be, tentatively, this. In perceiving the words or utterances, we are invariably conditioned to take in perceptually the meanings or the truth-conditions which constitute the other side of the language. It would be wrong to think of our linguistic competence merely in terms of our being able to make and react to sounds in a way one had been drilled to feel comfortable with. Use of a language does not mean simply blind responses to stimuli like perceptually grasped utterances which are expressive of thoughts. In addition, we are capable of, by our use of language, utterances which are expressive of such thoughts. Users of language, in this view, are also justifiers, reasoners, arguers and articulators.

7. JUSTIFICATIONISM, REALIABILISM AND THE CASE OF A COMPULSIVE LIAR

It has been argued (e.g., by E. Fricker, 1987) that the theory of testimony-based knowledge favours a certain Justificational conception of knowledge, as superior to any version of the Reliabilist conception, where the latter excludes any justification criterion. Justificationism is given a stronger version by Fricker through the inclusion of the requirement that a subject should be able to formulate and offer a suitable justification of his belief: 'knowers, on such a theory, must be . . . operators within the "space of reason;" not just optimally wired-up registrars of information, but moreover reasoners and justifiers, arguers, and of course, articulaters—users of a language'. (p. 62)

Now, it seems to me, if an initial belief-free understanding of what is testified to be is denied, and since brainwashing, deceit etc. are more frequent than we wish them to be, if belief and therefore knowledge-claims be said to be generated or derived from testimony, our alternative view would tend to accommodate *primarily* a Reliabilist conception of knowledge (a true belief is knowledge when acquired by a reliable method or in an accredited way), which need not make short work of justification. The Indian *pramāṇa* theory that was favoured by Nyāya can be seen as a version of such an account of knowledge, which sorts our different belief—or knowledge-producing causal processes, such as perception, inference and testimony. However, these accredited sources or causal processes were not often posed there as offering justificatory grounds, although on occasion a knowledge-claim that *p* might be defended partly by explaining how one had epistemic access to *p*, and partly by corroborative evidence or other tests, such as successful action or essential likeness with past knowledge-events. In other words, the notion of a reliable method or mechanism was the guiding principle which accommodated the justification requirement presumably by way of answers to a challenge to explain how it is that we know what we claim to know. There was thus a space which seemed to allow unchallenged and non-dubious true beliefs to be knowledge provided an accredited method had been in operation.

There is a further issue already indicated, that of the speaker's or the testifier's competence, sincerity and trustworthiness, which the upholder of Exclusive Justificationism tends to hammer at. Of course, specific knowledge by the hearer of these properties of the speaker may not be demanded except in a question-begging manner. Hence the Justification would be content to settle for a weaker condition, the hearer be in possession of a less than conclusive argument for justifying what is known. Otherwise, it would be giving in to two unpalatable extreme options, excessive scepticism on one side and honouring gullibility on the other.

The upholder of the given version of Reliabilism which does not preclude justification altogether may see this relaxation of the criteria as coming closer to the second line of thinking already noted, which discounts the contribution of a belief-free understanding to epistemology. It has already been noted that, in this view too, the testifier's properties such as competence and trustworthiness certainly constitute the ground or the guarantee for the emerging knowledge in the hearer. However, the conscious possession by the hearer of the knowledge of such properties ('I *see* the speaker is honest and sincere', 'I *know* that he does not usually deceive or lie', etc.) or the conscious use of such criteria in support 'within the space of reasons' is what is denied here. For true belief, and therefore knowledge of what is heard, may arise in the hearer even without such extraneous justification and reasoning, and a Reliabilist would not find it hard to account for the origin of such knowledge in so far as his conception of knowledge goes. Knowers, on this view too, are not *only* gatherers of beliefs following some normative patterns, but also capable of reflecting upon those patterns; these are both registrars of information and reasoners, i.e., justifiers. But these dispositions, on this view, do not show themselves unless and until a challenge is posed or a doubt infects the cognitive attitude.

The last point in the previous paragraph seems to answer also the charge of gullibility. As insisted already, the justification requirement, through causal explanation or other kinds of inference, is not completely left out of this account of knowledge. True belief arising out of an accredited way or reliable method (and testimony is one such accredited source) would amount to knowledge, if the condition for doubting its truth, sudden intervention of a contrary evidence or some such thing, does not arise simultaneously or immediately. There is a well-known caveat to this argument, which we may discuss briefly now. This is the case of a compulsive liar who happens to be misinformed on a given occasion (a case cited and discussed in the Indian tradition by Gaṅgeśa), or an accidental true belief from, say, brainwashing. Brainwashing is not a reputable source of knowledge, nor is the utterance of a compulsive liar who is known to be so, although both have some claim to have a superficial similarity with the process involved in the acquisition of knowledge by testimony. The Justificationist (Exclusivist) might score here a point over Reliabilism by arguing that she would not reject outright the knowledge-claim of such a belief, provided some acceptable justification can be given or a conclusive evidence of its truth is forthcoming, a disreputable causal history notwithstanding.

The Reliabilist who tries to maintain the second line of thinking would not find it difficult to resolve this problem or at least to get around it. There is, in the first place, something wrong in the purported claim that a subject derived even a belief, no matter whether true or false, from the process we call brainwashing if it is known to the subject as brainwashing. For our initial reaction to the liar's utterance of a sentence (when he is known to us to be a liar) will not be a belief in what he says, but a disbelief. The only thing we are certain of on such an occasion is that we have an awareness (a knowledge) that the speaker wants us to believe *p* where *p* is what is said). Knowledge or belief that *p* will not emerge in our consciousness, for mitigating circumstances or contradictory conditions exist. In the perspective of a causal theory of mental events, we can call such circumstances knowledge-stoppers or belief-stoppers. For example, if somebody *S* knows that the grass is green at a particular time and place, he cannot have a knowledge or even a belief that the grass is not green. In such cases we can say that knowledge that *p* is what *stops* emergence of belief or knowledge that *not p* in the same knower at the same time and place, and hence the former is a belief-stopper. Thus if we are faced with a statement from the brainwashing agency or even confronted with a compulsive liar, we will have in us a condition already present which is belief-stopper and hence knowledge-stopper. If later on we come to learn that the state of affairs reported by such disreputable agencies does obtain, we will have a knowledge that is arrived at by another reliable method and justified on different stronger evidence.

The rather intriguing case would be when the hearer does not have a prior knowledge that the speaker is a compulsive liar or belongs to the brainwashing agency and the reported state of affairs by such agencies does obtain only by accident. In this case, the hearer has a belief which is true and has it derived from, as far as he knows, a reliable method, and hence we have to accept that he has knowledge, this only means that knowledge by testimony does not depend always upon the intention of the testifier, but rather on what he testifies to, and how he does it. If, however, the speaker, knowingly or unknowingly, misinforms his audience, and the auditors are unaware of it, then the auditors are at his mercy. False beliefs will be generated and the auditors would not *know* that they are false until and unless further evidence comes to their notice. In this respect, however, testimony as a source of knowledge is in no way less reliable than perception and inference.

The Justificationist (Exclusivist) may insist that to fend off gullibility the hearer's possession of knowledge of the alleged properties of the speaker, competence, sincerity and trustworthiness, must be appealed to. For the opponent, in his argument against the case of brainwashing or a misinformed liar, has conceded that knowledge of the disqualifying properties of the testifier acts as belief-stopper. This is, he will say, only an indirect admission of the importance of qualifying properties. The Reliabilist, however, would demur. For he insists that the qualifying properties are important, but a knowledge on the part of the hearer of such properties of the speaker is not a pre-existing condition or factor for the emergence of knowledge by testimony. The hearers or auditors, on this view too, may not be just 'optimally wired-up registrars of information,' for they also have disposition to reason and justify. However, they gather knowledge or registrar information through the usual reputable and reliable mechanism unless a spanner is thrown in the works. When challenged, they reason and justify or search for good evidence. When conditions prevail, the relevant belief does not emerge. If contrary evidence is adduced, a previously gathered belief is given up. However, it is difficult to see how the properties of the speaker, such as competence and reliability, which are supposed to be perceptually grasped by the hearer could help us to determine the truth or falsity of the information gathered in the cases under consideration. On the other hand, it seems that by insisting upon the fitness condition negatively, i.e., upon the lack of knowledge of unfitness (knowledge to the contrary), Nyāya enjoys some advantage over its opponents (see also Matilal, 1990, pp. 65–8, 72–4).

Notes and References

Berlin, I. (1969), *Four Essays on Liberty*, Oxford: Clarendon Press.

Copi, I.M. (1972), *Introduction to Logic*, Fourth Edition (New York: MacMillan).

Fricker, E. (1987), 'The Epistemology of Testimony', *Aristotelian Society Supplementary Volume*, lxi, pp. 57–83.

Matilal, B.K. (1968a), 'Indian Theories of Truth and Knowledge (review of J.N. Mohanty's *Gaṅgeśa's Theory of Truth*)', *Philosophy East and West*, 18, pp. 321–33.

———. (1968b), *The Navya-Nyāya Doctrine of Negation*, Harvard: Harvard University Press.

———. (1971), *Epistemology, Logic and Grammar in Indian Philosophical Analysis*, The Hague: Mouton.

———. (1990), *The Word and the World: India's Contribution to the Study of Language*, Delhi: Oxford University Press.

———. (1991), 'Pluralism, Relativism and Interaction Between Cultures', in E. Deutsch (ed.), *Culture and Modernity: East-West Philosophical Perspectives*, Honolulu: University of Hawaii Press, 1991, pp. 141–60.

McDowell, J. (1981), 'Anti-Realism and the Epistemology of Understanding', in Herman Parret and Jacques Bouveress (eds), *Meaning and Understanding* (Walter de Gruyter, Berlin and New York), pp. 225–48.

Mohanty, J.N. (1966), *Gaṅgeśa's Theory of Truth* (Santiniketan: Visva-Bharti). Revised Second Edition, Delhi, Motilal Banarsidass, 1989.

———. (1992), *Reason and Tradition in Indian Thought*, Oxford: Clarendon Press. The remarks on *śabdapramāṇa* and the sense-reference distinction are revised from 'A Critique of *śabdapramāṇa* and the Concept of Tradition', Presidential Address to the Indian Philosophical Congress, October 1986.

12

A Realist View of Perception

Significant contributions have been made by Strawson to the philosophy of perception in several of his writings. The most noteworthy of them are, perhaps, his profoundly original essays, 'Perception and Identification', 'Causation in Perception' and 'Perception and Its Objects'. One has also to take into account his *loosely ruminative* and *comparative-historical* study in 'Imagination and Perception', as well as his view of the problem of perception in the more general perspective provided by his Woodbridge Lectures on *Skepticism and Naturalism.* Extremely sophisticated and finely balanced as all these writings are, there is very little doubt that it is a kind of realism rather than any alternative view of perception that their author defends. It would thus be worth our while to know how Strawson would react to the kind of realist view of perception which is presented in this paper.

It is impossible, says Richard Rorty, to step outside our skins—the traditions, linguistic and other, within which we do our thinking and self-criticism—and compare ourselves with something absolute.[1] Apparently a realist tries to do just that—step outside his skin and take what Putnam has called the *externalist* perspective,[2] a God's-Eye point of view. This is an old legacy which what we call 'science' has inherited in order to play the role of the divine observer. The realist believes that the world consists of some mind-independent objects, even discourse-independent objects. He believes himself also to be part of that world. But here complexity already sets in. He views his perception as an awareness-episode due to 'interaction' between his senses and objects or facts 'out there' (in the sense of being in space 'outside' or in the sense of being whatever we understand by 'mind-independent'). He also believes that whatever he is aware of, objects or facts, is external to the awareness itself. Such a view of perception was explicitly and somewhat rigorously formulated in classical India, in *Nyāyasūtra* 1.1.4, some time between 100 BC to

AD 100.[3] The aphorism in question adds three further qualifications: (a) the awareness must be non-verbal, though it may be verbalizable; (b) it must be non-deviating, that is, not falsifiable; and (c) it must be non-doubting, that is, not vacillating between alternatives. All these qualifications were important in the sense that they contained the ingredients for building up a strong realistic theory of perception, and thereby a sort of metaphysical realism.

The problems that the tradition of Nyāya faced over the ages may simply be of historical interest today. Metaphysical realism seems to have fallen into disgrace among modern philosophers. Of course we can mention a few notable philosophers today who have resisted the temptation of a tactical retreat from realism into old-style relativism or pragmatism. However, a sort of pragmatism, which is sometimes distinguished from old idealism or phenomenalism as well as from relativism, has leaped into popularity today, for it brings the 'liberating' message of insouciance and freedom from worries about 'unsolvable' philosophical problems. Hard-headed realism has often been discredited but it is hard to subdue it. It has been argued that metaphysical realism's assumption of a correspondence theory of truth and a God's-Eye, or a No-Eye, view of truth, is incoherent in spite of its powerful predominance for two thousand years. Michael Dummett makes the acceptance of bivalence as the all-important criterion for distinguishing realism (or 'reductionism' in his terminology) from non-realism or anti-realism.[4] A reductionist-realist may subscribe to the correspondence theory of truth, but what is important here is acceptance of the 'bivalence' strategy concerning statements within a given type of subject matter (these may include statements about the past, modal statements and moral statements, as well as mathematical statements). The realist accepts the principle of bivalence for such statements, and thereby assumes their truth-conditions to obtain independently of our knowledge or capacity for knowing that they do. He (the realist) endorses 'the belief that for any statement there must be something in virtue of which either it or its negation is true': it is only on the basis of this belief that we can justify the idea that truth and falsity play an essential role in the notion of the meaning of a statement, that the general form of an explanation of meaning is the statement of the truth-conditions.[5] The anti-realist, on the other hand, determines the meaning of such statements in terms of the conditions which we *recognize* as establishing their truth and falsity.

Although metaphysical realism has strong adherents even today, in view of the above, strong faith in its viability has been apparently undermined not only by neo-pragmatists like Rorty but also by such non-prag-matists as Goodman, Putnam and Dummett. The question is seriously asked whether realism is an old 'historical relic' or a straighforward belief-system of the common man which philosophers over two millennia have mistakenly tried to defend. The history of philosophy, however, is different from the history of, say, chemistry, for here the notion of a 'historical relic' is not easily available. Old problems raise their heads again, for problems are less seldom solved than resolved or rather shelved for the time being when the proponents get tired or bored. As Thomas Nagel has said, 'It may be that some philosophical problems have no solutions. I suspect this is true of the deepest and oldest of them. They show us the limits of our understanding . . . Unsolvable problems are not for that reason unreal.'[6] The insouciance of some modern philosophers seems to emulate the spirit of the old sceptics. The modern pragmatist knowingly or unknowingly sympathizes with scepticism. He is a sceptic without his *epoché* and he obtains his *ataraxia* by getting rid of all worries. He is not blind but he avoids the paradoxicality of the sceptical position by closing his eyes when necessary.

Transparency or (metaphysical) realism, it is perhaps rightly urged, demands some sort of what has been dubbed a correspondence theory, and/or reference theory underlining the 'tie' between words or thought-signs and the world, i.e., external things or sets of things. To be sure, some sort of correspondence or 'faithfulness' of the awareness with the world outside or the *word-world* marital tie should be the bedrock for distinguishing perception from misperception or 'factual' discourse from fictional discourse.

Almost all the different versions of the correspondence theory have been found fault with. But I am not sure whether all of them have been totally refuted or proven to be beyond any reformulation. The Indian Nyāya school defended a formulation which I shall call the theory of 'non-promiscuity' (or faithfulness between the world and its awareness that is generated in us). Non-promiscuity is not correspondence—in the strict sense of the term. Correspondence needs two terms—one that corresponds and the other to which it corresponds. And in this respect it is of a piece with such relations as comparison, similarity, even contradiction or opposition. Non-promiscuity, on the other hand, is a natural or general expectation in a marital tie, or it may even be likened to the quality of transparency of a transparent medium, if you look at it from another point of view.

A retreat from realism can take various forms, some of which are articulated as relativism amounting to incommensurabilism, guarded scepticism, a sort of pragmatism or solidarity within a cultural milieu (Rorty), context-dependence or even the internalist perspective (Putnam), although I am not sure whether the last named is really a significant retreat. Nor is it absolutely clear whether the anti-realist's rejection of bivalence only (and not *tertium non datur*) would not be compatible even with the realist's framework. Nāgārjuna (in India), for example, was explicitly prepared to give up *tertium non datur* and hence his retreat was a significant retreat from realism. It is difficult to have a common denominator for all these non-realist positions. We may dub them only negatively as 'non-realism'.

We shall try to present the view of Nyāya realism. In this context we need not sharply distinguish between epistemology and semantics, but follow the Russellian line of epistemologizing semantics. Besides, in our modern readings of ancient philosophers we do often attribute to them theories and views which are not expressed or formulated by them in exactly the same terminology as we prefer to use today. While epistemological issues such as that of sensation mediating between perception and the external world are well-entrenched in the ancient tradition, the semantic problem of 'reference' is of a comparatively recent origin. Nevertheless, the problem of the relation between thought-signs and what they stand for is quite old, which provides the rationale for the discussion of classical views in modern terms. This will be done here with regard to the classical Indian philosophers: The crucial qualifier in the *Nyāyasūtra* characterization is 'non-deviating' or 'non-promiscuous', which equals faithfulness.

The word for 'deviating' is also the word for promiscuity in Sanskrit, and hence negatively, the perceptual awareness-episode must be non-promiscuous, i.e., not unfaithful to the world out there. There need not be a 'tie', positively speaking, between the awareness and the relevant bits of the world, but there should be *lack of discord* between them. Discord marks off misperceptions from perceptions. One way of further understanding the notion of deviation or discord is to see the following. Each perceptual event selects some feature or features of the percept. It is conceded that such features may or may not be located therein or may not be included in the powers of the percept. A misperception misascribes, hence its verbal report is a false statement.

The above is the received doctrine of the alleged explanation of a misperception. But a Nyāya realist may put it in a slightly different way. It is, of course, true that each perceptual event selects some feature or features of the percept. However, it need not be conceded that such features, or at least some of such features may not be located in the percept itself. Before the event of a misperception, something else must happen, as a realist should insist. Our mind misconnects some of these features in a way not given in the relevant percept. But the realist must also insist that this does not always happen, not before veridical perceptual event. Such an event is an automatic happening without any further intervention. Lack of this misconnection means that we have a proper perception.

The intriguing element in this explanation is the notion of the deviant feature or the accidental misconnection: He is the intruder in the proposed marriage between the awareness and the world, he is responsible for the resulting promiscuity. Where form does this deviant feature come? We shall talk about it presently. But we may note that, according to this view, this deviant feature is *not* a mental image or a superimposition of a mental representation which lacks 'hooking up' with the world. (A pertinent question is: Where from does a mental image come if not from the world itself?) It *enters* into the awareness-episode and thereby into its verbal report, from the world itself. (This is, at least, the argument of the Nyāya realists.) It is just another feature present *elsewhere* or at another time, much as another real person, the intruder in a marriage.

The qualifier 'non-doubting' says that our perception or our judgement of perception should not vacillate between alternatives, i.e., given mutually exclusive alternative features, *A* and *B*, it must rest content with just one of them. This presupposes that confrontation between the world and the senses (physics and physiology) may generate a vacillating awareness, or uncertainty, the verbal report of which would be '*x* may be *A* or it may be *B*', when the evidence is not adequate, i.e., there is only a common evidence shared by both *A* and *B*. This also underlines the fact that perception on this view would be an inference from evidence—a point which the Buddhists were never slow to point out. This, as well as the other qualifier 'non-verbal', led to a vortex of controversy, eventually suggesting a radical distinction between conception-free or word-free *(nirvikalpa)* perception and conception-loaded, word-loaded (*savikalpa*) perception. In underlining the distinction in terms of such expressions as 'word-free' and 'word-loaded', the classical Indian philosophers mix epistemology with semantics, as I have already noted. But perhaps, this is not a serious drawback. For several centuries this issue became the most important chapter in the history of Indian philosophy of perception and marked the great divide between realism and idealism. We may also note that while the adjective 'non-promiscuous' ensured *physical* soundness of perception, in the sense that it would not be destroyed or falsified by 'the way the world is', the adjective 'non-doubting' ensured its *psychological* soundness so that it may be decisive. Absolute certainty is not what is necessary, but it must be *uninfected with doubt*.

Here again, the realist may add another point. Not all veridical perceptions occur after a doubting state of mind, as has been prescribed here. Only in some cases a doubting state may intervene. If a correct perception arises afterwards, on the basis of correct evidence, then the Nyāya realist must be drawing a very thin line of distinction between such perception and an inference. It may finally boil down to a terminological dispute, but I am not going to enter into it here.

I shall now comment upon the qualification 'non-verbal'. Its early meaning was obscure. But with the rise of a view championed by Bhartṛhari in fifth century AD, a view that asserted that all our awareness of the world is necessarily interpenetrated with the operation of words, or concepts, in fact, that it is a linguistic affair, the claim was made by the realists that wordless, concept-free perception is possible. This came very close to an early admission of the epistemological point about the distinction between receptivity and spontaneity, between passive and active parts in us, the former receiving the 'world as such' which the latter 'interprets' using concepts or words. The point (sometimes ascribed to Kant) was however differently taken by the Buddhists than by the Naiyāyikas, and neither of them was Kantian. Diṅnāga (the leader of the Buddhist *pramāṇa* school), for example, regarded the word-free, conception-free sensory awareness as perception proper, for here the 'world' is supposed to shine in its pristine purity, without distortion or manipulation (cf. *kalpanā*), and as far as Diṅnāga was concerned, interpretation with concepts or words is necessarily discourse-dependent and hence perhaps a distortion, though it is a convenient way for it is instrumental for our getting along with this world. It is not clear whether this attitude originated in the fear that discursive thought, or free flow of the mind's activity, if uncontrolled, will play us false and make us lose touch with the real, the ultimately real—a fear which Heidegger, it is said, has claimed to be typical of the Western philosophical tradition. (How can one claim something to be typical of the Western tradition without knowing much of the non-Western tradition?—a point to which my attention was drawn by my friend, Ninian Smart.) It should be noted here—a linguistic point but significant enough—that the word *kalpanā* or *vikalpa* in Sanskrit is also the word for poetic and playful fancy, the arbitrary use of language, or as the *Yogasūtra* defined it much earlier in the tradition, it is what is 'word-inspired'' as well as 'lacking in reality'. Kumārila asserted: words provide our access to fictional and utterly non-existent objects.

Bhartṛhari's point was that our verbal report or language 'carves up the world for us', our perceived world is also a manipulated/interpreted world, and therefore, the word-world tie is one of identity, or rather, the word 'creates' its own object (carves it out of the world) to refer to it. We do not 'deviate' but we 'create'. This was an attractive idea to Diṅnāga, the Buddhist. It was acceptable to him, for then one could easily *devalue* the assumed reality of the *interpreted* world captured in our normal, veridical perceptual judgements. For the Buddhist goal of diverting ourselves from desire-laden activity to quietude, it was all the more welcome.

The Naiyāyikas, however, criticized this theory which, they rightly feared, would lead to idealism or a Lockean kind of dilemma in representationalism, and the Sautrāntika apparently came very close to such a quandary. The problem before them was threefold, the same as seem to confront even the modern realist. First, we must have an acceptable theory of perceptual illusion, a theory that does not countenance mental images, representations, sense-data, etc., but like a Dickensian Scrooge (in *A Christmas Carol*), would be able to say to the hallucinated ghost: 'I do not believe in my senses because a slight disorder of the stomach makes them cheat, you may be an undigested bit of beef, a blot of mustard, a crumb of cheese, a fragment of underdone potato. There is more of gravy than of grave about you, whatever you are?' Second, we need a version of 'correspondence' or the *word-world* tie that would be intelligible and defensible. Third, while conceding the constructed nature of the structure of reality captured or revealed in our veridical perceptual judgements, one should try to undervalue, if not reject altogether, the privileged position enjoyed by structureless, construction-free perception, and along with it, one may try to avoid conceptual relativism, and deny the possibility of alternative interpretative frameworks mutually incompatible and totally unintertranslatable. For if we concede that our concepts or what is within us provides the structure for the neutral, structureless, material world, then we may side with the anti-realist. However, one can save realism by not only underplaying or not emphasizing the passivity of the mind receiving the structureless world, but also by recognizing at the same time the mind's active role in construction. If the mind's active role is externally *controlled* under all normal circumstances, then most beliefs thus acquired would be true beliefs, and a form of realism can be vindicated. This external control, if admitted, would also presuppose, however, that there are at least some mind-independent, non-discourse-dominated, non desire-laden universals, i.e., objective universals of natural kinds.

The later Naiyāyikas have tried to tackle all the three issues with varying degrees of success. I shall comment primarily on the first issue, and to some extent on the other two, for they are interconnected. Connecting epistemology with semantics we will have occasion to refer to the standard Russellian solution of the problem about universals as well as fictional discourse with his theory of descriptions and 'knowledge by acquaintance'. These problems have a distinct, though 'distant', Nyāya resonance, although in details Russell and Nyāya differed a lot, while both were trying to save realism.

A theory of error is also a theory of reality, for they are two[7] sides of the same coin. This view gradually became the conviction of most Indian philosophers from AD 800 onwards and hence a proliferation of different theories of error—i.e. about the status of the object appearing in perceptual illusion—followed, which underlined both realism and idealism in their various ramifications and combinations. During the time of Vācaspati (ninth to tenth centuries AD) there were at least five such theories prevalent (five hundred years later, about fourteen such views were recorded). Of these five, two were ascribed to the Buddhists, one to the Vedāntists and two to the realists, Naiyāyikas and Prābhākaras. The Buddhist view alternates between regarding 'objects' figuring in perceptual error as internal to and/or created by the awareness itself and regarding them as *unreal* or non-existent entities for which there is no objective support or foundation in the external world. Both, in Kumārila's description, are *nirālambana-vāda*, the view that regards all awareness as foundationless, i.e., lacking objective support in the outer world. The Buddhists may concede, as the Sautrāntikas did, that there is somehow a mind-independent world, for that is virtually presupposed in most of our rational behaviour,[8] and in this our experience may be somehow grounded. But we can form no absolute conception of this world for any attempt to characterize it or talk about it would lead to nonsense. Talk of the 'correspondence' between awareness and reality would be impossible on this view, for we have no independent access to reality to check such correspondence, and hence non-realism (which the Buddhists preferred) wins the day.

The third, Vedāntic, view is somewhat 'pragmatic' in the modern sense. It regards the object in perceptual illusion as neither real nor unreal, as neither part of the outer world nor an empty, airy nothing (for otherwise how can they be experienced?), but as having an indescribable, and inexplicable status. It is much like the object in Brentano's doctrine of psychological verbs, 'intentionally inexistent'. On the whole, however, this does not save realism; it only develops a tolerant attitude towards metaphysical realism to which I now wish to turn. (A realistic reading of Vedānta is, to be sure, possible, but that is not my concern here.)

One point of some significance, however, can be made here. This view also accepts the absolute duality of the *perceived* world (or the *interpreted* world, according to Bhartṛhari) and the world itself, i.e., the world that we perceive and the world that confronts us. The Vedāntin, it seems to me, wishes to point out that we generally use a set of terms to describe the bits and pieces of the world itself and then try uncritically to describe, with the same set of terms or sentences, the bits and pieces of the *perceived* world. Hence, the Vedāntin seems to argue, it is better to *prefix* such sets of terms or sentences of ordinary language or discourse to warn us that an illicit transition has been made in our linguistic act. The Nyāya realists would counter this argument by saying that the alleged *duality* is based upon an illicit generalization. There is practically no question of duality (leading to possible distortion) as long as the *natural* transparency of the media (perception or language) remains intact. If this quality is destroyed by a defect, it would be illegitimate to accuse all the individual members of the media. It is like accusing every spouse, even if only some of them are proven, as unfortunately some of them often are, guilty of promiscuity.

Both the Prābhākaras and the Naiyāyikas were metaphysical realists. Both assumed that the world out there consists of some fixed totality of mind-independent objects and that the structure of those objects can be revealed or grasped in our veridical perceptual judgement. Such perceptions, in other words, can say 'the way the world is', and misperceptions are regarded or explained either as 'confusions' of one thing for another or 'misplacement' of something real in another (something real). The Prābhākaras opt for the 'confusion' or 'fusion' theory while the Naiyāyikas prefer the 'misplacement theory.[9] The Prābhākaras believed that, practically speaking, there cannot be any illusion, only mixing or confusion of one mode of awareness (perceptual) with another (memory). That resists giving any separate status to *representation*. There is direct grasp of objects, there is perfect transparency. The world is a transparent text. Of course, there are institutional or cultural constructs which inform our perceptions. But there is, it is claimed, an infrastructure common to all rational humans which directly figures in our perceptions. If the verbal report of a so-called perceptual illusion is 'that is a snake', then both the terms 'that' and 'snake' have *ties* with the world we know best: 'that' refers to the object in front, the piece of rope, and 'snake' to a member of the snake-community inhabiting this world. The so-called illusory awareness does not *create* or grasp any 'form', image or 'appearance' of the snake (not even the sense-datum of the snake-appearance). It directly REFERS to (using 'refer' in the old, less entrenched sense) the world. The verbal report of the so-called illusory awareness is a blending of two different modes, a sensory perception and a memory-event, although their distinction remains unrevealed in verbalizations. There may be this distinction here between the cognizing faculty and the verbalizing faculty; the later may *miss* something which the former does not, hence the latter confuses or gives *mixed* signals which the former does not. The mind passively receives both the visual object and the revived memory, but does not receive enough to see that they are in fact two, not one. That is, their distinctness or lack of connection remains unrecognized. Or better still, we may say that the mind probably receives from them *as they are*, i.e., that they are two, not one, but the faculty of generating the verbal report misses this lack of connection and hence there is some fusion or confusion of the two as one. Notice that here we do not talk at all about sense-data, or sensory images, or mental representations, and thereby a lot of tricky questions regarding the ontological status of sense-data, etc., which have for long plagued the theories of perception are avoided.

Gaṅgeśa (AD 1300, in his *Tattvacintāmaṇi*)[10] has quoted a verse which summarily notes five main reasons for justifying the 'confusion' or 'no-illusion' theory of the Prābhākaras. The rather sweeping Prābhākara thesis is that all awareness without exception is object-corresponding (*yathārtha*), and that hence no explanation is needed for the so-called illusory appearance of objects, like the snake-image, etc., an explanation being needed only for the use of the term 'illusion' for a certain class of awareness. (At the semantic level, an explanation is needed for the application of the term 'fictional' to fictional objects such as Sherlock Holmes.) The five reasons stated in support of this thesis are as follows:

1. *Sākāra-pātāt*: If an awareness (perceptual) can arise about such an object as 'this snake' when there is no snake present, then we have to admit the ontology of mental representations or mental images (*ākāra*—cf. those who admit *ākāra* (= form) would face similar problems about sense-data as faced in modern Anglo-American philosophy). The Prābhākaras do not admit the idea of 'mental

representation'. Hence they argue that there cannot be any awareness that does not correspond or refer to any object. An awareness, on this view, refers to some object or other, an object belonging to the world itself much in the same way as a proper name (non-connotatively) refers to an individual. I have made a tongue-in-the-check use of the verb 'refer' in this context. If there is scepticism about the use of this rather well-entrenched term, we have to settle for the more metaphorical 'grasp' or 'reveal'. The idea is that there is direct grasp of the object by the awareness (naive realism), nothing intervenes. Since there cannot be any false awareness on this view, only 'fusion' of the two modes reflected confusedly in the verbal report, there cannot be any talk about the 'content' being divorced from the object. It seems that something happens between cognition and its verbal report (we should note that the verbal report may be inarticulate or indistinct or simply a concept-formation, as Bhartṛhari reminded us). The percept and the memory-object are fused together in such verbalization.

2. *Asato na bhānāt.* The Prābhākaras do not accept that an awareness 'refers' to or grasp a non-existent (unreal) object. Revived memory remembers the past snake and perception sights the rope; both being real, we cannot talk about any unreal objects. For if we do, we immediately subvert the claims of realism. If illusory objects are 'perceived' once, this could happen always. There would thus be no convincing argument against 'illusionism' which maintains that the whole world is an illusion (Vasubandhu) or an empty dream, or that we are simply brains-in-a-vat, or that all our experiences are being manipulated by Descartes' evil genius.
3. *Saṃvid-virodhāt.* A false awareness is usually explained as an episode which grasps an object (a snake) that is not present in the given spatio-temporal situation in addition to its grasping the object (the rope) that is present in the given situation. It is rather counter-intuitive (*saṃvid-virodha*) to maintain that when we are aware of *A*, a piece of rope in front, there is a contrary object, *B*, a snake, which is also captured in the same awareness. What captures *B* is a different awareness (remembering), and it is also object-corresponding in its own particular way, for we can remember that there were pieces of silver previously experienced.
4. *Hetvabhāvāt.* To admit that the senses can be wrong and/or that the mind wrongly interprets the data received is to say that they occasionally 'misbehave'. There is no causal explanation for this

misbehaviour of the senses or of the mind. It is the *nature* of the sensory faculty or of the mental faculty that they receive/grasp only what is presented by the world. Why should they act in a way that is contrary to their nature and grasp distant and past objects? It is impossible for something to change its *own nature*. Therefore, it does not stand to reason to suppose that our faculties should be supposed to have changed their *own nature* and inform us wrongly. The Prābhākaras believe that the *defect* (*doṣa*) does not affect the causal structure of the cognition but that of verbalization.

5. *Dhiyām anasvasabhayāt*. The real possibility of error or illusory perception must be denied. Our conscious activities are caused by our beliefs, awareness and knowledge. But such activities prompted by knowledge or awareness would be impossible. For if an awareness is not object-corresponding, but promiscuous or guilty of misdemeanour in the way illusions are supposed to be, what trust would we have in any awareness to prompt us to act in any way? All our actions would be infected with doubt and uncertainty.

To wit: Since our actions are caused by our beliefs, all our belief prompting actions must be *trusted* to be *true*, i.e., object-corresponding. Our failures in action show *not object-corresponding*, but that *more* knowledge (true-belief) was needed for our success. As I rush to pick up the piece of silver but fail, I realize what I did not *know* before, viz. the distinctness of the two cases of awareness or belief. I had an awareness in the past of the piece of shell as well as a revived memory (recurrence of an episodic belief) about a piece of silver. Our action fails because there was a *gap* in our knowledge, not because we had no knowledge. Not illusion but ignorance (lack of knowledge of the distinctness) causes this failure. We had a partial knowledge and hence we acted and failed; we did not know *enough*—such is the Prābhākara position. (Notice that it is much stronger than Davidson's point, according to which most of our beliefs must be *held* true, to use Davidson's terminology.) This also explains the usage: we apply the term 'illusion' when activity fails for no fault in our effort but due to ignorance of the kind already explained.

The Naiyāyikas accept all these points (and reject the 'mental representation' theory as well as 'universal illusionism' on similar grounds), but they admit, unlike the Prābhākaras, that perceptual illusions are facts, not just confusions and play of ignorance, for otherwise it would be highly counter-intuitive to call perceptual illusions nothing but mixing or co-occurrence of two modes of awareness. Instead of holding that there cannot be any false awareness or illusion, the Naiyāyikas agree with commonsense in holding that perceptual illusions are facts, not just confusion of verbal reports. A perceptual illusion is a unitary awareness-event in which we grasp the object in front, the piece of shell, as the location (*dharmin*) or the subject, and ascribe to it a feature that is absent there, but presented to the mind by memory (receiving it from past experience). The property of being a piece of silver is part of the furniture of this world just as much as a piece of shell is. No mental image is necessary for such presentation, for mind is not 'a wax tablet' here. Mind is like an instrument, by which we capture an object or a fact. Objects do not *enter* into our mind. However, past experience, a cognitive event, disappears, leaving behind another dispositional property in the person—this is called *saṃskāra* on this view. This dispositional property is retained by the person and it produces another cognitive event, this time it is called remembering what was grasped before or what happened before, provided adequate stimuli are present.

This is a good place to note briefly how both the realists, the Naiyāyikas and the Prābhākaras would react against a theory that is current and sometimes dominant in the Western world, the theory called *causal realism*. Very roughly this is the view that we *directly* perceive only sensations and can only *infer* material objects through some sort of a dubiously explained' causal relation. Even in its sophisticated formulation, in terms of 'sense-data' reductionism (even in the form: no physical object statements are true without some sense-data statement being true), the unsatisfactory nature of this position is not completely removed. One version of causal realism is rather widely accepted. This I ascribe to P.F. Strawson. It says: Since *X*'s perceiving *M* involves *X*'s sense-impression of the appropriate kind, the fact that it sensibly seems to *X* just as if *X* perceives *M* is causally dependent upon some state of affairs involving *M*. The Nyāya critique would be that the *connection* between *X*'s perceiving *M* and *X*'s having a sense-impression of the appropriate kind is only a *contingent* one, whereas the causal theory wrongly assumes it to be a necessary one. To put the matter in another way, the causal theorist may explain the connection to be causal in the sense that '*X* sees *M*' is true *in virtue X*'s seeing some visual datum *N*. Nyāya, however, contends that *X* may see *M* simply in virtue of the *presence* of *N*, where *N* is nothing but part of the physical reality, but it is not necessary to assume that seeing of *M* is always preceded (hence causally conditioned) by a sense-impression of *N*. In our most adult perception we see *M directly*. A sense-impression of *N*, if it is to be a cognitive fact as distinct from some pure physiological reaction, may occur and may very well precede our perception of *M* in some (initial) cases. But it does not happen always. In other words, '*X* perceives *M*' may be true without '*X* has a sense-impression of *N*' being about 'construction-free' perception being possible at *ādyapratyaksa*, child's perceptions, etc. (or *seeing* something after *pratyaksa*, child's perceptions, etc. (or *seeing* something after deep sleep, fainting spells, etc.).[11]

Pure sensory perception without any intrusions of concept (reception without interpretation) would, on this view, be impossible except, perhaps, the initial acquaintance of the neophyte with this world. Hence it accepts the supposedly Kantian point that each effable perception will have at least a minimal injection of concepts. There may be distinction between perception of things *unqualified* (e.g., perception of objective universals, such as cowhood, which is regarded on this view as a logical prerequisite for the perception of something as a cow) and perception of facts or propositional perception. At the semantic level, this implies that a word, say 'water', may be said to refer to the actual stuff water by virtue of its universal essence, waterhood. This means that when 'water' is uttered, the hearer understands the stuff qualified by waterhood, but the qualifying universal 'waterhood' must be grasped by the observer as unqualified! It must be *directly* 'captured'. In the Nyāya view, if the verbal report of a perceptual cognition is 'water' or 'it is water', then, the cognition captures the stuff water under the *mode* of waterhood, but waterhood itself is captured directly. The verbal report usually bears out what is directly captured in the awareness. If, however, waterhood is captured under another mode of presentation, the verbal report would mention 'waterhood', as, for example, 'waterhood is a universal'. This was believed to be enough to save the kind of realism they tried to defend.

The word-world link, in this view, is not exactly a 'physicalistic' or a metaphysical relation of reference (that was the view of Bhartṛhari, which was refuted here), but a very well-entrenched (cf. *samayika* in the *Vaiśeṣikasūtra*), determinate unique relation (well-entrenched because, as they put it, it was fixed by God). Words are invested, on this view, with a power (*śakti*) or dispositional property, to generate, as soon as they are uttered, an awareness of the objects they refer to in the hearer because both the speaker an the hearer share the well-entrenched conventions of a speech-community. Truth is not 'correspondence', but lack of promiscuity, aṣ indicated earlier. Truth is regarded as indistinguishable from knowledgehood or, we can say figuratively, knowledge 'captures' or 'reveals' truth. A sentence is said to be true when and only when it generates knowledge in the (ideal) hearer. An ideal hearer is one to whom the information given by the sentence is transparent enough, i.e. unambiguous enough, and in this case contingent factors such as inattention, lack of sensory ability, hypocrisy, would not present any problem. Episodic knowledge does not 'correspond' to reality, it *grasp* reality by being non-promiscuous or 'non-deviating'.

It may be said that there are other cases of perceptual illusion for which some sort of a 'representation' theory or 'visual data' theory has to be conceded, e.g., the blue dome in the sky, the blur at a distance and hallucinations. Hallucination (Macbeth's dagger etc.) could be explained by the Naiyāyikas as gripping memories of some traumatic experience which still haunts the perceiver. So this would be memory masquerading as perception, for generally the perceptual causal factors are present (eyes, open, vividness of experience/memory, etc.). For blue domes, blurs, apparent elliptical forms of discs, etc., the following explanation may be suggested. We may regard them as part of physiological-physical *data*. In other words, we may admit an ontology of a class of 'objective' external particulars. These *objective* external particulars are momentary, being dependent upon the percipient's perceiving. It is claimed here that an objective external reality is created *de novo* in these cases by several factors, and it is only misattributed to a real locus. They are created by a set of physical and non-physical causal factors. But among these causal factors, a mental event (sensing) is also included. This mental event is regarded as a crucial factor in the set of causal factors, crucial in the sense that the said external reality (which is newly created) lasts only as long as that mental event lasts. They cannot exist where no observer is present, but the physical (external) realities have the power or disposition in them to generate such properties with appropriate factors. This may seem to be very similar to the acceptance of external sense-data, or even secondary qualities, but not quite. They are not properties of the surface of opaque physical objects, but only attributed to them. Besides, such external particulars are not admitted to be present in every case of sensory perception. Only in the cases mentioned above are such particulars believed to have been generated. We posit such particulars only to explain the oddity of such erroneous perceptions. They may be like 'intentional' properties, provided it is admitted that an intentional property is created as long as it is intended by someone, i.e., as long as the episodic intention lasts. It is not all the time *there* to be intended, nor is it created simply by somebody's attitude, for other physical factors must and do cooperate, and it must disappear or die when nobody is intending it. Besides, these particulars may be shared by the agents while it is difficult to say that intended objects are shared by the agent. It may be pointed out that while we have pooh-poohed the theory of data, the immediately given, the given which are certainly known, we have now made a *volte face* and accepted a set of *queer* entities (which must be called mental). In reply, we must note that these so-called queer entities are sometimes intersubjectively verifiable. One would see the same or similar blur from the same vantage point as I do from here and now. And they are not *mental* (at least, in one important sense of the word 'mental') on this view.

Fictional objects or all objects of fictional discourse, on this view, are regarded as composite; they can be broken down to simples and to further simples until we reach the real elements of the actual world we know best. The mind's creative or active power needs materials to work upon and such materials cannot but finally belong to this world. But receptivity and spontaneity are always blended together. It would be futile to seek a distinction. We have seen that the Naiyāyikas believe in a sort of fallibilism and differ from the Prābhākaras in holding that perceptual illusions are facts. They also differ accordingly in their 'action' theories. According to Nyāya we act because of our beliefs or certitudes, even when they are false certitudes. Besides, even doubt may not deter us from acting. This answers the Prābhākara objection that if we admit perceptual errors to occur in our awareness we would not be able to act for we will have no trust in such awareness. For the Prābhākaras, there is no false awareness and hence our action in the case of so-called perceptual errors is prompted not by knowledge, but by the lack of it. We rush to grab a piece of silver due to our lack of knowledge of the distinctness (call it 'confusion') between what lies in front and what is desired by us. Hence, on this view, you have to accept the oddity that what generates actions is not a factual belief but the lack of it, for in the so-called errors, some right belief, belief about the disconnection, is missing. For Nyāya, however, false certitudes, i.e., false beliefs, or even doubts, generate action, not lack of them.

Finally, what could be said from the 'misplacement' theory's point of view about universal illusionism and universal scepticism? What if the entire external world is just within us, an empty dream? What if we are all simply brains-in-a-vat? Putnam has argued that some plausible assumption about the nature of reference shows that all sentient beings cannot be brains-in-a-vat. This anti-sceptical conclusion is welcome. But Putnam further thinks that for the metaphysical realist, or externalist, this 'brain-in-a-vat' is a real puzzler while his (Putnam's) internalism can dismiss it easily. I think it is possible even for a metaphysical realist to refute universal illusionism. According to the sort of metaphysical realism I wish to defend, the 'brain-in-a-vat' situation is indeed a possibility (it is not incoherent or self-refuting, as some philosophers apparently suggest). But the Naiyāyikas would say that this possibility has to be *parasitical* upon an actual world which must be rich enough, or at least contain a minimal number of *materials* required, for the successful construction of the overall experiences that we as brains-in-a-vat do experience. To put the matter another way: In order to imagine a *horned* rabbit (a favourite example of Indian philosophers) we need at least rabbits and the materials called horns, or an *alternative* list of actual items out of which a horned rabbit can be constructed (if, hypothetically, we live in a world where there are neither rabbits nor horns). To imagine a rabbit dressed as an Oxford don looking at his watch every five minutes, we need a world inhabited by rabbits, Oxford dons, watches, etc., not an empty world, that is, we must admit, at least a world with people, gowns and clocks, but may be no Oxford dons. This is the sum and substance of what the Naiyāyikas call the *vat-kāra katham* argument ('how this as-if-ness' argument). In a poor world where there are only vats and brains and a particular neuro-scientist with his instruments, how can I have the experience of tasting a mango, or the juicy tomato of H.H. Price, unless it contained in addition other materials to constitute such experience of a neuro-scientist who has had such experience or can imagine having such an experience? The existence of another actual world, whatever items it may or may not contain, is thus presupposed by this 'brain-in-a-vat' or 'life is an empty dream' argument and thereby its sceptical force is undercut. As Gilbert Ryle once put it, 'A country which had no coinage would offer no scope to counterfeiters . . . Ice could not be thin if ice could not be thick.'[12]

What is distressing about this sceptical suggestion is that it is a distinct possibility. It may just be that a god, or a mad scientist, is sitting there and playing tricks on us. Given our circumstances, we would never know that it is *not* so. It is a coherent idea. But, the realist may point out, coherence is not a sufficient ground for accepting it as true or actual. Hence we need not accept it. In either case, existence of some external world is not rejected, although our presumed knowledge of it may be infected with doubt from time to time. Scepticism is what we learn to live with, just as somebody said, 'Paradoxes are what we learn to live with'.

A metaphysical realist believes the world to be not only consisting of particulars but also to be already divided into natural kinds of particulars.

Here we come to our third problem which must be resolved, if we have to defend this sort of realism. There is this much truth in the traditional view that a realist must also admit reality of some universals. This is what Putnam has called the claim about the world that it contains Self-identifying Objects (the term was used by David Wiggins), i.e. 'the *world*, not thinkers, sorts things into kinds'.[13] I do not find this claim to be absurd or unjustified. *One can believe the world to be divided into natural kinds without knowing for certain exactly which are these NATURAL kinds.* We do, of course, try to sort them into kinds, but often go wrong, and, hence, Nyāya accepts fallibilism. We may not have the God's-Eye view, but we cannot deny that there may be such 'a view-from-nowhere'. Realism will be saved if we admit that there are objects in the world that are 'self-identifying' in this sense, even without our fully succeeding to tell exactly what they are and how many kinds there are. This may open up another possibility. The old realist doctrine that there is only one true and complete description of 'the way the world is' may be taken with a pinch of salt. There is one world, although it is possible to have several fairly faithful descriptions of it. For the language in which such descriptions are bound to be given, is a social-cultural fact and hence each description will necessarily tinge the objects described with different socio-cultural colourings or values. This much may be conceded without giving in to full-fledged (Putnamian) internalism where 'objects' are as much products of our conceptual invention as of the *objective* factor in experience. This is also to be distinguished from conceptual relativism or admission of alternative conceptual schemes. For the Davidsonian argument against what he calls the 'third dogma' of empiricism, namely, the dualism of scheme and content, or organizing system and something waiting to be organized, is acceptable to our realist. For it has not been conceded that any language will *distort* reality and that the mind can have a wordless grasp of the uninterrupted reality (a Buddhist position rejected by the Naiyāyikas). I believe there is a latent connection between this third dogma and the idea of the undistorted, wordless grasp of the 'uninterpreted' reality. We have argued that the active and the passive parts of the mind are not separable. Again, description of the world with different socio-cultural tinges does not amount to admission of completely or partially unintertanslatable, separate conceptual schemes. The realist's concession for different socio-cultural colourings is made to make room for effects of social conditioning, explainable disagreements and knowledge of explicable error. As Davidson has said, 'In giving up the dualism of scheme and world, we do not give up the world, but re-establish unmediated touch with the familiar objects whose antics make our sentences, and opinion true or false'.[14]

The above is also a far cry from the kind of pragmatism that Rorty has held. For one thing, it regards realism-idealism controversies as interesting and the coherence and correspondence theories *not* as non-competing trivialities. Besides, it is open to the full force of scepticism and tries to cope with it. The modern version of pragmatism trivializes scepticism, or it maintains a position akin to scepticism without the sceptical worries and emotions. The metaphysical realist (I prefer to call him the 'old-fashioned' realist) *has* the world, as Davidson underlines, and this is not a 'world well lost'. In fact, he can even joke as a cartoonist does, 'To be perfectly honest, I sometimes wish the news were not so factual.'

Notes and References

1. Richard Rorty, *The Consequences of Pragmatism*, Harvester Press, Brighton, 1982, p. xix.
2. Hilary Putnam, *Reason, Truth and History*, Cambridge University Press, Cambridge, 1981.
3. *The Nyāyasūtras of Akṣapāda Gautama*, edited by G. Jha, Poona Oriental Series, Oriental Book Agency, Poona, 1939. See also his Translation.
4. Michael Dummett, 'Common Sense and Physics', in *Perception and Identity*, edited by G.F. Macdonald, Macmillan, London, 1979.
5. Ibid., p. 14.
6. Thomas Nagel, *Mortal Questions*, Cambridge University Press, Cambridge, 1979, p. xii.
7. B.K. Matilal, *Perception*, Clarendon Press, Oxford, 1986, ch. 5.
8. Cf. *vyavahāra.*
9. I have used this terminology in my book, *Perception.* A better terminology for writers in English may be welcome.
10. T.C. *Pratyakṣakhanda*, vol. I, with *Māthuri*, ed. Kamakhyā Nātha Tarkavāgiśá, Calcutta, Asiatic Society, 1897, p. 474.
11. For Strawson's response, see P.K. Sen and R.R. Verma (eds.), *The Philosophy of P.F. Strawson*, ICPR, New Delhi, 1995, pp. 427–9. He says that 'the differences between Matilal's view and my own are, at most, insignificant or merely terminological' [Editor].
12. Gilbert Ryle, *Dilemmas*, Cambridge University Press, Cambridge, pp. 94–5.
13. Putnam, *Reason, Truth and History*, p. 53.
14. Donald Davidson, *Inquiries into Truth and Interpretation*, Clarendon Press, Oxford, 1984, p. 198.

PART III
Indian Buddhism

13

A Critique of the Mādhyamika Position

I. THE MĀDHYAMIKA POSITION—'EMPTINESS'

Suppose a man has committed theft. Another man, who does not, in fact, know whether the first man has committed theft or not, comes along and declares that this is the thief simply because he happens to take a dislike to him. Then, a third man, who has actually seen the first man committing theft, comes along to declare that this is the thief. Now, both the second and the third man make the same assertion about what happened in actuality, but yet the difference between them is very significant and important. It is the distinction between a liar and a truthful person, between falsehood and truth—a discrimination about all that matters in ethics. If we have understood this distinction between the third and the second person, we have then understood something important about a Mādhyamika Buddhist, who declares everything to be empty. This is exactly the way Candrakīrti wanted to explain the distinction between the 'emptiness' doctrine and scepticism, the essential difference between a Mādhyamika and a sceptic.[1]

The above parable, meant to underline the distinction between the 'emptiness' doctrine and scepticism is, in a sense, somewhat superficial and may be even misleading. For it might be argued that the assertion in both the cases is identical and the difference lies merely in what motivated such assertions. Thus, as a report on what is the case, both assertions will enjoy the same 'truth-value'! But this kind of argument only exemplifies how much one can be misled by over-extending the point of a parable. In fact, the usefulness of a parable no longer holds as soon as the relevant point is made. Thus, we have to understand, with great care and caution, the implication of the 'emptiness' doctrine. For it was Nāgārjuna himself who gives the following warning against any misunderstanding of the doctrine: 'Like a snake caught at the wrong end, or like a craft learnt in the wrong manner, the "emptiness" doctrine may destroy the stupid person when it is misunderstood by him!'[2]

The Mādhyamika is critical of all other philosophical systems. He refuses to believe in phenomenal plurality. Thus, his philosophic activity consists mainly in exposing the unjustifiability, and therefore the unreality, of the pluralistic order envisaged by our common experience and thought. That the pluralistic order of the universe is only a convenient myth and lacks essence or *svabhāva* in the ultimate sense is well expressed by the following Laṅkāvatāra verse.[3]

> Since the essence or 'own-nature' of things, when they are critically examined, cannot be established, such things have been declared (by the Buddha) to be inexpressible and without essence.

The Mādhyamika comes very close to the spirit of the Advaitin with regard to his attitude toward phenomenal plurality. But the Advaitin seems to me to be more committed to a metaphysical absolutism in relation to which he seeks to evaluate ordinary thoughts and experience. The Mādhyamika, however, tries to maintain a non-committal attitude in ontology.

The ultimate truth, according to the Mādhyamika, always eludes our ordinary experience and conceptual thought. But it is admitted to be accessible only to a direct but somewhat mystical experience, a sort of penetrating insight or *prajñā*. If this unlocks the door to mysticism in philosophy, my advice is to tolerate it. 'Mysticism', at least 'cognitive mysticism', need not be, it is argued, treated as a derogatory term. For, as we realize more and more the limits of language in our analytical struggle, the idea of something inexpressible may well dawn in our mind although it would be difficult to make a logical appraisal of this 'inexpressible'.

My point is that proper understanding of the Mādhyamika position ought to produce an incentive to strike a middle course between excessive naivete and excessive scepticism. The doctrine of 'emptiness', *śūnyatā*, is usually presented as the critique of all views, all philosophical systems. But the implication of this proposition can be misconstrued in two ways: one by the opponent and the other by the so-called proponent. An opponent might think that the Mādhyamika position amounts to nihilism. But this is wrong. A proponent might, on the other hand, think that the Mādhyamika *disproves* all views, all philosophy. But this too, is, in our opinion, wrong. If anything, the Mādhyamika critique is an attempt to show that it is neither proper nor is it strictly justifiable to regard any particular metaphysical system as absolutely valid. Perhaps in the same vein, T.R.V. Murti has remarked:

> The Mādhyamika dialectic is not refutation;... Refutation is the rejection of an opponent's view by an interested party having a view of his own to establish. A critique is the disinterested analysis of Reason by itself.[4]

Nāgārjuna makes a significant use of the earlier Buddhist doctrine of dependent origination (*pratītyasamutpāda*) to prove the 'emptiness' or 'voidness' of everything. The 'proof' has been summed up by Nāgārjuna as follows:[5]

> Here the dependent origination of things is what (we call) emptiness. Why?—Because it is devoid of 'essence' (or, 'own-being' *svabhāva*). Those things which are dependently originated have no essential nature (i.e., no being of their own), for they lack their essential nature. Why?—Because they are dependent on causes and conditions (*hetu* and *pratyaya*). For, if things existed through their essential nature ('own-being') then they would have existed (or, come into existence) without caring for their causes and conditions. But they do not originate that way. Therefore, they are devoid of their essential nature, and because they are devoid of essential nature, they are called 'empty' (or, 'void' *śūnya*).

Nāgārjuna puts his thesis succinctly as follows:[6]

> Whatever is dependent origination, (is what) we call 'emptiness'. That (again) is (called) dependent designation, (and) That is alone the Middle Way.

Candrakirti says that Nāgārjuna here establishes the following equation,

> Dependent origination = Emptiness = Dependent designation = The Middle Way.

meaning thereby that all these terms in Mādhyamika philosophy refer to the same thing, and are therefore interchangeable.[7]

Candrakīrti further notes that dependent origination is to be understood in this context as the lack of *natural* origination or origination by itself (*svabhāvena anutpādaḥ*). 'What lacks origination-by-itself lacks existence or origination or emergency (*astitva*), and having lacked emergence it lacks disappearance or destruction or non-existence (*nāstitva*).'[8] According to Candrakīrti, 'emptiness' is thus intended for the avoidance of the two extremes, existence or production and non-existence or destruction, and in this way 'emptiness' means the Middle Way.

In short, the Mādhyamika position can be interpreted, even at the risk of oversimplification, as exposing a conflict, or rather a contradiction, between two propositions—one of which we seem to assume *a priori* while the other we derive in some sense from experience. The former is: all beings have their own-being, all things have their 'own nature' or 'essential nature' (*svabhāva*). The latter is: all things are dependently originated. The contradiction between these two can be made obvious with a little bit of explanation. The first proposition implies that own-beings or essential natures cannot be created and hence they do not originate (or perish). In other words, own-being is *independent* and *changeless*. The second proposition implies that all things originate (and perish) through dependence on something or other. In other words, all things have *dependence* and undergo *change*. Now to reconcile the conflict between the two, the Mādhyamika concludes: Therefore, everything is devoid of its own nature, everything is empty.

II. TWO TRUTHS (*DVE SATYE*)

Nāgārjuna says:[9]

> The Buddhas teach *dharma* (the doctrine) by resorting to two truths: One is the conventional or provisional truth, the other is the ultimate truth.
>
> Those who do not comprehend the distinction between these two truths
> Do not comprehend the deep significance in the Buddha's teachings.

The conventional is called *saṁvṛti* or *lokasaṁvṛti*. Candrakīrti deliberates over the etymology of the term *saṁvṛti* and suggests three possible meanings: (i) complete covering or the 'screen' of ignorance which hides truth, (ii) existence or origination through dependence, mutual conditioning, (iii) worldly behaviour or speech behaviour involving designation and designatum, cognition and cognitum.[10] All three meanings reflect three different aspects of what is called *saṁvṛti*, the conventional level.

This doctrine of two truths may not be quite satisfactory to some philosophers. A realist may be rather suspicious of such bifurcation of truths into two levels. Accordingly, this doctrine has been seriously criticized by realistic philosophers like Kumārila and Bhāsarvajña.[11] But such criticism perhaps misses the mark if we do not take into account the soteriological significance of the doctrine.

The Buddha's teaching of the doctrine (*dharma*) may be seen as a claim to find a path (*mārga*), a means, of release or freedom from life's anxieties and frustrations. The first of his four Noble Truths equated life-experiences with pain and suffering. He was a practical teacher well aware of the problem of expressing the truth in a language that will be appropriate and intelligible to the particular hearer and his mental preparedness. It was only natural that a variety of truth statements made by the Buddha on various occasions will appear to be mutually contradictory. The later Buddhist teacher thus faced the problem of explaining away these contradictions by penetrating into the deeper significance of these sayings. Almost by a stroke of genius, these Buddhist teachers, among whom Nāgārjuna was most remarkable, introduced a level-distinction, in fact, a distinction between two levels of truth, the conventional (*saṁvṛti*) truth and the ultimate (*paramārtha*) truth.

This exegetical technique of 'level' distinction (distinction of contextual relevance) may not, however, be altogether novel in the Indian tradition as it might appear to be at first sight. A similar method is reflected in Brahminical exegesis of the Vedic scriptures (which combine the ritualistic injunctions of the Vedas and speculative philosophical questions of the Upaniṣads as one whole 'revealed' body of truth). The Brahminical teacher set the injunctive sections in the context of ritualistic action (*karmakāṇḍa*) where the religious goal is 'heaven' or some such limited end. But the speculative thoughts of the Upaniṣads (in which the same rituals are condemned as superficial and selfish acts) are set by the same Brahminical teacher in the context of a higher knowledge (cf. *parā vidyā* and *aparā vidyā*) with a nobler goal. Thus, *jñāna kāṇḍa* is contrasted with *karmakāṇḍa.*

The immediate purpose of the exegetical technique of distinguishing between two levels of truths is to maintain consistency in the whole body of the Buddha's teachings. But, in the context of the religious philosophy of Nāgārjuna, the affirmation of 'two truths' serves a deeper purpose. The teachings of the Buddha, four noble truths, five 'aggregates', eight-fold path etc., are all in this manner treated as practical advice given by a doctor to a sick person in order to get rid of his sickness, rather than as embodying the highest philosophical truth. As another Buddhist parable puts it, when a man is struck by an arrow and bleeding to death it is only practical and proper, at that instant, to pull the arrow out the administer medical care rather than look for the culprit to punish him or even teach the man how to avoid disaster in the future. Thus, the theory of 'dependent origination' or 'emptiness' (or 'essencelessness') which, according to the Mādhyamika, embodies the highest truth in Buddhism, does not ask one to reject any part of the Buddha's teachings, but to embrace all of them. Thus, Nāgārjuna writes:[12]

> For whom emptiness 'works', everything 'works' for him.
> For whom emptiness does not 'work', nothing 'works' for him.
>
> He who sees dependent origination, sees all these —
> Sufferings, origination, cessation and the path.

Besides, all these, the doctrine of 'two truths' makes the *exposition* of the highest truth, emptiness or essencelessness of everything, possible. The Ultimate Truth is beyond the scope of language. It is, in fact, inexpressible. But only through *indirection* can the Ultimate Reality be brought into relation with conventional means of communication. A discourse on 'emptiness' can be meaningful only in the light of this method of *indirection*. Herein lies the adequacy of the negative dialectic used by the Mādhyamika in his exposition or discourse,—a method already in use by the Upaniṣadic thinkers to communicate their idea of the highest truth. Thus, it has been said.[13]

> The highest truth cannot be taught without recourse to
> conventional language (*vyavahāra*).
> *Nirvāṇa* (Cessation) cannot be realised, if we do not realise
> the highest truth.

It should be conceded that the phenomenal world is not a mere fiction in the sense the 'son of a barren woman' is a mere fiction. The phenomenal world has a provisional existence. If the phenomenal world were a nonentity, all practical activities would have been impossible, and even ethical and spiritual disciplines, would lose their significance. In fact, phenomenal world (and phenomenal experiences) is what should lead us to the realisation of the ultimate truth. The character of the phenomenal world is thus declared to be neither real nor unreal, but logically indeterminable.[14]

III. 'EMPTINESS' AND LOGIC

The Mādhyamika uses philosophic arguments in support of his doctrine of 'emptiness', His 'court of appeal' is what is called *prasaṅga* 'reductio-ad-absurdum' as well as *vyavahāra* 'the common denominator of our phenomenal experience'. A *prasaṅga* type of argument, from which the name Prāsaṅgika is given to the sub-school of Mādhyamika of which Candrakīrti was the chief exponent, can be briefly characterized as follows. It is the argument that moves by extracting contradictory consequences or paradoxical results from the initial proposition or premise. If *P* is a given proposition assumed to be true by the opponent, a Prāsaṅgika-Mādhyamika will try to deduce from it such consequences as will be inconsistent with each other or with the original proposition. This may be called the logical absurdities that a position or a given proposition will lead to.

There is another kind of absurdity which a Prāsaṅgika sometimes tries to expose. Sometimes the deduced consequences of a given proposition run counter to our common phenomenal experiences or some tacit assumptions based upon such common experience. This is what I have called the Prāsaṅgika's appeal to *vyavahāra* as opposed to his appeal to logical contradictions or paradoxes. But in either case, the essence of a *prasaṅga* argument lies in the reduction to some absurd consequences.

In Euclidean geometry, a weaker form of reduction is used. In this system there are certain axioms and there are consequences derivable from such axioms. Here the truth of a theorem (*P*) is demonstrated by deducing from its contradictory (not *P*) absurd consequences inconsistent with the said axiom system. But the theorem is held true as long as the axiom system is held true. For the above argument simply proves that the said theorem and the axioms stand and fall together. Either both are true or both are false. But a *prasaṅga* exposes a proposition to be illegitimate because it has absurd corollaries. In short, *prasaṅga* is a sort of weapon in the hand of the Mādhyamika, the proponent of the 'emptiness' doctrine, by which he tries to demolish other philosophical assertions by exhibiting contradictions latent in them.

But although Nāgārjuna uses *prasaṅga* for destroying the opponent's position almost ruthlessly, his approach in philosophy does not seem to be dogmatic. He keeps the door open for arguments, for evidence and persuasion. He thinks that if the opponent can prove that he is wrong and supply evidence he will be glad to accept it. But since the opponent cannot supply evidence in favour of the unchanging *svabhāva* ('essences' or 'own beings') of things, his point remains. But more on this later.

The doctrine of 'emptiness' gives rise to an interesting paradox, a brief discussion and the stipulated solution of which will be instructive in this connection.[15] If all philosophical theories are 'empty' in the sense of being non-final and hence false then the theory of 'emptiness' is also empty and hence false. To put it in another way, if the Mādhyamika negates all philosophical doctrines on the ground of latent contradictions, his own doctrine can be subjected to the same criticism and shown to involve contradiction. This is how the early Naiyāyikas must have criticized Nāgārjuna. He tried to answer such criticisms in his *Vigrahavyāvartanī*.

The Mādhyamika claims that emptiness is the critique of all views of reality, but is not itself another view of reality. It is not a view of reality simply because it cannot be successfully negated or criticized. One simplified way of understanding the Mādhyamika point is as follows: Suppose *X* stands for reality and *P* is a variable for any view, i.e., a philosophic characterization of reality. The 'emptiness' doctrine says that no matter what *P* may be, it cannot be successfully applied to *X* because if *P* is applied to *X* it can be shown by *prasaṅga* that either *not-P* applies to *X*, or that some other absurdity follows. To negate this position successfully one has to show that there *IS* a *P* which applies to *X* without giving rise to absurdities. The Mādhyamika maintains that as long as such a refutation is not forthcoming, he cannot be persuaded to give up his point. But apart from this philosophic point, the motivation of the Mādhyamika in enunciating the doctrine of 'emptiness' is quite different, as we shall see in the next section.

IV. 'EMPTINESS' AND SOTERIOLOGY

The 'emptiness' doctrine has been propounded in the context of a religious philosophy. Hence we should not lose sight of the soteriological significance of the doctrine. Our ordinary and metaphysical knowledge and our various conceptual formulations are illusory to the extent they are formed with the assumption of an 'essence' or 'own being' (*svabhāva*). This assumption which binds a person to his emotional and conceptual habits is declared as necessarily a wrong assumption, in fact a form of *avidyā* in the context of a religious philosophy that seeks the cessation (*nirodha*) of all worldly sufferings, frustrations and pain, as the highest goal. Just because of this assumption, a man, so the argument goes in this religious philosophy, lives his everyday life in painful awareness of his frustrations. When one seizes something as one's own 'self' or 'soul' or 'essence' and construes some things as existent and other things as non-existent, some things as real and other things as unreal, frustrations due to this false assumption are reinforced all the more and painful mundane existence continues. The 'essencelessness' or 'emptiness' doctrine is supposed to provide the necessary antidote to this painful human existence. It is supposed to administer the change in the attitude necessary for overcoming the delusions about pain and for grasping the highest insight (*prajñā*). It is said to reveal the distinction between the *finality* and *non-finality* of purposes, between the *absolute* and the *relative* goals, between the conventional and the ultimate truths.

It should be noted that the Mādhyamika argument for 'emptiness' by using *prasaṅga* or the negative dialectic seeks to make a positive contribution, to provide an insight into the highest truth. At the same time, it helps to break our mental and emotional attachment to phenomenal realities. In fact, this negative dialectic is complementary to meditational practice to bring home the realization of the ultimate truth.

When the ultimate truth dawns in the mind, the 'emptiness' doctrine does not appear as a separate doctrine or viewpoint. Emptiness is the critique of all views, but itself is not another view. Thus, Nāgārjuna writes:

> If something were non-empty, something would also be empty. But nothing is non-empty, so how will something be empty?
>
> The victorious one (the Buddha) proclaimed the emptiness of all views. But those who take 'emptiness' to be a view, are called 'incurable (persons)'.[16]

Candrakīrti cites another parable in this connection. If a man goes to the shop to buy something, but the shop-keeper tells him, 'Look, there is nothing to sell, so I can give you nothing,' and if that man says, 'All right, then, please give me that *nothing,*' it becomes difficult to remove his delusion about buying. In the same manner, if someone thinks 'emptiness' to be a view (*dṛṣṭi*), his delusion is difficult to cure. Candrakīrti goes on to quote a *sūtra* reporting the dialogue between the Buddha and Kāśyapa:[17]

> 'O Kāśyapa, it is far better to resort to the 'soul' doctrine than to regard 'emptiness' as a view.'
>
> 'Why so?'
>
> Emptiness, O Kāśyapa, is the means of breaking away from, or getting out of, (*niḥsaraṇa*) all views. But if someone takes emptiness to be a view, I call him incurable. Suppose, Kāśyapa, someone is sick. The doctor gives some medicinal herb to him. And that medicinal herb, after removing all other 'defects' in the system, does not itself get out of the system. What do you think now, Kāśyapa? Will that man be relieved of sickness?
>
> Certainly not, O Honourable one. If that medicinal herb, after removing all defects of the system, does not itself get out of the system, then that man will be even more sick.
>
> The Honourable One said, 'In this manner, O Kāśyapa, emptiness is the means of "getting out" of all views. But if someone takes emptiness to be a view, I call him to be incurable.'

Thus, emptiness should, under no condition, be construed as a view (*dṛṣṭi*) or a position. It has the therapeutic value of curing delusions originating from all sorts of views or positions. When all such delusions are cured, emptiness vanishes into non-emptiness, *saṁsāra* vanishes into *nirvāṇa* and vice versa.

To take a position, or accept a point of view, in the undifferentiated totality, is to introduce a false distinction between that position and the rest of the whole. The therapeutics of 'emptiness', negative dialectic and meditation-practice of Buddhism are supposed to bring this point home. As soon as one is home, and totality is revealed, it would be foolish to construe 'emptiness' as a position. Thus, emptiness is the means by which our deepest delusions are purged out of our system whereupon the 'emptiness' doctrine resolves itself into the highest wisdom, the *Prajñāpāramitā*. Nāgārjuna describes it by eight Negatives (cancelling one another):[18]

> No cessation, no origination; no destruction, no permanence;
> no non-differentiation, no differentiation; no coming in,
> no going out.

It is said to be the state of perfect equilibrium, where all mutual forces are at rest. It is *śiva*, the state of perfect freedom, joy and bliss.

Notes and References

1. *Prasannapada*, 368.
2. MK. xxiv.11.
3. *Saddharmalaṅkāvatārasūtra*, 2/173; 10/167.
4. Murti, T.R.V., *The Central Philosophy of Buddhism*, Unwin, London 1953.
5. *Vigrahavyāvartanī* (ed. by E.H. Johnston and A. Kunst), *Mélanges chinois et bouddhiques*, ix, 99–152, 1951. Verse 22ff.
6. MK. xxiv.18.
7. Matilal, B.K., *Epistemology, Logic and Grammar in Indian Philosophical Analysis*, Mouton, The Hague/Paris, 1971, pp. 148–51.
8. *Prasannapadā*, 504.
9. MK. xxiv.8, 9.
10. *Prasannapadā*, 493.
11. B.K. Matilal, op. cit., 152–4.
12. MK. xxiv.14, 40.
13. MK. xxiv.10.
14. B.K. Matilal, op. cit., 155–7.
15. Ibid., pp. 158–62.
16. MK. xxiii.7, 8.
17. *Prasannapadā*, 248, 249.
18. *Prasannapadā*, 3.

14

Nyāya Critique of the Buddhist Doctrine of Non-soul

INTRODUCTION

Is there a soul apart from the body? It is an old, old question. This was one of the famous ten questions recorded in the Pali Canons. It has been asked in many other forms throughout the history of philosophy, east and west. Is there a person independent of the psychophysical complex? Recently this question has received renewed attention in the context of moral philosophy, thanks to Derek Parfit. Parfit's fundamental idea has been to convince moral philosophers today that much less is involved in being a particular person than we ordinarily assume, and that this shedding of ontological load, to some extent at least, ought to make us less concerned with ourselves and more receptive to a broadly utilitarian outlook that emphasizes the well-being of mankind as a whole.

A Buddhist would have been naturally delighted. For the original idea of Buddhism was to convince its followers that there is no ego or self or soul for whose pleasure or happiness we yield to the 'thirst' for becoming and perpetuate the cycle of suffering. This conviction is supposed to pave the way for the right style of living with right attitudes, right beliefs and thoughts, which, in turn, would facilitate the realization of *nirvāna* at the end. It may be noted that the kind of altruistic ethics which receives support from the Buddhist doctrine of complete egolessness can paradoxically receive similar support from the diametrically opposite doctrine of Advaita Vedānta, according to which every soul is identical with the One, the Universal Soul, distinction between one and the other being only an illusory appearance. If the distinction between self and others 'evaporates' in this way, then any self-regarding action becomes other-regarding and vice-versa, for the self here becomes all-pervasive, inclusive of all others. There will arise obviously some problems here, but

I am not going to go into them in this context. (Some interesting ideas along this line have been recently developed by Dr R.C. Gandhi).

The aim of the Buddhist or the Vedāntist however was directly different from the altruistic goal of the utilitarian philosopher. But there may be a remote resonance. In later Buddhist thought, the concept of a soul as a metaphysical entity was elaborately refuted. All other schools of Indian philosophy (except the Cārvākas, of course) believe in the metaphysical reality of the soul, although each have a different notion about its ultimate nature as well as about how it is or could be shown to exist. Śālikanātha[1] in AD eight century noted the following variety of views regarding the metaphysics of personhood. According to Advaita Vedānta, the self is identical with the one Universal Soul which inhabits every individual's body: the others (Nyāya, Sāṃkhya Yoga, Mīmāṃsā and Jainism) accept plurality and assign a separate self to each individual. Besides, many believe that the soul has a size or magnitude. Some contend that it is atomic, others say that it has a medium size (like the body), still others that each soul is an all-pervading ubiquitous entity. For Naiyāyikas and Prābhākaras, the self is inferable on the basis of evidence. For Bhāṭṭas and some Naiyāyikas, its existence is directly known through our inner perception. Others (Sāṃkhya, etc.) claim that the self is self-revealing. For the Jainas, the self is revealed in the *Kevala-jñāna* 'pure awareness' of the saints.

The ethico-religious doctrine of Buddhism, in spite of its radical difference in the metaphysics of self-hood from other Indian schools, should not be supposed to be very different or unique. In fact it is of a piece with the general, pan-Indian ethico-religious attitude. The structural affinity is unmistakable. The ultimate goal is the cessation of suffering; the means to achieve it must be a particular set of ethico-religious practices coupled with the real knowledge of the nature of the self. For the Buddhist, self-hood consists in a conglomerate and a realization of this knowledge must inform his religious practices directed towards the state of *nirvāṇa*. For others, self-hood constitutes a separate entity from body, mind, senses, etc., and such a realization must influence their ethico-religious activities.

Udayana[2] in the beginning of his *Ātmatattvaviveka* has underlined two types of 'doctrinal agreement' (*ekavākyatā*) among all schools of philosophy in India. First, cessation of the universal experience of suffering is possible through a means, and that means is, by universal consent, the knowledge of the truth or 'thatness' (or 'what it is all about') (*tattva*). Second, all agree that the natural or normal way of understanding the self does not constitute the required knowledge of the truth. The Buddhist will have to know the nature of self-hood in order to understand how this composite entity is to be dissolved in his vision of the *nairātmya* doctrine. The others will have to know how and in what way it could fit in their individual doctrines for achieving cessation of suffering.

1. THE UNDECIDABLE QUESTIONS

The Buddha's doctrine of non-soul can be seen to be related to one of the 'undecidable' *avyākṛta* questions. It may be that the Buddha did not intend to accept the stronger thesis. For '*avyākṛta*', though it has sometimes been translated as 'unanswerable' (Jayatilleke, p. 472) or 'inexpressible' (Murti, P. 36), should literally mean 'unexplained' or 'unanswered' (also Jayatilleke, p. 471). If we say 'these question cannot be answered', this seems to be a stronger claim. Today it may not be surprising to claim that some philosophical questions, the deepest and oldest of them, 'have no solutions' (Nagel, p. xii). For they show us the limits of our understanding. I believe the present question falls into this category. Whether answerable or not, this question is definately askable. It is not an unreal question.

Regarding the Buddha's questions, however, we may say that they do not have any easy answer, or that there is no definite or straight-forward answer to them. In free translations the ten 'unanswered' questions would be (according to another count there were fourteen such questions):

1. Is the world (universe) eternal?
2. Is it impermanent?
3. Is it infinite?
4. Is it finite?
5. Is the person (soul) identical with the body?
6. Is it different from the body?
7. Does Tathāgata exist after death?
8. Does he not exist after death?
9. Does he both exist and not exist after death?
10. Does he neither exist nor not exist after death?

(*Majjhima nikāya, Culamalmkya-sutta*)

Another formulation of questions 5–6 is:

Does he who acts also 'enjoy' (i.e. get reward and punishment)?
Is he who acts different from the 'enjoyer' of reward and punishment?

We cannot dismiss all these questions as unimportant. At least the pair 5–6 has not lost its relevance today. Even when we say that these are not important questions today we cannot deny that they are at least very disturbing, particularly because while no definite and decisive answers are easily available we feel that there must be some answers that will be true. There can be in fact several possible answers but such answers are often in conflict with each other. Accordingly philosophers over the ages have tried to give persuasive *a priori* arguments and/or find some plausible evidence in favour of one answer or the other. But such evidence often amounts to only plausible evidence, and *a priori* arguments are often inconclusive. Thus as philosophical argumentation goes, the rival view may gather equally plausible evidence and persuasive argument. Hence an *avyākṛta* may imply that there is no decidable answer.

We may set aside the question regarding survival after death. Most religious traditions believe in some form of 'post-mortem' existence. This is even true of Buddhism even though the doctrine of a surviving *soul* is explicitly rejected. What survives physical death is said to be the left-over *karma* (called also *saṃskāra*) which acts in conjunction with the congenital or 'beginningless misconception' (*avidyā*), and these become the condition for the consciousness series to be connected with another physical body series. This misconstrued personality series is exhausted only at *nirvāṇa*. This part of the Buddhist doctrine will not concern us in the present discussion. The question whether he who acts is the same as he who 'enjoys' is however deemed much more fundamental for any ethical or religious system. It seems undeniable that human actions, at least most of them, presuppose a sort of personal identity or at least a continuity which must be at the same time distinct from all other similar continuities. Otherwise nobody would sow the seed for others to reap the harvest. But this does not conclusively settle the question whether we (the person) are separately existing entities, over and above our bodies, sense-faculties and mind, over and above the causally connected series of physical and mental events. The non-Buddhist philosophers usually believe that persons are separately existing although about the nature of such entities, as I have already noted, there is a variety of views propounded by them. The Buddhist answer is of course that there are no such entities, for the concept of a person is easily analysable into physical and mental constituents—a set of five aggregates.

2. THE SĀṂKHYA THEORY OF TWENTY-FOUR ELEMENTS

A proto-Sāṃkhya analysis of a person may be given as follows. We may break a person into five sense-faculties, five organs of action, five sensory objects (the sense-givens), five elemental substances to be accessible only through the sense-given, and three other faculties which roughly constitute what we ordinarily call *mind*. The primary constituent of the mind is called *buddhi*, 'intellect', also called the 'great soul' or the 'great reality', the second constituent is 'I' awareness or *ahaṃkāra*, the third is a mental faculty through which the inner perceptions are received. These three constituents are distinguished by their separate functions, and taken together they constitute the psychological life of the person. All these twenty-three are then said to be the evolutes of the original unmanifest matter or the 'chief' (*pradhāna*). These twenty-four elements are supposed to exhaust the description of the person, although it remains complete only if we think that this is a mechanical analysis to which no purpose, no teleology has been added. Why does the 'chief' or the 'unmanifest' matter evolve the way it does? This question, if it is raised at all (and surely it was raised, as the history of Sāṃkhya philosophy undoubtedly shows), will make us recognize that our former description of the person has not been properly exhaustive. In other words, those who are inclined to raise such questions feel that something, in fact something very important, has been left out in our previous analysis of the person into its constituents. The material constituents of the person work in the way they do work, they are arranged in the way they are in fact arranged, because there is also a spiritual constituent of the person which transcends these material constituents and whose purpose the latter are trying to fulfil. The set of the material constituents are found in conglomeration (it is a *saṃghāta*). Similarly a chariot, a bedstead or a house, is a conglomeration. It is argued that usually such conglomerations are designed to serve some end. But the conglomerate itself can hardly *have* a purpose of its own. The bed serves the sleeper, its chariot the driver. Hence the need for admitting a spiritual constituent called *puruṣa*. In this way the Sāṃkhya theory has been allegedly rounded up, although it has generated an internal tension in the system which has been variously explained and resolved by successive philosophers.

The alleged internal tension of the Sāṃkhya theory is not our present concern. The Buddha (see Aśvaghoṣa) found it very unsatisfactory. For one thing, it was pointed out that if the spirtual constituent has to be admitted it would be almost impossible to explain the actual relationship between the two, their involvement or the entanglement of the spirit by the material constituents. If the entanglement cannot be explained, we cannot explain how and why the spirit could actually be free. For another, there does not seem to be any necessity for the conglomerate to have a purpose or to be guided by some purpose or teleology. Hence the Bud-dha's attempt was to knock down this spiritual constituent (called variously, *puruṣa, ātman*, soul, self) and remodel the description of the person, or suggest some alternative models, which he did in terms of five aggregates, or twelve bases or 18 base-elements (*pañca skandha, dvādaśāyatana, aṣṭādaśadahātu*).

We may note a couple of points before we leave the Sāṃkhya view. First, it is significant that within the material evolutes are included what we understand ordinarily by mental states and mental properties. Even the mental substrate, *buddhi* is said to be the first 'subtle' evolute of the unmanifest inert matter. Hence the usual opposition between the mental and the material has to be given up on this view. They do not constitute two different ontological categories or two different substances. Each of these material elements is characterized by some sort of activity. Causation is conceived here as only making explicit what was implicit before, manifestation of the unmanifest, modification of the appearances. On this view, therefore, the mental and the non-mental have a common origin, the 'chief', which proves that both have a material essence.

According to this style of philosophizing, many modern questions would seem to be irrelevant or unnecessary. The usual assumption of the mind-body dichotomy is avoided. There is no need to step into what is usually known as Cartesian dualism if we do not go into the spiritual constituent. And this spiritual constituent may very well be like the Kantian idea of a person, which explains the unity of a mental life, or Strawson's idea of a person as a primitive unanalysable concept. But this is arguable. The above also avoids the question whether epiphenomenalism is true, that is, whether mental properties can be causally idle. In other words, the above Sāṃkhya view seems to escape between the two horns of the dilemma, Cartesian dualism and mind-body identity theory. Instead of worrying about the relation, or the lack of relation, causal or non-causal, between consciousness and corporeal stuff, Sāṃkhya saw both as evolving out of a common causal source.

I concede that the above way of looking at Sāṃkhya is somewhat unorthodox and hence open to criticism. But my point now is to provide a philosophical background for the origin of the no-soul doctrine in Buddhism. So the lack of historical accuracy may be compensated by philosophical adequacy.

3. THE BUDDHIST WAY

When we consider the Buddhist analysis of a person we cannot but be struck by the resemblances with as well as the difference from the Sāṃkhya analysis. The proto-Sāṃkhya view is closer. But the fundamental difference emerges as we see that the Buddhist prefers to explain the phenomena of change and continuity as explicitly non-purposeful and mechanical. Unlike the Sāṃkhya, the Buddhist initially not only does not believe there to be any unchanging core or material essence underlying the ever-changing appearances, he also denies there to be any goal, telos, ends, purposes or values by which the ever-changing reality is ordered. Hence the question which led the Sāṃkhya to the doctrine of the spiritual constituent or soul was directly rejected by Buddhism as useless. Change is regarded here as the built-in nature of reality. It is automatic, non-purposeful, unteleological. A mechanical analysis of the concept of a person and an explanation of its continuity was deemed quite sufficient and satisfactory in Buddhism.

Like Sāṃkhya, Buddhism was also concerned with the origin of suffering and its cessation. The origin of *duḥkha* was located in desires, propensities to pleasures, etc., propensity to becoming. The roots of such desires were located in the psychophysical complex that we call the person. There cannot be any desire unless it is involved with notions of 'I' and 'mine' (*ahaṃkāra mamakāra*) '. . . desires . . .' etc. are two-place predicates, and hence require both a subject and an object to function. We must also note that in this metaphysical sense of desire, it is never set at rest permanently or allowed to cease finally through satisfaction or fulfilment. It is like fire that will burn as long as the fuel is supplied. Hence to destroy or completely eliminate it we can do either of two things. We may show that the objects of desire are only illusions. They are hollow or empty or do not exist. Or we may show that the subject is an illusion, does not exist. In fact the second way is the more radical way—a way that was first chalked out by the Buddha. In fact the claim is that the second way is also superior in the sense that it is infallible. It would be logically impossible to maintain the reality of a desire once we are convinced of the truth that the subject does not exist. It would be logically impossible for us to be attached to something if there is a discovery that there is nobody, no subject, who is supposed to be attached to the objects. If on the other hand we are shown that the objects of our desire are illusions, *māyā*, or magic objects, we can still be attached to or desire them, for even the 'dream' objects can satisfy the 'dream' desire and the run for it cannot be easily given up.

The Buddhist way was to say there is no real subject, no real 'I'. There is only a conglomerate of five aggregates, each element of which is pushing ahead on its own, but which jointly falsely create a sense of unity that plays the role of the subject. The continuity or flow of these five phenomenal series allows for the identity of the person over time. If the liberating insight shatters the unity of the subject in this way, desire etc. are thereby shattered altogether. And if the unity of the subject is lost into the multiplicity of fluctuating phenomena, the object to be grasped by perceptions and intended by desires, etc. are also automatically shattered into phenomenal pieces. In other words the Buddhist phenomenalism or the world-view that envisions a world of ever fluctuating phenomenal particulars is of a piece with the Buddhist view of no-soul or 'no unified subject'. The deep philosophical lesson that presents itself is this: if the unity of the subject is shattered, can the shattering of the unity of the objects and the objective world be far behind? There may also be, arguably, a clue here to the resolution of the 'subjective-objective' controversy. Objectivity requires persistence of a subject standing apart and 'grasping' objects. To argue for the latter in the absence of the former would be pointless.

We may derive another philosophical insight here. Some years ago when the terminology of sense-data was introduced in the discussion of the problem of perception and the perceived world, a controversy gradually became prominent: are these data material or mental? No straightforward answer to this question was found to be wholly acceptable. If we follow the Buddhist view here and dismiss the notion of the unity of the subject, it would seem that this sharp line of demarcation between physical and mental phenomena would disappear, and a sort of neutral monism would emerge. Each phenomenon would be a momentary flash and a series of similar flashes would be called continuity. On this view, the physical phenomena would be as much dependent upon the mental phenomena as the mental upon the physical. Strictly speaking, this view maintains that there are some neutral fundamental elements called *dharma*, out of which both mind and matter originate. It is significant to note that there is a distant resonance here of the view developed by William James and Bertrand Russell at some point, which was called neutral monism, which held that sense-data and images constitute a kind of neutral stuff, neither mental nor physical.

James put forward this view in his article 'Does 'consciousness' Exist?' in 1904. He described the subject as 'the name of a non-entity', 'a mere echo, faint rumour left behind by the disappearing 'soul' upon the air of philosophy'. This persuaded Russell to abandon the relational theory of sensation and propound a theory called neutral monism. Russell argued that so long as the 'subject' was retained there would be a 'mental' entity to which there was nothing analogous in the material world, but if sensation were only occurrences and not essentially relational in character, there would not be the same need to regard mental and physical occurrences as fundamentally different. On this theory, a sensation may be grouped with a number of other occurrences by a memory-chain, in which case it becomes part of a mind; or it may be grouped with its causal antecedents, in which case it appears as part of the physical world. This does not resolve all the traditional problems connected with the dualism of mind and matter. But Russell embraced it because it went a long way towards a resolution. The Buddhist position is not exactly the same as held by Russell and James. But the point was to illustrate that one of the consequences of adopting the view that the 'subject' is a logical fiction, not one of the actual ingredients of the world, is that one is led to not only phenomenalism but also a sort of non-dualism as far as the mind-matter dichotomy is concerned.

4. ANALYSIS OF SELF

The Buddhist analysis of self is usually given in three different ways. The three analyses are somewhat independent of each other. The first and the most common one is in terms of five aggregates or groups of elements which are also in perpetual flux themselves.

Table I: Groups

1. Aggregate of material forms or visible forms (*rūpa*) (This covers the physical elements.)
2. Aggregate of feelings
3. That of perceptions
4. That of dispositions or (mental) forces
5. That of awareness or consciousness in general.

We should note that there is no sharp line of demarcation between material and mental in this classificatory table. The theory states that a member of any group is in perpetual flux, it is by nature conditioned by members of all groups in the previous moment and is in its turn a conditioning factor of any member of all the groups in the following moment. Each is also connected with a member of its own kind by a causal nexus.

Table II: Bases

1. Faculty of vision	7. Colour and shape
2. Faculty of hearing	8. Sounds
3. Faculty of smelling	9. Odours
4. Faculty of taste	10. Tastes
5. Faculty of touch	11. Objects of touch
6. Faculty of mind	12. 'mindable' objects (64 *dharmas*, according to Vasubandhu)

Note here that nos. 1–5 and 7–1 1 are only detailed elements comprising the aggregate of material forms, i.e., no. 1 in Table I. Nos. 2–4 in the former table (I) is comprised under no. 12. There is however no real agreement among the schools whether no. 6 in Table II gives a real *dharma* or it is given simply for the sake of symmetry. 'Mindable' objects comprise an assortment of entities, volitions, feelings, birth, decay and even the unconditional elements such as space.

Table III: Base Elements

1-12: Same as before	13. Visual awareness
	14. Auditory awareness
	15. Olfactory awareness
	16. Gustatory awareness
	17. Tactile awareness
	18. Mental awareness

It is clear that Table III distinguishes the sensory objects from their respective awareness (sensations), while Table II combines them as one. But both tables are evaluated in the same way. It is not said that one is more fundamental or basic than the other. It is only an *upāya kauśalya* of the Buddha.

5. PHILOSOPHICAL ARGUMENT

We may now look at some philosophical arguments given in favour of these views, the Buddhist and the non-Buddhist. Belief in a soul apart from the body is very commonplace. Belief in the identity of the person, or the self is even more commonplace. Usually an argument against a well-known belief or a pervasive view takes the form of a challenge. The Buddhist, in proposing elimination of such a belief, went apparently against the wind. The main part of his argument consisted in plausible explanation of such apparently overwhelming evidence as points towards the separate existence of the self. Bits of such evidence are presumably unity of consciousness, memory, recognition of the previously experienced objects, self consciousness, motivated and sustained activity by us for future results, and so on. The Buddhist strategy is to deny the evidencehood of such phenomena for proving the thesis that there is a self apart from the psychophysical complex. His further strategy is to show that the acceptance of the 'soul' thesis would lead to absurd and undesirable consequences (*prasaṅga*).

I shall gloss over the first part of this strategy as far as this paper is concerned. Literature on it is quite substantial.[3] Instead I shall comment on the latter part. In order to do that, unfortunately, I have to introduce some banalities to clarify the nature of a philosophical argument as it was understood in the Indian *pramāṇa* theory. To prove that something does not exist is the hardest thing on earth. This is not simply because the apparent dilemma provides only an air of paradox that can be easily blown off. The difficulty lies at a much deeper level. That is why in spite of all the atheistic argument against God, theism has persisted. For each such argument has proven to be finally inconclusive. Theism therefore enjoys the benefit of doubt. This does not mean that to prove that something exists is in any way easier. Some philosophers have taken the question 'why is there something rather than nothing?' to be a fundamental question of metaphysics (Heidegger, for example). Others have maintained that this is not a proper question, i.e., it is ill-formed and meaningless, while still others think that it may be impossible to answer yet it is an inescapable question (Nozick). But this is not exactly the point here. I have noted that if it is almost impossible to show that something does not exist (unless it is obviously the case that it does not exist), it is equally difficult even to show that something exists, if it is not obviously so. Of course to prove the existence of something is not as baffling as to prove the non-existence of something.

To prove that *x* exists we have to have some evidence, an evidence that is logically connected with existence of *x*. Perception can be an evidence for the thing perceived, provided however, this perception amounts to what is called a *pramā*, a veridical perception. The old theory of evidence, or what is called the *pramāṇa-śāstra* in the Indian tradition, states that there are broadly speaking at least two kinds of evidence; direct, call it 'perception' (or *pratyakṣa*); indirect, call it the evidential, or inferential sign (*liṅga*) which leads to the knowledge of something besides itself. If God exists, or if *x* exists, we can prove that it exists either by direct evidence or by indirect evidence, i.e., an inferential sign. Observation, which in this context is only another name for perception or direct evidence, is the best evidence, provided it is a true one and we are not suffering from illusion, delusion, hallucination, mass hypnosis, etc. Hence if one can see God in this sense, then there must exist a God whom one sees. Further, if I see a ghost, I mean I *really see* it, then it, he or she must exist. Besides it must be admitted to be a perceptible object. But most objects, God, soul, ghost, spirit atom, power, etc. about which we raise controversy because we are in doubt, are not perceptible objects, at least not so in the ordinary sense. They are not directly evident. Hence let us note that while true perception or observation may establish existence of something, non-perception, or simple lack of observational evidence cannot establish non-existence. (This is how Udayana argued on a similar occasion in *Nyāyakusumāñjali*, Chapter III.) For this reason we admit indirect evidence or inferential signs for many important objects which we do believe to be there. We adduce indirect evidence even for many important beliefs we hold to be true. The logical evidence or sign must be critically examined to see whether it is logically faultless. This is not quite enough. For the concept of logical adequacy or faultlessness may be defined in various ways. A set of conditions or requirement are usually mentioned to ensure their adequacy or soundness. Sometimes a logical sign or reason may meet the requirements of adequacy or faultlessness, but may still lead to a belief that a found to be false. To avoid such problems, one needs to add such further conditions as that there is no other conceivable explanation of the cited evidence ('sign' = *liṅga*) besides its being logically connected with what is being proved and that there is no stronger evidence (direct or otherwise) to prove just the contrary.

The above way of characterising the inferential evidence was an issue among the *pramāṇa* theorists of India, and the details of it were disputed between the Nyāya and the Buddhist. Let us note further that this notion of logical evidence makes it also a 'positive' evidence in the sense that it is supposed to prove either the existence of something or truth of some belief, and only indirectly can it show that the contrary is not the case. We can call it the 'negative' evidence when it shows in this way that something is not the case. Besides these two types of evidence, philosophers often use what I shall call *a priori* arguments. Here we may note that to prove that something does not exist it is often expedient to show that admission of its existence or truth of the belief held leads necessarily to absurdities or inconsistent beliefs. The atheist therefore finds it convenient to show that the concept of God leads to inconsistency, and similarly the non-soulist or the Buddhist would like to show that the concept of soul leads to conflicting consequences. This type of argument is called the *prasaṅga* argument in the Indian tradition. But the theory of evidence or Indian *pramāṇa-śāstra* has made very little room for a *pirori* reasoning unless it is also directly or indirectly supported by a doctrine of evidence, i.e., empirical evidence, or it serves an important purpose for the theory of evidence itself.

The theory of evidence outlined here is primarily conceived as 'supporting' evidence that proves or establishes something. It can also be conducive to the notion of 'confirmatory' evidence, provided the belief in question has another *prima facie* evidence to support it. I shall refer to two important arguments variously cited to prove that a person is a separate, persisting entity. One is based upon the phenomenon of *pratisandhāna* and memory, which requires a persistent entity amidst the ever fluctuating factors. The other re-describes mental events as properties or qualities, i.e., locatees, and then argues for a substratum of them. The Buddhist has faulted both these inferences in their own ingenious way. Both these inferences are supposed to be based upon a *vyāpti*, i.e., a concomitant relationship between the 'evidential' property and the 'concluding' property, between what is adduced as evidence and what is proven. Such a relationship cannot be known *a priori*, hence we need empirical evidence to support it, i.e., an undisputed example for the co-incidence of the two properties, 'evidential' and 'concluding'.

Now we can see the limitation of the theory of evidence that has been delineated above. The supposed example must be undisputed in the sense that it must lie outside the scope of the conclusion, i.e., fall outside the cases that are to be covered by the inference. Hence presumably on this theory, I cannot prove that all human beings are rational on the basis of their being human, for to cite the empirical example in support of the concomitant relation between humanity and rationality, I have to consider the case of some human being. But this I cannot do because it is already included within the scope of what I am trying to establish: a truth about all humans. This of course does not preclude the possibility of the belief that all humans are rational being accepted as a piece of definition (*lakṣaṇa*) or an inductive generalisation. But this will raise many intricate logical issues which I wish to skip in this context.

The Buddhist has argued that both inferences are directly or indirectly based upon some sort of concomitant relationship, but a knowledge of such a relationship cannot be empirically derived from the citation of an undisputed example of the required sort. For instance, we cannot talk about memory and *pratisandhāna* in the strict sense (take machine 'memories' as figurative uses) without talking about a psychophysical complex; which is already to be covered by the scope of the inferential conclusion. Similarly an example of a mental episode is always associated with a body or a 'mind-body' complex and hence it cannot show that the person is a separately existing entity. Technically, the fault is called *sādhyasama*, where the evidencehood of the adduced evidence has not been established beyond a shadow of doubt. To put it simply, our concept of memory presupposes the concept of a persistent person, and hence cannot be used to prove its existence. Besides, what is ordinarily called 'memory' can be explained away in such a way as would neither presuppose nor entail the identity of the person as a persisting entity.

Denial of a persistent self leads to many problems such as explanation of memory and recollection, sustained and motivated activity for further results and unity of consciousness. The Buddhist has provided alternative models for explaining all these phenomena without assuming or presupposing the soul. Very generally, they are explained on the basis of *causal* relations ('causal' being defined in the Buddhist sense of *pratyaya*) in the 'stream' of the same psychophysical states (*kāya-citta-santāna*). Even transmigration is explained without assuming the existence of a persistent entity to transmigrate.

I shall refer to another powerful argument of the Buddhist. This seeks to prove that the very conception of a persistent, permanent entity called soul leads necessarily to inconsistent beliefs, to absurdities. This is the *prasaṅga* type of argument that I alluded to earlier.[4] All the ethico-religious systems (including Buddhism) believe in the doctrine of some sort of human bondage and freedom. In this background, the Buddhist argument can be presented very roughly in this form. If bondage (i.e., desires, pursuit of desire, resultant anguish, sufferings, thirst, etc.) is a *necessary* and *essential* property of the independently existing person then that person can never be free from it, for nothing can exist without its 'own nature' or essential properties. If the person on the other hand is by nature free, he would never have been affected by bondage. In other words, the fact of bondage runs counter to the conception of a permanent soul which should be, by definition, free and independent. Vasubandhu has therefore said in the beginning of the ninth chapter of *Abhidharmakośabhāṣya* where the 'self' is being examined: 'In any other theory that accepts a permanent soul, there cannot be any freedom possible.'

The concept of a person may very well be reduced to the 'stream' or the series (*santāna*) of the psychophysical complex. Different phenomena which presuppose a single persistent entity called soul can somehow be explained under a different model which would be free from such presupposition. This can certainly make the assumption of a soul metaphysically superfluous.

Udayana in AD eleventh century has tried to give an elaborate defence of the Nyāya doctrine of the Self against the Buddhist attack. He thinks that the reality of the self as an entity is threatened by at least four major metaphysical doctrines. 1. The flux doctrine or exclusive phenomenalism. 2. Indecision about the reality of the external world or immaterialism, 3. Non-distinctness of the quality from the qualified substances or the sub-stratum. 4. Simple empiricism or lack of any empirical proof. The

Naiyāyika would argue that neither the flux doctrine (i.e. extreme phenomenalism), nor the 'consciousness only' doctrine (or idealism or Buddhist immaterialism), can be maintained without running into problems. A sort of robust realism dictates that the substance or the substratum must be distinguished from the features, properties or qualities it holds. This would require a substratum for the so-called *mental* episodes and dispositions, awareness, desires, preferences, etc., and the body, because of its continuously changing nature, cannot be regarded as adequate for such a substratumhood. Lack of empirical proof has already been noted earlier. The Nyāya answers by constructing several proofs, a detailed analysis of which has enriched the philosophical literature of India over the centuries.[5] I will refer to a couple of age-old arguments.

Udayana first asserts that direct perception should be enough to supply the proof for the separate existence of the self. But then he says: '*kaḥ punar atra nyāya? pratisandhānam.*' Thus he believes that a proper analysis of *pratisandhāna* would be potent enough to establish the reality of self-hood. He continues 'What is it? It is the regular occurrence of cause and effect in one stream of awareness.' But this is to be understood, not in the Buddhist way, but as a certitude regarding the unity of the agency of the successive mental acts or awareness events. We cannot say the successive mental events are only causally related and hence appear (falsely) to belong to one substratum. For then the teacher's knowledge (a case of a mental event) being causally related to the student's knowledge would also have caused the (false) notion of the identity of the two continuous series. The debate continues for a long time and towards the end some analysis of the notion of *pratisandhāna* is extracted so as to justify the inference of the unity of the substratum (agency) for the causally related awareness-episode.

The other well-entrenched argument of the Nyāya school is that the soul-substance is a necessary prerequisite for locating such 'mental' phenomena (the so-called 'soul's' attributes) as desire, awareness, hate, pleasure and pain. The origin or occurrence of these phenomena can neither be located in the senses, nor in the body. They do not belong, on this theory, even to the 'mind'. For 'mind' or *manas* (and there is a terminological problem here) in the Nyāya vocabulary, which follows in general, the linguistic intuition of Sanskrit, stands for the 'instrument' for acquiring beliefs (awareness), desires, pleasures, etc., just as the outer sense-faculty, the eye, is the 'instrument' for visual perception. Thus it may be advisable to translate *manas* in its technical sense as the inner faculty or the 'inner sense' for sensing pleasure, pain, etc. That which is a mere instrument can be neither an agent nor a locus. A telescope, for example, is an instrument by which one sees, it does not see by itself, nor can seeing belong to, or be located in, it. Using such 'eliminative inference' (technically sometimes called *śeṣavat*, elimination of the available alternatives, senses, body and mind), Nyāya argues in favour of positing an additiional and distinct entity, a soul-substance, which standing apart, acts as both the causal substrate of such so-called 'mentally originating' phenomena, desire, etc., and the agent of such psychological verbs, desires, believes, knows, etc. An additional argument in support is what is called parsimony or simplicity. For acceptance of a separate entity here makes it simpler to account for various other matters, personal identity, continuity, unity of consciousness, memory, etc.

The situation seems to be as follows. Whether we admit the person to be a separate entity or not, it is incumbent upon us to rationalize our beliefs, our faith and make our experience or observational data compatible with such beliefs. But this can be done in a number of ways with different results. We can construct different ontological theories, and support different sets of beliefs on the basis of the same total evidence, the totality of experience. We have our total pie, the total evidence, the totality of experience, and it depends upon us how we can carve it our cut it and for what purpose. We can explain or interpret it in such a way as to support a belief in the separate existence of the soul. Alternatively we can devise an explanation that would support the Buddhist claim that soul is not a separate ontological entity, but only a psycho-physical complex with a structure. That this is possible may simply be a particular instantiation of the general 'indeterminacy' thesis—the thesis that claims that our theories are always underdetermined by the totality of evidence upon which we postulate theoretical entities in physics). But then if there is a change in paradigm, such postulation may be pointless.

Notes

1. Śālikanātha, *Prakaraṇapañcikā*, pp. 315–16 (ed. A.S. Sastri, Benares).
2. Udayana, p. 5 (ed. D. Sastri, Chowkhamba, 1940).
3. See S. Collins, *Selfless Persons* for the early Buddhist arguments; see also A. Chakrabarti, for the Nyāya argument from Uddyotakara.
4. See for further discussion on *prasaṅga*, Matilal, pp. 9–22.
5. For the most important philosophical arguments, see Vasubandhu's *Abhidharmakośa-bhāṣya*, ch. 9, Sāntarakṣita's *Tattvasaṃgraha*, Śrīdhara's *Nyāyakandalī*, Udayana's *Ātmatattvaviveka*.

References

Aśvaghoṣa, *Buddhacarita*, ed. E.H. Johnston, Baptist Mission Press, Calcutta, 1935.

Chakrabarti, A., 'The Nyāya Proofs for the Existence of the Soul', *Journal of Indian Philosophy*, 1982.

Collins, S., *Selfless Persons*, Cambridge University Press, Cambridge, 1982.

Jayatilleke, K.N., *Buddhist Theory of Knowledge*, Allen & Unwin, London, 1963.

Matilal, B.K., *Logic, Language and Reality*, Motial, Banarsidass, Delhi, 1985.

Murti, T.R.V., *The Central Philosophical of Buddhism*, Allen & Unwin, London, 1955.

Nagel, T., *Mortal Questions*, Cambridge University Press, Cambridge, 1977.

Nozick, R., *Philosophical Explanations*, Harvard, Cambridge, Mass. 1981.

Parfit, D., *Reasons and Persons*, Clarendon, Oxford, 1984.

Russell, B., *The Analysis of Mind*, Unwin, London, 1921.

15

Diṅnāga as Interpreted by Uddyotakara

PART I: UDDYOTAKARA'S EXPOSITION OF DIṄNĀGA'S *APOHA* THEORY

Diṅnāga was the originator of the *apoha* doctrine: the view that the meaning of the word is the *exclusion* of the other (see the *Apoha pariccheda* of his *Pramāṇasamuccaya*). The word 'cow' does not, on this view, mean cow-hood (the cow universal) nor does it mean the individual cow; it means 'what is not a non-cow'. This view was transformed into a full-fledged theory of non-objective universals (nominalism or conceptualism depending upon how we interpret certain terms) by Dharmakīrti (*Pramāṇavārttika, Svārthānumāna-Pariccheda*) but this lies outside the scope of the present essay. Uddyotakara was a Naiyāyika. But his *Nyāyavārttika* is in many ways an invaluable source wherefrom we get an account of Diṅnāga's (his opponent's) view on several important issues. The case of *apoha* was no exception. In fact, although he was an opponent, Uddyotakara gave, in my view, a most elegant exposition of Diṅnāga's argument in favour of *apoha*, quoting frequently from the text of the Buddhist master. I believe we can regard Uddyotakara as a commentator or an expositor (sometimes a better one) of Diṅnāga's text in so far as he presented the Buddhist master as his opponent (*pūrvapakṣa*). I shall substantiate this point below by giving an annotated translation of a section of Uddyotakara's *Nyāyavārttika* dealing with the *apoha* theory. Many scholars (Hattori, 1968, 1980; H. Kitagawa; S. Katsura, 1975 and Jambuvijayaji, 1961) have identified a number of citations by Uddyotakara from Diṅnāga's text, *Pramāṇasamuccaya*. Hence it is not necessary to repeat them here. Besides, there are two recent studies, one by R. Herzberger (1987) and the other by R. Hayes (1988). I shall skip the historical details already noted by these two authors.

Uddyotakara under Nyāyasūtra 2.2.66

Text 1: Some say that the meaning of the word cannot be individual, nor configuration, nor universal. Why? Because the alternatives cannot be upheld. The issue might be considered with respect to such a word as 'existent', for this word ('existent') is most generic (has higher generality than others). We ask: By the word 'existent' do you mean (designate) (a) the universal? or (b) the particular (thing)? or (c) the connection between them? or (d) that which possesses the universal?

Note: The Nyāya view that the word means all the three things, the universal, the particular and the configuration or form (*ākṛti*)[1] is challenged by the Buddhist here. Then, the four alternative views of word-meaning are enumerated, strictly following Diṅnāga. Diṅnāga rejected all the four alternatives one by one, and Uddyotakara reproduced his argument faithfully.

Text 2: In this matter (we say:) The universal cannot be designated by the word ('existent'), for it is appositional with the word for the individual. To wit: if the word 'existent' designated the universal then there would not have been the agreement between this word and the word designating the particular thing in respect of their taking the same (nominative) inflection, as in the expression: 'The substance (is) existent' (or 'the existent thing').

Note: It is difficult to translate '*sāmānādhikaraṇya*'. At the syntactic level, it means that the two words have the same syntactically connected *vibhakti* 'case-inflexion' (are in apposition); at the semantic level, it means that they are co-referential, have the same referent (*adhikaraṇa*). The first alternative is being refuted here. Diṅnāga's argument is this. Consider the expression: '*Sad dravyam*' ('The substance is existent' or 'The existent thing'). Both words here, 'existent' and 'thing', have the same 'locus of reference' (to translate the Sanskrit metaphorical expression). That is, they must mean, or refer to, the same object because they take the same inflexion. According to the dictum of the Sanskrit grammarians, the semantic correlate of having the same appositional inflexion is co-referentiality, or co-locatability. But this seems to be a counter evidence to the claim that the meaning of the word 'existent' is the universal existence. For then the two words would lack co-referentiality.

(1) The meaning of 'existent' is existence
(2) The meaning of 'thing' is the thing
But (3) The thing is not equal to existence

Text 3: We do not see that the two words will have the same syntactically connected inflexion when they have different loci of reference and hence we cannot find them used with the same appositional inflection in the same sentence. (For example, we do not say, 'The cow horse').

Note: This is the 'supporting example' of the above evidence. In Indian terminology, this is the negative *dṛṣṭānta* for the above negative argument. If 'existent' and 'thing' do not the same locus of reference, they cannot have the same appositional inflexion, But they do have such inflexion as in the perfectly normal expression: 'The existent thing.' Hence 'existent' cannot *mean* existence. No distinction is presumably made here between meaning and the locus of reference.

Text 4: If you say: the word 'existent' has the thing as its locus of reference, and this explains its 'appositionality' with the word 'thing', but the referentiality of the word is dependent upon a property i.e., existence, we still say: if two words are such that one designates a property while the other designates the locus of that property, then they are not seen to have the appositionally same inflexion, as in 'the white-colour of the conch shell'.

Note: Diṅnāga continues to argue that 'existent' cannot designate or *mean* existence, in the expression, 'The existent thing'. For one word would mean a property and the other would mean a locus of that property. To say this we would have to say 'the existence of the thing'. He refers succinctly to Bhartṛhari's *Vākyapadīya*, *Kāṇḍa* III, canto 14, verse 8, where it is stated that:

. . . where one word designates a property and the other a locus of that property, they do *not* as a rule have the same appositional inflexion. Hence, because of this rule, the two words, 'existent' and 'thing', would fail to have the same locus of reference.

This is how the verse was quoted by Uddyotakara, and presumably this was how it was quoted by Diṅnāga. But it is puzzling here to note that the extant editions of the *Vākyapadīya* have it with a variant reading of the second line: Thus,

sāmānādhikaraṇyasya prasiddhir dravya-śabdayoḥ

instead of

sāmānādhikaraṇyasyāsiddhiḥ sad-dravya-śabdayoḥ

The meaning of this verse in Bhartṛhari as explained by his commentator, Helārāja, was as follows. In the expression, 'The white-colour of the cloth', there is lack of appositionality between the words, one of which designates a property and the other a locus of that property. But (we have to supply from the context, that) in a compound with two co-referential words, as in '(a) courageous-man', either will designate its own meaning, a property in one case and a locus of that property in the other case, but by implication or through indirection, their co-referentiality will be understood.

Was Helārāja wrong? Which text did Diṅnāga have before him? Uddyotakara seems to have read the text in the same way as Diṅnāga.

Text 5: By similar argument, the connection between the particular and the universal is rejected as the meaning of the word.

Note: This rejects the third alternative.

Text 6: Nor is it proper to say that the word 'existent' designates the individual things, the particulars, for they are *innumerable*. We cannot say that we have established designative connection between the single word 'existent' on the one hand and numerous things (substances) and qualities on the other hand. And if a designative connection has not been established (between a word and some objects), it would be improper to claim that we cognize those objects (meanings) from the (utterance of the) word. For (in that case) from the (utterance of the) word we cognize the word-form i.e., the word itself.

Note: This is one of the two well-known arguments by Diṅnāga against the claim that words mean only the particulars. For Diṅnāga's argument, see *Pramāṇasamuccaya*, Apoha section, verse 2, quoted in full by Mallavādin: *ānantyāt* and *vyabhicārāt*. I wish to call them the 'innumerableness' argument and the 'deviation' or 'variability' argument. (It seems that Diṅnāga derived them from Bhartṛhari.) The point of the first seems to be this. Particulars are innumerable, and hence if a single word 'cow' is said to mean each of such innumerable particulars separately without any reference to their common property, we must say that it is impossible, for no one can learn the meaning of the word 'cow' in presence of each particular and then apply the word to that particular. To use modern terminology, this may be possible for what we call singular terms or proper names (provided we take them non-connotatively or as rigid designators), but not with common names or what Diṅnāga called *jāti-śabda*.

Text 7: Again ('existent' does not mean particular) because there will be deviation (or lack of invariance). (To wit): When the word 'existent' is heard, our cognition is in a state of oscillation among several alternatives, a thing, a quality or an action (for any one of these can be meant by the word 'existent'). If the cognition oscillates between alternatives (i.e., lacks certainly) after the word is expressed, then it is not proper to claim that such a word means such and such alternative objects. Therefore the word 'existent' cannot mean (simply) the particulars.

Note: This complete the other half of the argument. The point seems to be this: If we learn the word 'existent' as meaning a thing (when we learn the meaning of such a word) we cannot apply it to mean a particular quality or even a particular action and vice versa. The use of a particular word to mean something should not be variant from the thing in connection with which the word was learnt. If only the particulars constitute the meaning of a word, we will have to face this problem.

These two arguments, 'innumerableness' and 'deviation', are actually two side of the same coin. We cannot explain why common names are used to mean innumerable particulars unless we assume some common features among them to supply the basis. This is one of many strokes of genius of Diṅnāga. All the later philosophers from Uddyotakara onwards used this argument to refute the claim that the word means only the particulars. I believe, however, the source of this argument is *Nyāyasūtra* 2.2.61: *na, tad-anavasthānāt.*[2] Akṣapāda used this *sūtra* to refute the claim that only particulars are meant by the words. Unfortunately, Vātsyāyana's explanation of this *sūtra* was misleading and unclear. He only said that a particular alone, uncharacterized by a common property, cannot be meant by the word. He did not explain why. Uddyotakara fills up this lacuna by explaining the *sūtra* as implying that the word cannot mean only the particulars, for if it did, it would lack invariability. (That is, we learn the word in the presence of one particular and then cognize any other particulars indiscriminately.) I believe the *sūtra* can easily be taken to mean 'lack of invariance', which is being adduced here as an evidence to counter the claim that only particulars are meant by the word. Here, as in many other places, I have seen that we can have a better explanation of some of the *Nyāyasūtras* from our reading of the critical comments of Diṅnāga. I believe it worked both ways. Diṅnāga, in his turn, derived some of his important philosophic insights from his careful study of the *Nyāyasūtra*. For example, the word *avyapadeśya* in *Nyāyasūtra* 1.1.4, must have partly inspired him to define perception in the way he did.

Text 8: The word 'existent' does not also mean the substrata of the universal. Why? For there is 'lack of independence'. From the word 'existent' we do not understand (cognize) a pot or some other thing, therefore in the expression 'the existent pot', there would be lack of agreement in their appositional inflexion.

Note: According to Vācaspati, the word 'existent' cannot mean the substratum of a universal, such as, a pot, without the co-occurrence of it with such words as 'pot'. Hence it cannot mean the substratum independently.

Text 9: Or, the reason 'lack of independence' implies the following: the word 'existent' chiefly means existence and having meant that it is metaphorically transferred to mean the substrata (of existence). But if a word primarily means one thing and then by transference means (presents) another thing, the second thing cannot be the (proper lexical) meaning of the word. For example, the word 'cradle' means (primarily) a cradle but through transference it may present the child in the cradle (as in the expression: 'The cradle cries').

Note: The point of Diṅnāga's expression 'lack of independence' is faithfully described here. 'The cradle' may metaphorically present the child in the cradle, but we cannot for that reason accept the child as the (usual) meaning of the word 'cradle'.

Text 10: Further we have stated our objection already. What have we stated? Since the substrata of existence (or any other universal) are innumerable, they cannot be meant by the word 'existent'.

Note: This refers to the 'innumerability' argument mentioned above. In fact, the argument against the claim that the particulars are meant by the word is equally applicable to the claim that the substrata of universal are meant by the word.

Text 11: (Further arguments against this alternative:) Our awareness of existence or the primary meaning of the word 'existent' cannot be transferred to the substratum of existence on the basis of similarity of properties, as happens in the case of the word 'master' applied to the servant, (For example, when the servant behaves as the master, the word 'master' can be metaphorically applied to him). Nor can it be so transferred on the basis of the conditional ascription of the property, as in the case, 'the blue (piece of) crystal'. For there is lack of sequentially (as in the case of an actual metaphor, where first the primary meaning is cognized and then the metaphor). For simultaneity would be impossible (two meanings, the primary one and the metaphorical one, cannot be cognized jointly). For, the conditional ascription of the property would lead to the arising of errone-ous cognition. Hence the meaning of a word is not also the substratum of the universal.

Note: The last three arguments are from Diṅnāga to counter the position that the word 'existent' means the universal, existence, first (primary meaning) and then through metaphorical transference may be applied to the substrata of existence. This view is clearly formulated in *Nyāyasūtra* 2.2.60 and 2.2.62. Akṣapāda however rejected this view when he established his final view in *Nyāyasūtra* 2.2.66. This is presumably the view of the early Mīmāṃsakas (or of Vājapyāyana).

Text 12: It is also not proper to say that the word ('existent') means the exclusive particular having uniqueness (*svalakṣaṇa*). For then from the same word we cannot have cognition of another such exclusive particular. And there is no other way. Hence (Diṅnāga says:) the word excludes the contrary meanings. To explain: the word is said to mean what it means, when it excludes the other (contrary) objects—objects other than the one to which the word is applied.

Note: This is the conclusion of Diṅnāga: the word means what it means, only by virtue of its excluding all rival or contrary classes other than the one to which the particular belongs. But even this way of putting the thesis of Diṅnāga may be misleading. For it will raise such questions as: did Diṅnāga admit reality of classes (abstract entities) while rejecting the objective universals? Further do we have to talk about the reality of class abstraction if we formulate the thesis in this way? I shall put all these questions aside here. I believe Diṅnāga himself was non-committal.

Having described this as his opponent's view Uddyotakara goes on to give his elaborate refutation. The second part of this paper will consist of the translation and analysis of Uddyotakara's criticism of Diṅnāga's theory of *apoha*.

As far as the present part is concerned, we have established the following. First, Uddyotakara gave a faithful account of the *apoha* theory as it was propounded and developed by Diṅnāga. This will answer the criticism of some modern writers that Uddyotakara was only interested in misrepresenting Diṅnāga's view. It is true that he often quibbled. But that was part of the game at that time in philosophical disputation. When Uddyotakara got serious, he gave a brilliant account of Diṅnāga's argument, and threw more light on the philosophical problems involved.

Second, Diṅnāga often provided in a better way clarification of the arguments found in the *Nyāyasūtra*. For sometimes Vātsyāyana was obscure.

Finally, we cannot have a proper understanding of the philosophical debate in classical India unless we pay attention to these authors belonging to different schools, who criticized one another.

PART II: UDDYOTAKARA'S CRITIQUE OF DIṄNĀGA

In this second instalment I shall present a translation of portions of the *Nyāyavārttika* where Uddyotakara criticised Diṅnāga's formulation of the *apoha* doctrine. Diṅnāga, it should be remembered, criticised the Nyāya-Vaiśeṣika theory of universals, i.e., the theory of *jāti* or *sāmānya*, 'objective universals', as well as the idea of existentness (*sattā*) or 'existence' as the highest universal. As I have noted, Diṅnāga's formulation was the first formulation of *apoha*, the Buddhist theory of the universal. Uddyotakara's critique must have helped the later Buddhists to develop and round out the theory. Therefore the importance of Uddyotakara's critique can hardly be overestimated.

Text 13: (Uddyotakara continues): In this matter we have decided that the designate of such a word is the individual, the form or configuration as well as the universal, and established that there is no fixed rule as to what constitutes the principal meaning and what the secondary. The (above) faults are applicable to those who accept only one of the three (as the meaning of the word).

Note 1: Uddyotakara here repeats the view given in the *Nyāyasūtra* where all the three items are mentioned as the meaning of the word and no distinction was made there between what constitutes the principal meaning and what the secondary. The term *ākṛti* is very ambiguous. According to Kumārila Bhaṭṭa, *ākṛti* constitutes the meaning of the word. However, he gave a very different interpretation of the word, for which one may consult the *Ākṛtivāda* of his *Ślokavārttika*. In old Nyāya, however, the word means either the 'configuration' or the 'form'. The Mīmāṃsā notion of *ākṛti* is similar to that of universal.

Note 2: Vācaspati comments: We accept three items as meanings (as designata) of general terms like 'the existent': the individual (the lump), the form or uniformity, and the universal. The two ways in which there will be lack of dependence for such words (as pointed out above—see Diṅnāga's arguments in the first part) are ruled out. For the question of the primary and secondary designation is flexible. (a) It is not possible (to claim) that words (general terms), in order to generate cognition of the individual, depend, prior to it, upon the cognition of the universal. For both are necessarily cognizable by one cognitive state, and this being so it is improper to talk about priority and posteriority (which one is before and which one is after). (b) Nor can it be claimed that a general term generates an inconstant (fluid) cognition (i.e. the cognition that oscillates, grasping alternatively the individual and the universal) in the absence of an accompanying word designating the individual (as in 'the existent pot'), and that therefore to attain certainty, dependence upon a word for the individual is required. For the general term (in question will generate a cognition of its own designata and therefore the cognition will not be inconstant or oscillating. The 'object' i.e. (the designatum) of this term (general term) is simply the individual possessing the universal. Therefore this cognition is not inconstant or fluid. The restriction to a particular individual is with regard to the 'object' (the designatum or the whole), and hence inconstancy of cognition in this respect is not a fault. Consider this example. From a distance our perception grasps only an indefinite object, a substance with some height and breadth. We at this stage grasp neither the stump nor the man. Here cognitive inconstancy or fluidity (oscillation between the man and the stump) does not do any harm to our perception. Therefore the cognitive oscillation between the universal existence and the individual pot does not do any harm to the situation when the general term designates the individual as possessing or instantiating the universal. Also in this view, the general term is not really different from a term that designates the individual as well as the form. Therefore, we do not need the metaphorical transference. Nor is it the case that the use of the same suffix is not proper. For if both the general term and the term for the individual designate the same object, use of different suffixes will be improper. Here Vācaspati's comparison with a perceptual situation is illuminating.

Text 14: Nor are these really faults. Why? (Answer): You say that the word 'existence' does not designate existence. That is not true. For it is contradictory. 'The word is "existence" but is not a designator of existence'—this is a contradictory statement. If it does not designate existence why you call it the word 'existence'?

(Opponent): We call it so following your intention. We contend: in our doctrine the words such as 'existence' do not exist (meaning 'do not designate'?). But you imagine such designators (= words), the word 'existence' as well as words such as 'substance', 'quality', and 'action', and you use them (interchangeably). Therefore following your intention, we too utter (in speech only) words such as 'existence'.

(Answer): No, this does not resolve the contradiction.

Note: Words are designators. Therefore 'this word does not exist' could mean 'this designator does not exist' which would, in its turn, mean 'the designatum does not exist'.

Text 15: Words such as 'existent' are well established among people. What do they designate? This is the question for the debate between both of us. We say that the word 'existence' designates existence, and you say that the word 'existence' does not designate existence. When you say so, I refute you because your position involves contradiction. You, on your part, are not resolving the contradiction but merely saying 'I am following your principle.' Having said so you have not resolved the contradiction.

Note 1: Uddyotakara has used this convenient expression '*sattāśabda*' which I have translated as the word 'existence'. But the expression is ambiguous for it may mean either the word 'existent' or the word 'existence'. In fact Diṅnāga used the word 'existent', therefore Uddyotakara's use of the ambiguous expression is a bit tricky. And, perhaps, indirectly helps in the present argument.

Note 2: Vācaspati comments: what is called a contradiction here? *Sattāśabda*: a) it might mean the word designating existence or b) it might mean the word 'existence'. If we accept the first alternative then there is a direct contradiction: The word designating existence does not designate existence. In the second case, it contradicts the part 'it is not the designator of existence'. You designate existence by the word 'of existence' and in this part at the same time you claim that 'existence' does not designate existence. It is paradoxical to say, for example. 'The "existence" word is not the designator of existence.' This expression by its systematic ambiguity refers to both of the above paradoxes.

Text 16: (Uddyotakara continues): If you say, 'You have imagined (constructed) such words (designators) as 'existence', that is also not tenable. For you have not stated what is the object intended by such imagination, i.e. the subject matter on which the imagination rests.

Note 1: Imagination implies a duality: that which is imagined, and that on the basis of which it is imagined. Imagination cannot hang in the air. It must, according to the Nyāya theory, have an objective grounding. We imagine water looking at a mirage. Water is what is imagined to be the intended object of perception and its objective grounding is the mirage (i.e. the sun ray on the hot air-vapour).

Note 2: When one thing is imagined to be another then the first one is the one to which the properties of the second are attributed. In such cases the second object is technically called *pradhāna* ('the principal or the chief'). This is a technical use of the term *pradhāna* i.e. the object which is identified by mistake (or by imagination) with something else. The use of such terms is found in *Nyāya-sūtra* 4.2.37, where the first object is called *tattva* and second object is called *pradhāna*. In the 'rope-snake' illusion, the snake is called the *pradhāna*.

Text 17: When there is perceived a general feature (an object with height etc.), common to two distinct object A (= the man) and B (= the stump), we have an awareness of A (= the man) due to the attribution of A's property upon what is actually B (= the stump). This is the way we imagine something to be the man which is actually a stump. If these words (designators) 'existence' etc., are created by imagination, you have to state what is imagined here (what is the 'chief'). There cannot be imagination without what is imagined.

Note: The use of the word '*pradhāna*' (= 'chief') is technical, as already noted. Uddyotakara uses it in his arguments to refute the Yogācāra view of external reality. The analogy is between imagination of water, mirage, and the actual water on the one hand and designation, designator-word, designatum on the other. This seems to be the thrust of the argument.

Text 18: As regards what you have said, 'If two distinct words designate two distinct objects, then they should not have the same suffix,' this is not so. For you do not understand the meaning of sameness.

We do not say that the word 'existence' is co-referential with the word 'substance'. But (we say) by the word 'existent', which designates the principal *instantiator* of existence, are designated substance, qualities and action and by the words 'substance', 'quality' and 'action' are designated the very same objects, for the second set of words ('substance', 'quality' and 'action') are related to 'existent' as substantive to adjective. Under such circumstances, it is (only) proper to have the same suffix in the pair 'The existent substance' for they designate the same object. When the word 'existence', which designates principally existence, designates the instantiators in a subordinate fashion, there is no sameness of suffixes between the two ('existence' and 'substance' as in 'The existence of the substance.') Therefore, the lack of suffixes in the two words is not a fault. The following argument:

> Since the case-suffixes are necessarily different in the case of the two words, one of which designates an attribute and the other the owner of the attribute, the words 'existence' and 'substance' do not take the same suffix.

is answered here (by explaining why the two words have the same suffix).

Note 1: The text may be corrupt. The reference is to Diṅnāga and the quotation of Bhartṛhari is to be found in Diṅnāga. See *Vākyapadīya* III.14.8.

Note 2: The convenient expression '*guṇa-śabda*' presents some difficulties in translation. The word '*guṇa*' stands for both a property and something that is subordinate. But these two meanings are in fact intimately connected. For whatever is a property also becomes a subordinate element by the same token, for the subordinate becomes the property of the principal element. Both senses are intended here.

Text 19: This explains why the relation (that is the relation between word and object) cannot be designated by the word, Why? Not by the word 'existent' is the relation designated, but by some word for relation. A relation is, i.e., behaves as, an attribute. The word 'existence' is an 'attribute-word'. A word designating a substance (thing) does not take the same suffix as the attribute-word.

Note: The semantic difference between 'The existent substance' and 'The existence of the substance' is reflected in their syntactic difference. This is what is emphasized here.

Text 20: As for the opponent's argument 'a general term does not designate individuals or things because of the fault of innumerableness,' we ask 'who is claiming that a general term designates individuals?' You are only refuting a position which you have concocted yourself.

(Opponent): If the word (the general term) does not designate things, how is it that the substance, quality, and action are designated by such a word ('existent')?

(Answer): My dear friend, this (the word 'existent' and such others) is not a general name or a universal-word, but an individual name or a thing-name. A thing-name designates a thing and therefore nothing is contradicted.

(Opponent): How do you say that nothing is contradicted? For the word 'existent' is only one, a single entity, and there is innumerability of things, as pointed out earlier. It is not possible to learn from instruction or usage the relation of one with many. And if the relation is not learnt from instruction or usage, it is not possible to understand the object from the word.

Note 1: This is the implicit principle of the early theory of semantics. Compare with the *Mahābhāṣya: pratyartham śabdaniveśaḥ*.

Note 2: Uddyotakara argues that the word 'existent' is not word for universal but is designative of individuals. But the problem according to Diṅnāga is that this word is used to designate innumerable individuals. Uddyotakara says in reply (see Text 21, below) that, existence is a universal and as such it is a single, unitary property. Thus, whenever one recognizes such a property, in a substance, in a quality or in an action, one can use 'existent' because they all are substrata of the same existence. Therefore the fault of innumerableness will not apply. For a single word is being applied to innumerable individuals, by being tied to a single unitary property, existence, our recognition of this shared unitary property provokes the use of the single word 'existent' to such relevant cases.

Text 21: (Answer): No, The word (according to us) does not designate the bare things or individuals. Your criticism applies to one who says that the word 'existent' designates bare substances, qualities and action without any qualifications. In our view, substance, qualities, and action as qualified by the attribute of existence are designated (by the word 'existent'). Wherever one sees existence one uses the word 'existent.' Existence is one (a single entity), and since there is this awareness of unity that goes through each locus of existence, the innumerability of things (individuals) does not present a problem.

Note: Compare the modern dicta, intention determines extension, and sense determines reference, to avoid *ānantya*, the problem of innumerable designation.

Text 22: (Uddyotakara now argues against the formulation of Diṅnāga's argument): How do you formulate the relation between what is proved with what proves it? Your subject (of the conclusion) is a word ('any general name') and the reason adduced by you (i.e., innumerability) is a property belonging to a thing (a non-word). Suppose you say your conclusion to be proven is: 'Things are non-designable by general names.' Even so since your reason is 'because of innumerability (of things),' you cannot adduce any supporting example, either positive or negative.

Note: Diṅnāga's formulation of the argument is faulted here: A general name does not designate the individuals, because of the innumerability of the individuals. Vācaspati comments: The universal proposition supporting the conclusion may be stated as follows:

Whatever things falling in one group or the other innumerable in number are not designable by general names.

Here you cannot use a supporting example because all the things and groups are included in the extension of the subject term. We can infer that a particular place is on fire because of our seeing the smoke coming out of it, provided that the invariable relation of smoke with fire is empirically supported by an example, viz. another place having both smoke and fire. If your conclusion is a general proposition, your empirical evidence is included within the scope of your subject term and therefore loses its force as an evidence in a deductive process. You may re-state your conclusion: 'Whatever is designable by general name is not innumerable, such as cowness'—but your example is a fiction according to you—like a sky-flower.

Text 23: You may say, certain groups of things are non-designable by general names because of innumerability of the members (things) in each group, just as certain other groups of things are (you have split a general proposition 'All As are Bs' into two particular complementary propositions: 'some As are Bs' and 'All other As are Bs', and using the first as supporting the second). This is not tenable for it is incompatible.

Note: Vācaspati comments: You are saying 'none of the things are designable' but as there is nothing but things, you should say 'nothing is designable.' See Text 24, below.

Text 24: In this way, no object is (would be) designable, and no word would designate. If, in this way, the fact of designation is ruled out, any particular statement such as 'These are not designable' and 'These do not designate' will be without significance.

Note: There is perhaps a touch of sophistry here: however, it can be a serious objection. If no words designate, these words cannot designate either.

Text 25: You have said, 'Due to promiscuity a general name does not designate things'. This is not true. You have not understood the meaning of promiscuity. A reason/evidence is known to be promiscuous when it is not only present in its own subject locus (*pakṣa*) as well as in a similar case (*sapakṣa*) but also in a dissimilar case (of *vipakṣa*) (a good evidence is not supposed to be so). This word 'existent' certainly is not present in a dissimilar case, which should not be designated by it, viz. cases of non-existent fictions. Therefore, you have condemned a case as promiscuous improperly.

Note: The word 'existent' designates first one particular, a thing, and it is seen to designate something else, another particular, a thing, a quality or an action different from the first. You have called this behaviour of the term promiscuous, but as long as the word designates anything existent at different times on different occasions, and nothing that is non-existent, it behaves non-promiscuously. It has every right to designate one existent at one time and another existent at another time.

Text 26: (Your argument is untenable) also because we do not regard the word 'existent' as the inferential reason or evidence (for cognizing an object to be a substance, a quality or an action.) Who says that this is the evidence, i.e., existence is the evidence through which substances, qualities or actions are designated?

Note: Vācaspati comments: (In our view) the word is not an evidence on the basis of which an object is understood or cognized. Therefore the fault of promiscuity does not apply here. That which simply helps us to cognize a particular object need not be restricted to that object only. The eye helps us cognize blue-colour at one time and red-colour at another time, and this need not be condemned as promiscuous. True, we learn to use a word for designating particulars when we are confronted with one particular and then promiscuously (if you like) use the same word to designate other particulars. But still when we learn to use that word, we learn to use it to designate by it innumerable particulars that are circumscribed (*koḍīkaraṇa*) by an attribute shared by all such particulars. This is therefore not a condemnable view of promiscuity.

Text 27: Therefore this reasoning too is improper. If you refute that the words (general names) designate things, you cannot say there is co-referentiality between 'existence' and 'substance' (in 'the substance (that is) 'existent'). For that is incompatible. For first you say that no words (here) designate the things and then you say that both words are co-referential which means they designate (refer to) the identical locus or the thing.

Note: Application of the same suffix is justified when the words concerned refer and they do refer to/designate the same locus/thing.

Text 28: You have said 'The word "existent" does not designate the owner of the universal because of lack of independence. Certainly by the word "existent" things such as pot or a piece of cloth are not understood, and since the pot is not implied at all, there cannot be any locus/thing where the two attributes (designated by "pot" and "existent" as in "the pot which is existent", i.e., potness and existence) can co-exist or be co-present.'

This is not tenable. For the answer has already been given that since both 'existent' and 'substance' (in 'the substance (that is) existent') have the same object (for designation), they are coreferential and have the same suffix.

It is also improper to claim that things such as a pot or a piece of cloth as owners of the universal existence, are not implied or presented (by the utterance of 'existence'). For the word 'existent' does imply or helps us cognize the loci or instantiators of existence.

By a verbal utterance only you cannot claim that the word 'existent' does not present the substance, qualities, and actions. By the word 'existent' even the subordinate designata are to be understood.

The word 'existent' is the designator. What is its designatum? Whatever is understood/cognized/presented by (the utterance of) the word would be its designatum/object (*artha*). What is that object? There are three objects, existence, its relation to a thing, and a separate thing (that is existent). Now, as the speaker intends to make one principal and the others subordinate, we understand the instantiator/locus/thing as the principal designatum. Existence and its relation are subordinates. What determines which one is the principal while the others are subordinate? The object determines i.e., the way something behaves in a sentence is what determines.

When existence functions as an agent (in a sentence) it becomes the principal designator because it functions having recourse to other qualifying adjuncts (as in 'existence is present here in this pot'). Existence is subordinate when it causes us to cognize the principal, i.e., the instantiator. This is so because the object is specified or distinguished by existence (from what is not existent). For without a subordinate, an attribute to qualify, the object cannot be cognized. Where there is no qualifying attribute such as existence, a cognition such as 'existent' does not arise there. Therefore what you have said 'the owners of existence, such as a pot, are not presented,' is not tenable.

Text 29: You have said, 'The word "existent" designates primarily existence, and having designated it, it metaphorically designates the owner of existence.' That is not true. You have not understood the purpose of the use of the word 'existence'.

You do not know the purpose of the word 'existent'. Who says that the word 'existent' principally designates existence? I have already stated that the objects designated by the word 'existent' are substances, qualities, and actions, for they become instantiators of the existence.

Text 30: In the same way we answer the point based upon innumerability. The object or the scope of the word 'existent' is the instantiator of existence. And therefore the object/scope is one, i.e., whatever becomes the instantiator of existence.

Text 31: You have argued 'General terms do not designate the owner/locus of the universal, for the cognition (derived from utterance of the general term) moves or wanders towards the owner/locus (from the universal) on the basis of the similarity of attributes, as in the case of the word "(the) master" moving to apply to the servant.' This means: since the servant resembles the master, the word '(the) master' is used to designate the servant. We do not understand this: How can a cognition move/wander away? If this means that the servant has the property of being the objective content of the cognition which grasps the master, then it is wrong. For with regard to the servant the cognition of the master does not arise, but only having recognized the authority (*gurutā*) or popularity (*priyatā*) one applies the word '(the) master' in a secondary sense to designate that object (the servant, as 'master'). Therefore, since the servant functions as the master, the designation 'master' is transferred to him.

But the word 'existent' does not reside in/designate the substance etc. in this way (i.e. through transference). When the word is 'existence' derived from 'existent' in the sense of being the attribute of the existents, there that word 'existence' expresses/designates the property that qualifies the existents, and the qualification would be by transference. This also answers the point raised by saying, 'through attribution/transference of the property as in "The crystal is blue."'

Note: Uddyotakara makes the following point clear. 'Existent' and 'existence' are two different words. It is not proper to say that 'existent' designates primarily existence and then by metaphorical transference the existents, substance etc. One may call the servant 'the master' if he behaves as master but such designation is based upon metaphorical use of the word. But in the case 'existent' or 'existence' such metaphorical uses are not called for. For the crystal example, see Text 11 above.

Text 32: You have said, 'due to lack of sequentiality' and 'impossibility of simultaneity' (Text 11 above). This means as follows: The word 'existence' having designated (resided in) existence, designates by virtue of such designation the owner of existence. But we do not see this. It does not happen also simultaneously. The awareness of existence and that of substance does not arise simultaneously.

This is also not tenable. I have given my answer already. This has been answered by (my) saying that there is neither sequence nor simultaneity, for the awareness of existence implies the instantiator of existence (see Text 28 above).

By this (argument) is also answered the point made by saying 'for this will have the undesirable consequence of the arising of the cognition that is non-verdical' (see Text 11 above).

In this way, since the amplification of the bad arguments is refuted, it is established that the word designates the individual, the form as well as the universal.

Text 33: The (qualifying) word in "The words for universals, i.e. common nouns and adjectives, are not designators of the (individual) particular,' is meaningless. For in your view the word is recognized as designating the individual/particular. A qualifying word is used when there is an awareness of generality (unqualifiedness) along with what is to be qualified. Here there is nothing that could be qualified by it (the qualifying word 'the word for universal' or 'common noun'). It is not admissible (by you) that there is some particular object that is designable by the word for universal. Therefore it (the qualifying phrase) is meaningless.

Note: Technically this fault is called *vyarthaviśeṣaṇa*.

Text 34: The statement is also contradictory. If this word for universal were a designator of the particulars then it would not be called 'word-for-universal'. It is not proper (consistent) that a word is *for* one object while it will *designate* another object. If it did designate the particulars, why would it be called 'word-for-universal'? What you say, viz. The word-for-universal does not designate the particulars, is trivially/necessarily so. Who with a sane mind would admit the particulars to be designated by the word-for-universal? If the particulars are not designable by the word-for-universal, they become designable by other words. And if they are not also designable even by other words, they are neither designable by the word-for-universal nor by other word. Now if they are non-designable by either, what would be the force of the qualifying word in the statement: 'The word-for-universal does not designate particulars.' Therefore, you should say: The particulars are not designable. The words are non-designators (of particulars, reals).

Note: Diṅnāga did say that the particulars are non-designable (*anirdeśya*). Dharmakīrti elaborated the issue.

Text 35: You may think that you have to say in this way in the context of the views of the others, viz., 'The word-for-universal does not designate particulars.'

This is not tenable. For such a (putative) view is not admitted. There is certainly no philosopher (*tāntrika*) who accepts the particulars as designable by the word-for-universal. If you say that even the universals are not designable then it contradicts the word 'the word-for-universal.'

If something *x* is not designable by a particular word, it is not proper to call such a word as *the word-for-that x*. And the word-for-universal is not the designator of the particulars.

What would it then designate? For if it does not designate the particular, that it could designate something else is entailed thereby. And if you do not want it to designate anything else, then your qualifying statement is useless (when you say) 'The word for universal does not designate particulars.'

It is proper to say that all words are necessarily non-designators of objects.

Text 36: Now, words are non-designators, and objects are non-designable—this is an improper claim, for it is contradictory.

Words are non-designators and such a property of being a non-designator belonging to the words is conveyed necessarily by the words. Therefore, if the words are non-designators there is opposition in both the reason adduced and the thesis you are trying to prove. Your thesis is: The word for universal does not designate particulars. Your reason is: for there is innumerability. Both (the thesis and the reason) are designations/designators. And it is contradictory if both are (claimed to be) non-designators.

Note: There is an ambiguity in the word '*vacana*', meaning either 'designation' or 'designator'.

Text 37: If you accept that the words are non-designators, you should state some other means by which you can make other people understand your thought.

You may argue that you have made a different claim. You may say: 'We have claimed neither. Neither that the words are non-designators nor that the objects are non-designable. But what is accepted by you as the regulation concerning designator and designable, is being rejected by us. We say, on the contrary, that by words, the universal which is nothing but exclusion of other possibility, is being designated.'

Note: This is a reformulation of Diṅnāga's position.

Text 38: It is to be stated with proper specification, if the words, are (become) designators of objects in a different way. You should state with specification: 'The word for universal does not designate any universal apart from the kind of universal we have conceded.'

Text 39: You have also not stated the nature of such a universal. It is not possible to state the nature of the universal without referring to the ground of the awareness of sameness (or similarity). It is not possible to refute the awareness of commonness. That awareness cannot arise from the awareness of the particular (the specific) without any ground (cf. *akasmāt*). That from which arises such an awareness (of commonness) is called universal. In this matter there is no quarrel.

The fault lies here in the literal formulation of your statement.

You may say that the particulars are also to be the loci where the non-designability by the word-for-universal resides (and that is your reformulated thesis).

Even so, in the case of this reformulated thesis (statement), all previous faults of the debate (cf. *vākyadoṣaḥ*) would apply. In this way, even when only some members of a class are made loci of the property (non-designability by words), since the criterion for the qualifier and what is to be qualified would be inadmissible, previous faults would follow.

Text 40: You have said that there is co-referentiality between (the two words) 'substance' and 'existent' (in 'The existent substance'). This is not true. For there is contradiction.

It is contradictory to claim that there is co-referentiality between the words 'substance' and 'existent' on the one hand and that the words are non-designators of particulars on the other.

You may say that there is no contradiction for there is (metaphorical) transference (of meanings, which resolves the contradiction).

You may argue that both words 'substance' and 'existent' designate only metaphorically (not really and therefore they can remain non-designators).

If we ask 'How?' you may explain (as follows):

The word 'substance' excludes non-substances and the word 'existent' excludes the non-existents. These two, therefore, by virtue of excluding the non-substances and the non-existents (practically) designate the same object (i.e. are coreferential) and hence it is said that they are coreferential. But primarily no word is (in reality) positively a designator.

Note: Uddyotakara gives the actual position of Diṅnāga regarding reference or designation. 'Two names designate the same thing' means they by excluding certain other possibilities practically apply to the same object. Names are turned into predicates.

Text 41: We say No. For it is impossible to have the primary (*mukhya*). When the words 'existent' and 'substance' have *primary* designations, then on the basis of similarity (resemblance = *sāmānya*) they may be properly transferred to what is not primary (they may designate metaphorically something different from their primary designable). But for those who uphold your view there is no primary (designable, i.e. *pradhāna*). And without the primary designable metaphorical designation is not possible.

Text 42: In the theory where the universal is only exclusion of the others, there cannot be any metaphorical transference. For both words ('substance' and 'existent') are designators of the primary. For example, in the expression 'The boy is a lion' i.e., lion-like, just as the word 'lion' designates a lion by excluding the properties of being a non-lion, it also designates similarly the boy, for exclusion of the properties of being a non-lion is present equally in both. How then can be there a metaphorical transference?

Note: Properties of a non-lion would exclude power, energy etc., which are lion-like properties. And they are present in both, in a lion as well as in the boy in question. Uddyotakara points out that the theory of metaphor is not compatible with the theory of *apoha*.

Text 43: You have said, 'The word designates what is excluded by the designation (meaning) of other words' (see Text 12 above).

This is also not tenable. For there would be first awareness when and only when it is possible for a word to designate positively something.

If a word can designate anything positively, then the awareness of the positive designation of the word arises, and then it is proper to exclude (negate) that designation in others. But according to those who deny the positive designation of the word, how can there be an exclusion/negation without there being an earlier/a first awareness (of what is excluded or negated). As long as *the other* is not recognized, *the other* cannot be excluded/negated. For example the word 'cow' means what is not a non-cow. As long as the cow is not meant/designated, it is not proper to have an awareness of the cow, and as long as the awareness of the cow does not arise, the awareness of the non-cow cannot arise. And hence there is lack of awareness with regard to both (the cow and the non-cow).

Text 44: We further ask: Is this designation of the word 'cow', which is exclusion of the non-cow (i.e., what is not a non-cow), a positive category or a negative one. If it is positive, is it the cow, or the non-cow? If it is the cow, we have no quarrel (we agree with you). If it is claimed that the non-cow is what is designated by 'cow', Oh! It is then a great skill in assigning meaning to the word! If it (the designable) is claimed to be a negative category, that is not reasonable. For both awareness and command will not have any intended object. It is not true that by hearing the word 'cow' (in 'Bring a cow'), the command refers to something negative, nor does the intended awareness (in the hearer) is about something negative. The designable of the word is cognized (by the hearer) through an understanding of it. No one certainly understands a negative category (and absence, a lack) from the (utterance of the) word 'cow'.

Text 45: It is unreasonable to say that the word designates exclusion of the other. For it is non-pervasive (i.e., there are counterexamples). When there are two (mutually exclusive) sets of things, then through the (exclusion) negation of one set, the other set is understood. For example, from the word 'cow' the one set of things, cows, are understood and the other set, the non-cows, are excluded or negated. But this does not apply to the word 'all' ('All' is the supposed counterexample). There is no such thing as 'non-all' (The opposite set of the universal set designated by 'all' is the null-set). Hence there is nothing to be excluded by the designation of the word 'all'.

You may say that the designation of 'all' excludes such things as one and two and therefore it is not a counterexample. The 'non-all' means one, two and so on. All there are excluded by the designation of the word 'all'.

This is not true. For there will arise the fault of negating what is intended by itself (self-contradiction).

The word 'all' excludes one, two and so on. Now besides one, two etc., there would be nothing left (for the word 'all' to designate). If the members (*aṅga*) of a set are negated (individually), the whole set being not different from the members taken together would also be negated. Therefore the word 'all' would designate nothing, for it would exclude everything. By the same token, all collective words would have no designation, for they would exclude their parts (and thereby all parts) individually, and the collected whole is nothing but the parts taken together. The word such as 'two' are results of collectivity, and if they negate one etc., the negated ones being not collected, they would not designate anything.

Note: The word 'two' may designate, for example, the two balls before me. But if it excludes this one, because it is one, and that one because that is one took then there is nothing left for it to designate.

Text 46: Since exclusion is an act, you should state its own intended object. 'This is not a non-cow'—is this exclusion *about* the cow or about the non-cow? If it is *about* the cow, how can there be negation of cow with regard to the cow itself? If you think it is *about* the non-cow, how can there be exclusion about one object from which there is understanding *about* another object? If you are cutting the *khadira* tree there cannot be cutting in the *palāśa* tree.

You may say that you negate the non-cow with regard to the cow, 'the cow is not a non-cow'.

But how is there a possibility of the cow being a non-cow, which is now being negated by you? How also is it possible to negate something with regard to the cow if it has not been understood (positively) as a cow? Without an awareness of the latter object (the negated), we cannot find a negation (to be possible). We have already stated in this matter that the first awareness does not arise in this case. And without the first awareness, there is no negation (possible).

Text 47: The theory of exclusion (as designation) is also not tenable, for the alternatives are not defensible. To wit: Is the exclusion of the non-cow with regard to the cow itself distinct or non-distinct? If it is itself distinct, is it locatable or non-locatable? If it is locatable (or located) then it is a quality (an attribute) by virtue of being located. In this case, the word 'cow' designates an attribute, not the cow-individual. Then in 'the cow stands' there would not be identity (coreferentiality) between the designable of 'the cow' and 'stands'. If it is unlocated, then what gives the meaning of the genitive in 'The exclusion *of* the cow'? If it is (finally) non-distinct, then it is nothing but the cow itself, and hence you have not succeeded in establishing anything (more than what we admit). Is this exclusion one with regard to each thing or many? This must be stated. If it is *one* and connected with many cows (individuals) then it is (nothing but) the cowness. If it is many, then such exclusions are as innumerable as the particular things themselves. Then designation of each would be impossible to learn, awareness of the meaning from the word could not be reasonable.

Note: This is the *ānantya* argument again (see Text 6).

Text 48: You would have to face this question now: Is this e xclusion designable or non-designable? If it is designable, then it is not always the case that the designation of the word is exclusion of the other (for sometimes it is the exclusion of the exclusion itself?). Or, there would be an infinite regress. For the word 'exclusion' designates by excluding the non-exclusion, and the second word 'non-exclusion' will follow suit, and this will regress to infinity.

If you say, it is non-designable, it contradicts your statement 'the word excludes the designation by other words.' If you say that it is exclusion of the word, not what the word says, you would have to state what is its own meaning/designation apart from what the word says. If you say that (i.e. what the word says) is its own designation or meaning, then also it contradicts your (previous) statement. You have stated,

the word is said to designate as it effects exclusion of the designation by other words with regard to its own meaning.

The meaning of this sentence would, under this interpretation, be that the word designates by not designating others.

Note: Uddyotakara looks for contradiction in Dinnāga's own wordings—a common move.

Text 49: The word 'not-one' (= 'many') is about two, three, etc., and therefore the specific items should be resorted to for understanding the generic sense. If we do not resort to the specific, it is not proper for us to understand the particular from the general word.

The two words 'blue' and 'lotus' (in 'the blue-lotus'—a compound) are both primary, and it is improper to understand one as the qualifier and the other qualifiable. Grammar rules that the qualifier-word comes first in order (in the compound '(the) blue-lotus'), and now because both are primary (neither is secondary and hence only a qualifier) there would not be a use like '(the) blue-lotus'). (When exclusion is the meaning, both are on a par and one cannot be said to qualify the other.) This also explains the problem with the two words 'king' and 'man' (in the compound word 'the king-man').

Text 50: Those who hold the 'exclusion' doctrine must also explain the meaning of coreferentiality.

He who maintains that the word designates exclusion of the other, should explain how the two exclusions, that of the non-blue and that of the non-lotus, can be said to be coreferential.

He who maintains that the word designates positive entities, on the other hand, explains that the words 'blue' and 'lotus' designate the particular (lotus-thing) which is endowed with a quality and a universal. The universal (lotus-ness) and the quality (blue-colour) reside in the thing (substance), i.e., the particular, not the exclusion of the non-blue and the exclusion of the non-lotus. Therefore, there is no meaning attachable to the notion of coreferentiality (in the 'exclusion' theory).

Now, this theory of the exclusion of the other contradicts the established facts each time it is attempted to be understood with alternative interpretations.

General Comment: The argument of Uddyotakara against Diṅnāga touches upon a number of important issues in the philosophy of language. It is important to note the nature of the theory of the meaning which Uddyotakara is trying to develop while arguing against the *apoha* theory of meaning of Diṅnāga.

Notes

1. This enigmatic term is, however, differently interpreted in Kumarila's *Śloka-vārttika.*
2. See *Nyāyasūtra* with Vātsyāyana's *Bhāṣya*, Uddyotakara's *Nyāyavārttika*, Vācaspati's *Tātparyaṭikā* and Viśvanātha's *Vṛtti*, ed. by A. Tarkatirtha and N. Tarkatirtha, Calcutta: Calcutta University Press, 1936–44.

References

Bhartṛhari, 1966, *Vākyapadīya* with Helārāja's commentary, ed. by Iyer, K.A. Subrahmania, Deccan College Postgraduate Research Institute, Poona.

Dharmakīrti, 1959, *Pramānavārttika Svārthānumāna Parichcheda*, vol. II, ed. by Dalsukhbhai Malvania, Varanasi: Banaras Hindu University.

Hattori, M. 1968, *Dignāga on Perception*, Harvard University Press, Cambridge (Mass).

———, 1980, '*Apoha* and *Pratibhā*', in M. Nagatomi, Dimock, Masson and Matilal (eds), *Sanskrit and Indian Studies*, Dordrecht, D. Reidel.

Hayes, R. 1988, *Dignāga on the Interpretation of Signs*, Dordrecht: Kluwer Academic Pub.

Herzberger, R. 1987, *Bhartṛhari and the Buddhists*, Dordrecht. D. Riedel.

Jambuvijayaji, Muni. 1961, *Vaiśeṣika Sūtra*, Baroda: Gaekward Oriental Series.

Katsura, S. 1975, 'New Sanskrit Fragments of the *Pramāṇasamuccaya*', *Journal of Indian Philosophy*, 1975: 67–8.

Kitagawa, H. *Diṅnāga*, in Japanese (an English version in typescript made available to the author).

Mallavādin. 1966, 1976, *Dvādaśānanayacakra*, ed. Muni Jambuvijayaji, 2 vols, Bhavnagar.

Matilal, B.K. 1971, *Epistemology, Logic and Grammar in Indian Philosophical Analysis*, The Hague: Mouton.

Kumārila, *Mīmāṃsā-Śloka-Vārttika*, ed., R.S. Tailanga Manavalli, Varanasi, Chowkhamba, 1898.

Nyāyadarśana (2 vols), eds, T. Nyāya-Tarkatirtha et al., Calcutta. 1936–44.

16

Is *Prasaṅga* a Form of Deconstruction?

Prasaṅga is regarded by most as a philosophical method by which philosophical/metaphysical theses are critically examined and shown to be internally inconsistent. I shall compare this with a modern concept, deconstruction, and try to see whether or not such efforts make either concept a little more intelligible.

David Seyfort Ruegg has said in his book on Mādhyamika[1] that *prasaṅga* 'serves to relativize and deconstruct our artificially posited entities with their respective conditions, which are thus annulled ('zeroed') both as substantial entities and ultimately valid philosophical categories'. This was a casual remark in a book where the history of Mādhyamika thought in India and Tibet has been very carefully and meticulously discussed. Ruegg did not explain what he meant by 'deconstruction' (but obviously he was thinking of the very recent and well-known concept championed by Jacques Derrida and post-structuralists). Nor did Ruegg analyse the *prasaṅga* from of argument (usually called 'dialectics' by modern interpreters) in a way that would support the idea of its kinship with deconstrction. I have raised the question here, but I am not sure whether I can give a definite 'yes' or 'no' answer to it. But perhaps it is the nature of such philosophical questions that they seldom have any definite and straightforward answers. While we pose and ponder over such questions, certain muddles and confusions are cleared up, and that is all we can hope for. In the present case, I cannot say that we would proceed any further. In the Buddhist canonical texts, the Buddha is supposed to have identified and separated certain philosophically loaded questions, which, according to the Buddha, *need not be answered*. He called them *avyākṛta* 'not to be explained or analysed' or 'not to be answered'. (I differ from those who prefer the usual rendering of the term as 'unanswerable'.) These questions (e.g., 'Is the body different from the person or the soul? Or are they identical?') have been pondered over by philosophers over the millennia, but still we do not have any satisfactory answers.

The task, as I see it, is twofold. First, one should explain what 'deconstruction' is or how it is generally understood by modern post-structuralists. Second, one should give an analysis of the Mādhyamika 'dialectic' (*prasaṅga*) in such a way as to make it intelligible so that we would be in a position to ascertain its importance as a philosophical method. As I am not fully qualified to perform the first part of the task with any confidence, I shall concentrate on the second part. It is hoped that this would help to resolve to some extent the issues connected with not only the first part of the task but also with the main question in general.

Deconstruction, as I understand it (and I must quickly add that I do not understand it fully), is a form of philosophical criticism directed against the metaphysical or rhetorical structure of a 'text' or a discourse, or even a theory. The imagery is apparently reminiscent of the construction industry. The text is supposed to present a 'structure' in the structuralist's sense. A critic's choice is to 'dismantle' the structure. The idea, however, is not to demolish the edifice but to 'reinscribe' it in a way that would expose its lack of any transcendental significance or meaning. A text can be anything. A discourse can be on anything, philosophy, metaphysics, literature, linguistics, social anthropology. It is the structuralist's reading of the text that is relevant in our context. The deconstructionist's reading of the discourse is, I believe, implicitly 'Freudian' in its approach. The major preoccupation of the author, or rather the dominant concern of the text is shown to betray itself. Deconstruction is in a sense 'the interpretation of dreams'. Using implicitly the psychoanalytic technique, the critic exposes the 'return of the repressed' syndrome in the text. The text, much as the patient, is not destroyed thereby. It is a writing 'under erasure' (in Derrida's language). It is 'sous nature'. That is to write a word, cross it out, and then print both the word and deletion. As Gayatri Spivak explains, 'since the word is inaccurate, it is crossed out. Since it is necessary, it remains legible'.[2]

Perhaps some sampling is in order. Saussurian semiology, Derrida notes in *Positions*, by arguing that the signified was inseparable from the signifier, that they are two faces of the one and same product, turned against the metaphysical tradition which nurtured the concept of the transcendental *signified* and from which nevertheless Saussure borrowed the concept of sign. But the modern (Saussurian) linguist's preoccupation with the study of speech alone and his rejection of writing would be, in

Derrida's view, symptomatic of a much broader tendency which may easily give in to deconstruction. A deconstructionist would relate the *phono*centrism to *logo*centrism, would oppose subjectivity with objectivity thereby hinting at the undoing of the original position itself. It would be thus a writing under erasure. A deconstruction in this way criticizes 'metaphysics', i.e., a science of presence, and yet remains unabashedly within the clôture of metaphysics, for it is a process of effacing the presence of a thing and yet keeping it legible. This method is explicitly therapeutic. It is supposed to 'free us from and guard us within, the metaphysical enclosure' (Spivak, *Of Grammatology, xli*). If *prasaṅga* is to be related to deconstruction at all, then this feature seems to be more relevant.

Referring to decentering of the structurality of structure, which, according to him, is a symptom, particularly, in our era heightened by such critics like Nietzsche, Freud and Heidegger, Derrida remarks:

> But all these destructive discourses and all their analogues are trapped in a kind of circle. This circle is unique. It describes the form of the relation between the history of metaphysics and the destruction of the history of metaphysics. There is no sense in doing without the concepts of metaphysics in order to shade metaphysics.[3]

This seems to have, in the broader perspective of the demolition of metaphysics, a very significant resonance to Nāgārjuna's two main points of his critique of Nyāya metaphysics. One is circularity, and the other is his insistence that, short of circularity, we will end up with an irreconcilable difference and we have no language or concepts to explain this difference—*viśeṣahetuś ca vaktavyaḥ*. 'The reason for difference must be stated.' Both these points have been emphasized by Nāgārjuna in the beginning of his *Vigrahavyāvartanī*. Derrida also insists on the irreconcilability of difference that is made in the metaphysics of *presence* and the insurmountable problem of stating the destructive proposition. We quote from Derrida again:

> We have no language—no syntax and no lexicon—which is foreign to this history; we can pronounce not a single destructive proposition which has not already had to slip into the form, the logic, and the implicit postulations of precisely what it seeks to contest.[4]

Nāgārjuna also has conceded that there cannot be a *stated* proposition (in a logical discourse proposed by the critics; cf. *pratijñā*) to that effect.

Although the historical situations are different, places and other contextual factors also very considerably, I believe the intellectual crisis in one age in India here has a 'family resemblance' with the one that Derrida is referring to. Hence the resonances between them are not entirely superficial. Philosophically speaking, I believe it is fruitful to remember some historical antecedents, if there were any, even if they are from different contexts, cultures and geo-political situations. This is the purpose of this exercise.

A deconstructionist resorts to practical clues. In deciphering a text he would single out a word or a group of words which may 'harbour an unresolvable contradiction' or would choose the use of a particular word in a number of ways which would also expose the lack of its unified meaning, would select a metaphor that might inadvertently allow the opposite view to take a firm grip—the purpose of all these being the undoing of the text or the discourse, the revealing of its self-transgression, its undecidability. It is not the commentator's occasional grasp of a moment of ambiguity or irony which may be explained away. It is locating a place in the text, or a moment in the discourse, 'that genuinely threatens to collapse that system' (Spivak, *lxxv*). A deconstructive reading does not bring about the hidden implications or latent weakness but exposes its undecidability, opens up the horizon of manifold and indefinite meaning. It is a new form of exegesis.

A deconstructionist, according to the rule of the game, cannot claim a sacrosanct status for himself. He should realize that his choice of 'evidence' is arbitrary. The name of the game is criticism and self-criticism marked by a self-distrust. Otherwise we would invite a paradox. A deconstruction of deconstruction is required by the logic of deconstruction itself. Only provisionally might a deconstructionist 'forget' ('will to forget') her own vulnerability, might assume that she at least means what she says. But necessarily the critic's text is self-deconstructed, and this, as Spivak argues, creates the lure of freedom: 'The fall into the abyss of deconstruction inspires us with as much pleasure as fear. We are intoxicated with the prospect of never hitting the bottom' (Spivak, *lxxvii*). This fits very well with the contemporary mood, or the mood of what may be called post-modernism in thought—the insecurity resulting from the undecidability factor reigning in the arena of ethics, politics and social thinking today. With this rather simple account of deconstruction as a background, I shall proceed to the main part of my task: an account of the Mādhyamika dialectics with its historical underpinnings, and of the dispute among Buddhapālita, Bhāvaviveka and Candrakīrti. I have singled out only certain features of deconstruction, for there are some resonances with *prasaṅga* in these cases.

A philosophical school or system that develops over several centuries or more must also take account of and assimilate the history of its development within itself. Mādhyamika thought had a long history in India. It was systematized, and ramified into two substreams, for about half-a-millennium after Nāgārjuna, its founder. A synthesis of the Mādhyamika and the Yogācāra on the philosophical level took place primarily with Śāntarakṣita, and nearly about the same time Mantrāyana and the Tantric school of praxis developed out of the Mādhyamika.

Modern scholars have been dealing the Mādhyamika thought for nearly one hundred years (L. de la Vallée Poussin's edition was published in 1903–13).[5] The school has been variously described by modern scholars as 'nihilism, monism, irrationalism, agnosticism, scepticism, criticism, dialectic, mysticism, acosmism, absolutism, relativism, nominalism, and linguistic analysis with therapeutic value'.[6] We do not have to agree with all these varying descriptions. Some of these descriptions however do seem to correspond to some aspects of Mādhyamika thought. I wish now to add one more motivated description of the Mādhyamika, it is anti-metaphysical. It does not deny, in my view, the reality *out there*. But it definitely rejects any of our attempts to form a metaphysical system, any realistic or idealistic or relativistic account of such reality. For it claims that such systems would be internally inconsistent and hence such attempts would have little explanatory value.

We may raise a question. Why should a Buddhist concern himself with such a metaphilosophical issue? In search for a tentative answer, let us consider this. It is based upon the assumption of a simple theory of action. Our actions are guided by our inherent beliefs in the values and truths of the concepts that constitute our general conceptual scheme. Metaphysical realism tries to reify such concepts into substantial realities and thereby assign the value to them that we desire and prefer them to have. The Mādhyamika wants to expose the hollowness, in fact emptiness, of the mechanism of this evaluation, desire, and preference. A thing, we assume, has a nature or essence, it can thereby do us some good or harm us, and therefore we act to obtain it or avoid it. The Mādhyamika wants to show that such an assumption is entirely tentative and dependent upon our desire-orientated existence, our drive for pleasure, our drive for becoming. A *bhāva* or a thing is *only* evaluated to have an existence, an essence and a meaning or a purpose to serve. But actually it is *empty* of any assigned nature, its assumed value. Our desires and preferences assign this 'own-nature' to things and thereby generate our actions and thus perpetuate our existence. In the terminology of Buddhism it is described as follows. Our thirst (*taṇhā*) perpetuates our becoming. Hence, if it can be shown that what drives our life's activity is actually not what it is assumed to be, for it lacks its own nature, is devoid of any value, then such a thing will lose all its allure and our thirst is gone. If thirst is gone, suffering ceases, and Buddhism wins.

The Mādhyamika suggests a further reading of this message. The 'own-nature' of a *bhāva* or a *dharma*, can be read as the essential value that it is believed to have. Such a value may not simply by desire-generated but contextually conditioned. The evaluation may be simply non-absolute or non-ultimate (though not necessarily only subjective) because of its contextual conditioning (cf. *pratītyasamutpāda*) as well as our conditioned understanding (cf. *upādāya prajñapti*). The Mādhyamika argues that this conditioned origination itself would fully expose or unfold the *emptiness* (*śūnyatā*) or things, it would show that it lacks its nature and therefore its ultimate value. For our *a priori* understanding of 'own-nature' or the essential value of a thing runs counter to its being conditioned. Hence dependent origination of *bhāvas* proves their emptiness.

It has been claimed that the Mādhyamika re-established the Buddha's doctrine and fully brought about its philosophical implication. The doctrine of emptiness was a logical extension of the no-soul or *anattā* doctrine. The notion of an ultimate soul-substance distinct from the psycho-physical aggregate or complex (*skandha*) was found to be an *empty* concept, a hollow notion, for it was argued that in this kind of eternalism there would be no hope of obtaining ultimate freedom from suffering, i.e., the final cessation of suffering, *nirvāṇa*. If there is a soul and if it is as it seems to be, engrossed in materiality and steeped in suffering, then since nothing can change its own 'nature', such a soul can never be *free*, can never attain the unconditioned state. What is conditioned can be made to cease through de-conditioning. What is natural or non-conditioned remains as it is forever. If the person is devoid of its own-nature, that is if there is no soul, there is *pudgala nairātmya*. And if there is no soul can there be any way by which we can make sense of anything else, i.e., of all the *dharmas*? Do the *dharmas* have their own-natures? For the Mādhyamikas, this is only a rhetorical question. For the *dharma-nairātmya* is only a logical extension of *pudgala-nairātmya*.

So far I have shown how the sceptical dialectic was used by the Buddha himself as well as by the Mādhyamika to develop a destructive criticism of metaphysical realism. But the Mādhyamika was not a sceptic, although some scholars (R. Hayes)[7] might be satisfied with just that interpretation. We can call it the 'de-conditioning' of metaphysical beliefs, rather than the 'deconstruction' of metaphysics. The Buddha recognized the fundamental problems of suffering and the implication of the Buddha's doctrine of four great (noble) truths unfold this aspect. The Mādhyamika therefore realized the potential and real danger in accepting *theories* as truths, means as ends, concepts as real entities. If the dynamic nature of reality is not understood, if the 'own-nature' of things are not understood as empty (*śūnyatāṃ yadi na vetsi*), then there is no hope for changing anything, no chance of the cessation of turmoil and suffering, and then the revolutionaries, the visionaries and the Buddhas alike can give up all their efforts out of frustration. Hence Nāgārjuna's significant proclamation: the Buddha's doctrine is understood only if the emptiness of everything is understood.

Within 400 years after Nāgārjuna the school not only became systematized but also developed two sub-streams associated with Buddhapālita (AD 470–540) and Bhāvaviveka (AD 500–580). The schism did not have any doctrinal basis but rather depended exclusively on the method of philosophical reasoning to reach the same doctrinal basis, the emptiness as truth. Accordingly in the Tibetan tradition, these two sub-schools were referred to as *Prāsaṅgika* and *Svātantrika*. Buddhapālita's metaphilosophical point was this. The philosophical activity of a Mādhyamika is primarily and predominantly refutative and negative. To reach emptiness as truth, i.e., a position where emptiness would dawn upon us as truth, we must refute not only the *asserted* position or proposition but also the *implied* counter-position. And this type of double, triple or quadruple refutation can be done well with the well-known *prasaṅga* or *reductio* type of reasoning. For in this reasoning we refute a position because we are faced with the undesired or absurd consequences implied by the position. These implications may simply be logical implications and hence the refutation could be *a priori*. The famous ending of the arguments by Nāgārjuna was 'it does not fit' *na yujyate*' or '*nopapaadyate*' 'it is not understandable (i.e. incomprehensible = absurd)'. If we can refute both the position and the counter-position in this way we can maintain the Mādhyamika doctrine of emptiness.

Bhāvaviveka on the other hand thought that this type of *a priori* refutation is an inherently weak form of philosophical argument. He was quite impressed by the logico-epistemological method developed by Diṅnāga, where philosophical arguments must be fortified with a logical reason (*liṅga*) and empirical example in their support (a refinement of the old Nyāya method). Hence according to Bhāvaviveka, the Mādhyamika philosophical argument can be completely structured in this new way, where there will be a *pakṣa*—a position to be proved, and a *hetu*, a *dṛṣṭānta*, i.e., an example supporting the inferential connection.

I shall now use a section of Candrakīrti's text as the substratum for our discussion, *Prasannapadā* on I.3 of *Madhyamakaśāstra*. Candrakīrti's words will sometimes be reminiscent of some of the general comments made often by the deconstructionist today when he is faced with a given critique of the metaphysics of being. The original (*mūla*) text of Nāgārjuna attempts to develop a critique of the notion of *hetu* and *pratyaya*, roughly the 'metaphysics' of causation as it was understood by the *Ābhidharmikas*. Causation implies that something that was *not* there before has been caused to come into existence. Nāgārjuna argues that nothing can originate in this way for none of the four possible alternatives holds: (1) something *x* can be self-originating, (2) *x* can be originating from another, (3) *x* can be both, or (4) can be neither.

Buddhapālita explains the first alternative as follows. The beings or things do not originate out of themselves, for (a) if they did the 'origination' would be without any significance, and (b) if they did, there would be an undesired consequence. These two reasons, (a) and (b), are further explained. Reason (a) means: there is no need for the further origination of entities which already exist by themselves. Reason (b) means: If something that already exists may be allowed to originate then such origination cannot be 'temporal' (*kadācitka*), i.e. restricted to a particular time of origination. That is, without originating at a given time it should originate always!

Bhāvaviveka found this exegesis to be faulty. He mounted his attack as follows. The formulation of the argument by Buddhapālita, (i.e. Buddhapālita's 'text' itself) is improper. For, first, it does not mention the reason, nor does it cite an example to support the reason. Second, it does not refute the criticisms of the Mādhyamika by others. Third, being in the form of a *prasaṅga* (a type of *reductio* argument) is may establish the opposite hypothesis, that of non-self-origination which may imply origination from another, but since that is also refuted, we will end up with a contradiction where origination is both denied and then not denied. In other words, Buddhapālita has used a *reductio* type argument. 'Had it been *X*, then we would have an impossible, and unacceptable situation, and absurd consequence: something that originates must be originating all the time or it will never originate. The point of this argument is to deny *X*, i.e., self-origination. But the thesis of other-origination follows, and if that too is denied, then two denials clash headlong with each other. Such is the thrust of Bhāvaviveka's argument. Should we say therefore that he has successfully 'deconstructed' Buddhapālita? For being a Mādhyamika himself he cannot successfully demolish the original motivation of Buddhapālita: both are out to dismantle the *Ābhidharmika* edifice of *pratyayas*—'causal theory'. But this is still a premature question. Let us wait to see how Candrakīrti, the champion of the Prāsaṅgika school, 'deconstructs' (if I am permitted to use this term here) the above text of Bhāvaviveka's.

Candrakīrti begins, 'We consider all these criticisms to be inappropriate. How? let me explain.' He takes the first point about the lack of mention of reason and example, and declares it to be an unimportant charge. For the opponent of the Mādhyamika is the one who accepts self-origination, and he is asked, 'Is your 'cause' the same as that which originates?' And he asserts it to be so. To him then the Mādhyamika says (as Buddhapālita has done), 'we cannot find any need or purpose for re-origination of something that already exists. On the other hand we see an infinite regress being opened up if re-origination is conceded. You do not wish to assign the re-origination to something already in existence, nor can you embrace an infinite regress. Hence your discourse does not have the resolution that you intend it to have. Besides you would run into contradiction with what you have already accepted.'

The opponent (of the Mādhyamika) is here confronted with a threat that his preferred structure may collapse. Hence he may decide not to assert any further thesis. In that case, there would arise no need for citing a reason along with a supporting example. However, if he is 'shameless' and undaunted even by such a threat of contradiction in his own assumptions, he would not step back even by a counter-argument endowed with a reason and a (supporting) example. In that case, he appears to have taken leave of his sanity. Hence we would not like to quarrel with a mad man who would not listen to reason. In this way, Candrakīrti concludes, Bhāvaviveka's critique of Buddhapālita only exposes his own predilection for an inferential (syllogistic) form of argument. Bhāvaviveka wishes to fortify his argument with an inference (based upon reason and an example). However, for a Mādhyamika it is improper to construct an independent 'syllogistic' form of inference. Why? The Mādhyamika does not have a 'provable' position or hypothesis which can be reached as a conclusion of such an inference. As Āryadeva has said (Candrakīrti quotes from *Catuḥśataka* 16/25), if a position is not characterized by existence, nor by non-existence, nor by both, no one can refute or attack it, no one can blame it. In addition, Candrakīrti quotes two celebrated verses from Nāgārjuna himself, from his *Vigrahavyāvartanī* (1951 ed. by E.H. Johnston and A. Kunst):

If I had any statable (defensible) thesis thence could I be faulted. I do not have such a statable thesis, hence I cannot be faulted.

If I apprehended (asserted) anything through the evidence of perception etc., then I would have affirmed something or denied something. But since I did not, I cannot be blamed. (Verses 29, 30)

Bhāvaviveka might argue that it would be improper to say that the Mādhyamika would not have any thesis to defend nor any statable (syllogistic) inference based upon reason, etc. For the Mādhyamika does refute the Sāṃkhya opponent by formulating an independent thesis, viz. 'the internal' bases (faculty of vision, etc.) do not originate out of themselves'. Bhāvaviveka's critique can even go further at this point. Using the Sāṃkhya reply to Buddhapālita's refutative statement, Bhāvaviveka would repeat his second objection, viz. the Sāṃkhya criticisms of the Mādhyamika have *not* been answered and resolved properly. The Sāṃkhyas ask: what is exactly meant by 'out of themselves'? if the phrase refers to the products, i.e., the originating entities, then it is futile. For the Sāṃkhya already admits that the 'internal bases' evolve out of the 'unmanifest' matter. Hence the refutative statement on this interpretation would be establishing something (a negative thesis) that is already established for the Sāṃkhya. 'Establishing the established' is regarded a 'fault' of an argument, for it is redundant. If, however, the said phrase refers to the causes from which those entities originate, there the position would be threatened by a contradiction. For everything that originates, originates from being necessarily existent as a cause—this is the accepted doctrine of the Sāṃkhyas and hence the above refutative statement would run counter to this established doctrine. In short, the Sāṃkhya faults the Mādhyamika on two counts. On one interpretation the Mādhyamika's effort would be redundant, on another he would be threatened by contradiction. Bhāvaviveka now points out that Buddhapālita has not been able to answer these two points.

Having set up the position of Bhāvaviveka in this manner, Candrakīrti points out that Bhāvaviveka in his eagerness had forgotten that Buddhapālita did not assign a 'reason' to his refutative thesis nor mention supportive evidence for it. In other words, he was not formulating a proper (syllogistic) argument of the form: *A* is *B*, because of *C*, just as the case of *X* ('There is fire on the hill, because there is smoke, just as in the kitchen'). It was Bhāvaviveka who formulated the syllogistic form of argument, e.g. 'Things do not self-originate, for they are already existent, just as a pot'. When and only when arguments are presented in this form with a proper evidential reason (*hetu*) being assigned and an example being cited in support, then and only then one can find such 'faults' as redundancy or contradiction. But Buddhapālita did not take that way out. He presented only a *prasaṅga* or Indian version of a *reductio* agreement, where the position or a thesis could be refuted on pain of absurd consequence, contradiction or incoherence. Besides, even the third criticism of Bhāvaviveka has no foundation. For a *prasaṅga* argument is such that it is employed only to refute or *reject* a position; it does not involve the acceptance of the counter position or negation of a negative thesis. Those who employ only *prasaṅga* would not be prepared to concede any assertable thesis, positive or negative. In fact they would fault the negative or the counter thesis almost in the same way and almost as much as they fault the positive thesis.

This, then, is Candrakīrti's way of 'deconstructing' Bhāvaviveka's preferred form of argument. An illustration from *Karatalaratna* (chang-chen-lun) can be furnished. It summarizes the Mādhyamika doctrine in the form of a discussion on both levels, reasoning and meditation. This shows that the schism was not simply based on metaphilosophical ground, i.e., difference in their ways of arguing for the same doctrine, but also on difference in mental culture, or meditational praxis for meditating upon the Mādhyamika truth, emptiness:

> Conditioning things are *in reality* (*paramārthataḥ*) empty of *svabhāva* for they are conditioned, just as a magical creation. Unconditioned things are *in reality* not real for they are not produced, just as a sky-flower.[8]

What is important here is the qualification 'in reality'. The inferential subject and the inferable property belonging to it (*pakṣa* and *sādhya*), belong to different levels or realms of reality: the conventional level and the ultimate level. The proposition spans these two realms, selecting the subject from the phenomenal and the property to be inferred, i.e., the predicate from the ultimate. Candrakīrti finds this to be an irreconcilable double-talk which destroys the thesis itself. Things are 'conditioned' and so recognized as far as their phenomenal existence is concerned, whereas the property to be empty of *svabhāva* is how they are to be understood at the ultimate level. The abyss between realms, the ultimate and the convention, that is opened up by the insertion of the qualification 'in reality' can never be bridged, and hence the thesis would be unintelligible.

We cannot honestly form a proposition, or a *pratijñā* by juxtaposing the two. If on the other hand, the said qualification does not have such significance, it is redundant and pointless.

A logical reason (*liṅga*) is a technical term here. It is defined in Diṅnāga's system as one having *three* characteristics. It should characterize the subject (*pakṣa*), the locus. It should characterize a similar locus, a locus similar to the subject-locus. And it should not characterize anything that is a 'counter-example' where the property to be inferred is not present, a locus dissimilar to the subject-locus. It is usually supported by an example and 'counter-example' or a counter-case. This is in brief the structure which this type of inference must conform to. Bhāvaviveka in his formulation shows that his logical reason characterizes the subject-locus, for conditioned-ness is a character of every conditioned thing. But the proposition to be proven is a negative proposition. Hence a supporting example is possible, 'the magical creation' is a part of the group of conditioned things. But a counter- or negative example is not available. For it has to be something unconditioned. But such things are not to be found in this theory. Hence the only way we have to ascertain the logical relation that conditionedness implies emptiness is to have a positive case where both characteristics are present, i.e., the magical creation, for only such positive cases can warrant the generalization that all conditioned things are empty. A negative citation would have added to the degree of certitude belonging to this generalization. This would have increased its force for proving the proposition in question. In any case Bhāvaviveka thinks that this lack of negative example does not matter, for he has at least given a well-formulated argument distinct from *reductio* or *prasaṅga*, an independent inference, not simply an *a priori* implication. It is a *svatantra anumāna*, which proves the Mādhyamika truth beyond doubt. The Prāsaṅgika, i.e. the Buddhapālita School, neglects the virtue of the empirical constraint and hence there is a built-in weakness in the *prasaṅga* dialectic. This new type of reasoning to confirm the emptiness doctrine should also be internalized for meditational purpose.

Bhāvaviveka added another logical point to strengthen the Mādhyamika dialectic, to free it from the charge of contradiction or inconsistency or irrationalism. This is the point about negation. In order to maintain the middle course by avoiding extremes, the Mādhyamikas are bound to reject or refute sometimes both a proposition and its contradiction. 'Things do not have own-nature nor do they have other-nature,' '*Bhāvas* are neither self-produced nor other-produced, nor even both nor neither' (cf. *catuṣkoṭi*). This raises the question of incomprehension. For one may say that it violates what are sometimes called the fundamental principles of thought. Who can comprehend a statement if it says that something is neither A nor non-A, nor both, nor neither? The Mādhyamika dialectician can answer that that is precisely the point. The binary opposition is a principle of *vikalpa* or a product of our dichotomising thought. We have been trained that way to understand and organize our experience. This is, perhaps, the acceptable and convenient way to interpret our experience. But the Mādhyamika wants to move beyond this conventional truth, i.e., the conventional way of interpreting reality. This given way of interpreting experience has only a pragmatic, practical value for the Mādhyamika. This is not ultimate. This has only a provisional status. This rule of binary opposition, or contradicting pairs (of which we can accept only one, not both), is a fundamental principle, when and only when we accept the 'own-nature' theory. The emptiness doctrine destroys this *own-nature* theory. Hence violation of the principle of binary opposition is not a fault here but a necessary ingredient of the Mādhyamika thinking. This is how we transcend dichotomising thought.

Bhāvaviveka would, I think, accept such points of the dialectician. But he wishes to enrich the method of reasoning and meditation by adding another dimension to it. That is the concept of a special type of negation where a negation does not imply (nor does it *presuppose*) the opposite of what is negated (we may call it *presuppositionless* negation, following Hans Herzberger).[9] In Indian tradition, the grammarians (e.g. Patañjali's *Mahābhāṣya*), the Mīmāṃsakas and the Naiyāyikas from the very beginning talked about two senses of negation: *paryudāsa* and *prasajya-pratiṣedha.* Contextually one was nominally bound and the other was verbally bound (as explained in Matilal 1968).[10] Sanskrit grammarians noted that the former is *samāsa*-sensitive that is, allows the negative particle to be compounded with other words) while the latter is *samāsa*-resistant or compound-resistant (the negative particle is generally left to itself). On the basis of this, I have remarked elsewhere (1971, Section 5.9)[11] that in the former type the denial aspect is overridden by the commitment aspect while it is just the other way around in the latter type. In each act of negation, there is some implicit commitment to affirm something, the opposite (the contrary or contradictory) of what is negated. The 'denial' aspect overrides this implicit commitment in some negation more than others. Using a suggestion noted in Y. Kajiyama's paper in 1957,[12] I had noted in 1971 that Bhāvaviveka seems to have explicitly argued in favour of 'the strongest kind of negation' (cf. a special use of *prasajya-pratiṣedha*) where the negating act amounts to a *simple* denial which will completely contravene the implicit 'commitment' aspect, i.e., the commitment to implicity affirm anything even the opposite of what is negated.[13]

Hans Herzberger wrote a brilliant article in 1975, 'Double Negation in Buddhist Logic', where he developed a unique concept of the apohist negation suitable for the logical analysis of the Buddhist doctrine of *apoha*. In this connection, Herzberger suggested that the content of every sentence (which will include negative ones) can be factored into two components, roughly on the model:[14] presupposition and manifest content (p. 13). From this it may be suggested that Bhāvaviveka, in view of what has already been said above, will favour a special kind of negative sentence where the manifest content would simply include a denial and the presuppositional element in it would be completely removed. In other words, the negative sentences in Mādhyamika dialectics are expressive of such 'non-presuppositional' negation. This is not a very far cry from what I have called the 'no-commitment' denial that is most suitable for Bhāvaviveka. David Ruegg in his book *The Literature of the Madhyamaka School of Philosophy in India*, has used the term 'non-presuppositional' negation and ascribed the concept to Bhāvaviveka.[15]

In this connection I would add a brief comment on the relevance of the concept of 'zero' to interpret or translate the Mādhyamika concept of *śūnya* in *śūnyatā*. In 1971, I suggested (p. 152) with trepidation that while trying to translate the term '*śūnyatā*' of the Mādhyamika we might also consider the popular mathematical term 'zero'.[16] The idea was that since the symbol for zero is regarded in arithmetic as something that has a value when and only when it is attached to some other number (i.e., it has a value only for its position in a given natural number, a place-value), we may use this model to elicit an interpretation of the term '*śūnyatā*' in the Mādhyamika. (Incidentally this idea has nothing to do with the rather technical sense attached to zero in the philosophy of arithmetic, dealing with foundations of Arithmetic, for example, in the Peano postulates, where 0 is an undefined term and heads the list of non-negative 0, 1, 2 . . .). The Mādhyamika declared every *bhāva* to be *śūnya* (devoid of its own-nature) because it cannot have any absolute claim to existence or reality, but is only intelligible in relation to its causes and conditions (*hetus* and *pratyayas*). Hence the suggestion was that *bhāvas* are like zeroes, having a value (a claim to reality) only in relation to something else or to the position it occupies in a complex, and consequently no absolute value (claims to existence/reality independently).

This suggestion was criticised by some scholars at the time, and perhaps, rightly, because my cryptic comment did not make it clear that I was aiming at the popular, non-technical conception of zero. In any case the underlying point of the suggestion remains. Now it is rather a pleasant surprise to see that Prof. David Ruegg has in his new book (1981) as well as in an earlier article (1978) referred to an earlier paper by L. Mäll (1968) who used the term 'zerology' for *śūnyatā*.[17] I was unaware of this paper. Ruegg is, of course, right in emphasizing that the mathematical (that is, technical and sophisticated) notion of 'zero' should not be taken into account when we are trying to interpret the Mādhyamika *śūnyatā*. It is a different notion. The similarity which struck me in 1971 was only with the popular notion of zero, or a cipher obtaining some meaning and value only by being positioned in the proper manner, otherwise remaining a cipher. The word *śūnya*, unlike the arithmetical symbol for cipher, is always a relative term in the Mādhyamika writing. It is said that a *bhāva* is *śūnya*, i.e. 'devoid' of something, i.e., its *svabhāva*. Nothing is said to be *śūnya* or 'zero' *per se*. This only shows that the idea of the mathematical analogy does not work all the way.

To come back to Candrakīrti. He says that Bhāvaviveka's attempt to formulate a refutative inference 'syllogistically' to deny the metaphysics of causation is doomed from the beginning. It has been already noted that the insertion of the adjective 'in reality', 'from the ultimate point of view' (*paramārthataḥ*), in the thesis of the inference formula was disastrous. In the context of the refutation of the 'self-origination' view, Candrakīrti points out the 'bases' would not be accepted as self-originating even at the conventional level by a Mādhyamika Buddhist. The Buddha himself in the *Śālistamba-sūtra* made this point clear (and Candrakīrti quotes him). Rejection of both eternalism and annihilationism would be automatically dismissive of the self-origination theory. If the Bhāvaviveka thesis (which he wishes to prove by inference) is 'the "bases" (the eye, etc.) which are only *conventionally* or provisionally real lack self-origination from the ultimate level', we have already created the gap between the two levels, which dissolves the proposition itself and the philosophical argument cannot start. Besides, the provisional reality of the 'bases' (which constitute the subject term here) would never be acceptable to the opponent against whom the argument is directed. Hence from his point of view the inference suffers from the fatal defect of the 'empty subject term'.[18]

What exactly was Candrakīti after? The tradition answers that the *prasaṅga* form of argument is best suited for the Mādhyamika—this is the goal. Any other form would generate absurdities, inconsistencies. No affirmation and no denial may mean writing a proposition and crossing it out, and letting both, the sign and the deletion, stand. The repeated reference to the rejection of the binary opposition between eternalism and annihilationism may have the similar effect. But that is as far as we can go. Probably there is only a family resemblance between 'deconstruction' and *prasaṅga* dialectics. The goal is to dissolve the metaphysical enclosure and also to remain within it. The Mādhyamika would have agreed. For Nāgārjuna clearly says that between *saṃsāra* and *nirvāṇa* there is not even an iota of difference: *nirvāṇa* dissolving *saṃsāra* and at the same time remaining within it. Spivak (*lxxvii*) says that deconstruction shows us 'the lure of abyss as freedom' because we never 'hit the bottom'. The Mādhyamika shows also the lure of emptiness or 'substance-less-ness' or 'bottomlessness'. This is not very different from what has actually lured some, at least, of the modern Mādhyamika philosophers.

I have hinted at the purpose of my exercise in my initial remarks. I believe this has not simply been a juxtaposition of a few points from one cultural context and similar ones from another culture. Buddhism is still part of our global culture. Modern researchers give ample evidence to the vitality and attractiveness of modern Buddhism. Hence, I believe in this relevant context I have shown, or at least offered a glimpse of, the common problem that all critics of metaphysics face and are bound too face, and a useful device has to be only *provisionally* accepted, be it *prasaṅga* or deconstruction, for avoiding the problem of the inevitable circularity on the one hand and unbridgeable abyss of *viśeṣa* 'distinction' on the other.

Notes and References

1. *The Literature of the Mādhyamāka School of Philosophy in India*, Otto Harrassowitz: Wiesbaden, 1981, p. 10.
2. J. Derrida, *Of Grammatology*, John Hopkins, Baltimore (tr. G. Spivak), 1978, p. *xiv*.
3. *Writing and Difference*, tr. A. Ross, 1978.
4. Ibid.
5. L. de La Vallée Poussin, *Mūlamadhyamaka-kārikā*, St Petersburg, 1903–13.
6. Ruegg, *The Literature of the Madhyamaka School of Philosophy in India*, Wiesbaden, 1981, p. 12.
7. *Dignāga on the Interpretation of Signs*, Kluwer, Dordrecht, 1988, pp. 42–71.
8. D. Ruegg, op. cit., p 63.
9. Hans Herzberger, 'Double Negation in Buddhist Logic', *Journal of Indian Philosophy*, 1975, nos 1/2.
10. B.K. Matilal, *The Navyanyāya Doctrine of Negation*, Harvard, Cambridge (Mass.), 1965, pp. 156–7.

11. B.K. Matilal, *Epistemology, Logic and Grammar in Indian Philosophical Analysis*, Mouton, The Hague, 1971.
12. Y. Kajiyama, 'Bhāvaviveka and the Prāsaṅgika School', Nalanda, Mahavihar, 1957.
13. B.K. Matilal, 1971, pp. 164–5.
14. See Herzberger, 1975.
15. Ruegg, p. 65.
16. Matilal 1971, p. 152.
17. D.S. Ruegg, 'Mathematical & Linguistic Models in Indian Thought: The Case of *Śūnyatā*', WZKS 22, 1978, p. 174. L. Mäll, 'Une Approche possible du *śūnyavāda*', *Tel Quel*, 32, 1968, p. 54.
18. See Matilal, 1971, op. cit., ch. 4 for this problem.

17
What is Buddhism?

1. IS BUDDHISM A RELIGION?

Is Buddhism a religion? This has been sometimes denied by modern scholars. The concept of religion seems to imply invariably the idea of a deity and a soul that survives death. Buddhism explicitly denies both and does so emphatically. In the past, I have used the more general term 'soteriology' to hedge the issue at least temporarily. Is soteriology really a more comprehensive concept than religion? Those who use the term today seem to think so and some well-known Buddhologists have used this term. However, this has been vigorously disputed by others. It has been pointed out this term 'soteriology', which implies the aid of a saviour (*soter*), is hardly adequate to do justice to the Buddha's conception of *nirvāṇa* (Hayes, 1988, p. 34). While the point of this criticism can be readily granted, I believe a term sometimes gains an extended dimension in meaning by consistent use in a class of writings by a generation of scholars, and 'soteriology' has gained such sense by its use in the context of such Indian systems as Yoga, Sāṃkhya, and even Nyāya. The concept of a saviour is conspicuous by its absence in each of these systems.

The question 'what is religion?' has never been undisputably answered or decided. If soteriology is stipulated to be an essential mark of religion, then Buddhism, on such stipulative definition, would be considered a religion. However, this may be misleading to the common people. Soteriology is often thought as a 'salvational' system where human souls are saved from damnation. In this sense Buddhism can hardly be a soteriology. For *nirvāṇa* is not salvation, nor are there human souls, according to the Buddha, who could be saved. To call Buddhism a soteriology, we have to propose that there is an ultimate goal and that there are beings who can make an effort to reach that goal by following a particular path. If such vague and very general characterizations are allowed, and the ultimate goal if defined in terms of some form of self-etiolation or a total cessation of whatever is it that makes us tick, then we may be justified in calling Buddhism a religion and a soteriology. Or, if religion is, as Leszek Kolakowski once put it, only 'a lived allegiance to an order of taboos' (1982, p. 194) where breaking a taboo is associated with the consciousness of guilt, then Buddhism is also a religion. If one wants to be squeamish about 'taboo' in Buddhism, I would simply point at the first of the *śikṣāpada*, 'Let us not take the life of any being,' and enough will be said.

Each culture has its 'taboos', unconsciously agreed upon principles, which should not be broken. A rational basis or justification for such principles may or may not be found. The important thing about them, however, is that they are first accepted on faith, and only then some argument may be sought to satisfy our urge for a rational basis. They are the *givens* of the particular culture; without them, the culture will not hold together. Our moral principles are such taboos, and if they are viewed in this manner it would not matter much whether or not we can establish through reason a foundation for the ethics by appeal to God, or a divine mind or certain other religious dogmas.

Buddhism is such a system, with its own *given* principles which are accepted first on faith, and any violation of them would be 'non Buddhistic'. For example, one cannot claim to be following the Buddha's way and say at the same time that there is no such thing as *Karma* (or *Kanma*), moral causation perpetuating the *tṛṣṇā* (or *tanhā*), the thirst for becoming. I cannot be a Buddhist and claim in the same breath that cessation of the false 'personality' conception, or *nirvāṇa*, or *nirodha*, is not my ultimate goal. If I do, I would be a 'crypto-Buddhist', albeit not in the way Śaṃkara was accused of being one. If I take such a stance, I can at best claim to be a Buddhist-sympathiser. One cannot murder a fellow human being and also claim that one is only following the Buddha's way in such acts.

Buddhism is a religion in this extended sense, although it neither accepts a creator as God nor the ultimate reality of human souls which are supposed to strive for ultimate freedom or ultimate bliss. There is no doubt that, as a religion, Buddhism offers 'a lived allegiance' to an order of certain inviolable moral and non-moral principles.

How about the consciousness of guilt which comes from the violation of taboos? In the 'The Buddha's way', one might argue, this will be difficult to find. The presumption of this argument is the view that consciousness of guilt is very much a Western notion, dominant in the Judaeo-Christian tradition. Without being a Freudian convert, one may say that the idea of guilt is connected invariably and hence essentially, with the notion of a God the Father. This is, however, a wrong argument. Guilt is a universal cultural phenomenon in today's world. A Buddhist must also have feelings of guilt and shame, however indirect or transfigured, if he violates one of the cardinal *śikṣāpadas* or ethical virtues. In some cultures, it is more direct and undiluted than in other cultures. The frown of Father God is not the only way to make a child feel guilty. Other factors, such as loss of face before friends, can be equally potent in generating the same feeling.

A religion is invariably connected with the practice of certain rituals. Those who are intellectually attracted to certain principles and doctrines of Buddhism may argue that one need not associate any ritual practices with Buddhism. This is, however, not right either. Elaborate ritual practices, and *Mantras* and *Mandalas*, do constitute an integral part of certain forms of Buddhism, *Vajrayāna* and *Mantrayāna*. Besides, almost all known Buddhist communities in the world inherited, or gradually adopted, many ritual practices that are by now regarded as part and parcel of the creed. Burning incense, for example, when visiting a Buddhist shrine is not a totally unessential part of the practice. Hence, Buddhism qualifies as a religion even from this point of view. Intellectual sympathizers of Buddhism need not deny the point. It is one thing to be a Buddhist but another thing to be its intellectual sympathizer. It is the latter kind who do not find the rituals necessary.

Buddhism is underscored, and has underwritten, a rich and multiple valued philosophical tradition, which has developed along with the spread of Buddhism over the ages. Some modern scholars have claimed that Buddhism is a philosophical discipline, not a religious dogma. Again, this would be an overstatement. Without undermining the highly 'rational', or intellectual approach of the Buddhist way, we can appreciate the philosophical heritage of Buddhism. In fact, the deep philosophical underpinning of the Buddhist practice of meditation along with the eight-fold path is too pronounced to be missed. However, Buddhism, cannot be called only or exclusively a philosophy of life, or even a family of philosophical doctrines. Buddhism, or the Buddha's way, or what the Buddha taught, is both a religion and a matrix for philosophy. The Buddha was concerned with a very practical problem, which we may call the problem of life. Ageing, disease and decay are evitably, inextricably and unavoidable mixed up in the process that we call 'living' or 'becoming', and the question was: Is there a way by which we can resolve the puzzle of life, where 'growing' becomes synonymous with 'decaying'? The Buddha was supposed to have discovered an answer to this puzzle, a way, the Buddha's way. The answer was amazingly simple and yet had such a deep significance that it sustained its appeal and popularity over two millenia. The message acquired further depth and perhaps some new dimensions as it spread outside the boundary of India, the land of its origin. We may, however, record here a warning. In our study of world-religions today a common assumption may be made (and in fact has sometimes unwittingly been made) to the effect that there must be a common essence which all particular religions must share. It was Wittgenstein who pointed out that our use of common nouns or general terms for different objects, items or themes may be guided simply by what he called 'family resemblances', and not by the presence of some essential common property in those items. Thus, in the case of 'religion', what we are looking for may be simply a family resemblance, and not some essential religiousity. And yet it is sometimes disappointing to see that some comparativists (or professional scholars in the study of comparative religion) still today, under the influence of philosophers like Rudolf Otto (1923), search for concepts liked the 'numen' and the 'numinous' even in Buddhism. Either we change or extend the meanings of these terms to make them suitable for application to these subjects or we should discover a new set of terms appropriate for our discourse.

2. THE POPULARITY OF BUDDHISM IN THE WEST

Buddhism's popularity in the West has been an important contribution of the old Orientalists of the nineteenth century. It has been to some extent co-terminus with what Raymond Schwab has called 'The Oriental Renaissance'. Whether this was really an Oriental Renaissance or not may be debatable, but as Schwab notes in his Chapter 'The Buddhism of Wagner,' Buddhism apparently caught the imagination of that great composer, who wrote in *My Life*:

> Burnouf's Introduction to the *History of Indian Buddhism* interested me most among my books, and I found material in it for a dramatic poem, which has stayed in my mind ever since, though only vaguely sketched. I may still perhaps work it out. I gave it the title *Die Sieger* (The Victor).
>
> (Quoted in Schwab, 1950, p. 439).

Whatever weight one wants to put on such remarks, Buddhism has by now acquired a world-wide popularity. It is a subject that keeps, to a considerable extent, the Oriental Studies departments of Western universities in business. It attracts not only the academics and the students, but also the intellectual and the laity.

The earliest reference to the Buddha and Buddhism in the West is to be found in the work of one of the early Christian fathers, Clements of

Alexandria (150–215 CE). Afterwards, however, Buddhism was almost unknown until the rise of Orientalism in the nineteenth century CE Wagner's reference to Eugene Burnouf (1801–52) was not an accident. The New England Transcendentalists published part of Burnouf's French rendering of the *Lotus Sūtra* in English translation in their journal, *The Dial*, in 1844 (Ellwood, 1987).

The academic and scholarly interest in Buddhism percolated first to some intellectuals and philosophers in the West, facilitated by the steady publication of books on Buddhism and the Buddha.

Buddhism's elevating and humanizing character, as well as its monastic order, earned praise among the elite. However, the popularization of Buddhism, that is, its transfer from the cluttered desk of the academic to the people, was made possible through the publication of certain outstanding and popular books such as *The Light of Asia* by Sir Edwin Arnold. From the beginning of the twentieth century, various individuals in the West committed themselves to Buddhism, and gradually Buddhist *vihāras* or Churches were established in different places in Europe and America.

The abiding interest in Buddhism among Americans today has also a long history. However, it might have been helped by the influx of Chinese and Japanese immigration to the West Coast. In the post-war period, specially in the sixties of this century, when a fascinated admiration for various forms of Eastern religions and mysticism was visible among Americans, when, in other words, the American youth and not-so-young 'turned East', Buddhism had its share. It was not just the elitist Theravāda Buddhism (of the Thai, Sri Lankan and Burmese monks); there was a 'Zen-boom' (thanks to the writings of D.T. Suzuki, Christmas Humphreys, and Alan Watts), as well as the spread of Tibetan Buddhism (thanks to the works of W.Y. Evans-Wentz), the Soka Gakkai from Japan, Jodo Shinshu, and so on.

The new wave has not always been welcome. Scholars and Orientalists have mostly resented it. Sociologists and social anthropologists have found a new intriguing subject for study and research. The purists believe this to be a vulgarization of an authentic religious tradition. Sometimes it is identified as a direct result of the Western intellectuals' disillusionment with the limits of modern science and/or Enlightenment thinking, which leads a considerable number of Western people, young and old alike, to look to the East for a fresh transfusion of sacred feeling, or magic or mysticism. Sometimes, even the academics, such as Professor Harvey Cox of Harvard, are reluctant be totally dismissive.

It has been noted that Buddhism in the West is a highly diversified phenomenon. Apart from those who recreate the Theravāda monasticism, take to Zen discipline or Tantric shamanism, there are those who reject the original quietism and try to confront the contemporary social, ecological and moral issues with supposedly 'Buddhistic' solutions. Undoubtedly this can be called a sort of 'secularization' of Buddhism. But as Dr Brian Wilson (1989) has remarked :'It is a difficult conception of the location and the meaning of salvation, but one the practical relevance of which is likely to be recognized by many in the Western world.' Neo-Buddhism in the West in this way is not very far behind the 'Liberation Theology' of the Catholic Churches in some countries (cf. Gustavo Gutierrez, 1974).

If some forms of Neo-Buddhism seek to foster socio-political consciousness in Western societies today by being compatible with secular modes of Western thought, the Buddhism that flourished during the 'Theosophy' movement of Madame H.P. Blavatsky (1831–91) was by contrast not exactly the uncorrupted ancient wisdom of the Āryan Upaniṣads, though it was claimed to be so. In fact, in the nineteenth century West, although indological research made very important contributions to the knowledge of Buddhism, it was till enmeshed with the Western man's projection of the 'spiritual and holistic East'.

The point to note here is, of course, the vocabulary we tend to use, sometimes unconsciously, to get the message across, may be misleading to the uninitiated. Note that even Wilson uses the term 'salvation' while he is referring to *nirvāṇa*, although he is emphasizing that it is a different conception. This is the crux of the matter. We call it a soteriology, or say that it has a philosophical basis, although each time we have to underline, or put it in small print in our mental notes, that it is so or would be so in a different sense.

3. CAN WE TELL WHAT EXACTLY THE BUDDHA TAUGHT?

This has often been asked. The scepticism is not entirely groundless. However, there is no need for total despair. When the Buddha passed away into *parinirvāṇa*, the disciples were asked to recite and rehearse his original dialogues before an assembly of monks, whose purpose was to authenticate them. Admittedly, for a long time, the practice of memorizing (and not writing down) the canons continued. However, for those familiar with the ancient Indian culture, this is not at all a surprise. The Vedic 'scriptures' were called *śruti* ('Scriptures' is a term misapplied here, for originally they did not have a 'scriptic' basis), to be heard from the teachers and then memorized. This was the way the so-called scriptural texts were transmitted from generation to generation. Hence, ever if this practice continued for several centuries after the death of the Buddha, we would not expect a major corruption.

Available to us today are: (1) A complete 'canon' in Pali called *Nikāyas*, preserved, in fact, in South and Southest Asia, (2) A Chinese translation (more or less complete), representing a number of schools, of a probably earlier Sanskrit version, called *Āgama*, (3) A few scattered texts in Sanskrit or Buddhist Sanskrit, (4) The Tibetan translation of the 'canon' and ancillary works. These sources, as might be expected, do not agree one hundred percent. However, there are areas of unanimity, i.e., common factors, and, by collecting them together, a not-too-distorted picture of the original teachings of the Buddha as well as of early Buddhism, can be drawn. Most scholars find little to object in this matter. Hence our answer to the question in the title of this section is a qualified yes.

The *Sūtras* which are the reported dialogues of the Buddha on Dharma (the doctrine), are recognized (barring a few exceptions) as authoritative by all schools. The two different traditions which represent them, i.e., the Pali Nikāya and the Sanskrit Āgamas (in Chinese translations), have been compared and analysed, and this has revealed, fortunately for us, a common doctrinal basis. They are, as E. Lamotte (1958) has said,

> . . . the common heritage of all sects. Thus, the agreement between the Āgamas and Nikāyas over a doctrinal point—such as that of *anātman*—is the best, if not the only proof of the authenticity of the latter. Any attempt to reconstruct a 'pre-canonical' Buddhism deviating from the consensus between Āgamas and Nikāyas can only end in subjective hypotheses. (pp. 156–71, ong.)

Scholars would do well to keep in the mind this warning by one of the greatest Buddhological scholars of our time.

There is unanimity among different traditions that for about a century after the Buddha's passing away, the Buddhists remained united, and then schisms appeared. By about the first century BC, there were reportedly 'eighteen' schools there, each with its own recension of the 'canons'. However, the number 'eighteen' might be taken with a grain of salt in the Indian context. There are also certain texts available to us today, and they profess to be the recorded histories of Buddhism. They can be used with caution as checks on the material derived from other sources.

The problem of authenticity is not simply a problem of our day: even in early days, the Buddhist authors faced the question at different times. Their method of authentication was strikingly similar to ours. Candrakīrti (*c.* 600 CE), for example, once authenticated a dialogue of the Buddha, referred to by Nāgārjuna (*c.* 150 CE), by claiming that:

This *sūtra* (dialogue, viz. the Buddha's dialogue with Kātyāyana) is recited in the canons of all the schools.

(*Prasannapadā* under MK., verse 25.7)

Thus, consensus among the recensions of the schools is the most dependable guide in our search for the original Buddhism.

4. THE QUESTION ABOUT HERMENEUTICS

What we have before us is an enormous collection of texts, followed by a steady flow of writings, philosophical, exegetical, moral liturgical, historical and narrational, which continued for more than 1200 to 1500 years, until the rise of modern scholarship (and, in some places, like Tibet, the flow of exegesis never stopped but continued to the present century). These texts were written in not unfamiliar languages, which can be learnt and studied without a great deal of difficulty. The problem of interpretation, as may be expected, looms large behind, as it did even to the early exegetes. Modern scholars seldom agree on certain crucial issues. However, the situation is in no way worse than that in other traditions.

It is tempting here to cast a sidelong glance at the main thesis of modern hermeneutics, although it owes its origin primarily to the historical self-understanding of nineteenth and twentieth century Europe. It has been claimed that since the ideal of a totally 'unprejudiced' and presuppositionless understanding of a given text is a vacuous, i.e., an unachievable ideal, it would be better, if we follow Gadamer's advice, to be aware of one's own 'prejudice', or 'Vorurteil' and consciously assimilate it in the process. This may sound as the 'if you can't beat them join them' sort of advice, and it may also be argued that these principles of 'philosophical hermeneutics' may not be suitable for transcultural application. There is, however, this truth, or so I believe: that it is almost impossible to discover the 'virgin' meaning today of the type of texts under consideration here (the discovery of the 'virgin' meaning would be like the discovery of the 'soul' in a person, the 'soul' that animates the text, as it were, and Buddhism, if anything, would reject such an enterprise as useless!). The most we may expect is to find some meaning mediated through a tradition and consciously coloured by our historical (and, perhaps, geo-political) situation. The early commentators, perhaps unconsciously, aimed at the same goal. The argument for the main thesis of the philosophical hermeneutic is, of course, the claim that understanding or interpretation is not done by a transcendental ego, but rather by a historically situated *Dasein*, and hence there is very little scope for it to be entirely free from prejudices or 'fore-meaning'. Part of the argument seems to be sound, and perhaps the point about the unsuitability of the theory for transcultural application should be dismissed.

5. THE STARTING POINT

The dialogues of the Buddha used to be rehearsed collectively by those who remembered them, and endorsed as accurate by those who had been present at the event. A few centuries later, they were written down, although the oral tradition continued. The council of Rājagṛha, convened in the very year the Buddha entered into *nirvāṇa*, was the place where the *Dharma* and the *Vinaya*—the two main wings of the canon—were compiled. The *Dharma* stood for doctrine, and the *Vinaya* for disciplines. About a century later there was another Buddhist council (about 386/7 BC) at Vaiśāli, which criticized and condemned laxity in disciplines in various monastaries. This was the forerunner of the first important schism in Buddhism, although the community may have remained united even after this new Council.

The first Council supposedly gave us the text called *Tripiṭaka* ('The Three Baskets', although we do not know what 'Baskets' meant; an ancient substitute for the 'filing cabinets' of today?) At the request of Mahākāśyapa, who presided over the assembly, Ānanda, personal attendant of the Buddha, recited the dialogues on *dharma*, he remembered, and the assembly endorsed them as correct. The *dharma* or doctrine compiled came to be known as the *Sūtra Piṭaka* (collection of dialogues). Then Upāli was asked to recite the *Vinaya* 'The Discipline', which constituted the *Vinaya Piṭaka*.

How do we reach the number 'three' in *Tri-Piṭaka*? Some traditions do not mention the third recitation, although all the early schools had a third, the *Abhidharma Piṭaka*, 'Abhidharma' meaning the (philosophic?) discussion about *dharma* (where 'dharma' could have meant 'elements of reality' crystallized from the Buddha's teachings; see Vasubandhu,

Abhidharma-kośa, 1.1). It may be that it was derivative of the recital of Ānanda. It is also called the *Matṛka*, (meaning 'matrix'?) which was originally a list of headings for annotation, derived from the doctrine. In any case, the development of the *Abhidharma* constituted the philosophical basis of Buddhism.

6. THE DOCTRINE

I noted earlier that scholars are favourably disposed to that part of the doctrine that is common to all schools of Buddhism. The *Mahā-parinirvāṇa-sūtra* seems to provide us with a summary of the common factors (see A.K. Warder, 1970). However, to describe the essential points of the Doctrine, it is simpler to begin at the beginning, i.e., with the Discourse (or Sermon) at Varanasi, where, for the first time the Buddha, after enlightenment, revealed the Truths he had discovered to his first disciples. These are the Four Great Truths (*ārya-satya*) (I'm allergic to such translations as 'Noble' for '*ārya*', for there is no racial connotation or touch of class hierarchy here).

The Middle Way: The Buddha's teaching has been summed up by the tradition in one sentence. The Buddha discovered the truths about the origin of things and their cessation. This teaching was set up against the background of an advice to avoid two extremes, the unbridled pursuit of pleasure and the life of extreme mortification; hence, 'The Middle Way' is the name of Buddhism: *madhyamā pratipat*. The middle course between two extreme ways of life is the best course. And, as the later Mādhyamikas *read* it: Between two extreme (metaphysical) views, truth lies somewhere in the indefinable middle.

The two extremes were designated by the Buddha as 'eternalism' and 'annihilationism'. The exclusive pursuit of sensual pleasure was the principle advocated by the 'materialists' who thought the body was the soul or the essence of existence. This is 'annihilationism', for everything is thought to be annihilated with the annihilation of the body. The principle of extreme self-mortification was advocated by the 'eternalists', for whom the soul or the essence of existence was completely different from the body, the psycho-physical existence, and denial of the demands of psycho-physical existence (extreme acseticism) would lead to the ultimate goal of life. The Buddha's advice was the choice of the middle ground. The Four Great Truths and doctrine of 'Dependent Origination' avoid these extremes.

The Truth of Suffering: 'Duḥkha' is a pan-Indian word that does not always mean 'suffering' or 'unhappiness' or 'pain'. It means also the things that cause suffering or undesirable consequence at the end. In fact it is a term that combines both 'fact' and 'value', to use a contemporary jargon (Matilal 1982). Several philosophical concepts in classical India share the same features, as with B. Williams' 'thick ethical concepts' (1985, p. 129). Thus, the thesis of universal 'suffering', that everything is *duḥkha* is to be understood with a little bit of imagination. Not only suffering and the roots of suffering are suffering; everything, good as well as bad things in life, happiness, pleasure, joy, is suffering, undesirable, unsatisfactory and a disvalue. In the words of Buddha:

> This, O monks, is the Great Truth of suffering. Birth is suffering; so is the old-age, disease and death. Union with what we like is suffering, so is separation from what we like or love and so is the desire unfulfilled. In short, five aggregates for 'grasping' (five sets constituting our psycho-physical existence) is suffering.

This general thesis is stated in several places, such as *Anguttara I*, 286: 'all formations (*saṃskāra*) are impermanent, suffering (*duḥkha*) and devoid of self.' By 'formations' is meant all the psycho-physical phenomena of existence (see Frauwallner 1956, Schumann 1973). Hence the thesis can be restated, with a little bit of liberty as: all phenomena are evanescent and by the same token devoid of any worthwhile value (*duḥkha*) and devoid of any essence. The fragility as well as contingency of everything, good or bad, pleasure or unpleasure, constitutes its worthlessness. Now the question is, *why so*? That leads to the next item.

The truth of the origin of Suffering: The origin and disappearance of the phenomena of existence is governed by the fixed law of what is called dependent origination (*pratītya-samutpāda*). To avoid the paradox of an infinite regress of causal or conditional change on the one hand, and the oddity of an abrupt beginning of the succession of phenomena, it is said at the first level that suffering or the fruits of action is conditioned by a basic desire or instinctual drive called *tṛṣṇā* 'thirst', not only for objects of pleasure (*kāma*), but also for becoming or continuing to be (*bhava*), as well as for believing that death is the end of everything. However, this mutual conditioning of desire, action and suffering is claimed to be beginningless (*anādi*) and cyclical.

The full-fledged description of the chain of causation or dependent origination is given in terms of eleven or twelve items, which also explain the process or the cycle of birth and re-birth of individuals.

1. misconception (*avidyā*)
2. karmic forces (*saṃskāra*)
3. consciousness
4. psycho-physical existence (*nāma-rūpa*)
5. six bases of consciousness
6. contact (*sparśa*) with objects
7. feeling
8. thirst
9. grasping
10. becoming
11. birth (or re-birth)
12. old-age-and-death.

The twelve-membered causal-conditional chain looks backward as well as forward. The basic causal formula is of *passions* (thirsts) conditioning actions leading to perpetuation of *suffering*. In the above list of twelve, the preceding one is said to condition the succeeding one. However the first two, 1 and 2, relate to the previous existence (birth), one being passion, the other being the 'passionate' actions leading the present existence. Items 3 to 10 describe the present existence in some detail, from consciousness at the time of birth to gradual development (maturation of the fruits of previous actions) of the psycho-physical complex, and its reaction against the environment resulting in feeling or sensation, which leads to desire or thirst, i.e., passion, then action again. Item 10, 'becoming', stands for the general activity of the individual in the present existence. The last two, 11 and 12, look beyond, to future existence, and sum up the process in terms of birth, old-age and death to indicate the self-perpetuation of the process. Passions generate Action which generate in turn Fruit that matures in Passions again.

By identifying three kinds of thirst or instinctual desire, for pleasure, for perpetuation of being and a sort of obsession with death, the Buddha in one stroke preached against hedonism, against the eternalism which believed in the eternity of the souls, as well as against annihilationism, which is a form of materialism in that it believed only in the body, that ended with death. The Buddha's way, to repeat, was the middle way.

The twelve-membered chain of dependent origination was regarded as the hallmark of the Buddha's doctrine. Later on, it was generalized as the Buddhist notion of causality that gives a causal-conditional explanation of everything. The famous passage in the *Majjhima* (*I*, pp. 190–1) is:

Whoever understands it (dependent origination), understands the Dharma (doctrine); and whoever understands Dharma, understands it.

The Truth of Cessation of Suffering (nirodha/nirvāṇa): the conditionality of suffering (by which is meant all the phenomena of existence) presupposes its cessation also, through the removal or dissolution of its condition. If *A* arises depending upon, or being conditioned by, the arising of *B*, then with the removal of *B*, *A* will cease to arise at all. If thirst, craving, or instinctual desire, leads to passion-loaded actions resulting in birth and attendant sorrow and lamentation, old-age and death, grief and despair—in sum, *suffering*, then cessation of such desire will eventually lead to cessation of suffering. Cessation of suffering means extinction of existence. It is the escape, it lies beyond the causal-conditional chain. It is 'unconditional'.

Nirvāna has two stages: (a) The status of an *arhat*, the 'holy one', when desire is completely destroyed, the holy one has dispelled all future conditioning of rebirth. But the personality-conglomerate, the complex of corporeality, feelings, perceptions, volitions and consciousness, continues to be, as long as the person is alive. This state of an *arhat*, is called '*nirvāṇa*-with-residual-conditioning'. (b) After death, such an *arhat* achieves *nirvāṇa-without-residual-conditioning*. A flame lasts for a short while even when it is no longer being fed by a new supply of fuel etc. It lasts as long as the existing conditions, fuel etc., exist. It is extinguished completely afterward. This *nirvāṇa* is calm (*śānta*), complete peace, and 'excellent'—the ultimate goal of beings.

The Truth of the Way: There is, the Buddha asserted, the Way, which leads to the cessation of suffering. It is the Great Path characterized by the practice of eight virtues. This is called the Eight Fold, Path, having right view, right will, right speech, right action, right livelihood, right effort, right mindfulness and right concentration. There are three elements here: ethical behaviour, concentration, and wisdom or insight.

Ethical behaviour is the willful abstention from various misdeeds. The ten cardinal 'sins' are: 1. killing, 2. stealing, 3. sexual misconduct, 4. lying, 6. slander, 6. harsh talk, 7. frivolity, 8. covetousness, 9. ill-will, and 10. false views. Ethical behaviour is the essential first step for spiritual progress in the path towards *nirvāṇa*. This will falsify a claim that is often made by some ill-informed Orientalists today that religious practice in Buddhism (and in any other Indian religion) is decidedly 'amoral'. The alleged amorality, if there is any in modern society, must be a disease of modernity,—a disease that is overtly or covertly widespread in most modern world societies. What is unfortunate is that such an amoral stance, as well as its alleged presence in the history of such religions as Buddhism, received support and reinforcement from the misinterpretation of such intriguing phrases as 'beyond good and evil', describing the ultimate goal.

Ethics purifies external behaviour, and must be followed up by *concentration*, which purifies thought. Concentration aims for undistracted mental quietude by the successive practice of various mental cultures or meditaitons. When behaviour is pure and mind is freed, through various mental cultures, from all passions and impurities, wisdom as well as insight dawn upon the mind of the practitioner, and the *arhat* is on his way to arhatship or *nirvāṇa*.

Wisdom consists in the clear grasping of the thought: 'All relevant physical and mental phenomena of existence are momentary, painful or undesirable (*duḥkha*), and devoid of any self or substantiality'. This shows how wrong is our attachment to such *dharmas* and namings ('belonging to me'). Receiving such wisdom from the teachings is not enough, it must be reinforced by reflection and contemplation. Thus, the Buddha talks about three types of wisdom, based upon lessons (*śruta*), reflection (*cintā*), and contemplation (*bhāvanā*), and this was quite in line with the prescribed threefold practice of the Bṛhadāraṇyaka Upaniṣad: 'to be heard, to be minded and to be meditated upon'—common to later Hindu religious prescriptions.

It must be emphasized that the Buddha talked about *nirvāṇa* without talking about a person or a soul who enters *nirvāṇa*, for suffering exists but not the sufferer. The passage from *Visuddhimagga* (tr. H. Warren, p. 348) puts the point nicely:

> Suffering exists, but no one is afflicted; there is no agent, but activity is a fact; *nirvāṇa* is, but whoever has entered *nirvāṇa* is not; The Path exists, but no one treads it.

7. RELIGION AND SOCIETY AT THE TIME OF THE BUDDHA

Society

India, in the sixth century BC, was under Āryan domination, and, as the Buddhist, Jaina and Hindu sources show, the extended region from Punjab to Bengal, including some parts of Deccan, was divided into sixteen 'countries' (*mahā-janapadas*). The populations in the east and other places were, however, mixed with other local tribes; they were not dominated by the Āryans and not completely subjected to Brahminical or Vedic culture.

It seems plausible that the region where the Buddha was born (Kapilavatsu, a town, probably at the international boundary between present day India and Nepal) and the community of the Sākyas from which the Buddha came, both were comparatively free from being fully permeated by Brahminical culture.

It seems that we have reached a period in history when intermixture of Āryan and non-Āryan (i.e. indigenous Indian) elements has already taken place. The term '*janapada*' or '*mahā-janapada*' may be significant. The point has been made by scholars (Heesterman, 1979, p. 66) that the so-called major or minor 'states' in ancient India should be seen more as power-bases centred around a prince than as territorial sovereignties. The King was the Lord of the people (*narapati, nṛpati*), rather than the Lord of the land (*bhūpati*). So the word '*jana*' (people) in '*janapada*' may be important. The thesis that the King had power over a people rather than over a tract of land can be challenged, although it was clear that the Western concept of the ownership of land was something not known exactly in the same sense in ancient India. One can be misled by the negative thesis that the counterpart of the Western concept of *exclusive* ownership was totally absent in India for multiple ownership or multiple right was allowed. The king had the power on the produce of the land only. In view of such consideration, all that we can say is that we are dealing with a different conception of state in the Indian context.

Before the arrival of the Vedic Āryan or the so-called Indo-Europeans, India had a 'Bronze Age' civilization which, according to the archaeological evidence, flourished in about 3000 BC, i.e., about 2500 years before the Buddha. This is called the Indus Valley civilization. It appeared at the same time as other such civilizations in Mesopotamia or Egypt. However, this civilization disappeared and has very little relevance to the development of Buddhism. The Vedic Āryans are believed to have entered India at about the thirteenth century BC. They used an early form of Sanskrit, called Vedic, which was the linguistic substratum for the composition and collection of a canon of scriptures. These scriptures are called 'Veda'. There is archaeological evidence to show that the beginning of the Iron Age in India was at about 1000–800 BC.

Historians often conjecture that techonological innovations and the rise and spread of some religious movements or philosophico-religious thoughts are connected. With regard to Buddhism, as well as the Śramaṇa movements in general, the (hypo-)thesis is that (in Max Weber's language) it is 'the product of the time of urban development, of urban kingship and city nobles' (1958, original ed. 1921, p. 204). Early Vedic society seems to have been rural, centering around agriculture and the concern for rainfall. However, as the Āryans moved to the fertile area of the Gangetic plain, historians like D.D. Kosambi and R.S. Sharma have argued, there was an agricultural surplus, made possible by the use of iron ploughshares, leading to the development of cities and centres for trade and commerce, and small Kingdoms and principalities in the alluvium belt of the middle Gangetic basin. Rich iron deposits in the south of Bihar might have been a factor in the early use of iron ploughshares or other iron tools (Kosambi). Another factor for generating the surplus was the technique of wet paddy (rice) cultivation, the introduction of irrigation techniques and transplantation to increase the yield (Sharma). The 'causal' connections here are bound to be conjectural, and the plausibility of such hypotheses need not be annulled by the lack of archaeological evidence (in the case of the ploughshare, see Sharma). Besides, the doctrine of a plurality of causes teaches us at least that such causal connections are not unique, and that there may be different factors responsible for the surpluses, for the growth of principalities, power-centres and urbanization as it must have happened in other parts of the globe at different periods.

Whatever might have been the connection, or lack of it, between use of iron and ploughshares, plus new technology in rice cultivation, on the one hand, and the rise of cities and commercial centres on the other, by the time of the Buddha there were many major and minor 'states' with different types of government; some were monarchies, others republics. These Kingdoms or countries were frequently at war. The old empire under which Brahminism flourished seems to have disintegrated. The new wealth created by the exploitation of natural resources, development of industry and trade, generated in its turn new forces in the society. Coins were introduced and by the end of the fifth century BC, and they were widely used, which meant that a money-based economy had developed, replacing the old way of measuring wealth in kind, especially in terms of cattle (*go-dhana*). This inevitably led to conflict between the growing economic power of the new merchant class and the political or military power of the ruling class. Thus, according to some scholars (Warder, 1970, p. 30), there was a social and political crisis in sixth and fifth century BC India.

The intellectual climate of India at this period was notably brisk and lively with philosophical and ethical disputes, controversies and discussions. The old and extremely complicated Vedic rituals, and along with them, the domination of the priests, lost its hold on the people. The fanciful and mythological explanation of the different rituals was challenged and ridiculed. Even the corpus of the Vedic literature contained within itself doubts and questions about the efficiency of rituals and the existence of gods themselves. The philosophers and sages in the Upaniṣads, while they sometimes rejected Vedic rituals, developed their own cosmogenies. The dominant trend among the variety of views expressed therein, was the doctrine of Brahman or Being as the Ultimate Reality. Human souls were sometimes classified as, or identified with, the stuff of consciousness, the Ultimate Reality or Brahman. The origin of diversity and the material world was sometimes traced back to the non-dual reality, Brahman, and sometimes to an independent principle, called *pradhāna* 'the chief' or the 'unmanifest' (*avyakta*), as in the proto-sāṃkhya school.

The Renouncers (Śramaṇas)

The latter view might not have originated in the Brahminical orthodoxy although it was accepted and assimilated therein. Besides, there was a new movement by this time initiated by a group of 'free thinkers' called *śramaṇas*, who have been variously described as monks, wanderers or world-renouncers. The *śramaṇas* have sometimes been set in opposition to the *brāhmaṇas*, 'the priests of the Vedic Society'.

These 'renouncers' must have opposed the hereditary priesthood of the old society and the teaching (moral, social, ethical and philosophical) thereof, and they came from all ranks of society, not simply from the *brāhmaṇas*. They 'contracted out' of the ordinary society and of the existent social hierarchy, as well as of the assigned duties of the members of these social classes. Hence they were 'renouncers'. However, it must be mentioned that in the Buddhist canonical texts, the two terms '*brāhmaṇa*' and '*śramaṇa*' were often juxtaposed to form a frequently used expression *śramaṇa-brāhmaṇa* which referred to the teachers and philosophers in general, i.e., the so-called holy men, whom society paid respect to and regarded as teachers. These renouncers were engaged in ascetic practices, and, among other things, their livelihood depended upon begging food from householders, or by gleaning whatever they could from the fields. The man who came to be known as the Buddha, became first a renouncer, a *śramaṇa*, who gave up his this-worldly life as a prince, as a married man with a child, who renounced his kingdom and his pursuit of worldly happiness. He became the greatest of the *śramaṇas*—the *mahā-śramaṇa*.

This institution of renunciation has often been connected by scholars, somewhat inaccurately I believe, with the four so-called 'stages' of life—studentship, being a householder, retirement in a forest and renunication of all worldly pleasures—for which different life-styles were prescribed in the *dharmaśāstras*. These 'stages', called *āśramas*, were combined with the four ranks of social groups known as '*varṇa*'—the brahman or the priests, the rulers or fighters, the tradesmen, and the slaves or servants. Thus classical Hinduism has often been defined in terms of the prescribed duties and obligations of the four *varṇas* and the four *āśramas*. The schematic division of social groups was no doubt artificial, being an idealized version of a projected society—a piece of attempted social engineering of the ancient days. The fourfold division of the individual life-cycle (the *āśramas*) was also artificial, and in any case the *śramaṇa* movement, and the rise of Buddhism, must have antidated the practice. In sixth century BC, we believe, the contrast was between the householder and the renouncer, the early stage of education (scriptural and non-scriptural) being a preparatory stage for leading the life of a householder, a family life with all its duties and obligations. The vocation of a renouncer was open to any person from any social group at any stage of the individual's life cycle. The Buddha renounced the 'world' after being married and after he had a child. And there were thousands of other individuals who become renouncers in search of the ultimate meaning of life, through mediation and other mental disciplines, as well as through mortification of the flesh.

Some Philosophical Views of the Renouncers

By the time of the Buddha, there had been the establishment of organised communities of the renouncers, although the tradition of individual wandering teachers was still prevalent. The followers of the Buddha become an organized community following the same model. Besides them, the other main organizations were those of the Ājīvakas, the Lokāyatas, the Ajñānas (the Agnostics) and the Jainas. The leader of the Ājīvaka school was Gosāla, a contemporary of the Buddha, whose main teaching consisted in a doctrine of fatalism or a crude form of determinism. Common to all renouncers was the goal of permanent happiness or a state that is beyond suffering, which was interpreted as peace of mind or quietude. Besides Gosāla, there were two other teachers of the Ājīvaka group, Purāṇa (Kāśyapa) and Kakuda or Pakudha (Kātyāyana). All were identified as *heretic teachers* along with Ajita, Sañjaya or Sañjayia, and Nirgrantha or Mahāvīra Jina, in the canonical texts of early Buddhism.

Gosāla's main doctrine was that of *Niyati*, Fate or Destiny. It means that all events that happen to us are predetermined, that is, determined in advance by *Niyati*—a sort of 'what will be will be' determinism. This is the earliest formulation of the pre-determination theory in the Indian context, and although the Ājīvaka movement became defunct, this kind of Fatalism did not die away. It exerted a pervasive influence on the Indian mind at a popular level for a long time. *Niyati* was not Providence, nor was it understood as a god (although in later Hindu mythology it was personified as a god or a goddess). Purāṇa was credited with the view, called *akriyāvāda*, according to which, human action does not, because it cannot, have any effect on the course of events, and hence the idea of moral causation (good action produces good reward or happiness, and bad produces evil) was denied. It should be remembered that both the Buddha and the Mahāvīra rejected this view: they were called *kriyāvādin* and propounded, along with later non-*śramaṇa* teachers, the efficacy of human action as well as the theory of *karma*, or moral causation. The idea of *karma* 'human action' as influencing individual human destiny through sequences of rebirths was already present in rudimentary from in early Upaniṣads such as Bṛhad-āraṇyaka.

Kakuda's teachings consisted in claiming that the constituent elements of the universe are the *atomic* forms of earth, water, heat, air, happiness, unhappiness and consciousness (or *jīva* 'sensience'). In their atomic forms, they are uncreated and indestructible; they do not react nor can they be altered. Hence any action upon them would be ineffectual.

It is clear that all these three views fitted well with each other. Although they contained rudiments of a materialistic view of the universe, the Ājīvaka were not materialistic. They also believed that in billions and billions of years, each individual soul, after passing through billions of transmigrations, would attain the final bliss, for it is destined to attain it. It is like a huge ball of thread, which is constantly in a state of unwinding, until at the end the ball vanishes. Human experience of happiness and unhappiness is inescapable, and hence a spirit of resignation and quietude should be developed in life. They also believed in divination and prognostication, which fitted well with their view of determinism. The idea that sustained it was if the future is fixed or pre-determined, it is possible to know it.

The Lokāyatas were 'naturalist' or materialistic. They believed in the *svabhāva* 'own-nature' of things and claimed that everything happens spontaneously as a consequence of the inner dynamism of matter. They denied the existence of a soul that can transmigrate from one life to another. Besides, they also rejected the idea of moral causation (and here there was agreement with the Ājīvakas), for naturalism denied the evaluation of actions as 'good' or 'bad'. Happiness is the goal of beings, and the highest happiness, according to some protagonists of this school, lies in the gratification of the senses. Unlike the Ājīvakas, they recognized only four elements of the universe, earth, water, air and fire. Consciousness or sensience was understood as a compound, i.e., a special property that arises when the elements (themselves unconscious) are combined in a particular way in a living body. It is, they explained, like the property of being an intoxicant, emerging in a drink which has been fermented—a naturalistic explanation for the arising of sensience in a living body. As opposed to determinism, they preached, however, complete freedom of action, although it was not clear how that would fit their doctrine of naturalism.

The Agnostics or the Ajñāna school were concerned with the possibility of metaphysical knowledge, and knowledge in general. Does the soul exist? Philosophers debated this and other questions. But Sañjaya, their teacher, said that no knowledge was possible regarding such matters, and it is morally reprehensible to make such knowledge-claims. He defended agnosticism and scepticism for otherwise we would be lying and deceiving ourselves (*muṣavāda-bhiyā*). This provided the impetus for the sceptics later on in history, when epistemological inquiry was undertaken seriously.

The Jainas believed in the idea of a transmigrating eternal soul, and claimed that ultimate bliss was possible to attain after the cessation of this cycle of transmigration. Such cessation could be brought about by sincere human effort, through severe asceticism and self-mortification. They might initially have been a breakaway group the Ājīvakas. They propounded the doctrine, *kriyā-vāda*, efficacy of human action, free will and moral causation. This is the only *śramaṇa* school that survived, besides Buddhism.

8. LIFE OF THE BUDDHA

Birth

The child who later became the Buddha attained his *parinirvāṇa* at the age of 80 in, according to one group of scholars, 486 BC (A. Bareau, 'La date du nirvāṇa', 1953, pp. 27–62). This will put his birth at 566 BC, and his renunciation at 537 BC. This dating has by no means been uncontroversial. Although no certainty has been reached, scholars have occasionally reconsidered the question in the light of some new data, or sometimes from a novel way of approaching the problem. In his 1986 monograph, H. Berchert more or less agreed with Bareau's dating. However, in a symposium organized in Gottingen (by Berchert) in April 1988, a wide variety of views were expressed and enthusiastically argued for by scholars from different parts of the world (see Berchert, 1992). Old controversies have, however, been seldom resolved though new ones are multiplied. Convictions of the scholars here mostly derive from the trust they are persuaded to put in one source of evidence rather than another. For example, the importance of a straightened out 'Pali chronology' (which R. Gombrich largely depended upon in his 1992 paper) may cast doubt upon the date of *parinirvāṇa* as 486 BC, and require an 80 year forward correction (to 406 BC). It takes into account the references to the age of ordination and importance of the pupilary succession in Sri Lanka. However, the intervening gap has still to be filled up with conjectural material and imaginative devices, and 486 BC still seems plausible. The problem of fitting it with other non-Buddhist historical events in India seems less onerous. Since certainty is impossible, it is better to be modest about it.

There has been a surge of interest among scholars today in 'religious biography' or 'hagiography', for the simple reason that in such materials one can breathe a more familiar air about what it was like with the common people, and how the teacher was viewed by them as one with a compassionate and humane nature, rather than as a propounder of what appeared to be later on very abstract and highly intellectual doctrines, which it took generations of scholars and disciples to explain, and in so doing to amplify with still more abstract and intellectualized concepts and models. This section, however, would not be able to do justice to the newly recognized demand. A brief account of what we are in a position to gather about the life of this great teacher is the goal here. It has presented a great deal of problems for scholars over about a hundred and fifty years.

We know from the tradition that the proper name of the Buddha was Siddhārtha; his mother was Mayadevi, queen of the ruler of the Sākyas (a sub-Himalayan clan), and king Suddhodana was the father. He was born in the Lumbini Park near Kapilavastu, capital of the Sākyas. (The historical value of the tradition has been debated by scholars, for which, Winternitz (1927), Lamote (1958), Frauwallner (1956) and Bareau (1953) should be consulted. However, we will follow the traditional accounts here). Being a prince, he had a life of happiness and comfort, got married when he was about sixteen, and was blessed with a son called Rāhula. It is somewhat surprising this 'happy prince' became increasingly, and extremely, concerned about the common and unavoidable sufferings of beings, old age, disease and death, and developed a sort of 'indifferent and unaddictive' attitude (*vairāgya*, I am not in favour of such translation as 'disgust') toward pleasures.

An anecdote has been repeated with some minor variations by biographers to explain this reversal. It is said that he went out on his chariot with his charioteer to drive around the city and the countryside, in order apparently to get rid of boredom and restlessness due to the new attitude he was developing. Four such trips are mentioned. On the first day he saw the pitiable condition of an old, senile man. The charioteer, on being asked, informed him that every human being has to suffer in this way. On the second and the third day, he apparently saw a diseased person and a dead body, respectively, and there were similar questions and answers. The idea of the inevitability of suffering got firmly imprinted on his mind. On the fourth day, he met an ascestic, who had a calm and quiet appearance, apparently at peace with himself and engrossed in pleasant thoughts. The charioteer explained that the man was an ascetic, without family or social ties, who devoted his time in quest of the ultimate bliss, a sort of deliverance from the world of suffering to which all humans were subjected, and also tried to teach others how to escape from this inevitability.

The authenticity of this story need not detain us. It would be all right if we take it to be one of what I wish to call 'explanatory tales', which the Buddhist biographers invented several centuries later, in order to account for the young prince's final decision to be a 'renouncer', in search of the ultimate solution for what he thought to be the main problems of life, unstoppable suffering for any creature who would be born, ageing, disease and decay being repeated without cessation, if we believed in the transmigration doctrine, life after life.

Renunciation

The Buddha renounced his life of luxury and his family at the age of 29 (presumably in 537 BC). After this renunciation, which has been called by scholars 'the great departure', he is supposed to have travelled southward, crossed the river Anomā and reached Rājagṛha, the capital of Magadha. He apparently met king Bimbisar at that time. The Pāli canonical texts, not necessarily the earliest parts (Dīgha, I and Majjhimā I), form source-material for this biography. Wandering as a monk, he met Arāda (Aḷāda) Kālāma, another renouncer.

He studied what Kālāma had to teach but found it inadequate and unsatisfactory as far as his own search was concerned. He met also Udraka and Rāmaputra (perhaps both teachers were Yoga masters). He practiced how to enter into spiritual ecstacy, but doubted its usefulness to solve the problem of life. Afterwards, he went to Uruvilva and spent about six years in the company of five other renouncers, Kauṇḍinya etc., practising different forms of ascetic practice—austerities of an extreme kind, arresting of breathing, prolonged fasting, etc. Having realized, at the end, the fruitlessness of such self-mortification (according to the anectdotes, his life was in danger once, because of prolonged fasting, and he broke his fast by eating 'rice-custard' (*pāyasa*) prepared by a lady, Siyātā, daughter of a wealthy land-lord), the Buddha moved to another place.

Enlightenment

At a certain place, called Bodh-Gayā after the incident that followed, the Buddha sat under what was called later on the Tree of Englightenment, apparently a *ficus religiousa*, and engaged himself in deep meditation—a sort of mental culture different from that which he had been taught by his former teachers. He delved deeper into meditative thoughts, analysing the mysteries that had bothered him from the beginning, the problems of death, decay, and then rebirth, perpetuating suffering. On that night (531 BC), he succeeded in finding the answer—for he attained the perfect enlightenment (*bodhi*), the profound insight into the nature of the fundamental question and its answer. From this time onwards he was called the Buddha.

The texts graphically describe the process—how during the different watches of that night he obtained direct knowledge of how he was born many times before this life, of the mystery of rebirth of beings, successive rebirths being caused by desires (cf. *tṛṣṇā*) or thirst for 'becoming'. He realized this truth, for he also felt that his thirst for becoming had, on that night, been completely destroyed. In this connection the general doctrine of twelve-membered dependent origination dawned upon him, and this became one of the main constituents of his teaching.

Having spent weeks in meditation at Bodh-Gaya, the Buddha proceeded towards Vārāṇasī, and there at the Deer Park he gave his First Sermon before the five companions who formerly taught him, or perhaps simply witnessed his severe austerities, for six years. He unfolded the doctrine of Four Great Truths and the idea of Non-Self. This was called the *Turning of the Wheel of Dharma*. The wheel that was turned here continued in many parts of the country and he travelled extensively converting and recruiting disciples (as was the practice of other 'renouncers'). He established a new order of *śramaṇas* or *bhikṣus*. Many monasteries were eventually established in different areas through the generosity of such patrons as Bimbisāra, (King of Magadha), Anāthapiṇḍaka (a rich banker of Śrāvastī, capital of Kośala), Āmrapāli (a courtesan from Vṛji). In Rājagṛha he converted two young disciples of Sañjaya the Agnostic,

Śāriputra and Maudgalyāyana (previously called Upatisya and Kolita), who became his principal disciples along with a brahmin convert, Mahākāśyapa. The former two, though probably ranking higher in order, died during the Buddha's own life-time, and after the decease of the Buddha, the latter, Mahākāśyapa played a leading role in the order.

At Śrāvastī, it is reported, the Buddha had hostile debates, apparently, with the six *śramaṇa* teachers, called in the canons 'heretical masters'. It is said that the Buddha defeated all these opponents in the presence of king Prasenajit. This triumph was apparently marked by mircaculous happenings. Kosambi was another place where several monasteries were founded. The Buddha went to Mathura,—and also to Aṅga (Bengal), the latter place at the invitation of Sumāgadhā, daughter of Anāthapiṇḍaka. The Buddha also used to visit his native town, Kapilavastu, and converted some of his own family members, among them Śuddhodana, Yasodharā (his former wife) and Nanda (his half-brother); sometime later several cousins joined the order, including Devadatta and Ānanda. Ānanda became famous as a monk and was appointed his personal assistant. He was responsible, it is said, for changing the Buddha's mind into admitting women (nuns) in the order. He was also the one to receive the teaching of the discipline from the Buddha. He was with the Great Master for twenty-five years and remembered most of his teachings as he was endowed with an almost infallible memory.

The story of Devadatta was, however, different. He entered the order but soon had the ambition of replacing the Buddha and becoming its leader. He apparently insisted that the monks had been more lax in discipline under the guidance of the Buddha. When the latter disagreed, Devadatta hatched several plots (fortunately they were all unsuccessful) to assassinate the Buddha. In this, Devadatta received the support of the crown prince Ajātaśatru of Magadha, who later on regretted it and asked for the Buddha's forgiveness. Devadatta, however, managed to cause a schism and formed a separate monastery—a new community with 500 Vṛji monks. All these are reports from the Buddhist canons, and hence some modern scholars argue that Devadatta might not have been such an incarnation of evil. Perhaps he insisted upon more austere discipline among the monks, exhibiting a feature that was found in many established religious orders: conservatism versus liberalism.

Passing Away

The *Mahāparinirvāṇa-sūtra* describes in detail the passing away of the Buddha. After spending the rainy season in the retreat in Vaiśāli, he proceeded towards Kuśinagarī. On his way, he stopped in Pāpā, capital of the Malla country where he accepted the invitation of a smith Cunda and ate a dish of 'pork' which made him ill with acute diarrhoea. Somehow he continued his journey and reached Ruśinagarī (he already predicted his coming death while he was in Vaiśāli). In the Śāla Grove, lying on his death bed, he addressed the monks and comforted Ānanda, who was overwhelmed with sorrow. In the third quarter of that night, he entered *nirvāṇa* after going through various meditational stages, at the age of 80. He was cremated after seven days when Mahākāśyapa (who was not present at his death bed) arrived and set fire to the pyre.

Thus ended the life of a great teacher whose message is still relevant, nay inspiring, for most of us even today. Seeing that beings are torn between the nihilistic abyss of metaphysical despair, as enshrined in the Lokāyata materialistic hedonism as well as in the pietism of the Ājīvaka fatalism and Ajñāna Agnosticism, and the ever-elusive summit of the metaphysical promise of the Upaniṣadic Brahman-Ātman identity, the Buddha searched for a middle way—a way where despair is 'contravened' by a non-committed (sceptical) attitude to any metaphysical stance, and hope is infused through a prescription of praxis that is calculated to destroy the root cause of our *duḥkha*, our lack of contentment with, and of happiness in, the given state of life in which we find ourselves. The pursuit of happiness, however, is not the goal that the Buddha recommended. And this is the startling message. Pursuit of happiness develops into an obsession with most of us, and it necessarily and invariably involves unhappiness in the beginning, in the middle and in the end. Pursuit of a goal to end all such obsessive pursuits is what is *nirvāṇa*, which, as the extinction of all desires and obsessions, is asserted to be the Ultimate Reality—the goal of highest value.

Notes and References

Arnold, Edwin (1879), *The Light of Asia: or the great renunciation (Mahabhinshkramana); being the life and teachings of Gautama, prince of India and founder of Buddhism.* London: Trubner & Co.

Bareau, A. (1953), 'La date du Nirvāṇa', *Journal Asiatique*, 241, pp. 27–62.

Berchert, Heinz (1986), Die Lebenszeit des Buddha—das älteste feststehende Datum der indischen Geschichte.

———, ed. (1992), *The Dating of the Historical Buddha*, Göttingen: Vandenhoeck & Ruprecht.

Candrakīrti: *Prasannapadā* (1903–13), edited by La Vallée Poussin. Bibliotheca Buddhica.

Cox, Harvey (1979), *Turning East: The Promise and Peril of the New Orientalism*. London: Allen Lane.

Dīrgha Nikāya, edited in 3 vols by T.W. Rhys Davids and J.E. Carpenter. London: Pali Text Society, 1890–1911. Translated by T.W. Rhys Davids as *Dialogues of the Buddha*, Pali Text Society, 1899–1921.

Ellwood, Robert (1987), 'Buddhism in the West', in M. Eliade (ed.), *The Encyclopedia of Religion*, vol. 2, New York: Macmillan.

Evans-Wentz, W.Y., ed. (1935), *Tibetan Yoga and Secret Doctrines; or, Seven Books of Wisdom of the Great Path*, translated by Lama Kazi Dawa-Samdup, Oxford.

Frauwallner, E. (1956), *Die Philosophie des Buddhismus*, Berlin: Akademie-Verlag.

Gombrich, Richard (1992), 'Dating the Buddha: A Red Herring Revealed', in H. Berchert (1992), vol. 2, pp. 237–59.

Gutierrez, Gustavo (1974), *A Theology of Liberation: History, Politics and Salvation*. Translated and edited by Sister C. Inda and J. Eagleson. London: SCM Press.

Hayes, Richard (1988), *Dignāga on the Interpretation of Signs*, Dordrecht: Kluwer.

Heesterman, J.C. (1979), 'Power and Authority in Indian Tradition', in R.J. Moore (ed.), *Translation and Politics in South Asia*, New Delhi: Vikas.

Humphreys, Christmas (1974), *Exploring Buddhism*, Allen & Unwin, London.

Kolakowski, Leszek (1982), *Religion*, Fontana Paperbacks, Glasgow.

Kosambi, D.D. (1965), *The Culture and Civilization of Ancient India in Historical Outline*, London: Routledge & Kegan Paul.

Lamotte, E. (1958), *Histoire du Bouddhisme Indien*, Louvain: Museon.

Majjhima-Nikāya, vol. 1, edited by V. Trenckner, London: Pali Text Society, 1888. Translated as *Middle Length Sayings* by I.B. Horner, London: Pali Text Society, 1954.

Matilal, B.K. (1982), *Logical and Ethical Issues in Religious Belief*, Calcutta: Calcutta University Press.

Otto, Ruddolf (1923), *The Idea of the Holy: An Inquiry Into the Non-rational Factor in the Idea of the Divine and Its Relation to the Rational*. Translated by John. W. Harvey, London: Oxford University Press, 2nd edn., 1950.

Schumann, H.W (1973), *Buddhism: An Outline of Its Teachings and Schools*. Translated by G. Feuerstein. London: Rider.

Schwab, Raymond (1950), *The Oriental Renaissance: Europe's Rediscovery of India and the East, 1680–1880*. Translated by G. Patterson-Black and V. Reinking, foreword by E.W. Said, New York: Columbia University Press, 1984.

Sharma, R.S. (1959), *Aspects of Political Ideas and Institutions in Ancient India*, Delhi: Motilal Banarsidass.

Suzuki, D.T. (1950), *Essays in Zen Buddhism*, London: Rider.

Vasubandhu, *Abhidharmakośa* (1970–73), edited by S.D. Shastri, Varanasi: Bauddha Bharati.

Vinaya Piṭaka, edited in 5 vols by H. Oldenberg, London, 1879–83. Translated in 5 vols by I.B. Horner *et. al.* as *The Book of the Discipline*, Pali Text Society, 1938–52.

Visuddhimagga by Buddhagosa (1950), edited by H. Warren and K. Kosambi, Harvard: Harvard University Press.

Watts, Alan (1933), *Buddhism in the Modern World*, London: Watkins.

Williams, Bernard (1985), *Ethics and the Limits of Philosophy*, London: Fontana.

Wilson, Bryan (1989), 'The Westward Path of Buddhism', *Journal of Oriental Studies*, vol. 2, pp. 1–10.

Warder, A.K. (1970), *Indian Buddhism*, Delhi: Motilal Banarsidass.

Weber, Max (1958), *The Religions of India: The Sociology of Hinduism and Buddhism*. Translated by H.H. Gerth and D. Martindale. Glencoe. (Original edn., 1921.)

Winternitz, Moriz (1927), *History of Indian Literature*, English translation, Calcutta: Calcutta University Press.

18

The Perception of Self in the Indian Tradition

I

Holding as we do that, while knowledge of any kind is a thing to be honoured and prized, one kind of it may, either by reason of its greater exactness or of a higher dignity and greater wonderfulness in its objects, be more honourable and precious than another, on both accounts we should naturally be led to place in the front rank the study of the soul. The knowledge of the soul admittedly contributes greatly to the advance of truth in general, and above all, to our understanding of Nature, for the soul is in some sense the principle of animal life—Aristotle.

I begin with these two sentences of Aristotle's *De Anima*.[1] My purpose, however, is to talk about the perception of the self in the context of traditional or classical India. This is not directly addressed to the postmodernists. I shall instead talk about a premodern idea of 'self'. My suspicion is that there is an uncanny similarity between the premodern idea of self and postmodernist discussion of the same. The above quotation simply underlines a couple of notable phenomena. The first is the universality of concern among the philosophers in the ancient or classical (and premodern) world regarding the conception of the self. The second is the primary importance given to the knowledge of the self as well as its being the gateway to the knowledge of other things, to our understanding of Nature. In India, such pronouncements as 'know thyself' or 'knowledge of the self gives you the knowledge of everything' were frequently formed even in the Upaniṣads, when philosophical thinking was more poetically expressed and arguments achieved neither systematization nor sophistication. Some have claimed that the thoughts of the Upaniṣads influenced not only Buddhism but also, perhaps partly through Buddhism, the Neoplatonics, Christian mystics, and even Persian Sufis. Such a claim can hardly be substantiated, but the part about their possible influence upon Buddhism cannot be lightly dismissed. Even a late Buddhist text such as *Tattvasaṃgraha* summarizes the Upaniṣadic teaching about *ātman*, and its author, Śāntarakṣita, remarks that this teaching of *ātman* as the universal and eternal consciousness is *not totally* faulty (cf. *alpāpardaha*), for it has some merit. Kamalaśīla, the commentator, says that if the notion of eternality of consciousness is dropped, the Upaniṣadic teaching becomes more acceptable to a Buddhist who identifies the self with the momentary consciousness-series. The importance that the Upaniṣads put upon the knowledge of the self is well known. A single quotation from *Īśa*, verse 7, suffices to demonstrate this:

> He who sees unity in all diversities
> He who knows the self as the Universal soul,
> Is beyond all illusions and sufferirgs, beyond all losses and gains.

My express purpose is to talk about the perception of the self in India. I propose to do it in three parts. In the first part, I shall introduce briefly the classical Indian thinking about the trio—the self, re-birth, and ways to freedom. (The meaning of 'freedom' is intriguing. It changes according to the schools and religious sects. It also changes from age to age.) There is a bewildering variety of views regarding the details of their interrelationship, but there is unanimous agreement that these three concepts constituted the building blocks of what we may very generally call 'Indian soteriology'. In the second part, I wish to go a bit into the technical philosophical discourse about the ontological dispute between Nyāya and Buddhism over the existence of a soul-substance. In the third part, I wish to talk briefly about what possible lesson can we derive today from this age-old dispute and what relation could it have with the modern (and postmodern) discussion of personhood.

The task, at first blush, seems to be next to impossible. There are a variety of views about the self expressed in what we tend to call 'schools' and 'sub-schools', or rival systems or rival philosophers in classical India. And debates and arguments surrounding the self and nonself continued for about two millennia. One illustration will do. *Tattvasaṃgraha*, a Buddhist text belonging to circa AD 800, mentions the views of self of six different schools. Nyāya-Vaiśeṣika, Sāṃkhya, Mīmāṃsā, Jaina, Aupaniṣada (or the Upaniṣads), and the Vātsiputrīya, as well as several individual philosophers: four of them, such as Abiddhakarṇa, belonging to the Nyāya School, and Kumārila belonging to the Mīmāṃsā School. After refuting all these views, the author presents his own (Buddhist) view, which regards perception of the self as the misattribution of a false concept to the aggregates of material forms and mental events. However this rivalry indicates that they shared a common philosophical concern. Besides, philosophical concerns can be said to be conditioned to some extent by the cultural milieu. These rival views share certain common cultural presuppositions, which could constitute our starting point for giving an impressionistic account of the perception of the self in India.

One common concern has already been noted above from the Upaniṣad: they all accord prime importance to the knowledge of the self, which is supposed to unlock the door to 'freedom', or the highest good, marked by our flight from this 'prison house' of *conditioned* mundane existence, which is almost universally undervalued or devalued as *duḥkha*, 'suffering' or 'unhappiness' or 'unpreferred state'. It is an 'unpreferred state' because as it is *given* to us it does not have any ultimate meaning, any ultimately satisfactory value. By contrast, the attempts of all philosophers was to posit a goal possessing the ultimate value and ultimate meaning, and the claim was that only against the backdrop of such a covetable goal does this mundane existence of ours acquire any meaning.

Admittedly, the Buddha teaches how our false conception of the self has to be dissolved into the *analytic insight* (*prajñā*, literally, perfect wisdom) of the five personality aggregates or twelve bases of eighteen base-elements in order to achieve *nirvāṇa*. Here also the concern for the self is not absent. As Udayana (AD 1050) cleverly points out in his monumental work, *Ātmatattvaviveka*, even the Buddhist has to know the true nature of the *self* or soul, so that he can comprehend fully what it is that lacks ultimate existence or ultimate essence. In Udayana's language, in acquiring knowledge of the nonself, since the counter-entity is the self, knowledge of the counter-entity is presupposed in any knowledge of its negation. In plain words, expounding of even the no-self doctrine needs a lot of stage setting, a study of many common assumptions or perceptions of the self to serve as a foil.

I would like to make two further points at the outset. Another presupposition shared among the Indian philosophers in that ways of perceiving one's self not only (unconsciously) modifies one's perception of the nonself, by which I mean here the rest of the universe of which human beings are part, but also seems to distinguish the humans from other creatures. We are thus self-perceiving, self-interpreting, meaning-seeking, and value-discovering creatures.[2] Second, the manifoldness of ways of perceiving the self—*ātman*—is almost axiomatic because *ātman* is a technical term that is, in each case, a member of a set of technical terms, all of which are interlocked and thus constitute a system that we call a '*darśana*' in India. It has thus different shades of meaning in different *darśanas*. However, a common structure is nevertheless discoverable, and this is probably because of their common cultural and social background. Each *darśana*, for example, is concerned with an outline of what I have called 'the therapeutics of *nirvāṇa* or final release'—some more and some less. It is modeled after medical science. One quotation from the *Yoga-bhāṣya* will get us to the heart of the matter (under *Yogasūtra* 2.15):[3]

> Just a medical science is a system of four items—disease, causes of disease or sickness, health (cessation of sickness) and the medicine to cure, this *śāstra* likewise is a system of four: *saṃsāra* (suffering being caught in repetitious rebirth), causes of such suffering, its cessation (freedom) and the means for achieving that state of ultimate freedom.

Obviously, this is similar to the Buddha's teaching of four great 'truths': suffering, its origin, its cessation, and the Way. Even in the Nyāya, Vātsyāyana[4] (sūtra 1.1.1), while he says that knowledge of the self and the other realities eventually leads to the final goal or the 'ultimate good' (*niḥśreyasa*), also mentions that the *śāstra* is concerned with the system of four 'footings of reality' (*arthpada*); avoidable (i.e., future) suffering, its avoidance, means for such avoidance, and the destination or final freedom. Further documentation being unnecessary, I shall only point out that perception of the self or the non-self (cf. *nairātmya-dṛṣṭi*) occupies a central position in this so-called therapy. Hence, the sophisticated and hair-splitting argument to expose the exact nature of what it is to be a self or a person, which continued not for centuries but for a millennium in India, need not come as a surprise.

II

Recent renewed discussion in the West about the question of personal identity and the self has mainly centered around (what is now called) 'reductionism' versus 'nonreductionism'. The reductionist holds that the fact of a person's identity over time just consists in the holding of certain particular facts that can be described without the assumption that a persistent self exists. A person's existence means occurrence of a series of interrelated physical and mental events in a brain and a body. The nonreductionist, however, holds that there are some additional facts over and above those required by the reductionists. This new reductionist view has been claimed to mandate a change in self-perception that provides additional support for the moral theory of consequentialism by rejecting the classical self-interest theory. Since the Buddhist is sort of a reductionist in respect to his conception of selfhood, some Buddhological scholars have been delighted to see this new trend in the analytical tradition. I shall refrain from making any further comment on this issue but simply point out that the problems of such comparative philosophy, which, while they are very suggestive on the surface, at a deeper level become extremely complicated and involved, such that each comparison ends up necessarily in noting stark contrasts; only then does it become philosophically fruitful or rewarding.

It is true that the Buddha was reductionist and his soteriology was explicitly presented as deflationary. If the person's life experiences and his *saṃsāra* are by nature undervalued as suffering and pain, then the only possible way to the final and nonrecurring cessation of suffering is to perceive the person as a false, superimposed concept, which will disappear before the final liberating insight. I shall choose one particular school of Buddhism to discuss its detailed process and the argument. Among the nonreductionists, I shall present the counterargument of the Nyāya school in order to bring both arguments into sharp relief.

Almost all Indian philosophers, as well as the schools they belong to, regarded *darśana* as imparting the knowledge of the way by which one can change the existing life experience, which is, by all accounts, devalued in relation to the goal that is accorded the supreme value. Various pairs of terms are in use with the usual difference in their detailed explanation, although the basic pattern is the same due to their common cultural presuppositions (Table 1). The general assumption was that a true perception of the self (or nonself, as the case may be) will lead one from one stage (noted in the left-hand column) to the other (the right-hand column).

Table 1

bondage/*bandha*	release/*mokṣa*
constraints	freedom
dahana, tapa, pīḍa	*nirvāṇa*
duḥkha, bādhanā	*vimokṣa*
preya	*śreyas, niḥśreyasa*
slavery	liberation
pain, suffering	cessation, bliss

The Buddhists, however, had a chip on their shoulder. Although it is undeniable that the Buddha rejected the notion of a persistent self that transmigrates, he accepted the transmigration process as well as the *karma* doctrine, which involved action, motivation, and moral responsibility. Besides, a few of his *Dialogues* contained elements that might refer to a persistent self. Further, of the early Buddhist schools, the Vātsiputrīyas and the Sāmmitīyas accepted the concept of a persistent entity called '*pudgala*'. Since this concept came very close to the Brahminical soul, these schools were viewed as being heretical.

First, consider the often mentioned *Bhāra-sutta* of the *Saṃyutta-nikāya* (pt. 3, pp. 25–6, sutta 22):

> Bhāra have pañcakkandhā
> Bhāraharo ca puggalo
> Bhārādānam dukkhaṃ loke
> Bhāranikkepaṇam sukham.

Here the five personality aggregates, or the psycho-physical complex, are called the 'burden', whereas the 'person' (*pudgala*) carries the burden. Since the passage was frequently mentioned by rival philosophers, Śāntarakṣita[5] saw fit to explain it from the 'nonself' point of view. The commentator, Kamalaśīla, said that the 'bundle' of the psycho-physical event was identified as the 'person', such that the disciple might have recognized it as a 'nominally existent' entity (*prajñapt-sat*), not a separate and eternally real entity. A 'nominally existent' entity in Buddhism means a false and hence dispensable concept. Kamalaśīla also referred to a citation by Uddyotakara, the Naiyāyika, from the *Dialogues* of the Buddha, which might have had separated the self from *rūpa* ('material form'), feelings, perceptions, and so forth. Kamalaśīla explained it away by saying that such specific instructions of the Buddha were meant for those confused disciples who might have thought the bundle of feelings or the perceptions as the self.

The *pudgala* (person) of the Sāmmitīyas and the Vātsiputrīyas was not exactly the soul of the Brāhmaṇas; it was accepted, however, as a separate entity. Vasubandhu therefore elaborately refuted such a concept in the ninth chapter of his *Abhidharmakośabhāṣya*.[6] Śāntarakṣita summarized this argument in his *Tattvasaṃgraha*. He also added that the doctrine of universal flux would instantly refute any such persistent entity as the *pudgala*.

In the Yogācāra school the self was identified as the individual, but instantaneously emerging, awareness-series. It was divided into (Vasubandhu's *Triṃśikā*) eight:[7] five sensory awareness (called *pravṛttivijñāna*, for they cause motivation to act), 'mental' awareness, ego-shrunk' mind, and *ālaya* (storehouse) awareness. This *ālaya* doctrine was posited to explain the problem of linkage between one state and the other in the same personality series. I will comment more on this later.

Udayana[8] in his famous book, *Ātmattvaviveka*, identified four pairs of rival philosophical theses, one set of which refutes the claim that the self is something over and above the physical and psychological continuity, while the other set rejects the previous set, thereby creating the ground for our belief in a persistent self.

The first four theses, all ascribable to the Buddhists, are:

1. Everything that exists is momentary (the flux doctrine).
2. The assumed external objects are, in fact, created or given by our internal episodes. (The external object of awareness is in fact an object *in* that awareness.)
3. The attributes and their substratum are indistinguishable and hence identical.
4. No accredited means of knowledge is available to prove the existence of such an independent self.

The other set of four theses consists in the negation of these four. If everything is in a flux, the notion of a persistent self is by far refuted. If there are no external objects, we may not then cognize the self, for the self, which is distinct from internal awareness but recognizes external objects through such awareness, cannot be established. If the substratum-attribute distinction is not established, then the distinctness of the persistent self has to be sacrificed. Besides, we need evidence to prove the existence of a distinct, persistent self.

It seems, in Udayana's view, that we have here a package deal. The Buddhist perception of the nonself is interlocked with the above four principal philosophical theses. A Naiyāyika has to knock off all four, one by one, before he can hope to establish his belief in nonreductionism.

The 'flux' doctrine is argued on the basis of an abolition of any distinction between the capability or potentiality to *do* anything (causal potency) and actually doing it. This was the essence of Dharmakīrti's argument to prove the flux doctrine in his *Hetubindu*, which was later elaborated in various ways by his followers, such as Arcaṭa, Śāntarakṣita, Jñānaśrī and Ratnakīrti.[9] If a thing's potentiality is identified with its actually doing it, and if existence is defined in terms of the potency to do something, then the flux doctrine follows as the logical outcome. But a cook does not always cook, nor a teacher always teach. Hence if either capability or potency is defined in terms of causing something to happen when and only when all accessory conditions cooperate, then as Udayana argued, persistent objects must exist, which refutes the highly counterintuitive flux doctrine.

The argument to support the Buddhist challenge to not only the persistence but also the existence of external objects was formulated in various ways,[10] but one of Dharmakīrti's arguments became the most famous and a much-debated one. An external object, say a blue thing, and our cognition of that very object, are always and invariably cognized together. Given the truth of this claim, one can draw the conclusion that what appears to be *external* is in fact indistinguishable from, and hence identical with, what is *internal* to the awareness, that is, it is the awareness itself. The Nyāya reply, which Udayana formulates, basically uses the same kind of ordinary intuition of common people as evidence. Udayana says that whenever a cognition grasps a so-called (external) object, that very cognition itself cannot at the same time conceal the distinctness of the graspable from the grasping itself. Nyāya, however, disagrees that cognition of an object and the cognition of that very cognition arise together at the same moment. But even if this so-called togetherness is conceded for the sake of the argument, Nyāya points out that such togetherness is not a strong enough evidence to prove identity beyond all reasonable doubt. Besides, 'togetherness' itself implies a difference at a certain level. It takes two to tango.

The substance-attribute—or rather location-locative—distinction is so much ingrained in our ordinary experience of the structure of the reality that it would be highly counterintuitive to obliterate the distinction. From a distance we can see the substratum, for example, but because of our lack of seeing its attributes (leaves, etc., in the case of a tree, or hands and legs in the case of a person), we cannot have certainty. This shows that the substratum can be cognized as distinct from attributes. As regards the lack of any means of knowledge or evidence to establish the existence of a persistent self, Udayana claims that both perception and inference can supply the required proof of the self's existence. 'I'—awareness is a sort of inner perception that all creatures universally experience. Inference of the self is based upon the evidence of what is called 'recollective memory'.

The main argument for reductionism or nonreductionism turns primarily upon a proper interpretation of recollective memory and psychological connectedness, which is relevant for explaining personal identity not only over time but also, in the Indian context, over the birth, death, and rebirth process, which is perhaps misleadingly called 'transmigration'. The Buddhist had an additional chip on his shoulder, for he had to insist upon the said connectedness not only over some time but also from one birth to another. To explain transmigration without a transmigrating soul, one resorts, in Buddhism, to the theory of the twelve-membered 'causal' chain. In this chain, the preceding member is called a *pratyaya*, a 'condition' (in a very loose sense) for the arising of the succeeding member. The first two members belong to the previous birth, *avidyā* (false belief) and *saṃskara* (residual traces of *karma*; their being there causes the third member, *vijñāna*, to arise. This is explained by Vasubandhu as the origin of consciousness or awareness series at the time of the new life (i.e., conception in the mother's womb). Depending on this 'awareness', the psycho-physical complex arises, and so on. The point to note here is that the notion of *karma* combined with the set of false beliefs[11] (one of which is *satkāyadṛṣṭi*, perception of the body and mind as the self) perpetuates the continuity of the false personality aggregates from one life to another. Another crucial member of the causal chain is the 'thirst' or drive for pleasure or for continuing life. Life is continued because of the *hetu-pratyayas*, that is, as long as the causal conditions, such as false beliefs, *karma*, and the drive for becoming, perpetuate it. It is like the flame of a lamp that burns for becoming, perpetuate it. It is like the flame of a lamp that burns as long as it is fed with the *pratyayas*, such as the wick, and the oil and air. Just as it is not the *same* flame that goes on burning over a period of time (but each time a new flame arises), we have a false awareness of the identity of the flame of that lamp. Personal identity can be explained along the same lines.

We may at this stage take a closer look at the aggregate of awareness, which is usually the Yogācāra substitute for the self. It is interesting to note that in the Sarvāstivāda school, this is divided into six types of awareness (five sensory and one 'mental' or 'inner'), but although 'mind' (*mano-dhatu*) is mentioned, it is not considered an additional entity. Only the preceding awareness-moment is regarded as mind with respect to the succeeding awareness moment. In the Sthaviravāda school, however, the entity mind is distinguished by its three or more peculiar functions,[12] such as the adverting mind to any of the five 'doors' (i.e., senses) and two classes of acceptance of 'impressions'. The Yogācāra, as I have already noted, speaks of not only a mind (*Kliṣṭa-manas* = mind with defilements of ego-perception, etc.) but also an *ālaya*, the locus of all 'seeds'.

In the Maitriya-Asaṅga-Vasubandhu school of Yogācāra the *ālaya* became an all important concept. The Sthaviravāda had a concept of 'a current of consciousness' (*bhavāṅga-vijñāna*) linking the fluctuating and transmigrating stages. It was regarded as a backdrop against which 'thoughts' (*vithi-citta* in Sthaviravāda, *pravṛtti-vijñāna* in Yogācāra) arise and perish. Although this is said to be bound by birth and death, since death is a prelude to another birth, it must flow as a current from life to life. This, therefore, creates the false notion of the self that is supposed to maintain 'personal identity'.

The problem arises in the causal explanation of the continuity of thought-moments, where depending upon the preceding one, the succeeding one arises. For thought-moments are either good or bad, and hence a good moment cannot arise depending upon the preceding bad one. To avoid this quandry, the Sthaviras posited this 'undercurrent' of awareness, which is neither good nor bad, is itself in flux (*avyākṛta*), and can intervene between a bad thought and a good one. The Sautrāntika criticized this theory and posited their concepts of 'seed' and 'maturity'. Seeds of the evil may coexist with the seeds of the good and only one of them (from either group) can obtain 'maturity' at a time. Thus, good thoughts arise from good seeds, and bad ones from bad. In the context of this controversy and tension, the Yogācāra posited the *ālaya*, 'the receptacle', as a flow (or current) of awareness from which 'thoughts' arise like waves from water (Vasubandhu).[13] All thoughts leave their residual traces in the form of seeds, which await their respective maturity to generate further thoughts. Thus, *ālaya* is called the 'locus of all seeds' (they are also in a flux), and at death all other thoughts dissolve in the 'mental', which in turn dissolves into the *ālaya*, retaining the seeds for maturity in the next birth. *Nirvāṇa* is achieved when this *ālaya* dissolves or 'turns to itself' or 'reverses itself'.

The receptable (*ālaya*) awareness shares a lot of characteristics with the soul or the self of the non-Buddhists. Hence in the *Sandhisūtra* (where the doctrine was formulated as well as elaborated) the Buddha is supposed to have given the following warning:[14]

> The *ālaya* consciousness is the locus of all seeds, deep and subtle like the ocean. I have not revealed this notion (earlier) lest fools construe this as the 'soul' out of confusion.

In the later Yogācāra school, the *ālaya* doctrine was not given any prominence. However, that there was a tension within Buddhism itself has been illustrated by the above brief discussion. The Naiyāyikas found that the seed theory could be faulted in various ways. There was at least an argument made against the 'heaviness' of suppositions whereby at every moment millions of memory seeds and other *karma* seeds (residual traces) were said to continuously arise and die, for only a few seeds (or one seed) at a time could reach maturity to generate the next (particular) thought-moment or action-moment. There was no self or persistent substratum where such potentialities might reside until maturity. In fact, here the table was turned against the Buddhist, who originally blamed others for 'heaviness' in supposition (of an additional self).

The main (positive) argument of Nyāya for a permanent or enduring self, which will have not only transtemporal but also transmigrational identity, is based upon an evidence of a special kind of experience, *pratisandhāna*, which I have translated as 'recollective memory'. Vātsyāyana used this term, but the argument was first elaborated by Uddyotakara while he gave a unique interpretation of *Nyāya-sūtra* 3.1.1: 'For, the same object is grasped by seeing and touching.' Udayana also uses this as his principal evidence. *Pratisandhāna* is not simply memory or recollection, it is not even recognition of what was already recognized (= *pratyabhijñā*), as Udayana clearly states. It is usually verbalized as, 'This I (i.e., I myself) who saw the food am now eating (touching) it.' Uddyotakara said that this evidence is adequate to prove not only the stability of the external objects of our perception but also the persistence of the (internal) subject who grasps the object. In other words, it cuts both ways. It seems undeniable that we have such experience where not only the transtemporal identity of the object but also the same of the subject is witnessed. If the experience is not regarded as mistaken with regard to the object at least in the majority of cases, there is no adequate reason to regard it as *always* mistaken as regards the subject.

Notice that minimal criteria are needed to reidentify something over time. The rosebush that I planted five years ago is to me still the same rosebush although probably many cells of the plant have changed, multiplied, grown, and died. For one who does not believe in the flux doctrine it could be the same self or subject, just as it would be the same rosebush, or, for instance, the same chair that I bought five years ago.

The Buddhist, however, would have an easy answer. Being a believer in the flux doctrine, he would resort to the psychological continuity or connectedness between 'cause and effect' (in the special Buddhist sense) as an adequate ground for explaining the (illusory) appearance of the subject-identity over time. This cause and effect series must belong to the same (a particular) continuum, for otherwise, as Udayana points out, when the teacher's knowledge goes on in sequence generating the body of the disciple's knowledge, the above causal criterion will misidentify the teacher's person as that of the student. The unity of the causal continuum of psychological states is, thus, to be ascertained, the Buddhist may reply, on the basis of our lack of grasping the distinctness of the bodies. But this reply would be invalid. For this may guarantee transtemporal identity of the series, but not transmigrational identity, which the Buddhist admits and where, through a different body, the awareness-series is supposed to continue. The moral responsibility implicit in the pan-Indian *karma* theory pervades not just one life but a series of lives with different bodies, environments, and so forth. Besides, Udayana poses a tricky question.

Suppose a boy has never seen his father; then he would have a lack of grasping the distinctness of his own body from his father's. There is causal connection as far as bodies are concerned and, therefore, the above criteria for subject identity would apply. In fact, in the case of physical objects, causal connectedness is not an adequate criterion for object-identity in all cases, even when they arise in quick succession such that we cannot grasp the distinctness of their moments of occurrence. When an earthen pot is smashed into pieces all of a sudden, we do not have even a false sense of its identity.

The problem, as Udayana sees it, is this: the causal connection between the previous experience when I *saw* the object and the present experience when I *touch* it cannot be happily explained unless some additional factor is imagined. 'Belonging to the same continuum of awareness' is not an adequate explanation, because, without circularity how are we to identify the continuum? If it is done on the basis of the *ālaya*, that is not satisfactory either. For, as we have seen, the *ālaya* has to fluctuate at every moment, and this action is never registered in our awareness; what is registered there is the enduring subject-identity. It is this awareness of subject-identity over time that distinguishes one continuum from another. The theory of this being an illusion is based upon no other evidence (for we never directly experience that I am a *completely* different person at every instant) but upon such material object analogy of a river or the flame of a lamp. Even these examples can be challenged. If by 'a river' we simply mean some portion of water at a particular spatiotemporal coordinate, then, of course, we cannot step twice into the same river. But if it means a continuous water flow at a particular spatial location coming from the same fountainhead of water and perhaps also being emptied in the same lake or ocean, then we can step into *it* twice, thrice, and so on, for such an entity, whatever that is, will have well-known criteria for transtemporal identity. The Nyāya perception of the enduring self is similar to this: the self has both a transtemporal and a transmigrational identity, thereby taking care of the moral responsibility implicit in the *karma* doctrine. Short of accepting the doctrine of universal flux, it is possible to say that the universally felt common experience that I take a bath in the same *river* everyday is also veridical, unless it becomes part of the common universal illusion, which the universal flux doctrine upholds. The argument in either case seems to be evenly balanced: the idea of a multitude or 'heaviness' of suppositions (the other side of the parsimony argument) works both ways. The reductionist Buddhist is shedding off only one excess baggage, that of an enduring self, while he has to accept, as we have seen, other excess baggage. The flux doctrine, apart from being counterintuitive, is not by any means a simple doctrine. It is loaded with suppositions of various sorts, unsupported by common experience. Without the flux doctrine, the no-soul doctrine will lose at least one substantive argument in its favour. Then, of course, the coherence of the notion of the stability of material objects with that of an ever-fluctuating awareness-series recognizing those stable material objects, can very well be called into question.

III

Whether there is an enduring self or not, both the Buddhist and Nyāya agree that a perception of its *true* nature (which may be either a void or a substantial entity) is what adds ultimate meaning, value, and significance to our life, which otherwise appears to be full only of suffering, absurd and devoid of any value. The moral theory would be the same or similar in both cases in so far as they accept the *karma* doctrine and transtemporal and transmigrational moral responsibility. The ultimate goal is, for both, and cessation of *saṃsāra* through a sort of self-realization, the ultimate knowledge of what one's own self is.

Cessation of *saṃsāra* need not ensure a blissful state. Both Nyāya and Buddhism regard it as a negative state—a value but not necessarily, as any ordinary person may imagine, a state of happiness. This falsifies the usual claim that the goal of all human beings is a sort of ultimate happiness or bliss. Both are therefore committed to answer the common question, why, then, would people be inclined to look for such a goal? A commonsense answer is that if one is carrying a heavy burden for a pretty long time, would he not be attracted to a state where he is released and relieved of his burden? It is not a happy state certainly, but something that is still a desirable goal. In the postmodern context, we may understand the implication of this underlying soteriology in a slightly different manner. We are at liberty to choose our own interpretation. The gradually dawning self-knowledge or self-realization that makes one feel the valuelessness or essencelessness of everything we tend to attach value to, will lead naturally to self-etiolation and gradually self-effacement. This, in turn, is supposed to gradually attenuate the drive for life's pleasures and pain, which would make a glimpse of something beyond possible and within reach—a truth that the original Upaniṣads initially talked about. Why is such a nirvāṇic consciousness desirable, and is it a happy or blissful state? We may reply with a comment of Udayana (twice repeated): 'Why should we, small ginger-merchants, be concerned with big ocean-liners?'[15]

Buddhism, I believe, should distance itself from modern reductionism, for in spite of the allure of the moral theory it seems to endorse (if there is much less ego, there can be successful rejection of the self-interest theory), it seems to be of one piece with modern naturalism. Buddhism, therefore, cannot accept the whole package of Parfitian (modern) reductionism. Besides, I have shown that in the context of the transmigrational subject-identity or continuum-identity, and of the action theory and moral responsibility of the *karma* doctrine, the Buddhist and Nyāya may endorse a similar moral theory by which the classical self-interest theory may well be defeated. What is important, it seems to me, is to move away from the scientific-materialistic picture of the universe modeled after the canons that emerged in the seventeenth-century revolution of natural science, a view that I have called 'naturalism',[16] following Charles Taylor, and that may also be called 'modernism'. It is true that Derek Parfit's motivation was not to argue in favour of some form of behaviourism (in fact he was probably trying to find a way out of it). But, as I have noted, the dispute in classical India had some common presuppositions about one's understanding of the self. This type of understanding had features that added real significance to human beings and their agency, their actions and their self-understanding. It may be necessary to revive, within the modern Western analytical circle, the old classical Indian or the eighteenth-century Western (anti-scientist) 'premodern' concern for the dignity of human nature. To me, only in such a context would analysis and understanding of the different perceptions of the self in different non-Western traditions have true significance.

Our Indian poet, Rabindranath Tagore once said that there is a 'Surplus in Man'. In his nonphilosophical language, he said, 'However crude all this may be, it proves that Man has a feeling that he is truly represented in something which exceeds himself. He is aware that he is not *imperfect*, but *incomplete*. He knows that in himself some meaning has yet to be realized.[17] This may be regarded by some as the premodern view that has long been shattered by science. But has it been totally shattered? And where have science and technology brought us?

Albert Einstein in his conversation with Tagore once said: 'There are two different conceptions about nature; (i) the whole world as a unity dependent on humanity; (ii) the world as a reality independent of the human factor.' He added, however, that although the second was necessarily presupposed by natural science, no one had been able to prove it to be the true doctrine *scientifically*. Thus, while we need not attempt to undermine (or devalue), like some eighteenth-century thinkers, the value of natural science and the progress of modern technology, it may now be the right time to do some rethinking about what direction our serious philosophical activity should take. It may be that we badly need reconsideration of the old-fashioned and classical ways of perceiving the self as, to some extent at least, free agents invested with some self-conscious moral sensitivity. In view of the world situation today and some of the serious crises that modern science and technology have brought along with its blessings, it is this 'Surplus in Man', his own self-understanding and rational self-wisdom, that can save us from disasters. As the poet Tagore said a long time go, 'In spite of the present gloom we should not lose faith in humankind. For if that goes, we lose everything.'[18] Recent research in cognitive psychology takes into account the indeterminacy of the mental, but it treats a human being more as a computing machine. Why not reverse the metaphor and treat machines as simple models of human beings, thereby preserving the proper dignity of humankind and making the 'Surplus in Man' more visible to us in our perception of the self. Thus, perhaps, a new humanistic science can develop. If this still sounds old-fashioned, I might conclude with a comment, a rhetorical question, from Sir Isaiah Berlin:

> Yet what solution have we found, with all our new technological and psychological knowledge and great new powers, save the ancient prescription advocated by the creators of humanism—Erasmus and Spinoza, Locke and Montesquieu, Lessing and Diderot—reason, education, self-knowledge, responsibility—above all, self-knowledge? What other hope is there for men, or has there even been?[19]

The reason may also be given by another quotation from him:

> It is neither rational thought, nor domination over nature, but freedom to choose and to experiment that distinguishes men from the rest of nature.[20]

I conclude with the comment that I started with. There is an uncanny similarity between premodern and postmodern self. Analysis of some premodern (traditional) cultures, such as those of India and China, might help us to better understand the postmodern self.

Notes and References

1. R. McKeon, ed., *The Basic Works of Aristotle*, New York: Random House, 1941, 535.
2. This comment, in spite of its Sartrean overtone, can, with confidence, be ascribed to the premodern thought.
3. See Svāmī Brahmalīna Muni, *Yogadarśana*, Kashi Sanskrit Series, no. 201, Varanasi: Chowkhambha, 1970.
4. See A. Thakur, ed., *Nyāyadarśana*, Mithila, 1967; *Bhāṣya* under sūtra 1.1.1.
5. See Dwarikadas Sastri, ed., *Tattvasaṃgraha*, Varanasi: Bauddha Bharati, 1968, ch. on *Ātmaparīkṣā*.
6. See Dwarikadas Sastri, ed., *Abhidharmakośabhāṣya*, Varanasi: Bauddha Bharati, 1970–2. See also J. Deurlinger, 'Vasubandu's 'Refutation of the Theory of Selfhood' (*Ātmavādapratiṣedha*)' in *Journal of Indian Philosophy* 17, no. 2 1989, 129–87, for a new annotated translation and comments.
7. See S. Levi, ed., *Vijñaptimātratāsiddhi*, Paris: H. Champion, 1925.
8. See Pandit Dhundhiraja Sastri, ed., *Ātmatattvaviveka* (Varanasi: Chowokhamba, 1940), 5.
9. See also B.K. Matilal, *Logic, Language and Reality*, New Delhi: Motilal Banarsidass, 1985, 276–7.
10. See B.K. Matilal, *Perception*, Oxford: Clarendon Press, 1986, 229–40.
11. See Matilal, *Logic, Language and Reality*, New Delhi: Motilal Banarsidass, 1985, 319–32.
12. See Aniruddha, *Abhidhammatthasamgaho*, ed. R. Sastri, Varanasi, 1965.
13. See *Triṃśikā*, in *Vijñaptimātratāsiddhi*.
14. See Matilal, *Logic, Language and Reality*, 346.
15. See Sastri, *Ātmatattvaviveka*, 223.
16. See Charles Taylor, *Philosophical Papers*, 2 vols, New York: Cambridge University Press, 1985.
17. See the appendix to R.N. Tagore, *The Religion of Man*, Oxford: Oxford University Press 1920.
18. R.N. Tagore, *Sabhyatār Saṃkat*; see his *Collected Works* in Bengali.
19. See I. Berlin, *Four Essays on Liberty*, Clarendon: Oxford University Press 1969, 198–9.
20. Ibid., 208.

PART IV
Sanskrit Semantics

19

Some Comments of Patañjali Under 1.2.64

Patañjali made several very significant comments under Pāṇini-sūtra 1.2.64, which prescribes the grammatical operation called *ekaśeṣa* 'one-remainder' (by which, roughly, only one of the words having identical forms remains when the same case-inflexion follows). That these comments were very important from the point of view of semantics and philosophy of language had been noted by philosophers like Bhartṛhari and Helārāja, and several modern scholars have commented upon the issues in recent times.[1] My attempt here would be to reconstruct and criticize some of the theories that are apparently suggested by Patañjali. It is well-known that Patañjali introduces the philosophical dispute between Vājapyāyana and Vyāḍi regarding the primary denotation of the words, viz., whether by uttering a word we speak of the form '*ākṛti*' (universal?) primarily or we speak of the thing (which manifests the 'form'). The ambiguity of the word '*ākṛti*' is well-known,[2] and it is not always clear what the term stands for in Patañjali's writings, for he also uses the term '*jāti*' (universal). But later tradition seems to have identified *jāti* with *ākṛti* in this context and hence Vājapyāyana is called the Universalist (*jātivādin*) and Vyāḍi the Individualist (*dravya-vādin*). It is also not always clear whether the *dravya* in the context meant the thing or the stuff or the individual.

Patañjali apparently resolved the above dispute by striking a middle course between the two extremes. He said:

It is not that the thing/particular is not meant by the word for him who means the form/universal by the word, nor is it the case that the form/universal is not meant by the word for him who means the thing/particular by the word. Both are meant by the word for both philosophers. For either, one thing is primary and the other secondary. For him who means the form/universal by the word, the form/universal is primary and the thing/ particular is secondary. For him who means the thing/particular by the word, the thing/particular is primary, the form/universal is secondary.[3]

This passage seems to be amazingly simple although it raises further questions about certain fundamental issues. One can ask, for example, what is exactly meant by the 'form' (= *ākṛti*) that is supposed to be spoken about (*abhidhāna*) by uttering the word? Admittedly the paradigm example used in the context is what we today call a common noun or a common name, 'tree', 'cow', etc. But the theory is generalized to be applicable to other types of words or names. For instance, Patañjali elsewhere talks about four types of names depending upon the way they would present the object they name or denote (cf. '*catuṣṭayī śabdānāṁ pravṛttiḥ*' under 1.1. 2); although he uses *śabda* (word), the context and the classification force us to take it in the narrow sense of any substantival expression, generally, nouns and adjectives. The classification includes what we call today proper names as well as what we may call indefinite descriptions. It may be noted that Sanskrit lacks a definite article (and in this regard it resembles some forms of medieval Latin) and the Sanskritists did not develop any theory of 'definite description' (cf. Geach, 1962): 'The lack of definite article means, on the other hand, that no theory of definite descriptions may be looked for in medieval writers.'[4] In fact, Patañjali gives a primitive version of a theory about what Geach has called a 'referring phrase', of the form 'an A'.[5]

Patañjali was not concerned with the role of these expressions in the context of a sentence used to express a proposition, and therefore he was not concerned also with a theory that would involve the stating of the rules of inference from one proposition to another. His concern was with a theory of names (and all the four types should be called names), and outside the context of a sentence, such a name may be used to acknowledge the presence of the thing named.[6] This act of naming is distinct from a propositional act where we must attribute a predicate to something named by the name. The naming act could be correct or incorrect (according as we hit or miss), it cannot be true or false. But it expresses nevertheless 'a complete thought' (as Geach has insisted, p. 26).

The fourfold division of names says how they name when they do. For example, 'a cow' names the object it names through the basis of a natural kind. This is what is called a *jātiśabda*. The natural kind is the basis for the usage (cf. *pravṛtti-nimitta*) of the name 'a cow'. The second type is called *guṇaśabda*, such as 'white'. Can we use it as a name in the above manner? Even Geach's notion of a referring expression would stop here. But suppose I am using an evocative expression of a 'white' experience: 'Ah! White'. I am not naming the colour white which is an universal or even the white tints of the object I am experiencing. I am *calling* the object 'white'. I am not saying '(it is) white'. I am naming it 'white' on the *basis* of the white tint it has, which is a *guṇa* in Vaiśeṣika theory, or on the basis of white colour which is a universal. For the name 'white' must be the name of a particular thing.

The third type is called *kriyāśabda*, e.g. 'a cook'. I call somebody 'a cook' on the *basis* of an action he performs from time to time and performs very well. The required bases for all these three types are therefore a kind, a *guṇa* or attribute and an action. And a proper name is to be distinguished from these three. For in proper names, the basis is arbitrary. It is *yadṛcchāśabda*, such as 'Ḍittha' a name by which a child names, say, a toy elephant.

Kaiyaṭa (under 1.1.2, *Mbh.*) defines a proper name as a word which is used through only the will of the name-user and independently of any basis for usage that may belong to the object named. Nāgeśa comments that the will or wish to the name-user or name-giver does not create the connection between the proper name and what it names, for then the theory of natural/uncreated relation of word and meaning would be rendered false. Hence we must assume that the name-giver is only informing us, making it available for us, what is already there, i.e., the natural relation of the name to the object named (this 'relation' may be thought as the natural capacity or *yogyatā*) (cf. *Mbh. nityo hy arthavatām arthair abhisambandhaḥ*).[7] Nāgeśa also underlines the fact when a proper name is assigned to a person, it is usually to one person; the name is assigned by *saṅketa*.

Nāgeśa makes another comment about the proper name which is a bit difficult to explain. Assuming some philosophical discussion of his contemporaries, he says that in the case of such proper names 'Ḍittha' which names a single object, there is no additional basis for its use. In other words, in the case of 'a cow' the particular natural kind is the basis which is separately intelligible because several individuals belong to the same natural kind. But for calling Ḍittha 'Ḍittha' there is no separate basis, except, I presume, the stipulation of the name-giver. Nāgeśa seems to imply that when we call different individual cows by 'a cow' on different occasions, we need a common basis for such usage, for otherwise there will be the faults of 'innumerableness' and 'promiscuity'. But as long as there is only one single entity to be called 'Ḍittha' no such problem will arise (cf. *ānantya-vyabhicārayor abhāvāt*).[8]

This leads to another question discussed by Nāgeśa. Just as we can name the natural kind, the 'basis for usage' in the case of 'a cow' by adding the abstract suffix *tva*, (viz., *gotva* = cowness), can we name, in the same way, the said 'basis' in the case of 'Ḍittha'? The answer cannot be yes, for then it would imply that 'Ḍittha-tva' names the will of the name-user! Nāgeśa says that 'Ḍittha-tva' actually names Ḍittha! In other words, Ḍittha = Ḍittha-tva! This means that we do not have to worry, under this theory, about some intelligible, theoretically separable, property called Ḍittha-ness: the Ḍittha-ness is nothing but Ḍittha itself. The *essence* of Ḍittha is its essential identity! Nāgeśa also cites the authority of Patañjali to support this identification. For example, such technical terms as '*bha*' used by Pāṇini are on par with proper names. In fact, these technical terms are also regarded as *yadṛcchā-śabdas*, proper names. And Patañjali sometimes uses '*bha-tva*' to name nothing but *bha*, i.e., what '*bha*' stands for. In other words there is no additional property called *bha-tva*!

This type of 'nominalism' with regard to proper names was, however, not so uncontroversial in classical Indian philosophy, as it appears to us today. For example, the Naiyāyikas argued that the personal name such as 'Devadatta' is *used* on the 'basis' of Devadattaness—a sort of a universal or an invariant property, the personal essence (?), which runs through different stages of Devadatta's life (or Devadatta's body), although it was a person's (the name-giver's) will that brought together the name 'Devadatta' and the person Devadatta (when the name was being given). Besides, there are extreme realists who could maintain that even the unique property of some unique object is distinguishable and expressible adding an abstract suffix like '*tva*' to the name of the object. The sun is the sun because of its sunhood, for example. The sky is sky because of skyhood.

To come back to *ekaśeṣa*, it is indeed a very peculiar grammatical operation, if what the Pāṇiniyas say is true. Pāṇini says apparently (1.2.64) that when the same (similar) case-affix follows, of identical word-forms, only one remains. Since he says this about word-forms (*rūpa*) and not word-meanings, we may construe this as saying that only one word-form (e.g., *akṣa*) is retained to do the job for two or three or more such word-forms. (*Akṣa* is a homonym in Sanskrit.) It could then concern the problem of homonymy (one form with two or more meanings) rather than synonymy (two or more words with the same meaning). For example, the word-form '*akṣa*' in Sanskrit has at least three different lexical meanings which are apparently unconnected with each other. Now if we are trying to refer to all these meanings it is expected that we use three utterances of the form *akṣa* and perhaps all in the nominative singular so that the same case-suffix will follow. It is one of the features of the Sanskrit language that it offers an economy there. One can use '*akṣāḥ*' in the plural and this pluralization of only one occurrence of '*akṣa*' will indicate that all the three things are meant by it. Hence it may be said that Pāṇini noted this grammatical device of Sanskrit in 1.2.64.

Almost all commentators beginning with Patañjali (Kātyāyana), however, take 1.2.64 to mean a more general operation than the above. Thus, the *Kāśikā* example is: *vṛkṣaś ca vṛkṣaś ca vṛkṣaś ca vṛkṣāḥ* ('a tree and a tree and a tree = trees'), which is a case of simple pluralization of the form '*vṛkṣa*' when it is used to mean more than two trees.[9] There would be dualization of the inflexion when it is used to mean two trees (cf. *vṛkṣau*). Obviously the word-form 'tree' can hardly be called a homonym in these contexts. But Patañjali makes the implicit assumption of such an explanation explicit. The principle is or should be that for each object we should use some word (name) or other (cf. *pratyarthaṁ śabdaniveśaḥ*).[10] This apparently means that for each tree (i.e., in order to refer to each tree) there should be used a separate word-form 'tree' ('*vṛkṣa*'). Now, the *ekaśeṣa* operation says that we can eliminate other word-forms, *retaining* only one in such cases. This will finally imply that *ekaśeṣa* is a much more primitive grammatical operation (found in other languages too) supplying initially a ground for dualization and pluralizations.

It is possible to construe that dualization and pluralization would be enough to indicate that although one form of the word is used, more than one (two or more) objects are being referred to. The rules of grammar must follow the use of language by the people (*loka*). As Patañjali notes, 'People do use '*vṛkṣaḥ*' (= a tree)' to mean one tree, '*vṛkṣau* (= two trees)' to mean two trees, and '*vṛkṣāḥ* (= trees)' to mean many trees. If, however, people's usage is the authority in the correct use of words, why does Pāṇini undertake to prescribe *ekaśeṣa*?' (p. 142). In other words, the *ekaśeṣa* operation is highly redundant for it is natural to think that to indicate plurality (or duality) pluralization (dualization) is to be resorted to.

For another reason, *ekaśeṣa* in this general sense is highly improbable as an operation. The principle stated earlier, viz. each word-form for each object meaning, does not strictly imply that we use many word-forms of *vṛkṣa* to refer to many trees. For in that case the credibility of such a principle could be in jeopardy. The principle, when it is properly interpreted, requires us to use as many word-forms as is necessary to convey the intended meaning. Now the single utterance of the word form '*vṛkṣa*' would be enough to include as many trees as we wish in our intended meaning. One may counter, says Patañjali, that in this case word '*vṛkṣa*' becomes a word with multiple meaning (*bhavartha*). And the point of the *ekaśeṣa* operation would then be to indicate that words like '*vṛkṣa*' have a multiplicity of meanings. Now the question arises whether this property of having a multiplicity of meanings belongs to such words as 'tree' *naturally* or it is attributed by grammatical prescriptions (*svābhāvikī* or *vācanikī*). It cannot be the first, for then the *ekaśeṣa* prescription would be pointless. It therefore should be the second, in which case the *ekaśeṣa* prescription actually indicates, if I understand it correctly, that such words as 'tree', 'cow' are what we call today class-names or common names having a multiple denotation. And pluralization of such word-forms would indicate that more than one or two members of such classes are being referred to. I translate the relevant sections from Patañjali:[11]

This word ('*vṛkṣa*') does not have one meaning. What then? It has two or many meanings.

Q. If these words have multiple meanings then formulation of rule 1.2.64 is pointless. (*Vārttika* 28).

Here do the words have *by nature* multiple meaning or *by special rulings*? If they are so *by nature*, then

Vārttika 29. *Ekaśeṣa* is not to be prescribed, for one word-form will *tell* all others.

If one (word-form) 'names' the objects (multiply), the second use (of the same word-form) is not necessary,—for an already stated meaning cannot be stated again. If the word has multiple meaning by special ruling, then it should be stated, viz., 'one (only) is retained, and that possesses double meaning or multiple meaning'.

No, it should not be stated. It is given or established (indirectly) only through (the prescription of) *ekaśeṣa*.

How can we get the property of having double meaning or multiple meaning (belonging to the word), from the prescription, 'only one is to be retained'?

It is given by the *ekaśeṣa* operation. For (generally) an understanding of the meaning or the object does not arise, without the use of the word that means or names it. But we do see that understanding of the meaning/object arises even without the use of the word that means/names it. For example: '*agnicit*' or '*somasut*' (where the suffix is deleted but its meaning remains!). They resolve this problem as follows: Because of (the prescription of the rule) for deletion/elision (*lopa*), it is possible for the understanding of the meaning/object to arise without the use of the word that means/names it. Then (we resolve:) here (the same thing happens), because of (the prescription of the rule for) *ekaśeṣa* which says only one is to be retained, it is possible for words to have double or multiple meanings.

Patañjali uses the following argument tentatively: If a grammatical rule prescribed by Pāṇini seems to be redundant, it should be taken to make a special provision. The elision rule for '*agnicit*' implies that we can understand a special meaning (object) even if the word for it is not used. Similarly it is agreed that the *ekaśeṣa* rule is taken to imply that only one word-form is retained and it becomes a word with multiple meaning. This resolution is also rejected by the next passage of Patañjali, which shows the *ekaśeṣa* rule is really pointless:

'Then let it be stated (explicitly), (one word would have multiple meaning when it is so ruled as in "*jātyākhyāyām* . . .").' But it cannot be implied (by the *ekaśeṣa* rule). He who says 'a horse' meaning (thereby) a cow, or 'a cow' meaning a horse, may do so, but no proper understanding will arise thereform. Therefore, if one makes an effort to express multiple meaning (belonging from word) one should follow people's usage (cf. *lokaḥ*) in the last resort: (one should investigate) which words people use to express which meanings. People use '*vṛkṣaḥ*' to mean one (tree), '*vṛkṣau*' to mean two (trees), and '*vṛkṣāḥ*' to mean many. If the people's usage is the authority, for certain, in language, why is the *ekaśeṣa* rule prescribed? (Question:) Why then the elision rule is prescribed? (Answer:) The teacher (Pāṇini) prescribes elision rules (for suffixes) wishing to use some characteristics of the suffixes (that are elided). But then there is no such necessity for prescribing the *ekaśeṣa* rule.

The issue is further complicated by bringing in Vājapyāyana's view *vis-à-vis* Vyāḍi's view. If with Vājapyāyana we say that we use 'cow' to mean directly the common form of all cows (cf. *ākṛti*), then we have to sacrifice the theory of multiple denotation of such words as 'cow'. And, therefore, justification of the *ekaśeṣa* operation would again be difficult. In Vyāḍi's view, however, we may retain the multiple denotation theory, and thereby resort to the above justification. It should be noted that also in Vājapyāyana's view pluralizations can be easily explained as what indicates the plurality of manifestations (*vyakti*) of the common form of all cows.

Patañjali seems to resolve that the *ekaśeṣa* device is prescribed by taking Vyāḍi's view into account, not Vājapyāyana's. For he explicitly says so in the *Paśpaśā* section. But, as I have already argued, the resolution raises many intricate questions, answers to which are not all clear. First, it seems to be a very poor defence to say that *ekaśeṣa* is prescribed to indicate the obvious fact that there are in our language many words which are, not homonyms, but genuine names or words with multiple denotation.

Second, what is exactly meant by the principle: 'Each word for each object'? If it means that to refer to several trees we have to use several times the word-form '*vṛkṣa*' (in fact, a hundred times to refer to hundred trees, for example) and then by 1.2.64, we delete all others retaining only one of them, then it seems to be a very odd procedure and it is at least counter-intuitive. We may suppose that the fundamental relationship between a word and its meaning is that of 'naming'. But still it is conceivable that in order to *name* a multitude of trees, we need not use a multitude of names, but we use one name for tree plus a name for the multitude, i.e. the plural suffix. This seems to be intuitively simple.

Third, even if we accept Vājapyāyana's views that the word 'tree' *means/names* the common 'form' in all trees, pluralization in '*vṛkṣāḥ*' is not difficult to explain. For no universal or common form (*ākṛti*) is intelligible without any reference to its manifestations, and hence pluralization is done to indicate the plurality of such manifestations of the common form or universal.

Fourth, the *ekaśeṣa* rule of Pāṇini 1.2.64 is perfectly understandable (it is *sāvakāśa*) as a rule capturing a special feature of the Sanskrit language (perhaps of other languages too). This concerns homonyms. There are, for example, three Rāmas in the Hindu epics, three different persons, Dāśarathi, Paraśurāma and Balarāma. Now Rāma in this case acts like a homonym (cf. *akṣa*), and hence it is different from such words as 'cow' or 'tree' which are generic names having multiple denotation. In the latter case, the name is used to refer to multiple objects but such usage has the same '*basis*' in each case (cf. *nimitta*; see earlier passage from Patañjali). In the case of homonyms or similar words, the situation is different. It is a quite normal practice to use three 'Rāma' word-forms to refer to the above three persons in a context and then by 1.2.64, we can delete others and retain only one and use pluralization suffix. This could have been the original intention of Pāṇini (some extremists would however even try to discover some common *nimitta* in homonyms and similar words. See Kātyāyana in the concluding section of *Mahābhāṣya* under 1.2.64).

The above consideration seems to justify the doubt that has been expressed by some scholars. The doubt is that the original *Aṣṭādhyāyī* might not have contained the *ekaśeṣa* topic at all. The suggestion is that it was interpolated later on, perhaps, some time between Pāṇini and Kātyāyana. Thus, K.V. Abhyankar notes:[12]

The Daiva grammar has completely ignored this topic. . . . Some critics hold that the topic of *ekaśeṣa* did not exist in the original *Aṣṭādhyāyī* of Pāṇini.

My conclusion is slightly different from the above. Pāṇini rule 1.2.64 can be justified, if we wish to do so, by interpreting it as a rule tnat concerns the homonyms such as '*akṣa*' or '*Rāma*'. For in such cases, it is somehow arguable that we need to repeat the word-form thrice to mean three types of meaning that it apparently has as an accident of the Sanskrit language. And then the *ekaśeṣa* rule is needed to elide the other two forms, so that the pluralization here (as distinct from ordinary pluralization) would indicate that we refer to all three types of *akṣas* instead of many *akṣas* of one type.

Notes and References

1. See Kunjunni Raja (1969), B.K. Matilal (1971), G. Shastri (1959), M. Hiriyanna (1938).
2. S. Sharma (1957), thinks *ākṛti* in Patañjali means 'structural form' viewed in two ways, common form and particular form. The first would be closer to 'universal'. He thinks '*jāti*' means, in Patañjali, 'kind or class'—an abstract concept (1).
3. Patañjali, II (Haryana edition), p. 156.
4. Geach, P.T., p. ix.
5. Geach, P.T., pp. 47–8.
6. Cf. Geach, P.T., p. 26.
7. Patañjali, I, pp. 30 ff.
8. Ibid., p. 30.
9. *Kāśikā*, 1.2.54.
10. Patañjali, II, p. 117 (*Vārttika* I).
11. Ibid., II, pp. 140–42.
12. K.V. Abhyankar, *A Dictionary of Sanskrit Grammar*, p. 98.

Geach, P.T. (1962), *Reference and Generality*, Ithaca: Cornell University Press.

Hiriyanna, M. (1938), 'Vyāḍi and Vājapyāyana', *Indian Historical Quarterly*, 14, pp. 261–6.

Matilal B.K. (1971), *Epistemology, Logic and Grammar in Indian Philosophical Analysis*. Le Hague: Mouton.

Raja, K. (1969), *Indian Theories of Meaning*, Adyar: The Theosophical Publishing House, 2nd edn.

Sharma, S. (1957), 'The Words *Ākṛti* and *Jāti* in the *Mahābhāṣya*', *Adyar Library Bulletin*, 21, pp. 57–65.

Shastri, G. (1959), *The Philosophy of Word and Meaning*, Calcutta: Calcutta University Press.

20

On the Notion of the Locative in Sanskrit

It has been the general practice of modern writers to translate the Sanskrit term '*dharma*' as 'property' and use 'locus', 'substratum' or 'location' for the object called *dharmin* or *ādhāra* in which the *dharma* is said to reside. Such a translational scheme, although it is harmless at times, is not without its difficulties. One simple reason is that while all properties can play the role of some *dharma* or other, the converse is not true. The term 'property' in English is also, conveniently for us, infected with some sort of vagueness. A property can be said to reside in a locus, or a location, or an abode, or a place as much as *dharma* is said to reside in a place. This resident-hood or occurrent-hood is the common factor between a property and a *dharma* and hence it naturally misleads us to believe that we can go on using 'property' in lieu of '*dharma*' without any serious difficulty. However, the obvious difficulty arises as soon as we see that a Sanskritist is willing to call a tea-cup, when it lies on the table, a *dharma* of the table (cf. *bhūtale ghaṭaḥ*) but the linguistic intuition of no English-speaking person would be able to accept such a tea-cup as a 'property' of the table. Faced with such and other difficulties, I had once suggested the use of the pair 'locus and locatable' for '*ādhāra* and *dharma*'. This suggestion is, however, not entirely flawless. In any case, following the same line, I would use in this paper the pair of 'locatee and location' for '*dharma* and *ādhāra*'.

The use of a locative ending in Sanskrit is very pervasive. Pāṇini has ruled that the locative ending technically named as seventh ending is attached on account of the notion of what he calls *adhikaraṇa* (*sūtra* 2.3.36).[1] The notion of *adhikaraṇa* is explained as a sub-category of *kāraka*. *Kāraka* is said to be a grammatical category (cf. *saṃjñā*) in *sūtra* 1.4.23, of which *adhikaraṇa* is only one variety, a sub-category. *Sūtra*

1.4.45 defines *adhikaraṇa* as a 'location' or 'substratum' (cf. *ādhāry adhikaraṇam*). In short, the word expressing a 'location' would belong to the grammatical category of *adhikaraṇa*, a special case of a *kāraka*, and would thereby account for the use of the seventh ending.

A location or a place is generally connected with what is located, or purported to be located, upon it. We shall call this second item locatee. What is this locatee, with reference to which the object is being designated as a location? In the grammatical level, we may rephrase the question as follows: When a word is designated as the locative or *adhikaraṇa*, what is the locatee in reference to which the object denoted by the word would be called the location? The Grammarians' answer is that it is the verb, or the action designated by the verb, which should be the locatee of the said location, for, after all, *adhikaraṇa* is a *kāraka*, and the notion of *kāraka* invariably brings in the notion of an action designated by some verb.

A brief look at any well-known illustration of a locative will be enough to upset the above *prima facie* formulation.

'(There is) sweetness in honey.'

Obviously there is no action involved here. The verb expresses 'existence' and it would be too pedantic to say that the 'existence' (of sweetness) is the locatee of the location, honey. In 'the cat sits upon a mat', it is more reasonable to say that the mat is the location of the cat itself rather than its sitting. In 'He cooks rice in a pot', the pot is to be described more naturally as the location of the rice being cooked rather than the action of cooking. Faced with such objections, the Grammarians resolve that the 'location' is the location of action, or whatever is expressed by the verb, only indirectly, i.e., through the mediation of the agent (as in the case of the cat) or the 'patient' (*karma*, as in the case of rice). The obvious implication is this: what is denoted by the agent-word or the patient-word would be the 'natural' or 'direct' locatee of the location denoted by the locative word, i.e., *adhikaraṇa*. Bhartṛtari has said:[2]

In the *śāstra*, something is called *adhikaraṇa* when it is conducive to the successful functioning of the verb in the following way: The location holds the "action" (or whatever is designated by the verb) indirectly, being mediated by what is (designated by) an agent or patient.

There is another difficulty connected with the notion of *adhikaraṇa* which may be explained in this way. If the grammatical locative is guided, as it is claimed here, always by the ontological notion of 'location and locatee', then the following examples would be hard to explain:

1. The scriptures constitute an authority in righteousness (*dharme vedāḥ pramāṇam*).
2. The village is on the Ganges (*gaṅgāyāṃ grāmaḥ*).

It would be hard to maintain that *dharma* or righteousness is the 'location' of authority as it would be almost impossible to conceive the river Ganges and the location where the village is really located. The Grammarians' solution of this problem is amazingly simple. There are many ways of construing something as a location for a particular locatee. It is not always the physical location that is needed. The notion of 'location' could be extended from concrete to more abstract, physical to more conceptual, locations. In this way it is possible to construe *dharma* as the location where the authority is located. The Grammarians talk of three or four different types of location:

1. Pervasive occurrence, where the locatee is present pervasively in the chosen location (cf. *abhivyāpakādhāra*): There is sweetness in honey.
2. Partial occurrence, where the locatee is present in only a part or some parts of the chosen location (*aupaśkṣikādhāra*): The lion lives in the forest.
3. Transferred or metaphorical occurrence, where the locatee is closely connected with the location but cannot be actually (physically) located in that location (cf. *abhyarṇikādhāra*): The village is on the Ganges.
4. 'Object-hood' occurrence where the locatee is the object of some propositional attitude (cf. *vaiṣayikādhāra*): I have attachment to her (cf. *tasyāṃ mama prītiḥ*).

Righteousness is in this fourth extended sense, a location of which the authority is the locatee. We say that 'with regard to' righteousness the scriptures constitute authority, or that the scriptures' authority are above righteousness.

The first two cases of the above four constitute what is called *mukhya* location, i.e., location in the primary sense, while the last two constitute the *gauṇa* location, i.e., location in the secondary sense. The interpreters of Pāṇini's rule have sometimes resorted to several interpretative rules or guidelines (cf. *paribhāṣā*) in order to avoid infringement of rules by prevalent counter-usage (counter-examples). Such interpretative rules are deemed to be understood in Pāṇini's grammar, although the usefulness of many such rules has been doubted and rejected by later writers. One such rule is this: When a grammatical operation is possible (because it is so enjoined) in relation to both the primary members of a grammatical category and those which are only secondarily considered to be the members of that category, we choose only the primary member (*gauṇamukhyayor mukhya eva kārya-sampratyayaḥ*).

Patañjali under 1.4.42 says that a good principle that comes from commonsense is this: When the choice is open, choose the best.[3]

'Marry your daughter to a handsome person'—from this it is understood that we would marry her to the most handsome (if he is available), and would not marry her to one that is not handsome.

After stating this principle, Patañjali has argued that it was Pāṇini's intention to prohibit this principle of 'choose the better, the best' (cf. *tara-tama-yoga*) in the context of assigning items to the category of *kārakas*. Hence not only the chief and undisputed item (such as a location in the primary sense) would be assignable to one or the other sub-category of *kāraka* (such as *adhikaraṇa*) but also secondary and even remote items which will only tangentially have the required characteristics, would also be so assigned. Hence even an item like the river Ganges, which can only metaphorically be called a location for the village, would also qualify for the designation 'location' in the given case.

How do we know that Pāṇini had such an intention? Patañjali and following him other commentators, Bhaṭṭojidīkṣita and Vāmana-Jayāditya, give the following exegetical argument: Pāṇini has used a superlative suffix, *tamap*, in *sūtra* 1.4.42, in order to say that the most efficient causal element (cf. *sādhaka-tamam*) would be called *karaṇa* the 'instrument'. If, however, the general principle (which is commonplace), alluded to earlier, applies in this context, Pāṇini need not have taken the trouble of adding the superlative; for even without it, the *sūtra* in question may be understood in the same way. This additional effort on the part of Pāṇini has been taken by the Pāṇinīyas as an indication of a hidden intention of Pāṇini himself. He does not want us to appeal to the said general principle in the context of his formulation of the *kāraka* categories.[4]

It is clear that such an interpretation is a very strained one. One can obviously find fault with such exegetical arguments and reject the resulting interpretation. I shall not, however, go into this matter any further here. Instead, let us turn to the Naiyāyikas and what they have to say about the locative category, *adhikaraṇa*.

The Naiyāyikas such as Bhavānanda's *Kārakacakra* are, however, indifferent to the fact that a location that accounts for the use of the locative ending is to be always connected, at least indirectly, with a verb, i.e., whatever is meant by a verb. In other words, a location need not always hold (cf. *dhārayati*), as Bhartṛhari has claimed, indirectly the action or the meaning of a verb as its locatee. Something can be a location (*adhikaraṇa*), though not, perhaps, a *kāraka*, even when the meaning of a verb is not explicitly involved, e.g., 'the pot on the floor'. Here the floor is directly the location, abode, of the pot. This spells out the important distinction between the view of the Naiyāyikas and the Grammarians. The Grammarians have argued that there cannot be any sentence which does not have a finite verb in it at least implicitly (i.e., understood), while the Naiyāyikas believe that there could be sentences where even an implicit finite verb is absent, and they are nevertheless sentences as long as some judgemental awareness will arise from each of their utterances. Thus, in the above example, 'The pot on the floor' (*bhūtale ghaṭaḥ*), we do not have to argue that there is a finite verb '*asti*' ('is' or 'there is') understood in order to round up a theory. If no verb is uttered at all when the particular sentence is uttered, it may be simpler to assume that the sentence does not have any finite verb but two or more elements are linked syntactically without any intervention of a verb. In other words, in Sanskrit at least, according to Nyāya there may be verb-less sentences.[5]

Bhavānanda has said:

The seventh (locative) ending signifies either 'location-hood' or 'locatee-hood'. When it is syntactically connected with a verb, it is called a *kāraka* (otherwise it is not called a *kāraka*).

Therefore, according to the Naiyāyikas, from such verb-less sentence as 'The pot on the floor', a verbal (linguistic) awareness certainty arises, and it is of the form: 'The pot which is the locatee of the floor.

When a verb is used explicitly, we have a *kāraka*, according to the Naiyāyikas. Bhavānanda gives the following example:

He cooks rice in a pot in a kitchen.

The verbal awareness that arises from such an utterance can be identified by the following structural description:

A person is qualified by the effort conductive to cooking, of which the object is rice of which the location is a pot of which the further location is a kitchen.

In 'the pot on the floor', the seventh ending signifies location-hood. This location-hood is located in what is designated by the word with first ending (*ghaṭaḥ* = the pot). Thus, the resulting verbal awareness can be structurally described as:

(1) The pot determines the location-hood resident in the floor.

The above is, however, the view of the earlier (*prāñcāḥ*) Navya-naiyāyikas, according to Bhavānanda. The later (*navyāḥ*) Navya-naiyāyikas hold a slightly different view. Let me try to explain the point raised by the later Navya-naiyāyikas.[6]

First and foremost, we have to understand that a negation designates an absence (*abhāva*). Second, it is to be noted that in each absence there is an 'absentee-hood delimiting connector', which individuates such an absence from other absence. For example, a cat may be absent from the room but be sitting on the roof-top. In this case, 'the cat is not in the room' is true while 'the cat is not in contact with the room' is false. The cat-absence in the first case is qualified by a 'containment' connector as its absentee-hood-delimiting connector. In the second, it is qualified by a more general connector, called contact, as its absentee-hood-delimiting connector. It is therefore non-problematical to say that cat-absence; (1) obtains in the situation, while cat-absence (2) does not obtain. Now, it is argued that the absentee-hood-delimiting connector (*pratiyogitāvacchedaka saṃbandha*) potentially refers to a situation where the location-locatee connection obtains. In other words, if a negation designates an absence (i.e., the expression '*x* is not in *y*' designates the absence of *x* in *y*), then the corresponding (hypothetical) positive situation would involve a location-locatee situation (e.g., *x* is *in y*). For short, let us call it the 'locative' connector (cf. *vṛttyaniyāmaka saṃbandha*). The specific instances of such a locative connector are contact, containment, inherence, sitting on, lying upon, standing upon, characterizing, etc. The absentee-hood-delimiting connector in any particular case of an absence would be one such connector.

Now consider,

The pot is *not* on the floor.

To maintain parity with (1), this must be analysed as:

(2) The pot is qualified by the absence of location-hood resident in the floor. (Here the absentee-hood-delimiting connector is one of 'determining' *nirūpakatā* for the said location-hood cannot be a locatee of the pot.)

However, the connector which we have called 'determining' is not a 'locative' connector in our sense, for it does not involve a situation when we can say '*x* is IN or ON or AT *y*. Hence (2) would be a wrong way to describe the structural contact of our verbal awareness from the corresponding utterance.

The later Navya-naiyāyikas consider such objections and say that the seventh ending should be taken to signify locatee-hood rather than location-hood. This locatee-hood is to be connected with what is designated by the word to which the ending is attached through the connector of determining. This locatee-hood can then be a qualifier of the pot, the designatum of the word in the first (*prathamā*) case-ending. Hence the following 'analytic' descriptions (i.e., the structural descriptions of the corresponding verbal awareness) are in order.

(3) 'The pot is on the floor'—The pot is qualified by the locatee-hood determined by the floor.

(4) 'The pot is not on the floor'—The pot is qualified by the absence of the locatee-hood determined by the floor.

To return to the initial issue of the translation, a locatee, *dharma*, cannot be called a property in the usual sense of the term. It can be any occurrent entity, either an abstract particular (locatee-hood itself is one such abstract particular) or even a concrete particular (a pot), or an abstract generality (sweetness in sugar). The nature of a locatee (*dharma*) is to be determined by the linguistic intuition reflected in the use of locative endings in common (Sanskrit) speech. This is what is meant by such assertions as '*Vṛttimān dharmaḥ*' ('A locatee is what is occurrent in something else').

There is another characteristic of a locatee which it shares with a property. It serves as distinguisher (*vyāvartaka*). A locatee can be used to distinguish the location or the set of its location from others of which it is not a locatee. Put a cup on a saucer and this will distinguish the saucer from all such saucers on which there is no cup at the moment. It would, however, be wrong to say that all locatees are or can be used as distinguishers. For most Naiyāyikas admit locatees which are located in all possible locations. These are called ever-present or everywhere present locatees (cf. *kevalānvayin*). A discussion of this point is, however, beyond the scope of this paper.

Notes and References

1. *Saptamyadhikaraṇe ca*: 2-3-36.
2. See *Vākyapadīya* (Bhartṛhari, eds. K.V. Abhyamkar V.P. Limaye, Poona, 1965), verse 3-9-148.
3. See *Mahābhāṣya* under Pāṇini's rule 1–4–42 (F. Kielhorn's edn., vol. 1, R.N. Dandekar: Poona, 1962, pp. 331–2.
4. See *Kāśikā* and *Siddhānta-Kaumudī* under 1–4–42.
5. I have discussed this point at some length in 'Indian Theorists on the Nature of the Sentence (*vākya*)', *Foundations of Language*, 2, 1968, pp. 377–93.
6. See Bhavānanda's *Kāraka Cakra*, Chaukhamba, Benares, 1942, pp. 79–82.

21

What Bhartrhari Would Have Said about Quine's Indeterminacy Thesis

Since Quine's thesis of indeterminacy of translation was formulated and defended in his *Word and Object* (1960) about twenty-five years ago, it has generated various sorts of reactions and responses from philosophers. Barring occasional misunderstanding, the general point that this theory is of a piece with the thesis of underdetermination of natural science by all possible observation, or of theories by evidence, has more or less been sustained. Quine has recently undertaken the task of offering 'a succinct over-all clarification' of his thesis in 'Indeterminacy of Translation Again' (1987). He points out that his thesis applies first and foremost to sentences as opposed to terms (p. 9), and what he has challenged is 'just an ill-conceived notion within traditional semantics, namely, sameness of meaning' (p. 10). The old notion of *separate* and *distinct* meanings created a stumbling block for philosophers and linguists alike. It ought better be cleared away. And Quine's thesis does just that. Quine has also pointed out a difference between his indeterminacy of translation thesis and the underdetermination of science. His thesis, as he himself would like to see it, belongs squarely to philosophy of language, and dispenses successfully with the notion of separate meanings of sentences.

I wish to describe here an old theory of language prevalent in classical Indian writing, which from a slightly different point of view and on different grounds found the notion of meanings as *separate* and *distinct* entities unsuitable and superfluous. On the same theory one could have conceded the possibility of the indeterminacy of translation, not on the ground that even when everything is taken into account alternative ways of translating the native's sentence remain open, but on the ground that each translator's linguistic disposition is stimulated in some unique way and one need not match with the other. This theory was championed by Bhartṛhari in AD sixth-century India. In giving an outline of this theory of language and meaning, I shall try to show how this can be seen as a critique of Quine's theory by emphasizing that the elimination of the separate and distinct meaning-entities can be achieved even from a different set of hypotheses. There are many ways to skin a cat or a rabbit or a *Gavagai.*

Grammar was regarded as a central discipline in classical India. It was central to the study of the scriptures, rituals, logic and metaphysics. It does not take much to show the Indian grammarians' approach to the study of language or linguistics was implicitly behaviouristic. The model of language-learning that was provisionally accepted by almost all parties concerned was that of each child observing the overt behaviour (activities) of the young adults obeying the verbal commands and instructions of the old adults who are in a position to command. The situation envisioned in such a theory is behaviouristic, for the mental life of the learner does not figure in any significant manner. Hence this would nicely fit with Quine's view as re-asserted in the recent article, that in linguistics a behaviouristic approach is mandatory (p. 165). Even Max Müller much earlier (probably being influenced by his study of Indian linguistics) said: '. . . there is no such thing as intellect, understanding, mind and reason, but... all these are only different aspects of language' (1887, p. x, cf. p. 89).

Bhartṛhari was primarily a grammarian of the Pāṇinian school (and probably he was also a poet). But he was at the same time responsible for a fundamental re-appraisal of what we may call today philosophy of language. His major work is called *Of Sentences and Words*—a book that consists of three different volumes and the present extant version has about 2000 verses. (Some verses ascribed to him in later literature are not found in the present extant version.) I-tsing, the Chinese traveller, with his usual exaggeration, records that this book consisted of 3,700 verses. Bhartṛhari developed a theory of speech or language which was unique and it evoked strong criticisms from all quarters, the Naiyāyikas, the Buddhists, the Jainas and the Mīmāṃsakas. But still he exerted a strong influence on almost all later philosophers, if only indirectly. A very brief outline of Bhartṛhari's theory of language would be our first step. It is a very complex theory. For Bhartṛhari, language is also an activity—a type of activity in human beings. It is in fact an activity which all sentient beings engage in. The Sanskrit term for this activity is *śabdanā.* It is 'languaging'. In Bhartṛhari's metaphor, it is the very 'vibration' of our thought, our conscious life. He tells us that it plays an all-important role in our cultural life. It is the very basis of distinction between the sentient and the insentient. All thinking, in fact all awareness, is in his words 'intertwined' with 'languaging'. Language is not always sonorous, or the essence of language does not consist in its sonorousness. But at the same time it is not to be confused or conflated with other means of communication, gestures, etc. For Bhartṛhari writes elaborately about insonorous speech or the speech-seed which constitutes the essence of language. The idea may not also be as commonplace or 'the dialogue of the self with itself' (derived from the Platonic phrase) or the 'silent speech' of the early Behaviourists. For Bhartṛhari, it refers to a deeper fact.

Basic to Bhartṛhari's doctrine is a distinction which he calls the *sphoṭa-nāda* distinction in language. Earlier grammarians in India tried to capture this distinction in various ways, which Bhartṛhari refers to and criticizes. But perhaps, he got it right, or at least the later grammarians thought that he did. In connection with language, the 'expressive word', as opposed to noises made by beating drums, etc., one has to distinguish, he tells us, between two aspects: (1) the aspect which causes manifestation, makes the implicit power or disposition explicit, the utterance of a sentence and (2) the aspect which being then actualized communicates or conveys meaning to the hearer. Language, in this view, is a dispositional property of humans. In any linguistic community it is shared property. The 'expressive word' which is primarily for Bhartṛhari the sentence, is made explicit through a stretch of sounds uttered by the speaker and it is only this stretch of sounds that is received by the hearer, and the hearer understands the sentence. This stretch of sounds produced by the vocal organ corresponds to the former aspect, *nāda*, that makes the dispositional property explicit. It is like the striking of a match that produces fire, fire-potential being present there already though implicitly. The temporal and instantly destroyed sound-utterances have sequences and multiplicity and the hearer receives them in their multiplicity and sequentiality. But if the hearer has not grasped the unity and the sequenceless whole we call a sentence, he has not grasped the *linguistic* unit, the sound aspect above, which is called *sphoṭa*. We may say, in other words, that until this happens, linguistic communication has not taken place. To avoid constant reference to Sanskrit terms as well as the attendant metaphysical baggage, we may use 'linguistic unit' to refer to the latter (*sphoṭa*) and 'sound-stretch' to refer to the former. These two are, however, not separable, though distinguishable. We cannot separate vibration from the vibrating entity.

According to Bhartṛhari, the linguistic process goes through three stages. To make these stages clear, he uses the analogy of the painter. When a painter paints a picture he, (1) observes the different parts of the figure or the objects separately and individually, (2) he has a vision of the whole picture as he wants to paint it, and (3) he actually paints it part by part. The hearer perceives the whole linguistic unit only by perceiving its differentiated parts, phonemes or sound-stretch. But he perceives the whole nevertheless, as the speaker wants him to. The speaker on the other hand has no choice but to deliver sounds in sequences much as the painter has no choice but to paint the figure part by part.

In the background of such a theory we must understand Bhartṛhari's theory of meaning. The received doctrine which may be ascribed to Bhartṛhari's opponents, the Naiyāyikas, is that there is a dualism of the linguistic unit or the language and what it signifies or conveys, the so-called meanings. These meanings may be just external objects or facts, if we hold strictly to the reference theory of meanings, or thoughts or some mentalistic entities. There is a general consensus among common people to separate meanings from the meaning-bearer, the language, the message from the medium of the message. Language is often uncritically thought to be a vehicle of thought or meaning. From this flows also the pervasive idea that in a multi-lingual world, the same thought is or can be conveyed by different expressions which are distinguishable parts of different languages. The duality of word and meaning that is foisted upon us has generated the platitude that the *pure* meaning is what remains constant between different translations just as change is supposed to keep the value of the money intact. Viewed from Bhartṛhari's theory of meaning, this is a platitude that we should do well to give up. For Bhartṛhari the duality of language, of a linguistic unit and its meaning, is more a fiction than reality. It is a convenient fiction, a useful ploy, and in many ways, it seems to be indispensable. It is deployed to facilitate our understanding and explanation of the psychology of language learning, and in the order of explanation of the mechanism of language it has apparently a necessary part. If this aspect of Bhartṛhari's theory has any purchase then it requires us to give up the search for any independent, language-transcendent meanings as the translational constants, as the invariant part in variable languages, and yet the same view allows that there could be a situation which would create a meaning-myth to be correlated with different sentences of different languages such that the said sentences would be deemed as intelligibly equivalent. Since linguistic expressions are not viewed on this theory as conveyor-belts for thoughts or meanings, there cannot be any absolute transposition of virgin thoughts or virgin meanings from one language to another. Each meaning is already part and parcel of its so-called 'verbal' cloak. They are inseparable. To unclothe meaning is to destroy it. This may have the consequence that translation is always indeterminable, not based upon the notion of the so-called sameness of meaning, but an alternative device to bring about or evoke approximately the same total effect as intended by the original.

Translation is an activity about which philosophers, social anthropologists and historians of ideas can hardly afford to be indifferent. Some translational activity in a deeper sense is part of the accepted style of philosophizing. To put it blandly, 'translation' in a non-trivial sense is involved even when a philosopher tries, with whatever motivation, to *read* the writings of another philosopher, ancient or modern. The same materials can have different *readings*, and thereby inevitably different *meanings*, different interpretations. The rather platitudinous air of this very statement can be dispelled. If we take Bhartṛhari's view seriously, we need not, in fact should not, take 'meanings' or 'interpretations' too literally and assume them to be separate from the texts or sentences, nor should we presume there to be an essential difference between 'readings' and 'meanings'. Each *reading* is a creative formulation, and hence each translation based upon such a reading is a creative transformation. In fact, for Bhartṛhari there cannot be any real transference of the pure or virgin meaning of the text into another. The rather widespread idea that the meanings can stand in isolated glory apart from the text itself is a wrong idea as far as Bhartṛhari is concerned. Hence the 'transfer' of thought or meaning from one garb to another seems to be an impossibility in this theory.

All these observations are about translations in general, they do not concern particularly the notion of *radical* translation. Quine's indeterminacy thesis is, however, spun around a thought experiment of 'radical translation' where our linguists construct their manual of translation by using publicly observable situations as the only guidelines—manuals to translate from the ordinarily inaccessible native language to, say, English. Radical translation is a fact, though according to Quine, 'a near miracle' (1987, p. 4). But empirical constraints on the limits of possible data for preparing the (radical) translational manual almost force us, Quine claims, to accept the indeterminacy. After initial success (beginner's luck?), the preponderance of extravagant guess work at advanced stages, as well as of freedom of conjecture, would make it possible for different radical translators, working independently, to prepare two or more *good* manuals—good because they fit all check-points of verbal behaviour-and yet each manual might prescribe some translations that the other would reject. This thought experiment was supposed to be a critique of the traditional 'introspection' semantics, not of translation activity as such, nor of general semantics either.

Quine in his new essay has also underlined how the thesis of the indeterminacy of translation differs from the thesis of the underdetermination of science. Being a realist, Quine holds that even if natural science is assumed to be underdetermined by all possible observation, there is a fact of the matter, but this may not be uniquely revealed to us by all the possible empirical evidence that we can gather. In the case of radical translation, there is simply no such fact of the matter that will resolve the alleged indeterminacy, for the native's verbal behaviour has no bearing upon the disagreement between translators.

But let us grant the possibility that Quine envisions in his thought experiment. Why should we find this puzzling? We have seen that even in Bhartṛhari's way of looking at language and meaning, the traditional concept of a 'virgin' meaning, the meaning that is language transcendent, has to be given up. Besides, there is the commonly felt attitude towards translatability. If we insist upon a very strict concept of translatability, no *proper* translation between any two *natural* languages is possible. I emphasize both 'proper' and 'natural'. The notion of 'radical translation' has been developed as a technical concept within the context of the said thought experiment. The thought experiment regards, unduly I believe, the native language as a closed system, a completed totality where the growing process has been frozen for ever. But a natural language is like a living organism. It grows and modifies itself. If we arrest its growth and then ask whether we can prepare translation manuals in such a closed language, then of course it may be possible that two incompatible translations of the same sentence will be offered by alternative manuals, and we would be at a loss to decide either way on the basis of the native's behaviour. This follows from the way the thought experiment has been devised. But no natural language is a closed or frozen system in the way it has been conceived here. Even radical translation is made possible (Quine calls it 'a near miracle') indeed just because of this natural feature of any natural language—its tendency to 'grow' and change and modify itself. But then, one may argue that this is not quite the kind of radical translation that is envisioned here. In any case, Quine's thesis must be distinguished from the rather commonly accepted point (by some modern

European philosophers) that in the strictest sense, there is no proper translation between any two languages. The same view would allow that in a less strict sense translations are not only possible but also actual. It is claimed that every language can say anything which is said in any other, but in *its own way*. This 'way' alone is what is untranslatable (cf. Mohanty, 1989, p. 333). However, from the point of view of Bhartṛhari's doctrine of *sphoṭa*, even this is not acceptable. For according to him, the so-called 'way' is not easily separable from what is said, in fact it is a mistake to think they are separable at all in practice. Hence untranslatability would be implied by the essential properties of any natural language, if we strictly adhered to a version of the *sphoṭa* doctrine.

How exactly would Bhartṛhari have viewed the matter of so-called 'radical translation'? It may be understood as follows. Each translator presumably would have his own *sphoṭa* roused by the native's utterance which he believes to be 'matching' the *sphoṭa* of the native. Since this 'matching' can never be total (for it is only an identification based upon misperception aroused by recognition of similarity) the *sphoṭa* and hence the articulated sound-stretch (speech = *nāda*) of two translators could be and would be different from each other. Roughly speaking, the original *sphoṭa* (of the native) may provoke two different *sphoṭas* in two different translators and hence the sentence that makes these *sphoṭas* explicit (i.e. manifests them) may be different. A *sphoṭa* is not the meaning of the sentence. It is the sentence itself at an implicit level of language. How is this 'implicitness' to be understood? An explanation of 'levels' or 'aspects' of language, according to Bhartṛhari is in order here, to which I now wish to turn.

The uttered sound-stretch is only the last stage (of development of) the language, which is needed for the purpose of communication between people. Initially language resides in humans as speech potentials (*śabda-bīja*) in their inner speech faculty. It is there in its 'inarticulate' stage where the *nāda* 'sound stretch' lies undifferentiated from *sphoṭa* 'the linguistic unit' (a sentence). It is like the yolk of the pea-hen's egg where a full-grown and many-coloured peacock lies implicit and undifferentiated. This is called the *paśyantī* stage, a purely non-verbal stage of language. The sentence and what it is supposed to communicate (*artha*) are indistinguishable at this stage. Before full articulation, there is also an 'intermediate' (*madhyama*) stage, which is roughly comparable with our modern notion of an episodic but *unexpressed* verbal thought—thought that is totally verbal in the sense that if any one conceives it he would have a thought with exactly the same verbal content. It is still a private thought but the nearest thing to a public utterance (sentence). On this theory, there is no non-verbal thought and even a part of thought cannot be non-verbal. Therefore at this stage, if we take 'thought' to be the 'meaning' or *artha* or what the sentence purportedly communicates, we have to say that language in this stage (level) anchors thought and thought anchors language. To use Bhartṛhari's own imagery, thought is what 'vibrates' through language and language is what 'illuminates' thought. They would still be inseparable, though distinguishable. At the next the audible utterance completes the process of separation (only temporarily) of the 'medium' and the 'message', of the *nāda* and the *sphoṭa*, of the sentence and its so-called meaning. But this bifurcation is only a temporary though necessary one, for otherwise communication through language would have been impossible. The separation soon vanishes, because it is followed by a false identification by the hearer, a superimposition of the hearer's *sphoṭa* upon the *nāda* that he receives from the speaker. In other words, the hearer's *sphoṭa* is 'aroused' by the *nāda* he hears and he superimposes his *sphoṭa* upon (i.e. identifies it with) what he hears. This necessarily false identification does not matter in the context, for it is only instrumental to successful communication. A communication is deemed successful as long as the behavioural responses are all right. According to this view, one way to account for the widespread *false* belief in the duality of language and meaning is to see that people naturally take the most obvious, *nāda* aspect to be the language and hence require a separate meaning to be connected with it and conveyed by it. But this, Bhartṛhari asserts, is an illusion. How is our ordinary translational activity to be explained in this theory? I believe Bhartṛhari will say that the *sphoṭa* of the original speaker 'overlaps' the *sphoṭa* of the translator and hence he translates (in a less restricted sense). The indeterminacy of translation obtains because the respect in which the *sphoṭa* of one translator 'overlaps' with the original *sphoṭa* may not be the same as that in which that *sphoṭa* of another translator 'overlaps'.

The *sphoṭa* view of language need not be conflated with the well-known modern view of linguistic competence championed by N. Chomsky. Despite striking similarities, the *sphoṭa* is not akin to Chomsky's view about the contribution of innate ideas to language-acquisition. This notion of linguistic competence is the ideal speaker-hearer's knowledge of his language (the natural knowledge shared by the speech-community), which in an idealized situation (distractions, memory-limitations, errors, etc. being ruled out) would be reflected directly in the speech-performance, and a generative grammar purports to be a description of this intrinsic competence. This competence has to do more with the scale of grammaticalness as well as 'deep structures' or the logical forms of the language. Bhartṛhari's *sphoṭa* theory had a different purpose to serve; it was to get away from the prevalent idea, namely the relational view of meaning, which states the linguistic expression and their so-called meanings are connected conventionally by the time-honoured linguistic customs of the speech-community. The older grammarians and the Mīmāṃsakas held the view that the relationship between the word and its meaning is eternally fixed or 'natural' and uncreated (by any convention). Bhartṛhari reinterpreted this doctrine in terms of his *sphoṭa* theory, according to which the meaning-bearer and the meaning are related by a 'causal' relation. This 'causal' relation is interpreted as a 'transformation' of a former stage into a latter stage, the so-called 'cause' being non-different from the 'effect'. Thus the meaning and the 'meaning-bearer' are related by identity, being the two sides of the same coin.

I believe that in the case of natural languages where each grows mutually influencing each other in a situation of confrontation or contact, 'radical translation' in the preferred sense (as Quine's thought experiment) can seldom take place. Proper and adequate translation between natural languages has been made possible in spite of the lingering indeterminacy, provided we do not take translatability to be an *ideal* (like the perfectly smooth surface) that is never meant to work out. Translation, understanding and communication are all of a piece and are made possible by a commonly shared world, as well as by the creative power of each 'living' natural language. That is why the so-called 'radical translation' is not a miracle. The lingering indeterminacy is explained by Quine as being due to the lack of such mysterious entities as 'separate' meanings by which we could have once and for all decided in favour of one translation over another. In Bhartṛhari's view, the lingering indeterminacy is due to the nature of the 'overlap' that I have alluded to earlier. Let the *sphoṭas* of the two translators and the original speaker be S_1, S_2 and S_3. S_1 and S_2 may be utterly distinct, but their distinctness is mediated by S_3 with which both 'overlap'. The position occupied by the two translation manuals generating different translations in Quine's description may correspond indirectly to S_1 and S_2 when they do not 'overlap' at all but both 'overlap' S_3.

Notes and References

Bhartṛhari, *Vākyapadīya*, edited by K.V. Abhyankar and V.P. Limaye, Poona, 1965.

Chomsky, N., *Syntactic Structures*, The Hague: Mouton, 1957.

Mohanty, J.N., 'Phenomenological Rationality and the Overcoming of Relativism', in M. Krausz (ed.), *Relativism: Interpretation and Confrontation*, Notre Dame: University of Notre Dame Press, 1989, pp. 326–38.

Müller, Max, *The Science of Thought*, Longmans: London, 1887.

Quine, W.V.O., *Word and Object*, Cambridge: MIT Press, 1960.

———, 'Indeterminacy of Translation Again', *Journal of Philosophy*, vol. 84, no. 1, 1987, pp. 5–10.

22

Some Reflections on Sanskrit Semantics

Sanskrit grammar can be seen as basically a derivational system where correct forms of words are derived from a set of primitive word-bases and affixes (inflections). My attempt here is to introduce before non-Sanskritist linguists some fundamental ideas according to which the elements of a Sanskrit sentence can be analysed, and broadly categorized. It is well known that grammarians are concerned (and in this respect the Pāṇinīyas were no exception) with the *grammatical* correctness of an utterance or a sentence. The rules of grammar are therefore supposed to generate tentatively the correct forms—forms that people generally use or may use, and thereby reject such forms as may be recognized by any competent user of the language as ungrammatical or incorrect. What is grammatical or grammatically correct and what is not, are not however very easily definable. We generally depend upon the intuitive grasp of the competent language-user and the rules of grammar are tentatively attempts to articulate this 'intuition'. 'The competent speaker' is however an abstraction like 'the average man' and hence the so-called 'intuition' is not the private property of any individual. It is the commonly accepted and tacitly recognized understanding of the relevant linguistic community.

The rules of grammar are, however, empirically formulated. One has to look at usage under varying conditions and variable immediate environments in order to discover a pattern and then check again and again how far the pattern remains unmodified and when modification can be predictably recognized. This is the starting point for formulating a grammatical rule, but for actual formulations we need the aid of a number of already available concepts more generally known as grammatical categories. In all this the grammarian is concerned with the idea of telling us which grammatical category or type can be combined with which other type or types to generate a grammatically acceptable form. But he is not obliged to tell us whether all such possible combinations are used or could be used or are bound to be used by the competent speaker at some time or other. This is so presumably because the so-called grammatical types or concepts are more general and in a fundamental sense more abstract than the concepts that we deal with in our ordinary thought or language. Hence a rule of grammar may give a number of possible combinations, most of which we might have to reject when we look at the actual usage where people are trying to convey some thoughts to others or to represent reality. A competent speaker is therefore capable of not only recognizing what is grammatically permissible and what is, let us say, 'factually' possible but also of clearly distinguishing between them. For the latter he depends upon his acquired knowledge of the world and extrapolates whatever is allowable from such knowledge. (We have said only 'his acquired knowledge', but it has to be extended to include also, let us say, his *a priori* knowledge. But more on this later.)

Now let me illustrate what we have said in general terms so far. Suppose we have two very fundamental categories of grammar, noun and verb. And some rule (very primitive) of a primitive grammar requires that such verb be combined with a noun (to be called its agent). This means that any verb can be combined with any noun and such a combination will be grammatically correct, i.e., acceptable by a competent speaker as grammatically correct. But he will reject a great many of such combinations as unacceptable for his knowledge of this world would, if nothing else, *resist* all such possible combinations. For example, take the verb 'drinks'. It can be combined with such nouns as 'a man', 'John' and 'a boy' or 'a girl' but not with 'a table', 'honesty' or 'water'. If however the grammar is rich enough to sub-categorize the noun as 'inanimate' and 'animate' and so on then we would have a way to rule that 'drinks' can be attached to a special class of nouns, and therefore 'Honesty drinks' would be ungrammatical. But since primitive grammar is very primitive and poor we have to say that the combination 'Honesty drinks' or 'The table drinks' are not permitted (though correct according to the primitive grammar) because from our knowledge of the world (not knowledge of the primitive grammar) we cannot derive how what is *meant* by 'drinks' can be combined with what is meant by 'honesty' or 'the table'. It may be said that a verb is grammatically EXPECTED to be combined with a noun as its agent, but the object *denoted* by such noun must also COMPETENT for the action denoted the verb concerned.

Let me now illustrate from Sanskrit. Suppose again the primitive grammar has two categories: noun and verb. Further suppose that the verb can be combined with a noun in the instrumental case-ending (to be called 'instrument'). Take for example the verb 'wets'. We can grammatically combine it with such instrumental cases as 'with fire', 'with honesty'. But certainly our knowledge of the world would reject such combinations as *incompatible*. For one can only wet with water or some other liquid, but not with fire or with honesty. A verb with a noun in the instrumental ending may be grammatically EXPECTED, but some combinations would obviously be INCOMPATIBLE for the components denoted by the two words, (noun and verb) would be incapable of being connected in this way.

Sanskrit philosophers, specially the Nyāya philosophers, have tried to formulate two theoretical terms, *ākāṃkṣā* (expectancy) and *yogyatā* (compatibility) in order to underline the distinction that we have been talking about—the so-called distinction between grammatical matters and what we may call semantic matters. Obviously the competent speaker would recognize immediately when the combination of words would fulfil the grammaticality condition, and thereby the grammatical EXPECTANCY will be satisfied. But he would still claim that such combinations as 'wets with fire' are INCOMPETENT to convey any thought or meaning.

Now the grammarians will say that whether certain grammatically faultless combinations can, i.e., are *competent* to, convey any thought or meaning or not, it is not their business to formulate such rules, for that is semantics, and grammar is usually not connected with such matters. This contention is by and large timely and well taken. But a nagging doubt persists because it is to a large extent the grammarians' business to see that only such combinations are generated as would help to convey a thought. For otherwise grammar would be useless. The grammarians do want to generate such combinations as would form a larger class and only some members of this class would be such that they would pass the COMPATIBILITY test and convey some thought or other. This class cannot include combinations which would not have even the remotest possibility of conveying a thought or meaning. This point is borne out by the fact that in any actual grammar we introduce more and more categories and subcategories and formulate much more detailed rules of combination, and a minimal consideration for meaning as well as for how the matter stands in the actual world cannot be left out when we allow such sub-categorization and rules of combination. We have already seen this in the primitive grammar. If nouns can be sub-divided into concrete and abstract, then concrete into inanimate and animate (and then the latter with and without a mouth), we can rule that 'drinks' can be happily combined with such a noun which is animate (having a mouth). Similarly if a class of nouns can be grouped somewhere along the line as liquid then we can use any member of this group in the instrumental case to combine it with the verb 'wet'. But obviously this would be going too far. For ordinary rules of grammar never go this far but stop somewhere along the way by giving us only some broader categories and choices among a very wide range of combination. A vast number of combinations would be possible by such rules and the rejection of 'unusable' combinations would be left to the speaker or user. This will make grammatical rules at least manageable and teachable.

In what has been said above, I have willingly ignored other aspects of an ordinary grammar, specially phonology, morpho-phonemic rules etc. For my purpose is different. The attempt has been here to focus upon the combination of words or word-elements that are allowed in grammar and to see how we can set apart within this rather larger set, those which are though allowable in grammar, but nevertheless not usable or never used by the speakers for they baffle the purpose of the speech to convey a thought or a meaning. It seems that if there are any fundamental laws of thought, such as that of non-contradiction and excluded middle, then our thinking must obey them. Hence combinations that are blatantly against such laws could be rejected outright as unacceptable. In fact, contradictions of this kind, which we sometimes call logical contradictions are far more easily detectable, as long as we can simply locate a negative particle or negative expressions being combined with an item while the same item is used to be syntactically connected with it, e.g. 'a non-fiery thing having fire' (*nirvahniḥ vahnimān*). Besides these obvious ones, there are many other grammatically permissible combinations which cannot be entertained even in our thoughts. We cannot think of, for example, wetting something with fire or drinking bananas or making honesty rectangular unless we indulge in some questionable metaphors. We cannot have such thoughts because of the way the world is and also because of our thoughts being broadly conditioned by the way the world is. Besides the above two kinds, there is another kind of combination where only a milder form of opposition in thought is experienced. Some philosophers therefore claim that such combinations are 'possible' though non-actual as far as our knowledge of the world goes. Possibility in this case will also imply thinkability. We can think of rabbits having horns, and horses having wings to fly, although no such creatures have ever existed. This thinkability of course implies that we can still call a winged horse a horse and a horned rabbit a rabbit. Indian philosophers however would like to call even these combinations, 'the rabbit's horn' and 'the winged horse', *ayogya* 'incompatible' and treat them in the same way as the previous two kinds of combinations.

We may now ask: if we proceed along this line would we have anything, any combination, that would be only possible but non-actual? The answer would be this: we have to resort probably to missed chances and future contingencies to take care of our intuitive notion of possibility. Mitra is pregnant. She may have a boy or a girl. If she has a boy, she now missed the chance of having a baby-girl. In a possible world, Mitra has a baby-girl. Therefore we say 'Mitra could have a baby-girl'. So here the combination 'Mitra's girl' is not *ayogya* or incompatible, but only false because non-actual.

Let us note that those philosophers in West who think that 'the horned rabbit' or 'the winged horse' are unactualized possibles would have to say that the meaning of such words, 'horse' or 'rabbit' do not change even if such unusual but presumably non-essential features are added. In other words, a horned rabbit is also a rabbit and a winged horse is also a horse provided the former resembles the latter in all other respects, just as a lame or handicapped man is also a man, if a man had by chance a third eye on the forehead, we would still call him a man! But those Indian philosophers who would say that there are some incompatibilities (*ayogyatā*), however mild, in such combinations would probably claim that such extension of meaning, i.e., that of 'horse' to include winged horses, is not to be allowed, for lack of wings is not an inessential or unimportant feature of what it is to be a horse. We could invent another term if we happen to see such a creature. But this attitude would be rather too strict and rigid, for we do allow metaphorical extension of meaning when we call a man 'a tiger' provided he has tiger-like qualities. Of course, in calling a winged horse a horse we need a different kind of extension of meaning. In any case, if we want to say that 'the rabbit's horn' is an incompatible combination, here by 'compatibility' we mean more the actuality or truth of a combination rather than its possibility. Hence the concern is with the truth and falsity of an expression rather than with its possibility or impossibility.

PART V

Philosophy in India: Perceptions and Problems

23

Indian Philosophy: Is There a Problem Today?

I have found the expression 'Indian philosophy' puzzling more often than not. For one who has spent most of his life writing books and papers and editing journals on Indian philosophy, this is an odd admission. But one brief look at the titles of the papers presented in the subject, will vindicate the fact that the expression 'Indian philosophy' is utterly ambiguous and genuine doubt is entertained by many as to its exact significance. If we contrast 'Indian philosophy' with 'Greek philosophy' or 'Chinese philosophy' then we tend to have a particular understanding of the phrase. We may understand it in such a context as the philosophical thought of classical or medieval India, or the philosophical schools or systems called *darśanas*. But the study of Indian philosophy in this sense will be looked upon more as a mere philological exercise than a philosophical discipline. At best one can say that this belongs to the discipline of the history of philosophy, or perhaps more correctly to the history of ideas rather than to philosophy proper. I do not think this argument to be always valid.

The classical texts of Indian philosophy can be studied in a way that may fall under the discipline of the history of ideas. But often history of ideas is primarily *history*, and hence such a study will involve essentially a historical enquiry. But the history of philosophy is, as one modern philosopher has put it,[1] philosophy before it is history. Therefore, if the study of the classical Indian philosophy, or as the moderners call it, 'traditional Indian philosophy', is regarded as falling within the discipline of the history of philosophy, as opposed to the history of ideas, then it can hardly be separated from the general study of philosophy. I shall come back to this point later.

Sometimes, 'Indian philosophy' is contrasted with 'Western philosophy', and immediately the phrase takes on a new shade of meaning. This meaning is, however, by no means clear; it has, I venture to add, an amorphous nature. For some people, Indian philosophy has a distinct character, namely, it is overwhelmingly spiritual (and some critics say 'euphoric'), and, therefore, is in sharp contrast with the materialism of the West. Some say that it is other-worldly while the Western philosophy is this-worldly and hence scientific. The attitude toward this other-worldliness or the *mokṣa*-orientedness of Indian philosophy may vary from being one of over-enthusiasm to that of utter disapproval and condemnation. Over-enthusiasm for this other-worldliness need not detain us long. For this is generally found in un-informed dreamers who generally believe that Oriental mysticism is the answer to all the ills of modern Western civilization. In almost the same way, we may dismiss the other extreme view about Indian philosophy. For those who condemn Indian philosophy as not being philosophy at all but a bundle of dogmas and mystifying and unproductive statements about man and the world, are equally un-informed about the wealth of genuinely philosophical material contained in the classical texts of India.[2]

There are, however, some serious formulations of the above views about Indian philosophy, which cannot be easily dispensed with. For it is undeniable that the classical systems of Indian *darśanas* are *mokṣa*-oriented whereas the concept of philosophy has a different origin in the West. Philosophy, as the etymology of the word indicates, was connected with 'the love of knowledge' or 'the love of wisdom'. But a little investigation shows that each *darśana* holds that the so-called *mokṣa* or the ultimate freedom of man is achieved, directly or indirectly, on the basis of our knowledge of the reality (*tattvajñāna*). In other words, each *darśana* was engaged in constructing a metaphysical system and adhered to the belief that our knowledge of the reality (as captured in its metaphysics) leads to the ultimate freedom of man. Thus, the *darśanas* of India were not very strikingly different from the old-fashioned philosophies of the West.

Besides, from AD 400 onwards, Indian philosophers showed genuine interest in the analysis of knowledge and argument, in the criteria of knowledge that reveals reality, in the theories of logic and dialectics, in the search for a sound philosophical argument, and so on. The literature on these issues is very rich and varied. But unfortunately, most of this material lies buried under the treasure-chest of Sanskrit. This also proves that sound philological research is very useful even for genuine philosophical purposes. In my own view, to be sure, for research in traditional Indian philosophy, philological competence is almost indispensable. In any case, one thing is clear. The material that deals with the above issues cannot be but philosophical even in the modern sense of the term. Therefore, concern for *mokṣa* was not in any way detrimental to their philosophic interest. And some even argue that this concern actually adds to their special charm.

It may be argued that since the goal of *darśanas* was *mokṣa* or *nirvāṇa*, they were primarily therapeutics of *mokṣa*, and the philosophical, epistemological or logical issues discussed therein were only incidental. In other words, one may say, repeating an old argument, that the *darśanas* were 'therapeutics' first before they were philosophies, just as the history of ideas is history before it is philosophy. If this is conceded then, the argument continues, to the extent our concern for *mokṣa* diminishes or wanes in modern human societies, these therapeutics lose their value or usefulness, and, consequently, the philosophic discussions that sustained such therapeutics become myths or museum-pieces. It will not do to point out, as against this position, that much of medieval Western philosophy was inextricably mixed with theology, soteriology and religious beliefs, for that point is already conceded. The balance is said to tilt in favour of Western philosophy partly because of the 'resilience' of the philosophic issues discussed by the medievals and partly because of the rational reconstructions of the ancient and medieval doctrines that modern study of them demands and delivers.

I will cite two arguments to refute the above position. First, it is not true to say that *darśanas* where primarily *mokṣa-śāstras*, and hence philosophy was only incidental to them. For the ancient and medieval writers on *darśanas* were consciously and deliberately participating in philosophical discussions and using what may be called philosophical methodology. What Vātsyāyana says of *Nyāya-darśana* holds generally true of other *darśanas* as well. Referring to the four-fold classification of disciplines which form the subject matter of study, the Vedic scriptures (*trayī*), agriculture and commerce (*vārttā*), politics and law (*daṇḍaniti*), and philosophy (*ānvīkṣikī*), Vātsyāyana comments that each discipline has its own distinct *prasthāna* or method (Vācaspati glosses '*prasthāna*' as '*upāya*'), and this distinct method of the fourth one, *ānvīkṣikī*, or philosophy, is illustrated by its special examination of the sixteen categories which include means of knowledge, objects of knowledge, validity or invalidity of arguments, determination of truth and so on.[3] It may be said that I have taken here an unwarranted liberty in translating '*ānvīkṣikī*' as 'philosophy'. But this is not true. For Kauṭilya, who first talked about the four-fold classification of disciplines and from whom Vātsyāyana quoted, clearly used the term in the general sense of philosophy. For example, he cited three schools as examples of *ānvīkṣikī*; the metaphysical school of the Sāṁkhya, the twin school of Nyāya-Vaiśeṣika and the materialism of the Cārvākas.[4]

Vātsyāyana, in fact, argued that it is this distinct 'method' (*prasthāna*) that is essential to *ānvīkṣikī* (= philosophy), for otherwise this discipline would be indistinguishable from *adhyātma-vidyā* or *mokṣa-śāstra*.[5] I argue that this is true of the classical *darśanas* in general, not simply of Nyāya. The Vedic scriptures along with the Upaniṣads, undoubtedly, constitute the *mokṣa-śāstra*. But the *darśanas* followed a distinct methodology, and formed an entirely separate discipline. Thus, my point is that the classical texts of *darśanas* were not therapeutics for *nirvāṇa* but dealt with philosophy properly and in all seriousness that their time, society and environment allowed.

Second, it must be pointed out that, even if our concern for *nirvāṇa* wanes and consequently the therapeutics for such *nirvāṇa* lose significance, it does not necessarily follow that the philosophical bases of such therapeutics undergo total collapse or become automatically museum-pieces. In fact even a brief perusal of the contents of such texts as Dharmakīrti's *Pramāṇa-vārttika*, Jayanta's *Nyāyamañjari*, or Śrīharṣa's *Khaṇḍana-Khaṇḍakhādya*, shows clearly that the philosophic issues discussed by these classical thinkers are not altogether dead horses today. The concern of these classical Indian thinkers was genuinely philosophical even in its present-day sense, and their additional concern for *mokṣa* was hardly able to overshadow their genuine philosophical interest. Thus there is hardly any real reason, except, perhaps a parochial one, to argue in favour of the 'resilience' of the philosophical issues discussed by the medievals in the Western tradition, and the lack of such resilience in the case of the philosophic problems pondered over by the classic Indian thinkers. To put the matter strongly, if the study of Plato, Aristotle, Descartes, Hume and Kant, is useful for a modern student of philosophy, the study of Uddyotakara, Kumārila and Udayana is also relevant for him in the same way, provided of course, he can overcome 'the language barrier' that stands in the way. If a rational reconstruction of Descartes or writing a modern commentary on Aristotle's *Metaphysics*, is considered as part of creative philosophic activity today, I do not see why such a rational reconstruction of Diṅnāga or a modern commentary on Gaṅgeśa cannot be regarded as falling within the discipline of philosophy.

It must be noted that I have used the word 'philosophy' so far in a particular sense. This is the sense that is usually attached to 'philosophy' by the modern academic philosophers, specially by those who consider themselves as belonging to the modern analytic tradition in the West. But philosophy, it may be argued, is not just analyses and logic, epistemology and theory of meaning. It is also rational speculation and metaphysics, existentialism and phenomenology. It is arguable, however, that the study of certain classical Indian systems such as Advaita Vedānta or Mahāyāna Buddhism provides useful insights even when 'philosophy' is understood in this sense. But one does not need to labour this point any further.

This brings us to yet another sense that may be attached to the phrase 'Indian philosophy'. By this term we may be asked to record the recent philosophical activities in India. We may be required to consider what the Indian professional philosophers, academics, and thinkers today have been doing *vis-à-vis* their Western compatriots. What contributions, if any, have they made recently to the field of 'philosophy' by which one may understand simply Western philosophic tradition? The use of 'philosophy' in the exclusive sense of Western philosophy is quite widespread, and, therefore, such a question is quite reasonable for one to ask. Western philosophy, like Western education and Western science and technology, has after all, been studied by the Indian professionals for over a hundred years. In reply to the above question, one may point out that creative and critical writings by the Indian professionals on Western philosophy may be rare, but not altogether non-existent today. We have metaphysicians like Kalidas Bhattacharyya, phenomenologists like J.N. Mohanty (whose interest in Frege and Quine is also well-known), logicians like Sibajiban Bhattacharyya and P.K. Sen, Marxist-Socialists like S.N. Ganguly, and economist philosophers like A.K. Sen. One may understandably raise the question of the 'Indianness' of the writings of these philosophers. In reply we can say that at least some like Mohanty and Sibajiban have consciously indulged in creative-comparative thinking for they have sound grounding in the classical Indian systems. In the case of others one can probably talk about an unconscious influence of the Indian background of their authors, and such an influence is not always intractable.

Let me emphasize again that one does not need an apology for justifying the study of classical Indian philosophy today, nor does one need to puzzle about the 'Indianness' of any philosophic writings. As my own training and research have been in the field of classical Indian philosophy, I wish to comment briefly about the research method in this particular field. In an earlier writing[6] I had referred to two particular barriers for the modern student to the study of Indian philosophy: the language barrier and the prevailing misconception (not necessarily altogether Western) about what Indian philosophy is. I still believe firmly that sound philological scholarship is a highly desirable requirement. Besides this, it is necessary to have a good understanding of what counts as a philosophical problem discussed in the classical texts. Such an understanding should be supplemented by a reasonably thorough study of the relevant problems discussed in contemporary philosophical circles. Thus, a modern student of classical Indian philosophy need not fall between the two stools.

'Comparative philosophy' has acquired a bad reputation mainly because of the failures and lack of depth of the early comparativists. The early comparativists not only misunderstood the nature and the extent of the problem they were trying to grapple with but they also lacked insight and adequate preparation. But the task of explaining and translating classical Indian philosophical texts in a Western language by a modern scholar involves automatically a sort of comparison and contrast between the moderners and the ancients. I have called this method 'comparative philosophy in a minimal sense' in the absence of a better term. In fact, 'comparative philosophy' in this minimal sense, may be seen as falling within the discipline of the history of philosophy in the global sense. Since it has already been argued that the history of philosophy is philosophy primarily, the above task should also fall within the general discipline of philosophy.

The purpose of the Indian philosopher today, who chooses to work on the classical systems, is to interpret and thereby offer a medium where philosophers, using the word to mean those who pursue rationally arguable answers to meaningful questions, both Indian and Western, may converse. For such philosophical research I strongly recommend the above method, for I have taken time to convince myself that there does not exist a world of difference between a considerable portion of the problems discussed by the ancients and those discussed by the modern philosophers today.

Notes and References

1. Bernard Williams, *Descartes: The Project of Pure Enquiry*, London: Penguin, 1978, p.9.
2. Antony Flew. *An Introduction to Western Philosophy*, London: Thames & Hudson, 1971, p. 36.

3. Vātsyāyana on *Nyāyasūtra* 1.1.1.
4. Kautilya: *Arthaśāstra* (ed. R. Kangle), Bombay: Bombay University Press, 1960–65.
5. Vātsyāyana, op. cit.
6. B.K. Matilal, *Epistemology, Logic and Grammar in Indian Philosophical Analysis*, The Hague: Mouton, 1971, pp. 9–10.

24

On the Concept of Philosophy in India

One often faces, while talking about 'Indian philosophy', the following question:[1] 'Is there anything called 'philosophy' in India, specifically in the way the term is understood in modern West?' One common answer is to cite the Sanskrit term (*darśana*). However, I propose to answer it differently, for '*darśana*' in my view comes very close to the English word 'view', or maybe 'philosophical viewpoint'. I shall start with a counter question: 'Could we define 'philosophy' even in its modern Western sense, a definition that will be unanimously accepted by all philosophers in the West?'

The Greek etymological sense (*philein*, to love—*sophia*, wisdom) is usually referred to for a quick answer to the question: what is philosophy? And at a popular level, 'philosophy' still stands for private wisdom. At a technical level, however, the term is understood to mean the criticism and systematization of all knowledge (drawn from empirical science) as well as knowledge itself. Or, as a recent Western philosopher writes, it 'is characteristically argumentative and essentially directed towards the determination of what logical relations do and do not obtain' (A. Flew, *A Dictionary of Philosophy*, p. ix). This is not exactly 'love of wisdom', but not entirely unrelated to it.

Paradoxically, Sanskrit has a better term for 'philosophy' in the modern sense. I believe it is better to start with the term '*ānvīkṣikī*', a term used as early as Kauṭilya to refer to a discipline similar to what we call philosophy today. Kauṭilya, after enumerating the four main branches of learning, *vidyāsthāna* ('philosophy', religious education or Scriptures, trade-and-commerce, and the science of polity), defines '*ānvīkṣikī*' as follows (this view is repeated also in many places in the later literature such as Manu):[2]

Investigating, by means of reasoning what is good and what is evil in the context of scriptural/religious education, material gain and loss in the context of learning trade-and-commerce (*vārtā* = economics), what is good and what is not so as a policy in the context, of learning polity and public behaviour—philosophy (*ānvīkṣikī*) confers benefit upon people, keeps mind steady in prosperity and adversity and imparts proficiency in thought, speech and action.

The same term is explained by Vātsyāyana at *c*. AD 300 (repeated by Jayanta in *c*. AD 850 and others) as 'examination of what is obtained through perception (observation) and what is stated in the scriptures, by the *pramāṇas* (adequate evidence)'. In fact, it is the contention of Vātsyāyana that *ānvīkṣikī* is to be distinguished from other disciplines, specially from the 'spiritual' texts or the books of wisdom such as the Upaniṣads by virtue of its being characterized by a study of the *pramāṇas*, etc. For the Naiyāyikas, however, the term means the discipline that is called Nyāya-prasthāna. But if we are not parochial, like the Naiyāyikas, we can take it to mean any school of 'argumentative philosophy', as Kauṭilya did.

An incidental comment to guard against any misunderstanding here. The well-known German indologist, H. Jacobi[3] in 1911, interpreted the term *ānvīkṣikī* as philosophy and attempted to find in it a programme for an independent, theoretically-oriented 'science'. He was however severely criticized by P. Hacker,[4] in 1958, who argued that Jacobi in his conclusion was *wrongly* influenced by his own 'prejudice', i.e., his fascination for the Western emancipation of philosophy from theology. In other words, Jacobi, according to Hacker, wrongly superimposed a Western situation on ancient India. I do not wish to enter into the terminological dispute here, for I believe it to be a non-starter in this context. Nor am I searching for a Sanskrit term that would be exactly parallel to 'philosophy' in the West, for it is, by the very nature of the situation, bound to be an impossible task. In how many different ways has 'philosophy' been used in the West over a period of, say, a thousand years? Human beings decidedly are not so uniformly non-different from each other that we may expect to find an exact copy of one historical contingency of the Western tradition in another, in this case Indian, tradition. On the other hand, the point to be made is that reflective self-understanding and rational wisdom were present as much in the Occident as in classical India. And this gives us the rationale for talking meaningfully about 'philosophy' in classical India.

Two further observations in this connection would be in order. First, Hacker was wrong in his critique of the point (apparently made by Jacobi) that 'philosophy' (*ānvīkṣikī*) in India constituted an autonomous domain. For there was a stream of critical and reflective tradition in India, which might not admittedly have developed into a completely openended free enterprise of thought (as 'philosophy' in the West, particularly in the sense of the so-called Cartesian freedom from prejudice, is understood to have). However, even this idea of 'freedom from prejudice' in the Cartesian conception of 'philosophy' is a construction of the Western historiographers. This idea has recently been called into question. I believe the Indian thinkers beginning from the Buddha down to Raghunātha *perceived* themselves as 'free unprejudiced thinkers' as much as their Western counterparts, in the early, medieval and even modern periods, perceived (and still do consider) themselves to be such thinkers. Such self-perception, which is in part self-deception, is an indispensable ingredient of even a 'philosophical' mind. However, our task is not to delve into the psychology of philosophers, whether Western or Indian.

Second, it seems undeniable that there was a conscious and sustained effort on the part of a number of authors (whom we tend to call philosophers today) of ancient and classical India to re-define the scope of their *śāstras* 'treatises' and describe their method as rational, unbigotted and non-authoritarian. In some cases, there has been explicit denunciation of the religious rituals and the fruits they are supposed to bring about (see Īśvarakṛṣṇa, below). However, there were certain presuppositions, which we today in the later part of the twentieth century do, and those ancients and medievals did not, think as 'prejudices'. However, in our modesty, we may admit that although we, as moderners, are free from many 'prejudices' which the premoderners and traditional Oriental societies had unconsciously nurtured, we can hardly claim that we have no prejudice whatsoever. If modesty allows this much, then it would be too finicky to demand an exact word in ancient Sanskrit, whose meaning would totally coincide with whatever meaning we at this time in history, care to attach to the word 'philosophy'. What would be reasonable to enquire into and expect however is whether there was a tradition in India's intellectual history (of the classical period) which primarily concerned itself with rational inquiry and consciously wanted to avoid religious dogmas. This is what I will try to show.

In the opening lines of his celebrated *Nyāyabhāṣya*, Vātsyāyana Pakṣilasvāmin has remarked:[5]

Since there is success in activities based upon the knowledge of the object/goal (*artha*), the knowledge that is generated by *pramāṇas* (means or evidence for knowledge), (we can say that) the *pramāṇas* are connected (invariably) with the object/goal.

This rather important sentence has presented exegetical difficulties. There are five words in this sentence (in Sanskrit), of which two are compound words. There are about five terms which need explanatory notes because of their being slightly technical in nature. Of them, *pramāṇa* and *artha* are the two most difficult terms for the modern translators. In the above (translation), I have given the general sense of the sentence as far as practicable. It is a very condensed statement of an elaborate argument against the 'sceptics' (i.e. the Mādhyamikas). As I have argued elsewhere, the Mādhyamika fulfilled the role of the sceptics in the Indian tradition, although they were not sceptics themselves; they were Buddhists.[6]

Vātsyāyana gives the gist of his argument in a few sentences that follow, the opening sentence being a condensed version of it, almost 'aphoristic' (*sūtra*-like) in its nature:[7]

> There is no knowledge of the *artha* (object/goal) without a *pramāṇa*. (And) there is no success in activities without some knowledge of the *artha*. Having known the *artha* by *pramāṇas*, the subject (*jñātr* = knower) desires either to obtain or avoid that *artha*. The physical effort of that person (the subject) prompted (caused) by his desire to obtain 'success' of such activities means their connection with the results (fruits). Having desired either to obtain or to avoid, the subject makes 'physical' efforts and thereby either obtains or avoids the *artha*. The word '*artha*' means both happiness as well as its causal factors and unhappiness as well as its causal factors. The *arthas* of *pramāṇas* are in fact innumerable, the living creatures (to whom they belong) being also innumerable.

Saṃīhā has been translated as 'physical efforts', but the word itself is ambiguous and may in fact mean all *three* kinds of efforts noted by the Sanskrit philosophers, physical, mental and verbal (by speech).

Vātsyāyana, here, has himself explained the compound word 'success-in-activities' as well as the enigmatic '*artha*'. The concept of *artha* is based upon what we may call a tacit philosophical theory. The idea is that everything in this world, every object, every fact, can be the cause of the happiness or unhappiness of some creature or other in some way or other. Vātsyāyana also compares a *pramāṇa* with a lamp light (*dīpa*). Just as a lamp shows things are existent as well as establishes the non-existence of those that are not shown, similarly *pramāṇas* reveal those that are existent, and by implication establish the non-existence of those that have no *pramāṇa* or evidence.

Uddyotakara (*c.* AD 600), in the beginning of *Nyāyavārttika*, adds a few paragraphs where he deals with the question: what should a philosophical treatise concern itself with. In a clear and concise manner, he gives an outline of the nature of philosophy as a discipline, and shows admirably well how this theoretical discipline is connected with the practical life.

He argues that a theory of knowledge and evidence (*pramāṇa*) is an integral part of philosophy as a discipline and that such a theory is also connected with a theory of action. I quote these paragraphs in full:[8]

This 'treatise' (*śāstra*) speaks about what is good for human beings. The special purpose of a 'treatise' is to explain the true nature of such things (*artha*) as are *not* known through ordinary means of knowledge, such as perception and inference. And only such students are entitled to study this 'treatise' as are endowed with the intellectual capacity to comprehend the nature of things which they have not learnt through ordinary means of knowledge, such as perception and inference.

There are four kinds of people: those who have (fully) comprehended (the nature of things), those who have not comprehended at all, those who are in doubt, and those who have (completely) misunderstood. Among these four, one who has (fully) comprehended (i.e. one who *knows*) is in a position to teach; all the others have the need for knowledge, and hence are those who should be taught.

The latter group of people learn through perception when they depend upon sense-object contact; they learn through inference when they depend upon perception of evidence and remembrance (of the invariance relation). Finally with regard to matters (not amenable to perception and inference, e.g., the concept of the highest good), they require verbal testimony; this is supplied by the 'treatise' (*śāstra*).

In the above I have followed the text in Dr A. Thakur's edition. There is a variant preferred in two other editions, V.P. Dvivedin's as well as the Calcutta Metropolitan's, according to which the definition of 'a treatise' would be:

The special purpose of a treatise is to explain the true nature of such things as *are* (already) known through ordinary means of knowledge, such as perception and inference.

Thus this text drops the negative particle and the two editors of the Calcutta Metropolitan edition added a footnote showing preference for the variant without the negative particle in spite of the contrary evidence from a large number of manuscripts. Hence, apparently in their opinion, the *śāstra* or the treatise deals with matters that are already known (presumably to the teachers) through perception and inference. Since the students (the three latter groups of people) lack the required knowledge, the teachers teach them through *śāstra* what they (the teachers) already know.

However, let me continue with the remarks of Uddyotakara:

[What is good?] The good consists of both happiness and avoidance of evil. In fact there are two types of good: those that are perceived and those unperceived. The perceived good is pleasure or well-being. The avoidance of evil is unperceived. This avoidance again is of two kinds: the non-ultimate and the ultimate. The non-ultimate is accomplished through the removal of such temporary causes of evil (pain) as a thorn (or poison). The ultimate avoidance (of evil) is realised through the cessation of twenty-one perpetual sources of evil (unhappiness). They comprise: (1) the body, (2–7) six faculties of sensing and cognising, (8–13) six types of (the *given*, the sensibles and the thinkable), (14–19) six types of awareness (five kinds of perceptual awareness and the non-perceptual awareness), (20) happiness, and (21) unhappiness (evil).

Of these twenty-one varieties of evil, the body is regarded as evil because it is the abode of all unhappy experience; the faculties, the *given* objects and the awareness of them are so regarded because it is through their agency (or instrumentality) all unhappy experience (evil) arises. (Even) happiness is regarded as evil (a disvalue) because, it is invariably accompanied by some source of evil or other. And unhappiness is evil by its very nature. The cessation of all these is possible by the abandonment of their sources, viz., *dharma* and *a-dharma*. The future *dharma* and *a-dharma* (merit and demerit) can be abandoned by not engaging oneself in future (good and bad) action. The already acquired *dharma* and *a-dharma* can be 'abandoned' by exhausting them through the consequential experience of happiness and unhappiness.

Here it is interesting and at the same time important to note the thematization of the twenty-one items—all noted as *duḥkha*, the evil or the undesirable items which humans should try to avoid. Body etc. are instrumental for our mostly unhappy experience. Even the so-called happy experiences are invariably intermixed with unhappy ones. Hence 'philosophy' or 'treatise' is supposed to teach us the way to the ultimate good (*niḥśreyasa*). The *good* life, according to this philosophical outlook, is one that turns us away from these *duḥkhas*, the undesirables, and propels us permanently into the direction of the 'ultimate good'. It is useful to compare this notion of *ungood* or *duḥkha* with the three kinds of *duḥkha* in the Sāṃkhya school as well as the three-fold *duḥkha* of the Buddhists. However, let me continue further with Uddyotakara.

There are two kinds of people. Some are attached (to happiness etc.); the others are non-attached. Attachment means clinging to the objects (of enjoyment and suffering). The attached persons cling to such objects. Non-attachment means lack of clinging to such objects. The unattached persons do not cling to such objects. Accordingly, there are two types of activities: . . . the non-attached acts only in one way. He tries to avoid the 'undesirable' (what will cause bondage). He acts with the design 'I will avoid the undesirable'. He does not have any particular attachment to anything. The 'attached' person, on the other hand, acts in two ways. He tries to obtain the object he desires and shuns that which is undesirable . . . He acts from both motivations. He proceeds to obtain with the design 'I wish to obtain this desirable object' and he avoids with the idea 'I wish to shun this undesirable object'. Again, the action of the attached has two modes. One mode of action flows from *pramāṇa* and hence is crowned with success, and the other flows pseudo-*pramāṇa* (that which masquerades as a means of knowledge, but in fact a means of some erroneous judgement) . . . Both *pramāṇa* and pseudo-*pramāṇa* yield certainty about the generic character of the object (in both cases we ascertain 'it is an apple').

Both therefore lead to action. In the first case, it is successful (i.e. the desired object is obtained) in the second case, it is not.

All these statements are reasonably non-parochial and it seems to me that a general theory of what 'philosophy' means or what we would like to call 'philosophy' in the Indian context is outlined here very clearly.

In the Sāṃkhya, which was probably the earliest philosophical system in India, a similar notion of 'philosophy' or 'treatise' was present. For example, Īśvarakṛṣṇa (*c.* AD 400) begins his treatise by explicit reference to *duḥkha* as the necessarily given human condition and its possible amelioration.[9]

Being tormented by the three kinds of *duḥkha* (unhappiness: 1. pertaining to our body and mind, 2. caused by other beings, 3. caused by nature and the supernatural), there arises a desire to know (a question) about their causes. If these causes are due to the *perceived* (mundane) factors, we take care of them accordingly (by using antidotes). But no, the unhappiness does not vanish permanently (hence the desire to know the means of its cessation persists) (verse 1).

Even the scriptural acts are on a par with the perceived factors. For they are impure, unfair, and their results are perishable. Hence the opposite (imperishable state as the result) is better, which arises due to knowledge of the manifest and unmanifest (verse 2).

It is argued here that for the permanent removal of the persistent *duḥkha* or unhappiness, one should turn to the study of the 'treatise' or philosophical treatise, for neither ordinary measures to alleviate suffering nor the religious rituals or acts to reach heaven in the next life are capable of guaranteeing the permanent cessation of unhappiness. We may note that the first verse signifies that for removing mundane sufferings we do not resort to ordinary means to destroy their causal factors, but the persistent recurrence of sufferings persuades some of us to look for a permanent remedy. The second verse shows that turning to religion (Vedic religious rituals, etc. in this case) would be no better, for (a) some religious acts call for violence (in this case killing animals) and hence are *morally* impure, (b) some are unjust and iniquitous (for they supposedly make some people rich and powerful and others poor and weak in the next life), and (c) the projected outcome of all of them (limited time in heaven) is perishable. Hence the wise turn to *śāstras* (in this case, philosophical treatises) to find out a way to the ultimate good. Denunciation of the organized religion of the day is prominent here.

I shall now introduce Jayanta, who is somewhat parochial, but in presenting the *pūrvapakṣa* (opponent's position) he openly admits that: (a) *ānvīkṣikī*, which is *nyāyavidyā* or *nyāyavistara* is one of the *vidyāsthānas*, disciplines or subjects to be learnt (Jayanta quotes from *Yājñavalkya smṛti*), and (b) there were at least six different schools of *ānvīkṣikī* at the time, called *ṣaṭ-tarkī* (they were Sāṃkhya, Bauddha, Jaina, Cārvāka or Lokāyata, Vaiśeṣika and Nyāya).[10] It was significant that Haribhadra (who predates Jayanta) included all these six in his *Ṣaḍdarśanasamuccaya* (a collection of *six* systems of philosophy of *darśana*), but also added *Mīmāṃsā* or the *Jaiminīya mata*. Towards the end he tackles the question of the number 'six' mentioned in the title as follows:[11]

> Thus I have described briefly the philosophies of the *āstikas*. Verse 77 cd.
>
> Those who regard that there are only *five* systems of *āstika* philosophies, do not think that the Naiyāyika view differs from the Vaiśeṣika view. Verse 78.
>
> For them, the number 'six' in 'six philosophies' is fulfilled by adding the view of the Lokāyata. Hence I describe this view. Verse 79.

Thus I believe that at some point in history there was not much difference between the use of the term '*ṣaṭ-tarkī*' and '*ṣaḍ-darśana*', and hence the equation *ānvīkṣikī* = *darśana* (a *rūḍha śabda*) = philosophy was possible. The use of the word '*darśana*' in this context is intriguing. It may be that from this time onwards the word came to be used in the sense of a philosophical *view*. This is a far cry from the way some moderners and Westerners would like to interpret the term '*darśana*'. Taking a cue from the etymology of the word, they would translate it as 'vision' or 'intuition' and thereby they ride their hobby horse by arguing that Indian philosophy in this way is very different from the analytical and rational approach of Western philosophers.

To repeat Vātsyāyana, *ānvīkṣikī* was called *ānvīkṣikī* because of its special treatment of the theory of *pramāṇas* as evidence. A note on the word '*āstika*' is in order here. It does not mean a theist or a follower of the Vedas. It means only those views which acknowledge the existence of an 'after-world' (*paraloka*) as well as the moral principle that dispenses *pāpa* and *puṇya* (demerit and merit) according to good or bad actions. This is how the term has been explained in the commentary. The Lokāyatas were the only *nāstikas* for they argued that these entities, afterworld, demerit and merit, did not exist. In today's terminology, not simply an atheist, but any moral or religious sceptic would be called *nāstika*.

More important, however, is the omission of trade-and-commerce and polity from the list given by Yājñavalkya. Jayanta gives an answer to this puzzle. He says that this list of learnable subjects is compiled with the idea that they all should be teaching us about the four goals of human life (*puruṣārtha*), which include *mokṣa* as well as the doctrine of the *unobservable* fruits (demerit and merit) of our actions. The two, trade and polity, are squarely within the scope of *observable* results and purposes. Hence they have been left out in the list of Yājñavalkya. However, we should remember that Kauṭilya's treatise was concerned mainly with the *three* goals, *dharma, artha*, and *kāma* and this is also corroborated by the Mahābhārata account of the origin of *rājadharma*, in Chapter 5 of the *Śāntiparva* (Mbh. 12.5929).

Gaṅgeśa[12] (*c.* AD 1350) located *ānvīkṣikī* among a list of *eighteen* subjects of learning (*vidyāsthāna*), which included all the fourteen of the Yājñavalkya list and added: Āyurveda, Dhanurveda, Gāndharvavidyā and Arthaśāstra (see Mathurānātha's commentary). Gaṅgeśa asserted that *ānvīkṣikī* was the most honourable *vidyā* or subject of study (*abhyarhitatama*), which was only a resonance of Kauṭilya's favoured and oft-quoted pronouncement (see Rucidatta's *Prakāśa-ṭīkā*). In Gaṅgeśa's list however the two, *vārtā* (trade and commerce) and polity, will be included under *arthaśāstra*, and thus it avoids the anomaly of the Yājñavalkya list.

Gaṅgeśa wrote only on the four *pramāṇas*, his theology was only an appendix to the *Anumāna-khaṇḍa*. And this was recognized as an epoch-making book. Hence it would be interesting to see how he tried to connect his study of *pramāṇas* with the ultimate goal, *mokṣa*. In fact he says very little. The general idea was already expressed by Uddyotakara. The *śāstra* generates the right kind of knowledge of things (which includes knowledge of the self) and this is turn sequentially destroys the process of transmigration and the consequent sufferings or *duḥkha*. Mokṣa is thus automatically achieved in the way it has been described in *Nyāya-sūtra* 1.1.2.

Two points may be of some significance for us in the opening sentence of Gaṅgeśa. First, he mentions that the whole '*jagat*' (world) is steeped in suffering and hence 'philosophy' (*ānvīkṣikī*) provides the road to their release. The commentators disagreed about interpretation of this word '*jagat*'. Raghunātha said that it meant the souls that are in the process of transmigration (*jagat* = moving in). Mathurānātha[13] argued that the *rūḍha* meaning of *jagat* is any thing (*vastu*), any object not just souls. But certainly pots etc. are not suffering and hence would not be released. Thus, says Mathurānātha, the suffering state qualifies the things (*vastu*) and separates the suffering souls from those that are not suffering (pots etc. and free souls and God). And the release pertains only to the suffering souls, for whom the *śāstra* 'treatise' is composed. Second, Dharmarāja Rāmakṛṣṇa mentions an opponent's view (*pūrvapakṣa*) which has a sociological significance. '*Jagat*' means all sufferers and they must include the women and *śūdras* who have no right to study the Vedas. This view is clearly ascribable to Raghunātha, for he glosses '*jagat*' as '*saṃsāryātmajātam*', and this is quoted by Rāmakṛṣṇa. Hence according to Raghunātha's cryptic statement, Gaṅgeśa was saying that 'philosophy' or *ānvīkṣikī* is open to all, not restrictive to the male members of the three *varṇas*. Unfortunately such informal social critique often goes unnoticed by us today (specially by modern historians and sociologists). It would be stupid to neglect the strong undercurrent of criticism of religious and social practices by the classical thinkers. In the old Sāṃkhya of Īśvarakṛṣṇa we have explicit rejection of these practices. Raghunātha's tongue-in-check rejection of *caste* distinctions is also significant in this context. Rāmakṛṣṇa, however, being an orthodox *vaidika*, readily rejected Raghunātha's view.[14]

Gaṅgeśa's more significant statement (for our own purpose) comes at the end of the first paragraph. Referring to the sixteen categories (*padārtha*) enumerated in the *Nyāyasūtra* of Akṣapāda 1.1.1., he says:[15]

> I am going to deal with the nature of *pramāṇa* here (the first one) among these (sixteen categories) because on *pramāṇa* depends the establishment of everything.

Thus a rationale was given for his principal concern for *pramāṇa* or the source of knowledge. Mathurānātha comments that this exclusive concern with the theory of knowledge is vindicated by the fact that this is well in line with what is called *ānvīkṣikī* 'philosophy', which again produces the fruit of the right kind of knowledge that is instrumental to the ultimate goal of mankind, *mokṣa* or cessation of suffering.

The connection seems to us to be a bit tortuous, but not entirely fictitious. Obviously, there is a touch of parochialism here when it is claimed that knowledge of a particular system of metaphysics is *the* liberating knowledge. Even without taking notice of parochialism or sectarianism one can say that knowledge of things *as they are* (*tattva*) is the liberator, for knowledge gives control, specially control over our actions and if a particular type of action creates 'bondage', another type of action (or non-action) may lead to freedom or cessation of suffering. And if the liberating knowledge cannot be gained except through *ānvīkṣikī* or 'philosophy', then the position is proved.

I am inclined to treat *pramāṇa* as evidence for knowledge but not in the sense (at least not entirely in the sense) of the justificatory ground for knowledge. This may amount to a misconstrual, according to one view. *Pramāṇa* is what 'makes' knowledge. Since knowledge is always an episode (an inner event in Indian philosophy, in fact, a sub-category of mental occurrence) *pramāṇa* has also a causal role to play. It is the 'most efficient' cause of the knowledge-episode. Knowledge yields de-termination of an object *x* or a fact that *p* (*artha-pariccheda*) as the result, and a *pramāṇa* is 'instrumental' in bringing about that result. This is the causal role of a *pramāṇa*. Similarly when a knowledge-claim is made about *x* or about the fact that *p*, the opponent may demand a *pramāṇa* for the claim made. For example, the Buddhist will ask the Nyāya opponent 'what is your *pramāṇa* for the claim that the soul exists?' This question has been sometimes amplified as: is it from a perceptual *pramāṇa* or evidence (*pratyakṣataḥ*)? Or from an inferential *pramāṇa* (*anumānataḥ*)? In this context, *pramāṇa* is obviously fulfilling the evidential role. Hence a *pramāṇa* is both a cause and a 'because'—has both causal and evidential role.

In India, soteriology must be understood in an extended sense. It depends on one's seeing the world properly and acting according to its value. This is the general characteristic shared by all the systems. Such action is conditioned by the seeing. And *pramāṇas* are instrumental (*kāraka-pradarśaka*) in this seeing as well as 'persuaders' (*pravartaka*) in so seeing. In this second role, a *pramāṇa* is an evidence. In Buddhist philosophy too, Diṅnāga asserted in the beginning of his monumental work, *Pramāṇasamuccaya*, that in the person of the Buddha all the *pramāṇas* were realized and thus he connected soteriology with philosophy.[16]

What if this seeing or knowledge is called in question. If the knowledgehood of knowledge is doubted (as it could be in most cases), then, the Nyāya school says, we need an explicit evidence to establish the knowledgehood through an inference. It is in some of these cases that Vātsyāyana appealed to the test of 'successful activity'. There may be other ways[17] by which the knowledgehood may be inferentially established. Or, it may be self-established or self-evident, if we believe in the *svataḥ* theory. But in each case it seems that in knowing knowledge (i.e.

prāmāṇya-jñapti) *pramāṇa* has also an evidential role. According to the Nyāya position, knowledgehood is a contingent property of an awareness, and to *know that I know* I must know that this contingent property characterizes the awareness in question (and knowing simply the awareness itself would not do) and for this I need a *pramāṇa*, or an evidence. This is, however, not exactly foundationalism, nor the 'justified true belief' situation. Still, this is conceivably a new but totally intelligible model for epistemology which needs further exploration. On the whole, I believe it has been established here that there was a rich and multi-dimensional stream of thought in the Indian tradition, which was not entirely different from what has come to be called 'philosophy' in the West.

Notes and References

1. This happened, for example, in a conference during the *Festivals of India* in France, organized at the College International de Philosophie, Paris under the leadership of Jacques Derrida, during 23–26 October 1985.
2. Kauṭilya *Arthaśāstra* (ed. R.P. Kangle, Bombay), ch. 1.
3. H. Jacobi, 'Zur Frühgeschichte der indischen Philosophie', 1911, reprinted in B. Kolver (ed.), *Herman Jacobi, Kleine Schriften*, Wiesbaden, 1970.
4. P. Hacker, 'Ānvīkṣikī', WZKSO 2 (1958).
5. Vātsyāyana, *Nyāyabhāṣya* (ed. A. Thakur, Mithila, 1967), opening sentence.
6. Matilal, B.K., *Perception*, Clarendon, Oxford, 1986, pp. 46–65.
7. Vātsyāyana, op. cit., first paragraph.
8. Uddyotakara, *Nyāya-vārttika* (ed. A. Thakur), opening paragraphs. The Metropolitan edn. is from Calcutta University, edited by T. Tarkatīrtha and A.M. Tarkatīrtha. V.P. Dvivedin's edn. is from Chowkhamba, Varanasi, 1916.
9. *Sāṃkhyakārikā* (ed. R. Tripathi), Varanasi, 1970.
10. Jayanta, *Nyāyamañjarī* (ed. Gaurinath Sastri), Chaukhamba Sanskrit Series, Varanasi, 1982, pp. 9–10. See also *Yājñavalkya Smṛti* (1949, Bombay, ed. N. Acharya), ch. 1, verse 3.
11. Haribhadra, *Ṣaḍdarśanasamuccaya* (Chowkhamba, Benares, 1957), pp. 63–4.
12. Gaṅgeśa, *Tattvacintāmaṇi, Pratyakṣa*, with *Māthurī* (Delhi reprint, Motilal, 1973), pp. 114–16.
13. Gaṅgeśa, *Māthurī*, pp. 115–16.
14. Gaṅgeśa, *Tattvacintāmani, Pratyakṣa*, with Rucidatta and Rāmakṛṣṇa (Kendriya Sanskrtavidhyapitha, Tirupati, 1973), pp. 115–16.
15. Gaṅgeśa, *Māthurī*, p. 116.
16. See M. Hattori, *Dignāga, On Perception*, Harvard University Press, Cambridge (Mass.), 1968.
17. See Matilal, *Perception*, ch. IV.

25

On Dogmas of Orientalism

The rise of Orientalism as an *ism* is connected in its genesis with the subordination of Oriental societies to Western powers for the last four hundred years. Today the Indian subcontinent may enjoy political independence, colonial powers may have faded, the Suez Canel may have been Arabized, but the intellectual superiority of the West has remained unchallenged. Recently a thesis has gained some recognition, a thesis that has been put forward by some intellectuals of the Orient with some credible evidence, but either ignored or repudiated totally by Western scholars as irresponsible and unjust. The thesis implies that colonialism by the Western peoples, Western imperialism, and Orientalism are all of a piece. They are not, obviously, synonymous terms, but the claim is that they have a common origin. I believe that much of what this thesis has claimed is wrong and exaggerated. But it still contains grains of truth. It may be better to separate the kernel of truth from the chaff, cold facts from political and emotional overstatements and inflammatory comments.

It is undeniable that Orientalism began with the spread of Western powers to exploit and dominate the East. From the initial idea of collecting nuggets of information about the 'exotic' Oriental societies, much as the merchants and pirates collected gold, Orientalism became a full fledged subject for the classical scholars who switched from the study of Greek and Latin to that of Arabic, Persian and Sanskrit. This comment may be partly unfair, for there was one important and commendable difference in Western imperialist powers. They were not simply satisfied with collecting gold, extracting wealth and leaving the local societies undisturbed. They took to the study of the Orient in a systematic way. The original idea, to be sure, was not to learn anything new or of lasting value but to gather information that would be certainly useful for the administrators, legislators and rulers in their policy-formulations and decisive actions as far as the Orient was concerned. The goal was, as Sir William Jones clearly spelled out, to be Orientalists or Oriental experts. The result was both good and bad—not an unmixed bliss or unmixed evil. It was good and commendable for the interest the European scholars showed in the study of the Orient, as well as the scientific outlook and spirit they sought to maintain in their study. But it was bad for it went astray in its initial preconception. What could have been a successful and systematic *humanistic* study with scientific rigour playing an indispensable role, developed instead into a dry, so-called scientific study of facts and figures, of neat categorization and classification. The much acclaimed scientific curiosity was unfortunately characterized by lack of understanding of the human element in all these alien cultures and societies. The Orientalist's desire was to reduce the Orient to clear categorial structures, the resemblance was with the study of zoological species, and as a result, they often forgot that they were studying human beings, persons in their cultural and socio-political environments. Thus was the birth of Orientalism in the West.

Edward Said wrote a controversial book *Orientalism* some years back (London: Routledge, 1978). He propounded a very similar thesis in this book, but this thesis was far too sweeping and too sinister-looking to be true. Orientalism for him was an overarching concept with several meanings, an academic institution of studying the Orient in a certain way, the imaginative representation of a different cultural, religious and social mileau and the widely accepted pronouncements of colonial administrators. Neither do I accept the 'Said thesis' about Orientalism as such nor care much for its implications at large. But if we can separate some of the elements that constituted Orientalism and cut them loose from their original moorings, we will still be left with a mass of scholarship produced in the West about the Orient, which even in our present day enlightened situation would appear to be pretty much one-sided, distorted and false.

That the European knowledge of the Orient was gathered under the colonial domination is a fact that can hardly be ignored. The situation was such that despite their attempts at scientific objectivity, the European scholars unwittingly made many subjective judgements and drew improper conclusions based upon misperceived evidence, for many preconceptions, pre-judging and pre-commitments came to play a role. Of course, not all pre-judgements or subjective conclusions are harmful, and they have at least the validity of being what we may call the European *perception* of the Orient. But the problem is much more complicated.

If we turn to Said, we see that according to his judgement, for the colonial powers the Orient always appeared as bewitching, passive mysterious, unchanging, full of dangers, in particular sexual danger, and ultimately inferior. This may be very one-sided, and to some extent unfair, but if we make a distinction between the scholars who devoted their whole life to Oriental studies and the rulers or other writers who were responsible for Orientalism, and if we exclude the former groups, the above picture becomes to a large extent true. Now a believer in Said's thesis may be unimpressed by the presence of some seriously-minded Oriental scholars, for he might appeal to the truism that the exception proves the rule. Besides, a large number of Orientalists, or Indologists, despite their sincerity, objectivity and good intention, have often displayed an ethnocentric or Eurocentric outlook which distorted their final judgement. This is true of scholars even when they have been full of admiration for Oriental culture or when they are full of disgust for certain odd features of an alien civilization. The Said thesis may be very controversial but all controversialists have, in my opinion, something to draw our attention to—something that cannot be rejected outright. Controversialists usually grasp intuitively at some very fundamental truth. Their theses may be rejected wholesale, but part of them may be bought at retail price. Had it not been so, controversies would not have arisen in the first place. For the same reason, I believe such authors as Nirad C. Chaudhrui, V.S. Naipaul, and Salman Rushdie have generated controversies, and we may not always agree with their views but we must admit that they have something important to say—something that cannot be completely ignored.

One of the fundamental dogmas of Orientalism seems to be this. It has engendered a very strong binary opposition between the East and the West, between 'we' and 'they'. This has become almost a radical 'ontological' distinction. The Orientalists have always been ambivalent about making a straight forward judgement about the Orient because of their implicit and perhaps unconscious faith in this supposed 'ontological' distinction. They succeeded in unearthing a treasure house of knowledge and wisdom, a long tradition of human experience, man's experiments with his environments, a number of cultural and social systems—above all, a bewildering mass of information. But the ambivalence of the Western scholars is visible in both their occasional overenthusiasm and their unsympathetic criticisms. In fact both their overstatement and understatement, their ecstatic commendation and their unqualified condemnation, should be suspected. The Orientals, or the Indians, may feel elated at their overstatement or commendation, and may react unhappily to their adverse criticism. But at a deeper level, both attitudes are to be rejected as unacceptable and undesirable, for they are expressions of a very subtle ethnocentric sensitivity. In a way one should be more wary of overenthusiasm and admiration, for that is how the victims are unconsciously persuaded to join the victors. The victim's perception of his own state, of his own history, has often been coloured and clouded by the presuppositions of the victors.

A sinister result has followed from the above binary opposition which was presupposed in the study of Oriental subjects. This is embodied in the fact that the Orientals, with a few exceptions, were treated never as *persons* by the scholars who worshipped their Eurocentric selfhood. The Oriental man is either subhuman or superhuman, never human. He is either a snake-charmer, a native, an outlandish species, or else a Bhagawan, a Mahārishi, a Mahārāja, an exotic person, a Prabhupāda. The implication of the presupposition is that there cannot be any *horizontal relationship* between East and West. It has to be always vertical, either gurus or savages. I am not trying to flog a dead horse here. The olden days of romantic as well as imperialistic Orientalism might have passed. But its spectre seems to be still haunting us.

Let us concentrate on India in particular. As I have said, I do not agree with Said's too sweeping and provocative thesis about Orientalism. It is a seductive thesis, but I reject it. At the same time, I wish to note that there are elements that make up the 'seductive' body of this thesis—elements some of which are worthy of our attention and fit for our deliberation. A provocative thesis often validates itself in an indirect way. It can act as a corrective of our unconscious way of thinking. For unconsciously we absorb a number of preconceived ideas and prejudices which are prevalent in our midst. They come in the form of the established opinions and received doctrines of those whom we consider our superiors. These are seldom questioned but most of them may turn out to be dogmas. What is relevant in the path of knowledge is to obtain a sort of intellectual freedom from the established dogmas. We may emphasize that political and even economic independence is our goal but to achieve intellectual independence is entirely another matter.

A few illustrations of some general, widespread dogmas of Orientalism may be in order here. The 'Said thesis' should be rejected but a much less sinister view has been expressed by P.J. Marshall of Cambridge. He has shown how nineteenth-century Christian upbringing, nineteenth-century intellectual ideas and classical education, inhibited the Indologists in their study. 'Greece and Rome were the yard-stick by which India was measured' (*Journal of the Asiatic Society*, *XXVII*, 1985, p. 70). Besides, to the pioneer orientalist, William Jones, we owe the idea that Asians excelled in the sphere of imagination and poetic insight, while reason and argument were the grand prerogative of European minds. This idea later came to be known as the grand contrast between India and the West, and contributed to the genesis of the binary opposition between India's imaginative irrationality versus Western rationality. This has been repeated in various forms by later day scholars and uncritically accepted as valid by students and scholars alike before they study the subject or look at the evidence. Thus it is that when today one discovers the long tradition of rational discourse (cf. *śāstras*), sophisticated logical theories and serious philosophical arguments in India's classical texts of the premodern period, one becomes puzzled and uneasy.

The myths and half-truths manufactured by Indological scholarship have many facets, they take many forms. Sometimes, due to Indological training we have come to look upon our own past age as the golden age and the society in olden days is regarded as the garden of paradise which we have supposedly lost. In fact, the romanticism of some Western Indologists tends to infect our perceptions of realities in our past heritage. We tend to romanticize it for the wrong reason. To put it briefly, the Western Indologists were able to create two sorts of reaction upon their native counterparts. Some Indians, while showing equal excellence in scholarship turned into dogmatic traditionalists, dreamers who dreamt about the rejuvenation of the past glory, and into blind worshippers of what the Western Indologists described as 'spiritual' India. Others reacted against this glorification by rejecting completely the traditional values, traditional wisdom and traditional (Sanskrit) scholarship and thereby ventured to throw away the baby with the bath water.

The general outline of the dogmas of Orientalism (and even some modern Western Indologists are not entirely free from them) can be given as follows: (a) There is an Eastern Mind or at least an Indian Mind (I would be very much surprised if 800 million people had only one mind!). (b) The East is irrational and emotional, the West is rational and logical (this would mean that God made man and then sent Aristotle to Greece to make the Western man rational!). (c) India has an atavistic culture while the West nurtures a mature civilization based upon science and reason. (d) Indian culture is enriched with spiritual profoundity which makes up for its lack of logical thinking. (e) Such concepts on justice and fairness, privacy and individual freedom, are foreign to the Indian mind (sic), which is at best familiar with a sort of crude intuition as a guide to ethical and moral sensitivity. The culmination of this type of indoctrination is found in the articulation of the well-known binary opposition between Western materialism and Indian spiritualism, Western scepticism and Indian irrationality leading to mysticism. It does not take much to show today that all these claims are either false or they contain only half truths, which is worse. The word 'spirituality' has been used, misused and abused by the drug addict gurus of the West and by various Mahārishis, Mahāyogis, Mahārājas, and Mahābhagvāns such that today to call something 'spiritual' is already to censure it! This is but one extreme, a very paradoxical consequence.

At the other end of the spectrum, we see atrocious theorizing about Eastern or Indian ways of thinking. It has sometimes taken the following form: Ideas, concepts and things for which there are no exact equivalents in the Western world are looked upon as *deviations* from the occidental essences. And as deviations, they are regarded as either crazy ideas or contradictory (i.e. irrational) concepts.

There are, however, many notable exceptions in recent years among the Western Indologists who are comparatively free from the dogmas I mention, but that is not the issue here. Such exceptions cannot fail to unveil the general pattern; they also make the pattern more prominent. Let me emphasize that the dogmas as such may not always have harmful effects. The Orientals may also study the Occident with their own dogmas. In fact some dogmas, some preconceptions are bound to be present in any humanistic study. It is even doubtful whether even scientists are entirely free from dogmas or preconceived ideas. The dogmas of Orientalism have sometimes produced, paradoxically, good results. They have allowed the intellectuals of the Orient to see the other side of the picture. Because of the Orientalist's dogmatic and controversial assertions about us, we are able to see certain things in our own culture and certain elements in our civilization, which we could not have seen otherwise. Sometimes, things which are 'too close to our eyes' remain unseen and unobserved. Sometimes, in a very familiar landscape we cannot distinguish a line or a figure unless we are instructed to look at it in a particular way. And it is always good to know how our own faces would look from the opposite side. Our perception of our own selves would be enhanced and enriched if we could see ourselves also as others see us. Even a distorted and dogmatic description of our own heritage can be beneficial if it sets us to searching after the truth from proper and adequate evidence. This is how a culture develops its own self criticism. We become self-conscious. And self-consciousness is always preferable to self-deception.

Despite the above, past Indologists have done a great deal which we must admire. They had set standards for scholarly rigour and philological precision. This legacy we must accept. But there is also an increasing need today to study our Sanskritic past to challenge and expose the hollowness of the above myths and half truths. The Indologists popularized Indian philosophical thinking in the hey-day of German idealism, and gave it the colour of idealism and mysticism that was then fashionable in the West. They absorbed such thoughts as were congenial to them. Schopenhauer used Colebrooke's essays to round up a mythical picture of Indian philosophy which was so romantic that even our intellectuals today believe it to be true. The irrational element which was no doubt present in the tradition was so heavily emphasized that one modern scholar, my predecessor at the Oxford Chair (R.C. Zaehner), characterized Indian Philosophy as 'platonic madness and ecstasy'. To this we may add the effort of some of our own thinkers who, being faced with the challenge of modern civilization and superior technology, found an escape route in the aura of spiritual heritage. Our leaders, desperate in their search for an identity, accepted this rather distorted, if not false, image of their own heritage and were only too happy to do so. Paradoxically, to fight imperialism they were also victimized by the legacy of imperialism.

I believe the time has come now for us to till by ourselves the soil that we own, to conduct rigorous and unbiased research and study of our Sanskritic heritage—the heritage of Kaṇāda, Kumārila and Udayana, the Buddha, the Mahāvira and Śaṃkara, Kālidāsa, Bhavabhūti and Śrīharṣa, Ānanda, Abhinava and Kuntaka,—with scientific tools and objective goals in our mind. Only in this way, we can examine and challenge the ideas that the Indologists of the past had told us about ourselves. This will produce undoubtedly, more fruitful results, and we will have a better understanding of our own history and heritage and what we are today. For it goes without saying that our understanding of the present is rooted in our proper understanding of the past substratum; it cannot be the other way around. We may discover in this way that in the past we were not all really gods or spiritual dolls, but we were at least humans with all their glories and shortcomings, their ambitions and aspirations, their reasons and emotions. And this, I must add, will be a much better piece of knowledge for which we will not be sorry.*

*This was an invited address at the Department of Ancient History, University of Calcutta on 9 December 1985. I dedicate it to the memory of Professor D.C. Sirkar, who had done a great deal to make us free from the so-called dogmas of Orientalism.

26

Ideas and Values in Radhakrishnan's Thought

Dr Sarvepalli Radhakrishnan's approach to philosophy was syncretic. He wrote expositions on classical Indian philosophies, he wrote on the Advaita and Śaṅkara, but his major contribution lay in his independent treatises. There he was at his best. He was searching for a common bond, an underlying unity amidst the divisive philosophical disputations, amidst warfare and the gradual disintegration of creeds, sects and socio-political order. He was looking for a 'synoptic vision' and he thought it was the business of philosophy to discover it. In this regard, he was very close to the liberal democratic thinkers of Europe of the late nineteenth and early twentieth century. These liberal democratic thinkers also talked about the future possibility of a 'harmonious universe'—a kingdom of heaven on earth—brought about by the combined exercise of the rational self-wisdom of all human beings. The difference in Radhakrishnan's thought, however, lay in the emphasis he put not so much on rational self-wisdom, but on what he called the 'spiritual' side of man.

Whether such a 'spiritual' side exists or not has been a matter of debate among philosophers from the early age. Our poet Rabindranath Tagore chose a very interesting name for this side of humanity. He called it 'the surplus in man'.[1] It is what remains in men and women after the human being has been completely and exhaustively analysed and described by our material science, after the organism's biological and other needs—their desires, preferences, and satisfaction—have all been taken into account. It is believed that there is such a remainder, for the question is often asked, and only a human being asks such questions: 'Is that all?' Or, 'is there nothing else?' The question is asked because there is a sense of something lacking that is almost universally felt at some point or other. Only humans ask such questions, not the ants or the insects. Only humans ask for meaning and purpose of life, for values and goals even when material science and modern technology has provided for all our needs and comforts. In today's world, this may be regarded as a mild form of insanity. Where selfishness or self-love is the motto of life, where everybody is trying to strike down or elbow out everybody else for personal gain, it might be odd to feel sorry for the starving population of another country, to make efforts to alleviate the disease and untold sufferings of helpless men, women and children, with whom the members of the affluent society could possibly have no mundane connection except the common bond of humanity. Rare as it may be, it is still seen today that a pop star or some Hollywood film star, who does not have any particular lack or want as far as mundane pleasure or happiness is concerned, still goes out of his or her way to approach the other side of world, to reach out to the poor, the diseased and those suffering from starvation. This cannot be explained simply by an idle reference to Christian charity. Science does not exhaust the description of human beings completely: the moral being of man and woman, still remains unexplained. It is this 'surplus', which concerns itself with meanings, values and ideals.

Radhakrishnan believed in this 'surplus' side, and he in his own way even gave an outline of a *pramāṇa* theory to supply a philosophical basis of this belief. I will concentrate upon some passages from his *An Idealist View of Life*, and what follows is a sort of exegesis upon a part of his writing.

In *An Idealist View of Life*, Radhakrishnan distinguished three different senses of the word 'idea', from which the term 'idealism' has been derived. He acknowledged in the very first sentence that the term 'idealism' is decidedly ambiguous as it 'has been used to signify a variety of views'. The word 'idea' usually stands for a mental image or a thought grasped within a mode or consciousness. The philosophical view that is sometimes called idealism takes these 'mental' images, or the consciousness-stuff, out of which the real universe is made. Radhakrishnan also called it 'mentalism'. The general thesis is that the observer is not gathering knowledge of the real world through these ideas, for ideas are more real and more immediate to the observer than the real world. Here, matter is downgraded. The view can also be called 'immaterialism'. Radhakrishnan thought there was an agreement in this respect between the Buddhist *vijñāna-vāda* (or *citta-mātratā*) and some forms of British empiricism which 'reduce all knowledge to ideas in this sense'. Although he was well aware of the wide difference between the two traditions, it did not worry him, for his purpose here was to emphasize something else. He wanted to emphasize a third sense of the word 'idea' that suited his philosophical motivation.

There is a second sense of the word 'idea' by which we can bring general 'notions' or, concepts, or even the (Kantian) categories of thought under its domain. By such categories of thought, Radhakrishnan said (in Kantian vein), that the given, i.e. the 'uncategorized and un-idealized' datum, reveals itself to the finite mind. Referring to Benedetto Croce, he argued that our so-called objective form of knowledge is inescapably mixed up with the mind or mentalism, for mind is 'immanent in all cognitive experience as an active process'. Here is an important philosophic insight. A hard-headed realist can hardly escape the critique that he has to assume, without much evidence in favour of his assumption, that in a cognitive process, the mind has to stand apart passively in some (as Radhakrishnan put it) 'transcendent relation' to some extraneous object. Without some such assumption, it would be difficult to defend realism. However, Radhakrishnan was not interested in the age-old realist-idealist controversy in this context. Hence he moved forward to discuss the third sense of the word 'idea'.

The third sense of the word was indeed what Radhakrishnan wanted to drive at. This meaning lies behind such commonsense expressions as are sometimes made by an angry man: 'Now, what is the big idea?' Apparently, the person has not understood something, some meaning or some purpose behind some act. This idea of 'idea' is what Radhakrishnan was after when he expounded his *idealist* view of life. It is very different from mentalism or the other forms of immaterialism. In fact the mentalism-materialism controversy does not have any relevance to this view of life. This idea is value or purpose. In the words of Radhakrishnan:

> This idea or value is the operative creative force. An idealist view finds that the universe has meaning, has value. Ideal values are the dynamic forces, the driving power of the universe.[2]

This is not the idealism of Buddhism or Berkeley. In fact, this is the broad outline of a counterpoint to what used to be called in Radhakrishnan's days, 'the scientific view of the universe'. This is not, lest we misunderstand, a denial of the extreme importance of natural science in the domain of human knowledge. Radhakrishnan had always welcomed the outstanding achievements of modern science and technology. What he was raising here, however, was a more fundamental question: 'Is that all?' Such a question is often asked and has been asked over the centuries by the greatest of the philosophers. It comes from a deeply felt humility of the human heart: 'What else is there?', 'What gives meaning to all this? It arises from the not so uncommon Socratic pronouncement, 'The unexamined life is not worth living'. It was very common in the earlier part of this century to contrast, in the broadest possible terms, two opposite approaches to philosophy. This came about, for example, in a rather unusual conversation between our poet Rabindranath and one of the greatest scientists of the world at that time, Albert Einstein, recorded in the appendix to Tagore's *The Religion of Man* (the Hibbert Lectures, delivered at Oxford). Einstein described Tagore's concern for meaning, value and purpose of life as the 'humanistic conception of the universe' which he contrasted with the 'scientific conception of the universe',[2] which excludes such questions about value, meaning and purpose from its domain. Radhakrishnan argued for a synthesis of the two opposite viewpoints with the main emphasis upon values and ideals.

It may be mentioned incidentally that Radhakrishnan was deeply influenced by Tagore's thought. It was Radhakrishnan who saw the philosophical insight of some of Tagore's poetic writings and his later essays. Tagore's intuitive understanding of the synthetic philosophy of what we may call 'universal humanism' inspired Radhakrishnan to write about it. Besides, as Spalding Professor at Oxford, he represented Oxford along with Sir Maurice Gwyer (the then Chief Justice of India) and Mr Justice Henderson (of the Calcutta High Court), when on 7 August 1940, the University of Oxford held a special convocation at Santiniketan for the purpose of conferring on Tagore its doctorate (*honoris causa*). When the news of the death of Tagore reached Radhakrishnan's ear, he paid his tribute by saying, 'He was the greatest figure of the modern Indian Renaissance'.

In *An Idealist View of Life* (first published in 1932), Radhakrishnan went to considerable length to not only contrast intellect and intuition but also to set up an elaborate defence of what he called intuitive knowledge over and above scientific knowledge. Here he claimed that there are at least three 'different ways of knowing'. The distinction, according to him, is based upon the different ways by which each knowledge 'is produced'. This is what I have called his tentative *pramāṇa* theory. In fact, intellect versus intuition was a prominent issue in the philosophy of religion in the early 1920s, and 1930s. Radhakrishnan proceeded to deal with the issue in his own way.

The first of these three ways of knowing is, of course, sense-experience, which help us to know the features of the external world and thereby supply the data for natural science. The second is what Radhakrishnan called logical knowledge, which is obtained by a process of analysis and synthesis. Both enable us to acquire control over the physical world—our environment. About the possibility of knowledge through these two avenues, there can hardly be any disagreement among philosophers. Radhakrishnan, however, was more interested to argue in favour of the third avenue—intuition as the basis of knowledge—which was, and still is, decidedly the most controversial one. At the time when Radhakrishnan wrote, it was a matter of great debate, for the claim of many philosophers was that accessibility to certain truths belonging to ethics, religion and art, was only possible through intuition, a faculty that must be admitted to exist in humans, but should at the same time be distinguished from the immediacy of sensory experience. It is claimed to be as immediate and intimate as sensory perception, but the senses have nothing to do with it. It is said to be that state where the person's 'heart' is in direct contact with reality. Sometimes truths come to you through this avenue in a flash of understanding and you say, 'I know it, for I *feel* it in my bones'.

There is vagueness as well as ambiguity in the use of the word 'intuition' today. Obviously Radhakrishnan was not arguing in favour of such things as ESP, telepathy or clairvoyance. He was trying to show, as many did during his time, that the human being is fortunate to be endowed with the faculty of creative intuition, without which much that is covered by our scientific knowledge, i.e. by sense experience and logical deduction, would remain unexplained, even inexplicable. Radhakrishnan marshalled evidence in favour of his thesis from his extensive study of many outstanding philosophers from both East and West. He referred to Plato, who contrasted the world of eternal forms with the fleeting forms of sense-experience. But he mainly depended upon such Western philosophers as Bergson, Croce and Bradley. It was Bradley, who claimed that all intellectual analysis falsifies reality, since it breaks up its unity into a system of separate terms and relations. Ordinary thought distinguishes *that* from *what*, where the former refers to the reality and the latter to its abstract character. The unified structure of reality cannot therefore be revealed in such thought. It can be captured more in feeling, or what Bradley called the higher faculty, in which 'thought, feeling and volition are blended into a whole'. According to Radhakrishnan, in intuitive knowing, the knower and the known merge into one. It is a self-evident knowledge. It is like the artist's direct grasp of truth and beauty as a whole.

Radhakrishnan referred to Plotinus and the Neoplatonists, who asserted that logical knowledge alone was inadequate. He also referred to the classical Indian thinkers in support of his thesis about intuitive knowledge.

It is significant that he referred first to the hard-headed realist philosophers of the Nyāya-Vaiśeṣika school, who made room in their *pramāṇa* theory for such intuitive knowledge, called variously by such terms *ārṣa-jñāna, pratibhā, siddhadarśana* and *yogī-pratyakṣa* (a footnote quoted from *Vaiśeṣika-Sūtra* ix.2.13), and mentioned such Naiyāyikas as Jayanta and Viśvanātha.[3] Even the Buddhist talks about the supreme importance of *prajñā*, and the Buddhist *pramāṇa* theories like Dharmakīrti speak in detail about *yogī-pratyakṣa*. The Upaniṣads talk about the *brahman* experience, where knowing *brahman* and being it is said to merge into one undifferentiated blissful experience. The Vedāntins differentiate, as Radhakrishnan pointed out, intuitive experience, which is also direct and immediate, from ordinary sense-experience, by calling the former the *a-parokṣānubhūti* (non-sensuous integral experience).

There may exist a great deal of difference in the details of the *ārṣa-jñāna* or *pratibhā* of the Vaiśeṣikas and the *aparokṣa anubhava* of the Advaita Vedānta. But such difference does not matter much for Radhakrishnan's argument. His main purpose was to show that sense knowledge and logical knowledge are not enough to make certain deeper truths of life accessible to us. He argues in one place:

> The deepest things of life are known only through intuitive apprehension . . . In the sphere of values we depend a good deal on this kind of knowledge. Both the recognition and creation of values are due to intuitive thinking. Judgements of fact require dispassionateness; judgements of value depend on vital experience. Whether a plan of action is right or wrong, whether an object presented is beautiful or ugly can be decided only by men whose conscience is educated and whose sensibility is trained . . . Sensitiveness to quality is a function of life, and is not achieved by mere learning. It is dependent on the degree of development of the self.[4]

In another place, he claimed that some aspects of reality, for example, the domain of human emotion and love, can be amenable to only intuitive understanding, and not intellectual knowledge. He said:

> There are aspects of reality where only this kind of knowledge is efficient. Take, e.g. the emotion of anger. Sense-knowledge of it is not possible in regard to its superficial manifestations. Intellectual knowledge is not possible until the data are supplied from somewhere else, and sense cannot supply them . . . We know what it is to be angry by being angry. No one can understand fully the force of human love or parental affection who has not himself been through them.[5]

If philosophical wisdom is taken in its widest sense, and pictures are painted on a much broader canvas, if intuitive knowledge is understood in a larger context and in an extended perspective, then much of the above argument holds true. Intuition as a separate faculty for grasping certain truths is recognized even today by philosophers of different persuasions. But the tide of philosophical thinking as well as philosophical interest keeps constantly changing its direction over a period of time. Sometimes old problems come back for fresh reappraisals. Sometimes old truths are rediscovered. As Peter Strawson once said, 'If there are no new truths to be discovered, there are old truths to be rediscovered'.[6] This seems to be an echo of what Jayanta in our country said as early as AD tenth century in his introductory verse of the *Nyāyamañjarī*:

> *Kuto vā nūtanaṃ, vastu vayam utprekṣituṃ kṣamāḥ*
> *Vaco-vinyāsa-vaicitrya-mātram atra vicāryatām*[7]

Whereform could we derive the power to think of some new [philosophical] issues? [Hence, the readers, please] consider here the novelty of the ways of putting the words [to describe such issues].

It is also true that while old truths are rediscovered or revived for fresh discussion, sometimes current issues are somewhat unconsciously discarded. They are made to go out of fashion for the time being when they become overburdened with discussion, argument and counter-argument (and hence people get tired of them). Argument or concern for recognizing the presence of intuitive knowledge in humans is such an issue which has been thought necessary and important, as well as philosophically interesting, from time to time. During the time Radhakrishnan wrote, such concern was prominent in many quarters and some then raised the question whether Eastern wisdom could contribute further to the argument. Hence, in a way Radhakrishnan was riding the tide of his time. Interest in intuition, however, seemed to have abated immediately afterwards, and concern for further inquiry into the nature of logical knowledge, etc. occupied the centre stage for some time to come. But things keep changing, as they should. The style of philosophizing also changes, and in the midst of new ways of doing philosophy today, we can discern again the old concern for values, for meaning and purpose. Hence in this new century, it cannot be unrewarding to read Radhakrishnan. For it is only by critically reading the old-styled philosophy that we can create new styles and obtain new insights, perhaps also deeper insights, into the age-old problems. An *idealist* view of life, according to the new style, might take the form of 'an ethical view of life' or 'a value-centred view of life'.

I shall conclude by quoting a current example—an example that illustrates what I have argued in the last paragraph: the changeability of the philosophical cross-currents. Foundationalism, we know, has had its heyday and has run into disgrace in some quarters. Surprisingly, the discrediting of the search for the foundations or grounds of beliefs (in epistemology, ethics, or political theories) has come from two very different directions: from Continental philosophers such as Gadamer and Heidegger and from Anglo-American analytical philosophers, such as Wittgenstein and Quine. Richard Rorty has used this as his launching pad not only for raising his slogan for anti-foundationalism but also jettisoning 'the idea of universality' altogether and remaining content with bourgeois liberalism or the American status quo.[8] Rorty's pragmatism has been loudly proclaimed as Eurocentric or ethnocentric *ideology*. Anti-foundationalism, however, does not warrant Rorty's move to declare that all old philosophical controversies are obsolete and 'relics of the past'. Besides, it is also significant to note that while opposition to foundationalism from the Anglo-American philosophers is motivated by the idea that what is understood by foundationalism has not contributed to the progress of science their Continental counterparts, such as Heidegger, oppose it from their hostility to science and argue that this cultural legacy distorts truths (scientifically and methodologically) which seems to be irreconcilable (according to them) with the reality of human finitude. Anti-anti-foundationalists are also now at work pointing out that we may throw away the baby with the bath water in our zeal for overthrowing foundationalism. They believe that it is possible to develop an internal critique by which we can free the old view of its 'essentialist' and other objectionable trappings. Interest in the foundation of ethics and other age-old problems of moral philosophy are also seen to be gaining ground among certain philosophers today.

It seems, therefore, that a fresh quest for the foundations of morals and politics in the new styles of philosophizing will be with us for some time to come. Some believe that philosophy should be more closely connected with social, moral and political issues today. Others insist that philosophy should maintain its distance and concern itself with the critical examination of values that are inter-subjectively experienced (sometimes, we dare to add, by a common intuitive understanding) and approved. Such an examination, if carried out through rational self-wisdom, might uncover the universal applicability of certain basic values (not to be confused with the essentialist dogma) constituting the minimal moral fabric underlying all societies and all groups of human beings. Anti-foundationalists may recoil at the superficial implication of this suggestion, but it is still arguable that efforts should be made to develop a critical method (many are engaged today in doing just that) by which we can harmonize not only moral intuitions with moral principles, but also our intuitive knowledge with broad and substantive social theories. It may be that we should not look for the foundation of ethics or politics, for they can do without such grounds as God, reason, or human nature. But the issue still remains debatable, for many difficulties will still not have happy resolutions even under anti-foundationalism, unless we follow Rorty all the way and deflect our attention from moral and socio-political issues to champion the status quo of bourgeois liberalism, and reduce philosophy to mere conversation across the table in order to amuse ourselves.

What philosophy can do, and why it is worth doing, cannot be totally unaskable questions even today. At one time, we used to believe that philosophy would be able to answer such questions as, 'What is permanently true and real?' and 'What is permanently and universally valuable and desirable?' This has lost some credibility in today's atmosphere. But philosophical questions are still askable in some modified form, though not fully satisfactorily answerable. To this background, today, exploration of an ethical view of life based upon a sort of intuitive knowledge may still be a worthwhile enterprise, provided it is done in terms of the newly-accepted styles of philosophizing. If we can do that, it will be a good tribute to the memory of Radhakrishna.

Notes and References

1. Tagore, Rabindranath, *The Religion of Man*, Oxford University Press, Oxford, 1931.
2. Radhakrishnan, S., *An Idealist View of Life* (first published 1932), Unwin, Paperbacks, London, 1980, p. 105.
3. Jambuvijayaji, Muni (ed.), *Vaiśeṣika-Sūtras of Kaṇāda*, Gaekwad's, Baroda, 1961.
4. Radhakrishnan, S., *An Idealist View of Life*, p. 112.
5. Ibid., p. 109.
6. Strawson, P., *Individuals*, Methuen, London, 1959, introduction, p. 10.
7. Sukla, Suryanarayana, ed., Jayanta's *Nyāyamañjari*, Chowkhamba, Benaras, 1936, p. 1, verse 8.
8. Rorty, R., *The Consequences of Pragmatism*, Harvesters' Press, Brighton, 1982.

27

India without Mystification: Comments on Nussbaum and Sen

. . . it would be best of all if all human beings could come into an evident communal agreement with what we shall say, but, if not, that all should agree in some way. (Aristotle EE 1216).

When I started reading the Sanskrit novel, *Kādambari* in college, our teacher gave one piece of advice. The text contains long Sanskrit sentences which sometimes cover a couple pages of the book. The first sentence was one of the longest. The teacher's advice was: always start from the end to unfold the meaning. And it always worked. With this long paper (Nussbaum and Sen, 1989), I am going to follow the same advice.

The paper is concerned with both substantive and methodological issues. Nussbaum and Sen come to dwell upon the knottiest of problems: the relationship between cultural values and technological development in the third world, particularly in India. They outline the method of what they call 'internal' critique, by which old values may be rejected on the basis of new knowledge or understanding of old facts. This is supposed to fend against the fears of cultural conservationists about the undermining of traditional values (ways of life, etc.). Such undermining may be in the form of 'object failure' (where traditional craft is lost forever) or more seriously, in the form of a 'value-rejection'.

A Bengali couplet typifies 'value-rejection'.

Chede dilam patha, badle galo mattā
'I gave up that way because I changed my view.'

The term 'development' is more evaluative than descriptive. It presupposes a prior state of underdevelopment or non-development which is regarded as a disvalue. This accounts for the preference for development—a desire for change. The process of change, in order to qualify as 'development', must be assessed in terms of some pre-existing or external ends. Thus to discuss development we have to discuss values. This has been called the 'value-relative' nature of the concept of development. The substratum of development is provided by a whole culture, where values are not simply 'economic goods', but much more broad-based. Besides, a culture or a tradition is like a living organism, an on-going thing, never a static or frozen piece. It seems also to be 'self-conscious': it considers, decides and rejects. Hence a rational criticism can very well be *internal* to it. For a change to count as development, we need some sort of evaluation of values.

Many substantive issues arises here. As development can be a self-conscious choice should we let ourselves be blown off our feet by the stormy wind of technological development? Or should we let the wind blow but keep our feet firmly on the ground? (a metaphor once used by Mahatma Gandhi). The diversity, plurality and the dynamic (as well as evolutionary) nature of a culture (Indian culture, in particular) make the question of centrality of values further complicated. Development therefore cannot avoid evaluation and ranking of values in a culture, or a family of cultures. The first step in this process is therefore a deep understanding of the culture itself, perhaps from the inside.

The method of rational criticism suggested here is said to be Aristotelian as contrasted with Platonic. It should be internal *immersed, rather than detached*, and genuinely critical. This will fend against the objection that a *rational* criticism is usually detached and *icy cold* and therefore ineffective or insufficiently effective. Here a fundamental difference is underlined between the Platonic and the Aristotelian way, and it has important repercussions on ethical and political theory.

Plato's model for truth and value was a *mathematician's model*. It is dispassionate, a completely detached search for *true* values. The 'pure light' of the philosopher's soul sees, through the 'pure eye of reason', the true nature of values, justice, knowledge, good and the best life. The true values recommended on this view would be pure gold. But the criticism is that pure gold is never usable without some alloy. The closest analogy that comes to mind is the Sāṃkhya recommendation of values and the best life—one of complete detachment, fostered by the metaphysical knowledge of complete isolation of pure souls from 'material' entanglement. Īśvara Kṛṣṇa (*c*. AD 400) argues in the opening verses of his *Sāṃkhya Kārikā* that the three kinds of sufferings, physical environmental and mental, are all *caused*, and hence if the cause can be removed, the sufferings are removed—but *not* permanently. Hence there arises in us a search for the means of permanent removal of suffering (for the best life), and that is why people turn to philosophy:

> From the torment by the three-fold misery arises the enquiry into the means of terminating it; if it be said that this (enquiry) is fruitless, the means being obvious to us, we reply no, since in such means there is no finality.
>
> The fruits of actions enjoined by the Scriptures (traditional social life) are tainted with impurities, decay and hierarchy of gradation, and hence the best is what is the opposite (a completely detached life) effected by the knowledge of (isolation of, matter and spirit, and of) the distinction between what is manifest and what is unmanifest.

All this requires comment. But the point is that *mokṣa*, the highest value according to Sāṃkhya and Yoga, is the goal of complete isolation. This is irrespective of our desires and wishes, preferences and choices. It is where pure rationality leads. Another extreme example would be the Nāgārjunian idea of emptiness as the ultimate truth and the ultimate goal.

Reason reveals that everything is empty of its assumed 'own-character' (*svabhāva*), and hence the highest goal of life is the understanding (perfect wisdom—*prajñāpāramitā*) and achievement of this pure truth the essence of every reality or value is the emptiness of its assumed nature: 'Under rational scrutiny, each object dissolves into emptiness' (*yathā yathā vicāryante viśīryante tathā tathā*). Our hopes, desires and aspirations do not matter, for this emptiness is the truest of the truth revealed by a rational process. As I have elsewhere (Matilal, 1986) shown, this became a dominant preamble to mysticism with which India is so much credited (or discredited). If it was non-rationalism, it was heavily prefixed by an overemphasis on rationality, it is the use of logic and dialectics to debunk and demolish rationality as the end product (Matilal, 1977).

This concept of 'rationality' has been *challenged* also in the Indian tradition, and more so because in India it went to an extreme point at which it became palpably unfeasible and hence false. This challenge is found in the *pramāṇa* tradition and the *nyāya* method, where issues are discussed in the context of Indian epistemology and the concept of knowledgehood. An internal, practical critique of knowledgehood and reason can be developed without giving in to the circularity or the regress. Such was the conviction of the *pramāṇa* theorists in general and the Nyāya school in particular (Matilal, 1986). People are generally imperfect and have imperfect knowledge, but it is not a hopeless situation.

Now, the Aristotelian method in ethics takes *medical inquiry* as the model, not mathematics. There cannot be *pure* inquiries conducted in a void. Communities of human beings constitute the substrata of ethical virtues and values. Hence we cannot talk about values without 'humanizing' them. An 'unexampled' (*aprasiddha*) value is a non-value. Our conditions, ways of life, hopes and desires, pleasures and pains, almost weave together in our informal consideration and search for truth and values. Rationality is here *immersed* in human society rather than detached and standing 'on the rim of heaven'. This internal critique, Aristotle has apparently claimed, can yield truth and objectivity by achieving a degree of clarity, ordering and societal consensus. For in this way the subjective intrusion of people's fears, hopes and desires, which may distort and deform objectivity (which Plato was particularly afraid of), can be avoided. The internal reflection process that assesses values gradually reveals hidden inconsistencies, unclarities and confusions, and pushes its way ahead, leading to self-discovery on the basis of shared and sharable beliefs. It will be a self-discovery.

One may worry about 'truth' and 'objectivity' in this case. According to Nussbaum and Sen, this would be wrong, for 'Aristotle holds that all truth is in some sense internal and value-laden.' They refer to the Rawlsian view that Plato was correct about 'truth' in *natural* science while objectivity in human science would be more relevant to an account of ethical inquiry. In fact, *pure* truth if it means a *view from nowhere*, is as mythical as the round-square. Here Hilary Putnam's argument that ethics and science share almost the same notion of truth is recalled, which leads to 'internal realism'. This is also not without a parallel in the Indian tradition. The Sanskrit term *satya* means 'truth', and elsewhere I have argued that the term has been ambiguously used for both factual truths and evaluative exhortations (cf. *satya dharma, satya-rakṣa*). When the *sarvaṃ duḥkham* thesis, that everything, be it pain or pleasure, is nothing but unhappiness, is regarded in Buddhism as the first 'noble truth' (*ārya satya*)—it is more a prescription than a description (Matilal, 1982). It is a truth which is value-laden. An exploration of this notion of truth is necessary.

Another important component of the internal critique would be a conception of selfhood in relation to which values are to be understood. The authors recommend that the self be understood as a relational entity and its own ends as shared ends. For this will harmonize well with the communal goals and procedures of the reflective process that does evaluation and ranking in the developing nations. This view is certainly off-beat with the rampant individualism that is dominant in developed Western societies today. Here lies, I think, the root of a deep problem. It has been argued that rampant individualism is the price the West has paid for the growth of scientific knowledge and development, and it is also at the root of the society's malady and discontent. Enlightenment has spread disenchantment, loss of faith and scepticism, and with it indi-vidualism. Hence the *harmonious* view of selfhood, which existed in developing nations, may be completely undermined by the rampant indi-vidualism which development will no doubt foster. Hence there will be the loss of a central value, to be sure, and the worst fears of the cultural conservationists will be proven to be true. In this way, the so called inter-nal rational criticism will also be undermined. In reply, it must be said that there is no easy answer. Probably, the internalness of the critique will save it from being undermined. Man is a self-conscious and self-interpretive creature, and so is a living culture or a living culture-family.

Our poet Tagore once talked (1931) about an ontology of the 'surplus in Man', which he saw as an ontology of Hope to counterbalance the rampant individualism which has been the necessary precondition of progress, growth and development. The 'surplus in Man' or the 'Universal in Man' is what accounts for, according to Tagore, the 'other-regarding' activities. I believe this to be the poetic way of capturing the idea of self-hood as a relational social entity. Though not dominant in post-enlightenment Europe, the idea nevertheless finds expression today in our concern for the environment, for our future generations, for the health and survival of innocent children of poor countries. Hence it would not be difficult to argue for a richer conception of selfhood where both indivi-duality (required for our drive to change circumstances) and community would harmonize together. And such a conception of selfhood would also be part of the internal critical method by which a culture should decide between values. My ignorance of Greek prompts me to pose a question: is the above conception of selfhood imbedded in Aristotle's writings? If so, then it seems to me that in the modern discussion of selfhood and of ethical theory, this point has not been properly emphasised.

The Aristotelian method of Nussbaum and Sen departs in three other significant respects from the usual method followed in contemporary ethical discussion. It advises us to treat each of the values as qualitatively unique and incommensurable. It emphasizes that evaluative choice cannot be made unless the particularity of each context which presents the dilemma is fully taken account of. And it underlines the essential role of emotions and imagination in our correct perception of values, and thereby seeks to undermine the pitfalls of the Platonic conception of rationality.

Within the limits and reach of this method is noted its total commitment to a tradition of rational argumentation where the Patristic *Credo quia absurdum* ('I believe it because it is absurd') would not do. This tradition is also part of Indian heritage and has a long history there—a point that has been sufficiently shown and endorsed. Even the so-called mystically inclined philosophers participated in dialectics where they had a strong commitment to the law of non-contradiction. Even the Buddhist tetralemma or the Jaina seven-fold formulation of a proposition did not violate this law, for without it, dialectic would have been impossible (see J.F. Staal, 1975; Matilal 1981, 1982).

Problems posed by the plurality of cultures and heterogeneity of tradition must force us to extend the Aristotelian method to include the values of toleration, and of protection of minority rights. On toleration, the Indian religious traditions, Hinduism, Jainism, etc. are particularly expansive. Al-Biruni, the great Muslim Encyclopaedist, writing about the Hindus in the AD eleventh century, said:

> They [the Hindus] totally differ from us in religion . . . On the whole there is very little disputing about theological topics among themselves; at the utmost they fight with words, but they will never stake their soul or body or their property on religious controversy.

This has been sometimes noted as religious 'antipathy' among the Hindus (R.C. Zaehner, 1962). But this absence of dogma, which we need not overemphasize, was a fact. In the present context it need not to be a *dūṣaṇa*, a drawback, but a *bhūṣaṇa*, an ornament. Besides, the Jainas explicitly developed a metaphysic of the *many-sidedness* (*anekānta-vāda*) of reality. Truth is a many-faceted gem, the total view of which is accessible only to an omniscient being, not to imperfect humans—this is the slogan of Jainism (see Matilal, 1981). Hence I believe the native soil of India would be enough to allow the idea of toleration to be integrated with this method.

More interesting, however, is the point where the so-called 'internal' critique is supposed to transcend cultural boundaries. We need not quibble about the term 'internal'. But the argument seems to be based upon a holistic approach. Criticism leading to value-rejection often looks beyond the sub-cultural boundaries. Besides, knowledge of other cultures is easily available in today's world and such knowledge *ipso facto* may enter the process of the proposed internal critique. Since today's world is not cut up into self-contained bits, inter-cultural contacts (and conflicts, perhaps) may enhance the internal critique leading to value-rejection or value-acceptance or both. This need not always be a case of 'sour grapes'

(Elster, 1982), when an antecedent value is not necessarily less valuable than the consequent one. I shall mention a case in point.

Recently a Muslim divorcee in India, Shao Banu sued her ex-husband for alimony, but the husband argued that according to the Qu'ran this is not done. A great controversy arose when the Supreme Court of India ruled that alimony should be paid, no matter which religion they followed. The opponents argued that this was a violation of their rights of religious freedom. The case was further complicated when some Muslim religious leaders convinced the woman, Shao Banu, that she was guilty in the eye of God and accordingly she withdrew her demand for alimony. The Supreme Court, I understand, would let the ruling stand. Judging from the newspaper reports, letters, protests and demonstrations before courts and parliament house, it appears that the people in the Muslim communities are almost equally divided on this issues. To confound the issue, Congress (I), the party in power, passed a bill to overrule the Supreme Court decision, apparently to woo Muslim voters in the next general election. Now all my facts may not be exact here, on account of some information being second-hand, but we may consider this to be a hypothetical case. The point is that the internal criticism may in this way look across a cultural/religious boundary and struggle to reject or preserve a value. Besides, how about Shao Banu? Is her subsequent rejection a case of sour grapes?

The last point here is concerned with the concept of well-being seen in terms of the person's 'capabilities'. If we admit (as I do along with Nussbaum and Sen) that there is a basic similarity in the list of 'capabilities' for each person in different parts of the world (allowing possible difference in 'commodity bundles' answering the same capabilities), critical thinking for endorsement or rejection of values must benefit from looking beyond cultural boundaries. Enrichment of the critical evaluative thinking in this way within a culture would allow us to see why the argument that the Shao Banus of the Muslim community in India are quite 'happy' with the deal they have got will not have much 'bite' under this conception of well-being. The modern conception of the world is a holistic one where isolated cultural components are reacting and influencing (knowingly or unknowingly) each other constantly and over a period of time. Here bits and pieces will change and adjust themselves to the total picture through various forms of value-rejection and value-acceptance (various 'sour graphs'), but it is hoped, if development has the meaning it has for us now, the total picture will be increasingly free from 'sour grapes' situations.

I shall now turn to the first half of the paper. In the case of Indian culture (or the family of Indian cultures), perhaps the most confounding issue is the prevalence of the variety (and often conflicting) 'readings' or perceptions (mostly misperceptions) of India's tradition, which enter into the consideration about the relationship between value, technology and development. Nussbaum and Sen have identified such readings as those of the 'more mystical' East and the 'non-rational' in Indian culture.

To wit: India is believed to be a mysterious land of mysticism, where religious fervour and the consequent superstitions are believed to retard any progressive change, a land where the tradition is viewed as non-rationalistic and the present day culture viewed as unreceptive to modern rational approaches and technological wonders. Nussbaum and Sen have warned already against such a 'more mystical' reading of Indian culture, for there is a body of unmistakable evidence that belies such a simplistic and presumably wistful reading. The disciplined methodology of 'classical' Indian philosophy has just begun to become visible to us moderners. Materialism and scepticism were as much part of the Indian tradition as they were of the Occidental, though not always fulfilling the same function. The achievements of Indian mathematics, Indian polity and statecraft as found in Kauṭilya, Indian linguistics and grammatical theories of Pāṇini, pleasure and fulfillment in sensual activities and life (as found in the *Kāma-śāstra*), the teaching of practical wisdom and shrewdness through the literary media, *Pañcatantra*, invention and analysis of various games of skill (including chess)—have all been referred to in passing to underline the rather 'earthly' concerns which must have influenced traditional Indian values and living styles.

I simply add one or two details by way of comment.

(a) There was admittedly an over-abundance of mystical literature in India, but with a difference. They were tempered with scepticism. As I have already argued, many 'mystical' writers used logic and dialectics in much more sophisticated forms in order to foster a sort of scepticism about all the received doctrines, dogmas and views of reality and their mysticism came almost as the heightening of *ataraxia* into an illumination of 'truth'. Rationality was instrumental to the non-rational goal.

(b) As early as AD 700, Haribhadra wrote his *Saddarśana-samuccaya* which was a summary representation of the main tenets of the six rival systems of philosophy, of which Lokāyata materialism was one. Pleasure, including sensual pleasure, was declared in this system to be the goal of human life, and anything beyond the observable, such as god, afterlife and heaven, was regarded as a concoction prepared by the priests, or such things were labelled products of a false philosophical method nick-named 'wolf's foot-prints'. The commentator explains the implicit parable (by which this false method is illustrated) as follows: A man wanted to convince his very 'religious' wife that all this talk of the after-life, god and heaven was nonsense. So he took a walk with her before daybreak on a sandy beach near the village, and prepared some fake marks resembling the foot-prints of a wolf. Next morning the entire village was declaring: 'A wolf is in the village'. And then the man said that it was in the same way the philosophers cited (fake) evidence to prove the existence of god, afterlife and heaven. This was probably the beginning in the Lokāyata School's systematic critique of the adequacy of evidence on which any inference of unobservables was based.

(c) Kauṭilya (*c.* 300 BC) already mentions the Bhṛhaspatya school of *Arthaśāstra* (several times) which may or may not have been connected with the Lokāyata materialists, but which regarded only *vārtā* (economics, commerce, trade) and statecraft as subjects worthy of study, for the *trayī* (scriptures), and the philosophy derived from it, were nothing but a 'cloak' for people to hide the truth! Kauṭilya was not so radical and hence refuted the views of this school.

Throughout history 'Indian' culture has reacted, resisted and then assimilated a lot of 'foreign' or outside cultures and ideas. In this regard it has behaved as a living organism. Poet Tagore has said in a poem:

The sakas and the Huns, the Pathan and the Moghals—all came to be dissolved in one mass—(in India).

There is no need to over-emphazise this point. Perhaps the situation in the U.S.A. is not very different. But still we may note that India has a long history of mixing cultures, in which mixture of Hindu-Muslim ideas in religious rituals, social practices, arts and crafts, is perhaps the most significant one, a fact which is not at all emphazised today. This would reject outright any sort of monolithic account of the development of 'Indian' culture.

About the prevalent misreading of Indian culture, I shall venture a slightly different genetic analysis. In particular I wish to tackle the question: why would even an educated Indian today like to nourish or even relish the 'more mystical' images of India? I venture to suggest that the so-called 'images' of India, are in part products of two things, genuine ignorance and sometimes undiluted bias. But we have to answer the more important question: why? What could have been the genesis of these false 'images'?

A brief historical account of the genesis of these false 'images' may be in order here. I shall start with the Orientalists. Nussbaum and Sen have rightly pointed out that in the modern Western reading of Indian society and culture as a whole, the urban and the urbane parts of the culture have been systematically undervalued or ignored while they have been taken to be extremely important and central in the case of other cultures. But I would like to go further and point out that even the readings of the so-called urban culture have not often been without bias. They have been inadvertently or deliberately misrepresented more often than not. Elsewhere I have described them as Orientalists' dogmas (Matilal, 1988).

The Western powers in the seventeenth and eighteenth century were not satisfied simply with collecting nuggets of gold. They took to the study of the Orient in a systematic way to collect nuggets of information. Presumably such information was held to be useful for the administrators, legislators and rulers in their policy-formulations and decisive actions. And fortunately the goal was much wider: as Sir William Jones spelled out, it was to be Orientalists or Indologists, experts in the scientific study of the Orient. But despite good intentions, the Western Indologists and some modern social anthropologists unwittingly shared some common misconceptions. At least two possible reasons can be assigned. First, the fact that the Western knowledge of Indian culture was gathered under colonial domination can hardly be ignored. (The problem is partly exemplified in E.M. Forster's novel *A Passage to India*, particularly towards the end, the final chapter when the two characters Aziz and Fielding 'went for their last ride in the Mau jungles'—a scene unfortunately completely missed by David Lean's movie version). Second, they had started from the pre-conceived idea of a very strong binary opposition between the East and the West, between 'we' and 'they'. This became almost a radical 'ontological' distinction for them. Thus it is that when the Indologist succeeded in unearthing a treasure of knowledge and wisdom from a long tradition of human experience, the results of man's experiments with his environment, a number of sophisticated 'thought' systems, all these became a bewildering mass of information for them because, more often than not, it was incompatible with their implicit faith in the assumed 'ontological' distinction or binary opposition. As a consequence, their perceptions became highly selective, they came to see what they wanted to see and construct their theories accordingly.

A sinister result followed. The ambivalent attitude of the Indological scholars has been visible in both their occasional over-enthusiasm and in their unsympathetic criticisms, in their ecstatic admiration of Indian mysticism and their unqualified condemnation of the so-called non-rationality. Briefly, for these scholars who were much attached to their Eurocentric selfhood, the Oriental man was either sub-human or super-human, never human. He is either a snake-charmer, a native, an outlandish species, or a Bhagwan, a Maharishi, a Maharaj, an exotic person, a Parbhupada. The presupposition was that there cannot be any horizontal relationship between East and West. It had to be always vertical, either gurus or the savages. Although the olden days of romantic as well as imperialistic Indology have passed, the spectre seems to be still haunting us.

The pioneer Orientalist, William Jones, propounded the 'seductive' idea that the Asians excelled in the sphere of imagination and poetic insight while reason and scientific arguments were the grand prerogative of the West. This was the beginning of the grand contrast between India and the West, which led to the (false) theory of the binary opposition between India's imaginative irrationality and Western rationality and scientific outlook. This general theory, propounded on the basis of extremely inadequate evidence (since Indological research was just beginning), as well as on the romantic outlook of the scholars, came to be repeated in various particular forms by latter day scholars and uncritically accepted as valid by students and scholars alike (among them even the modern Westernized educated Indians.) They accepted the dogma even before they studied the subject or looked at the evidence. Hence when one is today confronted with a long tradition of rational discourse (in *śāstras* and *darśanas*), a highly sophisticated set of logical theories and philosophical systems (in the *pramāṇa* and *prameya* doctrines of various schools), traditions of rival literary theories and criticisms of art, dance, plays and literature (in the *alaṃkāraśāstras*), one becomes puzzled and uneasy, for one's conviction about the 'ontological' dichotomies of East and West has to be given up.

The myths and half-truths manufactured by Indological scholarship have many factors and many forms. They have created in general two opposite sorts of reaction upon the modern West as well as the modern educated Indians. Under the influence of the first sort of reaction, they romanticize India's past heritage for the wrong reasons. It is thought that the past age was a golden age and the society there was almost the garden of paradise which Indians have lost or are going to lose due to invasion of modern technology, etc. (This attitude may rightly be linked up with what Professor Appadorai has identified as the tendency of an absolutist form of relativist cultural protectionism.) It is the same tendency that finds mystical irrationalism alluring and modernization a positive evil. Under the influence of the second sort of reaction, we move to the opposite end of the spectrum. Following this tendency, people reject completely traditional wisdom and traditional values. In the name of progress and modernization, anything coming from the West will be uncritically accepted and embraced and any disruption of order and undermining of traditional wisdom and values will be regarded simply as necessary requirements for the operation. I have shown that the tacit valuation of cultural difference (between East and West) as an absolute end was itself a preconceived idea of the Orientalists. While we must admit that there is some difference between India and the West in cultural and aesthetic sensitivity, in certain religious presuppositions and moral commitments, this need not be overemphasized in the dynamic and holistic world of today where no man or woman and no community is an island or remains static for any length of time. In view of this, the preservationist's ideal is only an idle dream. It is also a repugnant dream in view of the commitment he has to justify a variety of inhumane and undesirable cultural practices that go along with the rest.

Despite what I have already said, I must add that past Indologists had done a great deal for Sanskritic scholarship, which we should also admire. They had set standards for scholarly rigour and philological precision. This legacy we must accept. Besides, I believe the Western Indianists have allowed the modern Indian intellectuals (at least a few of them) to see the picture from the other side. Sometimes, things which are 'too close to our eyes' remain unseen and unobserved. Our perception of our own selves becomes enriched and enhanced if we could also see ourselves as others do see us. Thus, even a distorted and dogmatic description of our own heritage can be beneficial if it sets us searching after our true selves from proper and adequate evidence (*pramāṇa*). This is how a culture develops its self-criticism self-consciously. And self-consciousness is always preferable to self-deception.

To add another dimension to the genetic analysis. The Indologists popularized 'Indian philosophy' in the hey-day of German idealism in the West and of necessity gave it a colour of idealism-cum-mysticism that was fashionable at that time. From the vast array of Indian philosophical writings in Sanskrit (and Pali) they absorbed only such thoughts as were congenial to their easy theorizing. Schopenhauer used Colebrooke's essays to round up a mystical picture of Indian philosophy which came to be very romantic and mystical (therefore attractive), so that even our Indian intellectuals today believe it to be true. And they either take pride in it or debunk it for the same mistaken reason. But this reading has been so heavily emphasized that it has undermined the outstanding and dominating presence of a very sophisticated rational tradition. Once my predecessor of the Oxford chair (R.C. Zaehner) characterised this 'brand' of Indian philosophy as 'platonic madness and ecstasy' and thought the tradition missed an Aristotle to put the matter right (Zaehner, 1972).

Study of Indian philosophy must travel beyond the Upaniṣads and other similar texts. These texts were simply not philosophical texts in our modern sense. They were only books of wisdom. Paradoxically, Sanskrit has a better term for 'philosophy' in the modern sense than what the word meant in old Greek according to its etymology (if 'sophia' means 'wisdom' in our sense). The Sanskrit form is *anvīkṣikī*, used by Kauṭilya and many others in order to distinguish what we call philosophy today from scriptural and religious education (called *trayī*). This term has been explained by the Naiyāyikas as 'examination of what is obtained through perception (observation) and what is stated by the scriptures, by *pramāṇas* or "adequate evidence".' Kauṭilya, after enumerating the *four* main branches of learning (philosophy, religious education or scriptures, trade-and-commerce, and the science of polity), defines *ānvīkṣikī* as follows (Manu and others also referred to this definition):

Investigating, by means of reasoning what is good and what is evil in the context of 'scriptural/religious' education, material gain and loss in the context of learning trades and commerce (*vārtā*-economics), what is good as a policy or principle and what is not so in the context of learning polity and public behaviour—philosophy (*ānvīkṣikī*) confers benefit upon the people, keeps mind steady in prosperity and adversity and imparts proficiency in thought, speech and action.

I believe I have said enough along with Nussbaum and Sen to underline its anti-mystical and rational nature and thereby not only to question but to reject the usual 'more-mystical' readings of Indian tradition. It is a tradition of the 'logical' empiricism of Akṣapāda, Uddyotakara and Udayana, of non-theistic ethics or virtues of the Buddha and the Mahāvīra, of the scepticism and agnosticism of Nāgārjuna, Śrīharṣa and Jayarāśi, of the analytical study of aesthetic experience by Ānanda, Abhinava and Kuntaka, of technical analysis of logical and philosophical concepts by Gaṅgeśa and Raghunātha, and of sophisticated materialism of the Lokāyatas. Books (in Sanskrit) covering millions of pages written over one and half millennia are available to us, thanks to the labours of the Sanskritists and Indologists. It is a culture for which there exists a vast body of elaborately written texts enriched by commentaries and subcommentaries over the centuries. A study of at least a small fraction of this literature must be important, in fact essential, for our understanding of the nature of modern India which is, it is true, still rooted in tradition but in a different sense altogether. There is no easy way out.

The most significant suggestion by Nussbaum and Sen regarding the methodology of the study of Indian values is that we begin by looking at a well-known and thoroughly studied case: the case of ancient Greek values. It has been mentioned that the Greeks did not make or anticipate the Kantian distinction between two sorts of values; the moral and the non-moral. Neither did the Indians. There was plurality even within the Greek culture.

Several types of evidence should be taken into account in order to study the Indian tradition:

1. The vast body of Indian literature has already been mentioned, not only the two great epics, but also other poems, plays, *kathās* (novels), *bhānas* (one-act plays where characters are usually courtesans, prostitutes, thieves or men about town).
2. *Dharma, Artha-* and *kāma-śāstras*: They all endorse a typically Indian division of values into the religious-moral, the economic-political and the one aimed at gratification of desire (sexual and other). It was argued that the economic-political is only instrumental to the other two. And various texts unanimously said that all three must necessarily be combined to ensure a good life. A fourth, *mokṣa*, entered into the discussion only later in history, and was regarded as the one with the ultimate value. But even Śaṃkarācārya re-emphasized that people in society are of many kinds, of whom only some would choose the path of renunciation and cessation, *nivṛtti-mārga*, while the majority opt for the path of action and non-cessation, *pravṛtti-mārga*. Thousands of epic stories and poems have illustrated this point.
3. Texts like *Kuṭṭanīmata* (Damodaragupta, AD 800) which discussed with illustrative stories what sort of virtues and values prostitutes should cultivate. For example, they should not fall in love if they are to succeed financially.
4. *Purāṇas*: Although they are fantastic tales, they reveal a lot about the contemporary ethos in the society.
5. The *vyavahāra* sections of Manu and Yājñavalkya, later commentaries, and still later Law-digests or *nibandhas* where various ways of settling disputes in courts, punishing offenders, criminals, what

counts as crime, the law of inheritance, special laws for settling gambling disputes—all these are discussed. A historical account of the development of social morality can be gleaned from this very interesting body of literature. Plurality of concepts and practices can be noted. (Matilal, in Bengali, *Desh*, 1986).

I will just cite two instances. The *dharmaśāstras* are usually regarded as responsible for patternization of life according to an hierarchical norm and restricting freedom in human behaviour. Yet in some areas they held a more liberal view than what our modern society allows. For example, transgression of married women unless it bore fruit was treated very lightly. Thus Yājñavalkya says (I.3.72) that such transgression of a married woman is purified by next menstruation. Besides, prohibition of primary and secondary sexual behaviour (kissing, etc.) was restricted only to married women, to girls of some higher castes, and to any girl against her wish. Apart from these, there was a fair amount of latitude of free love as is evident in all the sources. In the play, 'The Little Clay Cart', when Cārudatta was challenged as to how he, being a respectable person who was also married and had a devoted wife, could have a prostitute, said 'My youth has been faulted, not my character.'

Manu notes that there are twelve kinds of children—and the main division between them is not one of legitimate and illegitimate but one of having and not having the right to inherit. For example, the unwed mother's child cannot inherit, nor can anybody born out of lust in an extra-marital relation. Such children were *not* 'illegitimate' but only lacked the right to inherit properties. But, of course, the rigours of *dharma* advanced with time and tried to stifle free social behaviour. A careful analysis of the social history must be undertaken to deepen our understanding of Indian culture.

I shall conclude in a lighter vein citing two anecdotes which might throw some light on these issues. Our perceptions are socially dominated by our preferences. In an old Hollywood movie about the American south, a blackwoman (a maid) claimed that since God had said in the Bible that food should not be wasted but given to the poor and hungry, the cook should accordingly give the leftovers to the poor. The cook challenged: 'Now, where in the Bible had God said it?' the woman replied, 'I don't know, but if He didn't, He should have'. The other anecdote is about the problem nicknamed 'familiar-versus-foreign'. It is an inescapable bias of humans that we try to understand the unfamiliar by a sort of reductionism, in terms of the more familiar. Seeing a camel, a Sanskrit pandit asked 'What kind of animal is this?' 'A camel' was the answer from the Arab. Unsatisfied the Pandit asked again, 'what is a camel? Tell me, is it a *gaja-kṣaya* (diminution from an elephant) or a *musika-vṛddhi* (a mouse grown many times bigger)?' The problem of understanding becomes very serious in the case of a very rigid, preconceived categorization of the universe!

NOTES AND REFERENCES

Elster, J. (1982), 'Sour Grapes: Utilitarianism and the Genesis of Wants', in A. Sen and B. Williams (eds), *Utilitarianism and Beyond*, Cambridge: Cambridge University Press.

Gombrich, E. (1960), *Art and Illusion*, London: Phaidon Press.

Matilal, B.K. (1977), *The Logical Illumination of Indian Mysticism*, Oxford, Clarendon Press.

———. (1982), *The Central Philosophy of Jainism (Anekāntavāda)*, Ahmedabad: L.D. Institute.

———. (1982), *Logical and Ethical Issues in Religious Belief*, Calcutta, Calcutta University Press.

———. (1986), *Perception: An Essay on Classical Indian Theories of Knowledge*, Oxford, Clarendon Press.

———, 'On Dogmas of Orientalism', in K.K. Dasgupta, P.K. Bhattacharya and R.D. Choudhury (eds), *Sraddhanjali: Studies in Ancient Indian History, D.C. Sircar Commemoration Volume*, Delhi, Sundeep Prakashan, 1988, pp. 15–21.

Nussbaum, M. and Sen, A. (1989), 'Internal Criticism and Indian Rational Traditions', in M. Ķrausz (ed.), *Relativism: Interpretation and Confrontation*, Notre Dame: University of Notre Dame Press, 1989: 299–325. This paper (as well as the response) was originally presented at a conference entitled, 'Development and Technological Transformation in Traditional Societies: Alternative Approaches', United Nations University, World Institute for Development Economics Research (WIDER), Helsinki, 4–7 August 1986.

Staal, F. (1975), *Exploring Mysticism*, Berkeley, University of California Press.

Tagore, R. (1931), *The Religion of Man*, London: Allen & Unwin.

Zaehner, R.C. (1962), *Hinduism*, Oxford: Oxford University Press.

———. (1972), *Drugs, Mysticism and Make-Believe*, London: Collins.

28

Images of India: Problems and Perceptions

Martha Nussbaum and Amartya Sen in a recent paper[1] have raised the point that, as India enters the rank of modern industrial powers, her image seems to be threatened by mystification through mysticalization. I agree, and offer some amplification by way of pointing out the problems every Indianist faces today. I shall also note the propensity to prejudge some of these issues. The picture has been made more complicated by the recent writings of popular Indian writers like V.S. Naipaul, Nirad Chaudhuri, Khuswant Singh and Ved Mehta. The literary sensibilities of these writers are not in question, nor is their frequent intuitive grasp of the 'truth' of the matters that often touch very sensitive chords of the Indian mind. However, what they write is often constrained by the stereotypes of the literary genres in which they excel. Hence, many images of India emerge, and along with them the apparent incongruity of such images. Mystification continues.

We can identify certain substantive issues in order to point the way to some sort of de-mystification. At the risk of oversimplification, we can identify two contrasting images. Although the actual situation is much more complex and sometimes unimaginably so, we can nevertheless imaginatively talk about these two rival images, bringing each into sharp relief by way of contrast. One image is in accord with the perception of the enthusiastic, sometimes overenthusiastic, planners and development economists; the other is perceived by the sociologists and social anthropologists. The former image regards India as just another case, a country ready to be industrialized, ready with a big consumers' market, and a society divided only into the familiar 'economic' classes. The latter sees India as the homeland of mystifying pluralism, a society overwhelmed by hierarchy, with a bewildering variety of castes and status groups, where neither wealth nor power but 'ritual purity' becomes the decisive criterion. The latter usually call the former 'dreamers' and repeat the not-so-unrealistic prophecy of failure of Western-style development efforts. The former describe the latter as narrow-minded, non-progressive and non-forward looking.

The concept of development is value-relative. The substratum of development is provided by the fabric of a whole culture, where values are not simply 'economic goods' but much more broad-based. A culture or tradition, as I see it, is like a living organism, an on-going thing, never static or frozen. A culture may be self-conscious as well as self-critical, thereby displaying its vitality, variety and strength. Either due to confrontation with other cultures from outside or the internal tension derived from the in-built paradoxicality of the culture itself, its self-criticism helps it to consider, re-consider, decide, and reject old and new values. Indian culture, I believe, has been mostly self-conscious. The tradition was self-critical, and this helped it to survive. Its pluralism contributed also to its vitality, to tolerance and co-existence, to resistance to change as well as acceptance and assimilation of new ideas, no matter wherever they came from.

In the modern age, development has to be a self-conscious choice. In this context, the most pertinent question that the second group would pose before the first would be this. Should we let ourselves be blown off our feet by the winds of technological development? Or should we let the wind remove the cobwebs of the house but keep our feet firmly on the ground? The metaphor is borrowed form no less a person than Mahatma Gandhi, and perhaps he is the right person to start with.

Gandhi, it is well known, rejected industrialization. But still, as modern Western perceptions assert, Gandhi borrowed a great deal from Tolstoy and Ruskin and owed much of his inspiration to Western sources. Certainly he did. But what is often missed in such appraisals of Gandhi is that it took a traditionally-minded Gandhi to borrow from another culture, if it can be called 'borrowing'. This is of a piece with the social anthropologist's perception of the tradition-bound, hierarchical and tension-free Indian society where Gandhi was a revolutionary and where he had to borrow from Western culture in order to lead the so-called revolution. This perception missed more than it captured. The so-called 'traditional' outlook is in fact a construction. Indian history shows that the tradition itself was self-conscious and critical of itself, sometimes overtly and sometimes covertly. It was never free from internal tension due to the inequalities that persisted in a hierarchical society, nor was it without outside confrontation and challenge throughout its history. Hence Gandhi, Vivekananda and Tagore were not simply 'transplants' from Western culture, products arising solely from confrontation with the West.

Western Indologists and those who practise West-inspired Indology have often used the term Neo-Hinduism. This is also in line with the Western perception of the Hinduism of modern India. It is rather odd that, although the early Indologists' romantic dream of discovering a pure (and probably primitive, according to some) form of Hinduism (or Buddhism, as the case may be) now stands discredited in many quarters; concepts like neo-Hinduism, traditionalism etc.; are still bandied about as substantial ideas or faultless explanatory tools by the Western 'analytic' historians as well as the West-inspired historians of India.

What is being questioned here is the guiding principle in all these appraisals. The unexamined assumption in all this is that, to begin with, there is an unbridgeable gap between the ruler and the ruled, and it is the underdogs or the subjects who borrow, the subdominant group who always emulates the dominant, and side-by-side, the dominant and the more powerful can somehow maintain purity and remain unaffected and uninfluenced, for the confrontation is a 'one-way traffic' of influence and borrowing. This, one could say, even goes against the laws of physics. The guiding principle needs to be challenged if the balloon of complacency of the dominant group is to be punctured. If the principle is challenged, perceptions will also change.

I believe that a hierarchical society based upon inequality and injustice can seldom maintain a tension-free condition for any considerable length of time, and the Indian 'traditional' society was no counter-example to this general thesis. Well-known sociologists like Louis Dumont and his followers have constructed a picture of this hierarchical society and even given an admirable justification for such hierarchy, claiming it to be more 'natural' and more in accord with 'the order of things', and therefore a *value* as opposed to the ideal of equality plus individualism which is imposed by the so-called 'rational' society, which sees 'reason' only in the particular man.[2] Dumont is of course right in insisting, through his commendable structuralist construction, on the inherent hierarchy of Indian society. Once you come to see hierarchy as a *value*, many puzzles about Indian social behaviour today fall into place.

On the necessity of hierarchy, Dumont succinctly argues that 'to adopt a value is to introduce hierarchy, and a certain consensus of values, a certain hierarchy of ideas, things, and people, is indispensable to social life'.[3] This is not necessarily a sort of elitism, but something very similar. Of course we recognize that, in Plato's *Republic*, hierarchy was posited as a value. Dumont's point is probably this. The one-sided ideal of democracy and individualism, which no doubt has generated its own problems, may be balanced by putting adequate emphasis on the other value, hierarchy. Indian society consciously, though imperfectly, 'valorized' it; hence a study of such a phenomenon may also afford insight into the realities of modern societies. Dumont also thinks that hierarchy in India integrated 'the society by reference to its values' and engendered tolerance in Hinduism.[4] The Hindu, for example, accepts pluralism as a fact of life and when faced with a neighbour of a different sort, assigns him a rank, almost a rank within the cosmos, if you like; but Western individualism, so the argument goes, would either approve or exclude, thus intensifying tension.

If Dumont's perception is right, then within the context of the same vocabulary and style, Max Weber's characterization of caste-*dharma* as 'anti-rational', for it denied the 'natural equality of man',[5] must have been wrong. Dumont often refers to Weber with approval, for in the latter, according to Dumont, the sociological *apperception*, i.e., apperception of man as a social being, 'expressed itself in a very indirect fashion' (p. 8). It is not clear however whether Weber's footnote (quoted partially by Dumont) would be an *indirect* endorsement of a Dumontian kind of hierarchy as a value. But Weber no doubt came to appreciate the caste-*dharma* and its linkage with the *karma* doctrine albeit in an indirect way. In his terms, the linkage of *karma* and caste is a pure product or rational ethical thought. It was 'the most consistent theodicy ever produced by history' (op. cit., p. 121). Being excited about the implications of the *karma* doctrine, Weber quoted from the *Communist Manifesto*: '. . . (the proleltariat) have nothing to lose but their chains, they have a world to win'. The same holds for the pious Hindu of low caste; he too can 'win the world', even the heavenly world; he can become a Kṣhatrīya or a Brahmin; he can gain Heaven and become a god—not only in this life, but in the life of the future after rebirth into the same world pattern,' (p. 122).

Caste-hierarchy in Indian society is almost as old as the Vedas. It was, so to say, 'eternally' given. The reference to the castes (along with the evaluative hierarchy) in the *Puruṣa-sūkta* is not just accidental. Here Dumont is right about the fundamentality of the caste-hierarchy in India. The full-fledged *karma* theory was a latecomer in the system. Historically, probably the first reference to an esoteric doctrine called *karma* is found in the *Bṛhadāraṇyaka Upaniṣad*. The proper formulation of it however came later. Recently, J.C. Heesterman has said that the mixture of the two, caste, which Weber rightly described as 'anti-rational', and *karma*, which embodied an ethical rationality of 'just deserts', made the system as a whole 'volatile'. (As opposed to Heesterman, I claim that the social system in India was first 'volatile' and then the *karma* doctrine was introduced to stabilize the combination). Weber seldom mentions the 'paradoxicality' of the said combination. I believe the caste-system itself was already 'volatile' (to borrow the chemistry imagery of Heesterman) even before the introduction of the full-fledged *karma* doctrine was developed as an answer to the *internal* (as well as *external*, e.g. the Śramaṇa critique of Brahmanism) critique within the system; and then the mixture (which Weber referred to) was intended to stabilize the social system and make it coherent. But this stability was short-lived. The introduction of the *karma* doctrine was not entirely rational (*pace* Weber), but a rationalization of an irrational, but maybe 'natural' (Dumont), system. Dumont may be right about the naturalness of the caste-hierarchy but one can hardly agree if it is further claimed that what is 'natural' is always superior (in value) to what is rationally *imposed* ('imposition' is the right word). For everybody, except the lightweight existentialist today, would agree with our Bostonian who was the owner of a beautiful garden. It is said that once a clergyman congratulated him, saying that God above and he below had created a beautiful garden. Our Bostonian gravely replied that the clergyman should have seen what it was like when it was left to God alone. Nature to be sure includes all the three, the good, the bad and the ugly.

Rationalization can make a social system coherent for the time being, but since it always falls short of the ideal, i.e., a *rational* system, it becomes destabilized since it generates its own problems and reactions thereto. *Karma* falls under rationalization, and hence Weber's commendation of it was premature. The trouble started from the beginning. For if hierarchy is to follow the natural line of demarcation of virtues and functions, that of diminishing excellence, then heredity or birth becomes immaterial. But originally hierarchy was heredity-bound. Hence, as early as the *Mahābhārata*, criticism already raised its head. The following story illustrates this point.

In the *Vanaparva*, Yudhiṣṭhira had an encounter with a huge python or boa who was actually King Nahuṣa, one of Yudhiṣṭhira's forefathers. Nahuṣa, through his good deeds and piety, obtained as his reward the throne of heaven, but then his downfall started for he became too proud and forgot the distinction between *dharma* and *adharma*. He kicked at he head of the venerable sage Agastya, and was cursed by being turned into a python for thousands of years. He had been waiting to be saved by Yudhiṣṭhira through a *dharma* discourse. So he got hold of Bhīma and was about to kill him when Yudhiṣṭhira appeared in search of his brother. The fabulous power of Bhīma, that could kill an endless number of demons, elephant, pythons, boas etc., was of no avail. The python said to Yudhiṣṭhira, 'I will let your brother go, if you answer my questions on *dharma*'. So the discourse started. The first question was: what makes a brahmin a brahmin? Yudhiṣṭhira listed a number of virtues—truthfulness, generosity (*dāna*), forgiveness, goodness, kindness, self-control and compassion. A brahmin is one who has all these virtues. The python asked, 'But this goes against the principle of four *varṇas*. For even a *śūdra* may have all these virtues'. Yudhiṣṭhira replied in unambiguous language, 'Indeed, if a *śūdra* is characterized by all these virtues, he is then a brahmin by definition (cf. *lakṣya*). And if a brahmin lacks them, he is to be pointed out as a *śūdra* cf. *nirdiśyate*)'. The python asked again, 'But, if brahminhood is constituted by a number of virtues only, then birth (in a brahmin family) would be in vain'. 'Indeed', was the answer from Yudhiṣṭhira who continued, 'since through sexual urge (*rāga*) people copulate and produce children indiscriminately (in other words, copulation is not always between husband and wife of the same *varṇa*), birth is always a dubious criterion. Therefore, old sages depend upon good conduct (*śila*) as the indicator-reason of a better person. Even a *jātyā* brahmin, by his despicable conduct, would prove to be a *śūdra*'. Yudhiṣṭhira even referred to the 'self-originating' Manu as his authority.

What do we see here? Borrowing apologetically some terms from the so-called subaltern studies, I would say that I hear dissident voices loud and clear even at that early stage. The criticism of the sub-dominant group (in this case, the *śūdras*) surfaced in this manner in the literature which reflected the collective consciousness of society. We must remember that these groups were partially *muted* (to use an expression of a modern sociologist, Edwin Ardener). The language (as well as the literature), which was invariably the language of the dominant group (any language is an Orwellian 'newspeak' in this sense) lacked adequate expression and ways for giving vent to the dissident voices. Hence we have to depend upon oblique and not so oblique references. Viewed in this light, I would read the statement of Kṛṣṇa in the *Bhagavadgītā*, 'I have created the four *varṇas* depending upon the qualities (virtues) and conduct of the people', more as a criticism of the heredity-bound *varṇa* system than as an assertion of an already existing practice.

Another story from the *Rāmāyaṇa* may confirm the point. In the *Uttarakāṇḍa*, which scholars believe to be comparatively late in origin, we find a classic case where the rigidity of the caste-*karma*-oriented *dharma* was seriously challenged. Apparently, the child of a brahmin, in Rāma's kingdom, died a mysterious death. The *Rāmarājya* (Rāma's kingdom) is actually regarded by the tradition as an ideal kingdom where the system of caste-related *(varṇāśrama) dharma* used to operate with perfect smoothness, i.e., *ideally*, in a tension-free manner. This was the dreamland of the protagonists of hierarchical *dharma* in a holistic framework. The term conjures up an image of a perfect society in the Hindu mind. Even Dumont thinks of the ideal village economy system like this: a *jajmāni*-system; and even Gandhi frequently referred to it. But there must have been a serpent already in the paradise of the *Mahābhārata* as well as the *Rāmāyaṇa*.

The untimely death of the brahmin child in the *Rāmāyaṇa* highlighted the tension. Nārada came and unfolded the drama further. Not everything was running smoothly in the system. For, it was pointed out, a *śūdra*, Śambuka by name, was engaged in practising *tapas* (austerities) in the manner of the brahmin sages, in order to obtain a higher station in his next life. (Might he have seen the *Communist Manifesto* in his dream? as Weber anticipated). Anyway, such a transgression, Nārada insisted, created a disturbance in the system, and such disasters as the mysterious death of the brahmin child were bound to happen. Hence Rāma would now have to save the *dharma* system by inflicting death upon that transgressor, Śambuka, the *śūdra*-hermit. According to our *reading* of the text, the tension in the system has already surfaced here and come to a head, as it were. One of the sub-dominant group had already revolted. Hence Rāma, leader of the dominant group, must bring back order.

There was another significant admission from Nārada here. The story-teller further tells us that Nārada said that in *kāliyuga* the right to practise *tapas* or austerities would be given to the *śūdras*. Having obtained the right, they would then practice *tapas* with great enthusiasm. But in *tretāyuga Rāmarājya, śūdras* did not have the right yet. This is obviously a curtain-raiser in our view. Stripped of the *yuga* mythology, the story indicates the indisputable presence of the conflict, tension, the so-called transgression of hierarchy and eventual admission of some degree of equality (notice the concession in the *kāliyuga* that was predicted) in a society which was even hypothetically idealized as *Rāmarājya*.

Dark theocratic and reactionary tendencies are not unknown or lacking in India. In recent times, they are, in fact, more on the surface. In this situation, the social anthropologist's picture, as well as the claim of 'naturalness' and legitimacy that goes along with it, seems to support, no doubt unwittingly, such tendencies, an unfortunate result of which is the revivalism of fundamentalism in Sikh, Muslim and Hindu communities alike today. I see this as a backlash and it may give credence (and even the sense of desirability) to the picture or perception of the development economists. It thinks in terms of a market society that will soon break all unnecessary and outdated (uneconomic) barriers, creating only classes of rich and not so rich 'economic' men, the producers and the consumers, the buyers and the sellers, bowing down to the new social ethos of a presumably 'free for all' community.

The above exercise is not intended to be a critique of either discipline, social anthropology or development economics. I do well recognize that some social anthropolotists have succeeded in refuting the old criticisms, by exercising sufficient care and showing new subtleties and sophistication (Dumont would be one well-known example). Similarly there are sensible development economists who fully appreciate the *problems* of development and 'transfer of technology' and rapid industrialization in a third world society. The pictures I have painted are hypothetical constructs. But the point I am making is not directed against a straw man. For the intelligent laity of both India and the West face genuine difficulties in their perceptions. The problem is that the 'more mystical' reading persists, and the dream of the armchair economist or economic-planer is perpetuated. The middle ground is often lost between them.

If we go back to colonial history again and take even a cursory view of it, some of these points receive substantive support. For example, the Western ruler's perception was mostly infected with the problem of 'double vision', and the colonial subjects' perception of themselves suffered from the perils of fractured vision. First, let us take the colonial government. For administrative and legal purposes, the ruling group's reading of Indian society was guided by considerations of expediency, not ethics or morality or justice. They saw the society as a collectivity of such simple categories as landlords, ryots, traders, buyers and labourers. Notwithstanding whatever good the permanent settlement of Lord Cornwallis did, and also notwithstanding the fact that the rulers made efforts to understand the indigenous system by appointing Sanskrit pandits to collect, collate and produce such compendia as *Vivādabhaṅgārṇava* and *Vivādārṇavasetu* from the labyrinth of the *Dharmaśāstra* and the *Nibandhas* written over more than a millennium, the final settlement of land tenure was based upon a faulty reading which led inevitably to much disruption (the proliferation of *sati* within a short period certainly illustrated this). The pandits collected what they were indirectly asked to collect from the often confounding huge mass of *smṛti* literature. The nature of the questions put to them by the rulers already ensured the outcome.

The same colonial government, on the other hand, meticulously observed the caste and community divisions, and the rather complex web of relationships, when they distributed favours or political powers, e.g., recruited people for the army or other employment. The same policy was followed (later on) when they determined the franchise or made political concessions. Indian critics frequently refer to it as the 'Divide and Rule' policy of the colonialists. This is, however, taking rather a cheap shot at imperialism, a wrong-headed criticism indeed. The ambivalence of the colonial power was obvious enough. The economic man seeks for a homogeneous society of buyers and sellers. The administrators wanted a land-revenue system and landlord-tenant relationship which they could understand and control in the interest of the empire. So they had to disrupt the rather complicated web of the existing social order and impose a structure, presumably Western, which, after a period of initial violence and adjustment, took root and even acquired a local character. On the other hand, the same principle of expediency guided the rulers not only to sustain but also encourage the social divisions, hierarchies, community distinctions and the resultant tensions, where the idea of a free democratic culture, the implementation of which was regarded by the British liberals as desirable, became a myth. Even when the Montague-Chelmsford Reforms came, the same divisive nature of the policy persisted because political concessions were made on the basis of interest groups and their representations. The only reasonable excuse, if it needed one, was the perception that this was after all the *real* India with all its hierarchy, division, communalism, tension and clashes. Hence a sort of *paternalism* on the part of the law-makers and administrators dictated the *volte face*, although it was blatantly hypocritical.

The colonized people had their own share of misperception of their own society. To counter and criticize the ruler's disruptions of the social fabric in village communities, they portrayed and projected an ideal or idealized image of the Indian village community which was deemed to be based upon the principles of justice, if not equality. That is, they had to have respect for each other and have some degree of co-operation. The soil was believed to be community property, where exclusive and alienable freehold title (viz. the so-called Western concept of property) was unknown. Some English intellectuals and Indologists nurtured this image, and the Indians joined it. The Gandhian idea of an idyllic *Rāmarājya* (a slightly different conception from that of the *Rāmarājya* mentioned above) was also of a piece with this image. This, to be sure, was a gross oversimplification of a thoroughly complex phenomenon, if not an unwittingly fabricated falsification. Even a partial knowledge of the *Dharmaśāstras*, written in different centuries, would obviously prove that the 'Golden Age' never existed, but that it was a construction based upon extremely insufficient data. Nor need the *Dharmaśāstras* be regarded as Gospels; they were indeed various *projects* for social planning, or they recorded how the dominant group *wanted* to see the shape of society. In today's terminology, they would have even been blueprints for social engineering. A sober and critical reading of the *Dharmaśāstras*, in fact, contradicts the above *Rāmarājya*-like image, where, as Dumont argues, hierarchy could be a value, being 'natural' and based upon the 'order of things', for it marked 'the conceptual integration of a whole', 'its intellectual cement' (p. 252).

This was undeniably an effective counterpoint on the part of the liberals and Indians in order to embarrass the conscience of the colonial powers, to confront them with the two-faced nature of their policy. It also underlined the ambivalence of both the rulers and the ruled. The competitive force of different religions and ethnic communities, especially of the minorities such as Muslims, Sikhs and others, was boosted by fresh inputs of power and influence. This made inevitable the conflict and tension which no doubt existed already in various forms and at various stages of history, but perhaps not always as all-engulfing as what we saw a few years before the end of colonial rule. But paradoxicality is a central feature of politics. Thus the transference of power resulted in the transference of ambivalence and the earlier hypocrisy of the rulers to the new rulers. The national leaders who perhaps honestly felt that the divisive nature of the colonial policy hindered the emergence of a new India, a unitary and democratic state, themselves resorted to political expedience when they came to power. Without giving much thought to a new alternative and despite the creation of an *almost ideal* constitution, they had to continue the policy of expediency, of power-brokerage among the interest groups and divisive caste and class hierarchies. Of course, constitutional safeguards were initially introduced for protecting the interest of the scheduled castes and tribal people, a species of what today is called 'positive discrimination'. But gradually it became apparent that, not unlike their colonial predecessors, the new rulers were unable to shake off, despite their good intention, the hyporcritical tendency of following a two-faced policy, that of adjusting the new concept of a free democratic culture to be old caste and status hierarchies of society. By perpetuating the politics of interest groups and the distribution of favours and power, they were swallowed up by the tiger instead of riding it. In this we need not assume what apparently the Cambridge (South Asian) historians, John Gallagher *et al.* claim, namely that the professed ideology of nationalism of the old national leaders was simply a 'smoke screen', for their real interest lay in *power*. Without giving in to such a reductionist formula, one can say that the leaders vaguely, perhaps unconsciously, discovered their old misperception of a smoothly running co-operative village community (*jajmāni*-system) and all the rest, but that instead of riding the tide, they sacrificed their ideology and bartered favours for power and were swept off their feet. That things should have moved to some extent despite all these problems, that a modicum of free democratic culture at some level is also visible, in spite of the overall gloom, is itself a miracle.

The perceptions of the Cambridge (South Asian) historians were already heavily loaded against the ideology of Indian nationalism, and were inspired by the partial failure of the free democratic culture to take root in the post-colonial period, as well as by the new hypocrisy, arrogance and tyranny of the new leaders—all this led them to explode what they called the myth of Indian nationalism or the (phony) idealism of the (old) Indian National Congress. This was a rather harsh judgement, but in this, paradoxically enough, they emulated unconsciously to be sure, the Indian intellectuals of pre-Independence India who criticized the hypocrisy inherent in the so-called liberalism of the colonial policy. Of course these historians constructed and concentrated on a new category, power-motivation, and reduced all other hierarchies to this common denominator. The French structuralists would have been more cautious.

Bishop Berkeley once said that it was impossible to imagine (to have an 'image' of) an unperceived tree (*Three Dialogues*). This very general thesis may be debatable, but it nevertheless underlines the point that there are observational bases for most of our sustained images. Hence it has been argued that even the utterly false images must have some observational bases. This view predates the structuralist or the post-structuralist period, but I believe it still has some viability and is well regarded in some quarters. Therefore even when someone claims that the so-called 'images' of India were based upon faulty readings, they still must have had *some* observational bases. I accept this part of the argument fully. If Rudyard Kipling was firmly convinced of the essential difference between East and West and consequently inferred their mutual incompatibility, he must have rightly observed certain aspects (perhaps not too impartially) that reinforced his belief.

Caste-oriented loyalties, commitment to local and ethnic codes, religious superstitions, mystical beliefs and bigotry persist in India much as they persist elsewhere. But our perceptions naturally tend to be selective. As philosophers and art-historians have emphasized, we perceive or observe most of the time what we want or expect to observe. Even artists, painters, performers and magicians are well aware of this phenomenon. For example, we come to see the non-existent water flowing out of the performer's water jug on the stage. The perception of a colonial ruler, a modern social anthropologist, and even a disinterested onlooker, can be selective in this way. Hence the so-called images of India's tradition and culture are certainly not lacking in their observational bases. But to accept them as valid is to take a very simplistic view of a highly complex matter on the one hand and to ignore, or choose to be ignorant of, many other important and cultural characteristics of Indian thought on the other hand. A perception that is selective in a particular way at all times is bound to verge upon bias.

In conclusion we may identify a set of perceptions and conclusions that have questionable value:

1. The East is irrational and emotional, the West rational and logical.
2. India has an atavistic culture while the West nurtures a mature civilization based on reason and science.
3. Indian culture is spiritually profound, which makes up for its lack of logical thinking (William Jones).
4. Such concepts as justice and fairness, privacy and individual freedom, are foreign to the Indian mind (*sic*), which is at best familiar with a sort of crude intuition as a guide to ethical and moral sensitivity.
5. There is an 'Indian mind' which has all sorts of different conceptions and attitudes, not matched anywhere else.
6. The caste-oriented hierarchical society in India has remained well-integrated and thereby for a long time has been tension-free and stable.

Some of these are embodiments of 'half-truths' or problem-ridden perceptions, but all of them need to be revised in the light of modern research and scholarship.

'Half-truths' and problem-ridden perceptions can be regarded as part of the 'bondage' from which we need to free ourselves. The scholar's task, seen in this light, is an on-going work of liberation. The tentative results are in the nature of both critique and reconstruction, activities which, as Nikunja Vihari Banerjee always stressed, lie at the heart of the scholar's *dharma*.

Notes and References

1. Martha C. Nussbaum and Amartya Sen, 'Internal Criticism and Indian Rational Tradition', in Michael Krausz (ed.), *Relativism: Interpetation and Confrontation*, Notre Dame University Press, U.S.A., 1989, pp. 299–325.
2. Louis Dumont, *Homo Hierarchicus* (trans. Mark Salisbury), Weidenfeld and Nicholson, London, 1970, p. 253.
3. Ibid., p. 20.
4. Ibid., p. 252.
5. Max Weber, *The Religions of India: The Sociology of Hinduism and Buddhism* (trans. H. Gerth and D. Martindale), Glencoe, Free Press, *m.*, 1958.

29

Bankimchandra, Hinduism and Nationalism

1. WAS BANKIM A NEO-HINDU?

Was Bankimchandra Chattopadhyay a Neo-Hindu? The question is naturally dependent upon the answer to another general question: who can be called Neo-Hindu? I have always experienced some difficulties in understanding the exact significance of such terms as Neo-Hinduism or Neo-Vedānta. Some time ago, another such term expressed the Indologist's delight in, and fancy for, neo-logism. The offending term was 'Neo-logic', suggested as a monstrous translation of the well-known philosophical system called 'Navya-nyāya'. The translation 'Neo-logic' was misleading on two counts. The first element 'neo-' meant 'new', but this was applied to a philosophical system that was developed in the AD thirteenth century in India. There are of course such proper names in English as 'New College' which is the name of one of the oldest colleges in Oxford. But it may be better to listen to the class-room advice while translating from one language to another: Proper names may be directly borrowed rather than being translated into the second language; besides, a part of a proper name is usually a syncategorematic expression which does not have any meaning in isolation, and a word-for-word translation might create monstrosities. The second expression in 'Neo-logic' is also misleading, if not offensive. The word 'logic' has a specific connotation in current English, and it usually refers to a technical discipline in modern philosophical literature. The discipline is mainly concerned with deductive techniques, with set and model-theory with questions of consistency and completeness of formal systems. The term 'Navya-nyāya', on the other hand, denotes a whole system of philosophy. Although it lays emphasis on a certain theory of inference, it is chiefly concerned with a particular theory of knowledge and evidence (called *pramāṇa*), and an ontology based upon such a theory of knowledge. Besides, it made some innovations in the technical philosophical vocabulary of India. To call such a system simply a 'logic' is extremely misleading to the Western philosophers for whom the translation was supposedly meant.

There are, of course, certain well-entrenched terms in English, which are prefixed with 'neo-'. I have already used one above, 'neo-logism'. 'Neo-Hinduism' has obviously been coined by Indologists and historians following such usages. But I believe, as I shall argue below, that the expression is neither suitable nor adequate for expressing what it intends to express. Besides, it creates a false impression if we wish to characterize the religious belief of people like Bankim (presumably the beliefs he held in the later days of his life) as Neo-Hinduism. And we will see why.

Let us discuss first certain well-established expressions. One such term is 'Neo-classical' or 'Neo-classicalism'. It is used to refer to the revival of classical knowledge, specifically to such a revival of classical taste or treatment in the arts. It particularly marked the renaissance of art and letters between AD fourteenth and the sixteenth century in Europe. Now the term 'Neo-Hinduism' cannot be applied in this sense to what Bankim and his contemporaries apparently professed. For Hinduism had to be dead first in order to be revived. It would be presumptuous to assume that during the time when Bankimchandra wrote, Hinduism was dead and he succeeded in reviving it.

Another term is 'Neo-lithic' where the prefix 'neo-' means 'later' or the later period in history. 'Neo-lithic means, therefore, something belonging to the later Stone Age. Similarly, 'Neo-zoic' means something belonging to the later period of geological history. I believe the late nineteenth century Hinduism can hardly be called 'Neo-Hinduism' in this sense. It would be wrong to assume that it was the *later period* in the history of Hinduism. The Indologists certainly did not have that meaning in their mind.

There is, however, another term, well-entrenched in the philosophical literature, which might come closest to the intended significance that the Indologists and historians might have wanted to attach to their new coinage, 'Neo-Hinduism'. This term is 'Neo-Platonism'. It refers to a philosophical doctrine which flourished in AD third century. It was a sort of a revival of Platonism or Platonic ideas with a mixture of Oriental monism or mysticism. The synthetic as well as syncretic character of this rather short-lived philosophical movement might have acquired for itself the prefix 'neo-' in its title, but I am pretty sure the prefix focuses more on the aspect of revival of certain ideas of Plato than on anything else. 'Neo-Hinduism' during Bankim's time was certainly not a revival of certain old and out-of-fashion ideas of a dead religion. Hence the term is not a suitable one at least in this particular sense.

What I have said above may sound a bit fastidious. For one may say, 'What is in a name?' Indeed. It may be worthwhile at this stage to get down to the serious business. My objection to the use of the term 'Neo-Hinduism' to characterize the late nineteenth-century religious movement of which Bankim was part, is deeper than what has transpired in the above linguistic exercise. First and foremost, Bankim was not a revivalist. It is true that his search for the essential nature of Hinduism came later in his literary career. It may be that in the earlier part of his life he did not consciously engage himself in the critical analysis of his inherited faith. If I am allowed to make a somewhat facetious, but not entirely irrelevant, comment here, I wish to point out that this falls into the pattern of a scheme of life that traditional Hinduism upholds. People should start thinking consciously about their *paramārtha* or quest for a religious goal after the age of fifty. Instead of the adage 'Life begins at fifty', the Hindu prescription was 'Religious life begins at fifty'. Hence Bankim in his mature life was unconsciously following the pattern. I may add that even today we see some Hindus turning very religious all of a sudden towards the later part of their life. Naturally Bankim's interest in the examination of his own faith must be distinguished from some of these Hindus we see around us today. But the point is that Bankim's interest in Hinduism, in looking at it from a rational point of view when he was more mature in life, can hardly qualify him as a 'Neo-Hindu'.

The term 'Neo-Hinduism' in today's usage smacks of either fundamentalism or another not very different movement we see around us today: the 'Born Again Christian' movement. Fundamentalism is a worldwide phenomenon today, it is visible in different world religions with widespread social and political consequences which have a global perspective. It requires little comment. The rise of Hindu fundamentalism tries to match that of fundamentalism in other religions and has been turned into a tool in the hands of opportunist politicians. But we cannot call Bankim a fundamentalist in this sense, which the term 'Neo-Hindu' may imply in today's context. Nor was Bankim a 'Born Again Hindu' in today's sense. In the post-enlightenment period many intellectuals found their faith in Christianity slackened. Some openly denounced their faith. Even a philosopher like Russell had to write a book with the title, *Why I am not a Christian*. Interest among common people in going to churches and synagogues abated considerably. Some tried to find solace in the mystique of certain Eastern religions. Some theologians fought back and tried to moderinize and rationalise some of the Christian beliefs. However, the 'Born Again Christian' seems to be a very modern phenomenon in the West. It involves apparently going back to your roots and searching for a pure form of religion to which you have been born. But unfortunately it has become in most cases a matter of embracing blind faith, which many common people (and even some intellectuals) find preferable, and perhaps understandably so, to drugs or Eastern mysticism or an alien's religion. Again, we cannot call Bankim a 'Neo-Hindu' in this specific sense.[1]

2. HINDUISM AND BANKIMCHANDRA

Hinduism is a multi-faceted, multi-dimensional and multi-form religion. Its uniqueness lies in its infinite variety. It is like a *bodhi*-tree that has grown over the ages and provided shade in the form of religious aspirations for a variety of people and ethnic groups, for numerous communities, intellectuals, individuals and free-thinkers. There being no central or centralized authority or power-base, pluralism has constituted the very essence of Hinduism. Loyalty consists simply in conformity with a particular way of life. Conformity consists in active non-denunciation as well as in constant criticism of each deeply felt and deeply held belief over the ages, not necessary in going to a temple, nor in worshipping daily a particular deity, nor even in getting a guru in the later part of one's life. Living Hinduism has thrived throughout the ages for various reasons. Among other things, I wish to emphasize particularly two factors. One is the internal dynamism, by which I mean the stream of internal rational critique of dogmas and questionable practices, such as caste inequalities. This has found expression in various reform movements, in the rise of various types of *bhakti* cults and sects, from time to time, which often transcend caste or sex barriers, or in some forms of intellectual reformulation and reinterpretations of some basic tenets of Hinduism. The critique has remained alive and in its turn has kept Hinduism alive. The other is the response to, and the power of assimilation of, criticisms and attacks from outside. The *Śramaṇa* movement in general, and Buddhism and Jainism in particular, presented criticisms from outside, and there is enough textual evidence to show how Hinduism responded and re-adjusted itself to the changing circumstances. This dual force (from inside and as well as outside) kept Hinduism alive over the ages. During the time of Bankimchandra, no 'Neo-Hinduism' was formulated or preached. There was the challenge from outside, Christianity and the modern age, along with the internal *critique* which the Hindu intellectuals offered from the vantage point of the newly-gained knowledge of science and the social as well as political philosophy of the West. One of the sources of strength of Hinduism is that it can stand up to dissent. Bankim was one of those intellectuals, in late nineteenth century, who made a contribution that is worth examining today after a long period of more than a century.

Religion is not a matter of much importance to many intellectuals today. On the other hand, it is still a very serious and imposing force and a no less puzzling phenomenon today in world politics, in wars among nations, in civil conflicts as well as in terrorism and domestic politics. It is still a great mobilizing force to reckon with, a political power-base that can be hardly underestimated. This is true of both religious and various religious sects and sub-sects. In the context of all this, the academic study of religion has acquired a new significance in the West, and in many places, it has replaced interest in the study of old Christian theology. Unfortunately, in India, for reasons which are partly historical, the academic study of religion has long been neglected, and its aims and purposes have never been quite clearly understood by intellectuals. For mostly teaching is confused with preaching and hence is left in the hands of would-be proselytisers and priests. A rational approach to the study of Hinduism is thus hardly encouraged. A dogmatic assertion of blind faith, and more frighteningly, a sort of fundamentalism, lies at one end of the scale, while ignorance coupled with indifference, neglect and total rejection lies at the opposite end, and any effort for a rational inquiry falls between the two stools.[2]

What was happening to Hinduism toward the latter half of the last century has many parallels in the history of other living religions. Perhaps Christianity in the late twentieth century is a glaring example which is characterized by change, re-adjustment and vigorous re-thinking by religiously-minded intellectuals. A hundred years ago in the West, Darwinism smashed some of the certitudes of Christian belief. Much earlier even, Galileo's scientific discoveries contradicted some scriptural passages in much the same way. There was always initial violent reaction, but after a while both science and religion co-existed. In the course of time, religious people made compromises and re-asserted their faith in the basic Christian virtues, and in a Christian way of life which was not necessarily crippled with blind practices and superstitions. The century-old belief of some intellectual optimists in the West that science will gradually replace religion has now lost its substance. Freud's revolutionary ideas shook the foundation of certain beliefs, but today Freudianism is on the wane and although it has made some permanent contributions to the world of culture, it is admired more for its imaginative qualities rather than its alleged scientific goals. Even the therapeutic value of Freudianism has been assimilated and is being practised by some of the priests and rabbis with successful returns. I am not talking about the never-changing blind faith of the common people, but the informed activities of these intellectuals who are also believers. Even the 'God is dead' slogan has been theologized with some minute analysis. Last but not least, Marx along with his socialism that not long ago seemed to contain the liberating message, has now been embarrassingly discredited. USSR and China are gradually shedding their past precepts, and the doors of various churches are re-opening.

The Western challenge that Hinduism faced during the days of Bankim and his contemporaries is not very different from the modern challenge to Christianity. Bankimchandra, towards the later part of his life, was both an intellectual and a believer. He was incapable of embracing any blind faith and hence spared no pains to rationalize his deeply-felt beliefs. His early rejection of religion made the task all the more difficult and important. It is interesting to see how he came to assert the following:

> I think no religion has been formulated by God nor has it been divinely revealed. I accept that there is a natural basis for all religions. But at the same time, I admit that Hinduism is the best of all religions.[3]

The ambivalence, as well as the blatant contradiction, in these three sentence is obvious. In this essay, *Kon Pathe Jaitechi* he was trying to divide religions into two groups: those that are claimed to be revealed by God, and those that do not make this claim but have a basis in Nature (*nisarga*). In the first group he placed Christianity, Judaism, Islam and Brahminism. In the second group he placed Buddhism, Brahmo Samaj, Comte's religion and a sort of intellectual Hinduism which he himself believed in. His first category is well-known. Almost all religions are said to be divinely ordained, and his mistrust in such religion is re-assertion of his faith in human rationality and criticism. Rightly he separated Buddhism (but he forgot to mention Jainism), which did not make that claim. But it is slightly difficult to understand what he meant by 'natural' religion. Was he influenced by David Hume's use of the term in a similar context? It would be more useful to distinguish between the divinely-ordained religions and the rationally-based religions. Perhaps, this is what he had in mind. The error that consisted in making Vedic Brahminism 'divinely ordained' in the same sense as Judaism and Christianity is perhaps minor enough to be ignored. But contradiction lies in the fact that, on the one hand, he admirably insisted upon the rational-cum-natural basis of any religious faith, and on the other hand, claimed superiority of Hinduism to any other religion. It may be an admirable instance of his loyalty. Besides, it might have been aimed at some of his contemporaries who, under the influence of Western education, coupled with the complete ignorance of their own religious texts, lost faith, much like most post-enlightenment Christian intellectuals, in their own religious tradition.

Bankim himself was aware of the contradiction, and that is why he acknowledged the problem and proceeded to formulate an elaborate interpretation of various factors of Hinduism to show how they can be rationalized. What appeared reasonable and rational to Bankim towards the end of the last century may not, and most of the time does not, appear to be so to us today. But that is not the issue here. It is undeniable that he studied most extensively not only the works of well-known Western philosophers of his time, Comte, Herbert Spencer, J.S. Mill, and Bentham, but also the Vedas, the epics, the *purāṇas*, and the *dharmaśāstras*, in the search for a rational reconstruction of what he himself thought to be the *true* religion of Hinduism. He chose the theistic side of Hinduism and identified the monotheistic stream with Kṛṣṇa as the Supreme Being who is at the same time the Supreme Man. Hence, naturally, it is a sort of intellectual Vaiṣṇava devotionalism which has also a strong humanistic overtone. He expended a considerable amount of time and intellectual energy writing an almost modern commentary on the colossal epic, the *Mahābhārata*, to chisel out the character of Kṛṣṇa, the Supreme deity after his heart: *Kṛṣṇa-caritra*. His Kṛṣṇa was, however, a different kind of Kṛṣṇa; he was the Perfect Man, the Perfect Diplomat and the Perfect Upholder of Justice. He rejected in a somewhat high-handed manner everything else in the epics and the *purāṇas* about Kṛṣṇa (including the *Vṛndāvana-līlā*) as spurious or interpolations by later hands. In his words, whatever his late nineteenth-century sense of decency did not find congenial, was declared as only an *upanyās* (a fiction). Most of his arguments in his *Kṛṣṇa-caritra* would be found unacceptable and wrong today.

We must not, however, forget that Bankim's genius was a match for almost everything. His versatility was simply astonishing. He was, to begin with, a novelist, a writer, an essayist, as well as a literary critic. Rabindranath said about him that he was a *savya-sācī* who could use both hands with equal dexterity, one hand for creating the beautiful and the other for destroying the ugly. In other words, he was both a writer and a critic.

With one hand he was keeping the flame (of literary creation) alive, and with the other he himself took the responsibility of removing the cloud of smoke and ashes (i.e. of weeding out by criticism bad pieces of literature).[4]

In the role of social critic and social philosopher, he equipped himself adequately by studying almost all the available Western writings. Although he was deeply influenced by Comte and perhaps to a lesser extent by the classical Utilitarians, he never reproduced them in his own writings without the unmistakable marks of originality. Even in the world of thinkers he was not a 'copyist'. In *Kamalakanter Daptar* he wrote in a humorous vein a critique of Bentham's view by pointing out its lacunae. His concern for India's downfall and intellectual poverty (not to speak of the poverty as such of her people) led him in the earlier part of his life to study the classical philosophies of India in their Sanskrit originals. He admired the fact, unlike the popular belief, they were not all spiritual mythology or abstract and speculative metaphysics (a fact which he came to like sometime later in his life, although from a different point of view, and at a more sophisticated level) and that in Nyāya, Buddhism and Sāṃkhya, prime importance was given to reason and there was the rational examination of evidence called *pramāṇa-śāstra.* In his eagerness to discern a causal explanation of India's decline, he criticized that even these splendid potentialities (lying in the classical systems) to develop experimental science, and saw the material progress of the country as lost due to their subservience to the Vedas and a blind fascination for Nature myths, which subverted the empirical search for the means of material happiness.

3. THE NINETEENTH CENTURY AND INDIA

Whether he was right or wrong in this analysis is not a matter that should detain us here. Only a few years later he himself changed his opinion and acknowledged that there were some substantive issues discussed in classical Indian philosophy, and that Hinduism contained some elements which were 'superior' to similar elements in other religions. During Bankim's time, perception of the Western superiority in material culture, political power and social ethics was almost axiomatic and self-evident for any educated Indian. Equally self-evident was the comparative moral degradation and social inequality and religious superstition of India itself. Under such circumstances, the question naturally arose in the mind of *concerned* (Indian) intellectuals (and Bankim was one of them) about what could have been the root cause of India's decline and degradation. The interesting thing, however, was that the formulation of the question itself presupposed the answer. Was India really in decline at that time in history? If there was a decline, one may ask: Decline from what? Was the situation very different from pre-industrial revolution Europe? Were the social inequalities and social injustice very different from those in pre-enlightenment and, for that matter, post-enlightenment, Europe? (A caste system is not the only form of social injustice.) It is true that the progress in material science and the consequent advance in technology in Europe was not matched in India. But then few historical incidents can have parallels simultaneously in different parts of the world. Besides, there was no real centralized power-base in India before the establishment of colonial rule. There was also no aggressive nationalism. Nor was there any competent monarch with a well-established government as well as with an indomitable urge to build empires. There were many regional skirmishes between petty Nawabs and chiefs over small territorial disputes and occasional resistance from ridiculously small and weak chiefs or kings (each of whom again was engaged in internal fights, and never united against the British or the foreign rule). The empire-builders experienced very little resistance, which made it easy for the foreign power to colonize a vast area under a centralized power-base. In fact, there was no *real* India as we know it today or even as we dream of today.

Further, small chiefs and kings very seldom established or patronized educational institutions at that time. Due to the rigidity of the caste system, education was restricted to the upper class. But that was true also directly or indirectly of many Western nations. The important question is: what kind of education was available even to the upper class? Short of state patronage, education was left in the hands of denominational religious institutions and the pupils concentrated upon sectarian texts (various brands of Vaiṣṇavism and Śaivism in the case of Hinduism) and upon clever polemics against other sects. Education was mainly theocentric, except in the case of Buddhism, Jainism and Navya-nyāya, while the latter were engaged in abstract enquiries into logic and metaphysics rather than into physics or material science. Teaching of social ethics was in the hands of poorly paid priests, who were more after the patronage of rich people or small kings than anything else. Royal patronage or any other kind of monetary patronage from the rich used to come only to sycophants who would compose, for example, Sanskrit verses in flattery of the would-be patrons. Such a situation was hardly congenial to inspired scientific discovery and experiment with some inspired guesses about the properties of matter. All this shows that the simplistic assumption of the late (or mid-) nineteenth century intelligentsia (and Bankim was no exception), viz., that certain features of the Hindu intellectual tradition were responsible for India's decline, was somewhat wrongly headed. It seems to me to be a wrong answer to a wrongly formulated question.[5]

The other, and more pervasive, platitude in late nineteenth century India was to claim a monopoly of superior moral and spiritual values for the East to contrast with the Western conquest of the entire world in the political and cultural spheres. Here, again, it was part of a more universal phenomenon. As Raychaudhuri has remarked, 'Such claims, emphasizing moral rather than spiritual superiority, were part of a fairly universal response to the threatened victory of the West, political and cultural, in many parts of the world from Russia to Japan' (p. 137). Raychaudhuri, however, has rightly pointed out that Bankim's intellectual quest into India's past was too serious to fall for such 'simple clichés' as spiritual superiority. On the other hand, political subjection (under one superior Western power, which, inadvertently to be sure, contributed to the dream of a previously non-existent political unity under one *free* government) as well as the resultant desire for a sort of national regeneration, requires necessarily, among other things, a sense of pride. This pride again (in the case of India) has to be shared commonly by a very heterogeneous group of people with different backgrounds, having different ethnic origins and different languages. It has to be shared by the rich and poor, by the literate and illiterate alike, if all the members of this heterogeneous group are going to form a 'nation'. The commonness, which is another essential requirement for fostering the sense of unity, was superimposed by a force from outside, by the ruling power, upon heterogeneous groups of people, where each member together with the rest experienced in a similar manner, for a long time, whatever good or bad the colonial rule generated for the country. But this was not enough. An internal force must be at work to bring different groups of people under a common bond, a *nation*, even if that bond had to be forged. A sense of pride was well suited for the purpose. But a sense of pride in what? What else could it be, if not the pride in our own heritage—our 'national' heritage—and 'national heritage' for most of the nineteenth century Hindu intelligentsia meant the religious and philosophical past of India's oldest and most pervasive religion, Hinduism. Hence the Hindu intellectuals sought pride in their Hindu heritage to counterbalance the sweeping powers of 'copy-cat' Westernization of the educated people. However, they made the obvious mistake (for it was unfortunately *not* obvious to them) of taking a very one-sided approach to national regeneration and national unity by emphasizing the Hindu heritage and classical scholarship and thus ignoring the Muslim heritage. It may be said in their support that the idea of 'one nation' vs 'two-nation' theory was not yet formulated and hence it did not enter into serious consideration. However, even when the idea was formulated and the leaders still dreamt of an undivided 'free' India, the emphasis of those involved in the national movement on such slogans as 'Bande Mātaram' (conceived and popularized by Bankim), and on glorification of 'Shivaji Utsav', did not help at all the national unity (for they went directly against the Muslim sentiments). But this is going to take us away from our main topic.

4. NATIONALISM AND RELIGION

I believe an explanation has been given above about how intellectuals like Bankim, having first dismissed in their youth Hindu religion and mythology, holding it to be directly responsible for the *perceived* backwardness of the 'nation', and the resultant political subjection and humiliation, came back later on in their life in search of a basis for the required national pride. (A few years ago, the black intellectuals of America tended to get back to their *roots* in search of a similar basis for the pride needed to integrate the black movement.) The ambivalence (sometimes resulting in a lack of proper understanding) of the late nineteenth century Hindu intellectuals towards the largest minority, the Muslims, towards their ambitions and fears, has already been noted.[6] However, Bankim's re-discovery and glorification of the rational tradition of Hinduism was perhaps not simply the thought-process of a person who has entered (intellectually, at least) the *Vānaprastha*[7] stage of his life. It would be wrong, in my opinion, to take such a simplistic view. Rather, I believe it was part, and an integral part at that, of a larger programme he dreamt of, a sort of national regeneration or awakening against the colonial power. His own re-affirmed religious faith might have, as often is the case, cooperated, but that is not the issue here. Idiosyncrasy as an unconscious motivation often unlocks the door to something which has a greater scope and nobler purposes. It is significant to note that some recent historians have analysed the phenomenon of nationalism as a fusion of political and religious sentiments. In the history of the world, it has often been seen that nations are held together, sometimes, by religious ties alone. Salo Baron has noted in this context:

> Positively or negatively, religions served as the most powerful vehicle of both nationalization and denationalization, while receiving in turn enormous stimuli from the patriotic, ethnic and cultural loyalties of their adherents.[8]

This has been particularly true of colonized India, as a result of which partition took place (an example of de-nationalization, perhaps).

Bankim acknowledged clearly that nationalism was one of the few 'jewels' (*ratna*) which we had to learn from the 'thought-world' (*jñāna-bhāṇḍār*) of the West.[9] He was also very critical (in his later writings) of the limitations of rampant and uncontrolled nationalism. However, there was no doubt in his mind that a benign form of nationalism was needed in India if there was to be any hope for fulfilling her political ambition. He put his finger, rightly according to some, upon religion and identified the contribution that a nationalized and reformed form of Hinduism could make towards such an end. The same spirit gave us the song as well as the slogan 'Bande Mātaram'.[10]

Nationalism has many stripes. Under varying historical circumstances it has taken different forms, although originally it had an ethical basis. It was born of a humanitarian concern for justice and freedom for a particular group. For example, struggle against a colonial power generated one form of nationalism (India was a prime example), struggle against economic oppression, which generates an ideology of liberation from structured poverty and exploitation in a society, gave rise to another form of nationalism (witness modern nationalism as a social force in Mexico and other Latin American countries). Besides, struggle against a hegemony of foreign origin, which had a different stripe from that of colonial oppression, gave rise to the recent Polish Catholic nationalism. In Latin America, the movement has been called recently 'liberation theology'. Thus, the important factor to note in all these forms of nationalism is what is common among them—that the re-affirmation of an old religious faith had a role to play. In this sense, Bankim's intuition went in the right direction, no matter how much idiosyncratic and unacceptable his own 'reformed' or 'nationally reconstructed' Hinduism may seem to us today. Gandhi is another person who had an intuitive grasp of the effectiveness of religious sentiment in a political movement. In fact, Gandhi (although his method was very different from that of Bankim) believed, probably at the level of his unconscious, that fusion of religion and politics was essential for the birth of nationalism, which explained, in part at least, why he followed the path that he did follow in politics. Sometimes, nationalism grows out of ethnic separatism as well as economic oppression, where religion may not play any part. This was the case with

Bangladesh. If Bangladesh was an exception to the general pattern that I have tried to outline above, we must also recognize that an exception proves the rule. The baneful effects of nationalism, where it degenerates into militarism and new imperialism indulging in self-aggrandizement and most brutal forms of oppression, violence and genocide, are too obvious and too well-known to be repeated here.

5. BANKIM'S HINDUISM AND NATIONALISM

I have explained how Bankim's attempt at a rational reconstruction of Hinduism, which occupied most of his literary effort towards the latter part of his life, could have been at least partially connected with his unconscious wish to see a rise of nationalism in India, that would free her from colonial rule. He read extensively the works of the Western Indologists, and his purpose was to expose fallacies in their conclusions, for he rightly pointed out that, due to their Christian bias, they prejudged every issue, mistook hypotheses for conclusions and then went around searching for evidence selectively in their favour, ignoring, often, a massive amount of counter-evidence. It is true that the Indologists created some of their own concepts for explanatory purposes within their own theories. In fact, they created, to use current vocabulary, a *discourse* of their own. Although Bankim was critical of some of their theories in order to argue in favour of his *a priori* theories, he was in fact playing the 'same game'. Despite his vigorous effort for a project that had a laudable aim in view, Bankim's method, as well as the end product, was faulty on two counts. First, instead of questioning the explanatory principle of Indology as a whole he turned himself into an Indologist in order to argue with them. It did not occur to him that the prevalent Indology might not be suitable for his purpose: for example, what relevance, one may ask, had such topics as the historical date of the Kurukṣetra war, the historicity of the Pāṇḍavas and Kṛṣṇa? Second, he was guilty of the same offence as his opponents in another respect. He too had his own pre-conceived conclusions for which he selected his evidence; he rejected, as I have already noted, as 'spurious' or 'interpolations', almost all the sections of the *Mahābhārata*, the *Bhāgavata-purāṇa* and the *Harivaṃśa* that did not support or fit into the picture of Kṛṣṇa that he had in his own mind. His puritan mind had a very different picture of Kṛṣṇa, which he thought would be most suitable for his own brand of Hinduism. Although he was wrong in this matter, one feature stood out. His was a rational approach and he carefully avoided the extreme fantasy of some Hindu fanatics of his own time. Rabindranath noted in his memoir called *Jīvansmriti* how Bankim distanced himself quickly from the 'Neo-Hindu' movement of such pandits as Śaśadhar Tarkacūḍāmaṇi who wanted to show by their bizarre logic how every superstition of Hinduism was actually anticipatory of modern science and how the superstitious Hindu interpretation of every sneeze or the noise made by every house lizard was based upon advanced knowledge, which the West had just discovered as science:

> During this time at Calcutta Śaśadhar Tarkacūḍāmaṇi appeared on the scene. I first heard about him from Bankimbabu himself. I recall it was Bankimbabu who introduced me to him. At that time, the Hindus in order to prove the superiority of their own religion, tried to make fantastic claims by citing evidence from Western science; and within a very short period this movement became all pervasive. For a long time before this, however, it was theosophy which created the background for such a movement. It was not the case, again, that Bankimbabu was able to join this movement completely. No shadow of Tarkacūḍāmaṇi darkened the kind of explanation of religion that he was attempting at in the journal called *Prachār*; for this was altogether impossible.[11]

This shows that although Bankim was initially taken by this type of crazy attempt, the spell was very short-lived. Bankim's intellectualism was of a much higher order.

The cryptic comment of Rabindranath about the theosophists throws light upon another important aspect. Even today we hear a lot about the contrast between Western materialism and Indian spiritualism, as well as about the claim of India's superiority in the field of spirituality, which, our leaders have too often emphasized since the late nineteenth century, makes up for its lack of rationality and development of material science. The origin of this rather platitudinous attitude had obvious causal links with the euphoria about theosophy (declarations of such Western people as Mrs A. Besant and Madame Blavatsky about the great spiritual superiority of Hinduism), as well as with the glowing tribute paid to ancient Indian wisdom by Indologists such as William Jones and Max Müller. I seriously hold that this is only a platitude, which had gradually become pervasive and persistent, and it has perpetuated the common Western perception of the mysterious and mystical East. The fact of the matter is that materialism and spiritualism, rationality and irrationalism-cum-intuitionism, are monopolies of neither India nor the West.[12] It might also be noted that the above pre-conceived idea of the West about India's heritage has been so well-entrenched that, whenever there is a reference to classical Indian philosophy, even today, despite the fact that considerable progress has been made in modern research in this area and materials are available to some extent in some European languages, professional Western philosophers almost instinctively think of obscure and irrational claims about spiritualism, mythology, and at best some highly speculative metaphysics. For the same reason, the fact that a considerable portion of classical Indian philosophy contained a highly sophisticated rational tradition, that its method was empirical and epistemological, and that it had a serious concern for philosophical logic and philosophical semantics is often left out, unnoticed and unrecognized in modern philosophical parlance.

When the Western-style education system was introduced in India through the efforts of people like Macaulay, we should note that the emphasis was liberal arts, literature and the humanities (the idea was to create a number of excellent and loyal bureaucrats). There was much less enthusiasm about experimental science and technological development. For the industrial West needed a ready market in the colonies, as well as supply of raw material to feed its industries, not any competition in technology or in the production of goods from the colonies. Thus there remained for a considerable period of time a gap in the knowledge of experimental science and technology in colonial India. The point is that it is wrong to speculate and cite the other-worldliness of India's philosophical tradition as a scape-goat, i.e., as one of the possible causal factors explaining the gap in such knowledge and the lack of the spirit of experiment with material elements. There was indeed a lack of interest in the deductive method in their logical inquiry, and hence interest in discovering the theoretical foundation of mathematics was never developed. Besides, perhaps due to an undue separation of theory from practice, that is, lack of communication between the theoreticians or philosophers and the craftsmen or proto-technicians of the day (rigid caste distinctions might possibly account for this lapse), there was also an unfortunate lack of interest in the higher circle of classical Hinduism in practical and realistic calculation and measurement of the material elements. Hence Bankim, in a sense, was right when he remarked, referring to Torricelli and Pascal and their experiment which led to the discovery of atmospheric pressure:

> A Hindu philosopher in Torricelli's place would have contented himself with simply announcing in an aphoristic *sūtra* that the air had weight. No measure of the quantity of its pressure would have been given; no experiment would have been made with mercury; no Hindu Pascal would have ascended the Himalayas with a barometric column in hand.[13]

It is paradoxical to note that the lack of interest in deductive systems or formal science was compensated well enough by their avid interest in discovering the epistemic and empirical basis of logic, by their study of the theory of knowledge and the theory of evidence called *pramāṇa-śāstra* (which was more akin to the inductive method based on observation and citation of supporting example). Thus, contrary to the general preconceived idea (and Bankim himself held such an idea also), I must say that the philosophical background (reinforced by the doctrine of the *pramāṇas*) was favourable towards the development of experimental science (though not for formal science). Unfortunately, other external factors intervened and stultified the growth of the natural sciences, for the spirit of experiment stopped at a certain level, and the technicians or proto-technicians lacked the basis of knowledge and the principles of logic to grasp and spell out for others the significance of any intuitively gained truths or any practical knowledge and skill they possessed. There was a great divide between the 'theoreticians' and the 'practitioners'. Only in one area was this great divide partly bridged and some progress was hence achieved. This was the science of medicine and disease: Āyur-veda.[14]

6. CONCLUDING REMARKS

Bankim was an outstanding literary figure who wrote some of the best novels in Bengali literature. He was a patriot and, above all, a thinker. At the celebration of his 150th birthday, it is incumbent upon us that we re-acknowledge our intellectual debt to his genius, as well as re-examine his contributions. I have mainly concentrated upon his reconstruction of Hinduism and its possible link with his burning patriotism. Hinduism has meant many things to many people over a very long period. It is the very nature of Hinduism that it allows for such freedom of thought, for such diversities. Now-a-days, in the academic circles concerned with the study of religion, religious pluralism has for some time been a much discussed topic. Hinduism has been openly pluralistic. Bankim's reconstruction in the light of his newly-acquired knowledge from Western philosophy was not an entirely new phenomenon as such. Hinduism has been adjusting itself to new environments for many ages. For its internal critique has been alive, to accept and absorb the external challenges. This feature constitutes the essence of Hinduism. I shall conclude with a statement of Bankim which has a lasting value and with which I whole-heartedly agree:

Two and only two aphoristic statements may express the ethics of the human being. One is concerned with the self, the other with the others. What concerns the self may be called the root of self-purification. Since the latter concerns itself with the others, it may be called the root of religious ethics. 'Do not harm others, try to do good to others as much as you can'—this great statement contains the root of all religious texts (all scriptures), and they all also culminate in the expression of this great truth. What morality you may talk about, it will begin and end here. (Besides), the principle of self-purification can also be unified with this great truth of morality.[15]

This undoubtedly captures a very essential truth about morality and religion.[16]

Notes

1. It is reassuring to note that T. Raychaudhuri in his excellent book, *Europe Reconsidered*, also talks about his reservations, though very briefly, regarding the use of such terms as 'Hindu revivalism', pp. 9–10.
2. For a long time I had doubts as to whether the study of religion should be a 'university' subject in Indian universities; but in view of the present-day happenings in social and political fields, I am now sympathetic to the idea of opening departments for the study of various world religions.
3. This is from his 'Devatattva O Hindudharma', *Bankim-Rachanāvalī*, 1969, p. 792.
4. 'Adhunik Sahitya', *Rabindra-Rachanāvalī*, XIII, 1966, p. 894.
5. Tapan Raychaudhuri has rightly identified this platitude and put it as follows: there was, according to these thinkers, 'an obvious causal link between specific dimensions of the Hindu intellectual tradition and national decline' (*Europe Reconsidered*, p. 139).
6. Raychaudhuri notes that Bhudev was, to some extent, an exception. To put it facetiously, Bhudev was a *new* Mīmāṃsaka while Bankim was a *new* Naiyāyaka of late nineteenth-century Bengal. Hence it is not surprising that Mīmāṃsā-type orthodoxy would find orthodoxy in other religions also defensible. I believe Bhudev's recognition of Muslim rights, despite the touch of levity in the remarks just made, can also be explained.
7. A retirement in pursuit of the religious goal or the ultimate meaning of life.
8. S. Baron, 1960, p. 7.
9. 'Bharat Kalanka', last paragraph, *Bankim Rachanāvalī*, II.
10. An incidental comment: even this particular identification has a parallel in other parts of the world; the Soviet mythology of Holy Mother Russia is sometimes regarded as a more powerful force than Bolshevik ideology, although this may be debatable.
11. *Rabindra Rachanāvalī*, X, p. 115.

12. See my 'Images of India: Problems and Perceptions', 1990.
13. *The Study of Hindu Philosophy, in Bankim-Rachanāvalī*, p. 146. Dr Raychaudhuri also draws our attention to this remark (p. 157). I am however making a different comment here, as can be gathered from what follows.
14. Thus it is not surprising that the *Caraka-Saṃhitā*, the principal compendium on Āyur-veda, contains as elaborate chapter on *pramāṇas* and logic.
15. 'Bhālobasār Atyāchār', *Bankim Rachanāvalī, II*, p. 216.
16. I have made a brief explanatory comment on this passage in an article in *Desh* (a Bengali Weekly, 16 April 1988), entitled *Hindūdharma Bahujanasevita Baṭabrikṣer cchāyā*.

References

Baron, Salo W., *Modern Nationalism and Religion*, New York; Meridian Books, 2nd edn., 1960.

Chattopadhyay, Bankimchandra, *Bankim Rachanāvalī*, part *II*, ed. J.C. Bagal, Sahitya Samsad edn., Calcutta, 1969.

———, *English Works*, ed. J.C. Bagal, Calcutta, 1983.

Matilal, Bimal, 'Images of India: Problems and Perceptions', in *The Philosophy of N.V. Banerjee* (ed. Margaret Chatterjee), Indian Council of Philosophical Research, Delhi, 1990, pp. 1–15.

———, *Hindūdharma bahujana-sevita baṭavrkṣer chāyā*, *Desh*, 16 April 1988.

Raychaudhuri, Tapan, *Europe Reconsidered*, Oxford University Press, Delhi, 1988.

Tagore, Rabindranath, *Rabindra Rachanāvalī*, Janma-śata-vārṣik edn., Government of West Bengal, Calcutta, 15 vols, 1961–66.

30

Radhakrishnan and the Problem of Modernity in Indian Philosophy

In 1923, Bertrand Russell, in a review of Radhakrishnan's first volume of *Indian Philosophy*, commented:

His work is admirably done, though, perhaps, for English readers, it would have been well to give more account of the political history which accompanied the successive schools of philosophy. One of the main documents of Buddhism is the 'Questions of King Milinda,' this was the Greek King Menander, of the end of the second century B.C. The Western reader wishes to know what influence Greek philosophy had on Buddhism, the more so as Buddhist art suffered a powerful Hellenic influence; but on this subject the book contains no information.

This appeared in *The Nation and the Athenaeum* on 15 September, 1923. About 65 years later, the question that Russell asked still remains unanswered. In this regard, at least, we have not done anything better than Radhakrishnan did at that time.

The question had two distinct parts. Both parts, I venture to add most respectfully to Russell, whom I regard as one of the greatest philosophers of modern times, had originated unconsciously from a Western bias. Recently, when I have lectured at various philosophy departments in Western universities, I have frequently faced almost the same question, in almost identical language. It seems that with the majority of professional Western philosophers today, the Western understanding of Indian philosophy has not progressed much further.

The first part of the question relates to the political history of India and perhaps it is a valid question that springs from a genuine spirit of inquiry.

But the fact is that the so-called different *schools* of Indian philosophy did not originate under different political regimes, as far as we can tell. Or if they did, their history or pre-history is entirely lost to us. And it would certainly be of interest if we could, by a miracle, recover that history. But the question is why is that question important? I believe it assumes importance in the background of an implicit premise that those who are doing Indian philosophy today are at best historians of philosophy and at worst historians of ideas or cultural anthropologists. There is, of course, some truth in the idea that political and, of course, social realities exert an influence upon the philosophical doctrines that developed in a particular age. And this could be an interesting line of research, uncovering in it hidden peculiarities of such philosophical ideas. Russell's mistake, repeated by many today, was not to see that the basic philosophical systems developed within a very short span of time, if not all together, and that there was a continuous on-going philosophical dialogue among the upholders of different schools or positions for over a millennia, in fact for 14 hundred years or more; meanwhile political history in India was as varied and different as it could be. In such a situation, it is impossible to find any direct link between the political upheavals (such as the Muslim conquests, wars between small states, and despots coming to power) and the philosophical concerns of the age. This is a drawback and perhaps had something to do with the nature of philosophy in India in general, which was concerned with epistemology, logic and metaphysics, but not so much with moral or social philosophy. (Moral and social concerns, however, were not completely absent. Such concerns are often reflected in the literature, in different versions of the epics, and in the narrative literature. But this is another issue.)

The second part of the question is a non-starter. I have often faced it while talking about logic and epistemology: 'what influence Greek philosophy had on Indian philosophy.' The plain truth is that we do not know, and perhaps, there was not any influence either way. Had there been any, we could have found out by now. May be, some day, some Indologist will discover a Sanskrit text written in the beginning of the Christian era, which would be translation of Plato's *Republic* or Aristotle's *Metaphysics* or *Prior Analytics*. Then we would know. But until then let us assume that there wasn't any influence. Yes, the Hellenic influence on the Buddhist art is discernable. But in philosophy, Buddhism was an Indian product. Its origin has been well-documented.

In fact there might have been some influence, very indirect as it was, the other way around. Some have mentioned (although it has not been well-authenticated or proven beyond reasonable doubt) that Pyrrho (or Sextus Empiricus) was influenced by the Indian sceptics, or that the Neo-Plationists had absorbed some influence from the Mahāyāna Buddhism or the Upaniṣads. That is marginally possible. Russell's question was already loaded for he was moved by the Hellenic influence on the Buddhist art. However when I face today this question of possible Hellenic influence on Indian philosophy or Indian philosophers, and I have presented a paper or given a lecture on the contribution of an Indian philosopher of say ninth or tenth century AD to the ongoing debate on epistemology in India, I feel somewhat at a loss about how to answer or react.

The problem of modernity in Indian philosophy today cuts deeper here. A large section of those who are working today on Indian philosophy should be regarded not as mere historians of ideas, but philosophers in their own right who are deriving insights and inspirations from their close study of the classical Indian tradition. Many of those who are doing Greek or scholastic philosophy today are also regarded as philosophers in their own right. The same should hold for the Indian philosophers. And I believe such questions as those about Greek influence tend to deflect from the philosophical issues and hence the main points made in a paper or a book are thereby glossed over. (Russell did the same while reviewing Radhakrishnan's book, as noted above.)

There is another point to be made here. Historical issues are of course important within a tradition. And I for one would not dream of undermining them at all. But philosophical problems are in the habit of recurring at different times in different contexts, and it is interesting to see why they recur and how far they take on the contextual colouring and to what extent they transcend contexts. Study of Indian philosophy is also important in the light of these observations.

A brief comment on the problem of interpretation. Indologists for a long time have been taking others to task for distorting, misrepresenting and anachronistically reading new ideas in the old texts by taking them out of context. And surely there is a danger of misinterpretation if we do not keep within our view the age of the textual material. But the old Indological idea of discovering scientifically, through archaeological excavations, as it were, the *virgin meanings* of the texts, in their pristine purity, has by now been exploded. And some modern hermeneutic philosophers have gone so far as to say that there is no original meaning of the texts anyway, for the meaning is what you make of it today; or even that the meaning percolates through the mind of the reader, modern or ancient. While I do not endorse this extreme view completely, for I do not fully understand it, I believe this would have a sobering influence upon the Indological criticism of some modern interpreters' representations. Any outstanding philosophical text would be rich with ambiguities, so that it would admit of several, sometimes contesting, interpretations. Indian philosophical texts should be edited, re-edited, translated, interpreted and reinterpreted several times over by a number of scholars over a few generations; then and then only I believe would we be talking with confidence about such outstanding philosophers as Nāgārjuna, Dharmakīrti, Uddyotakara, Udayana, Śaṃkara, Kumārila, Vācaspati Miśra and Gaṅgeśa. Nowadays when we write a book on Indian philosophy we still talk in terms of different schools, as Radhakrishnan did: Vedānta, Nyāya, Bauddha, and Mīmāṁsā. A lot of spade work has still to be done. In the near future, if the research programmes are satisfactory, one may pay attention more fully to the individual philosophers I have listed above. This would be a welcome outcome of the kind of research started by Radhakrishnan along with many others a couple of generations ago.

I now move on to Sarvepalli Radhakrishnan. He was probably the only person in recent history who, from being well-known as a professional philosopher, came to be the head of a state, President of India; and I might add, without being unnecessarily reticent about my own country, that India is probably the only place where this could happen. A man does not have to devote his entire life in politics and public work in order to be the head of state. Plato's idea of a philosopher-king could be a distinct possibility in the case of India.

Radhakrishnan was primarily a philosopher concerned with such broader issues as whether the task of philosophy should be only *interpreting* life or changing it as well; what role, if any, religion should pay in contemporary philosophy, and what is the meaning of life, spirit and freedom. By his own admission, he was mostly influenced by Śaṃkara, Rāmānuja and Madhva of classical India, as well as by Plato, Plotinus and Kant in the West. In spite of his abiding interest in classical India, he was more a creative thinker than a classical scholar. He used the comparative method, being well-aware of its limitations as well as the difficulties involved in any adequate historical interpretation of Indian thought. But he realized, as most of us often do when we become well-acquainted with the classical philosophical texts of India, that this could not be simply an antiquarian's pursuit. He wrote:

> Ancient Indians do not belong to a different species from ourselves. An actual study of their views shows that they ask questions and find answers analogous in their diversity to some of the more important currents in modern thought.[1]

Radhakrishnan participated in the rather persistent debate about whether the Buddha was inclined towards the metaphysics of the Upaniṣadic soul, although the Buddha openly repudiated the notion of the empirical soul. Here he disagreed with his pupil, T.R.V. Murti, and gave a positive answer. With regard to the *bodhi* of Buddhism, he raised the question, which often seems pertinent: what can it be, if it is not the universal self? A tentative answer may be that it is exactly what the universal self is *not*.

With regard to the broader questions of philosophy and religion, Radhakrishnan held several distinct views. He believed that the human consciousness has three levels, that of perceptions, that of reason, and that of intuitive insight. The first helps us to collect observed data, the second to exercise rational reflection, and the third to add meaning, value and character to the observed reality. He defines the third as *ānanda*, a spiritual insight, and (using Sri Aurobindo's term) as 'integral consciousness'. He believes that scientific knowledge, where the first two levels are dominant, is 'inadequate, partial and fragmentary, but not false.' Our intuitive insight, he claims, is what gives fullness to man as a man, leads to his spiritual joy which is akin to aesthetic satisfaction, and brings about the fulfilment of his inner being.

The last point brings us to two other components of Radhakrishnan's thought: his idealistic view of life and his idea of a universal religion, i.e. a universal spiritual life for everybody. Regarding the first, he contributed to a worldview which he called 'idealism,' but refused to identify it with the usual meaning of 'idealism,' a sort of panpsychism or a pan-fictional approach to the world. The use of this term was perhaps unfortunate and confusing, as his critics pointed out. But his meaning was not entirely unclear. His 'idealism' has to do with the third level of human consciousness, what he described as the integral insight. It is what tries to make our life on this world neither 'an irrational blind striving,' nor 'an irremediably miserable blunder,' It is what is supposed to add meaning value and worth to our life. Without it, it is believed, our civilization would be bankrupt. 'It finds life significant and purposeful.'[2] We may rightly disagree about what worth, if any, we should assign to our life, but we cannot deny the presence of a worth-assigning component in human awareness. Radhakrishnan, I believe, referred to this component by his use of the term 'idealism.' Further, he believed that this part of human awareness, when properly cultivated, will take us away from the pursuit of materialistic pleasure towards the quest for the infinite joy of the Absolute. In this respect, he was an optimist.

When one reads this part of Radhakrishnan's philosophy, one tends to have a *deja vu* experience if one has read Rabindranath Tagore's *The Religion of Man* or some of his Bengali essays on such topics. That Radhakrishnan was deeply influenced by Tagore's thought, i.e., Tagore's poetic vision of the cosmos, is proven by the fact that he was partly instrumental in the process that led the University of Oxford to confer its Ph.D *honoris causa* to Poet Tagore at a special convocation at Santiniketan on 7 August, 1940. The university was represented on this occasion by Sir Maurice Gwyer, Dr Sarvepalli Radhakrishnan and Justice Henderson of the Calcutta High Court. This was exactly a year before Tagore died. He died on 7 August 1941, and at his death, Radhakrishnan said: 'He [Tagore] was the greatest figure of the modern Indian Renaissance.' Tagore's univeralism was not just an echo of the universalism that was prevalent in Europe at that time (in Goethe and others). It was less romantic and based more on pragmatic considerations. I believe Radhakrishnan's universalism was partly influenced by his reading of Tagore.

Radhakrishnan's idea of a universal religion has been criticized by many. Religions encouraged, if anything, respective dogmas and intensifying prejudices about other's religious beliefs. A true believer in one particular religion invariably and necessarily claims monopoly over truth and ultimate value. In the face of this state of affairs, how can one even hope to see common ties and underlying unity in different conflicting religious traditions? Radhakrishnan thought that this can be countered, for we can find a basis, the discovery of 'the World of Spirit' as he called it, which will enable us to ignore the concrete formulations of the Divine in different traditions and work towards a unity. For, according to Radhakrishnan, the Divine is 'formless and nameless and yet capable of manifesting all forms and names.'[3]

Whether this optimism or 'idealism' is justified or not, it certainly has a perennial charm for humans in all ages. Radhakrishnan was, however, well-aware that his use of the term 'philosophy' would not agree with that of others, especially those belonging to the Anglo-American Analytic Tradition. He was also far from being an Indianist, who would claim that India, and India alone, can save the world from disaster. For his search was for a universal religion (he called it philosophy too) which would be found in all lands and cultures, in the meeting point of the Upaniṣadic seers and Plato, Plotinus and Philo, Jesus and Paul. He believed that such a meeting point exists, and it resides in the spirit which alone can save us from meaninglessness.

Notes and References

1. Paul A. Schilpp, *The Philosophy of Sarvepalli Radhakrishnan* (New York: Tudor Publishing Co., 1952), p. 13.
2. S. Radhakrishnan, *An Idealist View of Life* (London: George Allen & Unwin, 1931), p. 15.
3. Paul A. Schilpp, *The Philosophy of Sarvepalli Radhakrishnan*, p. 796.

Index